Game Design: Theory & Practice

Richard Rouse III

Illustrations by Steve Ogden

Atomic Sam character designed by Richard Rouse III and Steve Ogden

Library of Congress Cataloging-in-Publication Data

Rouse, Richard.
    Game design: theory & practice / by Richard Rouse III ; illustrations by Steve Ogden.
      p.   cm.
    Includes bibliographical references and index.
    ISBN 1-55622-735-3 (pbk.)
    1. Computer games—Programming. I. Title.
    QA76.76.C672 R69   2000
    794.8'1526—dc21   00-053436
                                        CIP

Copyright Notices

Dedication

To my parents, Richard and Regina Rouse

Acknowledgments

Thanks to Steve Ogden for bringing Atomic Sam to life and providing the brilliant illustrations which enliven these pages.

Thanks to James Hague, Ian Parberry, and Margaret Rogers for looking over my work and providing me with the invaluable feedback and support which have improved this book tremendously.

Thanks to Chris Crawford, Ed Logg, Jordan Mechner, Sid Meier, Steve Meretzky, and Will Wright for graciously subjecting themselves to my endless questioning. To quote Mr. Wright, I'm "pretty thorough."

Thanks to Jim Hill, Wes Beckwith, Beth Kohler, Kellie Henderson, Martha McCuller, Alan McCuller, and everyone at Wordware for making this book become a reality.

For their help with this book, thanks to Benson Russell, John Scott Lewinski, Ari Feldman, Laura J. Mixon-Gould, Jeff Buccelatto, Jayson Hill, Laura Pokrifka, Josh Moore, Lisa Sokulski, Dan Harnett, Steffan Levine, Susan Wooley, Chris Brandkamp, Kelley Gilmore, Lindsay Riehl, Patrick Buechner, Scott Miller, Greg Rizzer, Lori Mezoff, Jenna Mitchell, Ericka Shawcross, Maryanne Lataif, Bryce Baer, Bob Bates, James Conner, Lisa Tensfeldt, Paula Cook, Donald Knapp, and Diana Fuentes.

Special thanks to Margaret Rogers, June Oshiro and Matt Bockol, Ben Young, Alain and Annalisa Roy, Gail Jabbour, Amy Schiller, Katie Young & Eric Pidkameny, Rafael Brown, Eloise Pasachoff, Mark Bullock and Jane Miller, Dave Rouse, Linda, Bob and Grayson Starner, Jamie Rouse, Alan Patmore and everyone at Surreal, the Leaping Lizard crew, Brian Rice, Lee Waggoner, Pat Alphonso, Clay Heaton, Alex Dunne, Gordon Cameron, Tuncer Deniz, Bart Farkas, Peter Tamte, Nate Birkholtz, Al Schilling, Cindy Swanson and everyone at MacSoft, Doug Zartman, Alex Seropian, Jason Jones, Jim McNally, Jeff O'Connor, Ira Harmon, Gordon Marsh, Chuck Schuldiner, Glenn Fabry, and Derek Riggs.

About the Author

Richard Rouse III is a computer game designer, programmer, and writer at Surreal Software (www.surreal.com). Rouse has been designing games professionally for over seven years and has played a lead design role in the development of games for the PC, Macintosh, Sega Dreamcast, Sony PlayStation, and PlayStation 2. His credits include *Centipede 3D*, *Odyssey: The Legend of Nemesis*, and *Damage Incorporated*. At Surreal he currently spends all his waking hours working on a secret PlayStation 2 action/adventure project, while also contributing where he can to *Drakan* for PlayStation 2. Rouse has written about game design for publications including *Game Developer*, *SIGGRAPH Computer Graphics*, *Gamasutra*, and *Inside Mac Games*.

Your Feedback

Your feedback to this book, including corrections, comments, or merely friendly ramblings, is encouraged. Please mail them to the author at rr3@paranoidproductions.com. You will also find the web page for this book, which will be used to track corrections, updates, and other items of interest, at www.paranoidproductions.com. See you there.

About the Artist

Steve Ogden has been an artist, illustrator, and cartoonist for almost 20 years, and miraculously, his right hand shows no sign of dropping off. Among his projects in the digital domain, he has worked on *Bally's Game Magic* casino game as well as *Centipede 3D*, and has just finished a stint as Art Director and Production Lead on Cyan's *realMYST* (while finishing the illustrations to this book during the few hours he was supposed to be sleeping). He is now gearing up for work on Cyan's next game, if they can catch him and chain him to his desk again. To see more of his work, both of the 2D and 3D variety, stop by his web site: www.lunaentertainment.com. You can reach him at ogden@ lunaentertainment.com. He is now going to crawl to a beach very far away and sleep for a while.

Contents Summary

Contents

Contents

Contents

Contents

Introduction

My earliest recollection of playing a computer game was when I stumbled upon a half-height *Space Invaders* at a tiny Mexican restaurant in my hometown. I was perhaps six, and *Space Invaders* was certainly the most marvelous thing I had ever seen, at least next to LegoLand. I had heard of arcade games, but this was the first one I could actually play. *Space Invaders*, I knew, was better than television, because I could control the little ship at the bottom of the screen using the joystick and shoot the aliens myself instead of watching someone else do it. I was in love. The irony of this story is that, at the time, I failed to comprehend that I had to stick quarters into the game to make it work. The game was running in "attract" mode as arcade games do, and my young mind thought I was controlling the game with the joystick when I was actually not controlling anything. But the idea was still mind-blowing.

This book is about developing original computer games that will hopefully have the same mind-blowing effect on players that *Space Invaders* had on my young brain. This book deals with that development process from the point of view of the game designer. Many books have been written about the programming of computer games, but I can remember my frustration in being unable to find a book such as this one when I was an aspiring game designer. In some ways, I have written this book for myself, for the person I was a decade ago. I hope that other people interested in designing games will find this book informative. In my humble opinion, it is the game designer who has the most interesting role in the creation of a computer game. It is the game's design that dictates the form and shape of the game's gameplay, and this is the factor which differentiates our artistic medium from all others.

What is Gameplay?

I hear you asking, "But what is gameplay?" Many people think they know what gameplay is, and indeed there are many different reasonable definitions for it. But I have one definition that covers every use of the term you will find in this book. The gameplay is the component of computer games which is found in no other art form: interactivity. A game's gameplay is the degree and nature of the interactivity that the game includes, i.e., how the player is able to interact with the game-world and how that game-world reacts to the choices the player makes. In an action game such as *Centipede,* the gameplay is moving the shooter ship around the lower quadrant of the screen and shooting the enemies that attack relentlessly. In *SimCity,* the gameplay is laying out a city and observing the citizens that start to inhabit it. In *Doom,* the gameplay is running around a 3D world at high speed and shooting its extremely hostile inhabitants, gathering some keys along the way. In *San Francisco Rush,* the gameplay is steering a car down implausible tracks while jockeying for position with other racers. In *StarCraft,* the gameplay is maneuvering units around a map, finding resources and exploiting them, building up forces, and finally going head to head in combat with a similarly equipped foe. And in *Civilization,* the gameplay is exploring the world, building a society from the ground up, discovering new technologies, and interacting with the other inhabitants of the world.

Though some might disagree with me, the gameplay does not include how the game-world is represented graphically or what game engine is used to render that world. Nor does it include the setting or story line of that game-world. These aesthetic and content considerations are elements computer games may share with other media; they are certainly not what differentiates games from those other media. Gameplay, remember, is what makes our art form unique.

What is Game Design?

What, then, is game design? Having defined what exactly I mean when I refer to gameplay, the notion of game design is quite easily explained: the game design is what determines the form of the gameplay. The game design determines what choices the player will be able to make in the game-world and what ramifications those choices will have on the rest of the game. The game design determines what win or loss criteria the game may include, how the user will be able to control the game, and what information the game will communicate to him, and it establishes how hard the game will be. In short, the game design determines every detail of how the gameplay will function.

Who is a Game Designer?

By this point it should be obvious what a game designer does: she determines what the nature of the gameplay is by creating the game's design. The terms "game designer" and "game design" have been used in such a wide variety of contexts for so long that their meaning has become dilute and hard to pin down. Some seem to refer to game design as being synonymous with game development. These people refer to anyone working on a computer game, be they artist, programmer, or producer, as a game designer. I prefer a more specific definition, as I have outlined above: the game designer is the person who designs the game, who thereby establishes the shape and nature of the gameplay.

It is important to note some tasks in which the game designer may be involved. The game designer may do some concept sketches or create some of the art assets that are used in the game, but he does not have to do so. A game designer may write the script containing all of the dialog spoken by the characters in the game, but he does not have to do so. A game designer may contribute to the programming of the game or even be the lead programmer, but he does not have to do so. The game designer may design some or all of the game-world itself, building the levels of the game (if the project in question has levels to be built), but he does not have to do so. The game designer might be taking care of the project from a management and production standpoint, keeping a careful watch on the members of the team to see that they are all performing their tasks effectively and efficiently, but he does not have to do so. All someone needs to do in order to justifiably be called the game's designer is to establish the form of the game's gameplay. Indeed, many game designers perform a wide variety of tasks on a project, but their central concern should always be the game design and the gameplay.

What is in This Book?

This book contains a breadth of information about game design, covering as many aspects as possible. Of course, no single book can be the definitive work on a particular art form. What this book certainly is not is a book about programming computer games. There are a wealth of books available to teach the reader how to program, and as I discuss later in this book, knowing how to program can be a great asset to game design. However, it is not a necessary component of designing a game; many fine designers do not know how to program at all.

The chapters in this book are divided into three categories. First are the twelve core chapters which discuss various aspects of the development of a computer game, from establishing the game's focus, to documenting the game's design, to establishing the game's mode of storytelling, to playtesting the near-final product.

These chapters discuss the theory behind game design, and what a designer should strive for in order to create the best game possible. The chapters also include discussions of the reality of game development, using examples from my own experience, to delve into the actual practice of game design.

There are five analysis chapters included in this book, covering five excellent games in five different genres. One of the most important skills a game designer must have is the ability to analyze games that she enjoys in order to understand what those games do well. By understanding these other games, the designer may then attempt to replicate those same qualities in her own projects. That is not to suggest that good game designers merely copy the work of other game designers. Understanding the reasons why other games succeed will bring the designer a more complete understanding of game design as a whole. Every game designer should take the games that she finds most compelling and try to examine what makes them tick. The examples I include in this book, *Centipede*, *Tetris*, *Loom*, *Myth: The Fallen Lords*, and *The Sims*, are all very unique games. And though a given project you are working on may not be similar to any of these games, a lot can be learned from analyzing games of any sort. First-person shooter designers have had great success in revitalizing their genre by looking at adventure games. Certainly, role-playing game designers have recently learned a lot from arcade game designers. Melding in techniques from other genres is the best way to advance the genre you are working on and to create something truly original.

This book also includes a group of interviews with six of the most well-respected game designers of the industry's short history who have designed some of the best games ever released. These are lengthy interviews that go deeper than the short press kit style interviews one finds on the Internet or in most magazines. In each interview the subject discusses the best titles of his career and why he believes they turned out as well as they did. The designers also talk at length about their own techniques for developing games. Throughout my own career in game development, I have found interviews with other computer game designers to be exceedingly helpful in learning how to perfect my craft. There is much information to be gleaned from these chapters, ideas that can help any game designer, regardless of how experienced he may be.

At the end of the book you will find a glossary. Though it is far from a complete listing of game design terminology, it does cover many of the more esoteric terms I use in the book, such as a personal favorite of mine, "surrogate." Every game designer has a set of jargon she uses to refer to various aspects of her craft, and this jargon is seldom the same from one designer to the next. If nothing else, the glossary should help you to understand my own jargon. For instance, it will tell you the difference between gameplay and game mechanics. Furthermore, readers who may find the content of this book to assume too much knowledge may find the glossary helpful in sorting out what an RTS game is and what the two different meanings for FPS are. Often, discussions of game design can degrade into questions of semantics, with no two sides ever meaning exactly the same thing when they refer to a game's "engine." I hope that the glossary will help readers to avoid that problem with this book.

Who This Book is For

This book is for anyone who wants to understand the computer game development process better from a strictly game design standpoint. As I stated earlier, there are plenty of books available to teach you how to program, or how to use Photoshop and 3D Studio Max. This book will do neither of these things. Instead it focuses on the more elusive topic of game design and how you can ensure that your title has the best gameplay possible. Though solid programming and art are both central to a game's success, no amount of flashy graphics or cutting-edge coding will make up for lackluster game design. In the end, it is the gameplay that will make or break a project.

I have written this book in such a way as to encompass projects of different scopes and sizes. It does not matter if the game you are working on is destined for commercial release, if you hope to someday release it as shareware, or if you are only making a game for you and your friends to play; this book should be helpful to a game designer working in any of those circumstances. Furthermore, it does not matter if you are working on the game with a large team, with only a few accomplices, or going completely solo. In the book I often make reference to the "staff" of your project. When I refer to "your programming staff" I may be referring to a team of ten seasoned coders commanding massive salaries and pushing the boundaries of real-time 3D technology, or I may be referring to just you, coding up every last aspect of the game yourself. When I refer to "your playtesting staff" I may be referring to an experienced and thoroughly professional testing staff of fifteen who will pride themselves on giving your game a thorough going-over, or I may be referring to your cousins Bob and Judith who, like you, enjoy games and would love to play your game. Good games certainly do not always come from the biggest teams. Even today, when multi-million dollar budgets are the norm, the best games still often result from the vision and determination of a lone individual, and he need not always surround himself with a massive team to see that vision through to completion.

Many places in this book make reference to you leading the design on the project on which you are working. Of course, not every designer can be in the lead position on every project, and even if you are the lead, you will often find yourself without the absolute final say on what takes place in the game. In this regard, this book is written from a somewhat idealistic point of view. But regardless of how much authority you actually have over the direction of the project, the important point is to always know what you would do with the project if you could do whatever you wanted. Then you should campaign for this direction with the other people on the team. If you are persuasive enough and if you are, in fact, correct in your instincts, you have a good chance of convincing them to do it your way. Projects are often led not by the people with the most seniority or who have the right title on their business card; projects are lead by the people who "show up" to the task, who care about their projects and are committed to them, and who are willing to put in the time and effort to make the game the best it can be.

Theory and Practice

Every medium has a unique voice with which it can speak, and it is the responsibility of the user of a medium to find that voice. Computer games have a voice that I firmly believe to be as strong as that available in any other media. Computer games are a relatively young form when compared with the likes of the printed word, music, the visual arts, or the theater, and I think this currently works against the likelihood of computer games truly finding their most powerful voice. This book is an attempt to help readers find that voice in their own projects. This can come in both the more theoretical form of questioning why it is that players play games, but also in the entirely more practical form of how to most effectively work with playtesters. To have any chance of producing a great game, the game designer must understand both the theoretical aspects and the practical necessities of game design.

Chapter 1:
What Players Want

"But when I come to think more on it, the biggest reason it has become that popular is Mr. Tajiri, the main developer and creator of *Pokemon*, didn't start this project with a business sense. In other words, he was not intending to make something that would become very popular. He just wanted to make something he wanted to play. There was no business sense included, only his love involved in the creation. Somehow, what he wanted to create for himself was appreciated by others in this country and is shared by people in other countries. ...And that's the point: not to make something sell, something very popular, but to love something, and make something that we creators can love. It's the very core feeling we should have in making games."

— Shigeru Miyamoto, talking about the creation of *Pokemon*

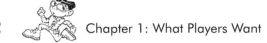

Game designers spend a lot of time concerning themselves with what game players are looking for in a computer game. What can they put in their computer games that has not been done before and will excite players? Often game designers are so bereft of an idea of what gamers want that they instead only include gameplay ideas that have been tried before, rehashing what was popular with game players last year. Surely if players liked it last year, they will like it this year. But therein lies the rub. Gamers generally do not want to buy a game that is only a clone of another game, a "new" game that only offers old ideas and brings nothing original to the table. Nonetheless, successful games can be useful, not for cloning, but for analysis. As game designers, we can look at the games that have come out previously, that we have enjoyed in years past, and try to determine a set of directives that explain what compelled us to try those games in the first place, and why they held our interest once we started playing them.

Why Do Players Play?

The first question we should consider is: why do players play games in the first place? Why do they choose to turn on their computer and run *Doom* instead of visiting the art museum or going to see a movie? What is unique about computer games versus other human entertainment pursuits? What do games offer that other activities do not? It is by understanding what is attractive about games that other media do not offer that we can try to emphasize the differences, to differentiate our art form from others. To be successful, our games need to take these differences and play them up, exploit them to make the best gameplay experience possible.

Players Want a Challenge

Many players enjoy playing games since they provide them with a challenge. This provides one of the primary motivating factors for single-player home games, where social or bragging rights motivations are less of an issue. Games can entertain players over time, differently each time they play, while engaging their minds in an entirely different way than a book, movie, or other form of art. In somewhat the same way someone might fiddle with a *Rubik's Cube* or a steel "remove the ring" puzzle, games force players to think actively, to try out different solutions to problems, to understand a given game mechanism.

When a person faces a challenge and then overcomes it, that person has learned something. It does not matter if that challenge is in a math textbook or in a computer game. So, challenging games can be learning experiences. Players will learn from games, even if that learning is limited to the context of the game, such as how to get by level eight, and so forth. In the best games, players will learn lessons through gameplay that can be applied to other aspects of their life, even if they do not realize it. This may mean that they can apply problem solving methods to their work, use their improved spatial skills to better arrange their furniture, or perhaps even learn greater empathy through game role-playing. Many players thrive on and long for the challenges games provide, and are enriched by the learning that follows.

Players Want to Socialize

I have a friend who maintains that games are antisocial. This is, of course, absurd, as nearly all non-computer games require a social group in order to function. Games arose as a communal activity many millennia ago out of a desire to have a challenging activity in which a group of friends and family could engage in. Computer game designers need to remember that the roots of gaming, and an important part of its appeal, are in its social nature.

For most people, the primary reason they play games is to have a social experience with their friends or family. I am not talking about computer games here, but rather board and card games like chess, *Monopoly*, bridge, *Scrabble*, *Diplomacy*, or *The Settlers of Catan*. People like to play these games because they like being with their friends and want to engage in a shared activity that is more social than going to a movie or watching TV. It is true that lots of people enjoy playing solitaire card games as well, but there are many more multi-player games than there are single-player. This is because people enjoy a social gameplaying experience.

But how does this apply to computer games? If one considers all the computer games ever created, the majority of them are single-player only experiences. But of course there are plenty of multi-player games, ranging from the "death-matches" found in *Doom* and its imitators, to the classic *M.U.L.E.* game of wheeling and dealing, to the persistent worlds founds in MUDs (Multi User Dungeons) or their commercial equivalent, *Ultima Online*.

Almost all death-match style multi-player games are basically adaptations of single-player games into multi-player incarnations. Though there are exceptions, such as *Quake III* or *Unreal Tournament*, these games usually provide a single-player (SP) game in addition to the multi-player (MP) game. The SP and MP games are played with nearly the same set of rules and game mechanics. But even in these single-player-turned-multi-player games, players like to socialize while playing. Anyone who has ever played one of these games over a LAN in a room with a bunch of their friends can testify to this. These LAN-fests are usually rich with conversation as players shout back and forth to each other, bragging over their most recent "frag" or proclaiming how close they came to being killed. Games such as *Quake* can also be played over the Internet, where the experience is quite a bit less social, since players may be miles apart and are thus only able to communicate through the computer. And the high-intensity and fast-action nature of these games

Unreal Tournament is an example of a game which focuses primarily on providing a multi-player experience.

doesn't leave players much time to type messages to their opponents, if they hope to survive for long. But these games do still provide chat functionality, and players, when they are in a safe corner, after they have died, or between games, can send conversational messages to each other. At more hectic points in the gameplay the messages are short and typed on the fly, consisting of only a couple of letters. The fact that players still try to chat with each other in these high-velocity games is testament to the players' desire to socialize.

A separate category of multi-player games is what has come to be called "persistent universe" or "massively multi-player" games. These games tend to be more in the style of role-playing games, where players wander around "virtual worlds" and meet and interact with the other characters in these worlds, characters who are controlled by other players. These games tend to be played over large networks such as the Internet, instead of over LANs, and as a result players only socialize with each other through what they type into the computer. Since these games are considerably slower paced than death-match games, there is a much greater opportunity for the players to chat with each other while playing. MUDs were the first popular incarnation of this style of game, which were played primarily by college students from the late 1980s on. At the time, college students were the main group of people with free time who were hooked to the Internet. These games are text-only, and provide their players with quests to accomplish in mostly fantasy settings. The quests, however, take a backseat to the socialization and role-playing, with players spending the vast majority of their time chatting with other players. A lot of people are drawn into playing these games as a way to interact with their friends, despite the fact that these friends are people they met online and who they have never seen in person. Indeed, the persistent worlds, MUDs in particular, draw in a legion of players who are not interested in playing any single-player computer games. These people play games in order to meet and talk to other people. The games are an activity these people can engage in together while socializing.

As multi-player games have become more and more common, many game developers have been quick to point out their advantages in terms of competitive AI. Human opponents are much more unpredictable and challenging than any AI that could be reasonably created for most games. This, they suggested, is why people are drawn to multi-player games. But the biggest advantage of these multi-player games is that they transform computer games into truly social experiences, which is one of the largest motivating factors for people to play games.

Players Want a Dynamic Solitaire Experience

Perhaps I have confused the reader by saying first that players want to socialize and then suggesting that players want a solitaire experience. Of course the two do not happen at the same time; some game players are looking for a social experience, and a different set are looking for something dynamic that they can engage in by themselves. Sometimes friends are not available, or a player is tired of his friends, or simply tired of having to talk to other people all the time. Similar to the difference between going to a movie theater with an audience versus renting a video alone at home, the antisocial nature of single-player games attracts a lot of people who have had enough of the other members of the human race.

But games are distinct from other solitaire experiences such as reading a book or watching a video since they provide the players with something to interact with, an experience that reacts to them as a human would, or at least in a manner resembling a human's reactions. But the players are always in control, and can start and stop playing at any time. Thus the computer game "fakes" the interesting part of human interaction without all of the potential annoyances. In this way, people are able to turn to computer games for a dynamic and interactive yet antisocial experience.

Players Want Bragging Rights

Particularly in multi-player gaming, players play games to win respect. Being able to frag all of your friends in *Doom* will force them to have a grudging respect for you: "Bob isn't very good in algebra class, but he can sure annihilate me in a deathmatch." Even in single-player games, players will talk with their friends about how they finished one game or about how good they are at another. Players will brag about how they played the whole game through on the hardest difficulty in only a few hours. If one looks at arcade games both old and new, the high-score table and the ability to enter one's name into the game, even if only three letters, provides a tremendous incentive for people to play a game repeatedly. Players who may not have much to brag about in their ordinary lives, who may not be terribly physically coordinated at sports or bookish enough to do well in school, can go down to the arcade and point out to all their friends their initials in the *Centipede* game. Even without telling anyone, players can feel a tremendous sense of self-satisfaction when they beat a particular game. When players are victorious at a challenging game, they realize they can do something well, probably better than most people, which makes them feel better about themselves.

Players Want an Emotional Experience

As with other forms of entertainment, players may be seeking some form of emotional payoff when they play a computer game. This can be as simple as the adrenaline rush and tension of a fast-action game like *Doom*. Or it can be considerably more complex, such as the player's feeling of loss when her friendly robot companion sacrifices himself for the player in Steve Meretzky's *Planetfall*. Sadly, many games' emotional ranges are limited to excitement/tension during a conflict, despair at repeated failure at a given task, and then elation and a sense of accomplishment when the player finally succeeds. It may seem strange that players would play a game in order to feel despair. But many people enjoy watching plays that are tragedies or movies that have sad endings, or listening to music that is out-and-out depressing. People want to feel something when they interact with art, and it does not necessarily need to be a positive, happy feeling. Perhaps the sense of catharsis people obtain from these works makes them worth experiencing. Many classic arcade games, such as *Centipede* or *Space Invaders*, are unwinnable. No matter what the player does, eventually the game will beat him. These games are, in a sense, lessons in defeat—tragedies every time the player plays them. Yet the player keeps pumping in his quarters. This is why a player's feeling of hopelessness as a game repeatedly bests him is not to be ignored. The player is feeling *something*, and some would say that is the goal of art.

Emotional range is not something computer games have explored as much as they could. The example from *Planetfall* I cited above is one of the very few examples in computer games of a player becoming attached to a character in a game, only to have him killed later on. Many developers are wary of making a game too sad. But in the case of *Planetfall*, the tragic story twist of that game was exploited for all the pathos it was worth by designer Steve Meretzky. It is a moment of tragedy that has stuck in many gamers' memories. Game designers would be wise to concentrate on expanding the emotional experience in games beyond excitement and accomplishment, into more unexplored and uncharted emotional territory.

Players Want to Fantasize

A major component of the popularity of storytelling art forms is the element of fantasy. Whether one considers novels, films, or comic books, many people experience these works to "get away" from their own "mundane" lives and escape to an altogether different world, one filled with characters who engage in exciting, interesting activities, travel to exotic locales, and meet other fascinating people. Certainly not all storytelling works portray exciting and glamorous protagonists, but there is certainly a large segment of works that is labeled "escapist." Some critics deride such escapist pieces of art, and indeed a lot of very good books, movies, and comics deal with more realistic settings and topics to great effect. The fact remains, however, that many people want to be transported to a world more glamorous than their own.

Computer games, then, have the potential to be an even more immersive form of escapism. In games, players get the chance to actually *be* someone more exciting, to control a pulp-fiction adventurer, daring swordsman, or space-opera hero. While in books or films the audience can merely watch as the characters lead exciting lives, in a well-designed computer game a player will actually get the chance to live those lives themselves. Even better, these fantasy lives are not weighed down with the mundane events of life. In most games, players do not have to worry about eating, needing to get some sleep, or going to the bathroom. Thus, a game can create a fantasy life without the tedious details. And, most importantly, the level of fantasy immersion is heightened from that of other art forms because of the interactive nature of gaming.

Another part of the fantasy fulfillment element of computer games is enabling the player to engage in socially unacceptable behavior in a safe environment. Many popular games have allowed players to pretend they are criminals or assassins. *Driver* is a good example of this. Though the back-story explains that the player is actually playing an undercover police officer, in *Driver* the player gets to pretend she is a criminal who must evade the police in elaborate car chases. There is a devilish thrill to outrunning police cars, especially for anyone who has ever been pulled over by one. Though most players would never consider driving in car chases in real life, there's something tempting and enticing about engaging in taboo activities. Computer games provide a good medium for players to explore sides of their personality that they keep submerged in their daily lives.

Players may also fantasize about events in history. If the player could have been Napoleon, would Waterloo have turned out differently? If the player were a railroad baron in the twentieth century, would he be able to create a powerful financial empire? A whole line of historical games, from wargames to economic simulations, allow players to explore events in history, and see how making different choices than the historical figures involved made will result in wildly different outcomes.

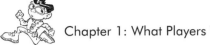

While many people spend their time dwelling on the past, wondering how events could have transpired differently if alternate decisions had been made, games can give players a chance to find out how history might have been different.

Even without the elements of excitement and glamour, even if another person's life is not actually that exciting, it can be interesting to spend time as that person. Good computer games can provide players with the otherwise unavailable opportunity to see the world through someone else's eyes. As millions of gamers can attest, it is fun to role-play and it is fun to fantasize.

What Do Players Expect?

Once a player has decided he wants to play a given game because of one motivating factor or another, he will have expectations for the game itself. Beyond the game not crashing and looking reasonably pretty, players have certain gameplay expectations, and if these are not met, the player will soon become frustrated and find another game to play. It is the game designer's job to make sure the game meets these expectations. So once they start playing, what do players want?

Players Expect a Consistent World

As players play a game, they come to understand what actions they are allowed to perform in the world, and what results those actions will produce. Few things are more frustrating than when the player comes to anticipate a certain result from an action and then the game, for no perceivable reason, produces a different result. Worse still is when the consequences of the player's actions are so unpredictable that a player cannot establish any sort of expectation. Having no expectation of what will happen if a certain maneuver is attempted will only frustrate and confuse players, who will soon find a different, more consistent game to play. It is the consistency of actions and their results that must be maintained, for an unpredictable world is a frustrating one to live in.

Fighting games are a particularly appropriate example of the importance of predictable outcomes from actions. Players do not want a maneuver to work sometimes and fail other times, without a readily apparent reason for the different outcomes. For instance, in *Tekken*, if the player misses a kick, it has to be because her opponent jumped, blocked, was too far away, or some other reason that the player can perceive. The player's perception of the reason for the move's failure is important to emphasize. It may be that the internal game logic, in this case the collision system, will know why the player's kick missed, but it is as bad as having no reason if the player cannot easily recognize why the maneuver failed. Furthermore, if only expert players can understand why their action failed, many novices will become frustrated as they are defeated for no reason they can understand. If a kick fails in a situation that closely resembles another situation in which the same kick succeeded, players will throw their hands up in frustration.

Pinball games are another interesting example. Of course, a pinball game is a completely predictable game-world, since it is based on real-world physics. An expert pinball player knows this, and will use it to his advantage. But the problem comes with the novice. Inexperienced players will often fail to see what they "did wrong" when the ball goes straight down between their flippers, or rolls down one of the side gutters. These players will curse the pinball game as a "game of luck" and not want to play anymore. Of course, the fact that players of different skill levels will have radically different levels of success at a given pinball game shows that it is not just a game of luck. But only those players who stick with the game through numerous early failures will find this out. I am not suggesting that pinball games should be abandoned or radically simplified, but one of their shortcomings is that they alienate new players who cannot see the connections between their actions and the outcome of the game.

Players Expect to Understand the Game-World's Bounds

When playing a game, a player wants to understand which actions are possible and which are not. He does not need to immediately see which actions are needed for a given situation, but he should understand which actions it is possible to perform and which are outside the scope of the game's play-space.

In *Doom II*, the player will not expect to be able to start a conversation with the monsters he is attacking.

For instance, in *Doom*, a player will intuitively figure out that she is not going to be able to hold a discussion with the demons she is fighting. The player will not even want to initiate a conversation with a demon during which she suggests surrender as the most logical course of action. The player understands that such interpersonal discussion is out of the scope of the game. Suppose that *Doom* had included a monster late in the game, a foe that could only be defeated if the player was friendly to it, winning it over with her witty conversation. Players would have been frustrated, since they came to understand, through playing the levels that led up to that level, that in *Doom* all that is needed for victory is to blast everything that moves, while avoiding getting hit. Talking is completely out of the scope of the game.

Of course, a chatty monster in *Doom* is an extreme example of a game having unpredictable bounds, but plenty of games break this design principle. These games have players performing actions and completing levels using a certain type of game mechanism, and then later on insert puzzles that can only be solved using an entirely new mechanism. The problem is that the player has been taught to play the game a certain way, and suddenly the game requires the player to do something else entirely. Once players come to understand all of the gameplay mechanisms that a game uses, they don't want new, unintuitive mechanisms to be randomly introduced.

Players Expect Reasonable Solutions to Work

Once a player has spent some time playing a game, he comes to understand the bounds of the game-world. He has solved numerous puzzles, and he has seen what sort of solutions will pay off. Later in the game, then, when faced with a new puzzle, the player will see what he regards as a perfectly reasonable solution. If he then tries that solution and it fails to work for no good reason, he will be frustrated, and he will feel cheated by the game.

This sort of difficulty in game design is particularly true in games that try to model the real-world to some degree. In the real-world there are almost always multiple ways to accomplish a given objective. Therefore, so too must it be in a computer game set in the real-world. Of course, a designer always provides at least one solution to a puzzle, and granted that solution may be perfectly reasonable. But there may be other equally reasonable solutions, and unless the designer makes sure those solutions work as well, players will discover and attempt these non-functioning alternate solutions and will be irritated when they do not work. It is the game designer's task to anticipate what the player will try to do in the game-world, and then make sure that something reasonable happens when the player attempts that action.

Players Expect Direction

Good games are about letting the players do what they want, to a point. Players want to create their own success stories, their own methods for defeating the game, something that is uniquely theirs. But at the same time, players need to have some idea of what they are supposed to accomplish in this game. Not having direction is a bit too much like real life, and players already have a real life. Many gamers are probably playing the game in order to get away from their real lives, to fantasize and escape. They usually do not play games in order to simulate real life on their computer.

Players want to have some idea of what their goal is and be given some suggestion of how they might achieve that goal. With a goal but no idea of how to achieve it, players will inevitably flail around, trying everything they can think of, and become frustrated when the maneuvers they attempt do not bring them any closer to their goal. Of course, without an idea of what their goal is, players are left to just wander aimlessly, perhaps enjoying the scenery, marveling at the immersive game-world. Yet without something to do in that game-world, it is pointless as a game. If the players do not know what their goal is, the goal might as well not exist.

SimCity 3000 is the third in a series of city simulation "software toys," which let users play without giving them a specific goal.

The classic example of the goal-less game is *SimCity*. In fact, Will Wright, the game's creator, calls it a "software toy" instead of a game. *SimCity* is like a toy in that the player can do whatever she wants with it, without ever explicitly being told that she has failed or succeeded. In some ways *SimCity* is like a set of Legos, where a player can build whatever she wants just for the thrill of creation. The trick, however, is that *SimCity* is a city simulator, wherein the player is allowed to set up a city however she wants. But since the game simulates reality (constructing and running a city), and the player knows what is considered "success" in reality (a booming city full of lovely stadiums, palatial libraries, and happy citizens), she will naturally tend to impose her own rules for success on the game. She will strive to make her idea of the perfect city, and keep its citizens happy and its economy buoy-ant. In a subtle way, the player is directed by her own experience with reality. If *SimCity* had been a simulation of a system that players were completely unfamiliar with, it would certainly have been less popular. Though the game does not explic-itly have a goal, the very nature of the game and its grounding in reality encourages players to come up with their own goals. And so, what starts out as a toy becomes a game, and thus the players are compelled to keep playing.

Players Expect to Accomplish a Task Incrementally

Given that players understand what their goal in the game-world is, players like to know that they are on the right track toward accomplishing that goal. The best way to do this is to provide numerous sub-goals along the way, which are communicated to the player just as is the main goal. Then, a player is rewarded for achieving these sub-goals just as he is for the main goal, but with a proportionally smaller reward. Of course one can take this down to any level of detail, with the sub-goals having sub-sub-goals, as much as is necessary to clue the player in that he is on the right track. Without providing feedback of this kind, and if the steps necessary to obtain a goal are particularly long and involved, a player may well be on the right track and not realize it. When there is no positive reinforcement to keep him on that track, a player is likely to try something else. And when he cannot figure out the solution to a particular obstacle, he will become frustrated, stop playing, and tell all his friends what a miserable time he had playing your game.

Players Expect to Be Immersed

A director of a musical I was once in would become incensed when actors waiting in the wings would bump into the curtains. She suggested that once the audience sees the curtains moving, their concentration is taken away from the actors on the stage. Their suspension of disbelief is shattered. They are reminded that it is only a play they are watching, not real at all, and that there are people jostling the curtains surrounding this whole charade. Perhaps exaggerating a bit, this director suggested that all of Broadway would collapse if the curtains were seen shaking.

But she had a point, and it is a point that can be directly applied to computer games. Once a player is into a game, she is in a level, she has a good understanding of the game's controls, she is excited, and she is role-playing a fantasy; she does not want to be snapped out of her experience. Certainly the game should not crash. That would be the most jarring experience possible. Beyond that, the player does not want to think about the game's GUI. If the GUI is not designed to be transpar-ent and to fit in with the rest of the game-world art, it will stick out and ruin her immersion. If a character that is supposed to be walking on the ground starts walk-ing into the air for no recognizable reason, the player will realize it is a bug and her suspension of disbelief will be shattered. If the player comes to a puzzle, figures out a perfectly reasonable solution to it, and that solution does not work, the player will again be reminded that she is "only" playing a computer game. All of these pitfalls and many others detract from the player's feeling of immersion, and each time the player is rudely awakened from her game-world fantasy, the harder it is to reimmerse herself in the game-world. Remember that many players want to play games in order to fulfill fantasies. And it is very hard to fulfill a fantasy when the game's idiosyncrasies keep reminding the player that it is just a game.

Despite all his fame, Mario does not have a very distinct personality. He is pictured here in *Super Mario 64*.

Another important aspect of player immersion is the character the player is controlling in the game. Most all games are about role-playing to some extent. And if the character the player is controlling, his surrogate in the game-world, is not someone the player likes or can see himself as being, the player's immersion will be disrupted. For instance, in the third-person action/adventure game *Super Mario 64,* the player is presented with a character to control, Mario, who does not have a very distinct personality. Mario has a fairly unique look in his pseudo-plumber getup, but he never really says much, and acts as something of a blank slate on which the player can impose his own personality. On the other hand, some adventure games have starred characters who acted like spoiled brats, and the player has to watch as his character says annoying, idiotic things over and over again. Each time the character says something that the player would never say if he had the choice, the player is reminded that he is playing a game, that he is not really in control of his character as much as he would like to be. In order for the player to become truly immersed, he must come to see himself as his game-world surrogate.

Players Expect to Fail

Players tend not to enjoy games which can be played all the way through the first time they try it out. For if the game is so unchallenging that they can storm right through it on their first attempt, it might as well not be a game. If they wanted something that simple they might as well have watched a movie. Remember that gamers are drawn to playing games because they want a challenge. And a challenge necessarily implies that the players will not succeed at first, that many attempts must be made to overcome obstacles before they are finally successful. A victory that is too easily achieved is a hollow victory. It is not unlike winning a fistfight with someone half your size.

It is important to understand that players want to fail because of their own shortcomings, not because of the idiosyncrasies of the game they are playing. When a player fails, she should see what she should have done instead and she should instantly recognize why what she was attempting failed to work out. If the player feels that the game defeated her through some "trick" or "cheap shot," she will become frustrated with the game. Players need to blame only themselves for not succeeding, but at the same time the game must be challenging enough that they do not succeed right away.

It is also a good idea to let players win a bit at the beginning of the game. This will suck the player into the game, making them think, "this isn't so hard." Players may even develop a feeling of superiority to the game. Then the difficulty must increase or "ramp up" so that the player fails. By this time the player is already involved in the game, he has time invested in it, and he wants to keep playing, to overcome the obstacle that has now defeated him. If a player is defeated too early on in the game, he may decide it is too hard for him, or not understand what sort of rewards he will get if he keeps playing. By allowing the player to win at first, a player will know that success is possible, and will try extra hard to overcome what has bested him.

Players Expect a Fair Chance

Players do not want to be presented with an obstacle where their only chance of surmounting the obstacle is through trial and error, where an error results in their character's death or the end of their game. A player may be able to figure out the proper way to overcome the obstacle through trial and error, but there should be some way the player could figure out a successful path on his first try. So, extending this rule to the whole game, without ever having played the game before the player should be able to progress through the entire game without dying, assuming that the player is extremely observant and skilled. It may be that no player will ever be this skilled on his first time playing, and, as we discussed, ideally the designer wants the player to fail many times before completing the game. However, it must be theoretically possible for the player to make it through on his first try without dying. Players will quickly realize when the only way around an obstacle is to try each different possible solution until one works. And as players keep dying from each shot-in-the-dark attempt they make, they will realize that due to short-sighted design, there was no real way to avoid all of these deaths. They will be frustrated, and they will curse the game, and soon they will not waste their time with it any longer.

Players Expect to Not Need to Repeat Themselves

Once a player has accomplished a goal in a game, she does not want to have to accomplish it again. If the designer has created an extremely challenging puzzle, one that is still difficult to complete even after the player has solved it once, it should not be overused in the game. For instance, the same painfully difficult puzzle should not appear in identical or even slightly different form in different levels of a 3D action/adventure, unless the defeating of the difficult puzzle is a lot of fun and the rewards are significantly different each time the puzzle is completed. If it is not a lot of fun to do, and the player has to keep solving it throughout the game, she will become frustrated and will hate the game designer for his lack of creativity in failing to come up with new challenges.

Of course, many games are built on the principle of the player repeating himself, or at least repeating his actions in subtly varied ways. Sports games such as *NFL Blitz* and racing games such as *San Francisco Rush* are all about covering the same ground over and over again, though the challenges presented in any one playing of those games are unique to that playing. Classic arcade games like *Centipede* and *Defender* offer roughly the same amount of repetition. *Tetris* is perhaps the king of repetitive gameplay, yet players never seem to grow tired of its challenge. The games in which players do not want to repeat themselves are the games in which exploration is a key part of the player's enjoyment and in which the challenges presented in any specific playing are fairly static and unchanging. After exploring a game-world once, subsequent explorations are significantly less interesting. While every time the player engages in a game of *Defender*, *San Francisco Rush*, or *NFL Blitz* the game is unique, every time the player plays *Tomb Raider*, *Doom*, or *Fallout* the challenges presented are roughly the same. Therefore, players do not mind the repetition in the former games while they will become quickly frustrated when forced to repeat themselves in the latter.

Game players' lack of desire to repeat themselves is why save-games were created. With save-games, once a player has completed a particularly arduous task she can back up her progress so she can restore to that position when she dies later. When a game presents a player with a huge, tricky challenge and, after many attempts, she finally overcomes it, the player must be given the opportunity to save her work. Allowing the player to save her game prevents her from having to repeat herself.

Some games will even automatically save the player's game at this newly achieved position, a process sometimes known as checkpoint saving. This method is somewhat superior since often a player, having succeeded at an arduous task, will be granted access to a new and exciting area of gameplay, one which she will immediately want to explore and interact with. Often, in her excitement, she will forget to save. Then, when she is defeated in the new area, the game will throw her back to her last save-game, which she had made prior to the challenging obstacle. Now the player has to make it through the challenging obstacle once again. However, if the game designer recognizes that the obstacle is a difficult one to pass, he can make the game automatically save the player's position, so that when the player dies in the new area, she is able to start playing in the new area right away. However, automatic saves should not be used as a replacement for player-requested saves, but should instead work in conjunction with them. This way players who are accustomed to saving their games will be able to do it whenever they deem it appropriate, while gamers who often forget to save will be allowed to play all the way through the game without ever needing to hit the save key. Indeed, automatic saving provides the player with a more immersive experience: every time the player accesses a save-game screen or menu, she is reminded that she is playing a game. If a player can play through a game without ever having to save her game, her experience will be that much more transparent and immersive.

Players Expect to Not Get Hopelessly Stuck

There should be no time while playing a game that the player is incapable of somehow winning, regardless of how unlikely it may actually be. Many older adventure games enjoyed breaking this cardinal rule. Often in these games, if the player failed to do a particular action at a specific time, or failed to retrieve a small item from a location early in the game, the player would be unable to complete the game. The problem was that the player would not necessarily realize this until many hours of fruitless gameplay had passed. The player's game was essentially over, but he was still playing. Nothing is more frustrating than playing a game that cannot be won.

As an example, modern 3D world exploration games, whether *Unreal* or *Super Mario 64*, need to concern themselves with the possibility that the player can get hopelessly stuck in the 3D world. Often this style of game provides pits or chasms that the player can fall down into without dying. It is vital to always provide ways out of these chasms, such as escape ladders or platforms which allow the player to get back to his game. The method of getting out of the pit can be extremely difficult, which is fine, but it must be possible. For what is the point of having the

Level designers for 3D action/ adventure games, such as *Unreal*, need to create maps which prevent the player from ever getting permanently stuck behind a piece of architecture.

player fall into a pit from which he cannot escape? If he is incapable of escape, the player's game-world surrogate needs to be killed by something in the pit, either instantly on impact (say the floor of the pit is electrified) or fairly soon (the pit is flooding with lava, which kills the player within ten seconds of his falling in). Under no circumstances should the player be left alive, stuck in a situation from which he cannot continue on with his game.

One of the primary criticisms leveled against *Civilization*, an otherwise excellent game, is that its end-games can go on for too long. When two countries remain and one is hopelessly far behind the other, the game can tend to stretch on past the point of interest while the dominant power tracks down and slaughters the opposition. Indeed, the less advanced country is not technically without hope. That player can still come from behind and win the game; it is not completely impossible. That player is not stuck to the same degree as the player trapped in the pit with no exit, but the player is so far behind that it might as well be impossible; the luck they would need to have and the mistakes the dominant power would have to make are quite staggering. The solution to this is perhaps to allow the AI to figure out when it is hopelessly overpowered and surrender, just as a player who is hopelessly far behind will do the same by quitting and starting a new game.

Players Expect to Do, Not to Watch

For a time the industry was very excited about the prospect of "interactive movies." During this period computer game cut-scenes got longer and longer. Slightly famous film actors started starring in the cut-scenes. Games became less and less interactive, less, in fact, like games. And the budgets ballooned. Then, surprise surprise, gamers did not like these types of games. They failed to buy them. Companies collapsed, and everyone in the industry scratched their heads wondering what had gone wrong. Of course the gamers knew, and the game designers were soon able to figure out what was amiss. The problem was that players wanted to do, they did not want to watch. And they still feel the same way.

I am not completely against cut-scenes; they can be a very useful tool for communicating a game's story, or for passing along to the player information she will need in order to succeed at the next piece of gameplay. That said, I do believe that cut-scenes should be stripped down and minimized to the absolute shortest length that is necessary to give some idea of the game's narrative, if any, and set up the next sequence of gameplay. Cut-scenes over one minute in length, especially those that fail to provide information essential for completing the next gameplay sequence, should be avoided. It does not matter if the cut-scene is text scrolling along the back of the screen, full-motion video with live actors, cell animation, or done using the game-engine, the entirety of this break in the gameplay should not take longer than a minute. If there is gameplay involved in some way, such as the player planning out troop placement for the next mission, then it is not really a cut-scene and can be as long as is necessary. And certainly, if the cut-scene contains information critical to the gameplay, the designer will want to let the player replay the cut-scene as many times as he desires.

The quality of the cut-scene really does not matter either. There have been many games with the most atrocious "acting" ever witnessed, usually as performed by the assistant producer and the lead tester. There have been games with Hollywood-quality production and content, some with even better. But in the end, if the game is any good, gamers are going to want to get back to it, and they are going to want to skip the cut-scene.

In short, the reason people play games is because they want something different from what a movie, book, radio show, or comic can provide. I did not include among the reasons why people play games "because the library is closed" or "because the TV is on the blink." Gamers want a game, and game designers should give it to them.

Players Do Not Know What They Want, But They Know It When They See It

One could see this as an argument against focus groups, but that is not quite it. Having playtesters is a very important part of game development. By playtesters, I mean people looking not for bugs in your game, but rather analyzing the gameplay and providing constructive feedback about it. A designer should have lots of people playing her game once it is at a stage in development where a majority of the gameplay can be judged.

On the other hand, having a focus group of gamers before a game has been created just to "bounce ideas around" is pretty much useless. Gamers are good, of course, at judging whether a game they are playing is any fun or not. They may not be able to explain in a useful way what exactly they like or dislike about a particular game, but they certainly know when they are having a good time, whether they are having their fantasies fulfilled, whether they are being appropriately challenged, or if a game gets them excited. But just because they enjoy a wide range of finished games does not mean they are qualified to critique raw game ideas. Similarly, game ideas they come up with are not certain to be good ones. It is the rare person who can discuss the idea of a computer game and determine if is likely the final game will be fun or not. People with these skills are those best suited to become game designers. Not all game players have these skills, so when asked what sort of game they might be interested in playing, gamers may not really know what they want. But, as I say, they will know it when they see it.

A Never-Ending List

Of course, this exploration of what players want could fill a whole book and could continue indefinitely. I encourage readers, whether aspiring game designers or those who have already had a number of games published, to create their own list of what they think gamers want. Think of what frustrates you while you play a game and what portions of a game deliver to you the greatest satisfaction. Then try to determine why you react to a game mechanic as you do. What did it do right and what did it do wrong? This will allow you to establish your own list of rules, which you can then apply to your own designs. Without feedback from playtesters it is often hard to determine whether your game is entertaining and compelling or not. But with a set of rules you can systematically apply to your design, you may just figure out whether anyone will like your game.

Chapter 2:
Interview: Sid Meier

   Sid Meier is certainly the most famous and well-respected Western
computer game designer, and deservedly so. In his nearly twenty years of
developing games, he has covered all manner of game designs and all
types of subject matter. He co-founded Microprose and at first focused on
flight simulators, culminating in his classic **F-15 Strike Eagle** and **F-19
Stealth Fighter**. Subsequently, he shifted to the style of game he is better
known for today, developing such classics as **Pirates!**, **Railroad Tycoon**,
Covert Action, and finally **Civilization**, this last game being one of the
most universally admired game designs in the history of the form. Most
recently, at his new company Firaxis, Meier created the truly unique RTS
wargame **Gettysburg!** What strikes one most looking back over his
games is their consistent level of quality and the fact that he never
repeats himself, always preferring to take on something new and different for his personal projects. If anyone has a solid grasp on what makes
a game a compelling experience, it is Sid Meier.

Your first published games were flight simulators. Eventually you drifted over to doing what you are now known for, strategy games. What drove you from one genre to the other?

It was not a deliberate plan. I think I've always tried to write games about topics that I thought were interesting. There are just a lot of different topics, I guess. A lot of things that I've written games about are things that, as a kid, I got interested in, or found a neat book about the Civil War,

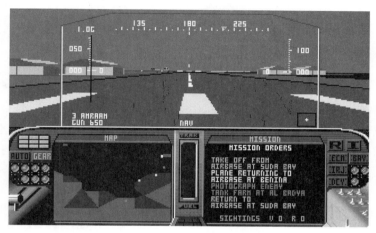

F-19 Stealth Fighter

or airplanes, or whatever. I think the other thing that drove that a little bit was the technology. That at certain times the technology is ready to do a good job with this kind of game or that kind of game. Or the market is ready for a strategy game, for example, or a game that you've wanted to do for a while but you didn't think the time was right. The shift, specifically from flight simulators to strategy, came about for two reasons, I think. One, I had just finished *F-19 Stealth Fighter*, which included all of the ideas I had up to that point about flight simulation. Anything I did after that would be better graphics or more sounds or more scenarios or whatever, but I didn't feel I had a lot of new ideas at that point about flight simulation. Everything I thought was cool about a flight simulator had gone into that game. And the other thing was that I had spent some time playing *SimCity* and a game called *Empire* which got me to thinking about strategy in a grand sense, a game that really had a significant amount of scope and time and a lot of interesting decisions to be made. The combination of those two factors led me to do first *Railroad Tycoon* and then *Civilization* after that, as kind of a series of strategy games.

I find it dangerous to think in terms of genre first and then topic. Like, say, "I want to do a real-time strategy game. OK. What's a cool topic?" I think, for me at least, it's more interesting to say, "I want to do a game about railroads. OK, now what's the most interesting way to bring that to life? Is it in real-time, or is it turn-based, or is it first-person..." To first figure out what your topic is and then find interesting ways and an appropriate genre to bring it to life as opposed to coming the other way around and say, "OK, I want to do a first-person shooter, what hasn't been done yet?" If you approach it from a genre point of view, you're basically saying, "I'm trying to fit into a mold." And I think most of the really great games have not started from that point of view. They first started with the idea that, "Here's a really cool topic. And by the way it would probably work really well as a real-time strategy game with a little bit of this in it."

So when you come up with your ideas for new games, you start with the setting of the game instead of with a gameplay genre.

I think a good example of that is *Pirates!* The idea was to do a pirate game, and then it was, "OK, there's not really a genre out there that fits what I think is cool about pirates. The pirate movie, with the sailing, the sword fighting, the stopping in different towns and all

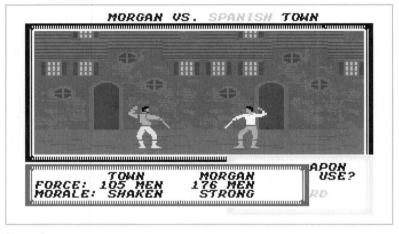

Pirates!

that kind of stuff, really doesn't fit into a genre." So we picked and chose different pieces of different things like a sailing sequence in real-time and a menu-based adventuring system for going into town, and then a sword fight in an action sequence. So we picked different styles for the different parts of the game as we thought they were appropriate, as opposed to saying, "We're going to do a game that's real-time, or turn-based, or first-person, or whatever" and then make the pirates idea fit into that.

I think it's interesting that *Pirates!* was designed with all those mini-games, but you haven't really used discrete sub-games so much since. Did you not like the way the mini-games came together?

Well, I think it worked pretty well in *Pirates!* It doesn't work for every situation. One of the rules of game design that I have learned over the years is that it's better to have one great game than two good games. And, unless you're careful, too many sub-games can lose the player. In other words, if you've got a good mini-game, then the player's going to get absorbed in that. And when they're done with that, they may well have lost the thread of what your story was or if any game is too engrossing it may disturb the flow of your story. Frankly, the mini-games in *Pirates!* were simple enough that you didn't lose track of where you were or what your objective was or what you were trying to do. But I wrote a game a couple of years later called *Covert Action* which had more intense mini-games. You'd go into a building, and you'd go from room to room, and you'd throw grenades and shoot people and open safes and all that kind of stuff and you'd spend probably ten minutes running through this building trying to find more clues and when you came out you'd say to yourself, "OK, what was the mission I was on, what was I trying to do here?" So that's an example for me of the wrong way to have mini-games inside of an overall story.

I've read that *Covert Action* was one of your personal favorites among the games you designed.

I enjoyed it but it had that particular problem where the individual mini-sequences were a little too involving and they took you away from the overall case. The idea was that there was this plot brewing and you had to go from city to city and from place to place finding these clues that

Covert Action

would tell you piece by piece what the overall plot was and find the people that were involved. I thought it was a neat idea, it was different. If I had it to do over again, I'd probably make a few changes. There was a code-breaking sequence, and circuit unscrambling, and there were some cool puzzles in it. I thought that overall there were a lot of neat ideas in it but the whole was probably not quite as good as the individual parts. I would probably do a couple of things differently now.

So *Covert Action* seems to have had similar origins as *Pirates!* You started with, "I want to do a covert espionage game..."

Right, what are the cool things about that. And unfortunately, the technology had gotten to the point where I could do each individual part in more detail and that for me detracted from the overall comprehensibility of the game.

In *Pirates!* and *Covert Action*, the player can see their character in the game, and the player is really role-playing a character. By contrast, in *Railroad Tycoon*,

Civilization, or *Gettysburg!*, the player does not really have a character to role-play. I'm curious about that shift in your game design, where the player used to be a specific character and now is more of a god-like figure.

It's good to be God. I think that's really a scale issue more than a specific game design choice. It's fun to see yourself, and even in a game like *Civilization* you see your palace, you do tend to see things about yourself. But the other thing is that a pirate looks cool, while a railroad baron doesn't look especially cool. Why go to the trouble to put him on the screen? I've never really thought too much about that, but I think it's probably more of a scale thing. If you're going through hundreds and thousands of years of time, and you're a semi-godlike character doing lots of different things, it's less interesting what you actually look like than if you're more of a really cool individual character.

So how did you first start working on *Railroad Tycoon*?

Well, it actually started as a model railroad game with none of the economic aspects and even more of the low-level running the trains. You would actually switch the switches and manipulate the signals in the original prototype. It kind of grew from that with a fair amount of inspiration from *1830*, an Avalon Hill board game designed by Bruce Shelley, who I

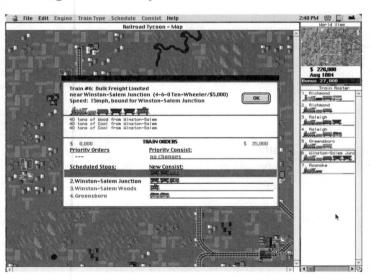

Railroad Tycoon

worked with on *Railroad Tycoon*. So, that inspired a lot of the economic side, the stock market aspects of the game. As we added that, we felt that we had too much range, too much in the game, that going all the way from flipping the switches to running the stock market was too much. We also wanted to have the march of technology with the newer engines over time, all the way up to the diesels. So there was just too much micro-management involved when you had to do all the low-level railroading things. So we bumped it up one level where all of the stuff that had to happen on a routine basis was done for you automatically in terms of switching and signaling. But if you wanted to, and you had an express or a special cargo or something, you could go in there and manipulate those if you really wanted to make sure that train got through on time, or a bridge was out and you had to stop the trains. But the origin of that was as a model railroading game and we added some of the more strategic elements over time.

It really was the inspiration for *Civilization* in a lot of ways, in terms of combining a couple of different, interesting systems that interacted continuously. The economic, the operational, the stock market, all interesting in their own right, but when they started to interact with each other was when the real magic started to happen. As opposed to *Pirates!* and *Covert Action,* where you had individual sub-games that monopolized the computer. When you were sword fighting, nothing else was going on. Here you had sub-games that were going on simultaneously and interacting with each other and we really thought that worked well both in *Railroad Tycoon* and later in *Civilization,* where we had military, political, and economic considerations all happening at the same time.

So in a way, you are still using sub-games; they just happen to all be in play all the time.

It's not episodic in the way that *Pirates!* was. Whenever you're making a decision you're really considering all of those aspects at the same time. That's part of what makes *Civilization* interesting. You've got these fairly simple individual systems; the military system, the economic system, the production system are all pretty easy to understand on their own. But once you start trading them off against each other, it becomes more complex: "I've got an opportunity to build something here. My military really needs another chariot, but the people are demanding a temple..." So these things are always in play and I think that makes the game really interesting.

In *Railroad Tycoon* you've got a very interesting economic simulation going, but at the same time the player has the fun of constructing a railroad, much as a child would. Do you think that contributed to the game's success?

It actually started there. And it was really the first game that I had done where you had this dramatic, dramatic change from the state at the beginning of the game to the state at the end of the game. Where, at the beginning of the game you had essentially nothing, or two stations and a little piece of track, and by the end of the game you could look at this massive spiderweb of trains and say, "I did that." And, again, that was a concept that we carried forward to *Civilization,* the idea that you would start with this single settler and a little bit of land that you knew about and by the end of the game you had created this massive story about the evolution of civilization and you could look back and say, "That was me, I did that." The state of the game changed so dramatically from the beginning to the end, there was such a sense of having gotten somewhere. As opposed to a game like *Pirates!* or all the games before that where you had gotten a score or had done something, but there was not this real sense that the world was completely different. I think that owes a lot to *SimCity*, probably, as the first game that really did a good job of creating that feeling.

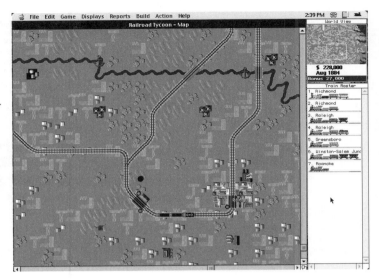

Railroad Tycoon

Were you at all inspired by the Avalon Hill board game *Civilization* when you made your computer version?

We did play it, I was familiar with it, but it was really less of an inspiration than, for example, *Empire* or *SimCity*. Primarily, I think, because of the limitations of board games. There were some neat ideas in there, but a lot of the cool things in *Civ.*, the exploration, the simultaneous operation of these different systems, are very difficult to do in a board game. So there were some neat ideas in the game, and we liked the name. [laughter] But in terms of actual ideas they were probably more from other sources than the *Civilization* board game.

A lot of your games seem to be inspired in part from board games. But, as you just said, *Civilization* would never really work as a board game. How do you take an idea that you liked in a board game and transfer it into something that really is a computer game instead of just a straight translation?

Before there were computers, I played a lot of board games and I was into Avalon Hill games, et cetera. I think they provided a lot of seed ideas for games. Often they are a good model of what's important, what's interesting, and what's not about a topic. But once you get into mechanics and interface and those kind of things, really there starts to be a pretty significant difference between board games and computer games. There's a lot of interesting research material sometimes in board games. Often they're interesting for "we need some technologies" or "we need to think about which units," et cetera. There's that kind of overlap in terms of the basic playing pieces sometimes. But how they are used and so forth, those things are pretty different between board games and computer games. I would say board games provide an interesting review of topics that are available and topics that are interesting. But once it gets into the actual game itself there is a wide difference between computer games and board games, in my mind.

One of the most remarkable things about *Civilization* is its addictive quality. I was wondering if that came about by luck, or if you planned it from the start.

We didn't really envision that. We intend for all of our games to be fun to play and hope that they are addictive to some degree. But *Civilization* had a magic addictiveness that we really didn't design, that we really didn't anticipate. I think any game where everything falls together in a really neat way is going to have that quality. I

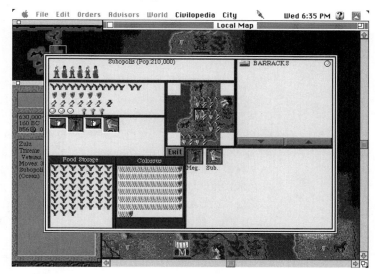

Civilization

think that it's really a result of how well the pieces fit together and how I think we picked a good scale, a good complexity level, a good number of things to do. I think we made some wise decisions in designing that game. And the sum of all those decisions is addictiveness. And I think that it was a good topic. A lot of things were right about that game, and that all came together to create this addictive quality. It was not something that we designed in, but it was something that we were kind of aware of. About halfway through the process we realized that, wow, this game really is a lot of fun to play. It was a pleasant discovery for us.

So you don't have any advice for how other designers can try to achieve that addictiveness in their own games?

I think in hindsight we know, or we think we know, why the game is addictive, or have our theories. One thing is what we call "interesting decisions." To us that means you are presented with a stream of decision points where the decisions are not so complex that you are basically randomly choosing from a list of options. A too-complex decision is one where you say, "Oh, I've got these three options. Yeah, I could spend five minutes analyzing the situation, but I really want to get on with the game so I'm going to pick B because it looks good." And on the other extreme there's the too-simple decisions: "It's obvious that I must choose A, because it is clearly better than all of the other options." In *Civ.* we try to present you choices where they are easy enough to understand, but in a certain situation you might choose A, in a slightly different situation B is a good choice, in another situation C is a good choice. So you're really saying, "Here are the three technologies that I can go for next." And you say to yourself, "Well, right now I'm about to get into a conflict with those no-good Romans. So I really need that technology that gives me the next cool military unit. But, well, that map-making looks kind of interesting. Next time I might take that because I want to do some exploring." So if you can create decisions where the player is always saying, "Next time, I'm going to try that one, because that looks interesting too," that creates this whole idea that there's this richness there that you're only scratching the surface of this time.

The addictive quality, I think, also falls out of the fact that you've got multiple things happening or in process at the same time. On the one hand you've got your next technology churning away over there. Your scientists are working on that. And this city is making that first tank that you're looking forward to. Over here is a unit wandering around to the next continent, and pretty soon he'll find something interesting. You've got different things that you are looking forward to in the game, and there's never a time when those are all done. There's never a reset state. There's always two or three things happening in the game that you are looking forward to when they finish. So there's never actually a good time to stop playing. I think that really helps the "you can never stop playing the game" phenomenon.

I know *Gettysburg!* was not your first real-time game, but it seems to have been in part inspired by the big hit RTS games like *Command & Conquer* and *WarCraft.*

I think the technology had gotten to the point where you could have a whole bunch of little guys running around doing stuff on the screen in real-time. And what you call "real-time," it's kind of a weird term because we've done real-time games forever, but we didn't think of them as real-time because it just seemed a natural

Gettysburg!

thing. But I guess when turn-based got to be its own genre, we had to make a distinction. I think *Gettysburg!* is a game that I wanted to do for a long time, but the technology didn't really lend itself to being able to do it until fairly recently. We finally got to the point where we could have a bunch of guys marching around the screen on a realistic-looking battlefield, loading their muskets, shooting and wheeling in different formations, and doing all that sort of stuff that I had visualized as what was cool about a Civil War battle. The time came along when that was doable.

It seems like it takes what *WarCraft* and the other, simpler RTS games did well, but then adds a deeper level of simulation, where you have flanking bonuses and other more traditional wargame features. Was it your goal to take a more complex wargame and merge it with the fast-paced RTS format?

Again, the idea was to do a Gettysburg battle game, and then the genre of "real-time" made the most sense. I'd always had a feeling in playing any other board game that something was missing. The sense that I get from reading the histories, the stories of the battles, is not captured in a board game or in any of the games I had played about Gettysburg. The time pressure, the sense of confusion, the sense of these different formations, et cetera, didn't make any sense until you actually had to make the decisions yourself. And then all of sudden you realize, "Boy, it wasn't quite that easy to do that obvious maneuver that would have won the battle if only they had tried it," or "Now I understand why they lined up in these formations that seemed pretty stupid to me before." A lot of things started to make sense when the battle came to life. And that was the idea, to include enough Civil War tactics like flanking, morale, and things like that to really capture the flavor of a Civil War battle without overwhelming the player with hard-core wargaming concepts. By representing the key factors that influenced the battle or that influenced tactics, you could naturally learn how to be a commander. You wouldn't have to follow a set of rules, but you would realize that, "Oh, if I give these guys some support they're going to be better soldiers, and if I can come in on the flank then that's a better attack." And you go through a learning process as opposed to being told how to be a good general. You learn that along the way. That was the intention.

I was wondering about the "click-and-drag" method you had the player use for directing his troops somewhere. It's very different from what other RTS games employ. Did you use it because you thought it was a better system, even though it was not the standard?

I'm not sure I'd do that the same way today. I think that click-and-drag made a certain amount of sense, especially since as you dragged we were showing with the arrow interesting things about the path that you would take. I'm also a big fan of standard interfaces, so if I had that to do today, I probably would try to go with more of the standard RTS interface. I think at the time that we were doing that, it was pretty early. *WarCraft* was out, but I don't think *StarCraft* was out, and *Age of Empires* came out at just about the same time. So the interface standard had not coalesced when we did that. I think that in recognition of that we gave the player the option to use the right-click/left-click way of doing things too. But if I had that to do today, I would probably make the standard RTS method the default and make the click-and-drag the option.

As opposed to *Railroad Tycoon* or *Civilization*, *Gettysburg!* has discrete scenarios: you play for a while and then that battle ends, you get a new briefing, and your troops reset. Why did you opt for that style of gameplay progression?

Well, I did that because the stupid battle of Gettysburg had too many units! [laughter] I would have preferred a complete battle at the kind of level that the actual game turned out to be. Basically, to make the game fun, I have found that you need to have somewhere between ten and twenty-five discrete units that you can move around. Unfor-

Gettysburg!

tunately the entire battle had seventy or eighty regiments, so it would have been totally out of control. We tried for a while actually fudging the scale, and saying, "You'll actually be given brigades but they'll act like regiments and then you can fight the whole battle." But it didn't feel right skewing the scale in that way. So, we got to the point where it was, "OK, the most fun and most interesting battles are of this scale. And that really means that it's a portion of the battle. And we have to accept that, and live with that, and make the best of that." And I think the scenario system was an attempt to do that.

I think that in an ideal world I could have picked the Battle of Hunter's Run or something where there were only three brigades and it was all capturable in a single scenario. But nobody's going to buy *The Battle of Hunter's Run*, they all want *Gettysburg!* So it's an unfortunate part of history that it happened to be such a large battle. And, I think it worked fairly well. But I understand when people say, "Well, I really want the whole battle." And we tried to give them that, and show them that they really didn't want that in this system. It was a case where history and reality didn't create probably the ideal situation for the game system that we had. But it was our feeling that, as opposed to either giving you the whole battle and over-whelming you with eighty units, or trying to play some pretty convoluted games to get the whole battle into that scale, we thought that the scenario system was the best compromise in trying to make it playable but also historically realistic. And I think there are some cool scenarios in there. It probably skews it a little more toward the hard-core, Civil War interested person but they can't all be *Civilization*.

So you are still working on your dinosaur-themed game. What are your goals with that project?

Well, the goal of the game is really the same as all the games that I've worked on: to figure out what is the really cool part, the unique part, the interesting part of this topic, and find a way to turn that into a computer game. I've thought that dino-saurs were cool for the longest time, and I think it's a topic that needs to be computer-motized. I try to take the approach of putting into the game a lot of things that are scientifically true or historically accurate, but that's not to be educational, it's to let the player use their own knowledge in playing the game. Most people know something about dinosaurs, or something about history, and if they can apply that knowledge to the game, then that makes it a lot more interesting and makes them feel good about themselves. It's not because they read the manual that they're good at the game, it's because of what they know. They realize that it's cool to have gunpowder and the wheel and things like that.

So in the same sense, people know that the *T. rex* is the baddest dinosaur. So we use things in the game to make it valuable to know some basic facts about whatever the topic is. We try and put that amount of realism and accuracy into the game. And then make it fun on top of that. In the same way that a movie gives you all the fun and the action sequences and all the important parts of a story and then jumps quickly over the boring things. I think the game has the same responsibility, to bring you to the key decision points and then move you on to the next interesting thing. We're trying to take that same approach with the dinosaur game, to bring them to life, to figure out what's cool and unique about them while cutting out all the dull parts. We're really in a "working that out" phase, and we don't have a lot to say about the specifics of that; hopefully in another few months we'll be able to talk a little bit more about how that's going to turn out.

Relatively speaking, you've been making computer games for a long time, since the early '80s. I was wondering how you thought the industry has changed over that time?

I think there's been a general, overall improvement in the quality of the games. I think there are some great games out there right now. I like *StarCraft*, *Age of Empires*, *Diablo*, *The Sims* I thought was really interesting, and *RollerCoaster Tycoon* was a hoot, a lot of fun. So I think those games compare very favorably to anything that's been done. I think they're overall better games than we were doing five or ten years ago. I think you can certainly see the improvement in presentation, graphics, video, and all that kind of stuff. The core of the games, the game design stuff, I think is a pretty slow evolutionary process. I think in terms of game design, games like *Pirates!* and *SimCity* and *Civilization* really stand up. I think they're really pretty strong designs, even today. I think they haven't been eclipsed by what's going on now. So I think that in terms of game design, the rule that says that things get twice as good every year, processors get twice as fast, et cetera, I don't think that applies. I think game design is a pretty gradual, evolutionary process, where we build on what's gone on before, and make it a little bit better, a little bit more interesting. Every so often a new genre comes along to open our eyes to some new possibilities. I think that will continue, but it's interesting to me that a three-year-old computer is completely obsolete, but a three-year-old game can still be a lot of fun.

As long as you can get it to run...

Right, as long as you have that three-year-old computer to run it on. There's a different pace, I think. Technology moves at one pace, a very quick pace, and game design evolution moves at a much slower pace.

Do you think that game design evolution has slowed since the early days of the industry?

I don't see a significant change. I think one phenomenon is that we only remember the good games from the past. The past seems like it had all sorts of great games, and the present seems like it has a few great games and a lot of crap. And I think there was a lot of crap in those days too, it has just all faded away. I think there is a lot of great game design work going on today. Before there was a lot more unexplored territory, and that gave us the opportunity to be a little more innovative. But with online technology and things like that, that opens up a lot of new areas for being innovative. So I don't see a substantial difference between the amount of good work being done today versus what was going on years ago.

You have worked at both small development studios, Microprose in the early days and Firaxis, as well as a big one, latter-day Microprose. Do you find that one environment is better at fostering the creation of good games?

I'm personally much more comfortable in the small environment. That may be more of a personal feeling than any kind of a rule about where good games happen. I think the trend certainly has been to bigger groups, bigger teams, bigger bigger bigger. And that may be just the way things are. If there's anything that makes me feel a little bit old it is the fact that I'm not as comfortable in the big group environment as clearly some of the other developers. I think some of the younger developers who grew up in that mode are much more comfortable with the big projects. I was in Los Angles for the E3 show, and the winner of the Hall of Fame award was Hironobu Sakaguchi who designed *Final Fantasy*, which is a massive, massive, massive game. It would totally frighten me to tackle something that big. But there are designers who just thrive on that. I think it's a personal preference for designers, and I think since I started in the time when there was no such thing as a gigantic team that I am comfortable in that smaller mode, while other designers prefer the larger projects. Primarily it's a personal preference.

Since you started in game development, development teams have grown from one or two people to a standard number of twenty or more. Do you think that has made games less personal?

I think it did, but there are still games today that have that personal touch. And I think those are the good games. I think that a lot of the games that are not so much fun are those that have this "designed by committee, programmed by a horde" feeling to them. And, yeah they look good, and they are kind of reminiscent of maybe one or two other games that were good. But they don't have that personal spark. To me, *RollerCoaster Tycoon* is a good example of a personal game. It really feels like somebody thought that was cool. Nobody said, "That's goofy" or "That's stupid." A lot of the ideas there are very clever, but if you brought it up before a committee they would say, "Oh really, won't people think that's silly?" And even *Final Fantasy*, in spite of its massive team, is really the product of one person's vision. And if you can keep that going in a big team, that's great. But I think that it becomes harder and harder the larger the team is to keep that personal vision alive and not get watered down by the committee approach.

You still serve as both lead programmer and lead designer on your projects. Are you happiest filling both roles?

I cannot imagine working in another way. It's just much more efficient for me to have an idea and just type it into the computer than to try to explain it to somebody else and see what happens. So, again, it's my personal style, but to me it's the most efficient way to get something done.

On most modern projects at other companies, you have one person who's the lead designer, and one person who's the lead programmer, and they're both very busy. It would appear that performing both roles you would be completely overwhelmed.

Well, I think they probably spend half their time talking to each other, which is something I don't have to do. I would see a certain efficiency in cutting out all those meetings. But certainly it works both ways. Either way can work, but my personal preference is for the designer/programmer approach.

Now that you are working on a larger team, how do you communicate your game design vision to the rest of the team and get them excited about the project?

Our primary tool is the prototype. In our development, one of the advantages of being a programmer/designer is that, within a week or two we can throw together something that feels like a game. That gives people the idea of what the game is going to be about, how it's going to work, the general parameters of it. Again, if we're working on a historical or scientific topic most people are half-way into it already, they know something about the topic. And then just talking, saying here's the kind of game I want to do, and here are the three or four really cool things that are going to happen in the game that are going to be the payoffs. Putting those things together I think gives people a pretty good idea of what direction we're headed. At that point you want people not to get the whole picture, but to figure out where they fit in and can contribute their own things that hopefully you hadn't even thought of, in terms of cool art or cool sounds or neat ideas. In a way you don't want it to be so complete that it feels done, because you want people to feel that they can make their own contributions above and beyond what you've already thought of.

So if someone else comes up with some cool ideas to add to your game design, you're happy to incorporate those even though you didn't come up with them.

I'm happy to steal those and claim they were my ideas years later. [laughter]

With your prototyping system, do you ever try out a game and then it just doesn't work out as you had hoped?

Yup, I have a whole group of directories on my hard drive that fall into that category. And many of the games that turned out to be products started in a very different direction. *Civilization*, for example, was originally much more like *SimCity*, much more zone this territory for farms, and place a city here and watch it grow. Initially it was much more of a stand back and watch it evolve approach; it only became turn-based after a couple of months. I mentioned that *Railroad Tycoon* started out as a model railroading game. A lot of times the prototypes will have to be radically modified to work. That's the whole idea of the prototype: to pretty quickly give you an idea of does the idea work, does it not work, and what are the major problems. It lets you focus on the big issues first, and hopefully straighten those out.

Your games seem very easy to pick up and learn to play. But at the same time they have very deep, interesting gameplay. How do you manage to accomplish both?

Civilization

The easy-to-play part is pretty well understood. I think interface conventions, and again getting back to the idea of a familiar topic helps people to get right into it because they know a little bit of what they should be doing. You want to give the players a lot of positive feedback early in the game to give them the idea they're on the right track. In *Civilization*, pretty quickly the people add something to your palace, and you get a population milestone, and your first city is formed. You want to give the players, especially in the early stages, the idea that they're on the right track, that everything they do, the computer acknowledges it, recognizes it, and thinks it's really cool. That gets the players into the game.

In terms of the depth, that's really because we play the games. The other advantage of prototyping is that if you have a game that takes two years to write, you spend one year and eleven months playing the game. You get pretty bored with the beginning of the game after a while. In one sense you are putting that depth in the game to keep yourself interested in writing this game. If there's twenty or forty hours of gameplay in a scenario, it's because we have played those scenarios for twenty or forty hours and found that, after about twenty hours, it gets a little thin. We have to come in with a new thing and make this problem a little more interesting, a little more complex at that point. So a lot of the depth comes out of the fact that we have intensively played the game for long periods of time.

Do you find that prototyping facilitates balancing as well?

Playing the prototype really facilitates balancing. It also really helps with writing the AI if you've played the game enough so that you really understand what are good strategies, bad strategies, and interesting strategies. Having played the game quite a bit helps to write the AI, it's good for the depth. The danger is that you lose sight of the beginning player. That's why we go back to playtesting at the end of the game's development. And we say, "Here's what we think the game is, try and play it." And we invariably find that they can't play it. There's just too much of that cool stuff in there. So we say, "All right, where are you getting stuck?" We're essentially unable to see the game in that light anymore. But you need to have both the depth and the ease of entry. Those are both important.

Your games all are grounded in history or real-life events, as opposed to many games which have fantasy or science fiction settings. Is this because you enjoy creating a game-world that the player is already somewhat familiar with?

I do think that's important. It does add a lot when you can apply your own knowledge to a game. I think that makes you feel better about yourself, and I think that's a positive thing. I think it also gives me a lot more to work with in terms of a historical or realistic situation. I probably grew up in a time also when there was less of the Middle Earth, the fantasy, the *Star Wars*, et cetera. Kids these days think these things are just as real as history. Space ships, magicians, and wizards are as real to a lot of kids as airplanes, submarines, and things like that. It's kind of an evolutionary thing, but in my growing up it was things like airplanes, submarines, the Civil War, and the Roman Empire that were interesting and cool things, and I try to translate those things into games.

I am curious about how you balance historical realism with the gameplay. *Gettysburg!* seems to be one case where you had to break the gameplay up into scenarios to keep it both historically accurate and fun.

That was one of the few times that we actually gave in to historical reality. In general our rule is if you come to a conflict between fun and history, you go with the fun. You can justify any game decision somewhere in history. Our decisions are made almost exclusively to the benefit, hopefully, of the gameplay as opposed to the historical accuracy. In *Gettysburg!* we came to a situation that we could just not fudge, though we tried. We tried as hard as we could to fudge that situation. In many other situations we come to an idea that we think is going to work well for the game and then we find the historical precedent or an explanation historically to justify it. In no sense do we try and stay slavishly accurate because, basically, we're trying to create a situation which is fluid where you're not just going down the path of history, you're creating your own history. Even though the pieces are realistic, you can take them off in a completely different direction that never really happened.

Certainly, part of the fun of *Civilization* is that the Zulus can take over the world, or the Mongols. Anybody can take over the world; it's not necessarily the Americans who are going to win in the end. We're not slaves to history.

Gettysburg!

At least since your days developing flight simulators, your games have not really been on the cutting edge of technology in terms of graphics. Was that a conscious decision on your part?

As I have said, in our prototyping process, things change almost up until the last minute. Most of the cutting-edge technologies are things that need to be researched from day one, and are gigantic investments in technology. And given that we're in a mode where things are changing constantly, it's practically impossible to merge those two approaches. The research project can't start really unless you know exactly what you want, or pretty much what you want. And we don't usually know that at the beginning. And we're not willing to put ourselves in that straightjacket in terms of game design. And I think a lot of times that's what it is. If you are committed to a first-person 3D viewpoint where you can see a certain amount, and you find out that to make your game fun you really need to see more, you really need to get more context for your location or whatever, you're kind of screwed at that point.

Often there's a conflict also between the functionality of the graphics and the loveliness of the graphics. A game that looks good but doesn't give you the information you need to play or doesn't give you the clarity, I think that's the wrong trade-off. We try and make games that we think look good. But in any good game the great graphics are happening in your imagination and not on the screen. If we tell you that the people have declared "we love the king day" in a certain town, if you're really into the game, that's a lot more meaningful, and you create a much more exciting image in your mind than anything we could show you on the screen. And vice versa, if you're not into the game, then anything that comes on the screen you're going to pick apart anyway. Our goal is to involve you in the game itself and have you create your own really cool mental images based on some suggestions that we give you on the screen.

You were one of the first game designers to get your name above the title on the box. I was curious how that came about.

Well, the way that happened goes back to *Pirates!* That was the first game that had my name on it. In those days I was working at Microprose and my partner was Bill Stealey who did the business/marketing side of things while I did the development/creative stuff. And the previous

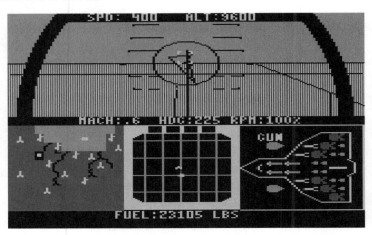

F-15 Strike Eagle

game before *Pirates!* was one of the flight simulator games, and I said to Bill, "Well, I'm going to work on this game about pirates." And he said, "Pirates? Wait a minute, there are no airplanes in pirates. Wait a minute, you can't do that." "Well, I think it's going to be a cool game." And he answered, "Well, who's going to buy a pirates game? Maybe if we put your name on it, they'll know that they liked *F-15* or whatever, and they might give it a try, OK." There was a real concern that there was this pirates game coming out, but nobody's going to be interested, because who wants a pirates game? People want flight simulators. So it was to say, "Sure, you want a flight simulator, but maybe you might want to try this pirates game because it was written by the guy who wrote that flight simulator that you're playing." I guess it was branding in a very crude, early form. It was because we were making this big switch in the type of game that I was working on, and to try to keep that connection between the games.

So it wasn't your lust for fame?

[laughter] No, no. Even today, fame is not a computer game thing. I think it's good. It's still a pretty non-personality oriented business. I think that people remember great games, and they know to a certain extent who's involved. But there's not a cult of Robin Williams or, you know, movie stars who really have a cult of personality. I think it's good. Once we get the idea that we can get away with anything just because we're who we are, that's not a good thing.

But that sort of confidence led to *Pirates!*, didn't it?

[laughter] Well, it was a good game. Had it not been a good game, that strategy would not have worked.

A lot of your games have had sequels of one kind or another, but you have never been the lead designer on one of them. Why is this?

I think they are a fine thing to do in general, especially if they're done well. I seldom go back to a topic primarily because I haven't run out of ideas yet, so I'd rather do a dinosaur game than go back to an older title. I don't have a lot of energy to get too involved in the sequels. Some of them turn out well, some of them turn out not quite so well. As opposed to letting the topic fade away, I think doing a sequel is often a good idea. In an ideal world, I'd like to be involved in everything, but I can't really do that. So I tend to be more interested in being involved in a new product as opposed to a sequel. It's certainly gratifying that people want another *Railroad Tycoon* or *Civilization*, et cetera, I think that's great. I'm happy that it can be done. On *Civilization III*, since it's being done inside of Firaxis, I'm able to take a more direct part in that, which I think is good. I would have liked to have done *Railroad Tycoon II* and do a new *Pirates!*, et cetera, if I had an infinite amount of time. But it's just not feasible.

I hear a lot of people talking about storytelling in games. Usually by storytelling they mean using cut-scenes or branching dialog trees or devices like that. Your games have never been very concerned with that side of storytelling.

To me, a game of *Civilization* is an epic story. I think the kind of stories I'm interested in are all about the player and not so much about the designer. There are players that are more comfortable in situations where they're making small decisions and the designer's making the big decisions. But I think games are more interesting when the player makes the big

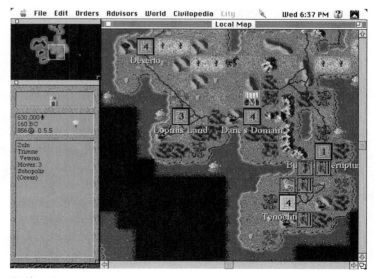

Civilization

decisions and the designer makes the small decisions. I think, in some sense, games are all about telling stories. They have a story created more by the player and less by the designer, in my mind. I think in *Civilization* there are fantastic stories in every game, they're just not in the more traditional sense of a story. We have, amongst our rules of game design, the three categories of games. There are games where the designer's having all the fun, games where the computer is having all the fun, and games where the player is having all the fun. And we think we ought to write games where the player is having all the fun. And I think a story can tend to get to the point where the designer is having all the fun or at least having a lot of the fun, and the player is left to tidy up a few decisions along the way, but is really being taken for a ride. And that's not necessarily bad, but our philosophy is to try to give the player as much of the decision making as possible.

Though *Gettysburg!* had a multi-player option, by and large your games have been single-player only for a long time. What do you think of the emerging popularity of multi-player gaming?

I think down the road I would like to get more into multi-player, perhaps even a game that is primarily multi-player. But I still enjoy essentially single-player games, so I'm not sure exactly when or how that's going to happen. Online multi-player gaming is probably the only revolutionary development in our technology we've seen since I started writing computer games. Everything else has been pretty much evolutionary. Better graphics, better speed, more memory, et cetera. But the multi-player online thing was a revolutionary change in the tools that we had to make games. I'm interested in doing something along those lines, but I'm not sure what it would be right now.

In an old *Next Generation* magazine interview, you said, "Games are going to take over the world. It's going to take a while, but there's something inherently more engaging about computer games than any other form of entertainment." Board games have certainly been around a long time, but have not yet taken over the world. I wondered what it is about computer games that you find so compelling.

Yeah, I think I stand by that statement. I think that it's the element of interactivity that makes them unique. They interact personally with you as a player, as opposed to movies, television, or music, which don't. There's this phenomenon of watching television and using the remote control to desperately try to make it an interactive experience, going from one channel to another... [laughter] But the interactivity of computer games is what differentiates it and makes it so very powerful. Now, we're still learning how to use that tool and in a lot of other ways we're not as good as television, movies, et cetera. But I think that as we learn to use the advantages that we have, they're more powerful advantages than the advantages of other entertainment media.

I think that board games are kind of interactive, but they require other players. The computer brings a lot of power to the equation that board games don't take advantage of. If anything, the advent of the Internet and multi-player play, that combined with interactivity seems to me like a really powerful combination. I think as we learn to use that element of our technology too, games can be very very compelling. The question that pops up is do people want games that are that interesting to play? There was the whole *Deer Hunter* phenomenon, and there was *Slingo* and things like that and I'm still working to integrate that into my model of the world, and I haven't totally succeed in doing that. But what that tells me is that there's a broader range of potential gamers than I am really familiar with. And part of our learning process is going to be to integrate them into the way that we design games and the way that we create games. But I still think we're going to take over the world.

Sid Meier Gameography

Hellcat Ace, 1982
NATO Commander, 1983
Spitfire Ace, 1984
Solo Flight, 1984
F-15 Strike Eagle, 1985
Decision in the Desert, 1985
Conflict in Vietnam, 1985
Crusade in Europe, 1985
Silent Service, 1986
Gunship, 1986
Pirates!, 1987
F-19 Stealth Fighter, 1988
Railroad Tycoon, 1990
Covert Action, 1990
Civilization, 1991
Colonization, 1994 (Consultant)
Civilization II, 1996 (Consultant)
Gettysburg!, 1997
Alpha Centauri, 1999 (Consultant)

Chapter 3:
Brainstorming a Game Idea: Gameplay, Technology, and Story

"You know what's the number one dumbest question I get asked when I'm out at some great university lecturing? I'm always asked 'Where do you get your ideas?' For about forty years I've been yanking their chain when I answer 'Schenectady.' They stare at me, and I say, 'Yeah, Schenectady, in New York. There's this idea service, see, and every week I send 'em twenty-five bucks, and every week they send me a freshly picked six-pack of ideas.'"

— Harlan Ellison

Harlan Ellison might scoff at the idea of trying to explain where ideas come from. Certainly, if you are a novelist having trouble coming up with ideas, it may be time to wonder if you have chosen the right profession. Similarly, a good game designer, at any given moment, will be able to come up with no less than five solid ideas he would like to try to make into a computer game. There is no shortage of ideas in the gaming world. Aspiring game designers often think they can sell their idea to a development company. They seem to be under the impression that game developers are just sitting around waiting for a hot idea to come around so they can spend several million dollars to make it a reality. On the contrary, the challenge in game development is not coming up with a good idea, but in following through and being able to craft a compelling game around that idea. That's what the rest of this book endeavors to explore.

In the arena of computer game design, the process of coming up with a game idea that will work is complicated by a number of factors fiction authors do not need to worry about. In part this is because computer game ideas can come from three distinct, unrelated areas of the form: gameplay, technology, and story. These different origins are interconnected in interesting ways, with the origin of the game's idea limiting what one will be able to accomplish in the other areas. So when a game designer starts thinking about the game he is hoping to make—thinking about it in terms of gameplay, technology, or story—it is important that he consider how that initial idea will impact all aspects of the final game.

Starting Points

Perhaps a quick example is in order. Say a game designer feels the need to create a game based around the specific stories of Greek mythology. This would be starting from a story. Immediately this limits the type of gameplay she will be going for. Chances are a *Civilization*-style strategy game is out, since that sort of game really has nothing to do with the classical stories of Zeus, Heracles, Ares, and so on. A real-time strategy game is out of the question as well, since it is not good at telling stories involving only a few protagonists. A high-end flight simulator is probably not going to work either. She could, however, still pursue it through an action game, a role-playing game, or an adventure game. Similarly, the technology is limited. In order to tell the story of the Greek gods, she will need some way to communicate a lot of back-story information to the player. There will need to be technology in place that can allow this. Furthermore, if she chooses the technology to be employed by the game at this point, this will have still further impact on what type of gameplay will be possible. For example, choosing an isometric 2D engine will best lend itself to an RPG or an adventure game instead of an action game. If a 3D technology is to be used, in order to tell the story of Greek mythology properly it will need to support both indoor and outdoor environments, which immediately eliminates a lot of 3D game engines.

For each decision the designer makes about the game she is hoping to create, she needs to understand how that limits what the game will be. If the designer tries to fit a type of gameplay around an ill-suited engine the game will suffer in the end: trying to do a *Populous*-esque "god-sim" using a first-person, indoor *Quake*-style 3D engine is a big mistake. Just as if one tried to tell the story of the Greek gods through flight simulator gameplay, the game would simply fail to work. Herein lies the difficulty with many "high-concept" ideas, often the brainchildren of marketing specialists who want to capture disparate markets with one product. If the parts do not work together, it does not matter how many markets the concept covers: no gamers will be interested in playing the final game.

Starting with Gameplay

Starting with gameplay is one of the most common starting points for game development, especially for designer or management driven projects. Thinking about a style of gameplay is often the easiest core for someone to latch onto, especially if that gameplay is similar to an existing game. "It's a racing game!" "It's a flight simulator!" "It's a 3D action/adventure like *Super Mario 64*!" "It's a first-person shooter like *Doom*!" Often a game developer will have enjoyed a game in one of these genres and will want to apply his own spin to it. With a general idea for a game that is interesting to him, the designer will want to work out what his particular game is going to accomplish in terms of gameplay. What type of racing game will it be? What aspects of racing are we trying to capture for the player? With a more specific idea of what type of gameplay he wants to create, the designer should start thinking about how that will impact the technology the game will require and what sort of story, if any, the game will be able to have.

Depending on the type of gameplay you are hoping to create for the player, you need to analyze what sort of technology that undertaking will require. Does the game need a 3D engine, or will 2D be enough or even more appropriate? What sort of view will the player have of the game-world? Will it be fixed or dynamic? Does the action transpire fast and furious with a large number of entities moving around on the screen at once? Are the game-worlds large or small? All of these questions and many more need to be analyzed to understand what the game's engine must accomplish in order to properly execute the gameplay idea. Of course the technology you choose to employ for your gameplay must be one that will actually run on the target system, whether it be the PC, a console, or a custom-made arcade cabinet. You must also ask if the game's programming team is up to creating the required technology. Technological feasibility may end up limiting the scope of your gameplay. Even worse, will the engine team's existing technology work or will they need to scrap it and start from scratch? Is there enough budget and time to trash it and start over? If you find that you need to adapt your gameplay to match the engine, you really are not starting out with gameplay as the origin of your idea, but instead with technology, as I will discuss below. If you are starting out with a gaming engine that must be used, it is in your best interest to not fight that technology with incompatible gameplay. Instead you should try to think up your gameplay idea in terms of what is well suited to that engine.

The type of gameplay your game will employ similarly limits what type of story can be told. An RPG can tell a much more complex and involved story than an action/adventure game, and in turn an action/adventure can tell a more substantial story than an arcade shooter. Certain types of stories just will not fit with certain types of gameplay, such as the Greek mythology in a flight simulator example discussed previously. Similarly, a romantic story might not fit with a strategy game, and a tale about diplomacy would not fit so well with a fast-action first-person shooter. Since you made the choice to come up with your gameplay style first, you need to ask yourself what sort of story is best suited to that gameplay, and try to tell that tale. Sometimes a designer will have both a story he wants to tell and a type of gameplay he wants to explore, and will attempt to do both in the same game, even if the two do not go well together. Do not try to cobble an inappropriate story, either in terms of complexity or subject matter, around gameplay that is ill suited to that type of narrative. Save the story for a later date when you are working on a title with gameplay that will support that story better. And while your technology is limited by what your team is capable of accomplishing in the time allotted, the story is limited only by your own ability to tell it. You should pick the story best suited to your gameplay and go with it.

Starting with Technology

Going into a project with a large portion of the game's technology already developed is also a fairly common occurrence. If this is not the development team's first project together at a new company, then it is likely that there will be an existing technology base that the project is supposed to build from. Even if the project is to use a "new" engine, this often only means an older engine updated, and as a result, the style of game best suited to the engine will not change significantly. Even if an engine is being written from scratch for the project, it is likely that the lead programmer and her team are best equipped to create a certain type of engine, be it indoor or outdoor, real time or pre-rendered, 3D or 2D, with a complex physics system for movement or something more simple. The programmers may be interested in experimenting with certain special lighting or rendering effects, and will create an engine that excels at these objectives. The designer is then presented with this new technology and tasked with coming up with a game that will exploit the sophisticated technology to full effect.

Other times it is predetermined that the project will be using an engine licensed from some other source, either from another game developer or a technology-only company. Sometimes the project leaders have enough foresight to consider the type of game they want to make first and then pick an engine well suited to that. More often, the engine licensing deal that seems to deliver the most "bang for the buck" will be the one chosen. Then, with an engine choice decided, the team is tasked with creating a game and story that will fit together well using that technology.

Just as starting with a desired sort of gameplay dictated what type of engine should be created, starting with set technology requires that the game designer consider primarily gameplay that will work with that sort of technology. If the engine is 3D, the designer will need to create a game that takes place in a 3D world and uses that world to create interesting 3D gameplay. If the engine is only 2D, a first-person shooter is out of the question. If the engine has a sophisticated physics system, a game should be designed that makes use of the physics for puzzles and player movement. Of course, the designer does not need to use every piece of technology that a programmer feels compelled to create, but it is always better to have your gameplay work with the engine instead of fight against it. Usually when a project is using a licensed game engine, that technology will often have been created with a certain type of gameplay in mind. The designer needs to seriously consider how far he should deviate from that initial technology, for it is surely going to be easier to make the engine perform tasks for which it was intended instead of pushing it in directions its programmers never imagined. For instance, the oft-licensed *Quake* engine was created for handling an indoor, first-person perspective, fast-action game involving a lot of shooting. Though some teams that have licensed that engine have tried to push it in different directions, the most artistically successful licensee thus far, Valve, retained much of the standard *Quake* gameplay that the engine excelled at for their game *Half-Life*. Certainly Valve added a lot of their own work to the engine, technology that was necessary in order to do the type of game they wanted to do. But at the same time they did not try to do something foolish such as setting their game primarily outdoors or using only melee combat. When technology is handed to a game designer who is told to make a game out of it, it makes the most sense for the designer to embrace the limitations of that technology and turn them into strengths in his game.

The technology can also limit what sort of story can be told. Without a sophisticated language parser, it is going to be difficult to tell a story in which players need to communicate with characters by typing in questions. Without an engine that can handle outdoor environments reasonably well, it is going to be difficult to make a game about mountain climbing. Without robust artificial intelligence it is going to be hard to make a good game about diplomacy. Without

The designers of *Half-Life* smartly used the indoor first-person shooter gameplay established by *Quake*, the engine licensed for the game's creation. Pictured here: *Quake II*.

compression technology that can store and play back large sounds, it will be hard to have huge amounts of dialog and hence hard to have characters whose dialects are important to the story. Without the ability to have large numbers of moving units on the screen at once, it will be impossible to tell a story where the player must participate in epic, massive battles between armies. The game designer needs to consider how the story line will be communicated to the player through the engine that he must use. Trying to tell a story with an inadequate engine is just as likely to compromise the game as tying a particular story to inappropriate gameplay. Again using the example of *Half-Life* mentioned above, if the team at Valve had tried to set their game in Death Valley and involve the player battling gangs of twenty giant insects at once, the *Quake* engine would have ground to a halt and the game would have been miserable to play. In the Death Valley scenario, Valve might have been telling the story they wanted to, but no one would have cared since the game would have been miserably slow and looked horrendous. For the greater good of the game, the story and the technology must be compatible with each other.

Starting with Story

Finally, it is certainly possible that the brainstorming for your game may start with a setting you want to employ, a story you want to tell, or a set of characters you want to explore. This is probably a less common starting point than technology or gameplay. Indeed, since many games have no story whatsoever, the very concept of a game starting with a story may seem strange. At the same time it is not unheard of for a game designer to think of a story she wants to tell, and only then start exploring what sort of technology and gameplay will be best suited to communicating that story. Any good game designer who thinks up such a story will have a tendency to think of it in terms of how it would transpire in a game, how the player can interact with that story, and how the story may unfold in different ways depending on the player's actions in the game-world. So a designer may not be thinking solely of the story but also of the gameplay. But the story can be the jumping-off point, the central vision from which all other aspects of the game are determined.

Of course the type of story to be told will have a dramatic effect on the type of gameplay the project will need to have. If the designer wants to tell the story of a group of friends battling their way through a fantastical world full of hostile creatures, a first-person shooter with teammates might be appropriate. Any sort of story which involves the player talking to a large range of characters and going on "quests" for those characters might be addressed with more RPG-style mechanics. Telling the story of the battle of Waterloo could be perfectly addressed in a project with wargame-style strategic play, with the gameplay adjusted in order to best bring out the aspects of Waterloo with which the designer is primarily concerned. Does the designer want the player to have a general's eye view of the game? In that case gameplay that allows for the tracking of tactics and logistics should be used. Or does the designer want to tell the story more from the view of the soldiers who had to fight that battle? Then gameplay that would allow the player to track and manipulate her troops unit by unit would be appropriate. If conversations with non-player characters (NPCs) are an important part of communicating the story, the designer will need to design game mechanics that allow for such conversations, using typed-in sentences, branching dialog choices, or whatever will work best. The designer needs to find gameplay that will allow the player to experience the most important elements of whatever story she is trying to tell.

Of course, the technology will have to match up with the story as well, primarily in order to support the gameplay the designer decides is best suited to telling that story. If conversations are an important part of communicating the story, the programming team will need to be able to develop a conversation system. If world exploration and discovery are a big part of telling the story, perhaps a 3D engine is best suited to the gameplay, one that allows the player to look anywhere he wants with the game camera. The designer may find that specifically scripted events are important to communicating aspects of the tale; the player must be able to observe unique events that transpire at specific times in different parts of the world. In this case, the programmers will need to give the level designer the ability to set up these scenes. The technology is the medium of communication to the player, and thereby the story is directly limited by what the technology is capable of telling.

Good examples of story-centered game design are some of the adventure games created by Infocom and LucasArts. All of the adventure games from these

Maniac Mansion was the first of the story-centered adventure games from LucasArts to use the SCUMM system.

companies used very standardized play mechanics and technology. The game designers worked with the company's proprietary adventure game creation technology, either the Infocom text-adventure authoring tool or LucasArts' SCUMM system. By the time the game designer came on to the project, his process of creation started with creating a story he wanted to tell. Certainly the story had to be one that was well suited to the adventure game format and that could be implemented using the existing tool set. Both Infocom's and LucasArts' tools were general purpose enough to allow the designer to create a wide range of games, with a good amount of variation in terms of the storytelling possible, even though the core mechanics had to consist of a typing-centered text adventure in the case of Infocom and a point-and-click graphical adventure for LucasArts. The game designers' primary driving motivation in the game's creation was the telling of a story, with the designing of game mechanics and the developing of technology much less of a concern. Just as a film director is limited by what she can shoot with a camera and then project on a certain sized screen at 24 frames per second, the adventure game designers at Infocom and LucasArts were limited by the mechanics of the adventure game authoring system they were using. Since for both the film director and the adventure game designer the mechanics of the medium were firmly established well before they began their project, their primary concern became the telling of a story.

Working with Limitations

Experienced game designers already understand the limitations placed on the creation of games by the technology, gameplay, and story. When they take part in brainstorming sessions these game designers have a good gut-sense of how making certain choices about the game in question will limit its creation further down the road. For each decision that is made about the game, many doors are closed. When enough decisions about the nature of the game have been made, it may be that there is only one type of game that can possibly accomplish all that the designers want. The stage for making major decisions is over, and now all that lies ahead are the thousands of smaller implementation issues.

For three of the games I have completed, *Odyssey: The Legend of Nemesis*, *Damage Incorporated*, and *Centipede 3D*, I began development from a different starting point. Coincidentally, one game started with story, another with technology, and the third with gameplay. Throughout each game's development I made every effort to remember where the game was coming from and what it was hoping to accomplish. The origins and objectives limited everything else about the game, resulting in only one acceptable game that achieved the goals I had set.

Odyssey: The Legend of Nemesis

Odyssey started with a story. I actually inherited this project at a point where a significant part of the 2D technology and RPG game mechanics were in place. Some story existed but it was by no means complete, and I was not terribly excited by it. As my first game project that was actually likely to be published, I immediately set to work rewriting the story into something in which I was personally invested. For years I had been wanting to get into game development in order to tell interactive, non-linear stories, and so I immediately set to writing just such a story, wherein the player would be presented with moral choices beyond just "to kill or not to kill." I wanted to create a game in which the choices the players made would actually change the outcome of the story in a meaningful way. So I charged blindly forward, with the story as my only concern.

Fortunately, the technology and game mechanics that were in place by and large supported this story I wanted to tell. Where they did not, I changed the game mechanics as necessary. When NPC AI had to function in a certain way to support the story, I made the AI work that way. When forced conversations became required, where an NPC could walk up to the player and initiate a conversation with him instead of the other way around, I implemented the appropriate game mechanic. The levels were designed with no other goal than to support the story. Since the levels were not designed with exciting battles in mind, combat situations in the game were not as compelling as they could have been. I was not interested in

Levels in *Odyssey: The Legend of Nemesis* were designed around the game's story.

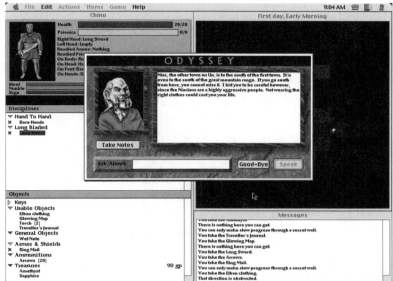

the combat so much as the story. The constant conflict with strange, marauding creatures was something people expected in an RPG and so it remained in, but I made combat such that it was very much secondary to exploring the story. This ended up turning the game into almost more of an adventure than an RPG, but that was fine with me, since it was what supported the story best.

Looking at it today, I can see that *Odyssey* has many flaws in it. But I do not think that these problems arose because it was a game whose development started with a story. This may be a rare way to begin game development, but it can still be a viable starting point. If I had possessed a better sense of game design at the time, I could have taken efforts to make the rest of the game as interesting as the story was, while never undermining or diminishing the impact of the game's epic tale.

Damage Incorporated

In the case of *Damage Incorporated*, the publisher, MacSoft, had obtained the license to a sophisticated (at the time) technology that they wanted to use for a game. It was the technology Bungie Software had created for use in *Marathon* and *Marathon 2*, two games of which I remain very fond. *Marathon 2*, in particular, remains one of the best first-person shooters ever made, easily holding its own against *Doom*. What *Marathon 2* lacked in fast-action battles and the atmosphere of menace that *Doom* created so well, it more than made up for with a compelling and complex story line, superior level design, and a good (though simple) physics model. As a result of my having enjoyed the *Marathon* games so much, I decided to make my game embrace the technology and gameplay that *Marathon* had established. I would craft my game around the technology that had been licensed and use that technology to the greatest effect I possibly could.

Damage Incorporated (pictured) had its origins in the licensed Marathon technology.

With a starting point of technology, I crafted gameplay and a story that could succeed using the *Marathon* technology. Of course, we added features to the gameplay and engine. The primary addition to the game mechanics was the player's ability to order teammates around the game-world, thereby adding a real-time strategy element to the mix. We added to the engine numerous enhancements which allowed for swinging doors, moving objects, and other effects necessary to create a game-world that more resembled the real-world. I was still concerned with story in the game, though not to as great an extent as I had been with *Odyssey*. Since having conversations with NPCs did not really fit in with *Marathon*'s game mechanics, I involved characters through the player's teammates, who would chatter amongst themselves as the player maneuvered them through the game-world.

One of the game's weaknesses was that at the start of the project I did not fully understand the limitations of the *Marathon* engine. It was best suited to creating indoor environments, so when it did create outdoor areas, they ended up looking fake, especially when they were supposed to represent real-life locations on Earth. Modeling the exterior of an alien world in the engine, as *Marathon 2* had done, was one thing, but creating environments that looked like the woods in Nebraska was another. Around half of the levels in *Damage Incorporated* are set outside, and none of these outdoor areas ended up looking very good. If I had understood the technology better, I could have designed the game to take place in more indoor environments, thereby better exploiting what the engine did well.

Interestingly, at the same time I was using the *Marathon 2* engine to create *Damage Incorporated*, MacSoft had another team using the same engine to create a game called *Prime Target*. The members of that team did not like *Marathon 2* as much as I did, and wanted to create more of a *Doom*-style shooter, with faster, simpler, more intense combat. Instead of starting with the technology and running with the type of gameplay it handled well, they started with a type of gameplay they wanted to achieve and modified the engine to better support that. As a result, the *Prime Target* team spent a much greater amount of time modifying the engine to suit their needs than we did. Because of this *Prime Target* became a significantly different game from either *Marathon 2* or *Damage Incorporated*. Not a better or worse game, merely different. The differences can be traced back to the origins of the idea for their game, and the way they approached using a licensed engine.

Centipede 3D

The *Centipede 3D* project was started when the publisher, Hasbro Interactive, approached the game's developer, Leaping Lizard Software, about using their *Raider* technology for a new version of *Centipede*. Hasbro had recently found success with their modernization of *Frogger*, and wanted to do the same for *Centipede*, the rights to which they had recently purchased. Producers at Hasbro had seen a preview for *Raider* in a magazine, and thought it might be well suited to the project. Hasbro had a very definite idea about the type of gameplay they wanted for *Centipede 3D:* game mechanics similar to the classic *Centipede* except in a 3D world. The team at Leaping Lizard agreed. At the time, not many new games were utilizing simple, elegant arcade-style gameplay, and adapting it to a 3D world would be a unique challenge.

For the development of *Centipede 3D*, the origin of the game's development lay in gameplay. Re-creating the feel of the original *Centipede* was at the forefront of everyone's minds throughout the project's development. When Hasbro set out to find a company with a technology capable of handling the game, they knew to look for an engine that could handle larger, more outdoor areas, because those were the type of locations a modernized *Centipede* would require. They knew not to go for a *Quake*-style technology in order to achieve the gameplay they wanted. Leaping Lizard's *Raider* engine was a good match with the gameplay, but not a perfect one. Much work was required to modify it to achieve the fast responsiveness of a classic arcade game. *Raider* employed a physics system which was by and large not needed by *Centipede 3D*, and so much of it was stripped out. Thus the technology was molded to fit the gameplay desired.

Centipede 3D's story was the simplest in any of the games I have worked on. In part this is because one of the traits of classic arcade games was their lack of involvement in any real storytelling. For games like *Centipede*, *Pac-Man*, and

The new, 3D version of *Centipede* was based on the classic "bug shooter" gameplay found in the original *Centipede*.

Space Invaders, setting was enough; all the games needed was a basic premise through which the gameplay could take place. Furthermore, everyone working on the *Centipede 3D* project had as their primary concern the gameplay, and story was simply less important. As we envisioned the game, it was the simple, addictive gameplay that would draw players into *Centipede 3D*, not the story. The classic arcade style of gameplay simply did not call for it. The primary effect of the meager story line was to provide a setup and to affect the look of the game, to explain why the player is flying around blasting centipedes and mushrooms, and why the game-worlds change in appearance every few levels. Just as the original *Centipede* used the setting of a garden and bugs to explain the game's gameplay, the new *Centipede 3D* used the story line only to support the gameplay. In the end, *Centipede 3D* was all about the gameplay.

Embrace Your Limitations

In many ways, developing a game is all about understanding your limitations and then turning those limitations into advantages. In this chapter I have discussed how the designer must understand where his game idea is coming from: gameplay, story, or technology. With this understanding, the designer must recognize how this limits the other attributes of the game—how a certain gameplay calls for a certain type of story and technology, how one story requires a specific technology and gameplay, and how technology will lend itself to specific types of games and stories. It is the designer's job to make all the pieces fit together, and to find the perfect parts to make a compelling game.

It is a very rare case indeed for a designer to be able to think of whatever game she wants and then search out the perfect implementation of that idea. In almost all cases, the designer is limited by the situation that is presented to her. The limitations may come in the form of the technology available, the team she has to work with, the budget available to develop the game, and the amount of time allowed for its creation. Though the producer is primarily responsible for making sure the game is on time and on budget, the designer must concern herself with all of the limitations she is faced with if she hopes to create a good game in the final analysis.

Established Technology

Often a designer at a larger company is required to work with whatever technology that company has. This may be an engine left over from a previous game, or it may be that the programming team only has experience working in 2D and as a result the only technology they will be able to viably develop in a reasonable time frame will be 2D as well. Even if the designer is fortunate enough to be able to seek out a technology to license for a project, that designer will still be limited by the quality of the engines that are available for licensing and the amount of money she has to spend.

If the developer is a lone wolf, working solo as both designer and programmer on a project, one might think the designer could make whatever he wants. Of course this is not the case, as the designer will quickly be limited by his own skills as a programmer and by the amount of work he can actually accomplish by himself. No single programmer is going to be able to create a fully featured 3D technology to rival the likes of *Quake III*, *IV*, or *XIII*. It is simply not possible. Functioning as the sole programmer and designer on a project has many benefits, but it certainly limits what one will be able to accomplish.

Even if a programmer is able to create the perfect engine for her game, what if it is simply too slow? If a large number of fully articulated characters in an outdoor real-time 3D environment are required for your gameplay, on today's technology the frame rate is going to be languid. Throw in some truly sophisticated AI for each of those creatures and your game will get down to 1 FPS, becoming, in essence, a slide show. If she must make that game, the designer has to wait until the processing power required is available, which may not be for years to come. Hearing that a project has been put on hold until the technology improves usually has the direct result of causing the publisher to stop making milestone payments.

The Case of the Many Mushrooms

When working on *Centipede 3D*, we were constantly troubled by our frame rate. Remember, for that game, our primary concern was to achieve gameplay which was in the spirit of the original arcade classic. But *Centipede*'s gameplay hinged on the presence of a lot of mushrooms on the screen at once, with similarly large numbers of other insects, arachnids, and arthropods flying around the world, threatening to destroy the player's little "shooter" ship. Furthermore, the gameplay necessitated a top-down view which provided a fairly large viewing area of the game-world, so that the player would be able to see the maneuverings of those deadly creatures. The end result was that there could be several hundred 24-polygon mushrooms, twelve 40-polygon centipede segments, and numerous other creatures all on the screen at once. On top of that, Hasbro wanted *Centipede 3D* to be a mass-market title, so the product's minimum system requirement had been predetermined to be a 133 MHz Pentium with no hardware graphics acceleration. On top of all that, *Centipede*'s fast-action gameplay required a similarly fast frame rate to be any fun at all.

While working on the project, we were constantly confronted with the problem of escalating polygon counts, with artists always attempting to shave a few polygons off of the much-used mushroom model. At one point, one artist suggested that perhaps if we could reduce the mushroom to two pyramids sitting on top of each other, we would have the absolute minimum representation of a mushroom, while using only six or eight polygons. Indeed, it was suggested, if all of the game's models went for a minimalist representation, we could use the polygon limitation to our advantage, creating a unique game-world filled with objects that looked as if they were created by a cubist. It would certainly be a unique look for a game, and would fit in quite well with *Centipede 3D*'s already somewhat surreal game-world. "Embrace your limitations!" I proclaimed in the midst of this discussion, not unlike a weary professor might finally proclaim, "Eureka!" All present thought my proclamation to be quite funny, but thinking about it later I decided it was actually quite true for game development. Unfortunately, we were too far along in development to convert all of our art to the minimalist implementation we had thought of, not to mention the potential troubles of trying to sell the publisher on the idea of a minimalist game.

In general, though, I still think that game developers need to embrace their limitations as soon as they discover them. When presented with an engine that must be used for a project, why go out of your way to design a game that is ill suited to that technology? Your game design may be fabulous and well thought out, but if the technology you must use is not capable of implementing it well, you will still be left with a bad game in the end. It is better to shelve an idea that is incompatible with your technology (you can always come back to it later) and come up with a design better suited to the tools you have. Once you have identified the limitations that the engine saddles you with, it is best to embrace those limitations instead of fighting them. This is not to suggest that a designer should always design the simplest game that she can think of or that sophisticated, experimental designs should not be attempted. If a shrewd theater director knows a given actor is interested in working with him, he will pick the best play to show off the particular skills of that actor. Similarly, a designer should consider what the technology lends itself to and use that as the basis for the game she designs and the story she sets out to tell.

The Time Allotted

Limitations that I have not discussed much in this chapter but which are nonetheless very important in game development are the budget and schedule with which a designer may be presented. Though these are primarily the concern and responsibility of the project's producer, the game designer needs to know how these factors will limit the project just as the technology, gameplay, or story may. When choosing the technology to be used, the designer must ask himself: can it be completed in the amount of time scheduled for the project? Can it be completed in time for level implementation and balancing? Does the suggested design call for the creation of such a large number of complex levels and heavily scripted behaviors that they cannot be completed in eighteen months by only one designer? Just as the timeline will limit the amount of time that can be spent on the project, the budget will affect how many people can be working on the project during that time. It may be that, given double the budget, the game design could be easily completed in a year and a half, but with only half the budget the designer will need to scale back the design to come up with something feasible. Again, if development is running six months late with no end in sight and as a result the publisher pulls the plug, it does not matter how brilliant your game design may have been in theory. No one will get to play your game because you failed to fully consider the logistics of implementing it. And if you fail to allocate enough time for fine-tuning and balancing the gameplay, your publisher may demand you ship a game you consider unfinished. What might have been a great game will be a bad one because there was not enough time to really finish it.

Lone wolf developers have it a bit easier in terms of time constraints and budgetary limitations. If a single person is creating all of the art, code, and design for the game, and is developing the game on her own time without relying on income from its development in order to survive, she is much more free to follow wherever her muse takes her, for as long as she likes. Of course, she is still limited by her own talents, by the quality of the art she can create, and by the limits of her programming skills, but at least these are the only limitations. In terms of creating art, there is a lot to be said for not being beholden to the person writing the checks.

If You Choose Not to Decide, You Still Have Made a Choice

So often producers, programmers, artists, and designers fail to consider the limitations of the game idea they are planning to develop. Whether it springs from notions of gameplay, suggestions of technology, or thoughts about a story, as soon as a game idea takes on form it begins limiting what the game can be if it is to be successful. Game developers need to understand that not every technology will work with every game design, nor every design with every story, nor even every story with every technology.

Often developers will try to take a bunch of compelling concepts and attempt to stuff them all into one game. The lead programmer may be interested in developing a cutting-edge inverse kinematics system. The lead game designer might have wanted to try a real-time strategy game ever since he played *Age of Empires* for the first time. The game's writer may think there's entirely too much violence in computer games and therefore wants to write a tale of romance. If the producer is a fool, she may even be thrilled that the members of her team are so excited about what they are developing and that, by combining IK, RTS, and romance, the result will be a breakthrough game.

Of course anyone with a whit of sense knows this game is doomed to fail. If, at the brainstorming session, the team were able to decide which aspect of the game they wanted to concentrate on, the team could work to make the game as a whole as good as possible. Suppose they choose the IK as what they all think would make for the best complete game. Then the designer can mull it over and realize a *Street Fighter II*-style fighting game would probably make the best use of an IK system. And the writer could come up with a story about a human fighting one by one through the pantheon of Greek gods, hoping one day to meet his true love, Hera. This game has a fighting chance of being fun to play, because all of the components are working together. In the end, you do not want your game to consist only of an excellent technology or a compelling story or a brilliant game design. If none of these components support each other your game will be just as bad as if you were working with a hackneyed story, a thin game design, and an incomplete technology.

Chapter 4:
Game Analysis: Centipede

Designed by Ed Logg with Donna Bailey
Released in 1981

ne can think of the classic arcade game as a form of the computer game, in the same way that a silent slapstick comedy is a form of film or the hard-boiled detective novel is a form of literature. The classic arcade game form fell out of favor with the commercial gaming companies pretty much as soon as the technology was available to move beyond it. However, many independent game developers still work on classic arcade games either for their own amusement or to be released as freeware or shareware titles. Many of these labors of love are imitations of established classic arcade games, but many others are interesting experiments in new gameplay. There remains something uniquely compelling about the form, and the fact that one does not need to have a sophisticated 3D engine to make a wonderfully entertaining classic arcade game helps to make the form an appealing one in which to work.

It bears mentioning that when I refer to the classic arcade game, I do not mean to imply that all classic arcade games are classics. Many of them are quite bad. As with any media, the old arcade games that are remembered and talked about decades after their release tend to be the best ones, thus creating the false impression of a "golden age." The bad arcade games have fallen between the cracks of history. The term "classic arcade game" refers to the form as a classic one, not to the games themselves, just as one might refer to "classical music." Surely the term "arcade game" is not limiting enough, since this would seem to include every game found in an arcade, including modern racing, gun, and fighting games, none of which are what I consider to be part of the form I am concerned with here.

The classic arcade game form had its commercial and creative heyday in the late 1970s through the early 1980s, when machines exhibiting the form lined the arcades. Looking at the games as a whole, one can come up with a series of traits that they all shared. Some of these aspects of the form may have been arrived at because of the commercial considerations of the arcades. The thought was to get a player to easily understand a game, so that by the end of his very first game he had a good sense of how the game worked and what was necessary for success. Second, a player's game, even the game of an expert, could not last very long, since any one player had only paid a quarter, and if the game only earned a single quarter in a half hour, it would not be profitable to operate. Players needed to be sucked in to replay the games, to keep plunking in quarters. As a result, in some ways the arcade games had to be more refined than home games are today. Once the player has purchased a home game, often for at least a hundred times the cost of a single arcade game play, the sale is completed. If he is not completely disgusted with the game he is unlikely to return it. Features such as scoring and high-score tables only served to increase the arcade game's addictive nature and encourage players to keep spending money.

In addition, the technical restrictions of the day limited what the games could do, and thereby influenced what the game could accomplish in terms of gameplay. Had the designers had the RAM and processing power to include fully scrolling game-worlds that were many times the size of the screen, they probably would have. If the games had been able to replay full-motion video of some sort, perhaps the designers would have incorporated more story line into the games. But the fact remains that a unique genre of computer games emerged, and if the commercial and technical limitations shaped the form, so be it. Just as early films had to work with the limitations of silence and short running times, computer game designers were limited in what they could create, and were able to come up with brilliant games nonetheless. Often, working within a series of strict constraints forces artists to focus their creativity in a fashion which leads to better work than if they could do anything they wanted.

Tempest is one of many classic arcade games that is centered on shooting at enemies which keep getting closer. *Tempest* is memorable because of the many unique twists included.

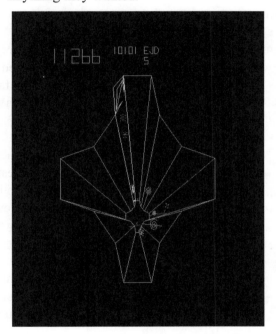

One key ingredient to many classic arcade games was their wild variation in gameplay styles. *Centipede*, *Missile Command*, *Pac-Man*, and *Frogger* are as different from each other as they possibly could be. Many classic arcade games featured variations on a theme: *Centipede*, *Space Invaders*, *Galaga*, and *Tempest* all revolved around the idea of shooting at a descending onslaught of enemies. However, the gameplay variations these games embraced are far more radical than the tiny amount of variation one will find in modern games, which are more content to endlessly clone already-proven gaming genres. Despite the wild variety of gameplay that can be found in classic arcade games, one can still look back on these games as a collective, as an artistic movement in the brief history of computer games. By analyzing the form's shared traits, modern game designers can learn a lot about how they can make their own games more compelling experiences for the player.

Classic Arcade Game Traits

- Single Screen Play: In a classic arcade game, the bulk of the gameplay takes place on a single screen, with the player maneuvering his game-world surrogate around that screen, sometimes only in a portion of that screen. This was done, no doubt, in part because of technological limitations. But it also has very important artistic ramifications on the game's design: the player, at any time, is able to see the entire game-world, and can make his decisions with a full knowledge of the state of that game-world. Obviously, empowering the player with that kind of information seriously impacts the gameplay. Many of the games in the classic arcade game form would include more than one screen's worth of gameplay by switching play-fields or modifying existing ones to create additional "levels." Examples of this include *Joust*, *Pac-Man*, and *Mario Bros.* Though these games may have included more than a single screen in the entire game, at any one time the player's game-world still consisted of just that one screen.

- Infinite Play: The player can play the game forever. There is no ending to the game, and hence no winning it either. This was done in part to allow players to challenge themselves, to see how long they could play on a single quarter. Players can never say, "I beat *Asteroids*," and hence players are always able to keep playing, to keep putting in quarters. At the same time, having an unwinnable game makes every game a defeat for the player. Every game ends with the player's death, and hence is a kind of tragedy. Having an unwinnable game also necessitates making a game that can continuously get harder and harder for the player, hence a game design with a continuous, infinite ramping up of difficulty. With the advent of the home market, game publishers no longer wanted players to play a single game forever. Instead they want players to finish the games they have and buy another one. This is one reason why it is rare to see a game with infinite play any more.

- Multiple Lives: Typically, classic arcade games allow the player a finite number of lives, or a number of "tries" at the game before her game is over. Perhaps derived from pinball games, which had been providing the player with three or five balls for decades, multiple lives allowed the novice player a chance to learn the game's mechanics before the game was over. Given adequate chances to try to figure out how the game works, the player is more likely to want to play again if she made progress from one life to the next. Having lives enables the game to provide another reward incentive for the player playing well: extra lives. Having multiple lives also sets up a game where dying once is not necessarily the end of the game, and encourages players to take risks they might not otherwise.

- Scoring/High Scores: Almost all classic arcade games included a scoring feature through which the player would accumulate points for accomplishing different objectives in the game. For example, in *Centipede*, the player gets 1 point for destroying a mushroom, 10 points for a centipede segment, 100 points for a centipede head, and 1000 points for a scorpion. Another classic arcade game component with origins in the world of pinball, the score allows the player to ascertain how well they did at the game, since winning the game is impossible. The high-score table was introduced in order to allow players to enter their initials next to their score, which would then be ranked in a table of scores so players could see just how good they were. The game would remember the table as long as it stayed plugged in, with some games, such as *Centipede*, even remembering the high-score list or some portion of it once unplugged. The high-score table enabled the classic arcade games to exploit one of the key motivations for playing games—"bragging rights." A player could point out her name in the high-score table to her friends as a way of proving her mettle. Friends could compete with each other (almost all of the games included two-player modes, where players switch off playing) to see who could get the higher score.

- Easy-to-Learn, Simple Gameplay: Classic arcade games were easy for players to learn, impossible (or at least very difficult) to master. Someone could walk up to a game of *Centipede*, plunk in his quarter, and by his third life have a good idea of how the game functioned and how he might play better. Why the player died was always completely apparent to the player. There were typically no "special moves" involving large combinations of buttons which the player had to learn through trial and error. There were few games with tricky concepts such as "health" or "shields" or "power-ups." Again, commercial considerations were probably a factor in making these games simple to learn. At the time of their initial introduction, there was no established market of computer game players and there were few arcades. The games wound up in pizza parlors and bars, where any person might walk up to one and try it out. These novice players might be scared away if the game were too complex or baffling. Of course, simple does not always mean "limited" or "bad" gameplay; it can also mean "elegant" and "refined."

- No Story: Classic arcade games almost universally eschewed the notion of trying to "tell a story" of any sort, just as many modern arcade games continue to do. The games always had a setting the player could easily recognize and relate to, many of them revolving around science fiction themes, though others dabbled in war, fantasy, and sports, among others. Many, such as *Pac-Man* and *Q*Bert*, created their own, unique settings, keeping up with the rampant creativity found in their gameplay. The classic arcade game designers did not feel required to flesh out their game-worlds, to concoct explanations for why the player was shooting at a given target or eating a certain type of dot, and the games did not suffer for it.

Even though the action in *Sinistar* did not take place only on one screen, it is still considered to be an example of the classic arcade game form.

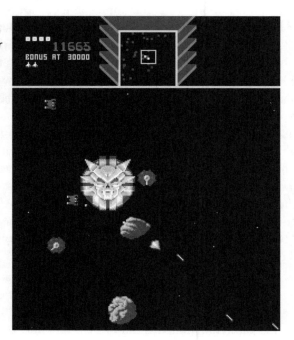

Of course, some games broke some of the above rules of the form, yet they can still be considered classic arcade games. For example, *Sinistar* and *Defender* both included scrolling game-worlds for the player to travel through, with the player unable to see all aspects of the game-world at any one time. Indeed, on first inspection, *Battlezone* seems entirely the odd man out among early classic arcade games. Yet, if one looks at the traits above, one will discover that it featured infinite play, multiple lives, and scoring, was easy to learn, and had almost no story. All three of these games included mechanics which, by and large, were adherent to the classic arcade game form. Thus we can still group them with games like *Space Invaders* and *Asteroids*, games which follow all the rules laid out above.

Being one of the defining games of the form, *Centipede* follows all of the aspects of the classic arcade game form listed above. Though not a very complex game by today's standards, the marvel of *Centipede* is how all of the different gameplay elements work together to create a uniquely challenging game. Nothing in *Centipede* is out of place, nothing is inconsistent, nothing is unbalanced. To analyze *Centipede* is to attempt to understand how to design the perfect game.

Input

One of the great advantages to working on a game for the arcades is that the designer has complete control over the type of device the player will use to control the game. On the PC, the designer can only count on the player having a keyboard and a mouse, while on a console, the designer must work with the standard controller that comes with that particular console. The arcade designer (budget constraints notwithstanding) is able to pick the best type of control for the game, and provide the player with that control system. The designer can then create the game around those controls, precisely balancing the game to work perfectly with that input method. *Centipede* does this expertly, providing the player with an extremely precise analog control device in the form of a trackball. This is ideally suited to moving the player's shooter ship around on the bottom of the screen. Players can move the ship quickly or slowly, whatever the situation calls for. For many fans of *Centipede*, the excellent controller is one of the first things they remember about the game.

The player's shooter in *Centipede* is more mobile than in *Space Invaders*, since it can move up and down in addition to moving sideways. Pictured here: *Centipede*.

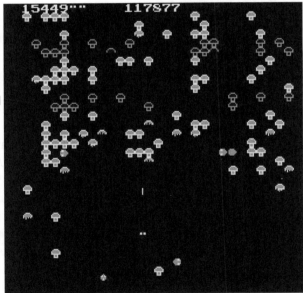

The shooter is extremely responsive to the player's manipulation of the trackball, with the player being able to easily and intuitively understand the relationship between her manipulation of the trackball and the shooter's movement. *Centipede* was no doubt inspired by other classic arcade games, such as *Space Invaders*, which feature the player's game-world surrogate locked at the bottom of the screen, allowed only to move left, move right, and shoot. *Centipede* takes that idiom one step further: the player is still trapped at the bottom of the screen, but the shooter can move within a six-row vertical space. This allows the player to avoid enemies that might be on the bottom row. At the same time, the shooter can still only shoot forward, so enemies that get behind the ship cannot be destroyed. Aside from the trackball, the only other control the player has is a button for firing the shooter's laser-type weapon. The game allows an infinitely fast rate of fire, but only one shot can be on the screen at a time which means the player has to think beyond just holding down the fire button constantly. If the player moves the shooter directly below a mushroom she can hold down the fire button and quickly shoot the mushroom four times, thus destroying it. But at the top of the screen, where the player cannot maneuver the ship, destroying a mushroom takes much longer, since the player must wait for each shot to hit the mushroom before another shot can be fired. If the player's shot is in the midst of traveling to a faraway target, she will be unable to shoot again in order to take out a divebombing enemy. The player must plan her shots carefully, a design element that adds more depth to the game's mechanics.

Interconnectedness

One of the great strengths of *Centipede* is how well all the different elements of the gameplay fit together. Consider the different enemy insects that try to kill the player. The centipede winds its way down the screen from the top of the screen to the player's area at the bottom, moving horizontally. The centipede appears as either a lone twelve-segment centipede or as a shorter centipede accompanied by a number of single heads. At the start of a wave, the number of centipede segments on the screen always totals twelve. Next is the spider, which moves in a diagonal, bouncing pattern across the bottom of the screen, passing in and out of the player's area. Then comes the flea, which plummets vertically, straight down toward the player. There is nothing terribly sophisticated about any of the movement patterns of these insects. Indeed, the flea and the centipede, once they have appeared in the play-field, follow a completely predictable pattern as they approach the player's area. The spider has a more random nature to its zigzagging movement, but even it does nothing to actually pursue the player. Therefore, once the player has played the game just a few times, he has a completely reliable set of expectations about how these enemies will attack him. Fighting any one of these creatures by itself would provide very little challenge for the player. Yet, when they function together they combine to create uniquely challenging situations for the player. With any one of these adversaries missing, the game's challenge would be significantly diminished, if not removed altogether.

Each of the insects in the game also has a unique relationship to the mushrooms which fill the game's play-field. The primary reason for the existence of the mushrooms is to speed up the centipede's progress to the bottom of the screen. Every time a centipede bumps into a mushroom, it turns down to the next row below, as if it had run into the edge of the play-field. Thus, once the screen becomes packed with mushrooms, the centipede will get to the bottom of the play-field extremely quickly. Once at the bottom of the screen, the centipede moves back and forth inside the player's area, posing a great danger to the player. So, it behooves the player to do everything he can to destroy the mushrooms on the play-field, even though the mushrooms themselves do not pose a direct threat. Further complicating matters, every time the player shoots a segment of the centipede it leaves a mushroom where it died. Thus, wiping out a twelve-segment centipede leaves a big cluster of mushrooms with which the player must contend.

In *Centipede*, fleas drop toward the bottom of the screen, leaving mushrooms behind them, while spiders eat whatever mushrooms block their movement.

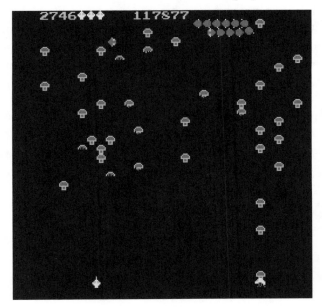

As the flea falls to the bottom of the play-field, it leaves a trail of new mushrooms behind itself, and the only way for the player to stop it is to kill it. The flea only comes on to the play-field if there are less than a certain number of mushrooms on the bottom half of the screen. This way, if the player destroys all the mushrooms closest to him, the flea comes out immediately to lay down more. The spider, the creature that poses the biggest threat to the player, has the side effect that it eats mushrooms. This then presents the player with a quandary: shoot and kill the spider or just try to avoid it so it can take out more mushrooms? Finally, the scorpion, a creature that travels horizontally across the top half of the screen and hence can never collide with and kill the player, poisons the mushrooms it passes under. These poisoned mushrooms affect the centipede differently when it bumps into them. Instead of just turning down to the next row, the centipede will move vertically straight down to the bottom of the screen. So when a centipede hits a poisoned mushroom, the centipede becomes a much more grave threat than it was before.

Once a scorpion has passed by, the player must now expend effort trying to shoot all the poisoned mushrooms at the top of the screen or be prepared to blast the centipedes as they plummet vertically straight toward the player.

So we can see that each of the creatures in the game has a special, unique relationship to the mushrooms. It is the interplay of these relationships that creates the challenge for the player. The more mushrooms the flea drops, the more mushrooms the scorpion has to poison. The spider may take out mushrooms along the bottom of the screen, getting them out of the way of the player, but it may eat so many that the flea starts coming out again. If the player kills the centipede too close to the top of the screen, it will leave a clump of mushrooms which are difficult to destroy at such a distance, and which will cause future centipedes to reach the bottom of the screen at a greater speed. However, if the player waits until the centipede is at the bottom of the screen, the centipede is more likely to kill the player. With the mushrooms almost functioning as puzzle pieces, *Centipede* becomes something of a hybrid between an arcade shooter and a real-time puzzle game. Indeed, some players were able to develop special strategies that would work to stop the flea from ever coming out, thus making the centipede get to the bottom of the screen less quickly and allowing the player to survive for much longer. It is the interplay of each of the player's adversaries with these mushrooms and with each other that creates a unique challenge for the player.

Escalating Tension

A big part of the success of *Centipede* is how it escalates tension over the length of the game. The game actually has peaks and valleys it creates in which tension escalates to an apex and, with the killing of the last centipede segment, relaxes for a moment as the game switches over to the next wave. One small way in which the game escalates tension over a few seconds is through the flea, which is the only enemy in the game the player must shoot twice. When it is shot just once, its speed increases dramatically and the player must quickly shoot it again lest the flea hit the shooter. For that brief speed burst, the player's tension escalates. In terms of the centipede itself, the game escalates the tension by splitting the centipede each time it is shot. If the player shoots the middle segment of an eleven-segment centipede, it will split into two five-segment centipedes which head in opposite directions. Sure, the player has decreased the total number of segments on the screen by one, but now he has two adversaries to worry about at once. As a result, skilled players will end up going for the head or tail of the centipede to avoid splitting it.

Most of the game's escalating tension over the course of a wave is derived from the centipede's approach toward the bottom of the screen and the player's often frantic efforts to kill it before it gets there. Once a centipede head reaches the bottom of the screen, a special centipede head generator is activated, which spits out additional centipede heads into the player's area. If the player is unable to kill the centipede before it reaches the bottom of the screen, which has already increased tension by its very approach, that tension is further escalated by the arrival of these extra heads. And those extra heads keep arriving until the player has managed to kill all of the remaining centipede segments on the screen. The rate at which those extra heads come out increases over time, such that if the player takes her time in killing them, additional centipedes will arrive all the faster, making the player still more frantic.

Once the player kills the last segment, the game goes to its next wave, and the centipede is regenerated from the top of the screen. This provides a crucial, temporary reprieve for the player, a moment for her to catch her breath. The player will feel a great rush at having finally defeated the centipede, especially if the extra centipede head generator had been activated. In addition, the newly generated centipede at first appears easier to kill, since it is generated so far from the player's area.

Over the course of a game of *Centipede*, mushrooms become more and more tightly packed on the play-field.

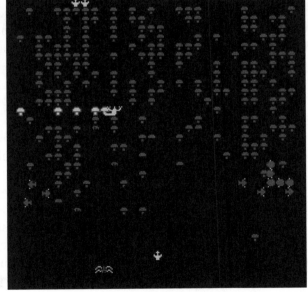

Over the course of the player's entire game, the mushrooms inevitably become more and more packed on the play-field. Once there are more mushrooms toward the bottom of the screen, the player feels lucky if he can just clear all of the mushrooms in the lower half of the play-field. He has no chance of destroying the mushrooms toward the top, since the lower mushrooms block his shots. Similarly, if the scorpion has left any poison mushrooms toward the top of the screen, the player has no chance whatsoever of destroying them, and as a result the centipede dive-bombs the bottom of the screen on every single wave. Far into a game, the top of the play-field becomes a solid wall of mushrooms. As the mushrooms become more and more dense, the centipede gets to the bottom of the screen faster. When the centipede can get to the bottom of the screen extremely quickly, the player's game is that much faster paced, and he is that much more panicked about destroying the centipede before it reaches the bottom of the screen. This increased mushroom density has the effect of escalating tension not just within a wave as the extra centipede head generator did, but also from wave to wave, since the mushrooms never go away unless the player shoots them.

Centipede also balances its monsters to become harder and harder as the player's score increases. And since the player's score can never decrease, the tension escalates over the course of the game. Most obvious is the spider, whose speed approximately doubles once the player's score reaches 5000 (1000 if the game's operator has set the game to "hard"). The spider also maneuvers in a smaller and smaller area of the bottom of the screen as the player's score gets really high, eventually moving only one row out of the player's six-row area. With the spider thus constrained, it is both more likely to hit the player and less likely for the player to be able to shoot it. Recall that the flea drops from the top of the screen based on the quantity of mushrooms in the bottom half of the screen. When the player starts the game, if there are less than five mushrooms in that area the flea will come down, dropping more as it does so. As the player's score increases, however, so does the quantity of mushrooms needed to prevent the flea's appearance. Now the player must leave more and more mushrooms in that space to prevent the flea from coming out and cluttering the top of the screen with mushrooms.

At the start of each wave, the game always generates a total of twelve centipede segments and heads at the top of the screen. This means that if a twelve-segment centipede appears at the top of the screen, that will be the only centipede. If a seven-segment centipede appears, then five other centipede heads will appear as well, thus totaling the magic number of twelve. The more centipedes that appear, the more challenging it is for the player to shoot them all, and the more likely one will sneak to the bottom of the screen. The game starts by releasing a single twelve-segment centipede. In the next wave, a slow eleven-segment centipede appears along with one head. In the following wave, a fast eleven-segment and one head combination arrive. Then a slow ten-segment and two heads appear. With each wave there are a greater number of individual centipedes for the player to keep track of and a greater escalation of tension. The game wraps around once twelve individual heads are spawned, but then the game becomes harder by only spawning fast centipedes.

The player's death also provides a brief respite from the tension. When the player's ship is destroyed, the wave starts over and hence the centipede returns to the top of the screen. Before this, however, all of the mushrooms on the screen are reset. This means that all the partially destroyed mushrooms are returned to their undamaged state. But also all of the mushrooms poisoned by the scorpion are returned to their unpoisoned state. Many waves into the game, the increased mushroom density makes shooting poisoned mushrooms all but impossible, and with those poisoned mushrooms in place, the player is bombarded by centipedes hurtling toward him in every single wave. Thus, a player is almost relieved when his shooter is destroyed and all those poisoned mushrooms are removed from the top of the screen. This causes the player's game to be much more relaxed, at least for the time being.

Centipede's frantic gameplay keeps the player tense most of the time, though it provides some breaks in the action during which the player can relax.

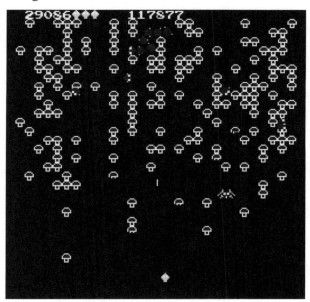

Centipede is marvelous at creating and maintaining a tense situation for the player, while still providing brief "breathing periods" within the action. Designers of modern games, who are always concerned with ramping up difficulty for the player, could learn much by analyzing how *Centipede* keeps the player constantly on his toes without ever unfairly overwhelming him.

One Person, One Game

Many may scoff at *Centipede* twenty years after its creation. There is no question that it is a less technically astounding accomplishment than more modern works, and those who do not examine it closely are likely to dismiss it as more of a light diversion instead of a serious game. But what *Centipede* does, it does with such facility, featuring game mechanics so precisely and perfectly balanced and gameplay so uniquely compelling, that it truly is a marvel of computer game design. One must remember that *Centipede* was created in the days of the one-person-one-game system, when the development team for a game consisted primarily of one person, in this case Ed Logg. By having one person in total control of a project, where a single talented individual fully understands every last nuance of the game, the final product is much more likely to come out with a clearness of vision and brilliance of execution. Of course, one person can create a terrible game just as easily as a large team, but one must wonder if the lone wolf developer does not have a better chance at creating the perfect game.

Chapter 5:
Focus

"Feel the flow... To become one with the flow is to realize purpose."
— Warrel Dane

Developing a game for two years with a team of twenty people can sometimes more resemble a war than the creation of art. Many would say that a decent amount of conflict can lead to great art, especially in collaborative forms such as modern commercial computer games. A stronger game may arise from the ashes of team members arguing over the best way to implement some aspect of gameplay. If the game merely becomes unfocused as a result of these squabbles, then a good game is not likely to emerge. Over the course of the many battles you must fight, skirmishes you must endure, and defeats you must overcome in the course of a game's development, with conflicts potentially arising with other team members or from within yourself, it is far too easy to lose track of just why you were creating the game in the first place. Is it possible that at one point the game you are working on captivated your imagination? Was there some vision you had for why this game would be fun, compelling, and unique? Is it possible that at one point you actually liked computer games at all?

Sometimes in the middle of a project it is easy to get sidetracked—sidetracked by technological obstacles that are thrown in your path, sidetracked by altercations between team members, or sidetracked when your publisher tells you features A, B, and C simply have to be changed. It is at these junctures where you come to doubt that your game will ever be fun, or whether it will even be completed. These periods of doubt are the ones that separate the good game designers from the merely passable ones. Good game designers will be able to overcome these difficulties and stay on track by remembering their focus.

The technique I will be exploring in this chapter is certainly not one that all game designers use, but I think it is one that all game designers could benefit from. Many designers may use the technique but not realize it. Others may have entirely different methods for assuring their game comes together as a fun, consistent whole. You cannot expect to go up to any game designer and say, "What's your focus for your current project?" and expect them to produce an answer in line with the method I explore in this chapter. But if you start being rigorous in maintaining focus in your projects, I think you will see very positive results in the final quality of your games.

Establishing Focus

A game's focus is the designer's idea of what is most important about a game. In this chapter I encourage designers to write their focus down in a short paragraph, since putting it down in writing can often clarify and solidify a designer's thoughts. However, it is the idea of the focus which is of paramount importance. In a way, a game's focus is similar to a corporation's "mission statement," assuming such mission statements are actually meaningful and used to guide all of a corporation's decisions.

As a game designer you should start concerning yourself with your game's focus from the very beginning of the project. When the project is in its infancy, before work has started on the design document and the project exists primarily as an idea in your head, you should ask yourself a series of questions about the game you are envisioning:

- What is it about this game that is most compelling?
- What is this game trying to accomplish?

- What sort of emotions is the game trying to evoke in the player?
- What should the player take away from the game?
- How is this game unique? What differentiates it from other games?
- What sort of control will the player have over the game-world?

By going over these questions, you should be able to determine the core nature of the game you are planning to create. If you have trouble answering these questions, now is the time to think about the game until the answers to these questions become obvious. Now—before there is anyone else working on the project, before "burn rate" is being spent and driving up the game's budget, before the marketing department starts trying to influence the game's content and directions—now is the time to focus. Only by firmly establishing the vision of the game early on will you have any chance of seeing it carried out.

If you do not have too much trouble divining answers to these questions, you may have written an entire page or more delineating the game's points of differentiation. But a page is too much. The focus that we are striving for needs to be succinct—a few sentences, a short paragraph at the most. It should be something you can quickly read to your colleagues without their eyes glazing over. You should take whatever notes you have in answer to these questions and whittle them down until they are short enough to fill only a few sentences, a mid-sized paragraph. Keep only your most compelling ideas. You do not need to list every single feature of the game, or even everything it does differently from other games. Keep only what is most important to your vision of the game, only those points which, if you took them away, would irreparably weaken the game.

You do not need to include the setting of your game if that is not inherent to the actual focus of the game. It may not matter if your game has a fantasy, science fiction, or 1920s crime fiction setting, if what is really at the heart of your game is exploring the relationships between characters in a stressful situation, or the subtleties of siege warfare. If the setting is not vital to what you want to do with the game, leave it out. Of course, your primary motivation for working on a project may be hopelessly intertwined with the setting. If you actually started with a setting you wanted to explore in a game, such as costumed superheroes in small-town America, and your vision of the gameplay formed around the idea of these characters in a certain environment, then you will want to include it in your focus. The focus is exclusively for the concepts that are most central to the game you are hoping to develop. All that should remain in your focus are the elements without which the game would no longer exist.

Your focus should be something that grabs you viscerally, stirs your creative juices, and makes you feel absolutely exhilarated. If it is not something that thrills you, even at this early stage, it is going to be hard for you to muster enthusiasm when your deadlines are slipping, your budget is skyrocketing, you still have three levels to create, and your lead artist just left for another company. Chris Crawford touched on the idea of a game's focus in his book, *The Art of Computer Game Design*, as he was discussing what he called a game's goal: "This is your opportunity to express yourself; choose a goal in which you believe, a goal that expresses your sense of aesthetic, your world view... It matters not what your goal is, so long as it is congruent with your own interests, beliefs, and passions." If you do not believe in your game, it is not going to be the best game you can make.

Even if you are working under the constraints of a license, a domineering publisher, or a prima donna lead programmer, make your own goals for the project. If the game you have been assigned to work on is not one in which you are interested, figure out some way to transform it into something you can get excited about. No situation is so bad that, given enough time, you cannot make something out of it that you find personally compelling. You want your focus to be something you will fight intensely for until the game finally ships.

Much of this chapter is written in a fashion that implies that you are in charge of your project, at least from a game design standpoint. Of course, this may not be the case. You may be one of several designers on the project. You may even be one of seven and you were just hired last week, so you are at the bottom of the seniority ladder. This does not excuse you from determining what your game's focus is and doing everything you can to keep the game on track. Hopefully the lead designer has already determined what the project's goals are and should have included this information in the introduction to the design document. If you cannot find it there, you may wish to go talk to your lead. Ask her what the project is really trying to do, not necessarily in a confrontational way, but just so you get a good idea of where the project is going, and how your contribution to the game can be properly aligned with that direction.

If it turns out the design lead does not really have a focus in mind, it may be held by another member of the team, say a lead programmer or lead artist. However, if despite your best research efforts, the project seems to be goal-less, you may need to take matters into your own hands. Try to figure out where the project seems to be heading, and start talking with people about it. Chat with the other designers, artists, programmers, and producers. Try to talk to them about what the game is all about, and try to get everyone to agree. Meetings may be a good place to do this; when everyone is present any conflicts between different perspectives or personalities on the team can be weeded out. You do not need to be in a lead position in order to keep your project on track. As a designer in any capacity on a project, it is ultimately your responsibility that the game always has a clear direction and that a fun game emerges at the end of the tunnel.

An Example: Snow Carnage Derby

Let us suppose you have a vision for a game involving snowmobiles and combat. What is it about snowmobile riding that excites you? Is it adventuring across Canada's Northwest Territories, trying to realistically simulate a great snowmobile trek? No? Perhaps what gets you going is that a snowmobile looks like a fun vehicle to drive, and you enjoy the idea of handling one in a safe game-world, where you can make jumps and spin donuts in the snow without actually injuring yourself. In this case, reality is not so much the issue as having fun with driving a snowmobile, in an environment that allows for plenty of cool maneuvers. Since the snowmobile component seems fairly central to your idea, you will need to include it in the focus. So your focus can start with a sentence that explains this: "The player's experience will revolve around the seemingly realistic physics of controlling snowmobiles, with the player being able to do fun and challenging moves and jumps in a snowy environment; the game will be balanced not for realism but for fun."

Now, what is it about this combat element that grabs you? You see visions of blood soaking into snow, snowmobiles ramming into other snowmobiles, riders hanging on to their snowmobiles for dear life, desperately clutching the handlebars to avoid being thrown. Why are these snowmobiles battling? That is not as important, you decide, as the excitement of the combat. Why it is happening is irrelevant. The vision of snowmobiles smashing into each other turns you on, with the violence cranked up to absurd levels. You may have trouble getting your game into censorship-minded retailers, but this is your vision. So include a sentence about the nature of the combat: "The game will provide a visceral thrill by allowing for the decapitation and otherwise crippling of enemy snowmobile riders, and said violence will be played out to maximum comedic effect."

What else about your snowmobile battle game is a central part of your vision? Do you want to realistically simulate fuel and snowmobiles breaking down? Is fixing your snowmobile an intrinsic part of your game? Not really; it seems that though that could be added to the game, it is not absolutely essential to your vision. Will the game be in 3D or in 2D? Well, actually, the game could work in either. To be commercially viable in today's marketplace it will probably need to be 3D but that is not central to your vision. In your focus, do not include aspects of your game that are more about getting the project funded and published than making the game you want to make. You can worry about commercial considerations later. Right now you are concerned with your vision, and if you start compromising your vision before absolutely necessary you are going to be blind at the end of the day. So you do not need to specify 2D or 3D. Indeed, maybe you have everything you need for the focus. Remember, the focus should not be very long.

Now is the time to put your two sentences together in a paragraph and name the game. Though it may seem premature, naming the game is actually a good idea at this point. You want other members of your team, the marketing department, and the business people to start liking your game as soon as possible, and having a name they can refer to it by is fairly important to that process. Can they really discuss it seriously as "this game idea Richard had"? Giving your game a name makes it real instead of just an idea, as ridiculous as that may seem.

Try your very best to come up with a name that you like and that could end up going on the final product. Often whatever name is given to a game early on will end up sticking with the game forever. It is especially important not to pick a purposefully idiotic name, since those are the kind most likely to stick. For instance, let us say you name it *Egyptian Rumba*. As your team keeps referring to the game as *Egyptian Rumba,* they will start to associate your cool game with this idiotic title, and your idiotic title will start to sound pretty good through association. Someone working on the art team may start giving the characters an Egyptian color scheme. Team members who are working on the story might spend a lot of time trying to figure out why the game should be named *Egyptian Rumba*, and will develop an especially clever story line around the name. If you later try to change the name they will be sad and possibly angry that their story no longer makes any sense. Even the "suits" will start to like your *Egyptian Rumba* title. They will think of how they can capture both the adventuring archeologist market and the Cuban dance market. And soon, if you even remember, you will say it is time to change the game's title, and everyone will say, "Why? We like *Egyptian Rumba*! It's a great name!" And you will be stuck. Then the public will see it on the shelves and will think, "What the heck is that? It sounds stupid," and quickly pass on to games with more reasonable titles.

So you finally choose *Snow Carnage Derby*. Perhaps a more exciting name will come up later, but you can live with this one. Now, assemble the pieces of your focus into one paragraph, and try to write it cleanly and succinctly. Refer to your game in the present tense, as though your game already exists. "*Snow Carnage Derby* is an exhilarating..." instead of "*Snow Carnage Derby* will be an exhilarating..." This lends your game a more concrete existence in the minds of those who read your focus. It is not just a game that may come about at some point in the future; it already is a game, if only in your head. Something else to avoid is using generic descriptions that do not actually provide the reader with any useful information. For instance, "*Snow Carnage Derby* is a high-quality, fun game that..." Of course it is supposed to be fun. Does anyone set out to make a boring game? Or a low-quality one? Edit out any sections of your focus that do not communicate important information about your game.

Putting together the parts of your focus, you will end up with the following:

Snow Carnage Derby *is an exhilarating, fast-action snowmobile demolition game. The player's experience revolves around the seemingly realistic*

*physics of controlling snowmobiles, with the player being able to do fun
and challenging moves and jumps in a snowy environment; the game is
balanced not for realism but for fun. The game provides a visceral thrill
by allowing for the decapitation and otherwise crippling of enemy snowmobile riders, and said violence is played out to maximum comedic effect.*
Snow Carnage Derby *provides fast-action thrills as the player tries to run
down the competition while avoiding destruction.*

The Function of the Focus

Your game may
be similar to
another game
such as *Tomb
Raider*, but in
your focus you
want to describe
the game on its
own terms and
avoid making
comparisons to
other games.

Try to keep your focus from referring to other games. You want the focus to
describe the essence of your game, and if your focus is, "*Voltarr* is like *Tomb
Raider*, but set on the whimsical planet Dongo and featuring many intense laser
gunfights," it is hard for someone looking at your focus to understand immediately
what parts of *Tomb Raider* you are hoping to emulate. Take a look at *Tomb Raider*
itself and determine what you think its focus may have been. Then take that focus,
remove whatever parts are not necessary for your game, and add in whatever new
ideas your game will incorporate. Chances are your idea of what was compelling
about *Tomb Raider* will be different from someone else's understanding. When a
member of your team reads, "It's like *Tomb Raider*," she is probably reminded of
some different aspect of that game's gameplay than you are. That's assuming that
she has played *Tomb Raider* at all. Since the focus is designed to guide your team
members as well as yourself, it needs to communicate the same ideas to everyone
who reads it. Even if the focus is primarily for your own use, the process of

analyzing *Tomb Raider* to determine what about it you want to replicate will help you to better understand your own game. You need to have a properly streamlined focus that can stand on its own, without demanding that the person who is reading the focus understand any other particular games. All the relevant information that is important to your focus must be contained within the focus itself, without outside references. Often when designers set out to create "It's like *Game X* but with . . ." games, they tend to lose sight of what made the game they are imitating so compelling in the first place. Then they proceed to make their own game top-heavy with tacked-on features that exist only to hide the fact their game is just like *Game X*. Removing references to other games from your focus will help expose the true nature of the project you are undertaking.

Establishing a focus for your project does not need to limit the scope of your game, and is not intended to do so. Your game can still be a massively complex game with an epic sweep. In fact, if appropriate, this complexity and depth should probably be mentioned in your focus, but you should still be able to describe the game in a few sentences in order to succinctly communicate what is most important about your undertaking. Your game can even include multiple styles of gameplay within the same game. Suppose your goal is to simulate the life of a pirate. You might want to include an exploration mode for navigating the seas, a tactical mode for engaging another ship in battle, a sword-fighting mode for fighting an enemy captain one on one, and even a trading mode for selling off booty. (Indeed, Sid Meier already made this game; it is called *Pirates!*) But having this multiple game structure does not mean that the focus could not still be, "This game re-creates the many different facets of a pirate's life through numerous different campaign modes, all designed to evoke the spirit of being a cutthroat. The player is able to explore the nature of being an outlaw, including the economic and physical risks involved." If your game is to have multiple separate modes, your focus should apply to all of the different sub-games within your project.

If you are working on a project solo or with a small team, you may think it unnecessary to actually write down your focus. After all, if you can just explain it to everyone who needs to know, what's the sense in writing it down? I would argue that writing it down is key to truly coming to grips with the nature of the game you are planning to develop. There is a world of difference between an idea that is kicking around in your head and one that is written down on paper in front of you. When it is on paper you can look at it and make sure that what is typed is really the core of your idea, that those sentences represent everything that is most important to you about the project. Unlike when you describe the project to someone, on paper you cannot say, "Oh, yeah, and there's this part, and this other aspect over here, and I really mean this when I say that." If it is not down on the paper, it is not part of the game's focus. Someone who reads the focus on paper should be able to understand your vision without you needing to explain it. I find that writing the focus down really helps to clarify and solidify what the game is attempting to achieve.

Though I did not know it at the time of the game's development, *Odyssey*'s focus was centered on telling a specific story.

When I worked on my first game, *Odyssey*, I had no grand plan to have a focus. Nor did I sit down and purposefully think it out. On the other hand, I seem to remember the primary goal revolving around a story. It was the story of a mad scientist-type character, a powerful sorcerer who performed experiments on hapless humanoid creatures. These were not biological experiments, but rather social ones—experiments where he would see how these humans would treat each other when under certain circumstances. Really, he was exploring the evil side of all sentient creatures. So *Odyssey*'s focus was to explore the mean and vicious ways different groups of people can treat each other in certain situations and to set up scenarios where the players witnessed this first-hand and would have a chance to make a real change in their lives. Non-linearity and multiple solutions were also at the forefront of my mind, so I set out to make sure players would be able to pursue different tactics to solve the problems they were presented with, with no solution being designated as the "right" one. And so I had my focus. Without really thinking of it in terms of a focus or vision, I had determined what I wanted to do with the game, and I was able to stick with that for the duration of the project. Since I was basically developing the project solo, I did not have to communicate this focus to anyone else, and if I had needed to I doubt that I would or could have. Though I knew in my head what I wanted in the game, at the time I could not define my goals in terms someone else could understand. Now, looking back, I can come up with the following:

In Odyssey, *the player explores a rich story line about the evil nature of mankind, and sees under what circumstances groups will treat each other in morally reprehensible ways. This is a simple RPG/adventure game. Though sword-and-sorcery combat will be involved, it never overtakes the story line. The story line allows for multiple solutions and non-linearity whenever possible, with the player able to effect real change among the NPCs he encounters in the game.*

Maintaining Focus

Once you have your focus down on paper and you are satisfied with it, when you can read it over and say, "Yes, certainly, that's what I'm going for," it is time to share it with the other members of your team. It is important that you get everyone on your team to sign on to your focus. You want them to acknowledge that, yes, this is the direction the team is taking, and to agree that they see a compelling game coming out of it in the end. If no one on your team thinks your focus is very captivating, and despite your best efforts to campaign for it no one can get excited over it, you can come to one of two conclusions. First, perhaps your game idea is not all that good. Hard as this may be to admit, it could be that your focus statement and possibly the game it describes are simply not original or enticing. If the idea in your head is still exciting to you, maybe you did not capture its focus properly on the paper. You should go back and try to figure out what about the game excites you but which did not come across in your focus. If you persist in thinking your game is compelling and that your focus properly reflects why, the second conclusion you can come to is that the team assembled is simply the wrong one to develop this game. Not every team can develop every type of game. A team that has been making sports games for years, likes working on sports games, and knows how to make a sports game fun is probably not the best team to enlist to create your nineteenth century economics simulation. If you have the option of finding a new team for your game, that is great. If not, you may need to come up with an idea that everyone on your team is going to like. It is important that everyone on your team like your focus idea. Because of the collaborative nature of modern, well-budgeted computer games, it is virtually impossible to create a good game if you do not have the majority of your team excited to be working on it.

If you are working on a project largely by yourself with others contributing significantly less to the game than you, you may not need to sell your focus at all. Indeed, games created by lone wolf designer/programmer/artists can be among the most focused of computer games. Since one person is creating the vast majority of the game's content, she is able to exert absolute control over every nuance. Solo game development is typically not something at which one can earn a living any more, but I know of a few who do. Of course, the fact that a game was created largely by one individual does not assure that the game is going to be focused. If that individual is scatterbrained and unfocused herself, chances are good the game will not be very focused either. Even if she is a more sane, organized person, if she does not keep track of her game's focus over the course of the project, her game may end up being just as unfocused as the most uncoordinated, over-budgeted, fifty-developer game.

If you are working as a designer on a game with a team, it is essential to make sure the other people on your project, whether artists, programmers, or producers, understand the nature of the game's focus. Without a strong focus to guide their actions, programmers and artists may have a misunderstanding of what the game is supposed to accomplish, and may be thinking of some other type of game as they work on yours. Through no fault of their own, their work may deviate from what needs to happen for your game to become a reality, and you will be forced to say, "No, that doesn't fit, redo it." If the team has a focus to follow, a focus they have signed on to, then they are far less likely to create work that is inappropriate for your game. Having a strong focus does not get you out of keeping a watchful eye on the artists' and programmers' work, of course, but it will save you the trouble of having to redirect them too frequently.

Fleshing Out the Focus

Once the team is enthusiastic about the project, has signed on to the focus, and has a clear understanding of what the game is supposed to be, you can proceed to more fully flesh out your idea through a complete design document. You may even want to make your focus the beginning of your document, as a sort of summary of the nature of the game that people can read quickly. (The nature and creation of design documents is more fully explored in Chapter 17, "The Design Document.") The design document should take the game suggested by your focus and expand on it, detailing how the goals in your focus will be accomplished by gameplay and how precisely that gameplay will function. You will also be sketching out the flow of the game, what the game-world will be like, and what sort of entities the player will encounter. Of course, while you are working on the design document, there will be countless points at which you have to struggle to come up with the correct solution to a given problem. Should the control system use method A or method B? What sort of environments will the player be interacting in? What sort of challenges do the enemies present? A properly designed focus will allow you to refer back to it to answer many of the questions you encounter during the design process. As these elements of the game are fleshed out, you should continually refer back to your focus to see if the additions you are making match with that focus. Through the focus, you can carefully consider if you are adding gameplay that takes the game in a new direction. It is important to identify which additions to your game cause it to deviate from the focus, and then to change or eliminate those erroneous additions.

You want to avoid having your game become too bloated with features, elements which may be "cool" in some way but that do not support the game's main focus or that distract the player's attentions. Using your focus as a tool, you can prevent this overexpansion by cutting away the chaff in your game design to leave only the core gameplay for which you were striving. Many of the ideas you or members of your team have may be fine concepts, but if they do not fit in with the game you are currently working on, they are not worth exploring or implementing. But do not throw these incompatible ideas away. Write them down in your notebook for the next time you are working on a game design. If they are good ideas, there is probably some game with which they will work well. If they are very good ideas, you may even want to design an entire game around them. But for the current project, by referring back to your focus you should be able to determine whether these extra, cool features are helping or hurting your game as a whole.

Once the design document is finished and other elements of preproduction are completed, full production can start on your game. Your team of programmers, artists, and other personnel will begin attempting to implement what you have set out to accomplish in your design document. As the project proceeds, there will be countless times where questions arise. Your design document will not cover everything needed to actually make the game playable; it cannot possibly. Questions will come up about how to implement a feature, in addition to new ideas about how to improve the game. For each of these, again, you should refer back to your focus to clarify your team's direction. Is the implementation that is being suggested going to keep the game on track with the focus? Or will it distract from the main thrust of a game? Is the distraction going to be too much of a diversion? Using your focus statement wisely throughout the course of the project will keep the game on the right course, and will result in an end product that is better because of it. Players will know the difference between a game that is properly focused and one that is not, even if they do not communicate their feelings in so many words. They will play and enjoy a focused game and will quickly cast aside one that is unfocused.

Changing Focus

Of course, either while working on your design document or when the game is in full production, it may become apparent that the goals of your game need to change. This can happen for a variety of reasons. You may come to see shortcomings or failings in your original focus. Through the act of creating your game, you may come to recognize a more compelling experience that the game can provide that is outside the scope of your original focus. Depending on where you are in the project's development, you may want to change your focus. This is particularly painless to do when you are still in the design document phase. In fact, you should expect your focus to change several times, if not on a daily basis, while you are working on the design document. There is nothing like trying to write down all the important information about your game to expose holes and failings in your original concept.

Even beyond the design document, when you are working on your game's first level you may begin to see weaknesses in your design, holes you had not anticipated when you were just working with an idea of the gameplay in your head instead of a playable game on the screen in front of you. At this point making changes to the focus is still not catastrophically damaging to your schedule and will not involve redoing much work. Better to fix problems in the game and your focus now than to be stuck with them for the rest of the project and end up with an inferior game.

When changing the focus, you should take the same care as you did when you initially came up with it. Make sure the focus fully represents your new vision for the project. Of course, if your focus changes radically, you will need to tell the team about the change and make sure they all agree with it. Remember, the team needs to be behind the project in order for it to succeed, and if you change the focus in such a way that the team is no longer interested in working on the project, you need to rethink that change.

For whatever reason or in whatever way you may change your focus, it is important to examine what parts of the game may already exist and see how far they diverge from your new focus. Look over the design document and realign it to your new goals. Consider whatever game mechanics may be in place and see if they are sufficient to carry the new focus. Look over whatever levels may exist (hopefully not too many have been created at this point) and see if they fit with the new focus. Whether it is in documentation, code, level design, or art, anything that does not fit will need to be reworked so that the new focus is properly supported.

If too many assets (levels, dialog, or art) need to be reworked, or if it is too close to the ship date to change them, or if there is not enough funding available to get them changed, you may need to rethink changing your direction. Is it really necessary? Will the old focus still result in an entertaining game, or is it inherently and thoroughly flawed? Can you make the change in direction less drastic, so that the old assets can still be used? The worst decision you can make is to create whatever new assets the game needs following a new focus, while the old assets still follow the inferior focus you had embraced previously. This will be apparent to the player, and instead of focusing the game, your two focuses will end up creating a game with a split personality, one that is entirely unfocused. Try your very hardest to come up with a refocusing plan for your project that will not put you over budget or schedule, if these are pressing concerns. Realizing your project is not as good as it could be, but lacking the time or money to fix it properly is a tough position to be in. Finding the best solution in such difficult situations can be extremely challenging and frustrating.

When I worked on *Centipede 3D*, we ended up changing our focus near the beginning of the project. This resulted in some amount of work needing to be redone, but it also led to a significantly stronger game in the end. *Centipede 3D* was something of a special case since it was a remake of a classic and much-loved game, the original Atari *Centipede*, created by Ed Logg. When doing a remake or a sequel, it makes sense to take a look at the original game you are working from, and get a clear understanding, for yourself, of what its focus was. This is necessary so you will have a good idea of what exactly you are remaking. Of course I was not present when Logg was making the original *Centipede* in 1979 and 1980, but I can try to figure out what his focus might have been:

> *Centipede is a fast-action shooting game involving a variety of adversaries that the player must kill in order to avoid being killed by them. The enemies move in completely predictable, predetermined patterns, but the combination of the movement of these creatures and other objects in the game-world creates a challenging experience for the player. The player can attempt to change the game-world to make the adversaries' movements more predictable, and the player can see the entire game-world at once. The game continues until the player dies a specific number of times, with points accumulating to represent how well the player did in that particular game; there is no winning or finishing Centipede.*

That focus is probably too long and too detailed to be a proper game focus, but it is hard for me to read Ed Logg's mind to know what his core concerns were when making *Centipede*. So I have included all of the crucial parts of the game I can find. Of course, the focus he used may bear no relationship at all to the one above.

The focus of the 3D version of *Centipede* was to create a game which captured the arcade gameplay of the original *Centipede* in a three-dimensional, level-based environment.

When development of *Centipede 3D* initially got under way, the idea was to take only the most basic characters of *Centipede*—the player's shooter ship, the centipedes, spiders, fleas, and mushrooms—and have them interact in a 3D world. Not much attention was paid to how the game mechanics or AI associated with any of these characters functioned in the original. The elements from the original *Centipede* were being used more for aesthetics than anything else. When our initial game prototype turned out not to be much fun to play, we decided to try to emulate more of the original game's gameplay in the new 3D version, wherever possible imitating and updating whatever the 1981 *Centipede* did in a 3D, level-based world. As we started pursuing our new focus, we found that the more we emulated the classic, the more fun the new game became. Though it was not written down at the time, you could say our focus was along the lines of the following:

> Centipede 3D *is a remake of the arcade game* Centipede, *and attempts to take what that original game did well and transplant it to a 3D environment. The original* Centipede *featured fast-action shooting combat in waves, with the player's deft maneuvering of the ship being the key to success, and with enemies that moved in completely predictable patterns. Instead of being on one level for the entire game as* Centipede *was,* Centipede 3D *takes the player through a progression of levels. The new game also embraces certain gameplay norms of modern console games, such as replayable levels, bonus objectives, and obstacle navigation. The action and combat portions of* Centipede 3D, *however, will be extremely reminiscent of the original game, employing identical AI wherever possible, and thus retaining the gameplay feel of the original.*

With our new focus, the game assets we had developed thus far were readdressed, and a number of levels had to be discarded, while others were significantly reworked. A small amount of coding that had been done had to be modified, but fortunately no change in the artwork was necessary. All told, our refocus resulted in some loss of work. However, in the end this lost work was worth it because the final *Centipede 3D* had a consistent, focused style of gameplay. And as a direct result, it was fun to play.

It is important to note that our focus for *Centipede 3D* was not a standalone focus as I advocated earlier in this chapter. The focus for *Centipede 3D* refers to another game, the original *Centipede*, and thereby does not stand completely on its own. Of course, *Centipede 3D* is a remake, and as such it makes sense to make reference to the game the project follows. The same would hold true when working on a sequel. For either a remake or a sequel, the game you are making has a direct relation to the other game you refer to in the focus, and a large part of whether the game is deemed a success or not will rest on how well it follows up its predecessor. As such, throughout the game's development, the team members should be asking themselves how their work relates to the original game, and whether what they are trying to accomplish in terms of gameplay is a logical and worthy successor. Since this is such a central concern, it belongs in the focus. In working on a sequel or a remake, your entire team should have played the original game through, and hence can be expected to understand it reasonably well. Note, however, that the focus for *Centipede 3D* includes a brief description of the primary appeal of the original *Centipede*, so that the focus can stand by itself better than if the central concerns of the classic game were assumed. If the focus must refer to another game, it is important to make sure everyone involved with the project understands the focus of that other game as well.

Sub-Focuses

It may be advantageous to take the focus technique to another level by including sub-focuses. This will allow you to start to flesh out your game idea while keeping track of your overall focus. A sub-focus is distinct from the main focus, and should be designated as such when presented alongside the main focus. You can see a sub-focus as a concept that supports your main focus, and which will help your game attain that central focus. A sub-focus alone is generally not enough to design an entire game around. It serves mainly to support your main goal, to break apart other objectives your game will strive for in an attempt to accomplish the central focus.

For an example of using sub-focuses, I will return to the *Snow Carnage Derby* example. As you may remember, you had come up with a focus for a game which allows the player to maneuver snowmobiles in a combat situation. Now that you have the central focus for *Snow Carnage Derby* squared away, you can consider what other goals the game may have. What other aspects of the game should the development team focus on to assure that our gameplay vision is implemented in the best way possible?

Now might be a time to explore what type of player you are thinking will want to play your game. Are you appealing more to the hard-core gaming crowd, or to people who maybe do not play computer games quite so often? This will have a direct effect on many aspects of the game, including what level of simulation will need to be created (the hard-core gamers will demand a more involved and complex gameplay experience), as well as the control system the game will use (hard-core gamers can put up with a more obtuse and convoluted control scheme, while more casual gamers will need something they can pick up quickly).

Arbitrarily, suppose you want to go for the more casual gaming crowd. This means you can create a sub-focus explaining what you will do to skew the game towards this audience: "*Snow Carnage Derby* appeals easily to more casual gamers." It makes sense to explain just what you mean by making the game appeal to casual gamers. Probably the biggest issue is control; you want *Snow Carnage Derby* to allow people to get in and play the game quickly, without confusing them with a lot of keys to remember to control their snowmobile. Your focus could read: "The game provides the simplest control scheme possible, with a player needing to use a small number of easily remembered keys to successfully play the game. Novice players can figure out how to play the game without reading the manual or using a training track, though an instructional level will be included." Note that you do not actually want to go into what the controls are here. Save that for the design document. Here you are just working on your goals for the game, not so much the specifics of how they will be implemented. You may also want to say something about the game's difficulty level. If you are aiming at casual gamers, you are probably going to want to make the game easier than it would be if it were aimed more at the hard-core market. You may want to specify that the game will play at various difficulty levels: "*Snow Carnage Derby* is of a relatively low overall difficulty, with the player able to specify difficulty levels in the game. Even marginally skilled, poor players will be able to play the game to completion on the easiest difficulty level, given enough attempts."

   It might make sense to talk about what type of engine and graphics your game will have in one of the sub-focuses. We discussed previously whether the game should be 2D or 3D, but decided that aspect was not central to our vision of the game. Therefore it was left out of the primary focus. It may, however, fit well as a sub-focus, something that will help further define how the game's development will carry out the initial vision. Now might be a good time to explain the visual style of the game as best you can, to give your art team an idea of what direction they should pursue, as well as your programming team what sort of technology your game will need to support. You can start with some summary of the overall look of the game: "*Snow Carnage Derby* includes a visually lush, high-contrast environment, with the bright colors on the snowmobiles and their riders contrasting with the snow and ice they are riding on." You may decide you want to pursue a 3D engine technology that handles physics well, since that can best help us to capture the excitement of maneuvering the snowmobile, and since the nature of the marketplace demands a 3D game. Within the 3D engine, perhaps a third-person view is the one that will work best to allow the player to control their own snowmobile and rider, along with keeping track of the competitors. Your focus statement could include: "The game uses a 3D engine that allows for a number of snowmobiles and riders on the screen at once. The player has a third-person view of his character and snowmobile to allow him the optimal control of his vehicle while watching out for the other snowmobile riders." It makes sense also to say something about the areas in which the player will be driving their snowmobile. Is it easy to see where to go and simple to navigate? Or is finding where the player is capable of going part of the challenge? You may want to consider our previous sub-focus here. It states that this game is supposed to appeal to the casual gaming audience, and that the game is supposed to be fairly easy to play. So, hard-to-understand courses and combat areas are probably out: "The design of the game-world is such that the player always understands where he is supposed to go and has no trouble understanding which areas can be navigated and which cannot."

Of course, there could be numerous other sub-focuses for *Snow Carnage Derby*, covering everything from gameplay mechanics to what sort of story line the game will have, to how long an average game should last. Always try to avoid putting in too much detail, however. That is for the design document. Here you are merely setting the project's direction, not actually implementing it. But for the purposes of our example, we have enough sub-focuses now, leaving us with a focus and sub-focuses that look like this:

> *Snow Carnage Derby* *is an exhilarating, fast-action snowmobile demolition game. The player's experience revolves around the seemingly realistic physics of controlling snowmobiles, with the player being able to do fun and challenging moves and jumps in a snowy environment; the game is balanced not for realism but for fun. The game provides a visceral thrill by allowing for the decapitation and otherwise crippling of enemy snowmobile riders, and said violence is played out to maximum comedic effect. The game provides fast-action thrills as the player tries to run down the competition while avoiding destruction.*
>
> ### *Audience*
>
> Snow Carnage Derby *appeals easily to more casual gamers. The game provides the simplest control scheme possible, with a player needing to use a small number of easily remembered keys to successfully play the game. Novice players can figure out how to play the game without reading the manual or using a training track, though an instructional level will be included.* Snow Carnage Derby *is of a relatively low overall difficulty, with the player able to specify difficulty levels in the game. Even marginally skilled, poor players are able to play the game to completion on the easiest difficulty level, given enough attempts.*
>
> ### *Visuals*
>
> Snow Carnage Derby *includes a visually lush, high-contrast environment, with the bright colors on the snowmobiles and their riders contrasting with the snow and ice they are riding on. The game uses a 3D engine that allows for a number of snowmobiles and riders on the screen at once. The player has a third-person view of his character and snowmobile to allow him the optimal control of his vehicle while watching out for the other snowmobile riders. The design of the game-world is such that the player*

always understands where he is supposed to go and has no trouble under-standing which areas can be navigated and which cannot.

Notice how the sub-focuses are set off by separate headings from the primary focus. This way readers of the focus can easily see what the primary, most important focus is and how the sub-focuses go into detail about specific parts of the game.

As you are working on your sub-focuses, it is important to always make sure that they jibe with your primary focus, as well as any other sub-focuses you may have. For instance, it makes sense that the Visuals sub-focus talks about the game providing a game-world that is easy to understand visually, since the Audience sub-focus talks about making the game easy to pick up and get into. If you are already contradicting yourself in the writing of your focus you are going to have a very hard time writing a whole design document that makes any sense at all. As the development documentation for your project gets larger and larger in scale, it also gets harder and harder to maintain consistency. Keeping your focuses supporting each other should not be a problem, however, since properly written focuses should be short, concise, and easy to understand.

Using Focus

The focus statement for your game may be quite handy in dealing with whatever marketing department you may be working with to sell your game. Often the marketing department wants to learn about the nature of the game long before the game is actually playable. Besides, many (though certainly not all) marketing people are not terribly interested in playing your game, and will be quite happy that you have a few sentences written for them which succinctly describe what makes the game so appealing. If generating a significant number of sales is one of the items on your agenda (let us presume it is not your primary motivation for working in games, for surely there are more profitable careers to pursue), then having the marketing people get excited about your game when they try to sell it is as important as having the programmers excited during the game's development. Marketing people will try to sell games they believe in and that they think are cool concepts, and your focus statement can serve to quickly explain to them what is so thrilling about your idea. Of course, marketing people also love comparative descriptions, such as, "The game's basically *Tetris* meets *Quake*." So, if possible, you may want to come up with some sort of comparisons that place your game within the context of already existing hit games, games the marketing specialists already know how to sell. But keep your focus devoid of unnecessary references to other games, in order to keep it as standalone as possible. Once the marketers think that *Tetris* meets *Quake* is a

pretty hot idea, they will want more information about your game, and your focus perfectly provides that.

Using your focus for your game's development is the primary reason you wrote it down in the first place. Many game designers do not have a focus when they are working on a game, and it shows. Of course, it is possible to make a good game without really having any idea of what your game is all about. It is also possible to win the lottery. When your livelihood, reputation, and the quality of your final game are on the line, however, you want something more than a random number generator to determine if your game works or not. Using a focus is one tool that will help you to create a solid, entertaining, and compelling game.

Chapter 6:
Interview: Ed Logg

Asteroids, **Centipede**, and **Gauntlet**. If there was ever an impressive track record for a game designer, that is it. Throw in some lesser-known classics such as **Super Breakout**, **Millipede**, **Gauntlet II**, and **Xybots** and you have a truly unequaled career. Ed Logg designed and developed all of those titles at Atari back in the heyday of the arcades. These days, designing games for the coin-op market seems to be a dying art form, with so much of the industry's attention shifted to the home market. Today Logg continues to work in game development, adapting popular Atari arcade games such as the **San Francisco Rush** series to consoles, including the Nintendo 64 and the Sega Dreamcast. To look at them, the classic arcade games seem quite simple, but it is that simplicity which forced their designers to refine them to the point of perfection. Logg's classic coin-op games remain some of the best computer games ever made, and the insight designers can gain from studying them is enormous.

What was it like working at Atari in the late '70s and early '80s?

We were young and energetic. I imagine it is very similar to the atmosphere at most Internet startups these days. We were a relatively small group in the Coin Operated Games Division. This allowed everyone to know everyone else. Ideas and pranks flowed freely. Since we were working on a new medium we could do anything and it would be "new." Even games like *Lunar Lander*, done by Rich Moore, which had been done originally years before, were new to our audience.

Where did most of the ideas for the games come from?

The ideas came from many sources. For example, Owen Rubin, another engineer at Atari, told me Nolan Bushnell had suggested to him an extension of *Breakout*. I took his idea and added many of my own to create *Super Breakout*, my first commercial success. The idea for *Asteroids* came from Lyle Rains, who was in charge of engineer-

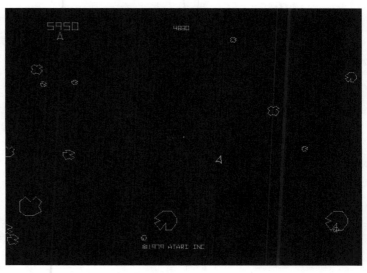

Asteroids

ing at the time. He got the idea from a previous coin-op game. *Xybots* came from a challenge by Doug Snyder, a hardware engineer at Atari. We wanted to do a multi-player *Castle Wolfenstein*-like game but we had no "bit-map" hardware. So I created an algorithm based on 8x8 stamps and he did the hardware. *Centipede* came from a list of brainstorming ideas. Atari would go off-site each year to think up new ideas. One of those ideas was "Bug Shooter" which was used as a starting point for *Centipede*.

Management had reviews where they would come in and play the game and give feedback. Sometimes the consensus was negative and a game could be killed. Most often it would continue until it could be "field tested." This meant it was left to the players to determine how much and for how long the game earned. However, sometimes good suggestions came from these reviews. The most important one of all was a suggestion made by Dan Van Elderen, who was in charge of engineering. He asked me why we could not shoot the mushrooms in *Centipede*. Yes, the mushrooms were originally static. It was his suggestion that led to the breakthrough that made this game fun.

Were you excited to get into game development at Atari?

Actually, I had been doing games for many years on the side, while in high school, at Berkeley in the '60s and also at my first job at Control Data Corp. I ported *Star Trek* and the original *Dungeon* game between Stanford's and CDC's computers.

I had built a home computer a year or two before joining Atari, just to create and play games. I had been to a Pizza Time Theater and played *Pong* and *Breakout*, so I was well aware of the coin-op business. I had also played games and was very inspired by a prototype of the Atari VCS (2600) at a Christmas party in 1977. So the change in employment seemed natural for me. At the time I thought it was great for them to pay me to create and play games.

Dirt Bike was your first game for Atari, but I understand it didn't make it into production. What sort of game was it?

This game was started by Dennis Koble who went on to do many consumer titles. It was a game similar to *Sprint* except you drove a dirt bike and the control was a set of handlebars that could be used to steer the bike instead of a steering wheel.

We field tested the game and it earned enough money to make it good enough not to kill outright but not good enough to make it into production. However, I had made *Super Breakout* at the same time I was working on *Dirt Bike*. No one at Atari had ever worked on two games at once before. *Super Breakout* had earned a large amount of money, and this probably led to the decision not to build *Dirt Bike*. I was not disappointed considering the success of *Super Breakout*.

What was the genesis of _Super Breakout_?

The original idea included six variations on *Breakout*. I envisioned three released games with two variations in each game. However, in actual play there was one overall favorite, Progressive Breakout. In the end we put three variations in one game: Progressive, Double, and Cavity Breakout. The variations that did not make it were more vertically oriented and I had to agree they were not as fun.

Were you given a lot of creative freedom on _Super Breakout_, or were you constrained since it was a sequel to a previous hit?

To me, *Super Breakout* was not a sequel. Remember the original game was not done in software. The code had to be created from scratch and the gameplay was completely different from the original even though we used the same controls.

I was given freedom because I was doing the title without any official sanction. It was not the last time I would do that, either. Games could be done in a short time in those days, which meant you could make something fun before anyone even noticed you were doing anything different.

Maybe I should explain how we were developing games in those days. We had one main Digital computer which had the cross assembler for our 6502 based games. We had several gals who would enter our handwritten pages into our programs and give us back a computer printout and a paper tape. Yes, you heard that right. We would then feed the paper tape through our

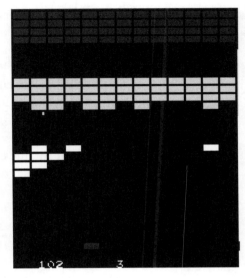

Super Breakout

development system into the RAM replacing the game ROM on the PCB. We would debug this using primitive tools and a hardware analyzer and write our changes on the paper printout. Since this process left time between the debug session and the next version, I used this time to develop a second game. I would just swap the graphics PROM (yes, we created the graphics by hand ourselves), and load the new paper tape.

That's really astonishing that you ever developed a game using such primitive methods. How did you manage to fine-tune your game with such a long time between versions?

Well, actually, I was very good at just patching RAM with new instructions, so it was easy to see what small changes did to the game. We also had an HP analyzer that we could use to trap on many conditions, which allowed us to find many bugs that many development systems cannot even do today. Actually it was possible to do some new coding while you were waiting for your last changes to be made, so less time was lost than you think.

But you would certainly agree that modern development tools have made game development easier?

There are several issues here. First, back then we often knew everything about the target hardware, which made it easier to see what was going wrong. Today, the target hardware is often hidden from us and there are several layers of software which can make debugging or doing what we really want to do difficult. So in this sense it is much harder now. Also these modern software or hardware layers are often not documented, documented incorrectly, or just getting in our way. Second, the hardware has gotten very complex with interactions between the many bytes causing all sorts of problems. Third, the processors have become very complex, causing all sorts of debugging nightmares, especially in dealing with the caches. Fourth, today there are many programmers working on a game and it is easy to mess up one of your coworkers.

Surprisingly, the development environment has not gotten any faster over the past few years despite the great increases in the computing power and RAM. As an example, some of my files on my 25 MHz Mac IIci with 6 MB of RAM compile and link in the same time or faster than files on a 550 MHz PC under NT with 512 MB of RAM. Even the same project on my 150 MHz Indy builds faster than my 550 MHz PC. I firmly believe that every tool developer should be given the slowest possible system to use to develop their software! Otherwise, we are doomed to continue to run no faster with each new upgrade.

The modern tools are so much better than the old method, it is hard to imagine how I could have done so well, but you mustn't forget how much time is spent learning each new software tool, processor, and operating system these days. In addition, the amount of time wasted chasing after bugs on new systems because I did not understand some other hardware or software is quite large. But I would not want to go back to the old tools unless the processors, hardware, software, game concepts, and team sizes were much simpler.

I've never seen your next game, *Video Pinball*. How did it play?

It simulated pinball by using a half-silvered mirror with a monitor below the mirror and the graphics for the play-field above the mirror. The monitor would show the flippers and ball, which gave the impression the white ball was on the play-field. The play-field actually had LEDs controlled by the program which simulated lit targets. In addition, the control panel was hinged, which allowed the player to "nudge" the cabinet to give the ball some English. I did not think this game up. I believe it was Dave Stubben's idea.

How did you hope to convince players to play *Video Pinball* instead of the real thing?

I did not believe *Video Pinball* would be successful and I was asking that exact question. However, there were places video games could go that a large pinball game could not. In the end, the game earned more than I had expected and it was a commercial success. I must say I was wrong on my first impressions, and that does not happen often.

Was it hard to work on a project that you did not think would be any fun? Did the final game turn out to be entertaining?

The gameplay was fun but no comparison to a real pinball game. I was surprised that it sold as well as it did. Yes, it was hard to work on an idea that I did not think would work well. But I was young and motivated… What else can I say?

Where did the idea for *Asteroids* come from?

Lyle Rains had suggested to me the idea of a game where the player could shoot asteroids because there had been an earlier coin-op game with an indestructible asteroid that the players kept shooting instead of pursuing the intended goal. I told Lyle we would need a saucer to force the player to shoot the asteroids instead of

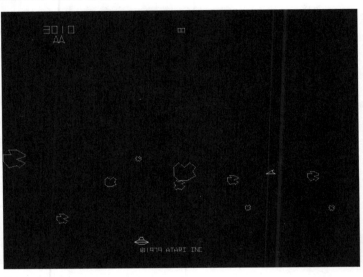

Asteroids

wasting time. I also suggested breaking the rocks up into pieces to give the players some strategy instead of just shooting the larger rocks first.

Lyle gave me the idea. People often attribute the success to one or the other of us. I would probably not have come up with the idea on my own and if someone else had done the game it would most likely have been totally different. So in truth, we should both be given credit for this idea. Come to think of it, without the vector hardware, *Asteroids* would not have been a success either. So there are many people and events that led to its success. I am very glad to have been there at that time and place.

The game changed very little in development from the original idea. I did make two saucers, one dumb and one smart. I made one fundamental change near the end of the project that had far-reaching implications. Originally, the saucer would shoot as soon as the player entered the screen. Players complained, and I agreed, this seemed unfair. Often the saucer was not visible just off the edge and if it started next to your ship you had no defense. So I added a delay before his first shot. This, of course, led to the "lurking" strategy. While testing, I had actually tried to lurk at one point and decided it was not going to work, which shows you how well the game designer can play his own game.

Were you surprised by *Asteroids'* success?

I was not surprised by its success. It sounded like a fun game when I played it in my mind. Even after the first few weeks, people would come by and ask when they could play. That was a sign your game was fun!

Even when we field tested the game for the very first time, I saw a player start a game and die three times within 20 seconds. He proceeded to put another quarter in. This tells me the player felt it was his fault he died and he was convinced he could do better. This is one of the primary goals a game designer tries to achieve and it was clear to me *Asteroids* had "it."

Back there you mentioned that you played the game out "in your mind." Do you find that to be an effective technique for predicting whether a game will be fun or not?

It is a skill which I find works well for me. I also play devil's advocate with my ideas: I ask myself "what can go wrong?" or "will players be confused by what I am presenting?" I find that some designers often are so married to their ideas that they will not accept the concept that maybe it just won't work. I cannot tell you the number of great ideas I have had that I "played out" in my mind that turned out to be bad ideas.

I am one of the few designers I have ever met that has actually killed many of his own games. I think this is a good trait. Why waste another year to two if the gameplay does not play like you expected?

Did you work on the sequel, *Asteroids Deluxe?*

I did not do *Asteroids Deluxe.* It was done by Dave Shepperd. I was promoted around that time into a supervisor role. I believe I was also leading the four-player *Football* project. So I was busy. I have no problems doing sequels if that is the best course of action. I had some new ideas, so I wanted to do *Millipede. Gauntlet II* was a logical choice since Bob Flanagan, my co-programmer, and I knew the code and this was the best game concept we came up with.

After *Asteroids* you didn't make another vector-based game. Did you not like working with the hardware?

Actually, I loved vector hardware for the reason it allowed me to put up high-resolution 768 by 1024 pictures. However, the industry was just moving over to color monitors at the time. Dave Theurer did do *Tempest* as a color vector game, but the color mask on color monitors did not permit high resolution. Besides, you could not fill the screen with color on vector-based games, so that medium died with the advance of color games.

Wasn't *Asteroids* the first Atari game to have a high-score table?

Actually, *Asteroids* was not the first game; there was another game that used it just prior. I thought the idea was a great way to preserve your score and identity for the world to see. So I added it to *Asteroids*. I see it as filling the role of graffiti. Now it is standard, of course, and the industry has added battery-backed RAM or EEROM to save it permanently.

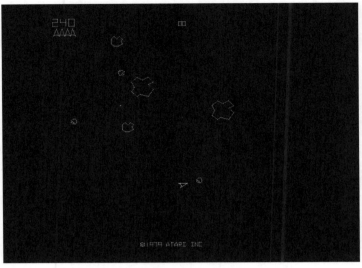

Asteroids

Around this time you created the *Othello* cartridge for the Atari 2600. I understand you studied AI while at Stanford. Did the *Othello* project grow out of your interest in AI?

No, actually *Asteroids* showed more influence from my Stanford experience. While I was at the Stanford AI Lab, I had played *Space War* on their PDP machines. I had also played a coin-op version of this in the Student Forum coffee shop. In my mind, this was the first video game. *Pong* certainly was the first commercial video game. Anyway, the spaceship design in *Asteroids* was a copy of the original *Space War* ship.

I had played *Othello* as a board game and I was intrigued by possible strategies. So I worked on this game at home and developed an idea that the game could be played by pattern matching without any AI. In other words, the computer does not look ahead at your replies to any of its moves, which was the standard AI approach at the time. So really the *Othello* game I did had no AI. It was good enough for the beginner and average player. It was not an advanced game by any means. Besides, the 2600 had only 128 bytes of RAM so there was not much space to look ahead.

In fact, Carol Shaw had done the hard part by providing me the kernel which drew the pieces on a checkerboard. The 2600 was extremely difficult to do anything complex on. It was intended to do *Pong*-style games. You spent all of active video counting cycles to draw the screen. This left Vblank to do any thinking or other work. There was limited RAM so nothing complex could be saved in RAM. *Othello* was 2,048 bytes. Most of this was the kernel. So I often spent time trying to eliminate a few bytes to add something new.

Was *Centipede* your next game?

No, as I mentioned I was a supervisor at the time. I was project leader on four-player *Football* and a kit to upgrade the plays on the original *Football* game.

On *Centipede*, I thought up the idea of the centipede segments and the way the legs moved. I do not believe it was mentioned in the original "Bug Shooter" brainstorming idea. In fact, no one has ever stepped forward to claim "Bug Shooter" as their idea. Maybe it was due to the finished product being so much different from the original idea. I had assigned a new programmer,

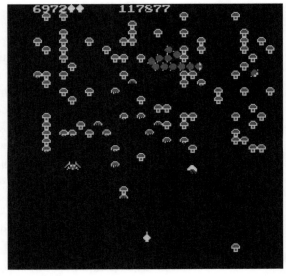
Centipede

Donna Bailey, to do the programming on *Centipede*. Partway through the project, I quit being a supervisor (I didn't like the job and it took me away from doing games) and spent time working on *Centipede*.

So Bailey was pretty important to the game's development?

I would guess she did about half the programming. The game design was left to me because she was working on her first project.

It seems that *Centipede* appeals to women more than most arcade games. Do you think Bailey had something to do with that?

I wish I knew the answer to that question. Someone could point out that no other game I have done appeals to women as much as *Centipede*.

Many theories have been suggested. One is that is was created by a woman. Another is that destroying insects fits well with a woman's psyche. I believe this game appeals to women because it is not gender biased like fighting games or RPGs or sports games. Other examples like *Pac-Man* and *Tetris* are notable.

I do know *Centipede* fits the basic criterion for a game that appeals to a wide audience. It has a new, appealing look (to get players to try it), an obvious goal (shoot anything), clear rules, an easy set of controls, a sense of accomplishment (kill the entire centipede before he gets you), dynamic strategies abound (trap the centipede and kill spiders or the blob strategy or channel the centipede or just plain straight-up play), enough randomness to make the game different each time, a goal to keep you going (a new life every 12,000 points), a clear sense of getting better with more play, and a sense that any death was the player's fault.

So you mentioned that *Centipede* grew out of a brainstorming idea. How did the brainstorming process work at Atari?

The brainstorming ideas came from anyone in the company. They were usually gathered weeks before the actual meeting which was held off-site, away from Atari. Often the ideas were just a theme. Most submittals had sort of a sketch or art to give the reader a little more info. Occasionally a full game description was submitted which explained the hardware, controls, art, and gameplay.

During the brainstorming session, each idea would be presented and then suggestions would be made for improving it. In addition, marketing would give a rundown of what was selling and the state of the industry. We would also break into smaller groups to discuss a specific type of game or talk about specific games themselves. In the end we would meet again to present any additional ideas from these smaller meetings and vote for the popular ideas. I would say we would get a majority from programmers and designers, but there were a significant number of ideas from artists and others in the company. I found many of the ideas needed a lot of work so it was not uncommon for the original brainstorming idea to get a major overhaul.

Atari Games Corp., now Midway Games West, still uses this process each year. But quite honestly, many of the recent coin-op games are just remakes of older games. For example, more versions of *Rush* or *Cruisin'*. The reason is often market driven: these are the games that have done well in the past and the company does not often want to risk taking a chance on a new theme.

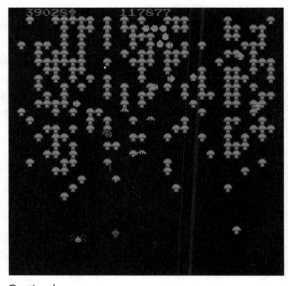

How did *Centipede* change over the course of the game's development?

I mentioned that Dan Van Elderen asked why the player could not shoot mushrooms. I realized early I would need some means to create new mushrooms. This led to one being left when a centipede segment was shot. I also

Centipede

created the flea which left a trail of them when he dropped to create more randomness in the pattern. In other words, I did not want the player to create the only pattern of mushrooms. The spider was always planned to be my "*Asteroids* saucer" which kept the player moving; the spider also had to eat mushrooms to keep the player area somewhat free of mushrooms. The scorpion was added to add a randomness to the centipede pattern and create a sense of panic when the segments would come rushing to the bottom of the screen.

Do you try to create games which allow different players to use different strategies to succeed?

I do strive to give the players as much freedom to create as many strategies as possible. So in a sense, yes, I guess I do encourage players to experiment and try different strategies. I do try to make sure that none of them work all the time or make the game too easy. But I want to leave the player with the impression that if he was only a little bit better he could pull it off.

Why did you choose to use the trackball for *Centipede*?

I believe we used the trackball from the start. I had experience with the trackball on *Football* but I wanted something that was not as heavy and physical to move around. That is how the *Centipede* trackball came about. The trackball, just like the computer mouse, provides a means for inputting arbitrary direction as well as speed. No other controller comes close. It was the clear winner for player controllability.

In my opinion, *Centipede* is one of the best balanced games ever. Was there a lot of experimentation to achieve such a balance?

I would not use the term experimentation in this case because nothing was tried and discarded. There was a grasshopper that we intended to add to hop onto the player, but the spider was sufficient in forcing the player to move so the grasshopper was never even tried. Of course, you can still see the graphics for the grasshopper if you look at the self-test graphics.

There certainly was a lot of tuning. The timing and speed of when things happened certainly was changed over the course of the project. The balance comes from the inherent rules of the game and the art of knowing when to leave the play alone and when to change something. This art is something that some people have and others just don't. I cannot define it other than to use the term "game sense."

Were you given freedom to do whatever you wanted for *Millipede*?

With my past record I was given more freedom than anyone else. Something most people do not understand is that half of the games I started did not make it into production. No one ever hears about the failures. Some of the games I actually

killed myself. That's something I
believe no one else at Atari did. Of
course, there are a few I tried to
kill but was not allowed to that
eventually died. These days you
would probably see them come out
in the consumer market anyway
just to get back some of the development cost. But in the coin-op
market there is no chance to sell
anything that isn't a clear winner.

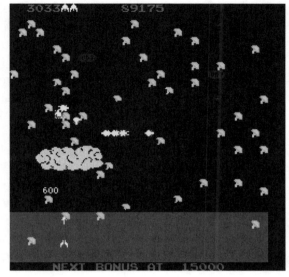

Millipede

Millipede **allowed players to start farther into the game, at 45,000 points, for
example. Was this an effort to shorten the games of the expert players?**

It was a way to increase the cash box. It allowed the good players to start at a
higher score where the gameplay was on a difficulty level that was probably just
above his level of skill. This often meant shorter game times but would allow higher
scores. In a sense I was doing this for marketing reasons. This was not a first for
Millipede. *Tempest* had this feature back in 1981.

**I particularly like the "growth" of the extra mushrooms in *Millipede*. Was this
done using a "life" algorithm?**

Yes, it is based on the game of life where two or three neighbors would create a
new mushroom and anything more or less would kill the mushroom. This has an
interesting history. Mark Cerny asked why I didn't do a life algorithm on the mushrooms. I told him I was busy but if he wanted to add it to the game he could. Of
course, Mark, being the sharp guy he is, looked at my code and quickly created this
feature. He also added the attract mode to demonstrate all the creatures.

**During the *Asteroids* to *Millipede* period, almost all your games were being ported
to a wide variety of systems: the 2600, the Apple II, and so forth. How did you feel
about these conversions?**

It was good business for the company so it made business sense. Of course it
always made me proud to see my game in many new places. I did have some concerns about several of the ports. I understand the limitations of some of the systems
but I wanted to make sure the company released the best possible conversion. In

many cases I was involved in making sure it had all the features but unfortunately not often enough.

Some of the conversions made improvements that were not possible in the coin-op market. For example, in *Gauntlet* they made a quest mode with a limited amount of health. This would not be possible in coin-op where the object is to get more money added on a regular basis. Another example would be to look at the number of variations of *Pong* included on the Atari 2600 cartridge. It just makes good sense to add value for a consumer title.

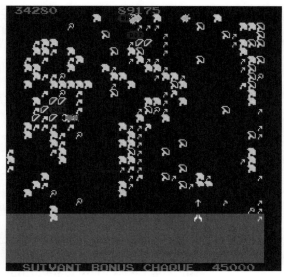
Millipede

Was *Maze Invaders* the next game you worked on after *Millipede?* I know it never went into production.

It was a cute puzzle-like game. I was not sad it didn't make it; it did not earn enough on field test. My son loved the game though and I still have one of the two prototypes in my garage. The other was purchased by an operator in Texas, I believe. He loved the game so much he talked Atari into selling it to him.

I believe I mentioned earlier that nearly half of my games did not make it into production. There were engineers that had a higher percentage, Dave Theurer in particular. But there were others who never had a game in production.

The name *Maze Invaders* suggests perhaps something inspired by *Pac-Man*. Was it?

Yes, in a way. It was a maze-like game but the maze changed dynamically. The main character was very *Pac-Man* like; he was cute. There were some parts that I found frustrating, such as when the maze would temporarily block me off. I could not resolve this frustrating aspect, which is probably why it failed.

I understand in 1983 you also worked on a *Road Runner* laser disk game. Was it based on the Warner Bros. cartoon character?

Yes, it was based on Road Runner created by Chuck Jones. The player played the part of the Road Runner who would try to have Wile E. Coyote fall prey to some trap. I had Time Warner send me all of the Road Runner cartoons. I watched every one and selected the best shorts to be included on a laser disk. So when you succeeded in getting Wile E. destroyed, the game would cut from the action to a similar scene from a cartoon where Wile E. met his usual fate.

I always loved the Road Runner and I thought I could bring him to a video game. When I started I had a vision of something unique. The game certainly met that criterion but it was not as fun as I had hoped. I certainly enjoying seeing all the old cartoons and meeting Chuck Jones but . . .

So the game was killed?

Laser disk games were failing in the coin-op world because of reliability problems. The game actually earned enough to warrant interest but not as a laser disk game. So when they asked me to port it to their new "System I" hardware, I declined, saying I had another idea I wanted to pursue. I am glad they let me pursue this new idea because this idea became *Gauntlet*. *Road Runner* was converted over to System I and actually was released.

Did *Gauntlet* follow your initial vision fairly closely, or did it change a lot in development?

I went back recently and looked at the original game design document and I was surprised how closely the graphics and gameplay matched the finished product. Of course, what did change during development was the hardware. I created an algorithm which would allow me to deal with 1,000 objects with-

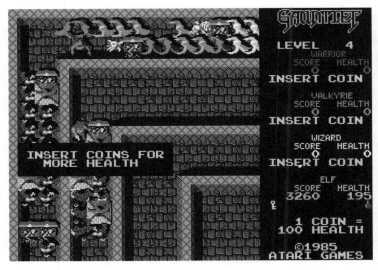

Gauntlet

out burdening the processor or slowing down the frame rate. I asked Pat McCarthy, the electrical engineer, if he could extend the existing hardware and he found a way to do this which would allow me to display all the objects I needed. In the end there were five patents issued for *Gauntlet*.

Because of the size of the PCB and the restrictions on PCB size for Japanese kits, we decided to use a four-layer PCB for *Gauntlet*. Atari had never laid out such a board nor had they ever used traces as small as we required. But in the end we paved the way for all future PCBs at Atari. So besides the success of the game in the industry, *Gauntlet* also made a giant leap in the way we did engineering and manufacturing at Atari.

To my memory of arcades in 1985, *Gauntlet* seemed to be one of the first action games to allow four players to play at once.

This was the first multi-player game which allowed players to end or leave at any time and the screen scrolling was controlled by their actions. This was not the first game to have multi-players. *Tank 8* allowed eight players on one monitor. But all the players had to start at the same time. The idea of using four players was designed into *Gauntlet* from the start. I suspect it was due to the fact that I could only put four players around an upright monitor.

I believe *Gauntlet* was the first game that allowed the player to buy in any time he wanted. I did not want the players to wait, like in *Tank 8*, for everyone to coin-up at the same time. The only solution was to have players come and go at will. Health was always planned from the start. I believe this idea came from *Dungeons & Dragons*, which was very popular at the time. So it was logical that money just bought more health. Since it is every coin-op designer's wish to have the players put as much money as they can into their game, I saw no reason why I would not have the players just increase their health with each coin. In hindsight, this is a wonderful idea because losing 2000 health was not as painful psychologically as inserting another quarter. Besides, the players would not need to reach into their pocket to find another quarter to insert before their character was lost.

Where did the idea to have the game say things like "Red Warrior needs food, badly" come from?

I do not remember. I suspect it was not my idea. It may have come from my co-programmer Bob Flanagan or from someone else at Atari. In any case we had a large list of phrases we wanted the "Dungeon Master" to say to taunt the player. There are several phrases that seem to stick in everyone's mind. My favorite is "the Wizard (me) seems to be eating all the food lately."

Many think the Valkyrie was the most powerful of the four characters.

Actually, the Hulk or the Wizard could be used to play forever. This was demonstrated first by players in Japan playing a one-player game. This was fixed later by reducing the amount of food on subsequent levels if the player had not lost enough health during the last level. The Valkyrie was designed to be the most balanced of the characters but shot power, shot speed, and strength proved to be more important than other attributes. This is why the Hulk and Wizard seemed to be the most powerful. Of course, the Elf was fun to play with for many players because you could always get more food or treasure than the other players.

Gauntlet II **allowed four players to all be playing Valkyries, or Elves, or whatever combination they wanted. Did this mean the character classes had to be more equal than in the first game?**

No, we actually did very little that I can recall to equalize the characters. This feature was added because some players wanted to play a particular character and I did not want them to wait until the desired position was open. So in essence I eliminated another reason for not entering the game right away.

Gauntlet II

Was *Xybots* **your next project after** *Gauntlet II?*

Bob Flanagan and I actually started another game which I quickly killed after the initial gameplay turned out to be less fun than I had expected.

Xybots, as I mentioned earlier, started out as an idea to do *Castle Wolfenstein*. I started the game as a two-player split-screen *Gauntlet III*. Partway through marketing said they wanted something other than *Gauntlet*. So I changed the characters and enemies to be more like *Major Havoc*. I still regret changing the theme and wish I had kept my original game concept.

Was it a great engineering challenge to create the game's 3D look?

I developed a very interesting algorithm for doing the 3D rotation using just 8x8 pixel stamps, as we call them. I don't know how to explain how this worked without getting my original sketches to visually demonstrate it. I could have had the player rotate other than in 90-degree increments, but it made the gameplay simpler to just allow only 90-degree rotations.

If I recall, the game had interesting and unique controls.

The controller was very unique because it provided the standard eight-way joystick as well as a knob on top which could turn left or right to indicate a rotation. This control made the game more difficult, which is often the kiss of death in the

coin-op market. As
with any 3D game,
players could not
easily visualize
where they were
despite the map
available to them. In
addition, it was pos-
sible to get shot in
the back, which
added to the frustra-
tion factor.

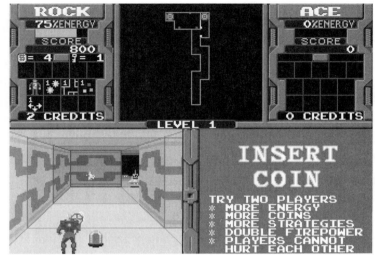

Xybots

How did you get involved working on the Atari *Tetris*?

I played a version of *Tetris* and was quickly addicted. I asked our legal counsel, Dennis Wood, to get the rights. Since I had just worked on reverse engineering the Nintendo Family Computer, which soon became the Nintendo Entertainment System in the U.S., I decided to create a version on the FC and NES and sell it through Tengen, which was Atari's consumer publisher. Dennis Wood got the rights and we showed *Tetris* first at the June Consumer Electronics Show. It was decided to improve the game so I redid the visuals and we released it at the following CES in January.

I should point out that I was working on another game at the time I was doing this, so I could not devote all my time to the *Tetris* project. It was this fact that made me need to turn over *Tetris* to Greg Rivera and Norm Avellar for the coin-op market. I did get my original code to run on the coin-op hardware before going back to my project. This is why my name appears on the credits of the coin-op version.

What did you like so much about *Tetris*?

It was just so addicting I knew we had to have it. In hindsight, I could explain why this game worked so well but I am not sure that would prove anything. Besides, the real question is "Why didn't I think of this idea?"

Was Tengen *Tetris* your only NES project?

I had *Centipede* and *Millipede* running on the FC before the lawsuit with Atari Corp. resulted in the ruling that they owned the rights to all our games prior to the sale of Atari to Tramiel by Time Warner. So we had to drop the work I did. So my previous work made *Tetris* very easy to do on the NES. I also added the two-player simultaneous feature which made this game better than all the other versions. Later you would see Tengen versions selling for $150 or more.

Why was Tengen *Tetris* eventually withdrawn from circulation?

You can read several versions of the story but I suspect the bottom line is the Hungarian who had the rights did a poor job of covering all the bases. The Russians accepted money from Nintendo when Nintendo created a new category of rights. Despite the fact we had the rights to computer systems, Nintendo claimed their Family Computer was not a computer even though they sold Basic and a keyboard and other services in Japan just like any other computer. I was certainly disappointed to see my work lost.

Why did you want to work on conversions of someone else's game?

As with many of my games, this was the best idea I could think of at the time. However, in this case, because I enjoyed it so much, it was an easy decision. What better way to play the game you like so much and make sure it comes out the way you like?

What did you work on next?

I eventually killed the game I was working on during the "*Tetris* Affair." I believe *Steel Talons* was my next project. I wanted to do a 3D Red Baron flying/shooting game but marketing thought World War I planes were not cool enough for teens, who were the prime coin-op target audience. Marketing wanted jets and I thought that was a dumb idea because who wants to see dots at a distance shooting at each other. I wanted something close where you can see the detail of the enemy you are shooting at. Helicopters were the logical choice.

Wasn't *Steel Talons* a fairly authentic helicopter simulator?

Steel Talons had all the regular helicopter controls: a rudder, a collective for controlling height, and a stick for turning. Of course flying a helicopter is difficult without some assistance, so I had computer assist just like real military helicopters. I added automatic collective control so the player would maintain level flight and any landing would be smooth. It would also increase height if the ground was sloping in front of the height. The "real" mode just disabled this helping code and increased the player's acceleration to compensate. This was a unique feature and Atari was issued a patent on this idea.

The game had another interesting feature that had never been used on a video game before. We installed a pinball thumper, often used to indicate a free game, under the seat. This was used whenever the player's helicopter was hit by enemy fire. During the first field test, the voltage for this thumper was higher than it should have been and the first players to use it nearly jumped out of their seats when it fired. The noise could be heard over the entire arcade.

The first field test also introduced a new problem that we never had before. I went out to check on collections and I tried to remove the coin box. If you have ever seen *Steel Talons*, you will see that the coin box is located at a strange angle requiring the operator to lift the box with his arms fully extended. Not the easiest position to lift any weight. Well back to the story. I tried to lift the box out but could not budge it. I thought it was jammed. I soon discovered that the box was so full and was so heavy it was nearly impossible to remove. This led to the strange instructions in the manual asking the operators to empty the coin box every couple of days.

On *Steel Talons*, didn't you work with *Battlezone* creator Ed Rotberg?

Yes I did. He was at Atari during the golden days of *Battlezone, Asteroids*, et cetera. He left Atari to do a start-up called Sente, before returning to Atari a few years later. He had just finished working on a *Tube Chase*-like game using the same 3D hardware that *Steel Talons* used. This hardware was a cost reduced version of the *Hard Drivin'* PCBs. So it was natural for Ed to work with me on this project. Another interesting feature of this game was fog. The original *Hard Drivin'* team did not believe me when I told them I could add fog to the world. I am still proud of this effect and they were surprised that it worked.

How did the *Space Lords* project come about?

I wanted to continue my ideas of multi-player play that I started on *Gauntlet*, and then continued on *Xybots* and *Steel Talons*. So I chose a 3D space environment with up to four cabinets linked together. Each cabinet had two monitors similar to *Cyberball*. I tried to keep the cost down by using Atari's "growth motion object" hardware which was cheaper by far than the 3D hardware used on *Steel Talons*. It could not draw 3D polygons, but it could grow or shrink flat textures.

I understand *Space Lords* did not do too well financially.

Space Lords had some strange earning patterns. At some arcades it earned more than $1,000 per week for two double cabinets. But at some small arcades it earned only $75 as a single cabinet. The bottom line is we had a difficult time selling it because of its cost and the limited number of locations it could be sold into. It was definitely hard to make a coin-op game using the concept of one player per monitor. Even though I added a second player as a gunner at half price, it was felt by many to be not as fun as being the pilot.

And *Space Lords* came out right around the time the fighting games were taking off.

The fighting games made *Space Lords* difficult to sell because they were often "kits," which sold much cheaper than a large dedicated upright. *Street Fighter II* had great earnings and continued to earn good money for a long time.

In fact, since the early '90s most arcade games have been in one of a very few, limited genres. What do you think of many of the arcade games that come out these days?

You are right, the coin-op market seems to be all driving, fighting, and shooting with an occasional sports title, like golf. There are reasons for this. Driving has universal appeal and usually earns for long periods. So it is often the most accepted game theme. Besides, most home units do not have steering wheels and gas pedals or give you the feel of being inside a car. So you cannot get this experience in the home. Fighting games are now difficult to sell in the arcades and I believe this is because you can get the same experience on most advanced consoles. At the time they were cheap and earned big bucks. Shooting games are still viable because guns are not the standard controller on consoles or PCs. So the only way a game player can get this experience is in the arcade.

So the bottom line is, most arcade games these days are not unique and fit very limited categories. I don't think the arcades are completely dead but they are not the destination places they used to be.

Did *Space Lords* turn out to be your last coin-op?

I was working on a shooting game prior to my departure from Atari. That game died but the gun was used later on *Area 51*. I joined Electronic Arts who were trying to start up their own coin-op group. My intention was to start doing consumer games. But EA had some old Atari friends and I decided to join them. I had done one puzzle game which I killed and was working on a shooting game when they decided to drop out of the coin-op market. Then I was even more determined to enter the consumer games business.

How did you come to start doing N64 programming?

I was looking for a project to work on, so I contacted many companies to see what they had to offer. I was planning to work with another programmer from EA but he decided to join some friends to start up a new company. Atari wanted the coin-op *Wayne Gretzky 3D Hockey* done on the N64 and I was looking forward to doing something on that platform. This was partly because the game promised to look better than the PSX but also because it looked like we could be the first hockey title available. So I joined a group at Atari and we started work on *Wayne Gretzky 3D Hockey*. This turned out to be more work than I expected partly due to the state of N64 development systems but also due to the fact the coin-op was not going to be done until just before we released.

As you mentioned, a lot of the appeal of playing an arcade game like *San Francisco Rush* seems to be sitting in the chair, having the gearshift, the steering wheel, the force feedback, and so forth. How do you try to capture that for the N64, which has none of these niceties?

You are right. The home does not have the environment of the arcade cabinets but we can do things on the home games we can never do in the arcade. We can provide more choices for the player, more tracks for them to learn, and more things to discover.

I try to keep the basic play the same but I always try to add value to the

San Francisco Rush: Extreme Racing for the Nintendo 64

product. This is one thing I made clear when I joined Atari. Atari wanted me to just do a straight port. That had always worked for them in the past. I did not believe this would work and told them I would be adding additional "stuff." For example, on *Gretzky* we added a full-sized rink, a new AI, instant replay, more players, full seasons, etc. In general, home games require considerably more work. I also believe we can do different games for the home market that we could never do in the arcade. So for me, this opens up new possibilities.

Arcade pieces must be easy to learn with rules that are obvious and provide entertainment that lasts ninety seconds. The home market is not bound by these rules. Instead you must provide more life for your product. Often this means it takes the player longer to "finish" the game. Even when the player has finished it, there must be reasons why he will want to go back to do it all over again.

Do you like the engineering challenges of doing home conversions?

I actually enjoy the "old style" of trying to get everything to fit. I also enjoy adding tricks to get the frame rate as high as possible. It was very interesting to get all of *SF Rush* into 8 MB, which includes around 3 MB of audio and all the graphics.

Do you miss doing original designs?

Yes, I do miss the old game designs. 2D worlds are so much easier for the player to understand. I also like the idea of creating a game with a fixed set of rules and enough randomness so that the player can create different play-styles and their own strategies.

I am not sure I could sell a game with an "old design." Players have different expectations now. They would expect 3D designs or Internet play or high-resolution textures and pre-rendered movies or highly developed characters... Besides, just about anything I do now will just elicit comments like "It is just a twist on game xxx with a little of game zzz." For the record, many of the old designs were based on previous game ideas. Remember, *Asteroids* came from a previous game with a little of *Space War* thrown in, even though many thought of this as an original design.

You have been working with Atari for more than twenty years now, so you must really like it there.

Yes, Atari has been very good to me. I have a deep sense of loyalty to the company and the people I work with. Besides, I like what I am doing, so I see little reason to leave. I think the loyalty is mostly due to heredity. Longevity comes from doing what I like.

Working on games requires something which many people do not have. Many cannot take the constant pressure to perform, the long hours, and the thought that their "baby" that they have been working on may get killed after eighteen months of hard labor. Others are programmers or artists who have found more interesting things to do.

I must admit I have often thought of doing something else. I just have not found anything else I want to do more than what I am doing now. That could change or I may find myself doing games until I retire.

In the last few years, *Asteroids*, *Centipede*, and *Gauntlet* have all been remade. How do you feel about the remakes?

Many are doomed to fail just like most game ideas. *Gauntlet* was a good case of a remake that worked very well. *Arkanoid* was a remake of *Breakout* that worked very well. So remakes can work, but it is difficult.

The real failure comes from comparing the gameplay to the original. For example, making a 3D version of *Centipede* makes the gameplay harder because the 3D information is not as easy for the player to process. Remember, designers have had twenty years to play these old games and come up with a new twist to make a new great game. The fact that they haven't done it yet seems to indicate that it is unlikely. Not impossible, but unlikely.

Which one of your games might you want to remake?

If I had the answer to that, and if I believed it was the best idea I had, I would be working on it. Besides, if I told you, then someone else would be doing it now, wouldn't they? In other words, I don't have any idea how to take some old classics and make them new and interesting in today's market.

Gauntlet Legends

How has the game development industry changed over the years?

The games industry has definitely changed, but it is still a video game industry. Video games were not a $7 billion industry when I started. With big business comes big money and that invariably brings with it control over how it is spent. So there is definitely more politics at the corporate level. The interference from management comes from their need to control the costs, but the real reason, I believe, is due to the evolution of the games themselves. By that I mean, we could design and program a game in three months in the early years. In three months you did not spend enough money for them to interfere. Games have evolved to the point where you cannot do a game with just one person in a realistic amount of time. It takes several programmers, several artists, an audio specialist, and someone to manage the project over a period from twelve to twenty-four months. The console market has changed too. You did not need to spend $1 billion to launch a new console in the early days, but it costs that much now. So with evolution comes longer periods for development and higher costs to produce a product. With the higher costs comes more money and hence more control (i.e., interference) over how it is spent.

For your original designs, you served as both designer and lead programmer. Do you enjoy working in both capacities?

Working as game designer and programmer is a good idea if you can pull it off. There are very few people who are good at both. So it is not a strategy I recommend today. For example, for today's complex multi-character and multi-level games, I am not as good a designer as I would be on other styles of games. So I would be willing to give up this role to someone else.

The programmer has to implement the design and if the designer's ideas are not communicated well enough, then the game is programmed differently than the designer expected. I believe it is often the programmer who can make or break the "feel" of a game.

You seem to have missed one point. I was also project leader on many projects. This is a role I am very good at but receive no acknowledgment. My projects are almost always on time and if there are problems, management is often told well in advance. No one outside Atari probably is aware of this. Unfortunately, I do not enjoy this role so I try to spend as little time as possible actually managing a project.

You even served as artist on your early games, didn't you?

Early on it was a good idea. There is no reason to train an artist to create a rock on graph paper and provide me with the coordinates so I could enter them into my game. When there was so little in the way of graphics or audio required, it makes no sense to have another special-ized person doing this. Today, it is an entirely different matter. Today it is absolutely required.

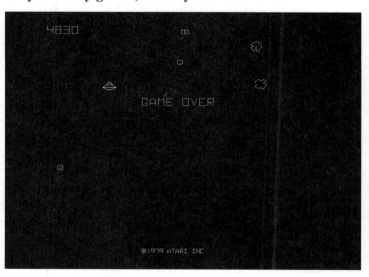

Asteroids

Do you feel that any of your games are underappreciated?

As a game designer, no, I do not feel I have any games that were under-appreciated. If the game design works, then the gameplay is fun and the game sells. As a programmer, yes, there are probably some game ideas or algorithms or pro-gramming speed which are underappreciated. Many programming tricks I do for personal enjoyment so I am not looking for external recognition.

In the early days you were pretty limited by the technology available to you. Did the technology limitations foster creativity?

Yes, I would have to agree. There were many times I spent thinking about how to do something on a given hardware and that turned into a game. *Xybots* was certainly one of those games. On *Gauntlet* we created new hardware to make the gameplay possible.

When working with an original game design, where do you start?

First, I try to come up with the game and then look at all the aspects of the play. From the market perspective: will it sell, is the timing right, licensing requirements, competition, et cetera. From the player's perspective: what makes this game fun and what is unique that will make it interesting. From the development side: what will it take to do this game in terms of people and equipment and will it be fun to do. Ideas themselves come from just about every possible source. I have mentioned how some come from previous games, brainstorming ideas, technical challenges, and other people's suggestions.

So, once you have your idea, do you start coding right away, or do you spend a lot of time thinking it through ahead of time?

With the large budgets and large teams these days, it is necessary to do a game design document and technical design document before the game gets too far into development. However, I try to start work on some critical aspect while the design documents are being drawn up. I believe it is extremely important to work on the aspect of the game that will make or break the concept. The front-end movies, story line, front and back end screens can all wait until the gameplay has been proven. Sometimes this prototyping phase is quick but often it can take several months.

Once you have proven the gameplay concept in a prototype, how does the rest of development progress?

Games go through four phases for me. The high at the beginning of a project of doing something new and the feeling that this will really be a great game. The project often makes giant leaps in short periods. The middle part of the project is mundane. The concept has been proven but there is often so much work to do and the game does not appear to change much for all your effort. The third phase is often full of panic and stress. This is the part just before release when you just want the project to end. The fourth phase is one of satisfaction after the game has been released.

With the current long projects I often feel I am getting diminishing returns for my effort, so I am happy to have the game end. In my case, almost everything I had planned for my game has been implemented, so I am happy to call it done. Except for finding those irritating last-minute bugs...

So after the prototype is functional, you don't really enjoy the development process?

Yes, I would say the bulk of the game is done after the core game concept has been proven. However, there are often parts that prove rewarding during the long development before the game is finished. But after doing so many games over the past thirty years, working on, say, the user interface just does not get me all excited.

No, I would like to do a prototype and leave it to someone else to finish. But I feel I still have the vision for the gameplay and I do not believe another person or group would continue the gameplay as I envision it. So in the end I would feel that the game was not what I expected, not mine anymore. I would always have the feeling that if I had worked on it to the finish, the game would be better than what anyone else could have done. I guess I would feel differently if I had not been as successful as I have.

What role do you think AI plays in games?

In the old games AI had no involvement. Often the enemy would follow a fixed set of rules with some randomness thrown in if necessary. These days it is entirely a different matter. It is becoming very important for modern games. Some people have recommended that, when appropriate, each project have one specially trained person dedicated to doing the game AI. And for some games, I would agree.

Why do you think the games require more sophisticated AI now?

I believe the theme and gameplay of most new games require more AI. The sim games, the shooters, et cetera, all try to give the real sense of intelligent life competing against you. If games do not try to mimic real life then a set of rules may do just fine.

How important do you think it is to make the AI in a game "real"? That is, to provide the AI only with the information the player would have in the AI agent's position?

It is not necessary but may lead to more believable enemy AI, so I would recommend it in some cases. For example, in *Steel Talons,* the enemy gunners would not turn or fire until they could see you visually. If there was a hill in the way or you were hugging the ground at the end of their range, then they did not see you. This is one case where it was necessary.

Lately, a lot of attention is being given to combining games and stories. Many arcade coin-ops, perhaps as part of their nature, have almost no story. What do you think about telling a story within a game?

I have never been high on stories. I feel it is absolutely necessary to have the player grasp the theme: setting, ambience, and goals. Sometimes stories help to make the goals easier to understand. Some games are made like a movie, so a story makes good sense: the player feels he is the main character that he is controlling. In a coin-op game, a story makes no sense unless it is shown in the attract mode. We do not want the player wasting his time watching something when he could be playing or putting in more money.

You mentioned before that you specifically wanted to get into doing games for the home market. Why was this?

I wanted to do home games instead of coin-op games because I saw more opportunity to do something new in the home market.

Do you not see any future for coin-op arcade games?

I suspect coin-op games in the arcades will tend toward cheaper simulation rides (physical movement or encompassing environment), just like you see now. They provide something you cannot get at home and are cheaper than the rides at Disneyland. I believe the coin-op arcade market is already there. The coin-op street market will always need to be inexpensive. So I see a consumer platform in a coin-op box or cheap PCBs with simple games that do not require long development times.

The arcade version of *San Francisco Rush 2049*

I believe the consumer market already dominates over the coin-op industry. I do not have the numbers, but it is clear to me by looking at sales numbers of hit games and the dollars they represent. It is sad to see the changes in the coin-op industry. I am sure glad I was a part of the industry. I feel I was definitely in the right place at the right time.

Ed Logg Gameography

Super Breakout, 1977
Video Pinball, 1979
Asteroids, 1979
Othello (for Atari 2600), 1979
Football (4-player conversion), 1979
Centipede, 1981
Millipede, 1982
Gauntlet, 1985
Gauntlet II, 1986
Xybots, 1987
Tetris (conversion to NES), 1988
Steel Talons, 1991
Space Lords, 1992
Wayne Gretzky 3D Hockey (conversion to N64), 1996
San Francisco Rush (conversion to N64), 1997
San Francisco Rush 2 (conversion to N64), 1999
San Francisco Rush 2049 (conversion to N64 and Dreamcast), 2000

Chapter 7:
The Elements of Gameplay

"We ended up with a game that I didn't know how to win. I didn't know which were the best strategies or tactics, even though I designed all the game's systems. That is what makes a good strategy game."

— Julian Gollop, talking about his game
X-Com: UFO Defense

What are the game design elements that make up a really good game? Of course, there is no definitive answer to such a question. Nonetheless, as a game designer you will be expected to intuitively know exactly what the answer is. Understanding game design, as with any art form, is very much an internalized understanding, a "gut" reaction, a "feeling" you might have. It may be that you will not be able to form that answer into words, but you will need to understand what aspects of a game are strong and which are weak, and how the latter can be replaced with more of the former. Experience plays a big part in understanding what makes a game fun, experience both as a game designer and as a game player.

Over my years of playing and creating games I have come up with my own answers for what makes a game great, and in this chapter I discuss some of those qualities. Some of these topics may seem fairly distinct from each other, yet to my mind they all play a crucial role in making a good game. Certainly I cannot hope to list all of the knowledge I have, since, as I mentioned, much of my understanding is more akin to a "sixth sense" than anything I could hope to write down in a book. But the ideas contained in this chapter should help to give you a starting point.

Unique Solutions

For me, one of the most exciting moments of being a game designer is when I hear someone talking about playing one of my games, and they explain a successful tactic for a given situation that I had never considered. This could be a solution to a specific puzzle, a way to incapacitate challenging enemies, or a method for maneuvering a perilous canyon. I see the games I develop as creating situations in which game players can utilize their own creativity to succeed. When the player's creativity can lead them to solutions which I had not envisioned, it shows me that my game is doing its job.

Anticipatory versus Complex Systems

Good designers will try to guess what players are going to attempt to do and make their game respond well to those actions. For instance, take an RPG that features a puzzle that involves placing weights on a series of pressure plates. (Having put such a puzzle in a game of my own, I would like to implore game designers to be a bit more creative than that, as pressure plates are surely one of the most overdone puzzle devices still in use. But I digress.) Suppose the designer leaves a conspicuous pile of rocks a few rooms over from the pressure plate puzzle. The obvious solution to the puzzle is to use those rocks on the pressure plates to achieve the desired results. But what if the player tries dropping his various weapons on the plates instead? This is a perfectly valid solution which should work equally well, provided the player has weaponry of the appropriate weights. What if the player has the

Summon Minor Threat spell which allows him to summon a variety of different small monsters? If the player summons those monsters onto the pressure plates, they might do the trick too.

Now the designer, having thought through the puzzle fully, can have the programmer add in code where the game reacts correctly if either rocks, weapons, or monsters are on the plates. This is the anticipatory school of game design, where the designer thinks what the player might do and hardwires the game to work well with those actions. I agree that this tactic is surely better than allowing for just one solution. However, what if the player thinks of some other weight he can place on the pressure plates? What if the player uses his Berkshire Blizzard spell on the pressure plates, causing snow to fall on them? Enough snow could conceivably pile up on the plates to have a significant weight. However, if the game has been hardwired only for rocks, weapons, or monsters, the game will not react appropriately. The player will have thought of a perfectly reasonable solution and the game will fail to recognize it.

Instead of hardwiring, however, what if the designer had the programmer come up with a system where every object in the game had a weight associated with it? This would include rocks, weapons, monsters, weather effects, blood, and anything else found in the game-world. If the programmer then made the pressure plates simply get the weight of all of the objects on top of them, regardless of their type, then this one, global solution would work for all objects. If each object was set up with a reasonable weighting, it would not matter what object the player tried to place on the pressure plates, as they would all work automatically.

This latter method is less of an anticipatory system of game design; it is more holistic in its approach. It relies more on creating reliable, consistent systems with which your game will function. Then, for a puzzle such as the pressure plate one described above, the designer and programmer come up with a series of success conditions for that puzzle. Instead of "the puzzle is solved if the player uses rocks, weapons, or monsters to offset the plates," the rule is "the puzzle is solved when the plates are offset by the correct weight being placed on top of them." Certainly the example of this puzzle is a simple one, but the same techniques can be applied to much more sophisticated and interesting systems which engender a wide variety of successful playing styles.

Emergence

It is the development of numerous robust and logical systems that leads to player-unique solutions to situations in the game. One could describe these solutions as "emergent" from the systems design of the game, a popular buzzword in game design circles. Establishing a game universe that functions in accordance with logical rules the player can easily understand and use to his advantage allows

The *Civilization* games are some of the best examples of complex gameplay emerging out of multiple consistent systems running in parallel. Pictured here: *Civilization II*.

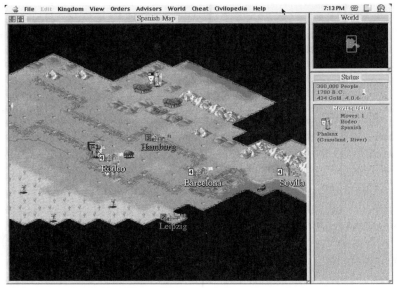

players to come up with their own solutions to the problems the game presents. Nothing can be more rewarding for the player than when he tries some obtuse, unobvious method for solving a puzzle or a combat situation and it actually works. The more complex systems that work correctly and concurrently with each other, the more interesting and varied the solutions to situations become. Consider the game *Civilization*, with its numerous systems running in parallel. These systems work together to create some of the most compelling gameplay ever pressed to disk.

Another example of this sort of emergent strategy can be found in the original *Centipede*. Anyone who has ever played the game knows that the piling up of mushrooms is one of the greatest impediments to a long game, and many players understand the importance of keeping the play-field as clear as possible. As the devotees of the game pumped quarter after quarter into the game, they began to notice some patterns. First, they recognized that the flea is responsible for dropping most of the problematic mushrooms, though destroyed centipede segments also drop them. Second, they saw that the flea does not come out on the game's first wave. Third, it was observed that the flea is triggered by the absence of mushrooms in the bottom half of the screen. Thus the famous "blob" strategy was developed, one that the game's designer, Ed Logg, never anticipated. To use the blob strategy, the player would clear all of the mushrooms from the board on the first wave, and then allow mushrooms to survive only on the bottom-right quadrant of the screen. If, through careful destruction of the centipede, the player only allows mushrooms to be created in that section of the screen, the flea will never come out, making the game much simpler indeed. This is an emergent solution to racking up a high score at *Centipede*, one which players no doubt felt quite proud of when it was discovered. Furthermore, it was a discovery that Logg, as the game's creator, did not even know was there to be found. That is good game design.

Non-Linearity

Non-linearity is another buzzword in the game industry, and well it should be. Non-linearity is what interesting gameplay is all about, and many designers forget this in their work. Non-linearity gives interactivity meaning, and without non-linearity, game developers might as well be working on movies instead. The more parts of your game that you can make non-linear, the better your game will be.

In general, when someone says something is linear they mean that it follows a line. A line is a series of points connected in either two- or three-dimensional space, where one can find any point on that line using a specific equation, such as, in a 2D case, $y = mx + b$. In layman's terms, this means that a line must be straight. If one considers any two points on that line, say A and B, there is only one way to navigate that line from A to B. There are no choices to be made; one simply must navigate all of the points between A and B. Outside the world of mathematics, we can consider reading a book to be a linear experience. If one is reading a 323-page book and if one does not skip pages or chapters, there is only one way to read the book: by starting on page 1 and reading all of the pages leading up to page 323.

Games, however, are non-linear works. In playing chess, there are multiple ways to capture the opponent's king, to move from the game's predetermined starting state to its conclusion. Indeed, there are a vast number of different ways to be victorious in chess, and that variety is what keeps the game interesting. These choices make chess non-linear. Suppose the chess board were one-dimensional instead of two, each player's pieces could only move in one direction, and each player had only one piece. This version of chess is a linear one, since there are no meaningful choices for the player to make and the outcome of every game is completely predetermined. And, of course, it is not a whole lot of fun either.

Types of Non-Linearity

So when we say we want our games to be non-linear, we mean we want them to provide choices for the player to make, different paths they can take to get from point A to point B, from the game's beginning to its end. We can mean this in a number of ways: in terms of the game's story, in terms of how the player solves the game's challenges, in terms of the order in which the player tackles the challenges, and in which challenges the player chooses to engage. All of these components can contribute to making a game non-linear, and the more non-linearity the developer creates, the more unique each player's experience can be. Furthermore, the different non-linear components can interact with each other to make the whole far greater than the sum of its parts.

- Storytelling: I discuss non-linear storytelling in more detail in Chapter 11, "Storytelling." Of course, a non-linear story line is necessarily tied to non-linear gameplay, and no one would bother to try to make a story non-linear if the game itself offered the player very little in the way of meaningful decisions. Storytelling is perhaps one of the most neglected parts of games in terms of non-linearity, with many developers allowing for non-linear gameplay while constraining their games to a completely linear story.

- Multiple Solutions: I discussed above how a well-designed game will enable the player to come up with his own solutions to the challenges the game presents. Not every player will think of the same way to go about solving a situation, and, given that these alternate solutions are reasonable, any challenge must have multiple ways for the player to overcome it. Having multiple solutions to the individual challenges within a game is a big part of non-linearity; it enables the player to have multiple paths to get from point A (being presented with the challenge) and point B (solving the challenge).

- Order: Beyond being able to figure out the solutions to challenges in unique ways, players will enjoy the ability to pick the order in which they perform challenges. Many adventure games have made the mistake of being overly linear by allowing the player access to only one puzzle at a given time. In order to even attempt a second puzzle, players must complete the first one. That is a linear way of thinking, which proves especially frustrating when a player gets stuck on a particular puzzle and, due to the game's linear nature, can do nothing else until that puzzle is solved. Giving the player choices of different puzzles to solve allows them to put aside a troubling puzzle and go work on another one for a while. After completing the second puzzle, the player may return to the first, refreshed and revitalized, and thereby have a better chance of solving it.

- Selection: Another way of making a game non-linear is to allow the player to pick and choose which challenges they want to overcome. Say that between point A and point B in a game there lies a series of three challenges, X, Y, and Z, which are non-order dependent, that is, the player can do these challenges in any order he wishes. What if, once the player surmounts challenge X, he does not have to go back and solve challenge Y or Z, he can simply move on to point B in the game, perhaps never returning to Y or Z? The same is true if the player initially chooses to tackle Y or Z instead of X. Any one of the choices will allow the player to proceed. The advantage is that if the player finds challenge X to be insurmountable, he can try challenge Y or Z. This greatly decreases the chance of the player becoming permanently stuck. It need not be the case that Y is easier than X; the mere fact that it is different may allow the player a better chance of getting through it, depending on his strengths as a player. Other players may find X to be easier than Y or Z, but giving the player a choice of which challenges he takes on allows the player to exploit his own personal skills to get through the game. Of course, after completing challenge X, the player may still have the option of going back and completing the Y and Z challenges, perhaps just for the fun of it or because overcoming those challenges somehow improves his chances down the line. Perhaps completing Y and Z gives his player character greater overall experience or riches. This type of non-linearity can also be used to add totally optional side-quests to the game. These challenges are not strictly required for the player to get to the end of the game, though they may make it somewhat easier or merely provide an interesting diversion along the way. Whatever the case, these optional challenges provide an extra degree of non-linearity, further customizing the player's experience.

Implementation

My first game, *Odyssey: The Legend of Nemesis*, is without doubt the most relentlessly non-linear game design I have ever done, and includes examples of all the types of non-linearity described above. *Odyssey* is an RPG and takes place on an archipelago that includes seven primary islands for the player to explore. Though the player is required to complete at least one quest on the first island before moving on to the rest of the game, there are two quests, each with multiple solutions from which the player may choose. Indeed, clever players can skip the quests

Odyssey is an extremely non-linear game, allowing the player to solve puzzles in whatever order he chooses and to select which quests he wants to go on. The game almost always provides more than one solution to any given puzzle.

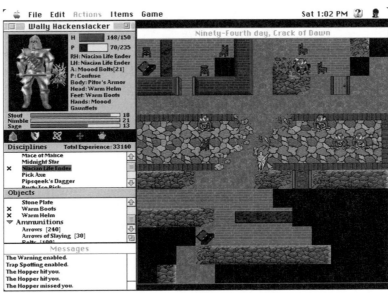

entirely if they figure out how to rob a particular townsperson. From there, the player is able to move freely about the next five islands, picking which ones he wants to explore and which he prefers to just pass through. Indeed, all that is required for the player to reach the seventh island and the end-game is for the player to successfully navigate each island, killing the monsters that get in his way. Of course, killing those creatures is made significantly easier if the player receives the rewards for completing the quests. But if the player so chooses, he can skip the entire middle of the game. Of course, few players have done this, preferring instead to explore the different quests and situations they encounter there. Nearly every single one of these quests has multiple ways for the player to solve it, with his actions having a direct impact on how each of the island's mini-stories resolves. Finally, the game itself has multiple endings for the player to explore, endings which suit the different overall goals the player may have: survival, revenge, or a sort of justice and harmony. Though the game had a very definite story, I am happy to say that I doubt very much that any two players ever experienced it in exactly the same way.

Non-linearity is an extremely powerful tool to use in designing a game, and the descriptions above of the types of non-linearity a designer can employ may seem obvious to the reader. What is astonishing, then, is how many games fail to provide any substantial non-linearity for the player, instead insisting that the player play through the game on a single line from point A to point B. One reason for this is that creating all of these non-linear elements can be quite time consuming. Consider that between point A and B, we have the aforementioned challenges X, Y, and Z, but the player only has to overcome one of these challenges in order to progress, say challenge X. The player can then continue playing through to the end of the game having never interacted with challenge Y or Z. As a non-linear game, that is the player's prerogative. The problem arises when a cost accountant looks at the game and tries to figure out where the game's budget can be trimmed. Well, obviously, if Y and Z are not strictly necessary, why bother having them at all? Why spend a lot of money on the programming, art, and design necessary to get Y and Z working when there's a chance the player will never see them? Unfortunately, accountants are often not in touch with the finer points of game design, and when you say, "But non-linearity is what makes this game great!" they are likely to dismiss you as "difficult."

Non-linearity is also often hard to pull off from a design perspective, certainly harder than simple linearity. This may be another reason why so many designers shy away from it at the first opportunity. Designing numerous obstacles that are different enough to provide variety for players while all applying roughly the same challenge is not an easy task. In the X, Y, and Z challenges example, if Z is significantly easier than X or Y, it is quite likely no one will bother with X or Y. In a way, a game with poorly designed choices for the player is nearly as linear as a game without any choices at all. The non-linearity your game provides must be

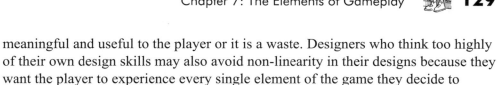

meaningful and useful to the player or it is a waste. Designers who think too highly of their own design skills may also avoid non-linearity in their designs because they want the player to experience every single element of the game they decide to include. "Why spend a lot of time on portions of the game that not everyone will see?" say these egotistical designers, starting to sound a lot like the accountants.

The Purpose of Non-Linearity

It is important to always remember that non-linearity is included in the game to provide the player some meaningful authorship in the way she plays the game. If forced to stay on a specific line to get from the beginning of the game to the end, the player will tend to feel trapped and constrained. The challenges along that line may be brilliantly conceived, but if the player has no choice but to take them on in order, one by one, the fun they provide will be greatly decreased.

Non-linearity is great for providing players with a reason to replay the game. Replaying a game where the player has already overcome all of the challenges is not that much fun. In replaying a more non-linear game, however, players will be able to steer away from the challenges they succeeded at the last time they played and instead take on the game's other branches. However, it is important to note that replayability is not the main motivation for including non-linearity in your game designs. I have heard some game designers complain that replayability is unnecessary since so many players never manage to finish the games they start playing anyway. So if they never finish, why add replayability? These designers do not realize that the true point of non-linearity is to grant the player a sense of freedom in the game-world, to let each player have a playing experience unique to himself, to tell his own story. If the player wants to replay the game again, that is fine, but the primary goal of non-linearity is to surrender some degree of authorship to the player.

Furthermore, the contention that players seldom finish games and hence the games do not need to be non-linear is a self-fulfilling prophecy. The reason players fail to finish games is often because they become stuck at one particular juncture in the game. This may be a boss-monster who is too difficult, a puzzle that is too confounding, or merely failing to find the exit from a given area. If the game were more non-linear, however, players would have much less chance of getting stuck at any point in the game, since the variety of paths available would increase the likelihood that the player's unique talents would be sufficient for him to make it successfully past one of them.

At a Game Developer's Conference talk entitled "A Grand Unified Game Theory," Noah Falstein suggested that when non-linearity allows the players to tackle a series of required challenges in whatever order they desire, completing one challenge should make the others easier for the player to accomplish. In the case of a collection of puzzles, this can be done by providing the player with a hint about the other puzzles once he completes one of them. In the case of a collection of battles of some sort, this can be done by providing the player with additional weaponry with which to survive the other battles. Whatever the case may be, using this technique increases the chance that the player will be able to overcome the challenges at hand and get on with the game.

A note of caution: all designers should understand that non-linearity is not about having the player wander around the game-world aimlessly. If the game is non-linear to the point where the player has no idea what she is supposed to try to accomplish or how she might go about it, the non-linearity may have gone too far. Often game designers talk up their in-development games by making statements like "In our game-world, the player can do anything they want; there are no restrictions. The game is completely non-linear!" Such a game would likely be completely annoying as well. Of course, by the time these "completely non-linear" games have shipped most of the non-linearity has been stripped out and the player is left solving puzzles on a rail. Somewhere between "on a rail" games and total freedom lies an ideal middle ground, where the player is left with a sense of freedom accompanied by a sense of guidance.

Modeling Reality

The desire to model reality in computer games is one that has driven game development for a number of years. The more real we make the games, the proponents say, the more compelling and immersive gamers will find them. But is this always the case? What would a greater degree of reality add to a game like *Tetris* or *Centipede*? Surely they could not be much more immersive than they already are. Consider a game such as *Civilization*, which is already modeled on reality. Would adding more reality to it make it any more fun? Actually, quite the opposite is true: adding a more realistic economic model or combat system would detract from the game's strengths as a macro-strategy game and quite possibly make the game more annoying than fun.

The trouble with modeling reality in games comes when the games get mired in reality to the point where they come to resemble real life a little more than players actually want. Alfred Hitchcock described films as "Life with the dull bits cut out." Indeed, games can be seen as modeling life or some aspect of life while leaving out the tedious and boring parts. If the designer, in an attempt to achieve a greater degree of reality, decides to include too many unnecessary and dull details, the game will likely become tedious to play. My favorite example of this is the use of food in RPGs. Many RPGs of the '80s were perpetually on a quest to make themselves more real than other RPGs, to up the ante with each new game that was released. One way designers attempted to do this was to add food, and to require the player to remember to feed his characters periodically, lest they starve to death. Here was a "dull bit" that did not need inclusion, especially as eating regularly scheduled meals is not the first thing that jumps to people's minds when they think of adventuring in hostile worlds.

Using reality as a basis for your game has its advantages, however. First and foremost, it provides players with a world they are instantly familiar with, a world in which they have some idea of what actions are reasonable and which are out of the question. Whether in *Civilization*, *SimCity*, or *Deadline*, a properly executed realistic setting gives players an instant "in" to your game-world. They understand or at least think they understand how it works and what they can do to be successful in it. Players can start playing the game and instantly have some idea of what they are supposed to accomplish. A more abstract game like *Centipede* or *Tetris*, on the other hand, has such abstract goals that players must be taught what it is they are supposed to do, either through reading the directions or by experimenting with the game-world.

Early first-person shooters such as *Marathon* did not allow the player to jump or crouch. But the realistic nature of FPS titles soon caused players to demand such features be added.

A potential downside to having a realistic world is that, since the game mimics a reality players are familiar with, players will expect certain game-world elements to work in a certain way and will be very quick to notice when something fails to do so. For example, many of the early first-person shooters, such as *Doom* and *Marathon*, did not allow the player character to jump. The worlds of these first-person shooters were more "realistic" than the worlds game players were accustomed to finding in computer games, so real that the players' expectations were raised and many were quick to complain that they could not jump over even waist-high obstacles. So the next generation of FPS titles added the ability to jump, then to crouch, then look up and down, and so on and so forth, making the games still more complicated with each element of reality added. Now, as the worlds possible with RT3D engines look more real than ever, players are constantly asking questions such as "Why can't I lie flat on the ground? I can do that in real life; why not in the game?" Some would say that, certainly for the novice players, these FPS games have grown too complex as a result of their attempt to model reality. Bringing in a certain level of reality raises players' expectations in a way that the totally abstract world of a *Centipede* or *Tetris* never does. Players never question their capabilities in these worlds because the boundaries were completely arbitrary in the first place.

So is there a definitive answer to whether or not you should model reality in your game? Of course not, just as there are no easy answers in all of game design, and as there are no easy answers in art. As a game designer you must strike the balance between reality and abstraction, weighing what your game needs from a gameplay standpoint with what your story and setting require and with what your engine can reasonably handle. What is vital to remember, and what many designers often forget, is that more reality is not always a good thing.

Teaching the Player

Attempting to model reality may be one way to give players an advantage going into your game-world; through their own life experiences, players will know to some extent what to expect of your game-world. However, even with the most realistic game, players need time to learn how to play your game, and this learning experience is often a crucial time in a player's overall experience with your game. The first few minutes a player spends with your game will often make the difference between whether she wants to continue playing it or not. Whenever a player tells a friend about your game, she will often remember those first few minutes and say, "Well, it was a little weird to get used to" or, preferably, "It was great. I jumped right into the game and found all this cool stuff."

In the past, many computer games relied on manuals to teach players how to play them. With some titles players literally had almost no chance of success in the game without first reading a large chunk of the manual. Today many games try to get away from this reliance on the player's reading ability, realizing that often the last thing a player wants to do when he has just purchased a new game is to sit down and read an extensive instructional manual. Players definitely have a strong desire to just pick up the controller and start playing the game. Now that so many games allow the player to do just that, the importance of allowing the player to "jump right in" has increased. If your game is too difficult to get a handle on within the first minute, the player is likely to put it down and try something else.

This does not mean that your game has to be dumbed down or simplified, merely that you must introduce the complexity of your game-world through the gameplay instead of through the manual. For example, at first your game should start out requiring the player to perform only the simplest of actions. Say you are creating a third-person over-the-shoulder action/adventure game akin to *Tomb Raider*. It makes the most sense to first teach the player how to move the player around correctly on the ground. Then, after the player has had a chance to become accustomed to the horizontal movement controls, you might introduce a section where the player has to jump to cross a canyon or climb up a cliff. After enough of that, you might want to introduce some simple combat challenges, where the player will learn how to use his character's weapons.

Prince of Persia carefully taught the player what to expect of traps such as collapsing floors and sharp spikes.

It is important that during the introduction of these controls the player is in a safe environment that engenders learning. If the player already has to worry about dying at every step and the game is generally unforgiving of the player's mistakes, chances are good that the player will become frustrated quickly. *Half-Life* did this particularly well, with an introduction to the game that provided a safe yet interesting environment and allowed the player to become accustomed to the controls without immediately threatening him. *Prince of Persia* was another game that was particularly good at introducing challenges to the player in a way that taught the player through example instead of by punishing him. For instance, when the player first encounters a break-away floor in *Prince of Persia* falling through it is non-lethal. Similarly, spikes are introduced in such a way that the player is very likely to notice them and to be able to survive them. Subsequent encounters with spikes will not be so forgiving, but by then the player has learned of the threat they pose to his game-world character, and if he is clever he will be able to survive them.

Rewards

During this learning period in the game, it is important to reward the player for even the simplest of accomplishments. This makes the player feel that, indeed, he is on the right track with the game and encourages him to keep playing. It is true that players do not want their games to be too simple and too unchallenging, but punishing them for blunders from the very start of the game is not the right way to produce this challenge. The key is to give the player success early on, to draw him into the game, to make him think that he knows what the game is all about, that he is better than it. "Ha ha, this game is easy, I rule!" he may say. And then, when the game becomes suddenly more challenging, the player will already have been drawn into the game and will be much more likely to see the challenge as a reasonable one, one that he can surely overcome. After all, this game is easy, right?

Recently, many complex games have started introducing the player to the gaming world through a tutorial level which exists outside of the game-world proper. The player can access this tutorial world through the main menu as an alternative to starting a "real" game. These tutorial levels are generally a good idea and are certainly an improvement over teaching the player about the game in the manual. The tutorial levels do one of the things that computers do best: provide an interactive learning experience. The one problem with tutorial levels is that they are seldom much fun to play, and as a result many players will skip them and head straight for the actual game. There is a feeling among players that the tutorial level is not part of the "real" game, and many players want to start playing this "real" game as soon as possible. If the designer includes a tutorial level because he wants to make his game difficult from the very beginning and avoid teaching the player how to play through the gameplay, players who skip the tutorial will become frustrated. Tutorial levels are good for players who want that sort of educational prelude to the game, but they must not replace making the beginning of the game itself easy to play. Again, *Half-Life* provided a tutorial level that taught players about the game-world, but the tutorial worked in conjunction with the beginning of the actual game itself, which was quite easy to play and had a friendly learning curve. Of course, making the tutorial level as entertaining as possible goes a long way toward encouraging players to actually play it.

Often these tutorial levels include instructions which explain what keys or buttons the player is supposed to press in order to achieve certain effects. Often voice-overs with accompanying on-screen text tell the player to "Press the spacebar to fire your primary weapon" or "Press and hold down the blue X for a super jump." Some games go so far as to actually tell the player during gameplay what

Console titles such as *The Legend of Zelda: Ocarina of Time* are good at teaching the player how to control the game.

the controls are, such as *Crash Bandicoot*. These detailed explanations of what the player is required to do in order to be successful can be quite a boon to making a complex game easier to pick up. Even beyond that, however, games like *Spyro The Dragon* and *The Legend of Zelda: Ocarina of Time* go so far as to have actual game characters tell the player character what the controls for the game are. "Spyro, press and hold the blue button in order to glide," the friendly elder dragon says in the former game. I think this goes too far and totally shatters the player's suspension of disbelief. The in-game characters should not know anything about the player and certainly nothing about a PlayStation controller. However, I do think it is helpful to remind players of the game's controls while they are playing, through more removed GUI displays and non-game character voice-overs. Many modern games include such sophisticated controls that they are likely to alienate non–hard-core gamers, and reminding novice players of what they need to do in order to perform a certain move is a good idea.

I would say that, in retrospect, all of my games have been too difficult, and certainly too hard for the player to get into. *Damage Incorporated* may have done the best job at introducing the player to the game-world through easy early levels. One game that erred in the opposite direction is *Odyssey*, my turn-based RPG. In it the player starts off shipwrecked on an island, without any weapons or possessions of any kind. I wanted the player to, immediately, be frightened and need to find a safe place to hide in a nearby cave. I achieved this by having a few monsters start charging in the player's direction a few turns after the player arrives on the beach. The player has no chance of defeating these creatures on his own, and needs to enter the nearby cave to survive. Originally, I had the cave hidden in the woods, making it hard for the player to find and thereby making the game even more unforgiving. Fortunately, my playtesters convinced me that the introduction was too hard, and I moved the cave out into the open where the player could easily see it. However, the problem remained that, before the player even has a chance to become familiar with the controls, she is assaulted by strange monsters, with no real idea of what she is supposed to do about it. I often wonder how many players were frightened away by this overly challenging introduction and never played the rest of the game as a result.

Input/Output

Your game's input and output systems are two of the primary factors that determine how steep the learning curve for your game is and whether a player will find it intuitive to play. Using the input/output systems you design, the player must be able to control and understand the game effortlessly. Designing these systems is one of the hardest aspects of game design, since, if they are designed well, the player will not even know they are there. But if they are designed poorly, players will become easily frustrated, complaining that the game's controls prevent them from doing what they really want to do in the game. Designing input and output systems are "invisible" arts in that the goal of their creation is for them to be transparent to the player. This can sometimes lead to designers failing to fully consider how to best make the I/O work in their game, a mistake you must avoid if you want your games to be any fun to play.

Controls and Input

Nothing is more frustrating than, as a player, knowing exactly what you want your game-world character to do but being unable to actually get him to do that because the controls will not let you. Good gameplay is never about trying to figure out the controls themselves; keep the puzzles in the game-world, not in the control scheme. The controls are the player's interface between the real-world and game-world. In order for the player to experience true immersion in the game-world the player must be able to manipulate the game-world exactly as intuitively as he manipulates the real-world. Every time the player has to think "Now, what button do I have to press to do that?" that immersion is destroyed.

Though the controls for many computer games seem to be getting more and more complex, particularly those for 3D action games, there is a lot to be said for keeping your controls simple. Indeed, a lot of the success of games like *Diablo*, *Command & Conquer*, and *The Sims* can be attributed to the fact that the player can play these games one-handed, controlling everything with only the mouse. The mouse is an extremely powerful input device when used correctly. Its great strength

The *Diablo* series' extremely simple controls make it one of the most easy-to-learn games available. Pictured here: *Diablo II*.

is that it is a control device with which most non-gamer computer users are already familiar. This makes mouse-only games very easy to jump into, since they minimize the time the user must spend learning controls.

A big part of designing a good mouse-based interface is making a system that does not look as sterile and business-like as the Windows file manager yet retains its ease of use. Making the interface look attractive is mostly a matter of well-conceived art, but making it attractive without losing any of its intuitiveness and functionality can be quite challenging. Whenever an artist suggests making a button look a certain way, the designer must consider if the new design takes away from the player's ability to understand what that button does. Often, you can borrow clearly understood icons from other interfaces, either from other games or from real-world devices such as VCRs or CD players. For example, everyone knows what a "fast forward" symbol on an audio device looks like, and using this appropriately in your game will mean that players instantly know what a given button does. Making buttons in your game that players can intuitively understand and that also look attractive is equal parts creativity and playtesting. If the people playtesting your game tell you your buttons are unobvious and confusing, they probably are, and you need to return to the drawing board.

A common game design mistake is to try to include too much. This applies to all aspects of gameplay, but particularly to controls, where sometimes the cliché "Less is more" really holds true. Every time you add a new button or key to your game, you must ask yourself if the complexity you have just added to the game's controls is worth the functionality it enables. When designing a PC game the temptation is particularly great, since the keyboard provides more keys than any game would ever need to use. Unfortunately, some games have tried to use nearly all of them, binding some unique function to practically each and every key. Complex keyboard controls favor the expert player while alienating the novice, leading to a radically decreased number of people who might enjoy your game. Due to the limited number of buttons they provide, console control pads are much more limiting in what they will allow the designer to set up. Unlike many other designers, particularly those making the switch from PC to console, I often feel that this limitation is a good one. Control pads force the designer to refine his controls, to cut away all that is extraneous, and to combine all of the game-world actions the player can perform into just a few, focused controls. This leads directly to games that are easier to learn how to play. Indeed, many of the most popular console games do not even use all of the controller's buttons. Because of the massive keyboard at their disposal, designers of PC games are not forced to focus the controls of their games in the same way, and I think their games may suffer for it. As I mentioned above, some of the most popular PC games have managed to squeeze all of their controls into the mouse.

Much of the increasing complexity of game controls can be attributed to the increasing dominance of RT3D games. These games, by trying to include the ability for the player's game-world surrogate to move forward and backward, up and down, sideways left and right, turn left and right, and pitch up and down, have already used a massive number of controls while only allowing the player to move in the game-world and do nothing else. In many ways, the perfect way to simply and intuitively control a character with total freedom in 3D space is still being explored. This is why very few of the successful 3D games released thus far have allowed the player total freedom to control his character. Indeed, the most successful 3D games, such as *Super Mario 64*, *Quake*, or *Tomb Raider*, have restricted movement to a ground plane.

One technique that can be used to make your controls intuitive to a variety of players is to include multiple ways to achieve the same effect. For instance, if one looks at the interface used by the RTS game *StarCraft*, players are able to control their units by left-clicking to select the unit, then clicking on the button of the action they want the unit to perform, and then left-clicking on a location in the world where they want the unit to perform that action. Players can also left-click on the unit to select it and then immediately right-click in the game-world, causing the unit to do the most logical action for the location the player clicked, whether it means moving to that point or attacking the unit there. Furthermore, *StarCraft* also allows the player to access a unit's different actions through a hot key instead of clicking on the button. This has the pleasant side effect of keeping the interface simple enough for the novice player to master, since it is all point-and-click, while the expert player can spend his time memorizing hot keys in order to improve his game. In many console action games, different buttons on the controller will

StarCraft provides the player with a very elegant interface which allows her to issue orders to her units using a variety of techniques.

perform the same action. A common choice to make, particularly on PlayStation games, is to allow the player to control character movement through either the left directional pad or through the left analog control stick. *Crash Bandicoot*, for instance, allows the player to move with either the directional pad or the analog stick, and also allows the player to access Crash's ability to slide by either pressing a trigger button or one of the buttons on top of the controller. Providing multiple ways for a player to achieve a single game-world action helps to ensure that a given player will enjoy using one of the ways you have provided.

There is a lot of room for creativity in game design, but controls are not one of the best places to exercise your creative urges. Your game should be creative in its gameplay, story line, and other content, but not necessarily in its controls. Some of the most successful games have taken control schemes which players were already familiar with from other games and applied them to new and compelling content. Sometimes the established control scheme may be weak, but often it is not weak enough to justify striking out in an entirely new direction with your own control system. As a designer you must weigh what is gained through a marginally superior control scheme with what is lost because of player confusion. For example, Sid Meier's RTS game *Gettysburg!* included as its default method for ordering troops around a "click-and-drag" system instead of the established "click-and-click" system found in other games. His system was quite creative and actually may have been a better way of controlling the game than the established paradigms. However, it was not so much better that it outweighed the confusion players experienced when first attempting to play the game, a fact he admits in the interview included in Chapter 2 of this book. Console games are particularly good at providing uniform control schemes, with fans of games in a particular genre able to pick up and immediately start playing almost any game available in the genre, even if they have never seen it before.

During the course of the development of a game, as you are playing the game over and over and over again, it is very easy to get accustomed to bad controls. Though the controls may be poorly laid out or counterintuitive, as the game's designer you may have used them so much that they have become second nature. However, as soon as someone plays the game for the first time, she will quickly be frustrated by these controls and is likely to stop playing as a result. A proper playtesting phase will include many players playing the game for the first time, and witnessing their initial reaction to the controls is crucial to understanding how intuitive your controls really are. Do not think, "Oh, she'll get used to it," or "What an idiot! These controls are obvious; why can't he see that!" Instead think, "Why are my controls bad and what can I do to fix them?"

Designing controls that players will find intuitive can be quite challenging, especially with such a variety of control setups for different games, particularly in the PC market. For example, it can be hard to determine what the "standard" controls for an FPS are when the last three successful FPS games each had a unique control scheme. Almost every PC action game released in the last decade allows players to configure the controls however they desire, and this is an absolute must for any PC game that demands the player manipulate a large number of buttons. That said, many players will never find or use the control configuration screens, either because of a desire to start playing the game immediately or a general lack of savvy with the computer. Many, many players will be left playing with whatever the default keys are, and this is why it is the designer's job to make sure these default settings are as playable as possible. You should never use a strange or confusing set of default controls for your game merely because the programmer in charge likes it that way or the team has grown accustomed to them. Always make sure the default controls are as intuitive as possible.

Particularly in action games, when your controls are perfect, the wall separating the player from the game-world will disappear, and the player will start to feel like he truly is the game-world character. This is the ultimate sign of an immersive game, and achieving this effect is impossible without strong controls. In a game where that level of immersion is possible, the controls must be completely invisible to the player. This can be frustrating to a designer. Why work so hard on something that, if implemented perfectly, will be completely invisible? In order to feel satisfied with a job well done, the designer must realize that it is the transparency of controls that allows the player to enjoy the rest of what the game has to offer.

Output and Game-World Feedback

While the player's ability to intuitively control the game-world may be key to a successful game, outputting information about that game-world to the player is just as important. Computer games contain numerous complex systems, commonly performing more calculations than a human would ever be able to track. Indeed, that is the area where computer games excel. Condensing that massive amount of data into its most representative form and communicating that information to the player is key to a well-designed output system.

Consider a strategy game in which the player has a number of units scattered all over a large map. The map is so large that only a small portion of it can fit on the screen at once. If a group of the player's units happen to be off-screen and are attacked but the player is not made aware of it by the game, the player will become irritated. Consider an RPG where each member of the player's party needs to be fed regularly, but the game does not provide any clear way of communicating how hungry his characters are. Then, if one of the party members suddenly keels over from starvation, the player will become frustrated, and rightly so. Why should the player have to guess at such game-critical information? In an action game, if the player has to kill an enemy by shooting it in a particular location of its body, say its eye, the player needs to receive positive feedback when he successfully lands a blow. Perhaps the enemy reels back in pain or screams in agony once an attack damages him. If the player does not receive such feedback, how is he supposed to know he's on the right track? Of course, all computer games conceal a certain amount of information from the player, and games cannot possibly communicate all of the information they have about the game-world to the player. But they must communicate what is reasonable for the player's character to know, and communicate that data effectively.

Almost all games present the player with a view of the game-world as the central part of their output system. Through this view the player sees the object he is currently controlling and its location and state in the game-world. Your game should try to communicate as much information through this view as possible. Consider a third-person 3D action game. Certainly the player sees the environment and position of her game-world surrogate, but what about the condition of the player-character? Perhaps as his health goes down, the character's animations change to a limp or hobble instead of moving normally. Similarly, the strength of the player's armor can be represented by texture changes on that character, with the armor appearing more and more deteriorated as it takes damage and nears destruction. The player's current weapon can be represented by the player seeing that weapon equipped on the character. If the player has a spell of protection currently in effect on her character, perhaps the character should emit a certain glow to easily communicate that to the player. Though the designer may also want to include this data in a Heads Up Display (HUD) of some sort, communicating it through the game's primary game-world view makes it that much more transparent and easy to understand for the player.

What the game-world view cannot represent is typically contained in some sort of a GUI which often borders the game-world view or is overlaid on top of it like a HUD. This GUI may be simple, such as the high score and lives remaining display on *Centipede*, the small potion-health display at the bottom of the screen in *Prince of Persia*, or the score/moves display in almost any Infocom game. For more complicated games, the GUI is also often more complex, such as the button bars used in any of Maxis' Sim games, the extensive status display in the original *System Shock*, or the extensive party data provided in many RPGs, such as the *Bard's Tale* games. Many GUIs in older games were created in order to block off a large portion of the screen. This was not because of any sort of design decision, but instead because the game's engine was not fast enough to handle rendering the game-world full screen. As engine technology has improved, games have attempted to make the game-world view take up the vast majority of the screen, with the GUI minimized as much as possible.

Oddworld: Abe's Oddysee did away with an in-game GUI entirely, giving the player an unobstructed view of the game-world.

A very few games try to work without any GUI whatsoever. One in particular is *Oddworld: Abe's Oddysee*. The game's director, Lorne Lanning, felt very strongly that any sort of GUI would distance the player from the game-world. As a result, Abe's health is communicated to the player through the way he animates. Since the game lets the player always have infinite lives, there was no need for a lives remaining display that so many console games now include as their only GUI element. *Crash Bandicoot*, for instance, only displays the lives remaining GUI if the player presses a button to bring it on the screen, defaulting to a completely unobstructed view of the world. Certainly, as technology has allowed it, the trend has been to get away from on-screen HUDs as much as possible, allowing the game-world view to take over the screen. The advantages of the immersion gained by a minimized GUI are obvious, and if the game-world can effectively communicate all of the information the player needs to play, there is sometimes no reason to use a GUI at all.

The most important part of designing a GUI is to try to keep it as visual as possible. In fast-paced action games in particular, the GUI is designed to communicate information to the player as quickly as possible, whether this is the player's current health, ammo available, or nearby monsters (through some sort of radar). If anything, the ascendancy of the graphical user interface as the dominant mode of controlling a computer, first through the Macintosh and subsequently through Windows, shows that most people think visually instead of in numbers or words. As a result, a well-designed graphical HUD in your game will be easier for a player to glance at and understand than one that contains a lot of numbers or words. This explains the superiority of the health bar instead of a health number or percentage. The artists will like a graphical HUD as well, since a health bar can look a lot more attractive than a big, ugly number.

The head at the bottom of the screen in *Doom* is a well-designed interface element because it communicates the player's current health visually.

A game element that is particularly well designed is the "head" used in *Doom* and *Quake*. This face, which appears at the center of the bottom of the screen, represents the player's approximate health completely visually. The face starts out healthy and snarling, ready to take on the world. As the player's game progresses and he loses health, the head starts to look bruised and bloodied, eventually looking all but dead when the player has almost run out of health. At any point during the game the player is able to glance down at the head and instantly get a sense of how much health he has remaining. If the health had been represented instead by a number, it would have been much more difficult for the player to comprehend his current health level just by glancing at it. The difference in time may be milliseconds, but in a fast-action game, that may be the difference between life and death.

Of course, the visual representation of data can also have a negative side effect if that representation is too obtuse for the player to easily understand. For instance, in *WarCraft*, the buttons for the different actions that a unit can perform are all represented by icons, which I would generally encourage. However, some of the buttons can be a little difficult to figure out at first. Fortunately, the game also displays text at the bottom of the screen when the player's mouse cursor hovers over a particular button, communicating what that button will do if clicked. What would have been even better is if the icons on the buttons were just a bit more obvious. Admittedly, representing a real-world action such as "guard" through a 32x32 icon can often be quite a challenge. The GUI for your game needs to balance the superiority of visual representation with the clarity of text, possibly using a combination of both as needed.

Audio output as a communication device to the player is something that is often underused in games. Not all of the information about the game-world needs to be communicated to the player through visual stimuli. For instance, in *The Sims*, the player gains a good sense of whether his character is enjoying a particular conversation based on the tone of the participants' voices. In *Command & Conquer*, the player knows that a particular unit has received a particular order by an audio cue provided by that unit: "I'll get right on it!" Similarly, when units off-screen are being attacked, the game communicates this to the player by saying "Unit attacked" or "Unit lost." Audio cues can provide an excellent supplement to on-screen information, or can work quite effectively as the sole way of communicating critical information.

A good output system for a game is both powerful and intuitive. It allows players to jump right into the game and understand what is happening in the game-world, but it also provides expert players with all the information they need to play the game effectively. Over time, the data the game communicates to the player should become transparent, just as the player's controls should become invisible once the player is familiar with them. Players should not have to think about understanding the world; they should just "know" what they need to by quickly looking at the screen and be able to react to it just as quickly through intuitive and responsive controls. As I have stated before, it is important not to get too creative in developing your input/output systems. The dominant paradigms from other games are often dominant for a reason: they work. The expression that "good artists borrow but great artists steal" is nowhere more true than in I/O design in games.

Basic Elements

In this chapter I have discussed just a few of the elements of good gameplay: unique solutions, non-linearity, modeling reality, teaching the player, and input/output. I feel that each of these components deserves serious thought as you set out to develop a game. Of course, this is far from a complete list, and as you work as a game designer you will accumulate your own personal list of elements which you feel contribute to good gameplay. No one can say for certain what the elements of good game design are. Each game designer must decide that for herself. This personal preference is part of what makes each game bear the distinct stamp of its author and lends the best games the individuality that makes them great.

Chapter 8:
Game Analysis: Tetris

Designed by Alexey Pajitnov
Released in 1987

ew games are as universally well respected by game developers as *Tetris*. Often when a game becomes as popular as *Tetris* has, with versions for every system imaginable and untold millions in sales, gaming professionals start complaining about what a poor game it is. *Myst* is a good example of this. On its release, the title received near universal praise from the gaming press for being a fun adventure game in a beautifully conceived world. Game developers themselves, though not quite as enthusiastic, still thought it was a good game. Multiple millions of copies later with years spent on the best-seller charts, the same gaming press found reason to start hating the game and its amazing continued popularity. Game developers are particularly loud in voicing their dislike for the game. Is the game worse now? No, of course not. Do gaming professionals, press and developers alike, resent the game for its sales? It would appear so.

But this is not the case with *Tetris*. *Tetris* conquered the world in terms of popularity, yet one is hard pressed to find anyone with a negative comment about the game. What is it about *Tetris* that makes the game immune to criticism? It would appear something about the game's simplicity and clearness of design vision make even the most cynical game developer concede the game's greatness. Contrary to what happened with *Myst*, when *Tetris* was first released, most of the gaming press dwelled on the game's origins in Russia and seemed underwhelmed, or at least unexcited, by the title's gameplay. The game was so simple, its technology so lacking in razzle-dazzle that, perhaps, the press found themselves incapable of writing enthusiastically about the game—at least at first. Now that the game is an undisputed classic, any game critic will be happy to tell you about the hundreds of hours she spent blissfully lost in the game.

Gameplay in *Tetris* is exceedingly uncomplicated. The game-world is a tall, rectangular, 2D box. Blocks appear at the top of the box. The blocks are made up of four squares arranged in every possible pattern where all the squares share at least one side with another square. The blocks then slowly fall to the bottom of the box, and the player is able to move these blocks to the left and right, or rotate the piece in 90 degree increments. Once the player hits an obstruction, either the bottom of the box or another piece, the block stops moving, the player loses control of the block, and another piece appears at the top of the screen which the player can now control. When the blocks at the bottom of the screen form a horizontal line across the rectangle, that line of squares disappears, and any squares above that line move down one row. The player's game is over once incomplete rows of the blocks fill up the rectangle and subsequent pieces are prevented from entering the play-field.

Puzzle Game or Action Game?

Tetris is often referred to as a puzzle game, and for good reason. *Tetris* has elements obviously reminiscent of a puzzle, with the player needing to find how blocks best fit together. In this way the game is similar to a right-angle jigsaw puzzle, or any number of other "organize these geometrical shapes in this small space" puzzles. An even better comparison would be the traditional game pentomino, from which

Tetris carefully
balances action
and puzzle
elements to
create a unique
gameplay
experience.
Pictured here,
and throughout
this chapter:
classic mode in
The Next Tetris.

Alexey Pajitnov, *Tetris*'s designer, is supposed to have drawn inspiration. In pentomino, one must take twelve different shaped pieces, each made out of five squares, and fit them into a square box. One can see the similarities, but at the same time *Tetris* changes the game into something entirely different, something entirely more challenging and compelling. Pajitnov could have just as easily made a direct adaptation of pentomino to the computer, as many other developers have done for jigsaw puzzles or "sliding number"-type puzzles. This might have been an entertaining program, though perhaps not as fun as the actual game itself since part of the fun of pentomino is the tactile nature of manipulating the blocks. But by taking the puzzle and changing it into a game that could only happen on the computer, Pajitnov ended up creating a unique new game, which is far more entertaining than the original.

Many times when members of the computer game intelligentsia refer to a game as being a puzzle game, they do so with derision. For them a puzzle game is one that presents a series of static puzzles to the player, puzzles which never change and never react to the player's actions. They argue that a game must provide a reaction to the player's actions, and an opponent for the player to compete against. Hence, the critics would say, these so-called "puzzle games" are not really games at all, but just puzzles. Furthermore, often the puzzles found in these games have only one solution, further limiting the player's interactive experience. Examples would include most all adventure games, such as *Zork*, *Myst*, or even *Grim Fandango*, games that, though they provide the player with a world to explore and challenging puzzles to complete, do nothing to create a unique experience for the player.

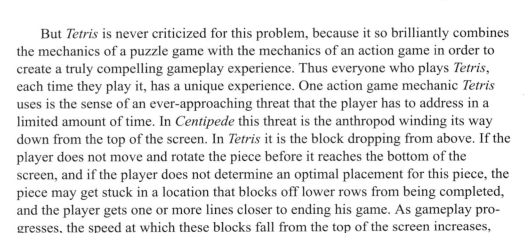

But *Tetris* is never criticized for this problem, because it so brilliantly combines the mechanics of a puzzle game with the mechanics of an action game in order to create a truly compelling gameplay experience. Thus everyone who plays *Tetris*, each time they play it, has a unique experience. One action game mechanic *Tetris* uses is the sense of an ever-approaching threat that the player has to address in a limited amount of time. In *Centipede* this threat is the anthropod winding its way down from the top of the screen. In *Tetris* it is the block dropping from above. If the player does not move and rotate the piece before it reaches the bottom of the screen, and if the player does not determine an optimal placement for this piece, the piece may get stuck in a location that blocks off lower rows from being completed, and the player gets one or more lines closer to ending his game. As gameplay progresses, the speed at which these blocks fall from the top of the screen increases, thus increasing the challenge for the player and ramping up the difficulty over the course of the game.

Another similarity between *Tetris* and action games that further distinguishes it from other puzzle games is the variety of gameplay situations *Tetris* can create: each game a player plays is unique. The play mechanics set up an infinitely large number of unique games, with each move the player decides to make influencing the rest of her game. The way a piece is positioned into the blocks already at the bottom of the screen directly impacts where the next piece can be placed. Should the player fill up the four-block-long slot with only two blocks from an upside-down "L"-shaped piece? Or should she hold out, waiting for that desperately needed "I"-shaped piece? The "L" will not fill the slot completely, but no one knows how long it will be until the "I" piece arrives. In other cases the player may have a number of different positions in which to put a piece, and the player must think ahead, figuring out if she puts a piece in a given slot what sort of slots that will leave available for later pieces. The player constantly has to consider where future blocks will or will not be able to fit. A player may learn to recognize certain piece configurations, but every game is sufficiently unique that no player can be completely prepared for the challenges she may face.

Tetris as a Classic Arcade Game

Indeed, there are many indications that *Tetris* is an example of what I call the "classic arcade game" form. This is despite the fact that it was not originally conceived for gameplay in the arcades (though its rampant popularity eventually led to its arrival there), and that it was created years after the classic arcade game form had stopped being used by professional arcade game developers. Looking over the list of classic arcade game qualities described in the *Centipede* analysis in Chapter 4, we can see just how *Tetris* fits the guiding principles of the form.

Despite being developed years after classic arcade games had fallen out of style, *Tetris*'s gameplay embodies many of the design principles of that genre of games.

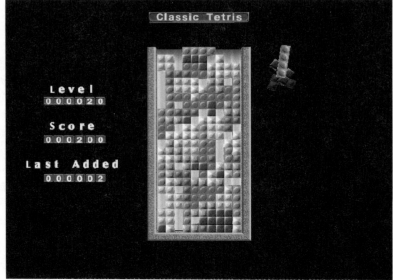

- Single Screen Play: Of course, *Tetris* takes place on only one screen. The player is able to view the entire game-world at one time and make informed decisions about what he wants to do with a given piece based on that. There is no exploration component to the game, no way to really surprise the player (beyond what piece appears next), so the player has all the information he needs to be successful at the game, and has nothing to blame but himself for failure.

- Infinite Play: *Tetris* allows the player to keep playing until, through her own bad decisions, the blocks reach the top of the box. Every game ends in defeat, and no one can truly say she has "beaten" the game. Players can always find ways to improve their *Tetris* playing ability. This is a crucial difference between *Tetris* and a traditional puzzle. Once a player has solved a puzzle, if she remembers how she did it the first time, the puzzle will no longer present any challenge to her. People usually do not enjoy doing puzzles multiple times, whereas a well-designed game can be replayed forever. *Tetris* is just such a game.

- Multiple Lives: Unlike most classic arcade games, the original *Tetris* implementation only offers the player one life. Once the blocks reach the top of the box, the player's game is over. The design of the game, however, allows the player to see that he is doing poorly while not defeating him instantly. As the blocks stack up at the bottom of the rectangle, the player sees the mistakes he is making and has time to figure out how to better line up the blocks before his game is over. So, while *Tetris* does not offer the player multiple lives, it does give him a chance to learn the game well enough to achieve some minor successes before forcing him to start over.

- Scoring/High Scores: *Tetris* uses a model for giving the player a score and recording it in a high-score table which is directly taken from the system used in games like *Asteroids* or *Galaga*. Indeed, since the game cannot be defeated, it is the possibility of achieving a higher score that can become the player's true impetus to play the game again.

- Easy-to-Learn, Simple Gameplay: *Tetris* truly excels in how simple and obvious its game mechanics are. The player really only needs three buttons in order to play the game successfully, and these all translate into obvious results on the screen. This means that virtually anyone, regardless of how familiar they are with computer games, can walk up to the game and start playing it immediately. However, a player will never be able to fully master the game due to the game's ramping-up difficulty and the potential for infinitely long games.

- No Story: *Tetris* has even less story than most classic arcade games, and is the case most often cited by people who want to point out that games do not need stories to be compelling for the player. The only sort of setting *Tetris* has is its origins in Russia, which has been used for various aesthetic effects in the different incarnations of the game. The first PC version of the game, as published by Spectrum Holobyte, included backdrops behind the gameplay that involved different scenes from Russian life, and the music sounded vaguely Slavic in origin. But once people learned what a great game *Tetris* was, subsequent implementations of the game, such as the one for the Nintendo Gameboy, had no Russian theme to them and had no setting or story at all. The game did not suffer one bit for this lack of story. Indeed, *Tetris*'s total lack of setting may actually be something that separates it from the classic arcade games, which all made an attempt to be grounded in a fantasy world of some sort, whether it was outer space in *Galaga*, insects in a garden in *Centipede*, or funky ghosts chasing a little yellow man around in *Pac-Man*. *Tetris* has no such pretensions, and thus stands out.

The Technology

Another similarity between *Tetris* and classic arcade games is that none of those games relied on their technology to impress the player. For CAGs, the graphics the arcade machines in the early '80s could produce were so lackluster compared to what players would find in other media, such as movies or television, that players had to be drawn in by something else. As a result, the gameplay had to be truly captivating for these games to survive. Despite the fact that much more sophisticated graphics were available by the time *Tetris* was released in the West in the late '80s,

the game did not need fancier graphics and stuck to a very simple 2D implementation. *Tetris*'s gameplay is so strong that it does not matter how technologically simple its implementation may be, the game is still wildly entertaining.

The implementation of *Tetris* is so simple that many aspiring game programmers start out by making a *Tetris* clone. Indeed, numerous companies have attempted to add fancy graphical effects to the game, including making it 3D. The first of these was probably *Welltris*, a sequel of sorts to *Tetris*, designed by Pajitnov. In *Welltris*, a 3D "well" takes the place of the *Tetris* box. *Tetris*-style pieces (though not always of four blocks) fall down along the sides of the well and must be lined up into rows on the bottom. The gameplay was considerably more complex without being particularly more fun or challenging. As a result, players were uninterested, and went back to the simplicity of the original. Many subsequent *Tetris* knockoffs attempted to make "improvements" on the original, either through fancy effects or special pieces of various sorts. None of these attempts were particularly successful, and players continued to want to return to the original.

The attempts to add technological sophistication to *Tetris* failed, not just commercially but also artistically. The enhanced technology added to these knockoff products was actually detrimental to the original game design, polluting its purity and making the game lose its elegance and fun in the process. Of course, the moral to the story is that enhanced technology is not necessarily beneficial to a given game, and game designers must be wary when the whiz-bang engine effects start to get in the way of what makes the game entertaining in the first place.

While *Tetris* may have not needed much in the way of computer technology to function, it is worth pointing out that there could be no *Tetris* without a computer. *Tetris* is not a game adapted from a pen and paper or board game, but rather something that only can exist in a world carefully controlled and governed by a computer. As mentioned previously, Pajitnov is said to have drawn his inspiration from the non-computer puzzle game pentomino. In adapting it to the computer, Pajitnov changed it into a form which could exist only on a computer. The descending of the pieces from the top of the screen at a steady rate, the way they can interact with the pieces already at the bottom of the screen, and the random way in which pieces become available to the player are all operations only a computer program could provide while still allowing for an entertaining experience for the player. These are all tasks the computer performs expertly, and it was brilliant of Pajitnov to think to add them to his game.

Artificial Intelligence

Tetris has a very limited artificial intelligence that randomly picks the blocks which fall into the play-field. Despite its simplicity, this AI provides the perfect challenge for the player.

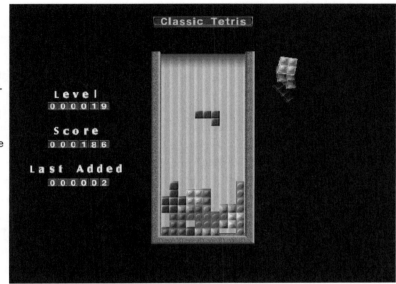

All the game has in terms of AI is the random number generator that picks the next piece to enter the play-field. However, the game mechanics are such that this random number is enough to completely change each game, presenting the player with unique challenges after every piece is dropped. Since the randomness ensures that the player never knows what the next piece will be, he is forced to play the piece in a way that is optimal for whatever one of the seven pieces comes along next. (Many incarnations of *Tetris* include a "next" feature, which shows the player the next piece that will come onto the play-field, a feature which does make the game a bit easier. Even when using this, however, players still do not know what the next-next-piece will be, hence they are still just making an educated guess as to where to stick the currently falling block.) If gameplay is about opposition, meaning an opponent providing a challenge to which the player must react, and if in solitaire computer games that opponent is the computer, then the fact that a random number generator provides all the challenge in *Tetris* demonstrates an important point. The AI the player faces only needs to be as smart as the game mechanics require. An AI needs to present the player with a situation that will challenge him, and it really does not matter how the AI arrives at that challenge. It could be as complicated as the AI for a deep strategy game like *Civilization*, or it could be as simple as the random piece picker found in *Tetris*. What matters is that the AI matches up with the game mechanics to sufficiently challenge the player.

The random nature of which pieces arrive at the top of the screen might suggest to the reader that success at *Tetris* is just luck. If the pieces a player gets are

random, how can different players' scores be compared against one another? The key point to realize here is that, over time, the randomness of the pieces evens out. Just as die rolls in a board game even out over the course of the game, the random pieces passed to the player in *Tetris* end up functioning as if they were not random at all. Since there are only seven types of pieces, none with more than four blocks, and since the player (at least initially) has a large space in which to manipulate them, the randomness keeps the game from becoming predictable while still making one player's game comparable to another's. Over the course of a game, a player will get a few hundred pieces. The number of times the player gets just the piece she was looking for is evened out by the times she does not get the piece she wants. It may be that the player will fail to get exactly the right piece at the right time and that, since the player's box is already full of pieces, the player's game ends as a result. However, in order to get to a situation where she could not use whatever piece was given to her, the player had already made a number of mistakes to put herself in such a perilous situation. In the end, the random piece picker found in *Tetris* provides a fair, consistent challenge to all players.

Escalating Tension

Tetris is very ruthless in the way it escalates tension throughout the player's game. Unlike a game such as *Centipede*, the player gets no reprieve when a wave ends, nor does he get the ability to "start fresh" when he loses a life. In *Tetris* the player "dies" when the box fills up with pieces that fail to make complete rows, and his game is over, period. This means that the player must be constantly on his guard, constantly considering what to do with a piece before it reaches the bottom of the screen. Even a fast-paced game such as *Doom* provides the player with plenty of respites from the action. In that first-person shooter, there are safe corners to hide in and rooms where, once all the threats have been eliminated, the player can wait indefinitely without being threatened. *Tetris* never lets up and constantly confronts the player with a new challenge that must be addressed.

The only reprieve the player finds in *Tetris* is when she "battles her way back" from a tricky situation. Say the player has dropped some blocks in bad locations, thereby blocking off uncompleted rows below. Now the player's game is harder because she has less space and time to manipulate her pieces before they are stopped at the bottom of the screen. The game's tension has escalated as a result of the player's mistakes. Now the player may be able, through careful placing of subsequent pieces, to erase the poorly placed bricks and finally complete the rows below. Now the game's tension has decreased and the player is back to where she was, with more space and time to manipulate the falling pieces. The player feels a sense of accomplishment and relief. She is able to relax momentarily, knowing she has a "clean slate" to work with once again. Of course, this only lasts until the player makes another mistake, and then the game's tension increases once again.

Further escalating the game's tension is the acceleration of the speed at which the pieces fall over the course of the game. When the player's score increases above certain specific amounts, the pieces in the game start moving at a faster rate, which makes the game more nerve-racking for the player. Since the pieces fall faster down the board, the player has less time to figure out the best position for a given piece, and also less time to manipulate the piece into that position. At the game's fastest speed, most players will be incapable of placing a piece in an ideal location, and with a piece in the wrong place the game only gets harder. Just before the speed increases, the player might start to feel that he has mastered the game and could play *Tetris* indefinitely. But when the speed increases, whatever sort of rhythm the player had established is thrown off. Now the player needs to do everything he was doing before, only faster.

Once the player starts making mistakes in *Tetris*, these mistakes compound, making the game harder and harder to play. As the player fails to create rows at the bottom of the screen, the player has less and less space in which to manipulate his pieces. When the player accidentally drops a piece in the wrong location, that piece may block rows below from being completed, and will make it harder to maneuver subsequent pieces around that ill-placed piece. When the player tries to hold out for an "I"-shaped piece to fill a narrow column of empty spots, the player will have to keep placing other pieces in perhaps less-than-perfect locations until that piece randomly arrives. In all these ways, *Tetris* penalizes the player for failure. Instead of giving the player a chance to catch up as some computer games do, *Tetris* just punishes her, making it even harder to come back from errors made previously. Further complicating matters are the bonus points the player receives for removing four rows all at once with an "I" piece. With this tactic, the game tempts the player into taking potentially game-ending risks.

Simplicity and Symmetry

Tetris, as has been discussed, is a very simple game. A big part of its success is due to its simplicity and that it is so easy to learn while being so relentlessly challenging. The player does not need to learn any special moves in order to play the game. There are a very small number of keys used by the game, and those keys produce very obvious results on the screen. It is interesting to look at the pieces used in *Tetris*. They are all composed of four squares, and, in fact, the seven different types of pieces used in the game represent every possible combination of four squares, where each square must share a side with another square in its group. Since the player can rotate the pieces to whatever orientation he wants, there are only seven truly unique combinations of squares possible.

All of the pieces in *Tetris* are composed of four squares, each of which shares at least one side with another square. This gives the game an inherent consistency and balance.

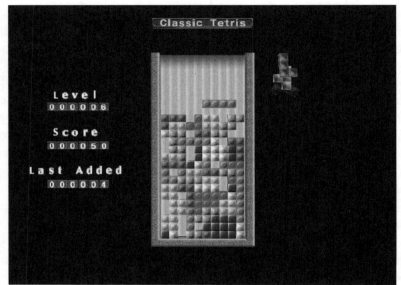

It has been reported that Pajitnov, in creating *Tetris*, originally considered using pieces consisting of five squares combined into twelve unique pieces. Indeed, the pentomino game from which Pajitnov drew his inspiration used twelve five-square pieces. Pajitnov soon realized that this was too many different pieces to have to manipulate in *Tetris*'s high-pressure setting, where the player has a limited amount of time to find a perfect fit for a given piece. Certainly a game using five-square pieces could have been challenging in its own way, and perhaps a slower falling speed and larger play-field could have compensated for the added complexity of the larger pieces. But would it have been *Tetris*? No. Would it have been as fun and addictive as *Tetris*? Probably not. At some point a complexity level begins to stifle the core nature of a game, and confuses players instead of challenging them. Using five instead of four squares ruined the simplicity Pajitnov was striving for, and as a result he reduced the number of squares a piece could have.

There are actually thirteen unique combinations of five squares possible, where each square shares a side with another square. So it would appear that the original pentomino game, with its twelve blocks, did not use a complete set of pieces. I have never tried pentomino, so I have no idea how much fun that puzzle may be. Part of what makes *Tetris* so elegant is the completeness of its pieces. Every possible permutation of four squares with squares sharing sides is used in the game. Remove any one of the pieces from *Tetris* and the game's balance would suffer. When playing, players will find themselves presented with situations that cry out for certain pieces. Certain arrangements of the blocks on the bottom of the screen leave holes that can only be perfectly filled by a specific *Tetris* piece. Part of what lends *Tetris* its balance is the fact that Pajitnov was wise enough to include each piece possible, thus providing a piece for every type of gap. The natural completeness and symmetry of the pieces available to the player in *Tetris* is a crucial component of its balance.

Ten Years On, Who Would Publish Tetris?

One must wonder, if *Tetris* were created today, what publisher would be willing to publish it. Originally *Tetris* was sold as "the game from Russia" and was attached to art and music of a similar nature, almost as a gesture to our new friends in what was then the U.S.S.R. Had *Tetris* been dreamed up by a kid in a garage in Iowa one wonders if it ever would have been published at all. (One would like to be optimistic and think that he would have been able to code it up, release it as shareware on the Internet, and the game's fame would still have been assured.) *Tetris* is the ultimate in low-technology gameplay, and many game publishers simply refuse to publish games that do not utilize the latest in computer graphics wizardry. After all, where will they find the pretty screenshots for the back of the box? The game lacks any sort of story or even setting, another absolute must for the people in marketing. What sort of copy will they write in their ads? Indeed, it is a testament to *Tetris's* brilliant gameplay that it cannot be adequately described in any amount of words, much less in a catchy one-liner. Even looking at a static screenshot of *Tetris* is a thoroughly unexciting experience, one which cannot hope to communicate the game's sublime art. Gameplay is an elusive subject for manipulators of the written word; it must be experienced to be understood.

Chapter 9:
Artificial Intelligence

"I'd basically watch the game play until I saw the AI do something stupid, then try to correct that and repeat ad infinitum. Over a long enough period that produced a pretty darn good AI. I have always tried to teach the AI the same successful strategies that I use in playing a game."

— Brian Reynolds, talking about the creation of the artificial intelligence for his games *Civilization II* and *Alpha Centauri* rtificial intelligence can mean a variety of different things in different contexts. In an academic context, artificial intelligence is sometimes defined as a system that can reliably pass what is called the Turing test. In the Turing test, a human is presented with a computer terminal into which he can type various sentences and can then see responses printed on the screen. If this user believes that the responses are provided by a human, even though they were actually provided by the computer, then that computer would have passed the Turing test and could be said to have artificial intelligence.

One could apply a similar test to computer games. If one is playing a game of *Unreal Tournament* and cannot tell if the opponent one is playing against is a human opponent or a 'bot, then one could say that the game passes a limited version of the Turing test and therefore possesses some sort of artificial intelligence. However, in actual practice, even if the game had failed that test, people would have said that the game has artificial intelligence, just not really good artificial intelligence. When game developers talk about artificial intelligence, they do not mean the computer's ability to trick the player into thinking he is playing against actual human opponents. Instead, game developers refer to whatever code is used to control the opponents the player battles as artificial intelligence. How the game reacts to the player's actions is determined by the game's AI. The reactions of the game may be completely random or completely logical; in either case the code which controls those reactions is referred to as the game's artificial intelligence.

If a player plays a game of *Unreal Tournament* and cannot tell whether the opponent is a 'bot or a human, the 'bot's artificial intelligence has passed the Turing test.

Consider a game like *Centipede*. The AI for this game is completely predictable, with the various insects moving in predetermined patterns, with a small amount of randomness thrown in. Some people would say that the game does not really have any AI. Indeed, the behaviors of the creatures in the game are exceedingly simple to implement. But at the same time, the game provides a great deal of challenge for the player. The difficult part of creating the AI for a game like *Centipede* lies entirely in the design of those creatures' behaviors, coming up with the movement patterns that will provide an interesting challenge for the player. The AI is more design than implementation. *Tetris*, perhaps, is an even more extreme example. The only AI the game could be said to have is the random number generator that determines which piece will drop into the play-field next. Yet *Tetris* is designed such that this is the only AI the game needs.

The reader may be wondering why I am talking about game AI in a book about game design. Surely AI is a programming task, and since this book is not about programming, the discussion of AI contained in this chapter may seem out of place. But determining what the AI will do and actually programming that behavior are two fairly distinct tasks. The first primarily involves creativity and the second consists of a whole lot of hard work. A game's designer should be intimately concerned with making sure the game's AI behavior is as well conceived as possible and performs the actions most likely to provide the player with a challenging and compelling gameplay experience. Part of designing a good game is designing good AI for that game, and a designer who just leaves the creation of the AI up to programmers better hope that they are good AI designers. If they are not, the game will likely not be much fun to play.

If a computer game is like improvised theater, where the player gets to be director of the primary character or group of characters, then all of the other actors in the play are controlled by the artificial intelligence. As the game's designer, you want to direct those AI-controlled actors to create the most stimulating experience possible for the player. These AI agents are not just the opponents the player might battle, but also any characters with which the player interacts. How will a town full of people behave? How will they react to the player's actions? Designing the AI is a big part of designing a game.

Goals of Game AI

Players have different expectations of the AI they find in different types of games. Players do not expect much of the AI in an arcade game like *Centipede* or a puzzle game like *Tetris*. As I have discussed, these games provide plenty of challenge to the player while using various simple-minded or outright stupid opponents. In a wargame like *Close Combat,* however, players expect a lot more from the intelligence of the opposing forces. In an RPG, players expect to move into a simulation of a living world, where characters move around in a town more or less "realistically." In a game like *The Sims*, the AI more or less is the game; with weak AI the

The Sims' success is completely dependent on the strength of its artificial intelligence.

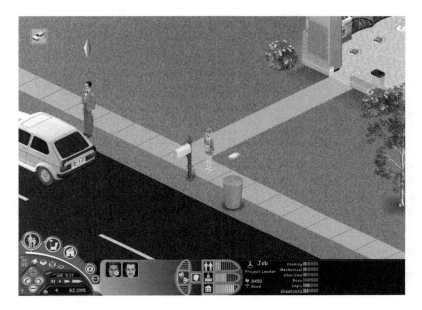

game would simply not be worth playing.

So different games provoke different expectations in the player of how smart the AI agents in those games need to be. However, we can still construct a general list of goals for any computer game AI, goals which change in importance as the design goals for a given game vary.

Challenge the Player

Providing a reasonable challenge for the player must be the primary goal for AI in any computer game. Without setting up a challenge of some sort, a game becomes unchallenging and therefore too easy to defeat. Worse still, a game that provides no challenge stops being a game entirely and becomes more of an interactive movie.

In a classic arcade game like *Robotron 2084* or in a first-person shooter like *Doom*, the challenge mostly comes from the player being overwhelmed by adversaries, and by the powerful abilities those adversaries have. For instance, in my oft-used example of *Centipede*, the bugs can kill the player by touching him, while the player must shoot the creatures in order to kill them. This puts the player at something of a disadvantage. The fact that there are multiple insects attacking the player at once does not help matters. As a result, the AI for these creatures can be fairly simple and predictable, yet the player is still challenged by them.

The same imbalance holds true in *Doom*, where the player may run out of ammo but his enemies never do, where the player is much more helpless in the dark while the enemies can detect the player just as easily as in the light, and where often the enemies, such as flying creatures, can go where the player cannot. The

In a classic arcade game like *Robotron 2084*, the challenge comes from the sheer quantity of opponents the player must fight.

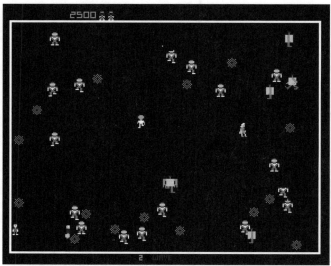

fact that the creatures far outnumber the player also tends to compensate for the reality that none of the creatures is very smart. The AI in *Doom* has to appear more sophisticated than the *Centipede* insects because the *Doom* world seems more real than the *Centipede* world, as I will discuss in a bit. The fact remains that primarily the AI provides a challenge for the player by being more powerful and numerous than the player.

Creating a challenging AI for a real-time strategy game like *StarCraft* is an entirely more difficult proposition. The expectation in games of this sort is that the player is competing with someone equivalent to him in strength. In your average real-time strategy game, both sides have a large number of troops to manipulate and the ability to build more as needed. Both sides usually need to mine a resource of some kind and use that to build more structures or troops. Basically, the AI in an RTS has to do everything the player does and seem smart while doing it. Often the AI is given an advantage by being able to see the entire level while the player cannot, and possibly having a larger number of starting units, an easier method for obtaining more, or a bigger pool of resources from which to draw. Nonetheless, creating a challenge for a player in an RTS game is quite difficult since it requires the AI to plan the movement of the units beyond the individual unit level, making the units appear to work collaboratively, as a player would use them.

The difficulties presented in creating a challenging AI for an RTS game are only magnified in a turn-based strategy game such as *Alpha Centauri*. Here the AI is supposed to operate just as the player does. Of course turn-based strategy games are some of the most thought-intensive games available, so that only amplifies the problem of creating a compelling opponent AI. Furthermore, the computer does not get to benefit as much from its extremely fast processing power; since the game is

Developing a challenging AI for a turn-based strategy game such as *Alpha Centauri* can be quite difficult since the player is supposed to be fighting opponents with roughly the same strengths and weaknesses as himself.

turn-based, the player has as long to think about a move as he likes. Often turn-based strategy AIs create a challenge for the player by cheating in various subtle ways, though I would certainly be the last to accuse any particular game of doing so.

Regardless of the game type, the AI must present the player with an interesting challenge. Without good AI, a game may become similar to playing chess with your (much) younger brother: somewhat pointless. The difference is, when you play chess with your kid brother, you hope to teach him the nuances of the game so that one day he may become a good player. You may also enjoy socializing with him, making an otherwise pointless game of chess worth it. Sadly, the computer game AI you battle has no hope of improving and is woefully inadequate when it comes to providing companionship. In order for a game AI to justify its existence, it must provide the player with a challenge.

Not Do Dumb Things

AI for a computer game must not appear overly stupid. Players love laughing at AI when it does something completely foolhardy. Nothing breaks a player's suspension of disbelief more than when an AI agent fails to navigate around a small obstacle such as a fire hydrant or a tree, or when an agent charges right off a cliff to its doom like a lemming. To the player, it is completely obvious what the AI should do in each situation. But what may look obvious to the player can actually be a fairly complex action for the agent to perform or understand. Nonetheless, for the game to avoid becoming a laughingstock, the game's AI must have a solid mastery of what seems obvious to human players.

When fighting aliens in a game such as *Marathon 2*, the player has lowered expectations of how smart these enemies will be.

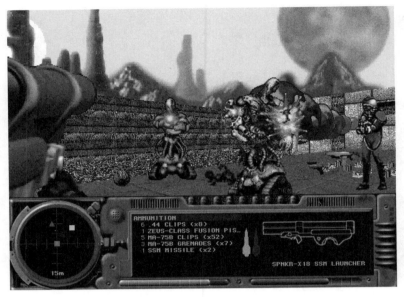

When fighting aliens in a game such as *Marathon 2*, the player has lowered expectations of how smart these enemies will be.

The number of dumb things the AI will be able to get away with has a direct relationship to what sort of intelligence the AI is supposed to represent. For instance, in my first-person shooter *Damage Incorporated*, the player is supposed to be almost exclusively battling human opponents. In *Marathon 2*, however, the player is battling a variety of alien species mixed with some robots. The enemies in *Marathon 2* are able to get away with appearing stupid since they are non-human creatures. In *Damage Incorporated*, conversely, since the enemies are all humans they must look much smarter. For another example, in *Damage Incorporated*, according to the game's story and the appearance of the levels in the game, the action is supposed to be transpiring in a real-world environment. On the other hand, *Centipede 3D* takes place in a whimsical fantasy world that bears only a tangential relationship to the real-world. Therefore, while the guards in *Damage Incorporated* need to appear to be tracking the player like real human soldiers would, in *Centipede 3D* it is less absurd that the centipedes are unable to make a beeline for the player and instead have to wind back and forth between mushrooms. AI stupidity is acceptable relative to the type of world the computer game is supposed to represent.

Be Unpredictable

Humans are unpredictable. That is part of what makes them good opponents in a game. This is one of the primary reasons that people enjoy playing multi-player games; a skilled person will be challenging to fight in a way a computer never will. A large part of that is the unpredictability of a human opponent. The same should be true of the AI opponents in a computer game. When the game gets to the point where the player feels with certainty that she knows exactly what the enemy forces are going to do at any given second, the fun of playing the game quickly wanes. Players want the AI to surprise them, to try to defeat them in ways they had not anticipated. Certainly multi-player games still have the advantage of including a social component, which is a major factor in their success, and the AI in your game will never be able to be a friend to the player in the same way another human can. But if you cannot provide the social component of multi-player games, you can at least strive to make the AI agents provide much of the same challenge and unpredictability that a human opponent can.

In all art, the viewer wants to see something she had not been able to anticipate, something that challenges her expectations. When, within the first ten minutes, you know the exact ending of a movie, book, or play, a big part of the thrill of experiencing that work is removed. The same is true for computer games. Of course, games can surprise players with their predetermined story, or what sort of environment the next level will take place in, or what the big boss robot will look like. But if the AI can also contribute to this unpredictably, the game gains something that no other component of the game can provide: replayability. Players will keep playing a game until it no longer provides them with a challenge, until they no longer experience anything new from playing the game. And an AI that can keep surprising them, and thereby challenging them, will help keep their interest high.

The only AI *Tetris* needs is a random number generator. Pictured here: classic mode in *The Next Tetris*.

Successful unpredictability can take many different forms in games. It can be as simple as the random number that determines what piece will drop next in *Tetris*. Surely this is a very simple case, and optimally we would hope many games could

provide deeper unpredictability than that. But at the same time, one must realize that for *Tetris*, it is the perfect amount of unpredictability. If players knew what piece was coming next, the game would lose a lot of its challenge. Indeed, with the "next" feature on (which displays the next piece to drop on the side of the screen) the game becomes significantly easier. Pure randomness is often a really good way to keep the player interested in the AI, to make them wonder, "What's it trying to do?" when in fact it is just being random. The randomness in *Tetris* provides the unpredictability required to keep the player challenged for hours.

Sometimes the goals of computer game AI can get confused, and in a quest for the holy grail of realism a designer or an AI programmer can end up making a very dull opponent for a game. Sure, the agent always makes a decision which "makes sense" given its current situation; it may even make the decision most likely to win the current battle. But if that logical decision is completely obvious to the player, how much fun is it going to be to fight that AI? If every time you run into a room in a first-person shooter, the Orc you find there is going to spin around, heave its club above its head, and charge at you while swinging wildly, the next time you play that room the situation will be much less challenging. What if sometimes the Orc is startled by the player's sudden arrival? Then the Orc might flee down the hall or go cower in a corner. What if sometimes the Orc decides to hurl his club at the player instead of trying to use it as a melee weapon? That would certainly provide enough spice to keep the player on his toes. You must remember that each human being is different and that many humans are known to act irrationally for any number of reasons. That irrationality keeps life interesting. If the player is battling humans or human-like monsters/aliens in a computer game, a little irrationality will result in making the opponents seem that much more real, believable, and interesting to fight.

"Fuzzy logic" is one method AI designers and programmers may try to use to keep the AI agents unpredictable and interesting. Essentially, fuzzy logic takes a logical system and inserts some randomness into it. In fuzzy logic, when the AI is presented with a given situation, it has several worthwhile courses of action to choose from instead of just one. Say the player is at a certain distance with a certain weapon while the AI agent is at a certain health level and is equipped with a certain amount of weaponry. There may be three reasonable things for the agent to do in this case, and they can each have different numerical values or "weights" representing how good a choice each is. Say that running up and attacking the player makes a lot of sense, so it rates a five. Doing a threat display in order to frighten the player makes a bit of sense, so it rates a two. And maybe trying to circle around the player in order to disorient him is also plausible, so it rates a three. Using these different weights, the agent can simply randomly pick a number from 1 to 10 (the total of the weights). If less than or equal to 5, the agent will run up and attack. If 6 or 7, the agent will try to frighten the player. And if 8 through 10, the agent will do its best to disorient the player. The weights represent the chance that the AI will make a given decision. If the AI has enough different plans at its disposal, the player will never be able to know exactly what the AI will do, thereby making the AI unpredictable. In the final analysis, basing AI decisions on randomness makes the agent look like it is performing complex reasoning when it is not. The player will never know that the AI in question just picked its action randomly. Instead, if the agent's action does not look too stupid, the player will try to imagine why the AI might have chosen to do what it did, and may end up thinking the agent is pretty sly when really it is just random.

Of course, the unpredictability of an AI agent in a game must not conflict with the other AI goals I have listed here. If an agent is so busy being unpredictable that it cannot put together a solid plan of attack against the player, it is not going to be much of a threat to the player and he will not be challenged. Ideally, unpredictability enhances the challenge the AI presents, instead of proving a detriment. If the AI randomly chooses to do something completely foolish when what it was doing was about to lead to victory, the player cannot help but wonder, "Why would the AI do such a stupid thing?" When working on the behaviors of the creatures in a game, it is always important to keep an eye on the bigger picture of what that AI is trying to accomplish.

Assist Storytelling

Game AI can be used to further a game's story. For example, in an RPG, a player may travel to a certain town which is home to a number of fearful residents who dread the arrival of outsiders. If the player only observes these people, they can be seen to be navigating the town, going to the stores, restaurants, and factories just as people in a real town would. This sets the scene for the town and makes it seem real to the player. But whenever the player approaches these people, they turn away, fleeing to safe areas to avoid interacting with the player. Why is this? What does it say about the town and the people who live there? Why are they frightened? The player wants to know why, and will start exploring the game's story as a result. English teachers are notorious for telling their students that it is better to show than to tell. This is especially true in a visual medium such as computer games. Instead of just seeing that the town's inhabitants are frightened of strangers in a cut-scene, a properly designed AI can actually show the player this interesting information.

Even the adversaries that a player might fight in a battle can be adjusted to aid in the storytelling process. Suppose that in a wargame the player is supposed to be fighting a general who is known for being compassionate about the welfare of his troops, perhaps more than is logical in a combat situation. The player could send in a few snipers to pick off several of the opposing force's troops that are serving as guards along the border between two contested areas. If the AI for the enemy general was properly designed, the slow drain of troops in that manner would start to enrage him. Once infuriated, the general would try a foolhardy attack to get back at the player's forces, thus putting him at the disadvantage. Here again, a bit of the game's story has been told through the AI.

In *Damage Incorporated*, the AI the player's teammates exhibit plays a crucial role in telling the game's story.

In my game *Damage Incorporated*, the player is a U.S. Marine Corps sergeant in charge of a fire-team of four men. Together with his men, the player storms through numerous missions against a variety of heavily armed opponents. The men each have different strengths and weaknesses. Some are headstrong and will charge bravely into a fight. Some of the squad members are more careful about firing their weapons than others, and as a result are less likely to hit the player or the other teammates. These personality traits are all communicated through the AI that these teammates use. Before each mission, the player gets to choose his team from a selection of thirteen different soldiers, each with a dossier the player can read. The dossiers provide a psychological profile of each of the teammates, which gives some insight into their personalities. Furthermore, when actually on a mission, the teammates are constantly speaking, either in response to the player's orders or just to comment on a given situation. This gives further insight into their personalities and how they will behave on the battlefield. If the player reads the dossiers and pays attention to the squad members' personalities carefully, he will notice warnings that some of the teammates may not be completely balanced psychologically. For some teammates, if they are taken on too many missions they will "crack" or become "shell-shocked" and attempt to run away from the battle. Other teammates, if taken on specific missions that they do not agree with ideologically, will turn against the player and his men. The AI, of course, handles these "shell-shocked" situations, which thereby helps to tell the story of these characters.

One area where AI is often avoided entirely by designers but where it can be quite useful is in dynamic storytelling. All too often designers cobble a story around a game instead of integrating the story and gameplay together. Furthermore, often designers want to tell static stories in which how a given character will react to the player is entirely predetermined, regardless of the player's actions in the game-world or how the player treats that particular character. While designers often strive to keep the battles and action sequences as dynamic and unpredictable as possible, they almost always want to keep the stories exactly the same every time the player experiences them. Why not have the player be able to affect the mood of the different NPCs he encounters? Maybe if the player says all the right things and does not ask questions about sensitive subjects, the NPC becomes friendly toward the player. Maybe the player can only coax crucial information out of a character after first becoming his friend. Perhaps the player's reputation precedes him, where the actions the player has performed elsewhere in the world directly impact how that NPC will treat the player. If the player has done less-than-good actions earlier in the game, maybe the player has to redeem himself in the eyes of a character before he can proceed in the game. Of course, there is a wide range of different effects that can be achieved using the game's AI to create interesting interpersonal relationships. Sadly this is something that has been all but unexplored in commercial games to date. Instead of telling static stories, we could be telling ones that, though not entirely procedurally generated, were subtly different depending on how the player played the game. Using AI to spice up and vary the story from game to game may make telling a story much more difficult, but what it can add to the game's non-linearity and replayability is enormous.

Create a Living World

In many games, the AI does more than just provide a threat and a challenge to the player. A game may even include AI agents that the player does not directly interact with at all. The AI can instead be used to inhabit the living world the game creates. A game-world may be infinitely detailed in terms of the objects it contains and how it looks and sounds, but players are used to a real-world which also contains living organisms that think for themselves and behave in interesting ways. Therefore, creating a sterile game-world filled with inanimate objects is not going to be a very authentic reality for the player. One does not need to go overboard in filling up the game-world with complex ambient AI agents; a little can go a long way. Whether this means a few birds that fly around in the sky, insects that crawl around on the ground, or humans that go about their daily business, adding ambient life to a world can do a lot to make the game-world seem more real to the player. And the more

real it is, the more likely it is that the player will be able to immerse himself in it.

There is a close connection between filling the game with ambient life and using the AI to tell the game's story. Creating these inhabitants does a lot to establish the setting for your game, and setting is a key part of telling any story. But ambient life in a game goes beyond just establishing that setting; it helps make the player feel less lonely in the game-world. How many times have you played a game where you felt like you were walking around a sterile wasteland, as if an exterminator had come through previously to eliminate any signs of life? Players love to see that the world has ambient life in it, creatures they can just look at rather than kill, and the depth it adds to the world can be invaluable.

The Sloped Playing Field

Often when programmers get together to talk about AI for computer games, they concentrate their discussions on how they want their AI agents to be on equal footing with the player. This was certainly the case at the AI round tables I have attended in years past at the Game Developer's Conference. These AI specialists want their AI systems to know only what the player would know, see what the player can see, and so forth. This, they suggest, will make the conflict between the AI and the player more realistic and therefore more interesting.

Of course, for years games have been giving the AI agents unfair advantages over the player. They have made the AI have more hit-points than the player. They have outnumbered the player a hundred to one. They have made the AI agents have a practically psychic knowledge of every location in the game-world, which allows them to know exactly where the player is at any given second, certainly an unfair advantage. Some game AIs have even been known to cheat. Surely this is unfair to the player, the AI programmers will say. The AI should be on equal footing with the player, they proclaim, and should triumph over the player through its wits alone.

But is it really better to put the AI and player on a level playing field? First and foremost, this is quite likely to lead to an AI that fails to provide much of a challenge for the player. The fact remains that a shrewd player is going to be able to outsmart even the most sophisticated game AI without that much difficulty. Trying to put the player and AI on equal terms will create a much larger challenge for your AI programmers. They will need to invest countless more hours in developing an AI that has even a slight chance of beating the player, time that cannot be spent improving other parts of the game. In the end they will end up with an AI that does not provide a captivating gameplay experience. In the worst case, the AI is too busy being "real" to avoid performing blatantly stupid actions.

A big part of what drives AI programmers to attempt a level playing field for players and AI agents is the programmers' own egos. These programmers pride themselves on their work and will assert that they can come up with an AI that will be able to challenge a player without having to resort to superior numbers, greater strength, or any sort of cheating. The programmers want the bragging rights of being able to say that their AI is as smart as a human. Often hours and hours are spent trying to come up with the sophisticated algorithms required for such equal versus equal competition, and in the end something has to be hacked together to make the game actually function. The goal of game AI is to support the game and enhance the player's experience, not to serve as a test-bed for artificial intelligence techniques.

Besides, there is something romantic for the player when he manages to defeat an AI opponent despite the fact that the AI's forces greatly outnumber his own, were better armed and equipped, and even had the benefit of prescient knowledge of the map. Just as the Hollywood action hero triumphs over countless foes, players want to overcome seemingly insurmountable odds for their own victories. Tipping the scales in the AI's advantage only makes the player's eventual victory all the more sweet. Unless, of course, the design ends up making the game too hard.

How Real is Too Real?

Another potential AI programming pitfall is creating an AI which, though it actually performs like a "real" person, ends up detracting from the gameplay as a result. In terms of the stories they tell and the settings they employ, games are often contrivances, strictly unreal situations that are specifically set up because they are interesting, not because they are authentic, and the AI must support this.

Consider the James Bond movies. These films are like many popular games in that they feature a lot of action and exciting situations with less of a focus on character development or meaningful stories. In nearly every film, Bond is captured at some point and tied down to a particularly hideous execution device. This device does not kill Bond instantly, but instead employs some slower method, such as a laser steadily burning a hole down the middle of the table to which James is strapped. Why does the villain not simply shoot Bond? Or simply aim the laser straight at him? Why does the villain almost always leave before the execution has actually been completed? And why does the villain reveal to Bond his entire mad scheme for world domination before he starts the execution device in motion? None of it is very smart behavior, but it is fun to watch, and fits with the overall style of the movie. It entertains the audience, which is the primary goal of the Bond films. Realism is much less of a concern.

And so it is with games. If the enemy AI is so smart, surely it should realize that it has no chance against the player, and should lock itself away in a safe bunker, refusing to open the door for anyone. It has, in fact, saved its own life by doing this, which is the smartest decision possible. But what has it done to the game? Now the player is stuck, since he has no way of getting to the enemy and

continuing on with the game. Another example might be a cowardly AI that runs from the player when sufficiently wounded. This is used to great effect in many games. But what if the agent was faster than the player, and better at dodging into safe locations? When quite wounded, the AI agent will start fleeing from the battle, with the player left with no other option but to chase after it. If the AI is speedier and better at navigation, the player will have a hard time catching up with it. What may have been a fun action game now becomes a tedious chase with a foregone conclusion, since the agent is mortally wounded and has no chance of recovering its health. And what of the deadly serpent boss the player must battle? With its protective armor coating, it is impervious to the player's attacks, and can only be damaged by being shot when its mouth is open. So the strictly logical choice might be to always keep its mouth closed whenever the player has any chance of getting off a shot. This is a decision it can make very easily. But now, of course, the player has no chance whatsoever of winning the battle. Is this fun?

The point again is that the AI must never overshadow the gameplay, and it must never distract the development team from the true goal of the project: to make a fun, playable game. If the AI is really very sophisticated but, as a result, the game is unplayable or extremely frustrating, a player is not going to remark on how smart the AI is. A player may notice advanced rendering algorithms which improve the visuals of a given title. He may remark on this and appreciate the game's aesthetic value even if the gameplay is poor, but a non-programming player is not going to appreciate sophisticated AI if the game that features it is not any fun to play.

AI Agents and Their Environment

Computer game AI cannot be designed or developed in a vacuum. For a game AI to turn out well, it needs to be developed in close association with the game's gameplay and the environments in which that gameplay is going to take place. The simple fact is that no AI agent is going to be smart enough to prevail in all situations. While an AI may be exceedingly good in wide open spaces, when it is thrown into a narrow canyon it will encounter problems its programmer never anticipated. If the AI programmer comes up with an AI that can handle the confined spaces, chances are it will not be as good out in the open. The best one can hope for is that the AI has a fighting chance in a specific type of gameplay situation. If the levels and AI are not developed in synchronicity, then there is little chance that the opponents the player faces will appear very smart at all.

This creates special problems in terms of how to best produce a game. Level design is often one of the last tasks to be carried out on a game, before it goes into final balancing, then testing, and finally ships. Similarly, AI is usually only worked on after the game's rendering is firmly in place, most of the mechanics for the player's movement are fully functional, and many of the other more critical programming tasks are mostly done. Now, if the same person who is designing the levels is also creating the enemy AI, it might be simple to integrate the development of the two, but this is rare if not unheard of in modern game development. As a result you have two teams—the programmers and the level designers—working in parallel. Unfortunately, the usual case is that each charges forward with their work without fully considering the other. The level designers do not have the AI yet, so they cannot tailor their levels to support it. It is just the opposite on the other side of the equation: the programmer does not have the levels yet, so it is hard for him to make AI that will function well in those levels. The situation is a catch-22. Once the levels are done in terms of architecture, the AI is finally added to them, and then it turns out that one or the other needs to be radically reworked if the game is going to be any fun. In the worst case scenario there is no time to rework either the levels or the behaviors, and the gameplay ends up suffering as a result.

Of course, the level designers will protest that the AI should be designed to fit the levels they create. And, similarly, the AI programmers will complain that the levels simply must be reconceived to work with the AI they developed. Since I have worked as both a level designer and an AI programmer, I may be in a special position to arbitrate this dispute. In my opinion, neither party is entirely right, and a little give and take is required on each side. I would advocate trying to make a simple, playable AI first. It does not need to be bug free or work perfectly in every situation. If it works fairly well in some situations, level designers can start making levels that facilitate what the AI is known to do well. As the level designers take this direction, the AI programmer can keep working on his AI, getting rid of any bugs while always keeping an eye on what shape the game-world is taking. The AI programmer must communicate to the level designer when he sees a problem emerging in a level, such as a situation the AI is unlikely to handle well. At the same time the design of the levels may give the AI programmer new ideas about what tricks the AI can pull off. Maybe ledges start showing up in the game-world that would be ideal for sniping. Or perhaps the structure of the game-world's architecture suits itself to large troop movements. If the AI programmer can then add functionality to his algorithms to allow the agents to identify these locations and behave accordingly, the AI will become stronger as a result.

A level designer must be willing to sacrifice cool-looking geometry if it does not allow the AI to function. If the AI is not functioning, the game is not any fun, and the primary responsibility of a level is to provide the player with a compelling and entertaining experience. In my game *Damage Incorporated*, the player is responsible for not only controlling her own player, but also for directing four teammates in a 3D environment. When I was working on that game, one of the greatest challenges I encountered was getting the teammate AI working in a way that appeared intelligent to the player. Fortunately, I had a rudimentary form of this AI working before any real level design began. This way I realized ahead of time

Getting the AI agents in *Damage Incorporated* to work properly required many changes to the levels.

that the teammate AI would not be smart enough to jump or swim to areas. This meant that the levels had to be designed accordingly, or the teammates would not be able to reach the end of a level with the player. Also, the teammates performed badly in tight, constrained spaces, often running into each other or blocking the player's progress. The levels had to be made with large, open areas so that the AI agents could have a decent chance of performing well.

But even with foreknowledge of the sophistication of the game's AI, once *Damage Incorporated* entered testing, endless problems arose with the AI. The teammates constantly seemed to be able to get wedged in tiny little spaces they were not supposed to enter. The end solution turned out to be about 25 percent code fixes and 75 percent reworking parts of the levels to eliminate the little nooks into which the AI agents jammed themselves. There were countless sections of levels that I had wanted to look a certain way but that needed to be scrapped because the AI simply could not function in those areas. I was sad to see those sections go, but not as sad as a player would have been when he managed to get a teammate stuck in a crevice. The AI and levels had to work together if the final game was going to be any fun to play.

How Good is Good Enough?

Damage Incorporated suggests another interesting point about the sophistication that will be required of AI in different games. What made the work on *Damage Incorporated* so challenging was the fact that the player was counting on the AI to perform certain actions for him. If the player ordered a teammate to move to a certain position, he expected that marine to reach that position and defend it. If the AI failed to do so, the player might die as a result, and would curse the AI for failing him. Even worse, if the player ordered the AI to relocate to a specific position and the trooper had difficulty getting there, the player would become frustrated, especially when the appropriate path to that location was completely obvious to the player. But if an enemy AI agent had trouble finding a path to a location, the player would never be the wiser. If an opponent got stuck in a corner on rare occasions, the player would be all too happy to exploit the AI agent's stupidity by mowing down the stuck foe with a blast of machine gun fire. However, if a teammate got stuck in a corner, he would be unable to follow the player to the end of the level. Since the player could not finish a level unless his entire squad was in the "Extraction Zone" for that level, the AI's mistakes would end the player's game prematurely. Nothing frustrates a player more than dying because of faulty teammate AI.

In a game with teammates, such as *Damage Incorporated*, the failure of the AI agents to work as the player expects seriously impedes the player's ability to play the game.

One can take a couple of lessons away from the problems I had with the AI implementation on *Damage Incorporated*. The first is to never do a game with teammates in a complex 3D environment. The other conclusion is that the amount of AI sophistication a game requires is dependent on how much the failure of that

AI will impact the player. If the AI screws up and the player's game ends as a result, that is very bad. If the AI makes mistakes and the only consequence is that the player's game gets slightly easier, then it is a failing the player can probably live with, as long as it is a rare enough occurrence. So when a designer is working on an AI system or critiquing a programmer's work, she should always keep in mind how important it is that the system function correctly. It is perfectly acceptable if only the development team knows of the AI's stupidity while the player is completely ignorant of its shortcomings.

It would be nice to make every system in a game as smart as possible, but the realities of the production cycle dictate that there is only so much time that can be invested in any given part of a game. Rare is the case that a programmer has finished all of the work needed for a game and still has time to "polish" everything that he would like. As such, spending a lot of time on overly sophisticated AI systems will directly take time away from other tasks which desperately need work. The reader will notice that when I listed the attributes that a game's AI needs to have, I did not list "be a respectable, academic-quality artificial intelligence." The AI for a game only needs to be good enough to challenge the player while not appearing overly foolish in its actions.

In his fascinating Game Developer's Conference talk "Who Buried Paul?" Brian Moriarty discussed the concept of "constellation" in games. This theory is of particular relevance to game AI. Roughly stated, the theory is that humans, when presented with some seemingly random data, will try to make sense of it, to put it into order, and to try to find meaning where there may, in fact, be none. For game AI, then, Moriarty suggested that having your AI perform seemingly random actions will cause players to think the AI has some grand, intelligent plan. A player might think something along the lines of the following: "Why did that platoon of tanks suddenly storm over that hill? There does not seem to be any reason for it. Maybe they know something I do not. Maybe they are regrouping with a force I cannot see." Players who are not game developers themselves will have a tendency to try to believe that game AI agents make intelligent choices. Of course, there is a fine line. If players see an AI agent pointlessly ramming into a wall they will know something is amiss. It is important to remember that players do not want to find bugs in your game, and will do their best to believe in the intelligence of the characters they see therein. By throwing in some random behavior, your AI agents may come out looking smarter than they really are.

Scripting

Of course, game AI does not need to spontaneously think up every behavior that is performed in the game. In some games, a combination of dynamic AI with predetermined paths and scripted behaviors may create the most exciting experience possible for the player. Usually scripted behaviors work best in games that have predefined locations and where players are not likely to play through those levels repeatedly. In these games, players are likely to come into a given area from a certain location, and therefore the designer can make assumptions about what plan of attack will provide the most interesting challenge for the player.

First-person shooters are a good example of a game genre that works well with somewhat scripted AI behaviors. *Half-Life* is perhaps the ideal example of a game that uses AI scripting to create opponents that players enjoy fighting. That game was widely praised in the gaming press for the strength of its AI, while in fact much of that perceived intelligence was accomplished using scripted paths that the AI agents would move to in specific situations.

Setting up scripted behaviors that are specific to a level is very much the concern of the level designer. The level designer already needed to concern herself with where the opponents should be placed to create maximum gameplay effect. But with scripted behaviors the designer needs to repeatedly play an area to figure out the most devilish places for the AI to hide, where it should retreat to when low on health, and how it should best reposition to have the greatest chance of defeating the player. Of course, the AI agent cannot only be on a path. The AI must still be used to enable the agent to determine which location it should try to get to in which situation. Furthermore, the AI must be able to realize when the scripted plans are not working out and when to try an unscripted, more general behavior. One might think that having AI agents that use scripted, predetermined behaviors will fail to produce the unpredictability I discussed earlier. One might wonder how a scripted behavior can be anything but predictable. For just this reason, scripted behavior should be used just to give the AI agent hints as to where good locations to duck and cover might be, not to specify where the agent must always go, regardless of the situation. The agent must still be able to react to the player's tactics in order to avoid looking too foolish.

Artificial Stupidity

The fact that games are often referred to as having not artificial intelligence but rather artificial stupidity is quite telling about the quality of AI present in many games. It is certainly true that the AI in almost all games is not something which in and of itself is impressive. However, when considered in terms of what it is intended to do—challenge the player—many of the best games really do present well-designed computer opponents. While multi-player games provide many avenues for interesting gameplay design and production, a large segment of the gaming population is still going to desire single-player games. Solitaire games provide a unique experience, and the game's AI is crucial to making that experience as fun as possible. It is the designer's responsibility to carefully conceive this artificial intelligence, and to make sure those who implement it have a clear understanding of what the AI must do to successfully challenge and entertain the player.

Chapter 10:
Interview:
Steve Meretzky

In the early 1980s, Infocom's games were quite unique; so much so that the company preferred to call them something else entirely: interactive fiction. Infocom's titles were totally separate and distinct from the arcade game clones and derivatives that so many other computer game companies were publishing at the time. Infocom's interactive fiction appealed to an entirely different and more sophisticated group of computer game players. The games' content was surprisingly literate and professionally made, with a consistent level of quality that has never been matched. Their text-only nature gave them a literary quality which lent them some degree of respectability, enough to garner a review of the game ***Dead-line*** in the ***New York Times Book Review*** and the admission of two of Infocom's implementors, Steve Meretzky and Dave Lebling, into the

Science Fiction Authors of America as interactive authors. The **Book Review** has certainly never reviewed a computer game since, and the SFA subsequently changed its rules to prevent the inclusion of any more interactive authors. Steve Meretzky remains one of Infocom's greatest talents, having worked both on one of Infocom's best-selling games, **The Hitchhiker's Guide to the Galaxy**, and on one of its most respected, **A Mind Forever Voyaging**. Since the demise of Infocom, Meretzky has continued the literary tradition in adventure gaming first with a string of titles for Legend Entertainment and subsequently with his own company, Boffo Games, which produced the lovely **The Space Bar**. Currently, Meretzky is involved with Internet game company WorldWinner.com. Of late, adventure games have fallen out of favor with publishers, game audiences, or some combination of both. One cannot help but wonder: what happened to the adventure game fans that made Infocom such a huge success?

What initially attracted you to computer games?

In the late '70s and early '80s, I was actually pretty repelled by computer games and, in fact, by all things computer-ish. I considered them nerdy and antisocial, and it seemed that whenever the talk turned to any computer-related subject, English went right out the window. Lots of people in my dorm were playing the original mainframe *Zork*, since it was being written at the Lab for Computer Science, and I found their preoccupation with the game pretty distasteful. I played a little bit of *Maze Wars* at the Lab, and I had a brief fling with *Space Invaders*, but that was about it.

Until, in '81 my roommate Mike Dornbrook was Infocom's first and, at the time, only tester. He started testing *Zork I* on an Apple II on our dining room table. When he wasn't around, I started playing a little and was soon very hooked. *Zork II* soon followed *Zork I* into our dining room "test lab." I reported all the bugs that I found, even though Mike was getting paid to find bugs and I wasn't.

So that lead to employment at Infocom?

At MIT, I majored in Construction Project Management, and that's the work that I did for the first couple of years after I graduated in June of '79. It was awful: tedious work, boring people, far-from-cutting-edge companies. So, in the fall of 1981, when my roommate Mike Dornbrook went off to business school in Chicago, Marc Blank (VP of Development at Infocom) needed a new tester for his forthcoming mystery game, eventually named *Deadline*. Since I had proven myself an able tester while testing *Zork I* and *II* for free, he hired me on an hourly basis as the replacement tester for Mike. At this point, Infocom still had no office, and just one or two full-time employees. I continued to test at home on the Apple II.

In January of 1982, Infocom moved into wonderful office space at the edge of Cambridge, and I started working out of the office, testing *Deadline* and then later *Zork III* and Dave Lebling's first post-*Zork* effort, *Starcross*. In June, I began as a half-time employee, having been just a contractor up to that point.

Even at this point, I didn't really have any plans to become a game author—I was just having a good time doing something fun for a change, and waiting to figure out what I wanted to do with the rest of my life. I had minored in writing at MIT, and had submitted some science fiction stories to various magazines, but didn't get anything published.

So how did you come to make the jump from tester to author? Did you have to prove yourself first?

Sometime late in the summer of '82, Marc Blank asked me if I'd be interested in writing a game. I agreed right away, pretty much thinking that, while testing games was quite a bit of fun, writing them was probably going to be even more fun. I didn't have to prove myself, for a few reasons. First, I'd known Marc for a few years at MIT; we were both involved with running the campus film program, so he knew that I was a pretty hard-working and creative person. Second, Infocom was still quite small and informal, with virtually no bureaucracy involved in such decisions. And third, in making suggestions while testing games, I'd shown that I understood the game and puzzle design process.

So what was your inspiration for *Planetfall*?

My main interest as a reader, and as a writer, was science fiction, so it was a foregone conclusion that the game would be SF. And since character interaction was what the Infocom development system was weakest at, an environment like a deserted planet seemed like a good idea. Beyond that, I can't really say.

What were your design goals with the Floyd character?

The idea of having a single, very well fleshed-out non-player character was a very early design focus of *Planetfall*. The Infocom games up to that point had usually had half a dozen characters each, such as the wizard, genie, dragon, princess, and gnomes in *Zork II*. Because of the large number of such characters, all were rather thin. I thought that by having just one other character (not counting the extremely brief appearances by Blather and by the alien ambassador during the opening scene) I'd be able to make that character more interesting and more believable.

I can't remember how I got from that point to Floyd, although "cute robot" was a very early decision. Perhaps the influence was the *Star Wars* trilogy, which was then between *Empire* and *Jedi*. The character of Willis, a cute alien in Robert Heinlein's book *Red Planet*, may have been another influence.

Did you always plan to force the player to allow Floyd to be killed in order to win the game?

No, that decision definitely came midway in the game design/implementation process. Floyd was turning out to be somewhat more humorous than originally conceived, and he was also turning out to be somewhat more sentimental a character than originally conceived: rubbing his head against your shoulder, getting his feelings hurt, discovering the remains of his old friend Lazarus, et cetera. It was clear that people were going to be very attached to him, and at some point the idea just clicked that I could create this really emotional moment.

Also—and this is a relatively minor influence on the decision, but still worth mentioning—at the time Electronic Arts was just getting started. They were running a series of ads meant to establish their stable of game designers as artists. One of the ads quoted one of their designers as saying something like, "I want to create a computer game that will make people cry." There was a little touch of a budding rivalry there, and I just wanted to head them off at the pass.

The Hitchhiker's Guide to the Galaxy was an adaptation from an already much loved radio series and book. How did you go about adapting a piece of linear fiction into interactive form?

It was actually quite ideal for adaptation, because it was a fairly episodic story line, and because it was an environment filled with all sorts of great characters, locations, technologies, et cetera, while the story line wasn't all that important. It was challenging, but good challenging, not bad challenging.

How was it working with Douglas Adams?

On the plus side, Douglas was already an Infocom fan and had played several of our games, so he understood what an adventure game was and he understood the abilities and limits of our system. On the other hand, he had never written non-linearly before, and that's always a difficult process to get a handle on. Also, I was somewhat awed to be working with him, and didn't assert myself enough at the start of the process. So I think you'll see that the beginning of the game is quite linear, including the destruction of Arthur's house and the scene on board the Vogon ship. Later, when Douglas became more comfortable with interactive design and when I got over my sheepishness, the game became one of the most ruthlessly non-linear designs we ever did.

It was quite wonderful to collaborate with Douglas. He's a very intelligent and creative person, and humorous as well. He's not a laugh a minute, as you might expect from his writing, but more wry with lots of great anecdotes. He was constantly coming up with ways to stretch the medium in zany ways that I never would have thought of on my own: having the game lie to you, having an inventory object like "no tea," having the words from a parser failure be the words that fell through a wormhole to start the interstellar war, et cetera.

How evenly was the work divided between you two?

The original goal was that we'd do the design together, Douglas would write the most important text passages and I'd fill in around them, and I'd do the implementation, meaning the high-level programming using Infocom's development system.

Douglas came to Cambridge for a week when we got started. Then we exchanged e-mails daily, and this was in '84, when non-LAN e-mail was still pretty rare. We also exchanged phone calls approximately weekly.

However, Douglas' single overriding characteristic is that he is the world's greatest procrastinator. He was slipping further and further behind on his schedule, and at the same time, his fourth *Hitchhiker's* book, *So Long and Thanks for All the Fish*, was about a year late and he hadn't written a word.

So his agent sent him away from the distractions of London and forced him to hole up in a country inn out in the western fringes of England. So I went over there to stay at this inn, which was an old baronial estate called Huntsham Court which had been converted into a delightful inn, and spent a week there completing the design. Then I returned to the U.S. and implemented the entire game in about three intense weeks, just in time for an abbreviated summer of testing. Douglas came back over in September for some final rewriting of key text portions, and it was done in time for a late October release. The game quickly shot to number one on the best-seller lists, and stayed there for months.

I've seen *Hitchhiker's* referred to as a particularly hard Infocom game. Was that your intention?

Douglas and I both felt that adventure games were becoming a little too easy, that the original *Zork* had been much harder than more recent offerings, and the 24/7 obsessive brain-racking was what made these games so addictive. So we might have overreacted and gone too far in the other direction. Certainly, Infocom's testing staff was strongly urging that the game be made easier.

On the other hand, the game's most difficult puzzle, the babel fish puzzle, became a revered classic, and Infocom even began selling T-shirts saying, "I solved the babel fish puzzle." So it's possible that, while some people were turned off by the level of difficulty, others were attracted by it. My feeling was, and continues to be, that people who find the game too hard can get hints, while people who find the game too easy are screwed because there's no way for them to make it harder.

Another contributor to the difficulty may have been the abbreviated testing schedule for the game, because an already aggressive schedule was made even more so by Douglas' spell of procrastination. More time in testing generally results in an easier game, because the inclination is that if even a single tester found a puzzle too hard it should be made easier.

***A Mind Forever Voyaging* is almost completely missing the humor you are so well known for in your other titles, yet I think it is one of your best works. Was your goal with that project to make a more serious game?**

Yes, partly that was a reaction to having just completed a purely comedic game (*HHGTTG*), and partly the feeling that interactive fiction was such a compelling medium that really "took over" someone's life for days at a time, it was an ideal way to put out a political/social message. It was my attempt to change the world, as it were. The goal was not just to make a work that was more serious and that had a message, but also to create a work that moved away from puzzles and relied more on its story.

The pretense for the player's existence in *AMFV* is very interesting and a change from other Infocom games. Did you feel the need to "break the mold" with this title?

I'm not sure what the inspiration was for the main character in *AMFV* being a self-aware computer, although I can remember the moment when the idea came to me, just sitting at my dining room table with one of my roommates, eating dinner. The navigational and interface differences just seemed like a natural extension of that initial decision. "Breaking the mold" in that way wasn't in my mind as much as "breaking the mold" in the game's content, as I mentioned earlier.

Did you meet much resistance from within Infocom to do the title, or did the success of your previous games grant you the freedom to do whatever you wanted? Were there fears that the game would be too different?

No resistance at all, and sure, the fact that my games to date had been both critical and market successes certainly helped. But the Infocom philosophy at the time was to do a mixture of games aimed at our core audience—the *Zork* games and *Enchanter* games, for instance—along with a few more experimental games aimed at pushing the envelope creatively and attempting to expand the audience for interactive fiction. Another example of this latter category were the "junior level" games like *Seastalker* and *Wishbringer,* which were an attempt to bring interactive fiction to a younger audience. There were some slight concerns that the game was a little too puzzle-less, and in fact we beefed up the puzzles in the last section—not in the epilogue section, but where Ryder comes and occupies the complex.

AMFV also pushed the envelope in the technical direction, being the first game in the "Interactive Fiction Plus" line, requiring 128K of memory rather than just 64K. It was also about twice as large as any other Infocom game to date.

As you mentioned, the moral implications of the game are particularly strong. Why have you not made a serious game since?

I would like to because I really enjoyed creating *AMFV*, and I still feel that computer games can have as much of an artistic component as books, movies, theater, etc. And I've gotten so much feedback over the years from people who were impacted by *AMFV*. A couple of people have mentioned to me that they went into the computer games industry because of playing it.

Unfortunately, even though *AMFV* had a pretty significant impact on the people who played it, there weren't that many people who played it or bought it compared to other Infocom games: about thirty thousand. And the sort of creative freedom that I had at Infocom has not been present since. With game budgets soaring into seven figures, publishers are not interested in anything that is in any way unproven or experimental.

A couple of years ago, I was involved in a group that was attempting to put together an adventure game whose purpose, in addition to entertainment, was to expose the plight of Chinese-occupied Tibet. One of the people involved was Bob Thurman, a Columbia University professor who is one of the leaders of the Free Tibet movement. He also happens to be the father of Uma Thurman, who would have been in the game and would have brought along a number of other Hollywood celebrities. Not just actors, but people like Philip Glass to do the score, et cetera. There was even the possibility of a cameo by the Dalai Lama. Even with all that marquee value, we couldn't find a publisher who was interested.

But it seems that serious works are allowed to exist in other media, alongside more "fun" or "light" works. Why do you think this is not the case in computer games?

I think one problem is that the games industry tends to be less profitable than other media. I've heard, for example, that it's very rare for a movie to lose money once everything is said and done, including foreign distribution, video, and all that. The vast majority of computer games lose money. So I think that as difficult as it is in cinema to get something made that is kind of experimental or a little bit different, it's way harder in the computer games industry. The executives in my industry are much more afraid of doing anything to shatter expectations.

I think another difference is that there is a path for the less expensive, artier films. There's really no similar path like that in the computer games industry. There are sort of signs that maybe something might be developing on the Internet. It's very encouraging that the Computer Game Developer's Conference has been running the Independent Games Festival. But for the most part there's nothing like a *Blair Witch Project* or a *Crying Game* that the computer games industry can really point to.

So, I think without an avenue for that kind of more experimental game, and with publishers being even more conservative than in other industries, the bottom line is publishers want the "safe game." And the safe games tend to be the ones that aren't serious or message-oriented.

So you think Internet distribution might lead to the creation of more serious works?

Well, I think that it may happen if a distribution channel coalesces, and the Internet does seem to be the best bet for that. And it's really not just distribution, it's also on the PR side. All the major magazines pretty much ignore everything except for the major publishers' games. In fact, I remember one tiny little blurb, and I think it was really just in somebody's column. It wasn't the magazine reviewing a game, but just one of the columnists mentioning that he'd run into a game that he liked and had maybe three column inches on it. And it was this very low production value game that was being distributed over the Internet as shareware, and it sounded really good, like the kind of game I would like. So I went ahead and I downloaded it. And it just really stuck out as a real rarity for a computer gaming magazine to have any mention of a game of that sort.

And certainly, in addition to having the distribution for something like that, you've also got to have some method for getting the word out to people. You can have a perfectly good distribution system, and if no one finds it, so what? But I think if something like that does coalesce, there will be an avenue for someone to do a relatively inexpensive game, something that could be done in a garage but that does have something really interesting, that does push the envelope in some way other than really high production values. It might be something that creates a new genre, like a *SimCity*.

How did *Leather Goddesses of Phobos* come about?

Quite a funny story. When Infocom was still pretty young and small, a few months after moving into its first Cambridge offices, it was decided to have a small beer-and-pizza party for our handful of employees and consultants, the board of directors, local retailers, and people from companies we were working with such as our ad agency or our production warehouse. It was a very informal gathering of just a few dozen people, but it was Infocom's first social function, and Joel Berez, Infocom's president, and Marc Blank were extremely hyper about seeing it come off perfectly.

The party was held in the large central room of Infocom's office space, which doubled as a meeting room and the "micro room" where we had our one Apple II, our one Atari 800, our one TRS-80, etc. One entire wall of this room was a single enormous chalkboard with a permanent handwritten table of all version numbers in release. Something like this:

	TRS-80 Model 1	TRS-80 Model III	Apple II	Atari 800	IBM PC	DEC PDP-11
Zork I	42	42	44	45	42	45
Zork II	17	17	17	19	17	17
Deadline	31	31	29	30	33	33
Zork III	10	12	12	10	13	13
Starcross	28	29	30	28	28	31

That is, every time a new version of a game was compiled in-house, it was given a new version number. When a given version number was released on a given machine, that number would be written up on the board. If the supply of, say, Apple II *Zork III*s ran out, we would order more with the latest approved version, and that particular number on the board would be updated.

So, to get back to the point of this story, shortly before this party I quietly went over to the board and added a line for a game called *Leather Goddesses of Phobos*. It was just a hack, and I just picked the name as something that would be a little embarrassing but not awful. As it turns out, Joel spotted it before anyone arrived and erased it in a panic. However, the name stuck, and for years thereafter, whenever anyone needed to plug the name of a nonexistent game name into a sentence, it would be *Leather Goddesses of Phobos*.

Then, at some point in 1985, I came around to the idea of actually *doing* a game by that name. After all, everyone loved the name, and had been loving it for years. I brought it up as a project that would be a little racy, but that was really more of a take-off on—and loving tribute to—SF pulp of the '30s. The idea was instantly accepted by Marc and the other game writers, as well as by Mike Dornbrook, my ex-roommate who by this point had graduated business school and returned to Infocom to head up marketing.

Upper management took longer to convince, particularly our humorless CEO Al Vezza, who was really only interested in the business products side of the company and found doing any games at all distasteful, even though they were wildly success-ful and were financing the database project. In fact, a year later, when *LGOP* was nearly done, and Infocom had been bankrupted by the business products effort, Infocom was in the process of being acquired by Activision. Activision's President, Jim Levy (who understood games and game development), was being shown around the offices by Al Vezza. *LGOP* came up, and Al quickly and nervously said, "Of course, that's not necessarily the final name." Jim roared, "What? I wouldn't call it anything else!" Naturally this made everyone feel a lot better about the acqui-sition. Unfortunately, Jim was axed by Activision's Board of Directors about a year after that.

How did you come to work on *Zork Zero*?

It was my idea to do a prequel to the game, and everyone loved the idea of calling such a prequel *Zork Zero*. It poked fun at the whole sequelitis syndrome that gripped and continues to grip the computer game industry. I had written *Sorcerer*, the second game of the *Enchanter* trilogy that can be unofficially considered to be *Zork V*. It was in the same universe as *Zork*, and as part of writing the game I compiled the first compendium of *Zork* history, dates, places, characters, et cetera, by combing through the *Zork* games and the first *Enchanter* game, and then attempting to tie them all together with a comprehensive geography and history. There was some initial resistance to this from the original authors, but it quickly became apparent how necessary—and later, how popular—a step it was.

So, I was pretty versed in the *Zork* milieu when *Zork Zero* began to be discussed. In fact, I think it's safe to say that I was more of an expert on *Zork*-related details than the original authors. *Zork Zero* had been on my list of potential next projects for a couple of years, and probably would have been my game the year that I did the *Planetfall* sequel, *Stationfall*, except that Brian Moriarty had just finished an adventure-RPG hybrid that we had decided to place in the *Zork* universe called *Beyond Zork*, and two *Zork* games in such close proximity wouldn't work.

As an aside, after finishing *Stationfall*, the decision was between *Zork Zero* and an idea that I had been tinkering with for years: an adventure game set on the Titanic during its maiden voyage. But Infocom's management finally decided, and I heard this many times over the next few years as I pitched this project to many publishers during my post-Infocom days, "people aren't interested in the Titanic." So when the Cameron movie came out and became the most popular movie ever, it was something of a bittersweet moment for me.

When the decision came down to go ahead with *Zork Zero*, the first thing I did was convene a brainstorming session with the original "implementors," or three out of four, at any rate. Marc Blank (who had long since left Infocom and moved to the west coast), Dave Lebling (still a game author at Infocom), and Tim Anderson (still a "senior scientist" special-projects programmer at Infocom) were all there. The fourth original author, Bruce Daniels, had long since moved on. The only thing set in stone going into this session was that the game would be a prequel, and that it would end "West of a white house." This session produced the very general framework for the game: the setting of Dimwit's castle, the reasons for the destruction of the Flathead dynasty, and the collection of artifacts belonging to each of the twelve Flatheads.

***Zork Zero* is a strange hybrid of a game: it's almost all text, with just some snippets of graphics thrown in. What was the general idea behind the design?**

At the time, Infocom was undergoing some stress and soul-searching. Our sales had been dropping for several years. Going into the 1987 product cycle, the thinking from Infocom/Activision management was "There are N thousand hard-core adventure game fans who'll buy any Infocom game no matter how many we put out. Therefore, the strategy should be to put out as many games as possible." We put out eight games during 1987, whereas in any previous year we'd never put out more than five. And all of them did pretty badly. So, going into the 1988 product cycle, the thinking was "Text adventures are a dying breed; we need to add graphics to our games."

Throughout Infocom's existence, we had always denigrated graphical adventures, and during the early and mid-'80s, this was pretty correct. While the early micros were pretty good at arcade-game-style graphics, they were pretty awful at drawing pictures, as seen in the graphic adventures of that time period. But then the Macintosh came out, providing much better black and white graphics than had been seen to date, followed by the Amiga, which did much better color graphics than anyone had seen before. IBM-PC graphics cards were also getting better. So graphics were starting to look reasonable and give all-text a run for its money. Infocom was a bit slow to come around to this truth.

So, in late '87 and early '88, Infocom's development system was being completely overhauled to handle the addition of graphics. At the same time, the game authors were collectively and individually wrestling with the issue of how to use graphics in games. Some people decided just to use them to illustrate occasional scenes, the way a book with occasional illustrations might use pictures. This is what Dave Lebling did with his IF version of *Shogun*.

Since the goal for *Zork Zero* was to be a classic puzzle-based adventure game on steroids, I decided that I primarily wanted to use graphics for puzzle-based situations, so I created five graphical puzzles: a rebus, a tower of Hanoi, a peg-jumping game, a pebble-counting game called nim, and a card game called double fanucci. But I didn't want the game to just look like an old-fashioned text adventure the rest of the time, so I designed the three different decorative borders: one for outside, one for inside buildings, and one for inside dungeons. I also gave every room an icon, and then used those icons for the on-screen graphical maps, which was a pretty good mnemonic device. Finally, I used graphic illustrations in the Encyclopedia Frobozzica, a book in the library that was basically an in-game version of the *Zork* universe compendium that I'd begun compiling while working on *Sorcerer*.

But none of the graphics games sold any better than the previous year's all-text games, and by mid-'89 Activision decided to shut Infocom down.

They didn't improve sales at all?

I would say that during the previous year, '87, all the games sold around twenty thousand. And the four graphical games that came out in late '88 and early '89 also sold around those same numbers.

So why do you think that was? LucasArts and Sierra seem to have been quite successful with their graphical adventures around that time.

Yes, at the time Sierra was selling several hundred thousand copies of their games. But certainly not Lucas nearly as much. Lucas was in fact quite frustrated that they were putting out games that they felt were technically pretty identical to the Sierra games and in terms of writing and content were really superior to them, and yet only selling a fifth or a third as many copies. And I don't really know what to think about that. It might just be that Sierra was doing a really good job producing games that were very well aimed at a middle-brow audience, at kind of the broadest audience. And much like many of the Infocom games, Lucas games tended to appeal to a somewhat more sophisticated and therefore smaller audience.

So that's why you think the Infocom graphical games didn't take off?

Well, no. I think it was much more that by that point the graphical games had become pretty sophisticated in terms of being not just graphical adventures but animated graphical adventures, like the Sierra and Lucas games of that period. And the Infocom games weren't really more than illustrated text adventures. Even though the graphics were introduced, I don't think it was perceived as being that much of a new animal from what Infocom had been producing up until that point.

So do you think Infocom might have been more successful using graphics if they had made them more integral to the design of the games?

It's hard to say what might have happened in '87 if Infocom had said, "We're going to go out and exactly imitate the Sierra adventure game engine the way Lucas did." On the one hand, it has always seemed to me that whoever gets to a market first kind of owns it. And I think that's another reason that Sierra really dominated Lucas at that point. There were certainly a lot of companies that came in, did text adventures, put a lot of effort into it and did some pretty good text adventures. For example, Synapse Software, in the mid-'80s, with their BTZ engine did a few pretty good games. But they got virtually no sales. It's just pretty hard to go head to head with a market leader, even with games that are just as good, because it's hard to make up for that head start. On the other hand, Infocom certainly had a name that was pretty synonymous with adventure games, so if there was anyone who could have made headway against Sierra's head start it probably would have been Infocom. But at this point it's completely academic, obviously.

The Infocom games all ran off of pretty much the same storytelling system, using nearly identical game mechanics from game to game. Do you think this shared technology and design worked well?

It worked extremely well for its time. It allowed us to get our entire line of games up and running on a new computer within weeks of its release. This was a tremendous commercial edge during a time when the market was fragmented between many different platforms and new, incompatible platforms were coming out all the time. For example, there was a time when there were about twenty-five games available for the original Macintosh, and fifteen of them were Infocom games. This annoyed the Mac people at Apple to no end, since we didn't use the Mac GUI.

Also, the type of games we were doing lent themselves well to a "line look," both in the packaging and in the games themselves. It gave them a literary feel: Infocom games all look similar in the same way that all books look similar.

But even today, engines are usually used for several games, particularly if you include expansion packs. And even though the final products appeared to be pretty similar, the Infocom library actually represents several generations of the ZIL engine. There was a pretty major revamping when the "Interactive Fiction Plus" line came along, starting with *AMFV*, and then another pretty major revamping around '87 with the introduction of an entirely new, much more powerful parser. And then, of course, there was a major overhaul for the introduction of graphics in '88.

A lot of effort was put into the Infocom parser, and it was well respected as the best in the industry. Did it ever get so good that you thought it couldn't get any better?

Certainly, by the time of the new from-the-ground-up parser circa 1987, I thought we had a parser that, while it could certainly be improved, was about as good as we'd ever need for a gaming environment. After all, we weren't trying to understand all natural language, just present-tense imperative sentences. The only area where I would have liked to see continued improvement was in the area of talking to NPCs. But the main problem with making NPCs seem more deep and real wasn't due to parser limitations, it was just the sheer amount of work needed to give a character enough different responses to keep that character from seeming "canned," even for a short while.

I personally loved and still love the text-based interface, both from a player and a game writer point of view. But I don't mind either reading or typing, and some people dislike one or the other or both, and that tended to limit our audience, especially as non-reading, non-typing alternatives proliferated. But I find the parser-based input interface to be by far the most powerful and flexible, allowing the user to at least try anything he/she can think of, and allowing the game writer to develop all sorts of puzzles that wouldn't be possible with a point-and-click interface. So many point-and-click adventure games became a matter of simply clicking every object in sight in every possible combination, instead of thinking through the puzzle.

What do you say to criticisms that the parser interface often proved more frustrating than intuitive, and that though the player may know what they want to do, he or she may have trouble finding the correct words for that action?

I think that's simply a poor parser. I can remember playing one Sierra game where there was what I thought was a horse on the screen, and I was trying to do all sorts of things with the horse, and it later turned out it was a unicorn. In those days, when the resolution was so grainy, I was simply not noticing the one pixel that indicated a horn. And so when I was saying stuff like, "Get on the horse," it wasn't saying, "There's no horse here," which would have tipped me off that maybe it was a unicorn. Instead it was responding with, "You can't do that" or something much less helpful. So to me, the fault wasn't that the game had a parser interface; the fault was that the game was not well written to begin with or well tested.

Certainly when someone sits down with even the most polished Infocom game, there tends to be, depending on the person, a one-minute or a half-hour period where they're kind of flailing and trying to get the hang of the syntax. But for most people, once they get past that initial kind of confusion, a well-written parser game isn't particularly frustrating. Even in the later Infocom games, we were starting to introduce some things that were really aimed at making that very initial experience less difficult: trying to notice the sorts of things that players did while they were in that mode, and make suggestions to push them in the right direction. The game would try to catch if they typed in an improper kind of a sentence, such as asking a question or using a non-imperative voice. It would try to notice if they did that two or three times in a row and then just say, "The way to talk to the game is," and then give a few examples.

And I think that the really critical thing about the parser interface has nothing to do with typing, it is being able to use natural language for your inputs.

Did you ever feel limited by the Infocom development system?

The system was extremely powerful and flexible, and could grow to meet the need of a particular game fairly easily. A minor exception was any change that required a change to the "interpreter." Every game sold consisted of the game component, which was machine independent, and an interpreter, which was a machine-specific program which allowed the game component to run on that particular microcomputer. Since there were twenty or more interpreters (one for the Apple II, one for the Mac, one for the DEC Rainbow, one for the NEC PC-800, et cetera) a change to the interpreter required not changing just one program, but changing twenty-plus programs. So that could only be done rarely or when it was extremely important, such as changing the status line in *Deadline* to display time instead of score and moves.

A more stringent limit was imposed by the desire to run on the widest possible array of machines, so we were always limited by the capabilities of the smallest and weakest of those machines. In the earliest days, the limiting machine was the TRS-80 Model 1, whose disk drive capacity limited the first games to an executable size of 78K. As older machines "dropped off" the to-be-supported list, this limit slowly rose, but even when I wrote *HHGTTG*, games were still limited to around 110K. Generally, this limit would be reached midway through testing, and then every addition to the game, to fix a bug or to handle a reasonable input by a tester, would require ever more painful searches for some text, any text, to cut or condense. At times, this was a good discipline, to write lean, to-the-point text. But often it became horrible and made us feel like we were butchering our own children. Okay, that's a slight exaggeration.

How did the development process work at Infocom? Were you fairly free to choose what games you made?

In the early days, things were pretty informal, and decisions were made by fairly informal consensus. In the later days, particular after the acquisition by Activision, decisions were much more mandated by upper management. Generally, the choice of a game was left up to the individual author. Authors with more of a track record, like Dave Lebling and myself, had more leeway than a greenhorn implementor. Of course, there were marketing considerations as well, such as the strong desire to complete trilogies or the opportunities to work with a licensed property such as *HHGTTG*.

One thing that was standard over the whole seven-plus years that I was at Infocom was the "Implementors' Lunches," or, for short, "Imp Lunches." These were weekly lunches at which the game writers would get together to talk about the games in development, share ideas, critique each other's work, et cetera. It was probably the most fun couple of hours of the week.

There wasn't too much oversight during the first few months of a game's life, while the implementor was working pretty much alone, other than at the Imp Lunches, any impromptu brainstorming, or requests for help/advice. But once the game went into testing, first among the other writers, then with the internal testing group, and then finally with outside "beta testers," the game was under the microscope for months on end. During this time, bugs and suggestions would often run into the thousands.

How fluid and changing was the design of an Infocom game?

This varied from implementor to implementor. My own style was to do a little bit of on-paper design before starting, mostly in creating the geography and any "background universe" documents such as a time line in the case of *Sorcerer*, or the rules of the deserted planet's language in *Planetfall*. But for the most part I would just jump right in and start coding with most of the characters and puzzles living only in my head.

The Infocom development system was terrific, compared to the graphic-based systems I've worked with since those days, because just the game writer working alone could implement an entire section of the game in only a couple of days, and then try it out and see how it worked. If it had to be scrapped because it wasn't working, it was no big waste of time or resources. This allowed for a lot of going back and rewriting big sections of the game, which is inconceivable nowadays, where such a decision might mean throwing away a hundred thousand dollars worth of graphics.

Was there a lot of playtesting on Infocom titles?

Lots of testing. Since the development system was quite stable during most of Infocom's life, the testing was able to concentrate on game-specific bugs and game content. There would ideally be about two weeks of "pre-alpha" testing where the other game writers would play a game, followed by two to three months of alpha testing with our in-house testers, followed by a month of beta testing with a couple of dozen outside volunteers. If time allowed, there was also a month of "gamma" testing, which was just like beta testing except that the idea was not to change a thing unless a really major problem was found.

Testing for both game-specific bugs and game content went on pretty much concurrently, although more heavily weighted toward content during the early days of testing, and more toward bugs in the later days, when it became increasingly less desirable to make any significant changes to game content.

The early testing period was probably the most fun and exciting time in the game's development. For one thing, after months and months of working alone, not having any idea if a game was any good other than my own instincts, all of a sudden a bunch of people are playing the game, usually enjoying it, and giving tons of feedback. It's a real rush. Also, we had an auto-scripting feature where our network would automatically make a transcript of each player's sessions, which I could read to see what everyone was trying at every point, so I'd often find things which were wrong, but which testers didn't necessarily realize were wrong. Or I'd find things that they'd tried which were reasonable attempts to solve the puzzle at hand and I'd try to reward such an attempt with a clever response or with a hint, rather than just a default message like, "You can't put a tablecloth on that."

It was during the testing period that games became great. Going into the testing period, the game was more like a skeleton, and the testing period, as one of our testers once said, "put meat on the bones." Lots of the humor, the responses to wacky inputs, the subtle degrees of difficulty, the elimination of unfair puzzles—these were all the products of Infocom's excellent testing group.

The packaging for Infocom games was really unique. Why did the company go above and beyond what so many other game publishers did?

When Infocom started, the standard for computer game packaging was something similar to a Ziploc bag. It was just a clear plastic bag with a Ziploc top and a hole to hang on a pegboard in stores; the bag would hold a floppy disk and an often cheaply photocopied manual. In fact, the early Radio Shack versions of *Zork* were in just such a package.

The original publisher of *Zork I* was a company in California called Personal Software. In fact, the product manager for the *Zork* line at Personal Software was Mitch Kapor, who went on to found Lotus. Shortly after they starting publishing *Zork*, Personal Software hit it big-time with a program called Visicalc, the first successful piece of business software for computers. They changed their name from Personal Software to Visicorp, and decided that they didn't want to waste their time dealing with games, and they gave *Zork* back to Infocom.

Rather than find a new publisher, Infocom decided to be its own publisher, and hired an agency to design the packages. The result was the "blister pack" packages for *Zork I* and *Zork II*, the first time such packages had been used for computer games. This is the type of package in which a clear piece of molded plastic is glued to a cardboard back, with the contents visible through the clear plastic, in this case the contents being the *Zork* manual with the disk out of sight behind it.

When it was time for the packaging design on Infocom's third game, *Deadline*, Marc Blank went to the agency with a series of out-of-print books from the 1930s, written by Dennis Wheatley. With names like *Murder Off Miami* and *Who Killed Robert Prentiss?*, the books were a portfolio of reports and clues, just like a police detective would be given when investigating a case: interviews with witnesses, typed letters, handwritten notes, railway tickets, newspaper clippings, a used matchstick, and lots more. The idea was that *you* were the detective, and after sifting through the evidence, you should decide who the murderer was and how they did it, and then open a sealed section of the book and see if you were right.

Marc was very influenced by those books in creating *Deadline*—in fact the original working title was *Who Killed Marshall Robner?*—and he wanted the agency to be very influenced by them in creating the packaging for *Deadline*. Marc wanted the player to feel like they were a detective being placed on a case from the moment they opened the package. Also, because of the strict limits on game size, having lab reports and suspect interviews in the package freed up space in the game for more interactive content. The *Deadline* package that resulted is very reminiscent of those Dennis Wheatley books, with a photo of the crime scene, interviews, fingerprints, lab analyses of things like the teacup found near the body, and even a bag of pills labeled "Pills found near the body." Those were actually white-colored SweeTARTS.

The *Deadline* package was a huge hit, even though we charged $10 more for it, $50 MSRP instead of $40 MSRP. We decided that great packaging was fun, was a great value-added, was a great way to "raise the bar" and make it harder for new competitors to enter our market space, and most importantly, it was a way to discourage pirating of our games. It was more difficult and less cost effective to need to copy a bunch of package elements as well as the floppy disk. Also, because the packages were so neat and so integral to the experience of playing the game, many people wouldn't have felt they owned the game unless they owned the complete original packaging.

The next games were *Zork III* and *Starcross*. *Zork III* just went in a blister pack to match its brethren, but *Starcross* was placed in a large plastic flying saucer, along with an asteroid map of your ship's vicinity. This package, while problematic for some stores because of its size and shape, was phenomenally eye-catching and popular. Recently, a still-shrink-wrapped copy of *Starcross* in this original packaging sold for *three thousand dollars* on eBay.

My favorite package of all the ones that I worked on was *LGOP*, with its scratch 'n' sniff card and 3D comic. The comic was a collaboration between me, a comic book artist, and a guy who specialized in translating conventional 2D comic drawings into 3D layers. For the scratch 'n' sniff card, I got several dozen samples from the company that made the scents. Each was on its own card with the name of the scent. So one by one I had other Infocom employees come in, and I'd blindfold them and let them scratch each scent and try to identify it. That way, I was able to choose the seven most recognizable scents for the package. It was a lot of fun seeing what thoughts the various scents triggered in people, such as the person who was sniffing the mothballs card and got a silly grin on his face and said, "My grandmother's attic!"

We, the implementors, had pretty wide latitude on the choice of package elements, as long as we stayed within budgetary parameters. But marketing often had good ideas too, suggesting that my idea for a book in *Zork Zero* become a calendar, and suggesting things like the creepy rubber bug in the *Lurking Horror* package. But most of the best ideas came from the writers.

The best package pieces were those that were designed in from the beginning of the game, rather than tacked on as an afterthought once the packaging process started in mid-alpha. Most other game companies had anti-piracy copy protection in their packages, but it was often completely obvious and mood-destroying, such as "Type the seventh word on page 91 of the manual." With the better Infocom package elements, you never even realized that you were involved in an anti-piracy activity, because the package elements were so seamlessly intertwined with the gameplay. And, of course, in the all-text environments of our games, the package elements were a great way to add visual pizzazz to the game-playing experience.

There seems to have been a clear difference between Infocom games and the games the rest of the industry offered, especially in terms of a consistent level of quality. Why do you think this was? How was this quality maintained?

Partly, it was the very early philosophy of Infocom, and even before Infocom, in the creation of *Zork*, which was to take a fun game, *Adventure*, but do it better. So there was always a strong desire to be the best. Also, partly it was because the people who made up Infocom were just a really smart and talented group of people. And partly it was luck. We had early success, so when we created each new game we could invest a lot of time and money into it, knowing that its sales would justify the investment, while many other companies couldn't assume that level of sales and therefore couldn't afford the same level of investment.

Our always improving development environment, parser, et cetera, was a big reason for the high level of quality. The talented testing group, and the time we scheduled for testing, bug-fixing, and general improvement, was another big factor.

Did Infocom's consistent quality level allow it to weather the "crash" of the mid-'80s pretty easily?

The mid-'80s crash began with a crash on the video games side, and then spilled over into the PC market. Many companies had a mixture of video game and microcomputer SKUs, but Infocom was entirely in the PC market. Also, our games were as un-video-game-like as possible. Another reason why the mid-'80s slump had little effect on Infocom's game sales was that we were on so many machines, and we could quickly get onto any new computers that were released. For example, the Mac came out in early 1985, and our games were extremely successful on the early Macs. And, of course, the high quality helped, because during any slump it's always the schlocky products that die first.

To me, it seems that Infocom games are the only titles from the early '80s that don't seem at all dated. Why do you think that is?

Well, graphics from games in the early '80s look awful, but text just looks like text. So time is kinder to text adventures. And, as we've already covered, the games were of a very high quality, which helps them hold up over time. And, once you've eliminated technical obsolescence as an issue, ten to twenty years isn't a very long time for a creative work to age well or not well. Think about books, movies, TV shows, et cetera from the same period. Only a very few that were unusually topical would seem dated today, and Infocom games certainly weren't topical, with perhaps *AMFV* as a lone exception. And it's certainly not unusual for people to continue to enjoy the best works long after their creation: *I Love Lucy* is forty years old, *Gone With the Wind* is sixty years old, the films of Charlie Chaplin and Buster Keaton are eighty years old, *Alice in Wonderland* is one hundred fifty years old, and Shakespeare's plays are four hundred years old.

Did the Infocom team think that text adventures would be around forever?

We certainly thought they'd evolve, in ways foreseeable and unforeseeable. While everyone had their own ideas, I'd say that around 1985 a composite of the thinking at that point would be something like this: graphics will improve to the point that they're worth putting in adventure games, there will be a growing emphasis on story over puzzles, games and game-worlds will get larger, there will be more realistic, believable characters in adventure games, many people who have been successful storytellers in other media, such as fiction writers and movie auteurs, will gravitate toward adventure games as the storytelling medium of the future. Looking back, only the first of those points came to pass.

But despite anticipated changes, I think everyone thought that adventure games would be around indefinitely in some form. I don't think anyone thought that by the end of the century all forms of adventure games would be virtually defunct as a commercial game type.

It's interesting that books seem to be able to coexist alongside television and film. Why do you think text adventures cannot seem to do the same thing?

There is still a fairly vigorous marketplace for text adventure games. There are still people writing them and people playing them, it's just not an economic market. The people writing them are not writing them for pay, they're just writing them for the joy of it, and the people playing them are mostly not paying for the experience. And I think one thing that's similar between writing text adventures and writing books is that it tends to be a one-person operation, assuming that you use an existing text adventure writing system. One person without too much specialized training can go off and in a few months write a text adventure game, just like someone with a typewriter, word processor, or big stack of paper and a pen can go off and write novels.

Perhaps it's just a matter of scale, as you mentioned before. The total number of people interested in playing a computer game is just a lot less than the number of people interested in other, traditional, non-interactive media.

I think that's probably true, though I don't know the numbers offhand. But I imagine a best-selling book is probably not much more than a million copies or something. I seem to recall that at the time we did the game, an aggregate of the *Hitchhiker's* books had sold seven million copies, so maybe a couple of million each? And certainly the number of people who watch television is certainly dozens of times more than that.

The interface for the *Spellcasting* series was interesting. It allowed the games to function exactly like the Infocom text adventures, but then added the ability for the player to use only the mouse to play by clicking on the list of verbs, nouns,

and so forth. What was the idea behind this new interface?

This interface came from the folks at Legend, particularly Bob Bates, who had begun working on this interface for his post-*Arthur* Infocom game *The Abyss*, based on the still, at the time, unreleased

Spellcasting 101: Sorcerers Get All the Girls

movie. The game was canceled when Infocom was shut down by Activision, and when Legend decided to start publishing their own adventure games, they continued developing that interface.

The impetus for the interface was not a particular feeling that this was a good/useful/friendly/clever interface for playing adventure games, but rather a feeling that text adventures were dying, that people wanted pictures on the screen at all times, and that people hated to type. I never liked the interface that much. The graphic part of the picture was pretty nice, allowing you to move around by just double-clicking on doors in the picture, or pick things up by double-clicking on them. But I didn't care for the menus for a number of reasons. One, they were way more kludgey and time-consuming than just typing inputs. Two, they were give-aways because they gave you a list of all possible verbs and all visible objects. Three, they were a lot of extra work in implementing the game, for little extra benefit. And four, they precluded any puzzles which involved referring to non-visible objects.

Also, the *Spellcasting* games went beyond *Zork Zero* by having full-on graphics. Did you make any changes to the way you wrote and designed your games as a result?

Not much. I think I could take any of my graphic-less Infocom games, get an artist to produce graphics for each room, and retrofit them into Legend's graphical engine. The menu-driven interface would be more problematic than the graphics. Conversely, all the games I did for Legend had a hot key which allowed you to turn off graphics and play them like a pure old-fashioned text adventure. So the graphics were always just an extra, not a mandatory.

In terms of the overall gameplay experience, what do you think was gained and lost by the addition of graphics to the text adventures?

There's the unending, passionate, almost religious argument about whether the pictures we create in our imagination based on a text description are far more vivid than anything created on even a high-

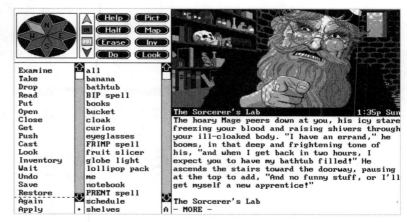

Spellcasting 201: The Sorcerer's Appliance

resolution millions-of-colors monitor. My own feeling is that there are probably some people who create better images in their imagination, and some whose imaginations are pretty damn feeble. Still, the change resulted in adventure games moving in a somewhat lower-brow, less literary direction.

Second, there were some puzzles precluded by graphics. For example, puzzles that relied on describing something and letting players figure out what it was by examination and experimentation. An example from *Zork I*: the uninflated raft that isn't called that, it's called a "pile of plastic." You have to examine it and find the valve and figure out to try using the air pump and only then do you discover that it's a raft. In a graphical game, you'd be able to see instantly that it was an uninflated raft.

Thirdly, and most importantly, graphics cost way way *way* more than text. As Brian Moriarty puts it, "In graphic adventures, you have to show everything—and you can't afford to show anything!" As a result, graphic games have far fewer of everything, but most important, far fewer alternate solutions to puzzles, alternate routes through the game, interesting responses to reasonable but incorrect attempts to solve a puzzle, fewer humorous responses to actions, etc. In other words, graphic adventures have a whole lot less "meat on the bones" than the Infocom text adventures. You get a lot more of those infuriating vanilla responses, like, "You can't do that" or your character/avatar just shrugging at you.

How did *Superhero League of Hoboken* come about? Had you wanted to tackle that genre for a while?

Well, I'd been wanting to make an RPG for many years, and at the time, the early '90s, RPGs were generally outselling adventure games. This was before the "death" of RPGs that lasted until the release of *Diablo*. But I thought that the usual Tolkien-esque fantasy setting and trappings of RPGs had been done to death, and it occurred to me that superheroes was an excellent alternate genre that worked well with RPG gameplay, with superpowers substituting for magic spells.

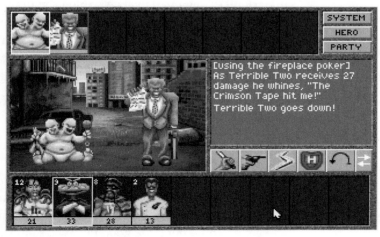

Superhero League of Hoboken

I originally planned to make it a full RPG, but Legend had never done anything that wasn't a straight adventure game and were therefore nervous, so the only way I could convince them was to make it an RPG/adventure game hybrid.

It's the only superhero game I am aware of that was not dreadful. Why do you think so few superhero games have been done?

I think that the dearth of superhero games is mostly a legal/licensing issue. Most companies probably feel that only one of the well-known superheroes is worth creating a game around, and such licenses are hard to come by. And even if a license is obtained, the cost of obtaining it means a lot less money in the development budget, which is why all licensed games, not just superhero games, are often so mediocre. I was able to get by with original content in *Superhero League* because it was a satire. I don't think I ever would have been able to convince Legend to do a "straight" superhero game in the same style and engine.

***Superhero League* is your only RPG. What made you want to try a game design in more of an RPG direction?**

I enjoyed and still enjoy playing RPGs a lot, and I always try to make games that would be games I'd enjoy playing myself if someone else created them. And I always prefer to do something that I haven't done before, whether it's a new genre as was the case here or a serious theme like *AMFV* or adapting a work from another medium like *Hitchhiker's*, or a larger scale like *Zork Zero*. Of course, that's just my preference. Publishers often have other ideas!

The game seems to automatically do a lot of things for the player that other RPGs would require the player to do for themselves. Was one of your design goals to make the RPG elements very simple to manage?

Because it was an adventure/RPG hybrid, we guessed that a lot of the players would be RPG players who were pretty inexperienced with adventures, and a lot of the players would be adventure gamers who were pretty inexperienced with RPGs. So I tried very hard to make the puzzles pretty straightforward, and we tried to keep the interface as simple and friendly as possible, given the highly detailed nature of RPG interactions.

***Superhero League of Hoboken* seemed to be pretty popular. I was wondering why you haven't done another RPG since.**

Well, it actually didn't sell all that well. I don't think it sold more than twenty, twenty-five thousand copies. And it was certainly pretty disappointing, because I spent somewhat longer on it, certainly longer than any of the other games I did for Legend. And it got quite good reviews, so the sales numbers were pretty disappointing. I think it was Accolade who distributed that, but at the time Legend was not doing all that well financially, so they didn't really do that great a job on the marketing side. As the publisher but not the distributor, their job was to handle all the advertising and PR, and they couldn't really afford to do all that much on either front. And Accolade as a publisher was certainly not as strong a publisher as someone like an EA might have been.

And I think something that really hurt *Superhero League* a lot was that the game was delayed about a year from its original release date. That was partly due to the delay of the previous games in the Legend pipeline ahead of it, and partly due to the fact that the game was trying to do some things that couldn't be done in the Legend development system, and this required some extra support. They hired a programmer to do that, and he kind of flaked out, and therefore it had to be rewritten by internal resources. So this served to delay the game, and it ended up coming out middle of '95 instead of middle of '94. And it was a regular VGA game. So, in the meantime, everything had become Super VGA. So by the time it came out it looked very dated. In fact, I remember another game that came out around the same time was *Colonization*. And I remember playing *Colonization* and being shocked at how awful it looked. I'm sure the experience was very much the same for people looking at *Hoboken* for the first time.

So would you ever want to do another RPG?

Certainly a lot of the projects that I started working on at GameFX were role-playing games, but of course none of those came to fruition. I certainly very much enjoyed working on *Hoboken* and I like playing role-playing games, so I definitely wouldn't mind working on another one.

Hodj 'n' Podj **was certainly your most different game up to that point. Were you trying to appeal to a new audience with the game?**

Well, I wasn't really trying to appeal to a new audience. As with all my designs the audience was basically me. I always just hope that there will be enough other people with the same likes as me to make the game a success.

Superhero League of Hoboken

The idea for *Hodj 'n' Podj* was at least five years old when it finally became a real project. I originally conceived of the game as a way to bring back all those fun, simple games which had pretty much disappeared, because the hard-core gaming audience which was driving development decisions wouldn't be satisfied by such simple games. This, of course, was before those classic games became ubiquitously available via CD-ROM "game packs" and more recently via the Internet.

At the time, I felt that a collection of such games would need a framework to tie them together to make them an acceptable economic package, thus the overarching board game and fairy tale back-story/theme. Of course, in the meantime, many companies released game packs with no connecting theme or mechanisms, and did quite well with them. Still, I'm very happy creatively with the decision to make the

Hodj 'n' Podj

Hodj 'n' Podj mini-games part of a larger structure.

It was only after the game was well into development that we began to suspect that it was going to appeal to a very different gaming audience. This was before the phrase "casual gamers" had really entered the industry vernacular. As outside testers, employees' friends and family, et cetera, began playing early versions of the game, we were surprised to find it appealing to people who didn't normally like computer games. We were particularly pleased and surprised to find how much female players liked it. And finally, we discovered that the game was appealing to another niche that hadn't really been identified yet at that time, "family gaming": that is, parents and children playing together. And, thanks to the difficult leveling mechanisms, parents could compete on a relatively level playing field with children, without having to "play down" to a child's level. It's still the only game I've ever written that I've been able to play myself for fun, and I still play with my kids every now and then.

How did *The Space Bar* project come about and what were your design goals for the project?

That's another idea that had been brewing for a long time. I think the genesis was actually back around 1986 or '87, when the *New York Times* threatened to sue Infocom because of our customer newsletter being called the *New Zork Times*. Our lawyer completely poo-pooed the threat, but when Activision began negotiating to buy Infocom, they insisted on all such "clouds" being removed, and thus we were forced to change the name of the newsletter. There was a naming contest open to customers, plus tons of discussions within the company, and the newsletter ended up being renamed *The Status Line*. But in the meantime, I suggested *The Space Bar* and giving the newsletter the ongoing fiction that it was being written by denizens of such a bar, and populated with ongoing characters who were "regulars" in the bar. I'm not sure exactly how, but at some point the idea made the leap from

The Space Bar

newsletter idea to game idea.

The main design goal for the project was to create an adventure game which was composed of a lot of smaller adventure games: a novel is to a short story collection as a conventional adventure game would be to *The Space Bar*. In addition to just a desire to want to try something different, I also felt (once again reflecting my own needs and wants in my game design) that people had increasingly scarce amounts of time, and that starting an adventure game required setting aside such a huge amount of time, many tens of hours. But if, instead, you could say to yourself, I'll just play this "chapter" now and save the rest for later, it would be easier to justify picking up and starting the game. Secondary design goals were to create a spaceport bar as compelling as the one in the first *Star Wars* movie, to create a Bogart-esque noir atmosphere, to be really funny, and to prove that you could make a graphic adventure that, like the Infocom text games, could still have a lot of "meat on the bones." As with *Hodj 'n' Podj*, I felt that just a collection of independent games was too loose, and required a connecting thread, thus the meta-story involving Alias Node's search for the shape-shifter, Ni'Dopal. Empathy Telepathy was just a convenient device for connecting the "short stories" to the meta-story.

At the very beginning of the project, Rocket Science was really interested in "synergies" to "leverage" their projects in other media: movies, action figures, board games, books, et cetera. I suggested that a great companion project for *The Space Bar* would be to commission an anthology of short stories by SF writers, with each one selecting one of the characters/races we created for *The Space Bar* and writing an original story about that race or character. Thus, it wouldn't be a conventional "novelization" of the game but an interesting companion piece. But, despite initial enthusiasm on their part and repeated reminders on our part, Rocket Science never did anything about it.

Correct me if I'm wrong, but it seems that *The Space Bar* was certainly your biggest budget project. Were you eager to work with such lavish production values?

Yes, it was more than twice the budget of *Hodj 'n' Podj*, which was my largest budget up to that point. But it was still a relatively small budget compared to other graphic adventures of that time; Boffo was a pretty lean operation that really got a great deal of bang for Rocket Science's buck, and the same is true for our primary art subcontractor for the game, Dub Media.

Even though it was a big budget, it certainly wasn't lavish, because there was never nearly enough money to do everything we wanted to do, so we were always cutting corners. Just one example: Alias' PDA was supposed to be an actual animated face, not just a disembodied voice. So in terms of what we wanted to do versus what we could afford to do, it was actually my most financially tight project. This is the big problem with graphic adventures, as discussed earlier, and the main reason why the medium is basically financially dead at this point.

But the project, while extremely stressful from a budgetary standpoint, was still a great time. Working with Ron Cobb as the conceptual artist was one of the real thrills of my career. *The Space Bar* team was the largest team I'd ever directed, which, of course, goes hand in hand with it being the largest budget, and it's pretty exciting having so many people contributing because almost everyone contributes beyond their narrow areas of expertise/responsibility. And I felt that despite the cut corners we substantially met every design goal, which was quite gratifying.

What led you to WorldWinner.com?

After about a year of canceled projects at GameFX/THQ, I was looking to get out and was working with a recruiter, and she steered me toward WorldWinner. The individual games will be very reminiscent of the kind of games in *Hodj 'n' Podj*, which was definitely

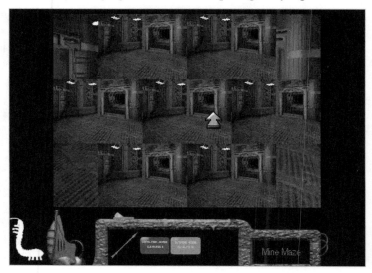

The Space Bar

one of the main attractions. Also, working in a multi-player online environment was a big lure, because I haven't done that before.

So do you think the Internet provides new possibilities for a wider breadth of games than is currently available?

Yeah, well I definitely think so in terms of providing an outlet for the more personal or more experimental kind of games. Other than that, for now, there are certainly negatives about it in terms of bandwidth. With the games I'm doing now, while there are really interesting and really fun things about them, it's certainly kind of annoying to be back in the days where 100K is really big, and in some cases too big. I had gotten away from that as we got into the CD-ROM days, where the size of things became, in most cases, completely inconsequential, and now all of a sudden it's back in spades. But yes, overall, there are certainly positives and negatives, but overall the positives are very promising and the things that are negative about it, like there are certain kinds of games we can't do because of bandwidth—well, people can still do those games via the normal, traditional channels.

Do you find writing or playing games more fun?

Playing. Writing games is sometimes a lot of fun, and sometimes a lot of drudgery, and sometimes it's really brutally painful, like when your company goes out of business. But playing games is always fun. Of course, the funnest parts of making games are more fun than the funnest parts of playing games.

So much writing in games is dreadful. What do you think is important to keep in mind when writing for a game?

All types of writing are different, and there are plenty of excellent novel writers who couldn't write a screenplay or vice versa. And writing for games is at least as different as those two. Of course, there are exceptions also. It helps to be a game player. You wouldn't expect a novelist to succeed as a screenwriter if he hadn't seen any movies! So a lot of the writing in games is bad because it's being written as though it is for another medium. Of course, some of the writing is bad just because the writers doing it are untalented. As with game design, programmers and producers often incorrectly feel that they're capable of doing the writing.

One thing that makes the writing in games so different is that it often comes in little disconnected chunks, one-word or one-sentence responses to various actions by the player. There is a difficult tradeoff between keeping such snippets interesting and keeping them terse. Also, writing has to be so meticulously crafted for gameplay and puzzle purposes—give away just enough clues, not too many, don't mislead—that the quality of the writing often has to take a back seat. And the non-linear nature of games is another obstacle to good writing. If you don't know whether Line A or Line B will come first, there often has to be a duplication of information, giving the appearance of being sloppy or overly wordy. And finally, there's the issue of repetition. In adventure games, you often see the same piece of writing over and over again, with familiarity breeding contempt for even very good writing.

How organic is the design process for your games? Did the onset of graphics end up limiting how much you could change your game?

Very organic, but you're right, graphics games are far more limiting in terms of how much the game can change once it gets beyond the original design stage. Of all my games, *AMFV* was probably the one that changed the most as the game's production progressed. Originally, it was a much more ambitious, much less story-oriented game, almost a "future simulator" where the player would be able to set parameters in the present and then travel N years in the future to see what world would result from those decisions.

I also think that development works best when the game grows during implementation, rather than mapping/plotting out the entire game to a fairly high detail level and then starting implementation. That is another big advantage of text adventures over graphic adventures. It allows me, in a game like *LGOP* or *Hoboken,* to find and then hone a voice/style while a lot of the game is still on the drawing board, resulting in better, more unified work.

A big issue for adventure games seems to have been difficulty. For instance, if the game is too hard, you are likely to frighten away new players. But if the game is too easy, the hard-core players will dismiss your game. Do you have any idea what a solution to this problem might be?

Difficulty was a constant problem. Our games got consistently easier, which didn't seem to help attract any new players, and definitely seemed to turn off our hard-core fans. Hint books and later in-game hints were definitely considered ways to keep the games pretty hard without discouraging newer, less sophisticated, less masochistic players. It's a pretty good solution, because if the game is too hard, hints can help, make the game a good experience for a weaker player, but if the game is too easy it's pretty much ruined for a stronger player. Another solution is to have multiple difficulty levels, with more in-story clues in the easier levels, but this is obviously a lot more work to design, program, and balance.

A frequent complaint one sees about adventure games is that they don't have a lot of replay value. As a designer, what do you do to add that replayability, or do you not consider it a big issue?

Yes, that became increasingly a big issue as my games were competing not so much against other adventures and RPGs, but against strategy games like *Civilization* and RTS games like *WarCraft.* To some extent, you can have replayability in adventure games. For example, *Suspended* was an extremely replayable Infocom game, as you strove to finish the game with the lowest possible casualty levels. Even with *Zork I*, I remember a New Jersey couple who used to write to us constantly with new ways to win the game in ever-fewer numbers of moves. Alternate puzzle solutions and "meat on the bones" responses to wacky inputs are other ways to extend play time. But for the most part, it's just a matter of making sure that it takes thirty or forty hours to play the game, and hoping that that's enough to get a person to spend forty or fifty dollars on it.

Did you ever want to forget about the puzzles and have a game that mostly focused on story? You seem to have done an "all puzzles" game with *Hodj 'n' Podj.*

My desire, and I think this goes for most adventure games writers, is to do more story and less puzzle, but puzzle is necessary to keep that thirty- to forty-hour playtime goal. Of all my games, *AMFV* was certainly the most in the story direction, and *Zork Zero* was probably the most in the puzzle direction. I certainly don't agree that *Hodj 'n' Podj* was all puzzles, as the board game certainly has a well-developed opening and closing story, and the gameplay fills in a little more between those bookends: prince rescues princess, prince confronts brother, et cetera.

Did you ever add puzzles to a game solely to make the game longer?

I have definitely added puzzles simply to prolong the gameplay. I'd say the whole third section of *AMFV* was partly that, and partly feeling scared that the game was too different and too puzzle free and that people would rebel if at least there weren't some puzzles in the game. I think *Planetfall* and *Stationfall* were definitely cases where, as the game went into testing, there was kind of an impression that the game was too easy and over too quickly. Some more needed to be put in to keep people from finishing the game in ten hours and feeling that they hadn't gotten their money's worth.

Do you ever fear that some people who might like the story elements of adventure games are scared off by the really hard puzzles?

Well, it is kind of a conundrum, because it seems like what makes adventure games so compelling and obsessive are really difficult puzzles that have you up all night, thinking about them even when you're not sitting down playing the game. Then, when you're away from the game, you're thinking about it and all of a sudden "Oh my God, the kumquat over in the hay shed seven rooms over, I've never tried that!" And you can't wait to run home and boot up the game to your save and run over to get the kumquat, bring it back, and try whatever. And maybe it works, and it's the greatest feeling, or maybe it doesn't work and it's the worst feeling, or maybe it doesn't work but at least it gives you some new direction or hint or something. And in a game with no puzzles or pretty easy puzzles you just don't get that same rush. But, on the other hand, particularly as time went by, it seemed there were more and more people playing adventure games who really really disliked very hard puzzles. It's very hard to satisfy both audiences. Attempting to satisfy the people more interested in the casual gaming experience seemed to, over time, dribble the audience away, because it resulted in a less compelling gameplay experience.

Did you also serve as a programmer on all of your games?

Through *Hoboken*, I did both design and programming, and since then just the design. I certainly prefer to avoid programming if possible; doing so was always just a necessary evil. Of course, it certainly has some great advantages in terms of efficiency and one hundred percent perfect communication between programmer and designer. But even if I loved programming, games these days are too complex for one programmer anyway, so I'd never be able to do all the design and programming myself anymore.

In adventure games and, in particular, text adventures, limiting what the player can do is a major part of the game. Players can become frustrated from seeing "you can't do that" too often. How hard do you work to eliminate this problem?

Part of this is limiting the geography of the game. The original choice of setting helps. This is why so many games are set inside a geography with very well-defined boundaries like a cave, castle, island, zeppelin, et cetera. It's less frustrating to not even perceive a boundary than to reach a boundary and be told "There's nothing interesting in that direction" or "You'd probably die of thirst if you tried crossing that desert."

Part of it is just rolling up your sleeves and putting in as many non-default responses as possible, based on initial guesses of what people will try, augmented by suggestions from testers and even more ideas from reading the transcripts of testers' game sessions. Adding such responses was only limited by time and, more often, by disk space. This was also a good way to put in hints; a player tries something which isn't the "Right Answer" but which is a "Reasonable Thing to Try." I'd make the response an explanation of the failure, but perhaps a clue for what to try. For example:

>GIVE THE SANDWICH TO THE OLD MAN
He looks too tired to eat right now.

And part of it is making the default responses as flexible and fun as possible. For example, in *Hitchhiker's*, the default response for the verb FILL was "Phil who?" Phil was Zaphod's alias during the party scene. For another example, in *Zork I* the default response to many "impossible" actions was chosen from a table, giving you a variety of responses. So instead of:

>TAKE ALL
loaf of bread: Taken.
knife: It's stuck firmly into the countertop.
countertop: You can't take that!
sink: You can't take that!
stove: You can't take that!
oven: You can't take that!

you'd get:

>TAKE ALL
loaf of bread: Taken.
knife: It's stuck firmly into the countertop.
countertop: What a concept!
sink: Think again.
stove: Not bloody likely.
oven: Think again.

Do you have a particular starting point when creating a new game?

Varies from game to game. *AMFV* started with the game's theme/message. *Sorcerer* started with the complex time travel, meet your own self puzzle and built from there. I've explained earlier what the seed ideas were for *Planetfall* and *The Space Bar*. Generally, I don't do all of one thing before moving on to the next. I don't write the entire story line, and then start on the geography, and then when that's done start writing some puzzles. Instead, I'll rough out a story line, then design the core part of the geography, start populating it with characters and puzzles, refine the story line, add a new scene with resulting geography, add in the two puzzles I thought of in the meantime, combine two characters into a single character, add a couple more rooms to that Laboratory section of the game, add a new puzzle to flesh out the end-game, figure out why Esmerelda ran away from home in the first place, and so forth.

Why do you think that adventure games are so commercially unviable these days?

Simply, the cost-revenue model for the average adventure game is so far from being profitable that almost no publishers will touch them, since almost all publishing decisions these days are being made on a purely commercial rather than creative basis. It's just one of the most expensive types of games to make, and the top N adventure games sell less than the top N games in almost any other category.

Of course, it can be argued that the adventure game isn't dead, but has simply evolved into action/adventure games, e.g., *Tomb Raider*, and platform games, e.g., *Mario*, *Crash*. Personally, I don't consider any game that relies on even a relatively small degree of hand-eye coordination to fit the bill of an adventure game.

I suspect that a major technical innovation could revive the genre, but I don't know whether that will be a voice recognition interface, Turing-proof NPCs, 3D-surround-VR environments, or what.

It's particularly distressing when a well-budgeted game that everyone agrees is well done doesn't sell very well. In particular I'm thinking of *Grim Fandango*.

Yes, *Grim Fandango*. I don't know the exact numbers, but I don't think it broke a hundred thousand. And that was everyone's pretty much unanimous choice for adventure game of the year. It was a wonderful game. I didn't think from a puzzle point of view it was that great, but from an art direction point of view it was probably the best adventure game I'd ever seen.

It seems strange that adventure games used to be among the best-selling games, and now they don't sell well at all. Maybe my numbers are off...

No, that's really true. Around the time of the *King's Quest* games of the very late '80s and early '90s, they really were the best-selling genre at that time. And the

Infocom adventure games, from circa '83 to '85 were too. There was a point when we had five of the top ten selling games for a given month.

So what happened to the players of adventure games?

Well, there are certainly genres that exist now that didn't even exist then. And there are other genres that may have existed then but have certainly come along quite a ways. So it may be that the people who were playing then liked an interactive experience, but they would have been playing the sort of games that are popular today if they could have then. And in 1985 there wasn't anything like a first-person shooter, there wasn't anything like a real-time strategy game.

It might be that there are still quite a few adventure game people out there but simply that the critical mass of them has dropped a little bit to the point where the ones who are left can no longer support the same degree of game. An adventure game that would cost two million dollars to make now would require ten times as many people to be interested in it as an adventure game that might have cost two hundred thousand dollars fifteen years ago. And maybe the market has even doubled since then, but it hasn't gone up ten-fold. So it has dropped below the critical mass that would make that kind of game economically viable.

What has kept you interested in games for as long as you have been? Have you ever considered writing a novel or writing for other non-interactive media?

I have often considered writing a novel or screenplay, particularly at the most discouraging moments in my game writing career: canceled projects, a company going under, a game selling very poorly. But game writing has always paid the bills, so other writing projects would have to be a moonlighting thing, and with parenting and other outside interests there just isn't a lot of free time for non-paying writing. But any frustrations and unhappiness with making games has been completely on the business side; I've never found the creative process of making games to be anything less than a blast. It's still a growing/developing medium, so it's pretty exciting to be helping to invent a new "art form." Because the pay in the industry is relatively low, everyone you work with tends to be really motivated and love what they're doing, and it's just a pretty cool way to earn a living. For example, how many dads can give their kids T-shirts for a canceled *WarCraft* adventure game?

Steve Meretzky Gameography

Planetfall, 1983
Sorcerer, 1984
The Hitchhiker's Guide to the Galaxy, 1984
A Mind Forever Voyaging, 1985
Leather Goddesses of Phobos, 1986
Stationfall, 1987
Zork Zero: The Revenge of Megaboz, 1988
Spellcasting 101: Sorcerers Get All the Girls, 1990
Spellcasting 201: The Sorcerer's Appliance, 1991
Spellcasting 301: Spring Break, 1992
Leather Goddesses of Phobos II: Gas Pump Girls Meet the Pulsating Inconvenience from Planet X, 1992
Superhero League of Hoboken, 1994
Hodj 'n' Podj, 1995
The Space Bar, 1997

Chapter 11:
Storytelling

"The danger for designers is that they get hooked into their story, and they forget that storytelling is a linear narrative-type thing. And the more you flesh out the story the more you remove the interactivity, and the more you remove the player from the game. It's kinda like 'Oh, the outcome has already been determined. So what's the point?'"

— Eugene Jarvis

S trictly speaking, computer games do not need to tell stories. Over the years there have been plenty of fabulous games that offered very little in the way of storytelling. Consider *Tetris*, which had no storytelling whatsoever, or *Centipede* and *San Francisco Rush*, where the only story found is in the game's setting. But other games, such as *Marathon*, *Command & Conquer*, and *Thief*, have taken a story and made it work as a key part of the gameplay, creating tales so rich that players find themselves sucked into the game-world more than if the games had been story-less. And still other games, such as *A Mind Forever Voyaging*, *Myst*, and the *Ultima* series, have made the story such an integral part of the game that one can hardly imagine them otherwise. So games certainly do not need stories, but it seems that when employed properly, stories can make games that much stronger.

The story is so central to *Myst* that it is hard to imagine the game without it.

In fact, the dream of interactive stories is what drew me into game development in the first place. Imagine all of the power of a story in a novel, with its ability to grab hold and captivate the reader, to make her care about the characters in the story, to change her perception of the world, and, in some special instances, to change the way she lives her life. Now imagine how much more powerful that would be if, instead of reading about the actions of other characters, the reader was the main character in the story and was able to make choices that would affect the shape, direction, and outcome of the story. This interactive reader could see the ramifications of different choices made in different situations, and since it was her own choices that determined the nature of the story, the interactive story's draw would be that much more compelling than a traditional story. The mind boggles at the possibilities. Of course this dream is still a long way off, with no available game close to achieving this ideal. But it does provide a compelling reason to keep experimenting, with the hope of one day achieving a truly interactive story.

Designer's Story Versus Player's Story

So what do we mean when we talk about a game's story? Many game developers consider a game's story to be a predetermined series of dramatic events, much like the story one would find in a novel or a film. These events are static and unchanging, regardless of the player's actions in the game-world, and the story is typically conveyed to the player between gameplay sections. For example, in *Command & Conquer*, the player is told the story of the conflict between the GDI and Nod forces between the different missions. The story determines in part where the missions take place and what the player has to do in them, but typically once the player has completed a level, the story can proceed in only one direction. The only potential endings to the story are success and failure, with success coming after the player has completed all of the predetermined goals in all the levels, and failure coming at any point where the player lets his forces be overwhelmed by the opposition. Some games allow some simple branching in their story lines, but each branch is still predetermined by the game's designer, and usually the branches are fairly limited in scope.

But there is an altogether different type of a story associated with a game. If what I have just described is the designer's story, we can call this other type of story the player's story. Returning to the example of *Command & Conquer*, each time the player plays the game, he generates a new story unique to him. Indeed, each level makes up a mini-story of how the player won or lost that level. For instance, let us say that the player started out his game on the GDI side, building a large number of Minigun Infantry, Grenade Infantry, and Humm-Vees. These forces, however, were nearly wiped out by an early Nod attack, during which the enemy's Flamethrower Infantry proved to be too much for the player. The player, however, was able to exploit a vein of Tiberium he found nearby and build an Advanced Power Plant and some Barracks. The player then concentrated on building only Rocket Infantry and Mammoth Tanks. When the Nod Flamethrower Infantry next attacked, the player was easily able to run them over with his tanks. A number of the infantry started retreating, and the player followed them back to their base with his tanks and Rocket Infantry. There the GDI infantry were able to bombard the Nod structures from a distance, with the Mammoth Tanks taking out any resistance they encountered. Thereby, the player won the level. This is the player's story.

Now, when many game designers talk about storytelling in games, they are most likely not talking about the player's story such as the one told above. However, the player's story is the most important story to be found in the game, since it is the story the player will be most involved with, and it is the story in which the player's decisions have the most impact. In most cases, once the player has defeated the level using cunning tactics, he will be much less interested in the prescripted, full-motion video (FMV) designer's story that comes up between the levels, explaining the next level to be played. There are certain advantages to having a designer's story, of course. It can contain interesting characters and situations and employ traditional storytelling devices such as building to a climax, creating tension, foreshadowing, and so forth. Unfortunately, the use of these devices is often at the expense of the interactive nature of the story. On the other hand, depending on how the player plays the game, the *Command & Conquer* player's story told above may not have much drama or narrative tension to it, and as a result may be somewhat limp as a storytelling experience.

The ideal for interactive storytelling is to merge the designer's story and the player's story into one, so that the player can have a real impact on a story while the story retains its dramatic qualities. There are two good examples of the ideal interactive storytelling experience. The first is an example Chris Crawford is fond of using: that of a parent telling a child a story. The parent has in mind a story to tell including what characters it will involve, what surprises it will contain, roughly how the story will unfold, and approximately how it will end. But as the child asks questions about the story, the parent will change the tale accordingly. The parent may use a book as a guide, but will stray from that guide as necessary. For example, the story might begin: "As the princess wandered through the dark forest, she was frightened by many different things she saw, including a large newt, a dark cave, and an old shack." As the parent tells the story, the child may ask questions. "What color was the newt?" "The newt was a strange shade of yellow, a color the princess had only seen in the royal spiced mustard." "What about the cave?" "From within the cave came a terrible smell, reminiscent of the smell of sulfur burning." "Maybe there's an old sorcerer in there, making potions. Does she go into the cave?" "She did enter the cave, taking each step carefully in order to avoid stumbling in the dark. And as she went deeper into the cave, she started to see a light, and a voice shouted, 'Who is it that enters my cave?' And as she got closer, the princess saw an old wizard with tattered robes . . ." There may not have actually been a sorcerer in the story as the parent had initially intended to tell it, but as the child asks questions, instead of answering "you can't go that way" or "there's nothing special about it" as a poorly designed computer game might, the parent adapts the story to the child, adding detail and introducing new characters and situations as necessary. The overall story arc and its main protagonists may not change that much, but the child has had a real role in determining what exactly happens in the story.

Another example of truly interactive storytelling is found in many pen-and-paper role-playing games, such as *Dungeons & Dragons*. In a game of *D&D*, the Dungeon Master (DM) leads the game, guiding the other players through the

game-world and telling them the story as it happens. The Dungeon Master plans out in advance the locations the players will be exploring, has some idea of what characters the players will meet in what locations, and probably knows what major conflicts will be presented. The players, though, are in control of what parts of the level they investigate, and how they conduct themselves with the different NPCs they may meet. For instance, the DM probably does not have a script of what the different NPCs will say when approached. Instead, he knows what their personalities are like, and how they are likely to respond. When a player asks an NPC a question, the DM is able to come up, on the fly, with a reasonable response. A clever DM will never have to say, "The NPC does not understand your question." As with the parent-child storytelling experience, the DM will be able to keep the players on track with the overall story he wants to tell, while allowing the players a considerable amount of freedom in how that story unfolds and perhaps even in how it resolves.

Of course, the problem in creating a computer version of an interactive storytelling experience such as the ones described above is that both require a human to be telling the story, since a modern computer will never be able to dynamically come up with story developments as well as a human can. So the best a game designer can do currently is try to re-create such an interactive storytelling experience, but, in lieu of dynamically generating the story line, anticipate all of the questions the player might ask, places he might go, and lines of dialog he might want to say. Of course, this is a Herculean task, and no matter how much anticipation the designer employs, she will never be able to think of everything a player might try. At the very least the designer must try to allow for different playing styles and levels of inquiry into the story-world, instead of pigeonholing the player into one way of playing the game and exploring its story. If a designer is interested in truly interactive storytelling, it is her responsibility to make the designer's story flexible enough to allow it to become the player's story as well.

Places for Storytelling

There are a number of ways in which a game can tell a story. Customarily, games use a number of different storytelling devices to communicate their story, with different games relying on some devices more than others. The type of story you hope to tell, what technology you will be using, and the gameplay of your game will determine what storytelling devices will work best for your game.

The simplest distinction one can make is in what context the storytelling takes place:

- Out-of-Game: This is any storytelling that is done on the computer while the game is running, but when the player is not actually playing the game. This includes any cut-scenes during which the player loses control of his character, such as the cut-scenes or mission briefings that occur between levels in *Command & Conquer* or brief non-interactive sections in *Super Mario 64*.

- In-Game: Logically, this is the opposite of the above, and covers any storytelling that occurs while the player is actually playing the game. This includes the setting of the game-world, the behavior of the player's opponents, any dynamic conversations the player may have, and any interactive pre-mission planning the player may do.

- External Materials: This includes any storytelling done completely outside of the computer, such as in an introduction written in the manual or any paraphernalia that may come with the game, such as a map or a collection of gems.

A given game may use only one or all three of the above types of storytelling. *Half-Life* is an example of a game that included only in-game storytelling; the player never lost control of her character from the beginning of the game to the end. The Infocom games are a good example of games that used both in-game and external materials to tell their stories. In addition to the conversations and descriptions of the game-world the player had in the game itself, the Infocom games always came with extra documents and knickknacks, which served to enhance the player's understanding of the game-world, in addition to sometimes being required to complete the game's puzzles. *Command & Conquer* used in-game storytelling through its settings and mission design, while much of the story line was communicated through the out-of-game, non-interactive cut-scenes. *Tekken* is an example of a game that tells its story, as insubstantial as it may be, almost entirely through out-of-game cut-scenes: one precedes the gameplay and one plays after the player has defeated the single-player game using a specific character. The settings of the various arenas have nothing whatsoever to do with the story line, and the characters themselves exhibit nothing of the personalities described in the scenes either, though their fighting styles usually relate to their nationalities. Indeed, it is unclear why the designers of *Tekken* felt compelled to include a story line at all. Perhaps they wanted to give the player something to reward them for defeating the game, and a cut-scene was the only suitable prize they could imagine.

Out-of-Game

Out-of-game storytelling is perhaps the most prevalent form currently in games, and it comes in a variety of forms. One can attribute the popularity of out-of-game storytelling to its similarity to storytelling in other media. For example, a cut-scene is very often like a film and uses established cinematic techniques, while a text briefing for a level is not unlike what one might read in a novel. These are both types of media that have been around for many more years than computer games, and both have an established syntax which allows them to tell stories very effectively. In a way, it is much easier to tell a story through these methods than it is through gameplay. But as a designer you must ask yourself, are non-interactive cut-scenes what games are supposed to be about? If your gameplay is any good at all, players will want to get back to playing instead of sitting through long cut-scenes. Players play games in order to interact. If they wanted a more passive experience, they would have gone to a movie theater or gotten a book from the library. Non-interactive storytelling may have its place in games, but designers need to be aware that it must supplement and not detract from an exciting gaming experience.

As I have discussed, there are a number of different methods that can be used to tell a story outside of the gameplay. A summary of the major methods is as follows:

● Cut-Scenes: What are commonly referred to as cut-scenes use cinematic techniques to communicate a narrative to the player. These may take place in 2D or 3D, and often involve cuts, pans, the "180 degree rule," and other devices that anyone who has watched movies or television will be familiar with.

● Text: Many games use text to describe the story or to give the player goals for the upcoming mission. The text may fill the entire screen and then flip to another screen as necessary, or text may scroll by at a slow enough speed that the player has time enough to read it.

● Images: Sometimes players are presented with simple images that communicate some part of the story line. These do not qualify as standard cut-scenes precisely, since they do not include camera cuts or other cinematic techniques, though a simple camera pan may be used to sweep across an image that does not fit on the screen. The image may be a map of an area, an "establishing" image of the challenges to come, or a recap of those the player has just accomplished. Images are often mixed with text, sometimes using comic book techniques but usually without word balloons.

● Audio: Sometimes players are given directives that are spoken dialog or other audio. This is usually when the budget did not exist to create FMV to go along with the dialog, or when the dialog is presented over other information the player is supposed to be looking at, such as maps, dossiers, or other documents.

One of the most important goals to have when working with cut-scenes is to establish a consistent visual appearance between the cut-scenes and the gameplay. If at all possible, the same engine should be used for the cut-scenes as for the rest of the game. In the mid-'90s, as games switched to CD-ROM as the distribution medium of choice, for the first time games were able to include actual video play-back in the games, even if these movies often could not fill the entire screen. Thus came into being the dreaded FMV game, such as *The 7th Guest*. Typically, these games presented long FMV clips with mini-games between them, resulting in products that were more movies than games. In these games the vast majority of the player's time was spent not actually playing the game but instead watching totally non-interactive cut-scenes, with these cinematic sections usually amateurish below what one would find on even the cheapest TV show. This serves to explain why the genre quickly fell out of favor with players. Other games, such as the aforementioned *Command & Conquer* and *Dark Forces*, used FMV sections between the levels that made up the actual game. These games were fortunate enough to actually include viable and compelling gameplay and thereby stood up as games regardless of the inclusion of FMV. However, the FMV sections of these games were created using live actors in worlds that looked nothing like the worlds that the gameplay took place in. Other games, such as *MechWarrior 2* and my own *Centipede 3D*, used super high polygon, pre-rendered 3D environments to handle these cut-scenes, creating an environment that looked nothing like the ones generated by the real-time 3D engines used for the gameplay. The result is a disjointed visual experience for the player, something that breaks whatever suspension of disbelief the player may have established. The use of cut-scenes is in itself already a very jarring experience for the player; one minute the player has an active role in the

Cut-scenes in *Karateka* are all handled using the game engine, resulting in a seamless visual experience for the player.

proceedings, the next he has to be passive, content to sit back and watch instead. Using cut-scenes that look nothing like the game-world only exacerbates matters.

Many games have successfully incorporated cut-scenes that use the same graphics as the in-game visuals, going back to 2D games such as *Pac-Man* and *Karateka*, up to such modern RT3D titles as *Legend of Zelda: Ocarina of Time* and *Drakan: Order of the Flame*. In these games, though the player may lose control of the game briefly, at least the player has a completely seamless visual experience. The artists may complain that the cut-scenes do not look as good; after all, they can only play with the number of polygons that can be rendered in real time. But what may be lost in terms of visual quality is more than made up for by the overall consistency of the game.

Another strange aspect of cut-scenes in many computer games is their non-interactive nature, which is indicative of the inability of the designer to understand the capabilities of the computer as an interactive device. Consider spectators at a movie or a play, or the nationwide audience watching a television show. The audiences for those productions are unable to interact with the proceedings in any way: the performance occurs and then it is over. On the other hand, someone reading a book, watching a video, or being told a story is able to experience the medium at whatever speed he wants. Pages can be reread in a book, videotapes can be rewound or fast-forwarded, and a child can ask his parent to further explain or reread part of the story he did not understand. The key difference here is that the audience of the first set of non-interactive media is a large group of people, while the audience for the latter set is a single person.

Consider the audience for a computer game. Is it a group or a sole individual? Obviously, for multi-player games the audience may be more than one, but multi-player games almost never bother with cut-scenes of any sort. No, the storytelling games that require cut-scenes are almost all designed as single-player experiences. Why, then, when the text scrolls by in the mission briefing for a game, is the user unable to rewind it? Indeed, why is it scrolling at all? Computers are excellent tools for giving the user control over her experience, and since the player is usually playing the game herself, who would mind if she read the text at her own speed, as controlled by a scroll bar or arrows on the keyboard? Similarly for cut-scenes: why can the user almost never rewind to watch the cut-scene again? What if she missed a part of the story she wants to hear, or just wants to enjoy the presentation again? It seems that the out-of-game sections of computer games are more user-unfriendly than almost any other solo experience medium. It seems likely that game designers may be thinking that they are movie directors and therefore want to create a movie theater-like experience, despite the extremely different nature of the medium with which they are working.

Some games are smart enough to allow the users to control the playback of cut-scenes. *The Last Express* in particular springs to mind, with its unique "egg" save-game feature that allows the user to go back to any point in his game and re-experience it. The game prided itself on transpiring in real-time or close to

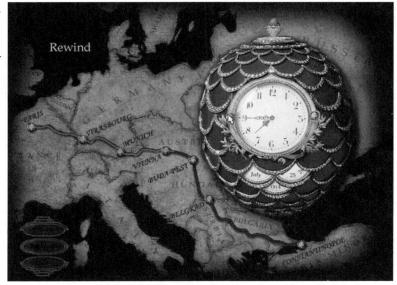

The Last Express' clever save-game system allows the player to turn back game-time in order to rewatch cut-scenes or play parts of the game again.

real-time, and hence the player was able to turn back the hands on a clock to any particular time he was interested in and the game would return him to that point, a feature which was essential for understanding the game's complex story. My own game *Damage Incorporated* used extremely interactive mission briefings in order to make sure the players understood what they had to do on a level. Players could use the arrow keys to flip back and forth between text and image documents. During these mission briefings there was also spoken dialog which supplemented the material printed on the screen. Players could pause, rewind, and fast-forward this spoken dialog as they desired using tape deck controls displayed on the bottom of the screen. In this way players were able to read the text at whatever speed they wished and relisten to portions of the dialog that they may have missed.

Unfortunately, the only interaction with the cut-scenes that many games include is the ability for the player to skip them entirely. This is essential, since many players will want to skip over the non-interactive sections of the game, as any playtesting session will reveal. Forcing players to watch cut-scenes is a totally unnecessary limitation no game should attempt to enforce. As I explained above, better than complete skipping is to allow players to skip forward and back through cut-scenes as they desire, watching and rewatching them at their own speed.

If one stops for a moment to consider the nature of out-of-game devices for storytelling in games, one will be struck by what a strange concept it is to disrupt the interactive experience with a non-interactive one. For instance, when you go to a movie, do the theater workers ever stop the film, bring up the lights, and direct the audience to read a book that they handed out? Sometimes text is shown on the screen, but never in a way that requires the audience to read more than a few words at a time. Instead, films present a consistent media experience for the audience. Games, on the other hand, still mix media in seemingly unnatural ways, forcing users who may just want to play a game to have to read a bit of a book, watch a movie, and only then actually get to play. Surely there is a better way to tell a story, convey a plot, and introduce characters from within the game itself that is far superior to out-of-game storytelling, at least in terms of maintaining a fluid experience for the player.

In-Game

There are numerous powerful techniques for telling a story during gameplay. *Half-Life* was universally praised in the gaming press for the strength of its story. However, if one looks at the game's story, it is not actually all that compelling, perhaps even hackneyed. Many other games, even many other first-person shooters, have contained stories just as compelling. What *Half-Life* did well, however, was to tell its story entirely from within the gameplay. The player never loses control of his character, even if he is locked in an observation room, stuck on a tram car, or thrown in a garbage compactor. The story is communicated through a combination of level settings, chatty scientists, announcements over the PA system, and NPC scripted behaviors. By the game's end, the player is under the impression that the story was excellent because of the compelling way in which it was told.

Some of the different techniques one can use to tell a story through gameplay are as follows:

- Text: A lot can be communicated to the player through text placed around the game-world. These can be signs explaining directions to locations, pinned-up notes left by previous inhabitants of a given area, graffiti on the wall, or books left lying around for the player to read.

- Level Settings: Almost all games use this technique, regardless of whether they attempt to tell a story or not. Consider the garden setting of *Centipede*, the hell-like setting of *Doom*, or even the art deco real estate setting of the board game *Monopoly*. What little story these games have is told entirely through setting, but setting can also be key to telling more complex game stories. The player's exploration of the game-world can lead to discoveries about the type of people that inhabit a given area, or inhabited it in years past. Instead of reading in a cut-scene that the land is run-down and decayed, the player can simply see that truth by navigating the game-world. Setting is a perfect example of showing a story instead of telling it.

- Dialog: Dialog with NPCs during gameplay is another massively powerful tool that designers can use to great storytelling effect. This dialog can be spoken during gameplay through conversations the player has with NPCs, where the player gets to choose his character's response to the NPC's dialog, either through a multiple choice of responses or by typing in his own response. Dialog can also happen non-interactively during gameplay, with NPCs, either friendly or unfriendly, speaking to the player during the game and thereby communicating more of the game's story. Dialog can also come from computer terminals, PA systems, or tape decks, to name just a few devices.

● NPC Behaviors: Of course, the NPCs should not just talk to the player; they should perform actions that back up the story line. For instance, say that the player fights two different races of aliens in the game, and according to the story line the two races bitterly despise each other. If the player is ever battling both at once, he should be able to trick them into fighting each other. In a peaceful village, if the player approaches the NPCs with his weapons drawn perhaps the NPCs will flee from the player. In a more hostile town, the NPCs might draw their own weapons and threaten to attack the player if he fails to stand down. NPCs can also be engaged in scripted behaviors that communicate to the player the nature of the game-world. For instance, say the people of a town live in fear of the Gestapo-like police force. As the player enters, he may observe a townsperson receiving a harsh and unjust beating from a member of the police.

The *Marathon* games used text expertly to communicate their story line while never taking the player out of the game. The game featured computer terminals scattered throughout the levels the player navigated. The player could walk up to one of these terminals and hit the "action" key to activate it. Then the player's view of the game-world would be replaced by a close-up view of the terminal. The player could then use the arrow keys to flip back and forth between different text screens which revealed more details about the plot and told the player what her objective was for the current level. The great thing about these terminals was that while the player was reading them, though she could no longer see the game-world, the game-world was still very much active and the player could be attacked by aliens or drowned by rising water. This sometimes gave the reading of the terminals a certain urgency, keeping the player's game-world tension active. Of course, the player was able to control the text by flipping forward and backward through the screens, rereading the text at whatever speed she wanted.

My own game *Damage Incorporated* used a combination of NPC behaviors and dialog to give the player some sense of character about the teammates who accompany him through the game's various missions. The player was able to pick from among thirteen different marines the four he wanted to accompany him on a given mission. Each of these marines had a distinct personality and would communicate this through the dialog he spoke during the missions themselves. This dialog might include the response to a directive from the player, a comment about the nature of the mission itself, or a response to the player's particularly effective

The *Marathon* games allow players to log onto computer terminals scattered throughout the levels, where they can read more about the game's complex story. Pictured here: *Marathon 2*.

killing of an enemy. Furthermore, different teammates could react differently to being taken on different missions. Some of the marines were less mentally sound than others and if taken on too many missions they would become "shell shocked" and run around the level at random, muttering gibberish all the while. Other marines would have moral objections to some of the missions on which the team was sent. As a result, these rogue teammates would rebel against the player and his other teammates in certain circumstances, shouting their disapproval for the task at hand as they went on a rampage. Thus, a combination of dialog and NPC behaviors created a group of teammates with real personalities, almost all of which was communicated during the gameplay itself.

One of the big concerns some people have with in-game storytelling is that the player may miss some of the story. What if the player fails to see the story being told? Since the player never loses control of the game with in-game storytelling, this makes it possible for the player to avoid talking to characters, witnessing scripted NPC behaviors, or reading signs. It is true that locking the player in front of a non-interactive cut-scene or scrolling text is one way to guarantee that she sees exactly what the designer wants her to see. But, as I have stated previously, one needs to remember that games are an interactive form, and that if the player does not experience every last element of the story, that is the nature of interactivity. If the player is interested in getting all of the story, it is the player's responsibility to seek it out. If the player would prefer to just charge through the game focusing solely on the gameplay, that is her choice to make. Indeed, having different layers of the story that can be discovered on playing the game a second time can be a significant incentive for replaying the game.

Almost everyone has had an English teacher who has emphasized the importance of showing instead of telling in creative writing. Instead of being told that the people are wealthy, readers should be able to read the author's description of an area and from that, deduce that the region is populated by a prosperous people. For games, in-game storytelling is the equivalent of showing, while out-of-game cut-scenes and other methods are telling. For in-game storytelling, players get to experience the story themselves instead of being told it secondhand. In addition to maintaining the player's immersion in the game-world, in-game storytelling shows the player the story instead of just telling it to him.

External Materials

Many games have used external materials to tell their stories. This was particularly true in the 1980s when disk space was severely limited and designers could not fit all of the story they wanted to include onto a single 400K or smaller floppy disk. Some designers used manuals to communicate the game's back-story, writing a narrative that would lead the player up to the point where she would start playing the game. Some games, such as the classic *Wasteland*, even used "paragraph" books, where the game would play for a while and then, when the player got to a storytelling juncture, would be instructed "Now read paragraph 47." Sometimes this referencing of the manual was used as a form of copy protection, in that the player would be unable to play the game without having a copy of the manual.

Arcade games also used external materials. Often the names of the game's characters were written on the side of the cabinet instead of in the game. Some cabinets even included a few sentences further explaining the game's setting and the player's mission. The artwork featured on the sides of arcade game cabinets used superior graphics to add a small amount of depth to what meager story lines the games may have had.

These days storytelling in manuals and other materials is generally frowned upon, and rightly so. We are certainly no longer presented with the technological limitations that necessitated storytelling through external materials. Furthermore, often the stories told in the manuals were not written by the game's designers or even with their consultation. Therefore these stories can hardly be considered a part of the game itself, but rather the marketing department's attempt to create a game-world they could hype on the back of the box. I would certainly never use a manual to convey the story in one of my own games since I believe it detracts from the continuous experience of playing the game on the computer or console.

That said, some games have used external materials extremely effectively. In particular, the Infocom games always included materials in the boxes which added to the player's gameplay experience in meaningful ways. Often the games referred to these materials, saying something to the effect of, "The magazine you find is the

same one as came in your game package." These materials were customarily prepared by or in conjunction with the game's author, thereby making them valid parts of the game itself. For more information on how Infocom used its packaged materials to add depth to the story and the motivations for doing so, consult the interview with Infocom author Steve Meretzky found in Chapter 10.

Frustrated Linear Writers

One of the primary story problems that many computer games have is that their stories are written by people who wish they were writing in a more linear medium. Sometimes failed screenwriters or novelists are hired to work on game projects. These writers often feel disappointed to have to work in games and see their game work as something they do strictly for the money, while simultaneously seeing themselves as above gaming as an art form. As a result of their training in linear writing and distaste for interactive writing in general, these writers use all of the linear writing techniques they have honed over the years and try to apply them to games, where they fail miserably.

Sometimes the game developers themselves secretly or not-so-secretly wish they were working in another medium and make their story writing choices accordingly. After all, for as long as games have existed, film has been a more respected, popular, and financially rewarding medium to work in, with mammoth cults of personality surrounding actors, directors, and sometimes even writers. Game designers can be sucked in by this allure and become envious of filmmakers. These designers often start emphasizing the cinematic nature of their games, sometimes attempting to deny that they are games at all by calling them "interactive movies." The games' cinematic cut-scenes become longer and longer, with the predetermined story line dominating the gameplay completely.

And in a way, the mistakes game developers make putting story into their games are forgivable due to the youth of the medium. For example, when the technology that enabled filmmaking was introduced, many of the first films that were made were documents of stage plays. A camera was placed in a fixed position on a tripod and the actors considered its frame to be their stage, just as if they were working with a live audience. There were no cuts, pans, or camera movement of any kind, because the language of film had yet to be invented. As time went on, however, filmmakers learned that their films could be more than straight transcriptions of stage plays, and they could instead take advantage of the strengths of their new medium. In some ways, games still suffer from the same problem, where established mediums, film in particular, are taken and just thrown into games without considering how a story might best be told in a language suited to interactivity.

What results from these frustrated linear writers are projects that try to be both games and movies, usually with the end result that they do neither very well. Using storytelling that is suited to an interactive experience is significantly harder than using traditional linear techniques, but the payoff in the quality of your final game will be more than worth it. There are a number of symptoms that arise in such a situation, and recognizing these problems as they come up is crucial to preventing them from ruining your game.

The first problem is forcing the player to experience the story in only one predetermined path. The linear writer often feels that there is only one way for the drama to unfold, and if the player tries to pursue anything else he, or at least his character, should be killed. The linear writer does not want to allow the player to discover different ways of navigating through the story space, when there is only one path that makes for the most powerful narrative. What the linear writer fails to realize is that games are about letting the player find his own path through the game-world, regardless of how uninteresting a path that may be. What the path may lose in drama it makes up for because the player feels ownership of it. It is the player's story instead of the designer's story.

Despite being perhaps the most famous computer game character in existence, Mario has a relatively undefined personality. Pictured here: *Super Mario 64*.

Linear writers also often try to force the player's character to have a strong personality. There is a popular misconception in game design that gamers want to have main characters with strong personalities for them to control, particularly in adventure and action games. But if one looks at the most popular entries in these genres, one will quickly notice that the player character's personality is often kept to a minimum. Look at *Super Mario 64*. Though Mario has a fairly distinctive look, what really is his personality? He does not actually have one, leaving him undefined enough for the player to imprint her own personality on him. What about Lara Croft in *Tomb Raider?* Again, a very distinct appearance, a very undefined personality. And if one looks at the space marine in *Doom* or Gordon Freeman in *Half-Life*, one will find no personality whatsoever.

The reason for this is simple: when players want to play games, they often want to play themselves. If the character they are controlling has a very strong personality, there is a distancing effect, reminding the player that the game is largely predetermined and making him feel like he is not truly in control of what happens in the game. Particularly frustrating are adventure games that feature strongly characterized player characters who keep speaking irritating lines of dialog. I remember one adventure game in particular where the player had to control a spoiled brat who constantly said annoying, idiotic things to himself and to the characters he met. Who would want to control such a character? The dialog for the character was actually quite well written and amusing, but not to the player who was forced to go through the game using that obnoxious character as his game-world surrogate. It would appear that the game's writer got carried away with this interesting characterization for the main character without realizing the detrimental effect it would have on the player's gaming experience.

I do not mean to suggest that your game cannot have terrific characters in it, and indeed, without strong characters your game will fail to have much of a story at all. Instead of trying to imbue the main character with a lot of personality, make the NPCs the player encounters in the game memorable and interesting. If the player finds these characters annoying that is totally acceptable; it means that they have enough personality for the player to feel strongly about them. But the player's character should be sufficiently amorphous and unformed that the player can think of that character in whatever way he sees fit. And fear not, after spending forty or more hours with that character, the player will come up with his own ideas of what motivates and drives his game-world surrogate. The character he creates in his mind will be one whom he likes and with whom he will want to continue to play.

Game Stories

As I have discussed, when writing a story for a game, it is important to stay away from the conventions of linear media, such as forcing the player to follow only one narrative and instilling too much character in the player's game-world surrogate. Beyond the pitfalls to avoid when creating the game's story, the game's scriptwriter should worry less about the overall plot and more about the situations in which the player finds himself and characters with which he interacts. Indeed, many film directors are keenly aware of this technique. For instance, in talking about his film *The Big Sleep*, director Howard Hawks said: "Making this picture I realized that you don't really have to have an explanation for things. As long as you make good scenes you have a good picture—it doesn't really matter if it isn't much of a story."

I have played countless games where the overall plot was completely lost on me; I simply did not care to follow it. Often in these games, I enjoyed the gameplay, the situations the game placed me in, and the interesting and amusing characters I met there. Since the characters and situations were interesting, it did not really matter if I knew who did what to whom and when. All I knew was that I was having fun playing the game. Often when games try to hit me over the head with their plot through long cut-scenes which go into minute detail about the reasons for the state of the game-world and the character's motivations for every last action, it becomes tedious. Remember that players want to play games. If the story enhances that experience, that is good, but if the story starts to get in the way of the gameplay, that is bad. Spelling out too much of the story is also a common failing of novice writers. Readers, viewers, and players alike are able to figure out much more than authors give them credit for. It makes sense for the author of the story to have all of the character's motivations figured out in detail, with all of the nuances of the different twists and turns of the plot detailed in her notebook, but does every last element of this story need to be included in the game? No, what is more important is that the story the player is presented with is consistent and could be used to put together the complete story. Players will not mind if every last plot point is not explicitly spelled out.

In Chapter 9, "Artificial Intelligence," I talked about Brian Moriarty's concept of "constellation" and how it could help to create more interesting AI. Constellation is a natural tendency that game storytellers can also use to their advantage. Moriarty has described constellation in media as the ability of an audience to fill in the holes or inconsistencies present in a storytelling experience, regardless of what form that story may take. For instance, if a storyteller only hints at the true appearance of an evil foe, the image conjured in the mind of an audience member may be far more frightening than what the storyteller might be able to describe to the audience. One can also look at the fan base for a TV show such as *Star Trek*. The slightest hinting at a bit of story by the writers of the show will lead to endless speculation among the audience members as to what the implications of that subtle hint are, and the fans will come up with their own explanation for what it might mean. This may or may not be the explanation the writer originally intended, but what is important is that it involves the audience in the work to a much greater degree, switching them from a passive mode to an active one. Of course, games are already much more interactive than television, and therefore it makes sense that game storytellers would not tell the audience every last detail of a plot. This will involve the players still more in the game as they try to figure out what exactly the story is all about.

Non-Linearity

Much talk is made of non-linearity in games, and storytelling in particular is a key area where non-linearity can be used to enhance the player's gaming experience. I feel the goal of game storytelling is to create a story in which the player feels he can play a significant role that may affect the outcome. Non-linearity is an essential tool for accomplishing that goal. In a way, in-game storytelling is non-linear. In-game storytelling allows the player to talk to some characters and not to others, to choose which signs to read and which to ignore, and to explore the game-world in order to reveal its relevance to the story line, exploration over which the player has control. With the player empowered to explore the story-space in his own way, some degree of non-linearity is unavoidably created.

One popular way to add non-linearity to the storytelling experience is through a branching story. With a branching story, at various points the decisions the player makes will have a significant effect on how the story progresses. This may mean if the player succeeds in defeating a certain adversary, the story will progress differently than if the player fails to kill that foe. In the latter case, it may be that the player will have to kill that foe later, or that the foe will summon a force to help him that the player will have to confront. Of course, branching stories increase the amount of content that will need to be created for a game, at least in terms of game design and dialog, if not also in art assets. This can sometimes make this technique unpopular with the cost accountants who see the creation of such assets as wasted money. What they fail to see is that if the branching story line is implemented properly, the gameplay payoff will be tremendous, hopefully making the game more popular.

Another technique that can be used to inject some non-linearity into the game's story is to allow the player to determine the order in which different story components occur. Suppose there are three sections of the story you need to tell. Perhaps the order in which the player experiences those components is not so important. With a little extra work, you may be able to give the player the choice of which section to do first, which to do second, and which to do last. If one thinks of this in terms of the "chapters" of a game's story, often designers find that, though the first and final chapters of the narrative must happen respectively at the beginning and end of the game, the other chapters in the game can happen in any order. Of course, issues with the difficulty of the sections may arise, since ideally designers want the difficulty of their games to ramp up continuously. This, however, is more of a game design question, and one that clever designers will be able to work around.

Of course non-linear storytelling in games goes hand in hand with non-linear gameplay: one can hardly imagine one without the other. Non-linearity is explored more in Chapter 7, "The Elements of Gameplay."

Working with the Gameplay

One of the most important parts of creating a story for a computer game is to match the story with the gameplay as much as possible. Earlier, in Chapter 3, "Brainstorming a Game Idea," I discussed how a game's development might start with either technology, gameplay, or, in more rare instances, story. If you are starting your game development process with gameplay or with technology, these are going to directly dictate which kind of story you can tell. If you try to fight the gameplay or technology with a story that is not suitable, you are going to be left with a poorly told story in a poorly executed game. There are infinitely many stories to be told, and infinitely many ways to tell a given story. Your job as game designer is to find a story and a telling of that story that will work with the game design and technology that you will be using.

Damage Incorporated's story was created to fit around the gameplay and technology.

For me, stories seem to naturally fall out of gameplay. I seldom think of a story independently and try to fit it into some gameplay. Instead, I see the constraints of the world with which I will be working, and start thinking of the most interesting content possible for that space. I do not see these constraints as a limitation on my ability to tell a story, but more as guidelines or even sources of inspiration. For example, in *Damage Incorporated*, long before the game had a story there was a technology and a game design in mind. From the game design, which centered around the player controlling teammates in an FPS environment, sprung the idea for the different teammates that would accompany the player, and how each one of them would have a distinct personality. What sort of men would be in the Marine Corps of the 1990s? How would they react to a combat situation? What would their reaction be when they saw their commander killed? These were the questions that ended up driving the development of the game's story. And these questions arose directly out of the limitations imposed by the game design.

The Dream

One could say that the goal of gameplay is to allow for different player strategies to lead to variable types of success, to reward player experimentation and exploration, and to empower players to make their own choices. All of these factors allow players to craft their own unique stories when playing your game. If you want to tell a more predetermined story through your game as well, it is important to do everything possible to make the player feel that it is her own unique story. The player should feel ownership over the actions in her game, and thereby ownership in the story that is being told.

Marketing people and game reviewers like storytelling in games because they are a much more easily understood and discussed subject than game design. A story makes easy copy for either the back of the box or the text of a review, something that is much easier to describe than gameplay. These days, game reviewers will be frustrated if your game does not have much of a story, regardless of whether it needs one or not. Games without stories are considered passé and archaic. The marketing people, and sadly sometimes even the game reviewers, truly will not care if your story is non-linear or allows for the players to make the story their own. Indeed, the business and marketing types will love a main character with a strong

Titles like *SimCity* allow players to truly tell their own story, with barely any guidance from the designer.

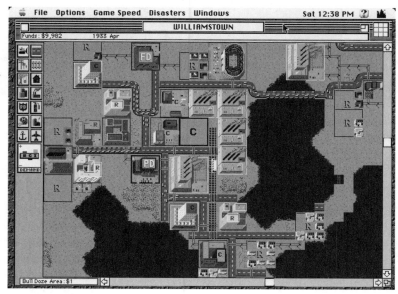

personality since it will better lead to licensing opportunities for action figures and Saturday morning cartoon shows. Never mind that the character's strong personality may alienate players from the game.

But as a game designer your ambitions must be higher than creating entertaining box copy or simplifying the job of game reviewers. Many great games dispense with traditional storytelling entirely. *Civilization* and *SimCity* immediately spring to mind as indisputably great games which allow players to tell their own story, with the designer providing only a starting place from which the tale can unfold. Games do not need prescripted stories at all, it is true. Nonetheless, a truly interactive story, where the narrative can change radically depending on the player's choices, while retaining the emotional resonance and power of a story told in a novel, is a very compelling idea. It is so compelling that it is hard to imagine any truly ambitious game designer who would not hope for it to become a reality.

Chapter 12:
Game Analysis:
Loom

Designed by Brian Moriarty
Released in 1990

For 1990, the year it was released, *Loom* was a decidedly different type of adventure game. Though it had many gameplay similarities to graphical adventure games that had been released previously by LucasArts, *Loom* endeavored to reduce the adventure game to its core mechanics from a storytelling standpoint and to cut away all that was extraneous. Looking in the manual, one finds that the game's authors were keenly aware that they were creating something different, as the following excerpt from the "About *Loom*" section indicates:

> *Loom* is unlike traditional "adventure games" in many ways. Its goal is to let you participate in the unfolding of a rich, thought-provoking fantasy. It is neither a role-playing game (although it incorporates elements of role-playing), nor a collection of brain-teasers. Its simple mysteries are designed to engage your imagination and draw you deeper into the story, not to frustrate you or increase the amount of time it takes to finish.

Later on in the manual in the "Our Game Design Philosophy" section, one finds still more references to how unique *Loom* is:

> We believe that you buy our games to be entertained, not to be whacked over the head every time you make a mistake. So we don't bring the game to a screeching halt when you poke your nose into a place you haven't visited before. Unlike conventional computer adventures, you won't find yourself accidentally stepping off the path, or dying because you've picked up a sharp object.
>
> We think you'd prefer to solve the game's mysteries by exploring and discovering, not dying a thousand deaths. We also think you want to spend your time involved in the story, not typing in synonyms until you stumble upon the computer's word for a certain object.

Reading the above, one gets the idea that perhaps *Loom* was a reaction by the game's author, Brian Moriarty, to what he saw in other adventure games as detrimental to the player's enjoyment. It is unclear whether Moriarty wrote these parts of the manual himself, but it seems likely that they at least represented his feelings on the subject accurately. *Loom* was going to retain the positive storytelling elements of adventure games and remove everything that conflicted with the player's enjoyment of the story. It succeeded admirably, resulting in a game that seemed to earnestly want the player to complete its interesting story.

Prior to coming to LucasArts to work on *Loom*, Brian Moriarty had worked at Infocom for a number of years, a company renowned for the unsurpassed quality and depth of their text adventures. There he had created two text adventures, *Wishbringer* and *Trinity*, and one text-only adventure/role-playing hybrid, *Beyond Zork*. While *Wishbringer* was designed from the start to be an easy-to-play game for beginners, both *Trinity* and *Beyond Zork* are massive and terrifically difficult games to complete. *Loom*, then, seems to be a change in direction from those titles, a return to a game which does not challenge the player merely for the sake of challenging him, but instead includes only those challenges that are critical to the story. Furthermore, *Loom* was Moriarty's first game to not involve a text parser, an input

method that he was all too happy to do away with, if one believes that the sentiments expressed in the manual are his own. Again, the simplicity of *Loom* seems to be a reaction to the needless complexity of older adventure games, both in general and Moriarty's own. In *Loom*, the story was king, and whatever stood in its way was removed.

Focused Game Mechanics

Loom seems to be a perfect example of a game that is completely focused in what it wants to accomplish. Instead of trying to include all of the game mechanics he possibly could, it appears that Moriarty thought long and hard about what the minimum game mechanics necessary for the telling of his story were. He then eliminated everything that did not truly add something to that story. This had the result of greatly simplifying the game, while at the same time making it considerably more elegant and easy to navigate.

Loom's game mechanics are focused on telling the game's story.

The game was developed using the SCUMM Story System which all of LucasArts' adventure games have used, in one form or another. Credited to Ron Gilbert and Aric Wilmunder, SCUMM stands for "Scripting Utility for *Maniac Mansion*," so named after the first game to use the system. Indeed, if one looks at the other LucasArts adventures, one will notice that nearly every one has much more in the way of gameplay mechanics and user interface than *Loom*. Both *Maniac Mansion* (1987) and *The Secret of Monkey Island* (1990, the same year as *Loom*) include inventories for the player to manipulate, in addition to allowing the player to click on a variety of verbs that can be used on various objects in the game world. Both games were created using the SCUMM system, indicating that inventory and verb systems were readily available to Moriarty via SCUMM if he wanted to use them. Indeed, inventories and verbs were a very common element of nearly all of the adventure games released prior to *Loom*. (Many adventures released since *Loom* have done away with both verbs and inventories, most notably *Myst* and its many imitators.) So Moriarty was making a tremendous break from both the SCUMM system and tradition when he left these mechanics out. Including an inventory and verbs could have added a lot of depth to the game if the story was reconceived to take advantage of them. But as it stands, the game functions perfectly without them.

Many other adventure games also feature branching dialog trees. In this sort of system, when the player's character is talking to another character, the player is presented with a list of different sentences her character can say. The player can then pick from those choices and some level of interactivity is achieved during the conversations. Again, *The Secret of Monkey Island* featured exactly such a system, used by the game's creator, Ron Gilbert, to enormous gameplay payoff, particularly in the classic sword-fighting sequences. But, as with the verbs and inventory, there are no branching dialog trees to be found in *Loom*. Instead, when the player talks to someone, the player just watches the conversation unfold as a non-interactive cut-scene, unable to control it. On one level, this would appear to remove a degree of player interaction with the game. But, in the final analysis, the branching conversation tree systems always contain a finite number of branches, and hence most such systems devolve into the player simply clicking on each of the options, one by one. (*The Secret of Monkey Island* is actually one of the few examples of a game that actually adds depth to the gameplay with branching conversations.) For *Loom*, Moriarty went with the cut-scene conversations since they were the most effective system for conveying his story. Again, Moriarty was focused on his storytelling goal, and he let no adventure game conventions stand in his way.

User Interface

The interface in *Loom* is the epitome of simplicity, requiring the player only to use her mouse and a single button. This, of course, makes the game very easy to learn and play for anyone at all familiar with a point-and-click system. This is in sharp contrast to many other adventure games, particularly the text-only adventures that had their heyday in the 1980s, including those that Moriarty had worked on. Nearly all of these games include a text parser which, ideally, allows the player to enter whatever she wants her character to do using natural language. "Get book," "Northwest," "Open door with red key," and "Look at painting," are all examples of common commands from such text adventures. The limitation, unfortunately, was that many text parsers did not feature a complete set of the words in the English language, nor could they properly parse complex sentences. In fact, Infocom, the company which published Moriarty's *Wishbringer*, *Trinity*, and *Beyond Zork*, had the best text parser available by far. Yet still the parser could be challenging to use. Especially frustrating was when the player knew exactly what he needed to do in the game, but he could not find the correct words to say it. Not to mention the fact that, for the system to work, the player is required to spell everything correctly, a task at which few people excel. At the very best, one could become used to the idiosyncrasies of a text parser over time, but to a beginner the dominant feeling was one of frustration.

Loom keeps its interface as simple as possible by having the player interact with the game-world by using only the mouse.

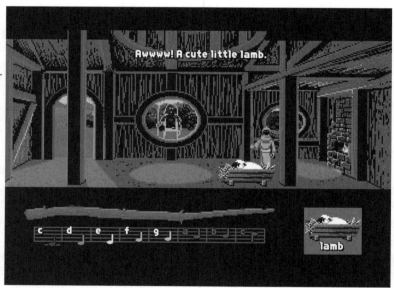

Indeed, in the excerpt from the manual included earlier, the text parsers of old are derided. It seems that Moriarty was ready to move on to a more intuitive and easy-to-learn interface. Of course, one of the primary requirements of any interface is that it be easy to learn. The challenges the player faces should be in the game-world itself, not in the controls he has to manipulate in order to affect that game-world. *Maniac Mansion* had already used an entirely point-and-click interface, and *Loom* borrowed a lot from that game's mechanics, at least in terms of world navigation. The player could move his character, Bobbin Threadbare, through the world simply by clicking on the location where he wanted him to go. This seems quite obvious to modern gamers who have seen countless point-and-click movement systems in games ranging from *Diablo* to *Grim Fandango* to *Command & Conquer*. Part of the beauty of the system is its obviousness; once one has seen it in action, one cannot imagine how else you would direct a character using a mouse.

However, *Maniac Mansion* and other graphical adventures had still included verbs for the player to click on. These verbs were basically a holdover from the text parsers, where the player would click first on an object and then on a verb in order to manipulate that object accordingly. Some other graphical adventures had replaced these verbs with icons which functioned identically to their text counterparts. Of course, in many cases there was only one verb/icon which would have any useful effect on a particular object, hence making the functionality of the icons largely extraneous. *Loom* eliminated the verbs entirely to allow the user to simply double-click on a given object and then have the game figure out what the player wanted to do with the object. If the player double-clicked on a person, Bobbin Threadbare would talk to him or her. If it was an object with text on it, Bobbin would read it. If it was a sheep, he would poke it. The game works with the player instead of against him, allowing the player to perform only the actions that will be useful to him. The double-click is an obvious extension of the single click. The single click moves Bobbin to that object; a double-click has him attempt to use it. Obviously, this input system is also identical to how point-and-click is used on the Macintosh and Windows platforms, so it has the added advantage that players are likely to understand it before they even start playing. The lesson to be learned here is that copying input ideas from established standards is almost always better than making up something new. Whatever slight gain one might achieve with a new input method is almost always negated by the frustration the player experiences while trying to learn it.

The Drafts System

While the game may do away with an inventory, verbs, and branching conversations, it does add a unique and well-designed game mechanic accessible through the player's distaff. This system allows the player to cast the equivalent of spells on various objects in the world. This system is quite different from spell-casting systems in any other games, and was especially revelatory in 1990. Again, the interface is entirely point and click, and it is a system which is very easy to learn.

The system is based around the player hearing different tones in different situations and then repeating those tones on their staff, in a manner reminiscent of a game of simon says. If the player double-clicks on a particular spinning wheel, a series of four tones will be played. These tones will also be reflected on the player's distaff, which is displayed at the bottom of the screen. Below the distaff are a series of musical notes that correspond to position on the distaff: c, d, e, f, and so forth, up to a full octave. When the player hears the tones for the first time, these notes light up to show the player visually what the different notes are. The player must then remember this series of tones (usually by writing it down), and then can repeat the tones in order to cast a particular "draft" or spell on a different object. The player repeats the notes simply by clicking on different locations of the distaff, a beautifully intuitive interface.

If the player plays the game in the expert setting, the learning of drafts becomes significantly more difficult. The musical notation is no longer present on the screen, and now the player only hears the notes; they no longer flash on the distaff. This forces the player to "play it by ear" in order to succeed. This, coupled with the fact that the tones required for a draft change with every game, gives the game significantly more replayability than many other adventure games. The musical nature of the drafts and of the entire game is a tremendous break from most other games that can be played with the sound completely off. Instead of just using music for sonic wallpaper, *Loom* beautifully makes the music an integral part of the gameplay.

The order of the tones can also be reversed to cause the opposite effect of playing the tones forward. The objects the player double-clicks on to originally learn the tones all correspond to the drafts they teach the player: double-clicking on a blade teaches the "sharpen" draft, double-clicking on water dripping out of a flask teaches the "emptying" draft, double-clicking on a pot full of bubbling dye will teach the "dye" draft, and so forth. Spinning drafts with the distaff is the primary method for performing actions on objects in the game. Sometimes the draft learned is not entirely obvious, and some creative thinking is required of the player in order to figure out which draft to use where. Drafts that are learned for use in one application will turn out to have related but different applications later. For instance, a draft that at first hatches an egg actually turns out to be quite handy for opening doors. A draft that heals a human can also be used to heal a rip in the fabric of the universe. All the connections are subtle yet logical. The manipulation of these drafts makes up the primary source of puzzles in the game, and they are used in such a way that the puzzles are never overly convoluted. *Loom* is one of the few adventure games where, once a puzzle is completed, the player never feels that the puzzle was arbitrary or capricious.

Difficulty

Once again, from the comments in the manual, one can infer that *Loom* was made from the start to be an easy game to play. One definitely gets the sense that the game truly wants the player to succeed, and hopes the player will see the end of its lovely story. Traditionally, adventure games prided themselves on vexing the player, on making him play the game again and again until, after much suffering, a reward was doled out.

Loom made a dramatic break from other adventure games by preventing the player from ever being killed or from ever getting stuck. Many adventure games included countless ways to die, thereby punishing players who had forgotten to save their game. Some adventure games would also allow the player to progress in the game even though she may have forgotten to do something fundamental earlier in the game. Then the player would get to a location, not have the object needed there, and have no way of going back to get it. In effect the player was dead, since she could not progress in the game, but this was a worse kind of death: it was death masquerading as life, where the player could still interact with the game-world but had no chance of actually winning the game. *Loom* set a standard which many subsequent adventure games have emulated: do not be unfair to the player.

Some cries were made by players that *Loom* was too easy. Indeed, the adventure game enthusiasts who had been hardened on the adventure games that came before *Loom* found it very easy to finish. They were used to dying around every corner and spending hours bashing their head against nearly incomprehensible puzzles. Indeed, many adventure gamers were accustomed to not being able to finish the games at all, at least not without buying a hint book. But the problem with making games that only appealed to the veteran enthusiasts was that it made it hard for any new players to start playing adventure games. If the player was not already experienced with these twisted and convoluted exercises in masochism, there was a good chance an adventure game would frustrate that player so much that he would feel no desire to try another one.

Story

With the game mechanics focused in order to emphasize the game's storytelling component, the entire game would be for naught if the story Moriarty wished to tell was not of the highest quality. Fortunately, it is. The story of Bobbin Threadbare, the chosen "Loom-Child" whose task is to restore the fabric of reality, is one of simple beauty and great poignancy. On his seventeenth birthday, Bobbin is summoned before the elders only to watch in amazement as they are transformed into swans. Dame Hetchel, the weaver who has been as a mother to Bobbin, explains to him the dire situation: the young weaver must discover what is slowly destroying the Loom and save it before it is too late. Thus Bobbin's adventure begins, with his trips to the various guilds of the land of *Loom*, drawing to a unique climax complete with a bittersweet ending. Along the way bits of the trademark, wise-cracking LucasArts humor are included (a style of humor found at its most intense in *The Secret of Monkey Island)*, though never so much that it dominates the story. Some players might see the story as strictly aimed at children, but *Loom* is a children's game in the same way *The Hobbit* is a children's book, *The Dark Crystal* is a children's movie, or *Bone* is a children's comic book. All contain enough sophistication and intelligence that one does not need to be a child to enjoy them, merely childlike.

Much of *Loom's* success rides on the strength of its fantastic and whimsical story.

The story is ideally suited to the gameplay that *Loom* includes, with navigation and the spinning of drafts being the player's only actions. At the same time the story never seems contrived for the sake of the gameplay, as many adventure game stories do. The text in the story is kept to a bare minimum, never going into excessive detail about anything, allowing the player's imagination to fill in the holes. It is a story that is told well visually, with the player's exploration and exper- imentation with the distaff matching the emotional temperament of the character he is playing, Bobbin Threadbare. Since Bobbin first acquires the staff at the begin- ning of the game, it makes logical sense that he would not yet be an expert at it. Thus the player's many failed attempts to use the drafts fit perfectly with Bobbin's character. This is in contrast to many adventure games where, though the player is controlling an intelligent, experienced character, the player must complete idiotic puzzles such as figuring out the character's password to log onto a computer sys- tem, when obviously the character being controlled would already know this information.

One problem with third-person adventure games, games where the player sees her character in the game instead of just seeing what that character would see, is that often the character in question has such a strong personality and appearance that it may be difficult for the player to feel properly immersed in the game. If the character is too much of a departure from one the player could see herself being, the player may become frustrated when that character speaks lines of dialog she would not say herself or performs other stupid actions. *Loom* works around this problem by putting Bobbin Threadbare inside a cloak, with the player only ever seeing his eyes. This keeps the main character anonymous enough that the player could believe that, in fact, it is herself inside that cloak. At the one point in the game where Bobbin takes off his hood the game quickly cuts away to a different scene, almost poking fun at the continued anonymity of the main character. And Bobbin's dialog is kept level and anonymous enough that he never says anything which might annoy the player. Many game developers and publishers speak of cre- ating strong characters, perhaps ones that can be used for action figures and movie rights later on. But what often keeps a game enjoyable for the player is a more anonymous character, one the player can sculpt in her mind into her own idea of a hero.

Loom as an Adventure Game

For all of its strengths, *Loom* is still an adventure game, and indeed a fairly linear one. Adventure games are the genre of computer games most concerned with tradi- tional storytelling, while at the same time often being the least encouraging of player creativity. The story being told in an adventure game is the designer's story, one that was clearly established ahead of time, and one that allows the player only to experience it without really being able to change its outcome. The critics of adventure games are quick to point out that, really, adventure games are not games at all, but merely a series of puzzles strung together with bits of story between them. The puzzles, regardless of their form, serve as locked doors between the different

parts of the story, and in order to experience the rest of the story, the player must unlock that door by completing the puzzle. Games, they say, are required to react to the player, while a puzzle provides a more static challenge, one that, once solved, is not nearly as much fun to try again. These critics suggest that once the story is experienced, because of its static nature it is hardly worth experiencing again.

Loom's gameplay centers on the player solving simple yet elegant puzzles. Once solved, the puzzles do not provide much replay value.

And *Loom*, for all its beauty and strength of design, still succumbs to some of the problems of adventure games. During the conversation cut-scenes, the game is completely linear and the player has no control of the game whatsoever. This might be more acceptable in smaller doses, but some of the cut-scenes in *Loom* go on for a significant amount of time. The game can also sometimes degrade into the player trying to click everything on the screen, just to see which objects can be manipulated. There is a good chance that, if an object can be manipulated, the player will need to do something with it to complete the game. This is both good and bad: good in that it limits the player's actions to useful ones instead of leading him down a false path after red herrings and pointless diversions; bad in that it severely limits the interactiveness of the world. And sometimes the game's landscape art is drawn in such a way that it is difficult to figure out where Bobbin can navigate and where he cannot.

But, truly, these are minor complaints. Is it so bad that *Loom* is a storytelling experience with a predetermined story? The game is only as worthwhile to play again as it is to read a book or see a movie a second time. Of course, repeat reading and viewing is something many people enjoy, if the work is good enough to warrant it. *Loom* may not be as interactive as *Civilization*, but does every game need to be that interactive? A game of *Civilization* may tell an interesting story of the rise of an empire and the advancement of technology, but to me there has never been a game of *Civilization* with a story as compelling and touching as *Loom*'s. Critics might ask, why not tell *Loom*'s story as a book or an animated feature? Sure, the story could work in those forms, but would the player be so drawn in as when he is allowed to explore and interact with the story-world in question? Through an adventure game like *Loom*, the player gains a certain emotional attachment to and involvement in the events that transpire that is impossible in other media. Perhaps it is not a game by an exclusionary definition, but that does not make it any less worthwhile.

Chapter 13:
Getting the Gameplay Working

"Those who wish to be must put aside the alienation, get on with the fascination, the real relation, the underlying theme."

— Neil Peart

Hollywood has a system. It is a well-known system with a well-defined goal, where the largest unknown is "where is the money coming from?" not "how will we ever make this film?" Hollywood producers and talent know how to go from a treatment to a script, through multiple revisions of that script, and then how to bring together the personnel that will make that script into a film, on time and on budget (usually). Hollywood as a whole has much less of a handle on whether the final film will be any good or not, but they do at least know how to get the film made. Seldom does a film already in production have its script completely rewritten, its personnel trimmed, or more people added willy-nilly to its cast and crew. Customarily, films are completed months and months before they are scheduled to be released. Granted, sometimes the film may never make it beyond the script stage or, once completed, may not get released as originally intended. But, overall, Hollywood has an efficient system for creating films.

On the other hand, computer game developers have no such system. The development of a game design is a chaotic, unpredictable process filled with problems not even the most experienced producer, designer, or programmer can foresee. Customarily, development on computer games continues until the absolute last possible second, with changes made right up to the time the gold master disc is shipped to the duplicators. For PC games, usually a patch follows shortly thereafter, since the game was never properly finished in the first place. Why is computer game development so unpredictable while film production is so predictable? Granted, Hollywood has been making movies for a lot longer than the computer game industry has been making games, which gives them a leg up. But beyond that, Hollywood is making a much more predictable product. Different movies may have unique stories and characters, and may even use a variation on cinematic techniques, but a lot of film-making is a known quantity.

Original games, on the other hand, are a totally new animal every time. Part of the problem is the shifting technology targets, where programmers must learn about new consoles, operating systems, and 3D accelerator cards for each project, and the fact that so many games feel the need to have a cutting-edge graphics engine. But purely from a design standpoint, a truly original game is far more unique compared with other contemporary games than a movie is from other films being made at the same time. Consider games like *Civilization*, *The Sims*, or *Doom*. The gameplay contained in these games was radically different from anything that came before them. Granted, many games are far less experimental and innovative than the games I just listed, and games that have followed more of a formula have had a much better success rate in terms of coming out on time and on budget. This includes titles such as the Infocom adventure games, the Sierra adventure titles, the annual revisions of sports games, or the new versions of arcade driving games. However, these are games which, though perhaps including new content in terms of

Doom offered gameplay so different from any game that came before it that the game's development was something of a bold experiment.

new stories and graphics, offer gameplay that is very much the same as the previous year's offerings. When a game tries to implement a new form of gameplay, even if it is only a variation on a proven theme, all hope of predictability in its development is thrown to the four winds.

Only really good designers have any hope of predicting what is going to be fun or not in a game, and even the most experienced designers will tell you that they use a lot of prototyping, experimentation, and general floundering around until they come up with the gameplay they want. These talented veteran designers do not have crystal balls; they only have an improved chance of anticipating what will make for compelling gameplay. They do not truly "know" more than anyone else.

The closest thing game development has to a reliable system for developing an original game is to get some small part of the gameplay working first, before moving ahead to build the rest of the game. This may be called a prototype, a demo, a proof-of-concept, a level, or simply the current build of the game. This is not merely a demo to show off the game's technology. Instead, it is something that shows off the game's gameplay, which includes all of the features described in the game's focus, as discussed in Chapter 5. This demo should be something any member of the development team can pick up, play, and say, "Yes, this is fun, I want to play this." By concentrating on getting a small piece of the game fully functional and enjoyable, the developer can get a much better sense of whether the final game is going to be any fun or not. If the gameplay just does not turn out as anticipated, the prototype provides an early enough warning that the game needs to either be redirected in a more promising direction or, in the worst cases, aborted entirely.

The Organic Process

In the games I work on, I prefer to keep the development process as organic as possible and I try not to plan anything out too thoroughly. This may be the opposite of the approach many development studios prefer, but I find it to be the most effective method for developing the best game possible. Due to the highly unpredictable nature of game design, which I discussed above, a more organic process leaves me room and time to experiment with how the gameplay will work. Instead of writing a mammoth document, I can first try to get some portion of the game to be fun before I start adding detail and length to the game. Adding too much content to the game too early can be very wasteful, if not actually restrictive. This obtrusive detail can take the form of an elaborate design document, a script for the game's dialog, detailed maps of the various areas the player will encounter, or even fully built levels for the game. It makes no sense whatsoever to create these elements of the game until you have a firm grasp on what the gameplay will be, and have a working prototype that proves the gameplay to be fun.

Too Much Too Soon

The problem with creating scripts, documents, or levels without a prototype is that these assets will make assumptions about how the gameplay will function, assumptions which may turn out to be incorrect once the gameplay is actually functional. If a designer builds an elaborate game design on principles which turn out to be flawed, that entire game design will probably need to be reworked or, more likely, thrown away. But if people have devoted large amounts of time to creating these flawed assets, they are going to be understandably reluctant to throw them away. If a designer gets too attached to those ideas, even if they later prove to be unworkable, he may try to cling to them. After all, a lot of work went into planning the game in advance with a long design document, how can it all just be thrown away? Cannot the assets be reworked to be usable? If you are not bold enough to throw away your inappropriate content, in the end you run the risk of producing a game that is patched together after the fact instead of built from the start with a clear sense of direction.

When I set about working on my first published game, *Odyssey: The Legend of Nemesis*, admittedly I had little idea of what I was doing. I had inherited a game engine and some portion of the game's mechanics from the previous developer. At the time, the project was very meagerly funded, and as a result, the publisher only requested a meager amount of documentation about where the game was going. I drew up a six-page document which described, in brief, all of the adventures the player would go on. First of all, none of these documents were very detailed, with just one page per major island in the game. That left me lots of room to maneuver.

Second, by the time I had implemented the first two islands, I had learned enough about how the game truly worked that I decided to throw away the last three islands and design them over again. Since I had only written brief outlines of the gameplay in the first place, I did not actually lose much work.

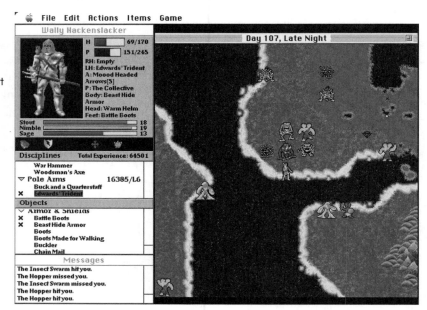

Keeping the development documentation light and using place-holder art kept *Odyssey's* development extremely organic.

Another interesting aspect of *Odyssey's* creation was that I developed the game entirely using place-holder art. Along with the game's engine, I had inherited a fair amount of art from another project, and kept using that as much as possible. Since the project was underfunded, I did not have an artist to work with during most of the game's development, so this decision was made more out of necessity than foresight. However, it did mean that by the time I had the money to hire artists to finish the project, all of the game's design was done and fully playable, and as a result the artists created almost no art for the game that went unused. Using the place-holder art had not hindered the game's development in the slightest. I concentrated first on getting all of the gameplay working, and then was able to focus on the visuals. Since I was not constrained by the thought of losing already created art assets if I changed the design, I was able to take the design in whatever direction seemed most appropriate while I was working on it.

On *Centipede 3D*, a significant amount of work was done before the gameplay was actually fun, and almost all of that work had to be thrown out as a result. The original idea for the gameplay had little to do with how the original *Centipede* functioned from a gameplay standpoint, and featured a more meandering, less-directed style of gameplay. Using this original gameplay conception, six levels were actually built and numerous other levels were planned out on paper. For various reasons, the gameplay simply was not much fun, and we began to look at what could be done about that problem. In the end, we made the enemy AI function more like the original game's enemies and adjusted the gameplay accordingly. When we tried it we were not sure if it would work, but that gameplay style turned out to work quite well. Unfortunately, much of the level design work that had been done was lost. All of the levels that had been designed on paper were thrown away because they were incompatible with this new style of gameplay. Of the six levels that had been actually built, three had to be discarded in order to support the new gameplay, while the others had to be changed significantly in order to play well.

Looking back, if we had focused on making the gameplay fun before making a large number of levels, we could have avoided a lot of extra work and wasted effort. With the gameplay functional, we were able to draw up documents describing how the rest of the game would function. For the most part, we were able to hold to those documents throughout the remainder of the development process, with only minor changes necessary. Of course it would have been catastrophic to the project if we had been unable or unwilling to throw away the work we had already done. If we had tried to keep all of the levels without changing them significantly, the game would have shown it and those levels would have been greatly inferior to the ones made with the proper gameplay in mind. If we had been foolish enough to stick to the initial design completely, the entire game would have suffered and the end product would not have been as fun as it turned out to be.

Keep It Simple

Early in development, it makes sense to work with only your focus instead of a long design document. The focus is short enough that it can easily be completely rewritten if your game changes direction. Yet, at the same time, the focus will give you a clear direction for what you are trying to achieve with the gameplay you are attempting to implement. In the prototyping stage, the focus may change many, many times as you shift the game's goals to match what you find to be working out in terms of gameplay. When your prototyping is done, you will have a solid focus that you can reasonably hope to follow for the rest of the game's development.

Unfortunately, you may not always have the option of keeping the game design process organic. If you are working at an established company, you may have a fully staffed team working on your project from the very beginning, and those people need to be kept busy making art, building levels, or coding up systems, even though there may not yet be a functional and fun gameplay prototype. It does not take a large team to get the initial gameplay working, and indeed such a large team may only get in your way as you try to keep them busy while experimenting with how the gameplay will work. You may also have demands from whomever is

funding your project's development, whether it is your employer or the publisher. Whoever is paying the bills may want to see a complete design document or script up-front, before a prototype of the game has been developed. You may be forced to abandon those documents later as the gameplay turns out to work differently than you had anticipated. Obviously, crafting these documents prematurely can be quite wasteful, yet you are forever beholden to whomever is providing the funding for your project. In some ways, if at all possible, it may make sense to self-fund the project until you have a fully functional prototype. Work on it "under the radar" if you are at a large company, or work on the gameplay prototype before you try to find a publisher. Besides, a playable demo will make the game easier to sell to a publisher or a green-light committee. Nothing proves to the financiers that your game is moving in the right direction better than a compelling prototype.

Building the Game

The best way to build your game is incrementally. Instead of working a little bit on all the different components of the game, you should try to complete one system before moving on to the next. Work on the most basic and essential systems first, and then build the systems that depend on that system. This allows you to implement a system, test it out, see if it "feels" right, and only then move on to the next system. That way, if you must change the underlying system to get it to work properly, your subsequent systems can be changed accordingly. It can often lead to disaster when you have a number of programmers concurrently working on coding up a variety of systems that work together. If one system has to change, other systems may need to be radically reworked. Better to build a solid foundation before trying to build on top of it. Programmers often enjoy working on their own isolated part of the code without fully considering how it will have to interface with the rest of the project. It is important for your programming team to be constantly focused on the big picture of making the game playable and fun.

Core Technology

Of course, all computer games rely on an underlying technology which has very little to do with the gameplay, usually referred to as the game's engine. Certainly you need to make sure that this underlying technology functions at a certain level before any work can be done on the gameplay. However, you do not need the engine to be perfect or feature complete before you can start building your prototype. Indeed, on a project with a cutting-edge engine, waiting until the engine is truly finished may be too late to spend enough time refining the game itself. The peril of working with unknown technology is designing around projections of the capabilities of the technology. If you design your game thinking you will be able to have ten enemies on the screen at once and your engine turns out to be only able to handle three, you will need to radically alter your design to accommodate this restriction. It should be no surprise that the best-designed games are often ones that did not use the most cutting-edge technology available when they were released.

If the technology is simply not ready, I know a number of game designers who start off prototyping their game using technology from a previous project. It is rare that technology will actually make or break a game design, though it may make or break the game itself. But technology, as unpredictable as it may sometimes be, is still more of a known quantity than game design, so it makes sense not to worry about it when you are first prototyping your game. Since the first few areas you create will probably be thrown away later anyway, it is not that wasteful to get them working using a technology that you will eventually throw away as well.

Incremental Steps

Once your technology is to a point where you can start developing the gameplay as I mentioned earlier, try to break down the game design into the most fundamental tasks that need to be accomplished and then the tasks which build on those. For example, suppose you are building an action game in which the player navigates a humanoid character around the game-world fighting insurance agents with a flyswatter while collecting kiwi fruits. Getting the player's navigation system working is a logical first task to tackle. First, get the character moving forward and backward and turning, allowing for basic navigation of the world. Work on this movement until it feels pretty good, until you find yourself enjoying playing the game in this simple, navigation-only way. Now you can build on that by adding more movement options, such as strafing, crouching, and jumping. As you add each new movement type, make sure that it does not break any of the previous types of movement and that they all work well together. Only once that is firmly in place should you try adding the ability for the player to use the flyswatter. With the flyswatter fun to use, at least in some limited way, it makes sense to add the insurance agents into the game. The AI's functionality can be broken down into building blocks just like the player's movement was. First, get the AI agents in the world so that the player can whack them with the flyswatter. Next, get the agents moving around the game-world before finally adding the ability for them to do their "audit" or "excessive paperwork" attack. Finally, you can add the kiwis to the world and the ability for the player to pick them up and launch them with his flyswatter. What is essential in this step-by-step process is that at each step along the way the game is still playable and fun. When you add something to the game that breaks a previous portion or simply makes it less fun, you must address this problem immediately. Now is the time to alter your design as necessary, before the game swings into full production.

Throughout the project's development, I think it is important to always keep a version of your game playable. Often programming teams will go for a long time coding up various pieces of the game without having a functional version that someone can sit down and play. It is very easy to lose sight of your gameplay goals when your game spends a lot of time in an unplayable state. Certainly the game can be broken in many ways, with various components that do not yet work as they are supposed to and with place-holder art used in many locations. But as long as you always have a playable game, team members are able to pick it up and play it, and see what they are working on and how it impacts the game. And if anything someone adds or changes makes this playable version of the game less fun, you can immediately discover this problem and rectify it.

A Fully Functional Area

Once you have many of the elements of your game mechanics working and you are happy with them, the next step is to make an entire section of the game that functions just like you want it to play in the final game. In many game genres this means one particular level of the game. You may think you have all of the components of your gameplay functional, but once you actually try to make an entire area playable you will quickly discover what you forgot to implement or failed to anticipate. Concentrate on getting this one level as close to a final state as possible before moving on to the creation of other levels. If you are observant you will learn many lessons about how level design must work for your particular game through the creation of this one level, lessons which will help to eliminate the element of guesswork from the creation of the other levels in the game. Once you are done with this level, it will no longer be the best you can do; you will have learned a lot, and subsequent levels you create will be better thought out from the beginning. Though you do not need to throw away this prototype level yet, keep in mind that you should probably scrap it before the game ships.

One example of this is from the development of my game *Damage Incorporated*. The very first level I created for the single-player game was done before I fully understood the game mechanics or the level creation tools I would be using. As a result it was far from fun to play and was quickly thrown away. The second level I made, though certainly not the best in the game, was good enough to make the final cut. The game also included death-match style networking, which used a completely different set of levels. Due to time constraints, I spent significantly less time balancing the network play than I would have liked. In particular, the first level I created for the network game, "My Mind is Numb, My Throat is Dry," ended up not being that much fun to play. It had a number of cool areas but they did not flow together very well and a number of sections in the level were unfair and unbalanced death traps. One of my playtesters even suggested it would be best to

The first network level made for *Damage Incorporated*, pictured here, was also the worst one in the game. It would have been better to scrap it and construct a new one.

throw it away and start a new level from scratch. Unfortunately, I did not have the time to make a replacement and it ended up shipping with the game. Fortunately there were seven other network levels that were significantly more fun to play. Nonetheless, it would have been better if I had completely scrapped my first attempt at a network level and made a new one instead.

Something you must be conscious of as you are building the first fully playable section of your game is how difficult the game is to play. Often difficulty can be adjusted and tweaked later in the development process, during playtesting and balancing. However, games also have a fundamental difficulty which is more intrinsic to their nature and which cannot be easily adjusted late in the development cycle. As you are working on getting your gameplay prototype working, try to look at it honestly in terms of how difficult it will be for novice players to get into. Bring in some friends or coworkers and have them play the game. Observe how easily they manage to pick up the game. It is much simpler to make a game harder than to make it easier. If you find that your game is turning out to be harder to play than you had hoped, now is the time to alter the game design in order to make the game easier to play, before it is too late.

Going Through Changes

A big part of the organic process of game design is being able to throw away your own work and, potentially, that of the rest of your team. This includes art, code, levels, and even general design itself; all of the game's content may need to change as

your gameplay changes. A particular asset may not be flawed in and of itself, but if it does not gel properly with the way the gameplay is working out, you may need to get rid of that asset and start from scratch. Many developers are unwilling to do this, and it shows in their games. Either their games are shackled to an initial design document which turned out not to work as well in practice as it did in theory, or their games retain a hodgepodge of components from before their direction was finalized. Once a designer decides that the game's direction needs to change, all of the assets of the game must be assessed to see if they can fit with that new direction. If they cannot, they must be reworked or remade.

As I have discussed, my project *Centipede 3D* changed course significantly in the middle of development, resulting in us having to throw away a large amount of work. Fortunately, no one on the team was unhappy to do so, since we all realized it was in the best interests of the project. With other projects I have worked on, I have been more stubborn and ignored the pleadings of coworkers and friends when they said something needed to be reworked or changed. I was reluctant to throw away perfectly good work, even though it no longer fit with the game. Sometimes the first step in fixing the problems with your game design is admitting that you have a problem.

Of course, you have to be careful not to go too far in the other direction by discarding content that does not need to be thrown away. As you work on a project, you are likely to become overly familiar with some of the content you have created, and familiarity can breed contempt. For example, after working with a level for a long time, a designer is likely to become sick of looking at the same geometry day after day. The designer may then feel the need to rework that level, not because it really needs it, but simply because it will be something new. This is wasted effort, since for the player playing the game for the first time, the level will be new and exciting. Changing your game's content just for the sake of changing it can lead to extra debugging time, delays in shipping your project, and general frustration for team members who do not know why perfectly good work is being thrown away and redone.

First impressions are very important, especially in game design. Always try to remember how you first felt when you played a level or tried to pull off a particular move. Was it too hard or too easy? Was it intuitive or confusing? Another big problem with working on a project for a long time is that the designers can grow accustomed to flaws in the design. Maybe the controls are unintuitive or a particular enemy attacks the player in an arbitrary and unfair way. As they play the game repeatedly, designers will learn to overcome and avoid these problems in the game design, giving them the false impression that nothing is wrong with the game. Playtesting is an essential tool for revealing the weaknesses in the game design that the development team has grown accustomed to, as I will discuss in Chapter 23, "Playtesting." However, before you get to the playtesting stage, try to always remember what your first impression of a particular aspect of the game was. Ask yourself if the problems you saw back then have been fixed or if they are still there, creating frustration for others who experience the game for the first time. It is best to fix these problems as soon as you observe them because, if you put them off, you are likely to forget about them.

Programming

This chapter is written from the vantage point of someone who is a designer and a programmer, as I have been on all of my projects. Being in such a position has many unique advantages, especially in terms of being able to experiment with gameplay. A designer/programmer is able to have an idea for some gameplay and then instantly be able to attempt to implement it exactly how she wants it. A designer who does not program is forced to first communicate her idea for the gameplay to the programmer and hope that he understands the design. Often the communication will break down and the designer will not get exactly what she wanted: the feature in question may have an inferior implementation than what the designer had in mind. As a result, either the game is weaker or the designer must go back to the programmer and try to explain to him how a particular feature is actually supposed to work. Since game design is such an iterative and experimental process, there must be a constant circle of feedback between the designer and the programmer. Obviously, this process is greatly simplified if the designer and programmer are the same person.

I often find that, as a designer who programs, I can try out ideas much more easily. In fact, many of the ideas I have I would feel bad trying to get someone else to work on, since I lack the confidence in them myself to waste someone else's time with them. But in the end some of these strange ideas turn out to work quite well in the game, and if I had never been able to experiment with the code myself, the ideas might never have been attempted.

A designer/programmer will also often be able to better understand the technology involved in a project, and be able to see what is easily accomplished and what is not. Often a designer who is not a programmer will suggest gameplay that is very difficult to implement in the engine. It may be that a different, though equally functional, type of gameplay will work better with the game's technology, and if the designer/programmer notices that, he will be able to greatly simplify the game's development. Say a designer wants a certain sword to have a particular behavior to communicate to the player that it is enchanted. The designer may request that the sword physically appear to bend somewhat within the player character's hand. The programmer assigned to set up this functionality curses the designer, knowing this is a practically impossible task given the constraints of the engine they are using. The designer does not realize that creating a fancy particle system around the sword is much easier to do, though he would be perfectly happy with that solution. As a result, the programmer, fearing to resist the designer's request, spends a lot of time on a challenging implementation, when a much simpler one would have satisfied the designer had he understood the technology better. Understanding the feasibility of ideas is a skill which comes with understanding how game programming fundamentally works, and how the engine you are working with is architected. Even if you are not actively programming on the project you are developing, you can better understand what can be easily accomplished with the technology and what feature will suck away resources for months without adding that much to the game.

Another problem arises when the designer and programmer have a different idea of what the gameplay for the project should be. I have heard one designer refer to this as the "pocket veto." A designer may come to a programmer with an explanation of how gameplay for a particular section of the game should work, and if the programmer does not agree, he can simply not implement what the designer has requested. He may even pretend that the designer's request is very hard or actually impossible to implement when it is not. A designer who cannot program will be beholden to the whims of often-temperamental programmers, which can be eternally frustrating.

I am of the opinion that it is worth learning to program if you want to be a designer. In fact, that is why I originally pursued programming. It is out of the scope of this book to actually teach you to program, and there are certainly plenty of books available to help you learn what you will need to work on games. Much of effective programming is a matter of discipline. And you do not even need to be a terribly good programmer to have it help your design out immensely. Indeed, almost all the designer/programmers I know will insist that they are not very good programmers, but that they are persistent enough to get what they want out of their games. As I have mentioned, knowing how to program will give you a better sense of what is easy to do in a game and what is hard. Furthermore, if you want your game design to turn out a particular way, often the only way to ensure that it turns out that way is to program it yourself.

If you are not going to be programming on your project, it is essential that you have a lead programmer with a good sense of gameplay, someone whose opinion you can trust. Indeed, you will be well advised to only have programmers on your team who have a good sense of what makes games fun. In the end, there are an infinite number of small decisions that programmers make which will have a profound impact on the gameplay, details that no designer can anticipate. These little details have an enormous impact on the final game, determining how the game "feels" to play. Often, unmotivated or disinterested lead programmers can be found to be behind games that seem like good ideas in theory but just do not turn out to be any fun. Many projects have gone from promising starts to dissatisfying final products as the result of programmers who merely implement various features from a specification and never take a moment to look at the whole game and see if it is any fun.

This book includes interviews with six people who are indisputably some of the most talented game designers in the history of the industry. It is interesting to note that of those six, all were programmers at one point in their careers and programmed in some capacity on their most respected games. Indeed, back in the early days of the computer game industry, the development process was of a small enough scale that one person was doing all the work, so there was no need to separate the role of designer and programmer. Nonetheless, three of the interview subjects still serve as the lead programmer on their own projects. This is not to say that one cannot be a great designer without being a programmer, but I think designers who are able to program have a leg up on those who cannot, an advantage which allows them to make better games.

When is It Fun?

Getting your gameplay working is one of the most essential parts of game design, yet it is also one of the most difficult to try to explain or teach. A lot of the process involves understanding what is fun about a game in a way that no book can ever explain. Indeed, a game's design changes so often during the implementation stage that I do not believe a designer who is not actively working on the game during that period can truly be considered to have designed it. If this so-called designer simply typed up a 200-page design document and handed it to the lead programmer to implement while the designer frolicked in Bora Bora, the lead programmer was then responsible for making the fundamental decisions which made the game fun or dull, stimulating or insipid, enjoyable or tedious. When the designer is AWOL during the implementation process, the lead programmer is the one who is actually designing the game.

So much of implementing your game design relies on personal "gut" reactions that it is no wonder people have great difficulty designing games for people other than themselves. This is why so many games that are aimed at the "mass market" but which are designed by people who are hard-core gamers turn out to be so terrible. The hard-core gamer doing the design wishes he was working on *Grim Fandango* but instead is stuck working on *Advanced Squirrel Hunting*. Even if he can overcome his contempt for the project itself, he will probably have no idea what the audience who may be interested in playing *Advanced Squirrel Hunting* wants in its games. Often features will be added to a game at the behest of marketing, over the protests of the development team. These features are always the worst in the game, not necessarily because they are bad ideas, but because the development team does not understand why they need to be added to the game or how they might improve the gameplaying experience. In the end, it is very hard to design a

Game developers do their best work when working on games they care about and enjoy. The excellent *Grim Fandango* appears to be a perfect example.

good game that you yourself do not enjoy playing. If you do not enjoy playing it, it is unlikely that anyone else will either, even if they technically fall into the demographic you were so carefully targeting.

The first step in designing a game is to get some portion of the gameplay working and playable. Once you have a prototype that you can play and which you find to be compelling and fun in the right amounts, you should step back and make sure that you have a firm grasp on what makes it fun and how that can be extended to the rest of the game. With that prototype as a model, you can now move on to make the rest of the content for the game, replicating the fundamental nature of the gameplay while keeping the additional content new and interesting. Now that you know that your game design is a good one, it may finally make sense to craft a thorough design document that explains that gameplay and explores what variations on it may be used for the rest of the game. This will provide a valuable guideline for the rest of the team in fleshing out the game. In some ways, once the prototype is working, the truly creative and challenging part of game design is done, and the rest of the game's development is simply repeating it effectively.

Chapter 14:
Interview: Chris Crawford

Today, Chris Crawford is probably best known for his contributions to the dialog of game design, including his founding of the Computer Game Developer's Conference, publishing the **Journal of Computer Game Design**, and writing the book **The Art of Computer Game Design**. In particular, **The Art of Computer Game Design**, though written in 1983, remains the best work ever published on the subject, and served as the inspiration for this book. The brilliance of Crawford's games cannot be denied either, including such undisputed classics as **Eastern Front (1941)**, **Balance of Power**, and Crawford's personal favorite, **Trust & Betrayal: The Legacy of Siboot**. For most of the '90s Crawford devoted himself to his labor of love, the interactive storytelling system called the Erasmatron, a tool which shows great promise for transforming interactive stories from mostly pre-written affairs into truly dynamic experiences.

What initially attracted you to making a computer play a game?

That actually started back in 1966, when I was a high school sophomore, and a friend of mine named David Zeuch introduced me to the Avalon Hill board wargames. We played those, and I thought they were a lot of fun. I played them into college, though I didn't have a lot of free time during my college years. When I was in graduate school, I ran into a fellow who worked at the computer center, and he was trying to get *Blitzkrieg*, an Avalon Hill game, running on the computer. I told him he was crazy. I said, "That can't be done, forget it." But that conversation planted a seed. I thought about it, and about a year later I decided I was going to attempt it. So I went to work and it turned out to be nowhere near as difficult as I had feared. So I ended up putting together a little program on an IBM 1130 in FORTRAN. It actually ran a computer game, a little tactical armored simulation. The debut of that game came early in 1976 when I showed it off at a little wargame convention that we held. Everybody played it and thought it was a great deal of fun. So then I bought myself a KIM-1 and redid the whole thing around that system. That design was unmatched for many years, because you had genuine hidden movement. I had built little tiny terminals, as I called them, and each player had his own little map and little pieces, and a screen to divide the two players. Two guys played this wargame, each one unaware of the position of the other. It was a lot of fun, and that was 1977 or '78.

What made you at first think it would be impossible?

The difficulties of organizing the artificial intelligence for it. I thought, "That's just going to be impossible." And the hex-grid motion, I figured that was probably computable, and in fact it turns out it's not that difficult. But I figured that doing armored tactical planning on the computer, at the time, seemed ridiculous. Now, you have to remember that was twenty-five years ago, and given the state of AI back then, I was really on rather solid ground thinking it impossible. But as it happens I solved that problem, marginally, within a year.

What made you think it would be worthwhile to put games on the computer?

I was driven by one thing and that was "blind" play. I was very concerned that, no matter how you looked at it, with board games you could always see what the other guy was up to. And that always really bothered me, because it was horribly unrealistic. It just didn't seem right, and I thought the games would be much more interesting blind. And, in fact, when we did them, they were immensely powerful games, far more interesting than the conventional games. And as soon as I saw that, I knew that this was *the* way to go. And board-play technology has never been able to match that simple aspect of it. It was so much fun sneaking up behind your opponent, and, as they say, sending 20 kilograms up his tail pipe. It was really impressive stuff, very heady times.

So from that early work, how did you come to work at Atari?

Well, actually a bit more transpired first. I got a Commodore Pet and programmed that in BASIC with some assembly language routines to handle the hex-grid stuff. I had shown my tactical armored game at some wargame conventions and everyone had been very impressed. So then I actually made *Tanktics* into a commercial product and sold it on the Commodore Pet for fifteen bucks. And then I did another game called *Legionnaire*, also on the Commodore Pet. And based on that I got a job at Atari, doing game design there. Actually, I was one of the few job candidates they had ever had who had any experience designing computer games. It's hard to appreciate just how tiny everything was. The very notion of a computer game was, itself, very esoteric.

What was the atmosphere like at Atari then?

It was heady. Again, it's very difficult for people nowadays to appreciate how different things were just twenty years ago. I remember a conversation with Dennis Koble. We met one morning in the parking lot as we were coming into work, and we were chatting on the way in. And I remember saying, "You know, some day game design will be a developed profession." And he said, "Yeah, maybe someday we'll be like rock stars!" And we both laughed at how absurd that thought was. There were, in the world, a couple dozen game designers, most of them at Atari. And everybody knew each other, at least everyone at Atari, and it was all very cozy. And many of them did not consider themselves to be game designers.

For example, I remember a meeting where the department manager said, "All right everybody, we need to print up new business cards for everybody, and we need to select what kind of title you want." And there was something of a debate among the staff whether they wanted to be listed as "Game Designer" or "Programmer." I remember people saying, "Gee, you know, if we put our titles down as Game Designer, we may not be able to get another job." And I think we ended up going with "Game Programmer." But game design was nowhere near the thing it is today, it was just a very obscure thing. I remember telling people when they'd ask me, "What do you do?" And I'd say, "I design games for Atari." And they'd say, "Wow. That's really strange. How do you do that?" It was a very exotic answer back then.

Were you able to do whatever you wanted in terms of game design?

It depended on what you were doing. If you were doing a VCS [Atari 2600] game, then you talked your games over with your supervisor, but there was considerable freedom. The feeling was, "We need plenty of games anyway, and we really need the creativity here, so just follow your nose, see what works, see if you can come up with anything interesting." And in general the supervisor gave you a lot of latitude, unless you were doing a straight rip-off of somebody else's design. So in that area we had lots of freedom. But once you got your design complete, there would be a design review where all of the other designers would look it over and make their comments. This wasn't a marketing thing, it was a design level review.

Everybody wanted to program the computer [the Atari 800] because it was so much more powerful than the VCS. So at the time I started, in 1979, the policy was that you had to prove yourself by doing a game on the VCS first. And only then could you go to the computer. Well, I mumbled and grumbled; I didn't like that idea at all. But I learned the VCS, and I did a game on it. However, another policy they had was that all games had to be done in 2K of ROM. They were just coming out with the 4K ROMs, but at the time those were rather expensive. And so the feeling was, "You can't do a 4K ROM. You've got to prove yourself, prove that you're a worthy designer if we're going to give you all that space. We've got to know you can use it well." So I had to do a 2K game.

And I did one called *Wizard*, which I think was rather clever and worked in 2K. Although I got it done in record time, I finished it just as Atari was starting to get its 4K games out. Everybody started realizing that the 4K games were not just a little better, but immensely superior to the 2K games. So there was a feeling that anything that was marketed is going to be compared against the 4K games, and my design as a 2K game just couldn't compare with a 4K game. So the other designers ended up saying, "This is a very nice design, for 2K, but it just doesn't cut it." They wanted it redesigned for 4K. I could have redesigned it for 4K and gotten it published, but my feeling was, "OK, look. I've done my game on the VCS, now I'd like to move on to the computer. So let's not screw around here." So I argued that, "Look, this was designed as a 2K game, we're not going to simply add features to it. If you want a 4K game, we start over; that's the only way to do it right." And mumble-mumble, I was able to sneak past it and be allowed to go straight to the Atari 800. So that game was never published. And I had no regrets.

So your biggest commercial success while at Atari was *Eastern Front (1941)*. But I understand that you had trouble convincing people that a wargame would be successful. Were you confident a lot of people would like it?

No no, I didn't really care. My feeling was, this is the game I wanted to design, so I did it in my spare time. This was nights and weekends. Meanwhile, I was doing plenty of other stuff at work. In October or November of 1980 I was promoted away from game design. I was basically the first hardware evangelist. I did for the Atari what Guy Kawasaki did for the Macintosh. And, actually, I was successful at that. I did a very good job of attracting people to work on the Atari, because it was so much better than the Apple and all it needed was a good technical salesman. So I traveled the country giving these seminars, handing out goodies, and so forth. And I generated a lot of excitement among the programmer community, and the Atari really took off. There was this explosion of software about a year after I started that task. I take primary credit for that.

So anyway, I started that task in October or November of 1980, and as part of that I was putting out these software demos to show off the various features of the Atari. And I told myself, "I'm finally going to take the time to teach myself this scrolling feature that everybody knows is in there, but nobody has actually gotten around to using." So I sat down and started messing around with it, and within a couple of weeks I had a very nice demo up and running. I built a big scrolling map and I thought, "Boy, this is pretty neat." And by the standards of the day this was revolutionary. It went way way way beyond anything else, just mind-blowing. And I remember taking that to S.S.I. which, at the time, was the top wargame company working on the Apple. And I showed it to the fellow there, and he was very unenthusiastic. He said, "Whoop-de-do, this will never make a good wargame." I think it was some kind of prejudice against Atari, that "Atari is not a real computer." I was kind of disjointed, and I thought, "Jeez, what a narrow-minded attitude." So I decided, "I'll do it myself." I did this game in the classic way that many games are done nowadays: I started off with a cute technical feature and said, "How can I show off this wonderful graphics trick?" So I said, "Let's build a game around the scrolling." I went to work and built *Eastern Front*. I had it working by June of '81, but the gameplay was awful. It took me about two months to finish up the gameplay. We released it through APX [the Atari Program Exchange] in August of 1981 and it was a huge success. It was generally considered to be the second definitive Atari game, the first being *Star Raiders* of course.

So you actually made the fancy graphical effects first, and then built the game around that?

That's a phase every designer has to go through. You start off designing around cute techie tricks, and as you mature as a designer you put that behind you.

So you ended up releasing the source code for *Eastern Front (1941)*. What motivated you to do that?

It was an extremely unconventional act. My feeling was, this is a fast-moving field. I'm good. I'll have new, wonderful technological discoveries by the time other people start using this. I'll be on to something else. I didn't feel any sense of possessiveness: "This is mine, I don't want anybody else to know." My feeling was and continues to be that we all profit more from the general advance of the industry. But I'm not an intellectual property anarchist. I do believe people have rights to claim certain things as theirs. I just feel that this should be done with great restraint, and only in situations where there is something very big which took a *lot* of work. I felt this was just a little techie stunt, no big deal. So I gave it away.

It's funny. There were a number of technologies that I gave away that nobody really used. The scrolling one was a good example: there were a couple of attempts to use it, but they were all half-hearted. Then the other thing, I never could get anybody to learn a wonderful graphics trick that was shown to me by Ed Logg, and I sort of picked it up and ran with it. I did a number of extensions which took it well beyond what he showed me. But it was a wonderful thing for doing dissolves, a variety of transitions, and it was beautiful. Very clever code. You applied this to a bitmap and, wow, you could get fantastic things happening. And I used that a number of times and nobody else ever seemed to bother to use it. But I think lots of people did look at the *Eastern Front* source code as a way of realizing that games aren't that hard to write.

So did your evangelism work take away from the amount of time you were able to spend developing games?

Well, I was software evangelist for only a year. I was then asked by Alan Kay to join his research team. In fact, I was the first guy he invited. For about three months the Atari Research Division consisted of Alan Kay, myself, Alan's administrative assistant, Wanda Royce, and my employee, Larry Summers. And the only place they could put us back then was in the executive suites, there was a spare room there. And there were Larry and I doing programming in the executive suites. Ray Kassar, the Atari president, was a very stuffy, straight-laced guy. And he really resented our being up there. I mean, it really bothered him. So we got a new building real quick.

I'm curious about another game you did during your Atari days, *Gossip*. Was that game ever released?

Yes, it was released, but it was released just as Atari was going down in flames, so nobody had any opportunity to see it. *Gossip* was an immensely important game in that I tackled interpersonal relationships. I had realized very early that computer games had an emotional sterility about them, and I spent a long time thinking about that. I finally decided that the crucial factor was the absence of characters, of people. And I remember writing an essay, way back then, entitled "People not Things," arguing that computer games were very thing oriented, and that we had to focus our energies on people. So I attempted to design something around people and interpersonal interaction. And *Gossip* is what I came up with. A very simple design, but way ahead of its time in terms of its goals.

So what was the gameplay like?

It was solely about what I call circumferential relationships affecting radial relationships. Basically the idea was that you had a group of eight people, and your goal was to be popular. This was just before the high school prom, and you wanted to be elected king or queen of the prom, and so you were doing your politics. And the way you did this was by calling people up. It had a really cute interface. There were eight people sitting in two rows of four; they looked like panelists on a game show.

You were the one in the upper left corner. And you would use the joystick to select one of the other seven players, and then you pushed the button and the telephone would ring at that person's station. He'd pick up the phone. Then you would use the joystick to point at another person. And then, once you'd selected that other person, you'd push the joystick up or down to show a facial expression ranging from a big smile and nodding your head up and down all the way to a big frown and shaking your head from side to side. These were expressions of how much you liked or disliked this person. So you'd point to someone and say, "I like them this much," and then your interlocutor would say, "Well, I like them this much." Then your interlocutor would tell you things about what other people were saying. "This person likes him this much, and that person likes him that much." And the idea was, you would try to read the social clustering and decide which clique are you going to join so as to ingratiate yourself to everyone else. To some extent this involved a certain amount of deception. You'd tell everyone, "Oh, I like you very much" and you'd say, "Oh, if you hate him, then I hate him too." But you could get caught at it, and that would really hurt; you did have to be quite careful in all of this. It was a very interesting little game.

What was the mind-set like at Atari during the video game crash?

There was a sense of catastrophe. It turns out that it was solely a matter of momentum. That is, all that really happened was that Atari went bust. Atari did a lot of things really wrong, and those are what led to its going bust. It's just that in going bust, it discredited an entire industry, and so many companies that hadn't done anything wrong and were perfectly healthy, they went bust too. It was just a matter of an industry collapsing because its lead company was greatly discredited. It was kind of silly in many ways. Everyone just convinced themselves that bust was upon us and everyone decided, "Oh, we're all going to die, so let's just die." The underlying forces had not changed by much.

So things were able to pick up. Unfortunately, the recovery surprised everybody by its shape. The initial collapse discredited video games, but not really computer games as much. Unfortunately, at the time, most computer games were just copies of video games. Hence, many computer game companies that were deriving all of their sales from video games collapsed. It was really bad for a while there. I couldn't get a job, I couldn't get anything. There were two new things for me: *Balance of Power* and the Macintosh. I had some serious discussions with the people at Amiga, as to whether I wanted to do software evangelism for them. And really this boiled down to a choice between platforms. Which platform am I going to run with, the Mac or the Amiga? I gave that a lot of thought, because I realized you hitch your star to a platform. I chose the Macintosh, which turned out to be the right decision.

I went to work on *Balance of Power*. My big hope then was that we could maybe rebuild the industry along more rational lines. And, you know, there was a real chance there. That was the crucial moment of truth for the computer games industry, the period from '85 through '87.

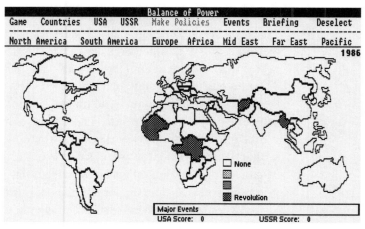

Balance of Power

And it took the wrong turn. Actually, 1990 was when the fate of the industry was sealed. And if anything sealed it, it was Chris Roberts' *Wing Commander*. But we had a real opening there for a while; it looked like we might pull it off.

How do you think *Wing Commander* sealed the fate of the industry?

The big question for the industry in 1985 was what, if anything, will sell? Nobody seemed to know for sure, but there were a few strands. The fact that *Balance of Power* was a huge hit suggested to people that perhaps serious games might have a future, or at least games that weren't video games. And there was a lot of excitement about exploring some of those ideas. The other games that were a big success back then were the whole series of Infocom games, which continued to do well right through the crash.

Because they were clearly different from video games.

Yes. And you put those two together, and it pointed strongly in one direction. So there was a lot of effort in that direction. The industry was still torn because it was so much easier to design the video games, and they did seem to sell to a group of people who weren't affected by the crash. We really teetered on that fence. Which way are we going to go? Video games, or a broad range of game possibilities? What sealed it was *Wing Commander*, for two reasons. The main thing that *Wing Commander* did that doomed the industry was that it bought market share. That is, *Wing Commander* was a hugely expensive program to write. It's funny, Chris Roberts has denied that it cost much, but that's because of some creative internal accounting. Back in those days, around 1990, a typical budget for a game would be $100,000 to $200,000. There were some done cheaper, but $300,000 was a very expensive game. *Wing Commander* probably cost about $1,000,000. By the standards of the day that was considered absurd. And in fact, I've been told by an Origin insider that *Wing Commander* by itself never paid back its investment, but that the follow-ups and add-ons did. But what they were really doing was spending so much money that it would only work if it became the top hit. It did. The problem then was, they've raised the bar for the whole industry, we all have to produce $1,000,000 games, and unfortunately they can only work if each one is the number one game. And you can only have one number one game. So that, in turn, forced the industry to become much more conservative. We've got these huge expenses, we simply can't make money turning out a number twenty game. Anything less than being in the top ten will lose money. So very quickly it became a hit-driven business. That was already starting in the late '80s, but *Wing Commander* sealed it. So once it became a hit-driven industry, the whole marketing strategy, economics, and everything changed, in my opinion, much for the worse. The other thing was that *Wing Commander* also seemed to reestablish or reconfirm the role of the action game as the wave of the future. And basically that's where the industry solidified, and the cement has now set.

It was right before the crash that you wrote *The Art of Computer Game Design*, wasn't it?

Yes, actually I started that as soon as I joined Atari Research. It's funny, one of my goals at Atari Research was, "Let's really sharpen up the whole field of game design." So I, in essence, tried to create a computer game developer's conference within Atari. I tried to set up a Friday afternoon seminar. And some politics got in the way. I sent out invitations to all the designers throughout Atari, and some pig-headed guy who was running the software group at coin-op was furious that I didn't route it through him. I didn't follow the hierarchy properly, and he therefore sent out a memo forbidding any of his employees to go. That's one of the reasons why Atari collapsed; there was a lot of pig-headed ego crap going on. So the seminars never really came off. I therefore decided, "OK, I'll write these ideas down." I started working on the book. I finished it in 1982, but Ray Kassar, the CEO, was also pig-headed and insisted that he personally approve the manuscript before we sent it out to a publisher. So I sent it to him, and he sat on it for a year.

Do you still look back on the book positively?

I certainly have come a long ways. Had I known that fifteen years later people would still be reading it and deriving some benefit from it, I would have been flabbergasted, and I simply would not have believed it. I still get e-mails referring to it. There's no question it's still providing people with some benefit. And that says some very bad things about the whole games industry and the games community, how little thinking there is going on. It's shameful.

There's really no other book like it at all.

Yes, all the other attempts just turn out to be programming books. It is shameful that no one has gone beyond that book.

Ever since you published that book, you have been very concerned with sharing your thoughts about game design with the community. I'm curious why that is.

There are two very separate reasons. First, sharpening my own thinking through writing, which I do a great deal of. And second, communicating ideas to others. There is some overlap. Most of the time I write for myself. I have reams and reams of little design essays on particular designs, where I muse with myself on design issues. However, I will sometimes write an essay solely for public consumption, put it up on the web or something, and that is done with a very different purpose. But I often write with both purposes.

So did your writings about game design lead to your establishing the Computer Game Developer's Conference?

I had started off by founding the *Journal of Computer Game Design*. That turned out to be quite a success; it rose up to one hundred to one hundred fifty subscribers rather quickly. And by the time it reached that level, I realized that it really would be possible to have a conference, there were enough people out there. So I decided to have a little miniature conference at my home. I just put a little notice in the *Journal*, saying, "I'm going to put together a conference, it's going to be at this date. And anybody who wants to come, contact me." We ended up having twenty-six people show up to this conference, one day long, and we all sat in the big room upstairs and talked about game design. It was a very exciting experience! Everybody agreed, this is great, this is wonderful, we've got to do this again. They all turned to me and said, "Chris, do it again." I said OK. I thought about it for a while and then I decided it would be really good if I broadened participation in this by recruiting some other people to help me. I decided the only way they were going to be really involved was if they had a sense of ownership. If I brought them in as assistants to me, it would never really work. So I decided to create a corporation with a board of directors, and I invited five other people to be on the board. And to give them a sense of ownership, even though I owned the whole thing free and clear and had gotten it rolling with my own money, I basically just gave away ownership. Everybody had an equal share in the conference. We set up the conference, and it was a huge success, and it just grew and grew every year.

Did you foresee it growing to be the mammoth event it is now?

No, and to some extent that reflects a violation of my initial intentions. We had some clear disputes within the board: is this a show, like E3, or is this an academic conference, like AAAI? My feeling was that the core of this is the exchange of ideas among developers. We can have a show, but it's got to be a side show. It's always tucked away in a corner. This conference is designed around people sharing ideas, and that's why I came up with the idea of the round tables. Unfortunately, it is now a show, and the conference is now a secondary activity.

So after Atari you became an independent game developer. Why did you do that instead of opting to return to a big company?

Well, at first it was forced on me. But then, once I got going, I was working on *Balance of Power* and it was an independent project. It was more inertia than anything else.

Do you prefer being independent?

Yes, I am very much a solitary worker. I am very concerned with my efficiency and how much I get done. When you're working with other people, you spend a lot of time just holding their hand, explaining things to them, helping them out, rather than actually getting anything done. I felt I had a lot of ideas, and if I really wanted to explore them I had to explore them alone.

So what originally started you working on *Balance of Power?*

It was a sort of a culmination. My interest in wargames arose because I was part of the Vietnam generation. While a lot of people wanted to resist the war, I wanted to understand war so that I could ultimately do something about it. I felt that protesting in the streets was very ad hoc, a very temporary solution, and not very

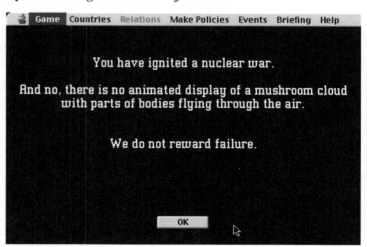

Balance of Power II: The 1990 Edition

effective either. I was asking questions like, how do wars get started? All through the early '70s and early '80s, I was very much a student of warfare, learning everything I could about military history. Finally, by 1984, I felt I had figured that out well enough that I could design a game around some of those concepts. I would say that the emotional support for the game was the Bob Dylan song "Blowin' in the Wind." You know, "How many times must the cannonballs fly before they're forever banned?" That was the thing that gave me the emotional inspiration to continue with the project even though there were many points where it looked impossible. I was taking a completely different approach to design and exploring new territory and there were many times when it looked hopeless. It took a lot of emotional toil to get over those problems and carry on.

But you thought the concept was compelling enough to be worth it?

Yes. I really wanted to do an un-wargame. We have plenty of wargames.

And in *Balance of Power* when you get to the point of having a war you have lost.

Yes, that was very much the point of the game. I don't know if you remember, but if there was a war, the screen would go black, and it would say, "We do not reward failure." That was very much a surprise to many people.

At any time were you concerned that the game was too different?

I did not expect it to become a hit, but I felt it was important to do. This was exactly the same thing that happened with *Eastern Front*. I did *Eastern Front* for myself and then, lo and behold, everybody loved it. Well, that's very nice. I did *Balance of Power* for myself and, gee, everybody loved it. But I also did other games for myself that were dismal failures, commercially speaking.

How did you go about balancing realism with the gameplay in *Balance of Power*?

People talk about realism versus playability as if it's a dilemma. I see it more as a matter of sharpening things. An artist, painting a portrait, will deliberately accentuate certain components of the face that he feels bring out the character of the subject. They don't see that as realism versus playability, they see that as art. In the same way I felt that I needed to sharpen up, editorially and artistically, those elements that I thought clearly showed the issues at stake. So I certainly made the world a much more dangerous place. I took out a lot of the boring complexities, simplified it down, and sharpened it up to a game about pure, direct geopolitical rivalry between the two superpowers. And that's all it was, clearly showing that conflict.

I've read that *Trust & Betrayal: The Legacy of Siboot* is your favorite of your games. Why is that?

Every game I have done has been original, with the exception of the second *Balance of Power*, which I did at the urgent request of my publisher. With that one exception everything I have done has been a new design. But with *Siboot* I went much further out than with any other game, that is, in terms of just how far I took the design beyond the conventions of game design. *Siboot* was easily the most advanced. I explored ideas with *Siboot* that people still have not even come close to.

We were talking about *Gossip* as in some ways ahead of other games. *Siboot* went way, way beyond *Gossip*. The other thing about *Siboot* was it wasn't just one good idea. There were at least three major ideas in *Siboot*, each one of them worthy of a game all by itself.

And then there were lots of other little ideas. Here's an example of a little idea. There's now a user interface concept called "tool tips." If you put the cursor over something and leave it there for a few seconds, it pops up some descriptive text. I anticipated that and came up with something vaguely similar,

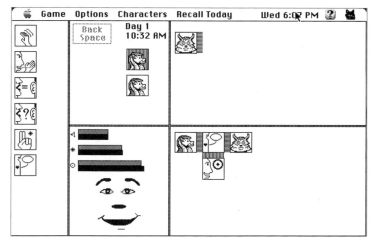

Trust & Betrayal: The Legacy of Siboot

where you could click and hold on a button to see its functionality. That was four years before tool tips were first noted as a user interface item in the PC world. That wasn't a major idea on my part, I considered it to be just a minor little thing, but at the time, nobody had anything like that.

So what were the three major innovations?

First, the language, use of language as the primary interface element. You talk to the other creatures. I see this as completely different than the text parser approach, because I really don't think that's linguistic communication, that's something very different. Second, it used an inverse parser. Actually, the core concept behind the parser was patented by Texas Instruments in 1979. I didn't know that at the time. However, my implementation was different enough that we were never concerned with any patent infringement issues. TI's approach was more menu driven. Mine, in the end, boiled down to being functionally similar to a menu, but technically it's called a palette. So I didn't invent that concept, but I developed its implementation and showed very clearly how to do that kind of thing. That was a major innovation, and I'm sad to say that nobody seems to have run with that concept. The third major game innovation was the use of non-transitive combat relationships, which has been used in some games since then. That was basically just an extension of the rock-scissors-paper idea. That basic concept of non-transitive relationships has enormous potential for development; you can build whole games out of extensions of that. And there's no reason why non-transitivity has to be applied to three components. You can have a ring that has twelve components and then the implications of victory or defeat in the non-transitive ring can be interpreted many, many ways. It's a huge area of game design to explore. This would be easy to implement. It's just that nobody is thinking along lines that unconventional.

Do you think the unconventionality of the project hurt *Siboot's* popularity?

Well, yes and no. Actually, it was only sold on the Mac. There was never a PC version done. I think we sold about four thousand copies on the Mac, which by the standards of the day was disappointing but not horrible. The general rule back then was that you'd sell five to ten times as many on the PC as you'd sell on the Mac. So we're talking twenty to forty thousand copies if there'd been a PC port. But the publisher opted against doing so.

So, as with *Gossip*, was your goal to put people in the games?

Yes. And I took that concept of "people not things" much, much further with *Siboot* than with *Gossip*. Another innovation was the interstitial stories that pop up. They weren't irrelevant, they actually did tie into the overall game.

So you did *Balance of Power II* solely at the insistence of the publisher?

Yes. I had done *Siboot*, and they had published it, and it was obvious that it wasn't going to make money for them. They were obviously disappointed. They'd been asking about a sequel. They pressed me hard this time, and I felt I owed them one. So I did the *Balance of Power* sequel.

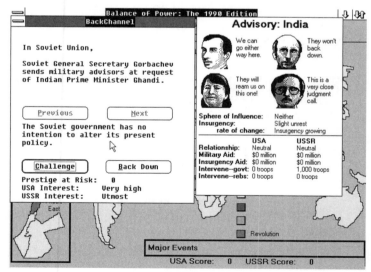

Balance of Power II: The 1990 Edition

So you didn't have great hopes to better the original?

No, and in fact I felt that *Balance of Power II* was little more than a clean-up of *B.o.P. I*. It's funny, though. By the standards of the industry, it was a major new version and deserved to be called "Second Edition." But by my standards it was just tidying up, adding some bells and whistles, but in terms of gameplay it didn't do much.

So where did the idea for *Guns & Butter* come from?

At about the same time, the three best game designers in the world, independently, all got the same idea. Each of us said, "I'm going to do a conquer the world game, an *Empire* game." (Those three were Sid Meier, Dan Bunten, and myself.) It is interesting how each of us took a completely different route. We all know how Sid took his, and it was an immense success. Sid, Dan, and I got together at one point to discuss how the three of us approached our designs. Sid had a very clear notion: he was going to make it fun. He didn't give a damn about anything else, it was going to be fun. He said, "I have absolutely no reservation about fiddling with realism or anything, so long as I can make it more fun."

My approach was to make it educational, and Dan's approach was to make it social. Dan came up with this wonderful little game, *Global Conquest*, where you really interacted with the other people playing. I think that game was an undiscovered jewel. It bombed even worse than *Guns & Butter*. He had endless trouble with Electronic Arts, I don't see why he stuck with them, because they kept wanting him to put shoot-'em-up elements into his games, especially *M.U.L.E.* I consider *M.U.L.E.* to be, probably, the greatest game design ever done. That is, in terms of the platform he had to work with, and the design expertise of those times, *M.U.L.E.* was definitely the greatest ever done. And it is a brilliant game, it is loads of fun, and it has never been ported onto a modern machine. That's a tragedy. And the reason why is that Electronic Arts insisted that the players be able to go shoot each other up.

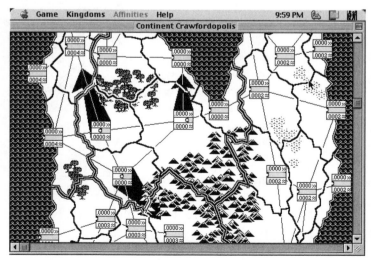

Guns & Butter

Dan refused, just said flat out, "That will not happen." And *Global Conquest* was the same way. It was not so much about shooting as about teamwork.

My conquer-the-world game, *Guns & Butter*, was really more about macro-economics. In fact, during development, it was called *Macro-Economic Conquest*. I think it's reasonably successful as a game to teach about how history really develops, but that's all. It was certainly one of my poorest games, no question. It really didn't have that much creativity. There were some cute ideas, but where that game had cute ideas, *Siboot* had thunderclaps of genius. For example, *Guns & Butter* had this nifty little algorithm for generating continents. I also developed a wonderful algorithm for giving names to states and provinces, and I'm very proud of that algorithm; it's very clever. But this is mere cleverness, not creative genius.

Guns & Butter has some interesting ideas about balancing complex systems. But you think it did not work?

No, it didn't work, largely because I completely blew the handling of trade and alliances. That was a disaster. I think if I'd given that game another six months it probably would have worked out just fine, but I rushed it.

Balance of the Planet seems to be an extremely educationally oriented game. Was that your intent?

Oh, absolutely. I had no intent whatsoever to make something that was fun. My feeling was, "OK, there are all of those shoot-'em-ups and so forth, and I'm not going to try to compete with those things. I'm going to do a game that taps into another area of humanity. So I'm going to do pure simulation, and I'm

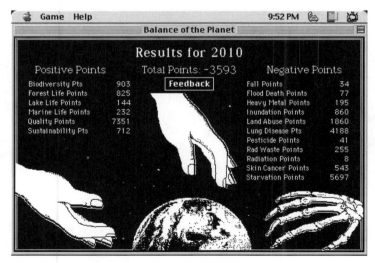

Balance of the Planet

going to make that simulation very realistic and very educational as well." We knew Earth Day 1990 was coming up, and we thought, "We're going to release this thing in time for Earth Day." And I felt that would be one of my contributions. Again, Vietnam generation, Earth Day, and all that jazz. *Balance of Power* was about the Vietnam War, and *Balance of the Planet* was about Earth Day.

Will Wright's *SimEarth* came out just shortly after *Balance of the Planet*. It's interesting to compare the two. Of course his is more of a toy, and yours is much more goal oriented.

SimEarth was not one of Will's better efforts. He's done brilliant stuff, but I think he didn't have a clear purpose with *SimEarth*. It was kind of, "OK, here's this planet, and here are these geological processes, and here are these life forms, and . . . " There was no design focus to it. He seems to have said, "Let's take *SimCity* and do it to the whole Earth." That kind of extrapolatory approach to design never works well. And it didn't work well for him. It was certainly more successful than *Balance of the Planet*, because it was a lot better looking and had plenty of cute features. But it was not as educational as *Balance of the Planet*.

ic*SimEarth* had a lot of interesting systems in it but it was difficult to understand what was going on.

It was more that all of the different systems, they sort of didn't add up to anything. He had all of these simplifications, but they weren't purposeful simplifications. They were simplifications to make the internal systems accessible, but they didn't really add up to anything. The model for the way living systems develop didn't seem to make any sense to me, even though it was easy to see its results.

I've heard *Balance of the Planet* criticized for not being a lot of fun. Do you see fun as the sine qua non of game design?

That's exactly the problem. Many people do see fun as the sine qua non. That's one way that the game design industry has gone down the wrong path. Basically, computer games and video games are now one, and in fact they're all video games in the sense of cute shoot-'em-ups, lots of graphics, splendiferousness, and emphasis on fun in the childish sense. I see no reason why computer games needed to constrain themselves in this fashion. It's rather like somebody saying, "I went to go see the movie *Das Boot*, but it wasn't any fun, so it's a crummy

Balance of the Planet

movie." Well, I'm sorry, but *Das Boot* was not meant to be fun. I think we could agree that *Saving Private Ryan* is not a fun movie, but it is a damn good one. And the same thing goes for *Schindler's List*. And, sure, there are plenty of fun movies. *Star Wars* was lots of fun. But Hollywood doesn't constrain itself the way the games industry does. I suppose that was the whole thrust of my efforts all through the '80s and into the early '90s, to help the games industry become a broad-based entertainment industry, rather than a kiddie, fun industry. I failed at that. It is now most definitely not an entertainment industry, and never will be. They've painted themselves into a corner from which they can never extricate themselves. It's rather like comics. It's a shame to see the medium of comics used brilliantly by people like Spiegelman and McCloud, yet it is relegated to the comic book stores where the kids chewing bubble gum come. Not enough adults take graphic novels seriously. Some progress is evident, but it's a slow, slow process. I'm not sure they'll ever pull themselves out of that dump.

So you think the games industry has reached that same point of stagnation?

Yes. Only they're not even trying to get out; they haven't even realized yet that there's a problem.

So I guess that's what led to your leaving the games industry and starting work on the Erasmatron.

Well, there were two factors in that. Yes, I had been steadily drifting away from the games industry. The hallmark of that was the "Dragon Speech" I gave. That lecture was ... I'll just tell you how it ended. In the lecture, I'd been talking about "the dragon" as the metaphor for this artistic goal. And, right at the end of the speech, in essence I stopped talking with the audience and had a conversation directly with the dragon. I said, "And now that I have finally devoted myself heart and soul to the task of pursuing the dragon, all of a sudden, there he is, I can see him brightly and clearly." I began talking to the dragon, and that was intense. I can't remember it exactly, but I said something like, "You're mighty, you're powerful, you're beautiful, but you're oh so ugly. Yes, yes, you frighten me" and then I screamed, "You hurt me! I've felt your claws ripping through my soul!" I wasn't lecturing any more, this was much more acting. I let out that line "you hurt me" with great passion, and it frightened the audience. They weren't used to that level of passion in the technical lectures that they were familiar with. And then I said, "I'm not good enough to face you, I'm not experienced enough, so I'm going to do it now. I've got to go face to face with you, eyeball to eyeball, and I'm going to do it now, here." I reached over and I pulled out a sword and I kind of hunkered down and shouted in a battle cry, "For truth, for beauty, for art, charge!" I went galloping down the center aisle of the lecture hall, and I never came back.

This was at the Computer Game Developer's Conference?

Yes. A lot of people thought, "Well, Chris gave his swan song, he'll never come back." But in fact I came back the next year, and I had every intention of continuing to lend my expertise. "I'm going off in this other direction, but you guys need my help, and I will still be there." Unfortunately, a whole ugly incident with the conference board members put an end to that. What was so hurtful was not just the behavior of the board members, but also the attitude of the community, which was, "Hey, this is Silicon Valley, you just gotta fight to get yours. If they play hardball, what's the big deal?" My reaction was, "I just don't want to be a part of this nasty community." It was so bitter an experience, that moving to Oregon was an imperative. I had to get out of Silicon Valley. And it's funny, every time I go down there now, I can see the Silicon Valley greed all around me. It really bothers me.

So that drove you into working on the Erasmatron?

I had been evolving in that direction. But what made it a negative move was A, the industry was editorially going in directions I did not like, and B, the industry was going in moral and social directions that I did not like.

So how did the Erasmatron project come about?

I set out to do interactive storytelling. I said, "I'm going to go back, and I'm going to do my King Arthur game now." Because I had done a King Arthur game at Atari that I was proud of, that had a lot of good ideas, but I felt it did not do justice to the legends, so I felt that I owed something to those legends. I started all over to do a completely new approach. That led me up to the storytelling engine. However, everything was hand-coded and it was enormously difficult. We had gone the rounds to all the big companies trying to interest them in it and nobody was interested.

Just about that time, I ran into a lady named Edith Bjornson, who was with the Markle Foundation. She suggested that I take the technology in a different direction, as an enabling technology to permit non-technical people to create their own story-worlds. I very much liked the idea. So Markle funded me, and the fundamental strategy of the project was expressed in the slogan "Unleash a tidal wave of creativity." Thus, I was building three pieces of software. The Erasmatron, which is the editing software for the engine, the engine, which actually ran everything, and finally the front end, which delivered it to the user. It was a huge project and I had to do it in two years. Unfortunately the problem turned out to be much bigger than I anticipated. What I got working after two years was nice, and indeed technically adequate, but I don't think it was commercially adequate.

How do you mean?

It takes too much effort to create a sufficiently entertaining end result. Laura Mixon worked on *Shattertown Sky* for nearly eighteen months. But *Shattertown* just didn't work. It was not entertaining, it was not even finished. There were places where it would just stop. Yet she worked longer and harder on it than she was expected to. There wasn't any failure on her part. The failure on my part was underestimating the magnitude of the task. I thought that a year would be sufficient. Well, first, she didn't get fully operational software for at least six months. And second, the tool she had was so weak that she spent a lot of time doing busy work. The conclusion was that the Erasmatron needed to be souped-up, and there were a few embellishments to the engine that came out of that. But they were actually comparatively minor. Most of the work I have been doing since that, on the Erasmatron 2, has been to make the whole process of creating a story-world easier.

So you haven't concluded that making a story-world is just an inherently hard task? You've found ways to make it easier?

Well, there's no question in my mind that creating a story-world with Erasmatron 2 is immensely easier than with Erasmatron 1. Erasmatron 2 dramatically cleans up the process of creating a story-world, cutting the time required roughly in half. You see, with Erasmatron 1, we were shooting in the dark. I had no idea of what the process of creation would look like. I don't feel bad that Erasmatron 1 was a bad design, in fact it was much better than the original design document. I'd made quite a few improvements, but they weren't enough. I think that, using Erasmatron 2, people can create excellent story-worlds with an adequate commitment of time, which I consider to be at least six months and probably a year, but I haven't proved that. That is what's stopping the whole project: I need proof.

Is that something you're hoping to provide with the *Le Morte D'Arthur* project?

I don't know. I've had some kind of writer's block with that project and I don't understand why. I think one factor is a sense of demoralization. I've put nine years into this project, and so far it's been a failure. With the exception of the Markle funding, nobody's interested. There are always a few pots bubbling. Right now there are three separate groups who have expressed interest in this. So it's not as if I ever reach a point where I can say "it's dead." There's always something going on, and there's always the hope that it will go somewhere, but these things never go anywhere. I'm definitely getting discouraged.

What would an ideal Erasmatron storytelling experience be like?

I'll describe it in two ways, tactical and strategic. Tactical being what the audience experiences moment to moment, and strategic being the overall experience. Tactically, the audience will see a static image on the screen representing whatever has just happened. It will show the face of the person who just did whatever happened, as well as anybody else who's on the same stage. It will have some text explaining what has happened. The other thing I want to use is something like a comics technique. That is, comics show action between frames very well. So it might require two frames. But I want to use the artistic styles that have developed in the comics. In Scott McCloud's book, *Understanding Comics,* he has that triangle that represents the amount of abstraction.

With the smiley face in one corner and the photo-realistic face in the other.

Right. My guess is we would want to move on that triangle far away from the photo-realism corner. We'd want to be somewhere much closer to abstraction and representation. So I think we're talking about a more abstract type of display. And then there will be your menu of choices, expressed as complete sentences. This is what the player is permitted to say or do. Strategically, the big difference is that all story-worlds have a very meandering character to them. "Barroom Brawl" doesn't, because it's a single scene. "Corporate Meeting" is a single scene and even it meanders a bit. We have figured out how to cope with that problem. I had thought that plot points would do enough, but Laura and I have now come up with a scheme. I don't want to describe this as a new discovery; rather this is a concept that has been slowly brewing for several years now. We're putting flesh on its bones and I think it will work.

The idea is that there is something like a core plot that is beyond the control of the player. However, the player does control lots of interactions that will not just influence but ultimately determine the final outcome of the plot. For example, consider a murder mystery, such as *Shattertown.* Basically at some point, time is going to run out, and either the clans are going to go to war or Sky will unmask the murderer or Sky will get caught by the murderer. That ending has been established, and events will force that ending. The thing is, what ending you get depends critically on all the things you have done up to that point. Same way with *Le Morte D'Arthur.* The basic design says, very clearly, that the end game is going to have Mordred revolt. No matter what happens, Mordred is going to revolt at some point. And when he does, all the other actors are going to choose up sides. Some of them will go with Mordred, and some will stay with you. There will be a big battle, and the side with the bigger battalions wins. The decision to go with Mordred or stay with you will be based on all the things you've done up to that point.

I've come up with another concept for *Le Morte D'Arthur* that I'm tempted to go with, which would incorporate some of the elements of the current *Le Morte D'Arthur.* In this one, you're not playing as Arthur, you're playing as Merlin, and you're a transplant from the future. Your task is to modernize Arthurian society and thereby prevent the Dark Ages from happening. You're trying to build up this society and get it operating on a more efficient basis and teach them a little bit about sanitation and education and so forth. Along the way all the nobles are developing their resentments against you, and they try various plots to discredit or kill you. And, once again, Mordred revolts. The end result feels more purposeful, less meandering.

So the player is led in a direction more than in the current version.

We're not asking you to be creative or come up with new social innovations, we'll simply present you at various points with opportunities to initiate new innovations, to say, "All right, do you think it's time to teach these people sanitation, or do you think it's time to teach them how to use the stirrup?" And each one takes time. And there's still this steady plot that develops as you help this society pull itself up by its bootstraps. But there's still an awful lot of interaction going on. What we're developing here is a concept of "semi-plot" or "pseudo-plot" or a "skeletal plot" that can proceed in the way that a plot is supposed to. You still have a plot, but it doesn't hijack the whole story and dominate it as it does in a conventional story.

So the player has more involvement than they would reading a book, but not total freedom either.

Yes. The idea is that you want to use dramatic constraints, not artificial constraints. This is a drama. It's got to evolve by certain rules. We're going to apply those rules here. It should not incur resentment on the player's part that he can't pick his nose while talking to Arthur. That's not dramatically reasonable. Some argue that, if you don't give the player full freedom to be creative, it just doesn't work. I disagree with that entirely. So long as you give him all dramatically reasonable options, or even most of them, you're doing fine.

So you're quick not to call your Erasmatron system a game of any kind. Why is that?

The differentiation is two-fold. The first reason is marketing. Right now, computer games mean *Quake, Command & Conquer*, or something like that. The associations with that term are all about shoot-'em-ups, resource management, and those associations are very clearly defined in the public's mind. If I call this a game, they're going to apply associations that are misleading. Moreover, the term "game," if you look it up in the dictionary, has more column inches than most words. I compared it with words like "do" and "eat" and "have" and I found that it's bigger. Because that word is a semantic imperialist, it just goes everywhere. It can be used for many many different meanings, all completely different. But then there's sort of a switcheroo that happens. You can apply the word "game" to a whole bunch of products and activities, but then as soon as people associate it with a computer they say "computer game!" and all the semantic meaning collapses down to this little bitty point. Maybe I should call it a web game, get the whole thing on the web. Or if

I do it on the Mac maybe I can call it an iGame. But I don't dare call it a computer game or a video game.

Why do you think facial expressions are so important for storytelling?

Because facial expression is one of the fundamental forms of human communication. It's funny, other people think graphics where I'm thinking communication. What goes on between user and computer is primarily a matter of communication. I am deeply desirous of optimizing that communication. That means designing the

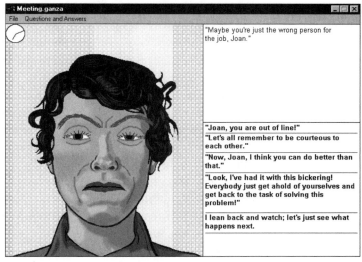

The *Corporate Meeting* story-world in the Erasmatron

computer display to most closely match the receptive powers of the human mind. And the two things that we are very good at are facial recognition and linguistic comprehension. Accordingly, those are the two things that computers should emphasize. Computer games have neither and that appalls me. Facial expression and linguistic comprehension are the two most important areas of development for the time being. Nowadays you can get excellent 3D facial models, although the expressions on them are still crappy. This is largely because the people who design them aren't artists, they're engineers, and they've come up with these anatomically correct heads. Every cartoonist in the world knows that you never ever, draw a face the way it really is. For this type of thing we've got to use cartoon faces and not real faces.

When I was playing with the Erasmaganza, sometimes it would present me with three different actions to choose from, and I wouldn't want to do any of them. In that way, it feels a bit like an old adventure game with a branching dialog tree. Do you see that as a problem?

The real issue is not "Gee, you only get three things." The real issue here is that you're not permitted to say dramatically reasonable things, and that's a flaw in the design of the story-world. Both of the demo story-worlds have that problem, because they're very tiny story-worlds. If you want to get away from that you must have a much larger story-world. "Brawl" has about fifty or sixty verbs and "Meeting" has about a hundred. I used to think that five hundred verbs was the threshold for entertainment value. I now think it's more like a thousand verbs. But "Meeting" just doesn't give you very many options because it's so tiny.

As to whether the user will ever be satisfied with the finite number of options he's given, I don't see a problem there at all. Certainly you're not permitted nuance in such an arrangement. But you should have all dramatically reasonable options. Besides, if we gave you some system where you could apply nuance so that you could say, "I'm going to say this with a slightly sarcastic tone of voice," the infrastructures for that would be ghastly. It would make the game very tedious. So I feel that the only way to do this effectively is to confine it to a menu structure. In fact, there are some games that have implemented nuance as their primary modality of interaction. In these games you're interacting with someone and you've got these sliders: one is for forcefulness, one is for humor, and another is for charm. But that's all you get. You respond to someone with this much forcefulness, this much charm, and that much humor. I've been tempted for quite some time to build something like that into the Erasmatron. But the problem is, first, coming up with some generality, and second, keeping the interface clean and usable. Right now, with the simple menu you need merely look, see, and press. I think that's important for a mass medium. The sliders for tone are for game aficionados.

The system that *Siboot* uses to construct sentences with icons and the inverse parser is an interesting one. Why did you opt not to use a system like that for the Erasmatron?

Because the vast number of sentences in *Siboot* are self-completing. In *Siboot*, you could click on just one icon and often the rest of the sentence would fill itself in because that's the only option available. The way to do that nowadays, by the way, is with pop-up menus. I could do this with the Erasmatron. For

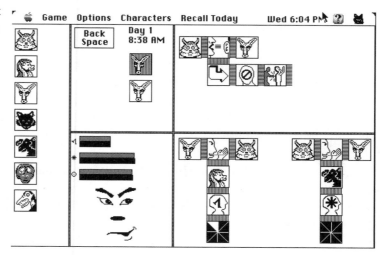

Trust & Betrayal: The Legacy of Siboot

example, suppose you had a conventional menu item that said, "I'll give you my horse in return for that six-gun." The words "horse" and "six-gun" could be in pop-up menus providing other options for the trade. This would require some expansion of the Erasmatron system, but nothing very serious. The only reason I haven't done it yet is my unwillingness to add complexity. I believe that the system has all the complexity it needs and then some. It's always easy to add complexity to the design, but I'm thinking in terms of simplification.

Have you had a chance to play *The Sims?* It seems that a lot of people succeed in using that game as a sort of tool for interactive storytelling.

The Sims is not an attempt to produce interactive storytelling. I had some e-mail with Will Wright about *The Sims*, and he acknowledges that it isn't an interactive storytelling platform, but he pointed out that many people use it that way. *The Sims* is exactly what it claims to be, a simulation, not a drama. No drama simulates the real world. In Shakespeare's play, in the middle of Henry V's speech to the soldiers at Agincourt, he doesn't say, "Just a minute, guys, I have to take a pee." However, in *The Sims*, he does. Once, when I was playing *The Sims*, a little girl couldn't get to sleep because there were spooks coming and frightening her. The spooks are a very nice touch, by the way. They kept her awake all night long, and she wandered all around until she fell asleep, because a sim who stays up too long is overcome with drowsiness. She happened to fall asleep on the floor of her parents' bedroom. Morning came, mommy woke up, stretched, got up out of bed, and walked to the bathroom, stepping over the inert body of her daughter! This is a good simulation of the physical processes of daily living. It is an atrocious simulation of the emotional processes of daily living.

Will built an excellent physical simulator. But it has no people content. It's a direct violation of my "people not things" argument in that it focuses on the things aspect of life, on all the mechanical details. Going to the bathroom is a major module in that program, whereas emotional processes simply aren't there. I don't want to criticize a brilliant product: Will set out with a clear goal and he achieved it, and that's wonderful. But he didn't set out to do what I'm doing and, lo and behold, he didn't achieve it. I refuse to criticize *The Sims*, because as a design it is magnificent. It has a clear purpose and it achieves that purpose brilliantly. It's just a different product, and it's not interactive storytelling.

So what makes you want to pursue interactive storytelling?

It's a hell of a lot more relevant. Furthermore, I think it's a hell of a lot more interesting than game design. The design problems of computer games nowadays bore me, because they're not very involved problems. They tend to be very small models, quite easy to calculate. I continue to be appalled at the low level of intelligence in a lot of these games. The computer opponent is really stupid, and that's about the only element that still interests me. I might like to do a game with some really good AI, where the computer opponent can really outsmart you, and I don't mean that in the sense of chess, I mean that in something complicated like a wargame. But wargames themselves are obvious. I feel that I have mastered that form and so why should I continue to indulge in it? There are so many other, more important tasks, such as interactive storytelling. This is a challenge! Something I can really sink my teeth into. Unfortunately, it appears I have sunk my teeth into the tail of a tiger.

Do you ever fear that you will always be dissatisfied with the Erasmatron?

I consider this to be my life's work, this is the culmination of everything I've been leading up to. I have no doubts that if I continue working on this I can continue to improve this technology. I have major doubts as to its commercial feasibility right now. That is, I'm quite certain that twenty years from now people will realize that interactive storytelling is a commercially wonderful thing and, golly gee, we ought to do it. I believe we can make products that people will find far more entertaining than computer games, because they'll be about drama instead of resource management. Unfortunately, I don't think people quite see that yet. Certainly the games industry does not and will not. They will feel that *The Sims* represents the correct step in that direction. They can continue to get more polygons in the faces and have them dance better and so forth. But in terms of dramatic resolution, they haven't even begun.

Maybe it would be good if they go down that path, leaving the real problem area free for me and the other people who are serious about interactive storytelling. There are indications of a hankering for dramatic content. For example, Sony calls the chip in the PlayStation2 "The Emotion Engine." Well that's bull, total bull. It's a graphics processor and has nothing to do with emotional modeling. But it shows that they would sure like to have some honest emotional content. They're just not willing to make the product-level commitment. Then there's the twin factors of the Internet and Hollywood. Between them, there's a strong desire to establish an identity untainted by computer games. So between the Internet and the Hollywood people I think that we really ought to get interactive storytelling. There are lots of indications in that direction. Six years ago, when I went hat in hand to almost all the majors in Hollywood trying to get them interested, and I struck out, that was because they had all just recovered from the experience of getting burned by having their own games divisions. So nowadays they're starting over with web-based things that have a completely different outlook, and they might be interested.

I wonder if you have an answer to the critics who say that telling a story interactively is somehow at odds with the fundamental structure of storytelling. Obviously, you don't find this to be an issue.

Not at all, and in fact I'm surprised at the shallowness of that argument. The easy refutation is the example of grandpa sitting down with his little granddaughter to tell her a story: "Once upon a time, there was a girl who had a horse." And the little girl says, "Was it a white horse?" And grandpa does not say, "Shut up, kid, you are ruining my carefully constructed plot!" He says, "Oh yes, it was very white, white as snow." He develops his story and the little girl interacts with him. He embraces her participation and incorporates it into the story, which makes the story that much better. This kind of storytelling has been around since the dawn of human existence. We've long since proven that, yes, you can have the audience intervene in the story without damaging it.

In your games work, you created both the content and the technology, whereas with the Erasmatron you're focusing on creating just the technology which will allow other people to create the content. Why did you shift your efforts in that direction?

There are lots of people who could provide artistic content, but I'm the only person who can provide the tool. I therefore have a moral obligation to concentrate on the talent that is unique to me. However, there are still some other things I want to do. There's so much going on, I have to very carefully allocate my time, and a lot of good projects are sitting on the back burner.

So as a result you don't get much chance to work on *Le Morte D'Arthur*.

Right, I have to just let it burble around in my subconscious for a while longer. And it may never come out, I don't know.

So what's next for the Erasmatron technology?

Well, the basic technology is, I feel, ready to go commercially right now. We still need to build a front end and so forth, but we are ready to begin the commercialization process immediately. My next primary task is to commercialize this technology. I'm not sure how to proceed on that point.

Would you ever be interested in working on a more traditional game again?

At this point I would be interested and willing to consult with people on various game designs. That is, I wouldn't mind going in and looking at a project and identifying fundamental design problems in it, or assisting. But I don't think I would want to accept responsibility for creating a commercial product for the games industry at this time. I'm happy to help somebody else do it. But that's such a political and

nasty process, and less and less time is spent on the creative aspects and more on the political aspects that don't interest me.

Chris Crawford Gameography

Tanktics, 1978
Legionnaire, 1979
Energy Czar, 1981
SCRAM, 1981
Tanktics (updated for Atari 800), 1981
Eastern Front (1941), 1981
Legionnaire (updated for Atari 800), 1982
Gossip, 1983
Excalibur, 1983
Balance of Power, 1985
Patton vs. Rommel, 1986
Trust & Betrayal: The Legacy of Siboot, 1987
Balance of Power II, 1988
The Global Dilemma: Guns & Butter, 1990
Balance of the Planet, 1990
Patton Strikes Back, 1991

Chapter 15:
Game Development Documentation

"Omit needless words. Vigorous writing is concise. A sentence should contain no unnecessary words, a paragraph no unnecessary sentences, for the same reason that a drawing should have no unnecessary lines and a machine no unnecessary parts. This requires not that the writer make all his sentences short, or that he avoid all detail and treat his subjects only in outline, but that every word should tell."

— William Strunk in his book ***The Elements of Style***

Many a game designer will proclaim himself better than development documents, and will make them only to suit the managers who demand their creation. Game design, these obstinate designers may insist, is something one cannot write down on a piece of a paper. And these designers are partly correct; writing quality development documentation is very difficult. Much of the development documentation you may come across seems to have been written merely for the sake of it, perhaps to placate a publisher who demands to see something on paper. Nonetheless, documentation does have a legitimate place in the creation of modern computer games, and it is the designer's job to make sure those documents are created and used effectively.

The necessity of game development documentation is a side effect of the increasing size of game development teams. In the early days of game development, when a development team consisted of one multi-talented individual, documenting the functionality of the game was less important. If that one person was able to establish and implement a vision for the project's gameplay, it did not especially matter if she wrote it down or not.

As development teams grew from one to five, from five to ten, from ten to twenty, from twenty to thirty, and onward and upward, maintaining the project's focus became more and more of an issue. As members of the team became increasingly specialized in certain areas, a reference document they could turn to in order to see how a given system was supposed to function and how their work fit into the project became necessary. And so, points of reference came to be used, such as the design document, the art bible, the technical design document, and numerous other reference works for guiding the creation of a game's content. Development documents can be a key way of "holding the reins tightly" on a project, to make sure it does not spin out of control because of the impractical ambitions of team members. Writing down ideas and story components is a helpful way to quickly realize when a game is being overdesigned and if there is no way the project will ever be done on time.

Good documents have benefits not just for the production side of game development, but also for improving the game design itself. Chris Crawford has written more about game design than probably anyone else, as a visit to his web site (www.erasmatazz.com) will reveal. Crawford uses documents to refine and sharpen his own ideas and to track how a project evolves over the course of its development. Personally, I use a steno pad to keep all of my thoughts for a given project. I find that I can later go back and review these notes to see how I arrived at the design I did, and to recall good ideas I had but that I have long since forgotten.

Of course, it is entirely possible to go too far in the other direction, to spend all of your time working on the documentation and none of it actually developing the game. And having a massive amount of repetitive documents is certainly not beneficial, especially if the team feels as though they are adrift in a sea of documentation, with none of it actually practical to their work. It is also possible to make games without any sort of documentation, but if one hopes to work at a development house that makes commercially viable, professional computer games, getting used to working with documentation is an absolute necessity.

Document Your Game

As a game designer, you will be primarily concerned with what is commonly called the design document, which I will explore in Chapter 17. However, there are many other pieces of documentation used in the creation of modern computer games. Even though you may not work with all of these documents, it is important nonetheless to understand what each of them is supposed to contain and how the different documents are interrelated. So before delving into the nature of design documents, a survey of the different types of documents is appropriate. Different people at different companies or in different situations will invariably call the documents listed below by a variety of different names, so you should be aware that the naming convention I employ here is not universal, but the types of documents used are quite common throughout the game development industry.

Concept Document or Pitch Document or Proposal

These are usually the first formal documents created for a given game. Often they are written in order to sell the idea of a game to a publisher (if the author works at a developer that does not publish its own work) or to upper management (at a company which publishes internally developed projects). In short, this document is shown to the green-light committee, the money, the suits, the decision makers, or whatever one may call them, in order to convince them to spend a lot of money on the idea, thereby funding its development. Concept documents are usually short in length, customarily no longer than ten pages, and usually include plenty of concept art. Concept documents are commonly written by committee, typically involving the game's producer, lead designer, lead programmer, whatever marketing people may be on hand, and the lead artists who contribute a variety of sketches, conceptual pieces, and screen mock-ups. Concept documents discuss all aspects of the game idea in question, including how it might be positioned in the marketplace, budgets and development timelines, what technology will be used, what the art style of the game will be, mini-bios of the team who hope to work on the game, and some broad description of the gameplay. These documents are not much use in the game's actual development, though they can be a springboard for creation of other documents, such as the design document or the art bible. Since concept documents do

not apply very much to the game's actual development, I will not go into further detail about them.

Design Document

In other parts of the software development industry, the equivalent of the design document is often called the functional specification. Indeed, some game developers refer to the design document as the functional specification. I prefer "design document" because it is the more widely used term and because it better represents the contents of the document. The design document's goal is to fully describe and detail the gameplay of the game. For large team projects, the design document serves as a vital reference work for how the different aspects of the game need to function, with, ideally, team members referring to it throughout the game's development. Producers will often use the design document as a springboard from which to schedule the project. A well-written and complete document can also be of vital importance when a game is subsequently converted to another platform by a different development team. The document can serve as an ideal reference tool for this new team to understand how the game is supposed to function as they start porting it to a new system.

Whereas a functional specification for, say, a spreadsheet application can be extremely detailed and complete, a design document for a game is necessarily less complete because of the more organic, dynamic, and iterative nature of game development, as I discussed in Chapter 13, "Getting the Gameplay Working." As a designer working on a large team project, the design document will be the primary specification with which you will need to be concerned. The guts of a design document are the detailing of game mechanics: what the player is able to do in the game-world, how they do it, and how that leads to a compelling gameplay experience. Design documents typically also include the main components of whatever story the game may tell and a detailing of the different levels or worlds the player will encounter in the game. Also included will be lists of the different characters, items, and objects the player will interact with in the game-world. One can think of the important aspects of the design document as not dissimilar from what a journalist looks for in a news story: what the player does (which actions the player can perform), where he does it (the game's setting), when he does it (at what time and in what order the player must perform different actions), why he does it (the player's motivations), and how he does it (what commands are used to control the game).

The design document can also be defined by what it does not include. Most of the content contained in the other documents listed in this chapter should not be found in the design document, including the bulk of the information found in the script, the technical design document, and the art bible. In particular, a design document should not spend any time describing the game's development from a technical standpoint. Platform, system requirements, code structure, artificial intelligence algorithms, and the like are all topics that should be covered in the technical design document and therefore avoided in the design document. The design document should describe how the game will function, not how that functionality will be implemented.

Similarly, discussions about the marketing of the game, explorations of how it will be positioned compared to other games in the marketplace, and sales projections are all inappropriate in the design document. In addition, schedules, budgets, and other project management information should be left out. This information should certainly be recorded in some documents, such as the pitch document or project schedule, but it should be strictly excluded from the design document. I would think that such an exclusion would be obvious to anyone undertaking a design document, but I have seen many design documents that spent half their pages considering how the game will be sold. The design document needs to describe how the game functions so that someone working on the development team can see exactly what she needs to create. Including materials which are more about the business side of the game's development will only get in the way of more appropriate information.

The design document and its creation are discussed in more detail in Chapter 17, "The Design Document."

Flowcharts

Flowcharts may often be included as part of the design document or as separate documents. In my experience, flowcharts are not actually all that useful in the game design process, though they may be handy for communicating to the other members of the team or the publisher how the gameplay is supposed to progress. In game development, flowcharts have two primary uses. The first is to track the player's navigation of out-of-game menu options, such as those the player uses to start a new game or load a saved one. Flowcharts can also be used to chart the areas the player progresses to and from in the game, particularly in level-based games. Flowcharts can be either handmade or developed using various flowchart creation tools, such as Visio. Primarily, I have found that flowcharts impress the publisher, while the development team seldom refers to them.

Story Bible

For games that tell stories, some amount of that story must be included in the design document. Certainly a summary of the game's overall story is essential, and a thorough description of the game-flow will need to include parts of the story, but the design document cannot include it all. This is especially true if the game being

developed involves a complex story line with a variety of characters and locations, or if the game takes place in a universe with a specific history. A story bible may be the best place to document this information. Often the author of a game's story will have in her mind a vision for the universe and its inhabitants beyond the scope of the game, such as where game characters come from and what their motivations are, and how the game-world came to be in the state it is in when the player encounters it. What the player experiences may be only the tip of the proverbial iceberg, with the story's author having in mind ten times more detail about the game-world than is actually communicated to the player through the gameplay. Other aspects of the universe may only be hinted at. By having a complete plan for the game's back-story, even if the player does not directly learn all of it, the story's writer will have a much better chance at keeping the game's narrative consistent and plausible.

A story bible, then, is a good place to document a game's potentially extensive back-story. Separating this information from the design document proper avoids burdening it with a lot of information that is less central to the game's creation. Weighing down a design document with a lot of back-story is an easy way to give it perceived depth and completeness, but can hide the fact that the specification fails to fully cover game mechanics and other more vital information. Nonetheless, the back-story is still important, and hence the value of its documentation in the story bible. Once a story bible has been created, when an artist wishes to learn more about the character he is modeling, he can turn to the bible and find out about that character's childhood. He can make his art better by making it fit with the back-story. When a voice actor wonders how she should play that same character, if she has read the story bible she will be working from the same information base as the artist. Properly used, a story bible can add to a game's consistency.

Should there ever be a sequel or spin-off made from the game, the game's story bible becomes all the more useful when the development team for the derivative project tries to understand what sort of new story line can be crafted. Since the story bible included more content than was actually used in the original project, it will provide the new team with plenty of unexplored areas of the game's universe. If the story bible is followed properly, the new game will fit in perfect continuity with the original. As that team creates the new game, the bible can be expanded and updated, so that future projects will be just as consistent.

The format for a story bible is fairly open, and the bible's author should make the format best fit the information she is planning to include. Often the story bible consists of a number of different historical narratives of varying lengths. One narrative might describe the history of the game-world, detailing the major events that have led the world to the state it is in when the player starts his game. Similarly, the document could include narratives for the different major characters the player encounters in the game. Topics discussed would include the character's childhood, how he rose to whatever position he has in the game, and what motivates the character to act as he does. By having a sense of the character's background, when it comes time to write the game's script, the game's writer will be better equipped to create compelling and believable dialog for the different characters. Of less importance but perhaps still appropriate for the story bible are the histories of the various major items or locations the player finds in the world. A powerful sword might have a colorful history, which NPCs may hint at when they talk of the object to the player. A particular shrine might have a colorful history all its own. However, the author should always be careful to try to keep in mind how much information is actually going to be useful to the game's creation, and should not feel obligated to fully explain the lineage of every last character and object in the game. Include only the information which you think will be important to the game's creation.

The writing style of the story bible should be in more of a prose style than the bullet-point style of the design document itself. A team member using a story bible is more likely to want to sit down and read a few pages at once, and will appreciate bible content that reads and flows nicely. Breaking the document down by character, item, or major event is still useful to the reader, so using a good quantity of appropriately titled headings is a good idea. You may also wish to include various diagrams in the document to supplement the written content, such as timelines, event flowcharts, or character-relationship trees. These charts can prove useful in allowing the reader to understand a particularly complex game-world.

On the other hand, even with a complex game-world, you may not need a story bible at all. If the author of the game's script is able to keep track of characters and their motivations in his head, and if the likelihood of a sequel worked on by another team is low, the creation of a complex story bible may not be a good use of anyone's time. It all depends on the working style of the team, particularly the lead designer and scriptwriter, who may or may not be the same person. Certainly many great authors have managed to write novels far more complex than your game is likely to be without keeping more than a few scribbled notes to themselves, if that. Many complex films have only had a script to go on for their stories, with the actors responsible for interpreting their characters' motivations based only on the lines they are supposed to speak. It may be that the script's author created a story bible for her own personal use, and never saw fit to share it with anyone else. The story bible is a tool which can help in the creation of the game's story, but it may not be a tool that every script writer or game designer feels the need to use.

Script

If a game has a story, it is quite likely that at some point the player will be asked to listen to narration, hear characters talking, or read information about upcoming missions. This dialog and the accompanying descriptions of the situations during which

the dialog occurs (stage directions) should be contained within the game's script. A game's script may be written by a variety of people: a designer, an artist, the game's producer, or someone whose only role on the project is to write the script, someone who was specifically hired for his dialog writing skills.

The script may take on different forms depending on what type of game events the dialog will accompany. For instance, if the game has film-style cut-scenes, the script may closely resemble a movie script, with descriptions of the action the player witnesses and rough indications of what the camera is looking at for any given instant. Or the script for these cut-scenes may be more like that of a play, focusing primarily on the dialog. For in-game conversations, the script will focus primarily on the dialog, since the player is still in control of the game and thereby in control of what direction the game's camera is pointing. But a script for the in-game dialog might include descriptions or "stage directions" for the accompanying character animations, to assist the artist in creating the appropriate artwork to accompany the dialog.

For instance, here is an excerpt of a script that could be used for a cut-scene in an adventure game:

> When the PLAYER approaches ROGET and BARTLET after resurrecting the TREE OF PLENTY, ROGET will be visibly thrilled at the player's arrival. He immediately bursts into effusive praise for the player's accomplishments:

ROGET: That's just the solution we have been praying for! You have saved our great Tree, and nothing we can do could ever thank you enough. Please accept this token of our appreciation...

ROGET tosses a BAG OF FLIMFLAMS at the player's feet. BARTLET steps forward:

BARTLET: [Apologetically.] We know it's not much, but...

ROGET: [Interrupting.] It's all we have!

BARTLET: [Cowering.] Please do not hate us for our poverty...

The non-linear nature of games demands that the script be organized and presented differently from a play, movie, or television script. If the player has branching conversations with NPCs, as he might in an RPG or an adventure game, the script will need to take on a special form conducive to the non-linear nature of the interchange. Here a script might use a small amount of pseudocode, using IF-THEN-ELSE or SWITCH-type syntax to communicate when the player would hear different pieces of dialog.

Returning to our adventure game example, here is one possible layout for a more non-linear conversation. This game uses the old "keyword" conversation system, where the player types in a word and the character being talked to may or may not have information about that subject:

IF the player asks about "FLIMFLAM":

ROGET: A FlimFlam is a drop of dew, fallen from the morning sky, carefully wrapped in a baby leaf from the Tree of Plenty. It has special curative properties for Humanoids, when rubbed on the back of the neck.

IF the player asks about "TREE" **OR** "PLENTY":

ROGET: The Tree of Plenty has been my people's source of life since before any of us can remember. Without the shade it provides, my people grow exhausted in the noon-day sun. Without its leaves we have nothing to eat. Without its strength my people are weak.

DEFAULT, if the player asks about anything else:

ROGET: I do not know of what you speak, stranger. We are not the most intelligent of peoples; we are not as wise as a great traveler, such as yourself.

In-game dialog may be randomly varied between a number of expressions which communicate the same information, but say it differently. Simple OR statements between different lines of dialog can communicate to the reader of the script that the game will randomly choose between several different lines of dialog.

Once again returning to our adventure game, here we have a sample of dialog that the player might hear during actual gameplay:

When the player bumps into ROGET, he says:

"Oh, excuse me, begging your pardon."

OR

"Oh dear, I seem to be blocking your way."

OR

"My mother always said I was born to get in her way."

There is no industry-standard syntax that dictates the form of an interactive script. It is up to the designer, producer, and scriptwriter to come up with a form that best documents the dialog they will need to use in their game.

The game's script is also where one might find the text of what the character reads in a mission briefing or in a book they might find. Any text that is contained in the game, from signs and posters on the walls to the commands issued to the player from an off-screen commander, is all contained in the game's script.

As games try to incorporate more and more story, scripts documenting all of the dialog they include have become necessary. The most important thing to remember when working on the script for your game is that people are usually playing your game not for the dialog, but for the gameplay. If they had wanted to watch a movie, they would have done so. Instead they booted up your game. They may enjoy hearing some clever dialog while they are playing, but they are usually not so interested in listening to long, drawn-out cut-scenes that delve into endless back-story. If the gameplay is any good at all, players are going to want to get back to it as quickly as possible. If players find themselves more captivated by the dialog in your game than in the gameplay, you need to wonder why you are bothering to make a game at all.

Art Bible

The art bible is often composed primarily of concept sketches and other resources that artists can refer to as they are working on creating various visual assets for the game. Sometimes text accompanies these images, whether in the form of handwritten notes on concept sketches or text descriptions describing the parameters artists should follow when coming up with new elements for the game. The art bible is usually not compiled or written by the designer, but instead by the lead artist working with his team. Of course, the information contained in the art bible needs to correspond and be consistent with the story and characters described in the game's other documents, including the design document, script, and story bible. Therefore, when constructing the art bible, the artist will work closely with the designers, writers, and producers to make sure their work is going to fit with the overall vision for the game.

The art bible is the place where the look and feel of the game is comprehensively established in detail. Descriptions of the art style to be employed in the game (art deco, animé, Warner Bros. cell animation, Lovecraftian, and so forth) will be found in the bible accompanied by sketches which communicate the game's style better than words ever could. It is important to keep the descriptions of the game-world's art style in this document instead of in the design document, to allow each document to stand on its own as a comprehensive reference tool. Of course, designers on a project should read over and be familiar with the art bible, if for no other reason than to make sure it is on track with the rest of the game. An art bible may also contain technical guidelines that artists need to follow to create assets that will work with the game's engine, as detailed in the technical design document. This may include polygon limitations to be followed or the duration and number of frames involved in different animations.

Storyboards

Storyboards are an established film and television device for sketching or mocking-up shots before they are actually filmed. Storyboards may be included as part of the art bible or can stand alone as their own separate document. Storyboards are most handy for mapping out non-interactive cut-scenes, which are quite cinematic in nature and are thereby well suited to storyboarding. This allows members of the development team to provide feedback and corrections on those cut-scenes before someone goes to the trouble of filming or rendering them. Storyboards can also be used as concept sketches or mock-ups for how the game-world will appear to the player if the game's engine is not yet ready to be used. Such storyboards can be useful both for making the entire team understand at an early stage where the game is heading, as well as convincing financiers to fund the project's development.

Technical Design Document

A technical design document is the sister specification to the design document. Whereas the design document focuses on how the game will function, the technical design document discusses how that functionality will be implemented. Sometimes called the technical specification, the technical design document is customarily written by the lead programmer on a project, and is used as a point of reference by the programming team. Here is where the code's structure is laid out and analyzed. The technical design document is where programmers on the project can turn to figure out how they should implement a specific system. The document may include the overall code structure, what major classes will be used, descriptions of the rendering architecture, details of how the AI will function, and any amount of other implementation-side information. Pseudocode is appropriate, though not required, in the technical design document. Though the technical design document may be a good idea, many projects manage to have perfectly successful development cycles without a technical design document ever being created. Indeed, none of the projects I have worked on has had one, nor do I know anyone who has actually worked on a project which did.

As I have mentioned, the technical design document is used primarily by the programming team. Nonetheless, a designer with any sort of programming experience would do well to look over the technical design document for her project, since it may contain general descriptions of how AI and other algorithms will function, along with other information critical to the gameplay. Just as looking through the art bible is important for a designer to do, reading through the technical design document, even if she cannot understand all of it, will give the designer a chance to make sure the programming team is on the right track.

Schedules and Business/Marketing Documents

I include these in my list of game development documents in order to emphasize that schedules, budgets, and marketing projection information does not belong in the design document. On many occasions, I've read design documents which had whole sections about how the game might be sold. Indeed, some so-called design documents are little more than dressed-up marketing plans. Such business-oriented information is inappropriate in the design document, nor does it belong in any of the other documents I have discussed here, except for the concept document. The design document is about the game's functional design, not how it will be advertised or sold at retail. It is best to separate out such marketing plans and business data into distinct documents, where it can best be reviewed by the people concerned with such information.

When working on a project with a large budget and which hopes to at least recoup its capital investment, it is important to have well-thought-out marketing projections, budgets, schedules, and any number of other documents that will assist press relations people, sales representatives, and advertising artists when they are working on your project. The lead designer on a project should offer her services to help in the creation and maintenance of these documents in whatever way she can, though the writing of these documents usually falls on people more attuned to selling and managing rather than creating. Often it is the responsibility of the game's producer to develop and maintain these documents. Still, it is the designer's moral responsibility to make sure that the people funding the project know what sort of a game they are getting. This makes them less likely to become upset down the road when the game is done and it fails to match the advertisements and box art they have already spent large amounts of money creating. And when the suits are happy with your game, they are far less likely to demand changes or, even worse, cancel it. If the business people are really happy with the finished product, they are much more likely to be enthusiastic about promoting and selling the game, which can only mean more people will end up playing it.

No Standard Documentation

Different companies may have different standards for what documentation they create in order to assist and guide a game's development. Though they may have different names for the documents than those I have used above, I think the categories I have delineated cover the vast majority of documents that companies will create. Some teams may split the design document into two separate documents, one containing only gameplay information and the other containing only story and level progression descriptions. Some development teams may create only a design document, having no need for a story bible. Some programming teams may find that they do not need a technical design document. Some art directors may make it through a game's development without a formal art bible. Some teams working on multimillion-dollar projects may even get through a project without any documentation at all, though this is increasingly unheard of as publishers demand documentation so that they have some idea of exactly what game they are financing. Furthermore, publishers like to have some tangible proof that the development team has a good idea of what they are doing. Usually, how much documentation a publisher requires is inversely proportional to how trusted and experienced you and your team are as developers. The newer and more unproven your team, the more assurances the people funding your project will want to make sure you are not throwing their money away.

The Benefits of Documentation

Beyond making the suits happy, good documentation really can help make your game better, regardless of whether you are developing it alone in your basement or with a team of thirty other developers. As a game designer, you should be involved and interested in the creation of all of the documentation described above. As a lead or senior designer, the creation and maintenance of the design document, story bible, and script are all your responsibility. Each of these documents may be written by an individual or worked on collectively by a number of people. For example, you may not actually write the script yourself if there is a writer available more qualified to compose compelling dialog. Yet as the lead designer, you must still be concerned that the story, script, and gameplay all fit together appropriately. Making sure that all of the various documents are consistent with one another and are in line with the vision and focus of the project is something the designer needs to take very seriously.

Chapter 16:
Game Analysis:
Myth: The Fallen Lords

Designed by Jason Jones
Released in 1997

Designer/programmer Jason Jones' games have always exploited technology in ways no one else has quite managed. His first title, *Minotaur*, was a network-only game before such things were fashionable (1992). It created a uniquely stimulating game by using networked human opponents who could not see each other's screens. *Pathways into Darkness* took simple 3D technology and applied it to an action/adventure hybrid to create an immersive, story-driven world. *Marathon* and *Marathon 2* improved that 3D technology and applied it to an action game setting, but with a more thought-provoking game-world than was found in other first-person shooters of its day. Most recently, *Myth* went off in entirely new gameplay directions, immersing players in epic battles of strategic combat as no other game had. What is most important to note, however, is that in none of these games does the technology come to dominate the gameplay, as is so often the case when a game uses cutting-edge technology. Instead, in Jones' games, technology and game design work together to accentuate each other's strengths and create uniquely compelling experiences.

All the way back to his second game, *Pathways into Darkness*, Jason Jones' games have exploited technology to create new gameplay experiences.

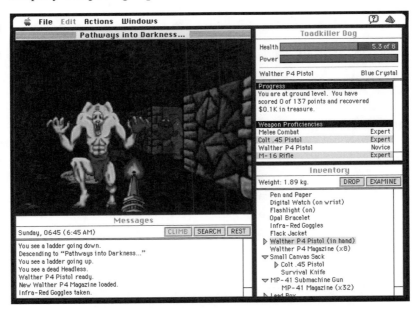

Use of Technology

Myth is a good example of taking an established genre and then adding new elements to it in order to transmogrify it into something new and unique. The original genre in question here is real-time strategy games such as *WarCraft* and *Command & Conquer*, titles which had risen to tremendous popularity a year or so before development on *Myth* began. The games were popular and seemed simple enough to develop from a technological standpoint that suddenly every publisher had to have one. A sea of clone games soon flooded the market. Most of these games attempted to function nearly identically to *WarCraft* and *Command & Conquer*, with minor

improvements such as way-point systems for unit movement and production queuing. These changes were far from revolutionary, however, and as a result, these games failed to offer any compelling reason for the public to purchase them. Consequently, they disappeared without a trace.

In a way, *Myth* was a part of the real-time strategy bandwagon, but Jones was too smart to just clone the success of RTS games. Instead, it would appear, he examined the games differently and questioned how they could be altered and improved on a more fundamental level. What if, instead of the 2D graphics technology that all of the games to date had used, a game used a truly 3D engine? With the sole exception of his first game, *Minotaur*, Jones' games to date had all been 3D, so it made sense for him to continue to use that technology for his new project. The 3D component would not be added merely for visual flair, however. As with id Software's *Wolfenstein 3D*, which years earlier had taken a relatively simple action game and, by incorporating 3D technology, dramatically changed the nature of the game design itself, *Myth* took strategy gameplay and molded it to suit the new technology. The result was an entirely new game design, not merely another clone.

However, it appears that the 3D technology used was not completely dictating the game's design direction. The 3D engine developed is one uniquely suited to modeling outdoor environments, and hence supporting RTS gameplay. Instead of taking the technology from his previous game, *Marathon 2*, and trying to make that work with a real-time strategy game, Jones wisely started over with a whole new engine. *Marathon 2* had used a *Doom*-style BSP engine, a technology suited for simple indoor, non-organic environments, but not so conducive to the needs of RTS games, which require wide-open, outdoor environments to play well. So a new terrain engine was created that was uniquely suited to the gameplay requirements of a 3D RTS project.

With the 3D technology in place, certain game design changes could be made to the fundamental RTS form as established by *WarCraft* and *Command & Conquer*. In *Myth* the elevation of terrain the combat took place on would have a dramatic effect on how well the player's units fared. Place the archers at the top of a hill for maximum effectiveness. Place them in a gully and watch them get slaughtered. *Myth* also uses a simple but effective physics system which serves to emphasize the 3D nature of the landscape. When the player sends a dwarf scurrying up a hill to throw one of his Molotov cocktails at an enemy atop that hill, he should be prepared for the bottle to possibly roll back down the hill before detonating. Should the projectile hit its intended target, the player can marvel as the ground at the explosion point ripples in a visually interesting way, altering the landscape for the rest of the game. Of course, if the target is killed, the player can expect the body parts of that destroyed enemy to roll back down the hill toward the dwarf.

Using its 3D terrain engine, *Myth* added new gameplay elements to the real-time strategy genre.

Another significant improvement that results from the 3D engine is the ability of the player to see the battlefield at a level of detail not possible in a top-down or isometric 2D game. The player can rotate the camera in order to see past objects that might obstruct her view, or merely to find the perfect angle for a given battle. Furthermore, the player can easily zoom in and out on the action. The zooming in has little gameplay benefit, and is almost exclusively useful for the visceral thrill of seeing a battle close-up, immersing the player in the action in a way 2D RTS titles simply cannot. The angle of view is significantly different as well, being at a much lower angle relative to the battlefield than any strategy game that proceeded it. The camera's position was no doubt chosen partly for aesthetic reasons and partly for gameplay considerations. Regardless of the motivations, the result of *Myth*'s close-up view of the battle is a decidedly more intimate experience for the player, where the individual units become more important and more real than they ever do in an RTS game with a more removed perspective. Thus, the intimacy of a first-person shooter such as *Marathon* is married to the tactical gameplay of a strategy game, resulting in an entirely new type of gameplay experience.

The 3D engine employed by *Myth* is not all that sophisticated, especially by the standards of just three years later. The characters on the landscape, for instance, are simple sprites instead of being fully 3D polygonal beasts. This was no doubt important so that a great number of units could be on the screen at once. What fun would an RTS game be if one could only have three units on the screen at any one time? Even today, rendering a large number of fully 3D, humanoid creatures on the screen at once would bring most PCs to a crawl.

In *Myth*, every bit of technology is used to its greatest gameplay effect, as is typical of projects run by designer/programmers such as Jones. This hybrid developer understands what the technology can do perfectly while also understanding what would be compelling in terms of gameplay, making for very economical game development. Thus, when the technology does something that can enhance the gameplay, the designer/programmer instantly notices it and is able to exploit it to its maximum effect. This differs greatly from so many projects where programmers implement complicated functionality that is never used because the designers never fully understand it.

Of course, adapting gameplay from 2D to 3D is not without its drawbacks. For instance, despite being able to zoom in and out in *Myth*, one is never able to zoom out from the action quite as much as one would like. This is in part because of the precedent set by other RTS games, which, because of their 2D engines, can have a much more distant viewpoint, a viewpoint that lends itself to tracking and moving large numbers of units. A patch was released for *Myth* shortly after its publication which allowed players to zoom the camera out farther, but with the side effect of decreasing their frame rate, since more landscape and hence more polygons are now in view. Of course, the engine could probably support viewing the landscape from still farther away, but the amount of polygons on the screen would quickly become prohibitive, decreasing the game's overall speed unacceptably. Thus, the limitations of a 3D engine come to limit the gameplay choices the designer can make. Another gameplay drawback that results from the technology is the often confusing camera. Though the camera is able to rotate to view whatever side of the action is desired, this camera rotation can often become jarring and disorienting, causing the player to lose track of where different locations and units are on the map. For a novice, a casual gamer, or anyone without a good sense of direction, the camera's movement would probably be altogether unmanageable.

Game Focus

Myth is also a good example of a well-focused game design. As mentioned previously, *Myth* came out several years after the success of two other RTS titles, *Command & Conquer* and *WarCraft*. In both of those games, the player builds structures which exploit the terrain's natural resources in order to create additional units. The player is then able to direct these units against his opponent in a combination of ways. Thus, those trend-setting RTS games are a mixture of gameplay—part resource management and building, part combat. Many of the subsequent RTS titles, both the successes and the failures, copied this general model, dividing the player's efforts between unit creation, resource exploitation, and strategic unit deployment.

Myth's gameplay is entirely focused on tactical combat, leaving out the resource management found in many other RTS games.

Six Vulture Dog Star *(Journeyman)*
Told of the rearguard at Bagrada in 1158: "Not a palm's breadth free of wounds on his body, Five Moon Heron knelt to kiss the earth, and drawing strength from her rose to charge the thickest

But *Myth* does not feature any resources to be mined or structures to be built. Instead the player is focused entirely on the tactical side of the game, on the combat experience. The player starts out on a level with a given quantity of units, and for most of the levels in the game those are the only units she gets for that entire level. In some levels, additional units are acquired later in the level, but those levels are the exceptions rather than the norm. *Myth* does away with everything except for the combat elements of RTS games, which gives its gameplay a unique focus.

This tactical emphasis has several ramifications on the overall game design. First, by not needing to worry about developing a resource exploitation system, Jones was able to focus on making the combat model as good as it could be. This resulted in more sophisticated and detailed combat than was found in any other RTS game at the time. In *Myth*, unit facing, formation, and placement matter more than they had in other strategy titles. Because the developers did not have to worry about how the player would use resources, more time could be spent on the physics system and other technologies that would enhance the combat experience. For example, this attention to detail meant that archers needed to worry about finding a clear shot through the trees, how the weather would effect the trajectory of their arrows, and how their vertical placement on the landscape would impact the distance they could shoot.

The lack of ability for the player to build additional units also affects the care he will take in using the units with which he starts a level. In *WarCraft* one can make a very substantial blunder early on in a level and still be able to win by wise resource usage and unit creation. In *Myth*, such an error is often fatal, with the levels becoming less and less forgiving as the game progresses. The player's only

recourse when his plan of attack fails is to reload the level. This makes for a very different kind of gameplay than is found in *WarCraft*. In *Myth*, the player must think through his actions fully instead of just trying whatever first pops into his head. The units the player has are much more precious and, as a result, the player starts caring for their welfare. Since more can be made easily, the units in *WarCraft* may seem like just so much cannon fodder. Conversely, in *Myth* a particular unit may be crucial to finishing a level, and there is no way to bring him back once he is killed.

Storytelling

Despite its exemplary game design, a large component of *Myth* is its storytelling, which is conducted using a number of well-integrated devices. First are the cut-scenes which appear sporadically throughout the game, outlining major plot points and setting up certain levels. These are often used more as "teasers" than to really advance the story significantly. Second are the mission briefings which precede each level. These contain a large amount of detail about the progression of the war between the Light and the Dark (the game's two opposing forces). They also give meaning to the level the player is about to play, making the mission objective more than just some arbitrary task picked by the level designer.

Third, and most interesting, are the in-game storytelling devices that are used. Of course, the levels are set in locations that match the needs of the story line, whether it be a frostbitten, barren mountain area or a smoldering lava pit. The battles and missions contained in the level match up with the story as explained by the mission briefings. But the player can also see and hear exchanges within the game between different characters. For instance, a townsperson may advise the player of the location of a traitor. Your troops may provide advice such as, "We'd better get back to the bridge!" Though the player never loses control of his units, the game is able to trigger these bits of dialog at different key points in the levels. In one mission, as the player's troops approach an insurmountable mass of Myrmidons, the Avatara the player has been guarding steps forward and proclaims, "Let me handle this." He begins a conversation with the Fetch leading the opposing forces and the story line unfolds right there in the game-world during game-time.

In contrast to the majority of games which use storytelling as little more than an add-on to an already existing group of levels, *Myth* makes the story line, levels, and gameplay dependent on each other, strengthening each as a result. Players enjoy games because they enjoy the gameplay, not because the games are accompanied by long, non-interactive cut-scenes. Yet players do enjoy having stories in their games, since they can give the gameplay meaning. The best way to communicate a deep story is by making it integral to the gameplay and by revealing a little bit of it here and a little bit of it there during actual game-time, something *Myth* does

Myth tells a compelling story through a combination of mission briefings, level design, and gameplay.

expertly. Of course, the fact that *Myth*'s story line is top-notch, the script is well written, and the voice acting is professional certainly helps. Telling a story line through gameplay will not do a game a bit of good if the plot is hackneyed, the dialog is contrived, or the voice acting is amateurish.

Hard-Core Gaming

Myth is a game design by hard-core gamers for hard-core gamers and makes no apologies about it. Far from trying to capture the "mainstream" or "casual" gamer market that so many companies have tried to court, *Myth* is a game that would quickly frighten away anyone who is not already familiar with other RTS games and who does not have the quick-clicking skills required by *Myth*. There is nothing wrong with this, of course, and it is pleasing to see a game which has the artistic conviction to know its audience and to stick to it. Indeed, since the game's developers are among the ranks of the hard-core gamers, it only makes sense that they will best know how to make a game that this audience will like. Often, when a group of hard-core gamers try to make a game that the mythical casual gamer will enjoy, they end up making a game they themselves do not like very much, and that the casual gamer does not care much about either. It is very hard for an artist to make art that appeals to sensibilities which are at odds with her own, the end result often being works that are without appeal to any group or demographic.

But *Myth* did not have this problem; its developers created a game which no casual gamer would ever be able to pick up. One reason for this is the incredibly sophisticated and challenging set of controls. For instance, consider the control of

the 3D rotating camera. As opposed to other RTS games at the time, where the camera could only move horizontally along with the terrain, *Myth*'s camera can move horizontally, zoom in or zoom out, rotate around a point, or orbit around a point. Even experienced game players find it somewhat challenging to get used to this system. However, once one masters the camera's movements, one finds that they are expertly designed and provide all of the freedom one could reasonably expect given the technology the game uses. The game is also littered with special keys for different actions, such as formations, special actions, and alternate attacks. Again, these commands, once mastered, provide the player with a large degree of control over how her units move and attack, but do take some time to learn. Indeed, these keys make the game impossible to play with only the mouse, something almost all other RTS games focus on. The "gesture-clicking" is another interesting feature, used for pointing units in a certain direction when they reach a given location. The system for gesture-clicking is quite powerful yet nearly impossible to learn without being taught in person or by practicing a great deal. Nonetheless, for the hard-core players who are willing to put in the time to learn the controls, the end result is an extremely enjoyable game-playing experience.

Myth is also an inherently hard game. Even for players experienced at RTS titles, the game will prove to be extraordinarily difficult from the get-go. Customarily, games include a few simple levels toward the beginning of the game, in order to give the player a fighting chance while they are still learning the controls. *Myth* does not. Immediately, players are presented with barely accomplishable goals, where one mistake may make the level virtually unwinnable. The loss of a particular unit will often cause the seasoned player to conclude that the level is now too hard to beat, so why bother? They will just restart the level instead. The sad thing is that, despite their great difficulty, the levels toward the beginning of the game are the easy levels, with the levels becoming exponentially harder from there. However, this is the sort of challenge that truly hard-core game players thrive on. It is not that the challenges are unfair, arbitrary, or unpredictable, at least not always. In most cases, players can beat the levels on their first time through; it is just extraordinarily difficult to do so.

Myth is the kind of game that many publishers would demand be simplified so that non-hard-core gamers would not be frightened off by its complex controls or sadistic level of difficulty. But if the game were simplified significantly, would it still be as compelling as it is now? Probably not. For whatever small number of casual gamers might be gained, large numbers of hard-core gamers would be lost.

Multi-Player

As with the *Marathon* games before it, Bungie created *Myth* to excel both as a single-player game and as a multi-player experience. What is most notable about this is that Bungie manages to do both so well. Many games are criticized for emphasizing one over the other. *Quake* and *Quake II*, for instance, were both praised for their solid network play while being lambasted for their lackluster single-player games. Many other games seem to add multi-player support as an afterthought, hoping to get another bullet point on the back of the box. *Centipede 3D* is a good example of this, where multi-player was added late in the project as a marketing consideration, and almost no design time was spent making it any fun.

Bungie's well-publicized strategy for making a game that excels in both the single- and multi-player arenas is worth noting. After they have established the core engine technology for their game, getting the networking functional is the next step. Once it works, the entire team starts playing network games, and keeps playing them until they are fun. At this point no work has begun on the single-player game, and the team is entirely focused on enhancing the network play experience. Only after the networking game's core design is completed does the team start work on the single-player game. However, this is not to say that the single-player game is rushed. This merely means that the entire team knows what "works" and makes the game fun before any solo levels are even created, resulting in less reworking on those levels and leading to more entertaining levels in the final product.

It is because the team has spent so much time playing the multi-player game that the net games have the depth to hold up over time. If the team were creating a shallow experience they would quickly grow tired of it. *Myth*'s multi-player allows players many different game types with a variety of goals, all of which require different playing styles. The interesting pre-game unit trading system allows players to think up their own "killer" team, much like a player of *Magic: The Gathering* spends time developing the perfect deck of cards. Team play, where multiple people control one set of allied units and go up against another team, opens up many possibilities for strategies too complex for a single person to pull off. It is because of the time Bungie's development team spent playing the multi-player game that it has the impressive staying power it does.

Overall

Myth's developers paid a lot of attention to detail, which helped to create a deep gameplay experience.

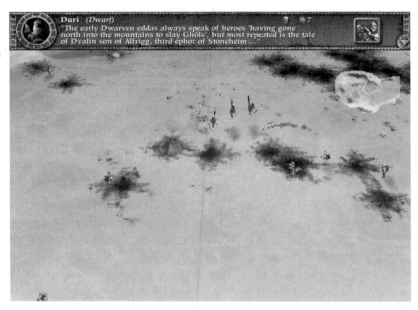

Duri *(Dwarf)*
"The early Dwarven eddas always speak of heroes 'having gone north into the mountains to slay Ghôls', but most repeated is the tale of Dvalin son of Alfrigg, third ephor of Stoneheim ..."

Myth is also littered with little design touches that add a certain luster to the solid foundation of the core design. Whereas missions in other RTS games exist as separate, self-contained play-spaces, in *Myth* the missions become a part of the whole due to the use of "veteran" units. These units, if they survive a given battle, will be available for the player to use on the next level, and their skills will be noticeably stronger than the greenhorn units. This makes the player treat those units with special care, expending the greenhorns on more dangerous exploration. Another nice touch is the ability of the units to leave footprints in the terrain, which adds an interesting element to tracking down enemies on snow-covered levels. The variety of missions available provides a much more diverse set of goals than many other RTS games, causing the player to modify his gameplay style drastically from level to level.

Of course, *Myth* is not without its problems, even if one can accept the challenging controls and staggeringly difficult levels. Clicking around the overhead map sometimes causes the camera to rotate in ways the player does not expect, possibly throwing off his orientation in the world. The overhead map is actually translucent and drawn over the play-field, which can sometimes cause players to click in it by accident. The desire to see more of the play-field at once is a valid one, even if it is a limitation of the technology. Nevertheless, these are truly minor flaws in an overwhelmingly impressive design. *Myth* represents how a great game can grow out of the marriage of technology and gameplay. This is not a shotgun wedding, however, but instead one where the bride and groom have carefully thought out how they can happily live together, enhancing each other's strengths, thus creating something new and exciting in the process.

Chapter 17:
The Design Document

"It wasn't until *Ultima IV: Quest of the Avatar*, that *Ultimas* really started having compelling, purposeful stories, and it was the first game in the series to have a social commentary subtext. Not only did I want to build worlds that were large, epic, and meaningful, I also wanted to add a subtext to each game which might not necessarily be obvious in the actions your characters took in the game, but one which ultimately would give the game a more lasting meaning. So in *Ultima IV* you had to prove yourself to be a good person, one who could be an example to the people of Britannia. The game acted like a 'Big Brother,' requiring gamers to behave in a 'heroic' fashion in order to win the game. I thought that design was pretty cool, since gamers were accustomed to pretending to be the hero yet they would beat up all the townsfolk in order to become powerful enough to beat up the character who was supposed to be the big bad guy, even though he generally didn't do anything bad in the game."

— Richard Garriott

For some years, while I was still an aspiring professional designer, I wanted someone to tell me what the official format for a design document was. I knew that Hollywood screenplays had a very precise format, and I figured there must be something comparably rigorous for design documents. What sort of information is it supposed to include? How should it be laid out? What format should it use? Only recently, after numerous years as a professional, did I figure out the big secret, and it is one that I am happy to pass on to you in this book. Yes, here my years of experience in the gaming industry will impart on you the precious information.

There is no format! Everyone who writes a game design document just makes up their own format! Have you ever heard of anything so incredible? Whenever I have asked people what format I should be using for a particular document, they invariably answer "well, you know, the standard format." No one really knows what this mythical "standard" format is, yet all refer to it. In the end, as long as it communicates the nature of the game effectively and in sufficient detail, whatever you hand over to the people who will review your document will be regarded as the "standard" format. There is definitely a certain type and quantity of information that belongs in a design document and which must be included for it to be useful, but there is no standardized form you must use in documenting that data.

Certainly within some companies, especially large ones, there may be an agreed-upon format that all of the in-house designers must use for their documents. Your design document will end up standing out if it diverges too much from other design documents in the industry. It makes sense for you to get your hands on every official design document you can, just as you might seek out practice exams before taking major standardized tests. Optimally, you will be able to obtain some documents that were used for games that were actually published. Or, at least, you will want to review documents written by designers who have completed and shipped games. This is hard to do, since gaming companies are fanatical about protecting their intellectual property and do not want to reveal how chaotic their internal development may be, but see what you can find. The *Atomic Sam* design document included at the end of this book is a good one with which to start.

A design document is all about communicating a vision for a game, for mapping out as much information as possible about how that game will function, what the player will experience, and how the player will interact with the game-world. Organizing and structuring all of this information into appropriate sections is one of the key challenges in writing a good design document. Again, many companies may prefer their documents in a format different from what I describe here, and you should certainly organize your data in the form desired by the people for whom you are writing. If the development team is familiar with navigating design documents written in a specific format, you should mold your data to fit that format.

Remember, the design document is not the end result of your efforts; the game is. As such, the format of the design document is relatively unimportant. As long as the format allows for the effective communication of the pertinent information, the design document will be a success.

The Writing Style

Before we delve into which sections your design document should contain and what areas it should cover, it is worth discussing the style you should employ when writing your document. The design document is meant to be a reference tool and, as such, you want to make it as easy for people to search and refer to as possible. A big part of this will be maintaining a good Table of Contents, as we will discuss in a moment. In writing the text of your document, you will want to break it up with lots of titles, headings, sub-headings, and so forth. This will make it easier for the reader to skim over the document and zoom in on the information he is seeking. Breaking your information into lists, either numbered or bulleted, wherever possible will further allow readers to easily realize what different attributes a given part of the game will need to include. It is actually more difficult to write in a bullet-point style, as it requires you to constantly be shifting indentations around and bold-facing titles instead of just including all your ideas in a single narrative paragraph. You may find it easiest to write out your document first, and then go back and format it properly. That way you get all the content down, and when you go back to edit the document, you can simultaneously properly format it. Though writing in a bullet-point style may involve more work for you, the end result is a more useful document to the members of your team. Furthermore, the managers and executives will appreciate it, since it makes the document that much easier to skim.

Some designers use special writing tools for composing their document. These might be applications better suited to writing text with lots of headings, subheadings, bulleted lists, and so forth. These various applications may allow for the auto-formatting and indenting of text, which could save you a lot of the time you would spend in a regular word processor dragging around indentation markers and tab stops. That said, I have never used such a tool, nor have I ever worked with someone who did. The primary problem with these tools is that once your document is done, you will need to pass it around electronically for everyone to read. Chances are slim everyone will have this unique formatting tool. Instead they will have a regular word processor. This will be read by everyone from the other members of your development team to the people in management to the executives at your publisher. You cannot expect all of these people to have installed whatever eclectic design document authoring tool you have chosen. If the tool you use provides an exporter to a standard word processor file format such as Rich Text Format (.rtf), that will usually solve this problem, but make sure the exporter actually exports a document that matches the one you have composed. Still, I have always been quite content using standard word processors for my own needs, and have not felt the need for a more capable tool.

Though there is a great temptation to do whatever is necessary to "bulk up" your document in order to make it seem more thorough and complete, you want to avoid repeating information as much as possible. This is challenging as you talk about an element of gameplay that directly relies on another system which you discussed ten pages back. Instead of redescribing the system, refer your reader to the system's original definition. This is important since, as you find yourself updating the document over the course of the project's development, you will need to change data in only one place instead of several. Often, if the same gameplay mechanism is described in detail in more than one place, when it comes time to make a change, only one of the descriptions will get updated. This leaves the other description out-of-date, thus resulting in an internally inconsistent document. Nothing is more frustrating to the reader than to find contradictory information in the design document. Inconsistent information in a specification can also throw up a red flag for producers, who will begin to question your competency to develop a game when you cannot seem to keep your facts straight.

Many people like to read design documents on their computer, as it allows them to search for words and navigate the document more easily than with a large heap of paper on their desk. For these people, it makes sense to include hyperlinks wherever appropriate. Most modern word processors make it easy to create links from one part of your document to another, allowing the reader to quickly navigate to another relevant section. This can be quite helpful as you try to avoid repeating any

Though comparisons to existing games, such as the oft-cited *Super Mario 64*, may be appropriate in the design document, the designer should be careful to fully explain what she means by the comparison.

more of your design than is absolutely necessary. Instead of repeating, include a hyperlink to the pertinent location so that the reader can jump there if they need to remember how a specific system functions.

As you write your document, you want to write as well as you possibly can, but keep in mind that the design document is supposed to be a reference document for the creation of an entertaining game, not an entertaining document in and of itself. You want your writing to communicate the information necessary in as concise and succinct a manner possible. Do not spend a lot of time worrying about making the document stimulating reading. No one is looking for excitement when reading the bulk of a design document; they are looking for information. I usually try to make the Introduction and Story Overview the most readable sections of the document, where someone could actually sit down and read through those sections and be interested while doing so. But for the rest of the document, you will be successful if you simply manage to include all of the information necessary. Spending a lot of time dressing it up with fancy verbiage will do nothing to improve your game. Similarly, though you should try to write as correctly as possible, do not spend too much time worrying about editing the document for grammatical mistakes. If the readers of the document, the members of your team, are able to read it and get the information they need, they will be happy. They really will not care if you used a gerund correctly or not.

As you write your document, it will be awfully tempting to compare elements of your design to other games, certainly ones the readers are likely to have played. Though in Chapter 5 I discouraged you from using such comparisons in your focus, in the design document comparisons can actually be useful, but with a caveat: you must fully explain your system, even if it is "just like the mechanic found in *Super Mario 64*." A comparison to a popular game can provide the reader with a starting point to understanding a complex game system you are describing. If they can remember that game, they will instantly have some idea of what you are talking about. Of course, to prevent any confusion, you must still include a thorough description of that aspect of your design. Comparisons are almost always not useful enough to replace a thorough explanation of how a system is supposed to work. Therefore, do not rely on a comparison as a crutch to save you the trouble of documenting some gameplay. Nonetheless, having started with the comparison, your readers will have a better chance of understanding exactly what you are driving at when you go on to fully describe and document the system.

The Sections

The game design documents I write typically break down into the following major sections. Within each of these, there will be further subdivisions, and not every game may require that all of these sections be used.

- Table of Contents
- Introduction/Overview
- Game Mechanics
- Artificial Intelligence
- Game Elements
- Story Overview
- Game Progression
- System Menus

Table of Contents

The reader may laugh to think that I list this as an important part of the document. Of course a document over fifty pages in length and containing multiple sections will have a table of contents—why even mention it? What bears emphasis, however, is the nature of the Table of Contents. Since creating an index is a time-consuming task for a large body of text such as a design document, it is unlikely you will have time to make one. In the absence of an index, the Table of Contents ends up as the tool people use to navigate your document. When a member of the development team needs to find a specific piece of information in your document, she will be inclined to look first in the Table of Contents to try to find where that information is most likely to be. So the more detailed and inclusive your Table of Contents, the more likely she will be able to quickly find the information she needs.

No simple novel-style table of contents will do in the design document—in other words, no listing of only eight separate sections with the reader left to navigate the pages within the sections on his own. The Table of Contents must include sub-sections, sub-sub-sections, and perhaps even sub-sub-sub-sections. We have already discussed how you will need to use bolded headings throughout your document to make it easy to navigate. In addition, any commercial word processor will allow you to turn these headings into entries in a table of contents. These entries will then automatically update for you as those headings move around within the document. Most word processors even allow someone reading the document on his computer to click on an entry in the table of contents and be taken directly to the appropriate part of the document. Making a detailed Table of Contents for your design document is crucial to making it useful.

Introduction/Overview or Executive Summary

It is a good idea to have a single-page overview of your game's design at the beginning of your document. This summary is not very useful to developers actively toiling away on the project, who, as you may remember, are the target audience for the document. However, for new team members who come on board the project, a summary will be a good starting point for understanding the game. Indeed, for anyone reading the document for the first time, be they a producer, an executive, or a marketer, getting an idea of the game's "big picture" through a one-page summary can be quite helpful. Even if whoever reads the Introduction is not going to have time to read the rest of the document, this one-page summary should allow them to understand the essence of the gameplay.

The Introduction should limit itself to a single page. Longer than that and the Introduction stops being an effective summary. Any information that does not fit on a single page is simply not part of the game's core design. If you find yourself going over the limit, figure out what is least important among the data you have in the summary and cut it. Repeat this process until the summary fits on a single page. Think of the summary like your resume: longer than a page and you may lose your reader. Write a gripping first paragraph which sums up the entire game, with the following paragraphs filling in the structure outlined in the opening.

Before writing the design document, you should have worked on defining your game's focus, as I explored in Chapter 5, "Focus." That focus is an excellent starting point for your summary. Recall that the focus is a summing up of your game's most compelling points in a single paragraph. Start with your focus as the opening paragraph of your overview, and then use the following paragraphs to go into more detail about each compelling part of your game.

One of the body paragraphs of your overview should sum up the game's story, if any. In this paragraph, focus on the adventures the player will experience during gameplay, while not dwelling so much on the back-story or history of the game-world. Follow the game through to the story's conclusion, mentioning the different types of worlds the player will navigate and characters they will encounter. Always keep in mind that this is just a summary, so it does not need to go into that much depth. Just touch on the high points of your story and move on to the next paragraph.

The other body paragraphs of your summary should discuss different aspects of your gameplay, using the key parts as outlined in your focus. What features of the gameplay are most central to the game and will be most instrumental in making gamers want to play your work for hours and hours? Of course, you should not focus on features that all games have ("Project X includes the ability to save the player's game at any time!") but rather on features that will make your game stand out, the parts that define your game as a unique and compelling experience.

The conclusion should then come in and sum up the entire overview, with a special emphasis on why this game will be so compelling to the user, what this game does that no other game has. The reader should finish the page on an up note, enthusiastic about the project. Think of this page summary as rallying the troops, psyching up the team, and getting people excited about the project without forcing them to read over the entire document.

Game Mechanics

The Game Mechanics section is the most important part of your document. It could also be called the "gameplay" section, since it describes what the player is allowed to do in the game and how the game is played. By describing what sort of actions the player can perform, the Game Mechanics section defines the game itself. As a result the Game Mechanics section is one of the hardest to write in the design document. Describing gameplay is an extremely challenging proposition, and as a result many bad game design documents skip this section entirely, preferring instead to focus on story, visuals, or menuing systems, all of which are easier topics to write about. The old saying goes, "Writing about music is like dancing about architecture." Writing about gameplay is just as challenging and imperfect, yet it must be done for your design document to be useful to the team who will create your game.

Sequels, such as *Thief* and *Thief II*, are often able to use an identical or extremely similar Game Mechanics section in their design documents. Pictured here: *Thief II*.

Except for necessary references to the player's character, you will want to avoid detailing any specific game-world objects or characters in the Game Mechanics section. Save those descriptions for the relevant content sections later in the document. For instance, you will want to describe the possible effects of the different weapons the player might pick up, and how the player will control those weapons, but you will want to save the actual list of the different weapons found in the game-world until later in the document. The specific weapons represent instances of the functionality you describe in the Game Mechanics section. You can think of it in the following fashion: many different games could be made from what you lay out in the Game Mechanics section. For instance, the design documents for the *Thief* games follow a nearly identical Game Mechanics description. It is only the weapons, items, levels, and enemies that change from *Thief* to *Thief II*. The core game remains the same, and it is the core game you are documenting in the Game Mechanics section.

It makes sense to introduce the player's different capabilities in the same order someone playing the game for the first time would experience them. For instance, start out simple. What are the most basic moves the player can do? Say you are working on a game where a player controls a game-world surrogate (be it another human, a spaceship, an airplane, a robot, or whatever your imagination may have concocted). You should probably start with how that character moves forward and backward, turns left and right, and so forth. After you introduce the simpler moves, introduce more complex ones such as jumping, crouching, rolling, and so on, as appropriate. If your game is more of an RTS game or *Diablo*-style RPG, it may be that the player moves his surrogate(s) using point-and-click, and you will want to describe precisely how that works. How good does the player character pathfinding need to be? What does the game do when the surrogate cannot reach the place the player clicked? Do you have separate buttons to select a character and then to move it, or is it more of a one-button system?

As you describe the character's movements, you will want to list the physical commands the user needs to perform to pull off those movements. For instance, "To move forward, the player will need to press and hold the Forward Button. If the player just taps the Forward Button, the player character will only move a tiny amount." It is probably a good idea to name the different keys or buttons the player has as her controls instead of referring to them specifically; use "Forward Button" instead of "Up arrow" or "Blue X Button." This keeps your description of the player's controls more platform-independent and allows you to change which keys do what later, without making you change a lot of instances of "the Up arrow" in your design document. A programmer who is implementing your control system does not care so much what the literal key assignment for a command is, but she needs to know how many different commands the user will have and what game-world actions are associated with which commands.

Once you describe how the player commands his game-world surrogate, the next logical step is to describe the surrogate's movement model. Does it follow a realistic physics model or something more simplistic? Does it ramp up to full speed slowly or does it achieve terminal velocity immediately? Does it move slower up inclines than on flat surfaces? Is its responsiveness quick and tight like *Quake* or slow and precise like *Tomb Raider?* How does it react when it bumps into an object—slide off, turn, or just stop? These are the sort of details you will need to consider and describe in depth.

It may be that moving game pieces or player surrogates around is not the key operation in your game. Think of what a player starting a game would do first, and describe that. If you were describing *Railroad Tycoon*, for instance, you would want to talk about how the player lays down track and the rules governing that. If you were writing the design document for *Lemmings*, you might want to describe how the player can change a regular lemming into a special lemming, such as a blocker or a digger. If you were describing *SimCity,* you would want to explain how the player zones an area.

RPGs such as *Diablo II* often start the game with the player creating her character. Of could this will need to be fully described in the design document.

If your game starts out with the player needing to create her character, as she might in an RPG such as *Diablo*, you will want to describe that process, summarizing the significance of each statistic the player must choose. What does "strength" or "dexterity" represent? Later on in the Game Mechanics section, when you are describing an action that is affected by a particular statistic, you will be able to refer the reader back to that particular statistic's original definition.

Having started with the basics, you can proceed to the player's more complex actions, trying to logically structure the document so that each subsequent action builds on the previous one as much as possible. You want your different game mechanics to flow one into the next so the reader can see the structure of the game building. And, of course, you want to avoid referring to mechanisms you have not yet defined or detailed.

Certainly the sort of topics you will cover will vary widely depending on what type of game you are creating. If your game involves combat, you will need to go over that in detail, explaining how the player uses different weapons and what the possible effects of those weapons are on the game-world. If the player's surrogate is able to pick up and manipulate objects, you will want to explain fully how it picks them up, how it can then access them, how inventory management works, and so forth.

The Game Mechanics section is also a proper place to lay out what sort of puzzles the player might encounter in the game-world. Indeed, if your game is a puzzle game this will take up a large portion of the mechanics section. You will want to describe how puzzles function, how the player is able to manipulate them, and give direction as to how the puzzles will be created, without actually listing specific puzzles. As with descriptions of specific weapons, save lists of puzzles for the content sections later in the document. For instance, say you were describing puzzles in the original *Prince of Persia*. You would want to explain that puzzles can involve hitting pressure plates, hidden knock-away ceilings, falling floor segments, gates which can be raised and lowered by the pressure plates, spikes that spring out from the floors and walls, special potions, certain types of magical effects, and whatever other components the game-world allows. You will not actually list any specific configurations of these components that will be found in the levels. Save that for the level-specific sections later in the document, or for the level designers to figure out on their own. Here you should list the palette of objects and behaviors from which the puzzles can be created.

Describing the variety of puzzle components found in a game such as *Prince of Persia* is appropriate in the Game Mechanics section.

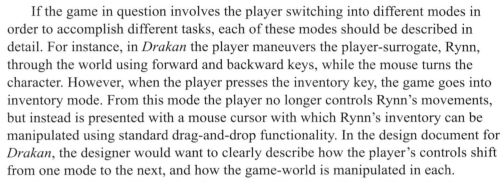

If the game in question involves the player switching into different modes in order to accomplish different tasks, each of these modes should be described in detail. For instance, in *Drakan* the player maneuvers the player-surrogate, Rynn, through the world using forward and backward keys, while the mouse turns the character. However, when the player presses the inventory key, the game goes into inventory mode. From this mode the player no longer controls Rynn's movements, but instead is presented with a mouse cursor with which Rynn's inventory can be manipulated using standard drag-and-drop functionality. In the design document for *Drakan*, the designer would want to clearly describe how the player's controls shift from one mode to the next, and how the game-world is manipulated in each.

Some sections of the design document will be dependent on the technology the game will be using, whether 2D or 3D, indoor or outdoor, real-time or pre-rendered. Though one tries to separate the technological aspects of the game into the technical design document and keep them out of the design document as much as possible, what is being created is still a computer game, and as such it is inherently tied to the technology it will use. Writing a design document without having any sense of what sort of technology the game will have access to is usually impossible and at the very best impractical. You do not need to know how many polygons per second the engine will be able to handle, or whether it will support NURBS or not. However, you do need to have some base understanding of the tools that will be available to the designer. Designing a control or combat system that works in a 3D world and one that works in a 2D one are completely distinct and different tasks. You want to play to the strengths of the technology the game will use while dodging the weaknesses.

For example, the Game Mechanics section will need to describe what the player sees while she is playing the game. This includes how the player sees the world, what sort of camera view will be used, and how the player will be able to affect that camera's position. In order to write about this, you need to know what the camera will be capable of doing, which is entirely dependent on the game's engine. It may be that the engine will only support a first-person view, only a side view, or any number of other limitations. Nonetheless, how the player sees the world is such a central part of the game's design that you must discuss it in the Game Mechanics section.

The in-game graphical user interface (GUI) is of critical importance to your game, and therefore, it should be described in detail in the Game Mechanics section. You should describe any data that is overlaid on the depiction of the game-world, such as, for an action game, the player's health or other statistics needed during gameplay. The GUI section should also cover any other GUIs which are part of gameplay, such as what the player sees when his surrogate becomes involved in a conversation or when managing inventory. Describing the graphical interface is even more important for games like *Alpha Centauri* or *The Sims* which

The GUI is extremely important to games such as *Alpha Centauri*, and will need to be thoroughly described in the design document.

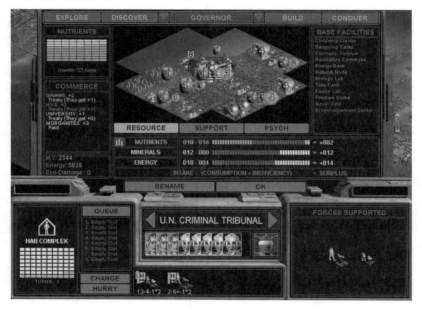

include many different GUIs and in which the player constantly uses the GUI to play the game. The descriptions of these GUIs can either all be included in one part of the Game Mechanics section, or can be detailed during the description of the system to which they are relevant. Remember that you want your design document to be as reader-friendly as possible. If the art director is looking for the different GUIs that need to be created and they are scattered throughout the Game Mechanics section, some may be missed. On the other hand, a programmer might prefer to find the GUI for a particular system included with the description of that system. You need to decide which approach is in the best interest of your document and the project. In the Game Mechanics section, you want to describe only the GUIs that are used in the game and are thereby relevant to gameplay. Any of the front-end GUIs used when the player is starting a new game or loading an old one are not really part of the gameplay. As such, the front-end GUIs should be separated into the System Menus section, which I will discuss later in this chapter.

It is easy to assume a lot when writing a Game Mechanics section, but a good designer will avoid assuming anything. For instance, a designer may be working on a first-person shooter in the *Quake* mold. He may make the assumption that when a player runs over an object, her character will automatically pick it up. The designer has played so many first-person shooters that it is totally obvious to him that this is how he wants it to work. But if he fails to write it down in the document, the programming team may assume it will function some other way, copying their own favorite game. Do not assume that the same gameplay components that are obvious to you will be obvious to whoever is reading your document. Spell everything out explicitly so there is no room for confusion.

You can almost think of the Game Mechanics section as an extremely detailed first pass on the manual. You are describing in intense detail how the player will accomplish every different action in the game-world—what commands the player will use and what the results of those commands will be. If you are writing your game design document as a journalist might write a news story, in the Game Mechanics section you should be concerned with the "what" and "how"—what the player does in your game and how he does it. Later in the document, you will get to the "where," "when," and "why."

Artificial Intelligence

If the Game Mechanics section describes how the player can interact with the game-world, then the Artificial Intelligence section documents how the world will react to the player's actions. How will the opponents the player faces in the game-world behave? What will they do in which situations? This section may also describe how the game-world behaves when the player is not doing anything. For instance, it could discuss ambient behaviors such as how townspeople go about their daily business.

In games such as *Doom II*, the player mechanics and the behavior of the AI agents are discrete enough to be described in separate sections of the design document.

Some design document authors may prefer to include the Artificial Intelligence section in the Game Mechanics section, but I prefer to keep them separate if possible. Whether to include the Artificial Intelligence section within the Game Mechanics section depends on the nature of your game. For a game such as *Lemmings*, where the player controls and the AI are tightly intertwined, it makes perfect sense for the author of the design document to discuss them in the same section. But for a game such as *Doom*, where the player's manipulation of his game-world surrogate, the Space Marine, is relatively distinct from the behavior of the enemies he fights, it makes sense to split up the information into two sections. Such separation makes the programmer's navigation of the document easier, since the process of working on the player's movement and the creatures he will battle are customarily separate coding tasks.

In the AI section you will want to do your best to fully describe how you expect the game to behave for the player. If you are working on a game where the player moves her character around in a game-world where she encounters other characters, you will want to describe how those characters react. Do they ignore the player until she initiates a conversation? Or are they attracted to the player? Can they pathfind around the area in an apparently intelligent manner, or are they walking on predefined paths? Some NPCs may initiate combat with the player; when and why do they decide to do this? Is it based on seeing the character? Hearing her? Or are they activated by level-designer specified triggers? Or all three, in different situations? How smart are the characters? Are they able to hide around corners, sniping at the player from a safe location? Do they flee when wounded? There are a number of questions you should answer in the AI section, enough to give the AI programmer an idea of what he needs to implement. The more questions you answer, the more likely the programmers will create behaviors in the game that match your expectations and vision.

Describing the collaborative tactics the AI will use is very important in the design documents for strategy games such as *WarCraft II*.

Designing an AI for a strategy game can be a significantly more involved process. Suppose you are working on an RTS game like *WarCraft* or a turn-based strategy title such as *Civilization*. What sort of strategies will the enemy use to overwhelm the player's units? How will the units work together? If applicable, when will the computer player decide to build more units, and how many will it make? Will the AI pick up on and defend against different attack types performed by the player, such as a flanking maneuver? Is the enemy AI supposed to be a real match for the player, or is balance achieved because the computer simply has more powerful equipment? If necessary, you can provide a walk-through of a specific game, and how the enemy AI would behave at different junctures of that game.

Working on the Artificial Intelligence section is a good place to enlist the help of programmers on your team. Find out what sorts of AI they have experience working with, and explore how that might be applicable to your project. Find out what is difficult to accomplish and what is easy. It is often hard for a designer (especially if he is a non-programmer) to comprehend that getting an AI agent to flee when wounded is a trivial task, while getting it to pathfind up some stairs and jump over a ledge can be extremely difficult. Instead of going for pie-in-the-sky notions of what you would like the AI in your game to be capable of, work only with real, accomplishable goals. Remember that a programmer who reads a design document that is filled with descriptions of implausible AI that is in no way grounded in reality is likely to become irritated at the document, and it will be a challenge for that document to be taken seriously in the future. Having a programmer work with you on the game's AI documentation will help make that section of your document that much stronger, as well as assuring that the AI programmer really understands what is expected of the agents in the game.

In working on your Artificial Intelligence section, try to follow the same rules you did when writing the Game Mechanics section. Do not refer to specific NPCs in the game, but rather to general behaviors that different agents may exhibit. You will get to the specific NPCs and what set of behaviors they will use in the Game Elements section later in the document. Again, try not to assume anything. Put in as much detail as you can about how the agents in your game will behave, even if it seems obvious to you.

Game Elements: Characters, Items, and Objects/Mechanisms

If you think of the level designers on your team as painters, then the game elements are the colors they have on their palette. These elements are the different parts of your game that will be brought together in the levels to create a compelling experience for the player. The designers will be able to take these elements, and, combining them in unique and interesting ways, create a variety of levels which will keep the player interested for hours. Of course, not every game has levels, but nearly every game has game elements. Whether these elements are the various types of foes the player fights in *Robotron 2084,* the different sorts of special buildings that can be created in *SimCity*, or the different blocks in *Tetris*, the game elements need to be listed and detailed in the Game Elements section.

Now that you have spent a good many pages focusing on the more general game mechanics and artificial intelligence capabilities of your game, it is time to move on to specific content. Remember that you kept the Game Mechanics and AI sections general enough that one could make many different games using them. These sections may even remain relatively unchanged for a sequel, should your game have one. But the enemies, NPCs, objects, items, and mechanisms the player will encounter in the game-world will probably be unique to this game. This content is usually closely tied to the story, which you will delve into later in the Story Overview and Game Progression sections of your document. It is actually a toss-up if you want to list your characters, items, and objects before or after the story sections. It is up to you to determine what makes the most sense for your particular document and game.

I customarily use three classifications of game elements: characters, items, and objects/mechanisms. You may wish to create a separate section in your design document for each of the classes, or you can make each class a different sub-section in one all-inclusive Game Elements section.

- Characters: The characters class includes all the enemies the player will battle, all the personalities he might meet and potentially have conversations with, and all the different types of AI agents in the game. Think of the character grouping as containing all of the active, non-player-controlled elements in the game.

- Items: The item class includes any entity that the player can pick up and use or manipulate in some fashion. Certainly any weapons the player might use would be listed here, as well as any items that might make their way into the player's inventory, such as armors, keys, or health elixirs.

- Objects/Mechanisms: The third group contains what I call objects or mechanisms. These elements are entities that appear in the game, that are not AI driven, and which the player cannot pick up but can operate in some way. This would include doors, switches, puzzle elements, or other objects which can be manipulated through the course of the game.

Again, depending on the type of game you are working on, you may not need to use all three classifications. A shooter like *Half-Life* would have all three: the aliens the player fights would be among the characters, the weapons he finds would be listed under items, and the different game-world mechanisms the player encounters, such as the redirectable laser beams, would fall under the third classification. An RTS game like *StarCraft,* however, might instead have a units listing (which is essentially a combination of characters and items) detailing all of the different units that the player or enemy can control, along with an objects/mechanisms list which details any objects the player interacts with, such as doorways or teleporters. If the RTS being designed is one in which units could pick up objects, however, you might want to create a third classification after all. An RPG such as *Diablo* might add fourth and fifth groupings for listing the player's skills and spells respectively, since these are game elements that do not really fall into any of the three classifications I have discussed. Try to separate your game-world elements, whatever they may be, into the most logical groupings possible. Depending on the nature of your game, it is not unreasonable to have only one class or as many as ten; compelling games can be created in either case.

The design document for *Diablo II* might contain separate Game Elements sections for describing the player's spells and skills.

Within each class, try to list the objects in the most logical order possible and group different sub-classes of objects together. For instance, if you are working on an RPG, you might want to list all of your potions in one spot, all of your bladed melee weapons in another section, and all of your ranged weaponry in another. An RTS might want to separate its units into offensive, defensive, and construction, or perhaps static and mobile. Again, take a look at the kind of game you are making, and try to divine the method of representation that best suits the data you are presenting and that makes it easily navigated and understood by readers. The Game Elements section should provide information for both the art and programming teams. The art team will need to make sure art assets get created for all of the elements you describe. The programming team will want to read the Game Elements section in combination with the Game Mechanics and AI sections to get a full understanding of what the game will be expected to do. (Of course, ideally, if the Game Mechanics and AI sections are thoroughly written, the programming team should not have to look at the Game Elements sections at all.) Keep both the artists and programmers in mind as you work on cataloging the game's characters, items, mechanisms, and whatever other classifications your game may demand.

In listing and describing these game elements, you want to avoid assigning actual statistics to any of them. This level of detail about the items or enemies is simply not something you can predict before you have a functioning game in which you can test the behavior of the AI or weapons and balance them properly. Statistics that you come up with in pre-production, where you have no real chance of play-balancing or trying them out, are a waste of your time as well as that of anyone who might have to read them over.

Instead, try to write descriptions of the game elements in question and their relation to the other elements. How do they compare in difficulty to each other? What traits does a particular AI agent have? Is this one more or less likely to run away in combat? Which AI capabilities will this element use and to what intended effect? How do the entity and its various effects appear to the player? How big is it compared to other objects? Include enough information for a programmer to understand what code will be required for the entity, and sufficient description that an artist will be able to make a concept sketch. You want to provide as much useful detail as possible without overdoing it. Readers, whether artists, programmers, or other designers, will know when you are just documenting for documenting's sake, in which case your document stops being practical and useful. Do not waste their time by making them read through reams of fluff to get the information they need.

Story Overview

Though not strictly necessary for a design document, I think having a brief Story Overview can be quite helpful in a design document, assuming your game has a story at all. Properly written, the overview provides all of the document's readers with an easy-to-read narrative of what transpires in the game. Much like the design document's overview, the Story Overview is a quick way for everyone on the team to understand the story's "big picture." To achieve this, you must keep the overview to an easily readable length while trying to include all of the major story points. A couple of pages should be sufficient, though this may vary depending on the complexity of the game's story; a shooter might only require one page, while an RPG might take a few more.

Certainly you do not need to include all of the game's sub-quests or describe every conversation the player will engage in or every character the player will meet. Try to make the Story Overview as compelling and readable as possible, so people will want to read it. While the Game Mechanics section may be difficult to read with its bullet-point lists and attention to detail, your Story Overview should be a pleasure to read. Indeed, if it is not a pleasure, try to figure out why not. Is it because your story is not that compelling? Do you need to refine and improve it in order to make it more interesting?

Game Progression

Depending on the nature of the game, the Game Progression section may well turn out to be the longest in the design document. This is where the game designer breaks the game down into the events the player experiences, and how they change and progress over time. This section will provide a guide for both the art team and the level designers as to what type of environments they will need to create for the game. The level designers take this section as a guideline for what each level is supposed to include and then fill in all the details as they build out each level, bringing all of the components of the game together.

For many types of games, including RPGs, RTS games, first-person shooters, action/adventures, and mission-based flight simulators, the Game Progression breakdown will be best done by level. For each level, you should describe in detail what challenges the player will face, what story (if any) transpires on them, and how the levels will appear aesthetically to the player. Figure out and describe what the major challenges will be on a given level: fighting with a horde of enemies at location A, meeting and talking to a specific character at location B, and solving a gameplay puzzle at location C. You certainly do not need to break down the level to the point where every single conflict is listed in minute detail. As with the character statistics, this is something that you will only be able to do when you are actually working with the level, when you are able to try the conflict a certain way and test it out. Explain how the appearance of the level will communicate the game's story, if applicable. What objects and items must be in what locations for the story to progress properly? Also discuss which elements from the game's "palette" will be available on this level. Which types of enemies will the player expect to encounter and what types of items will he find along the way?

More than anything, try to put into words how the level should affect the player, not just in terms of how difficult the level will be, but what sort of gameplay experience the player will have. Should the player feel constant conflict and challenge, or is this level more slow-paced and centered on exploration? Is the story at a climax in this level, resulting in increased tension, or is the level more slow-paced, focusing on filling in the game's back-story? As you write your Game Progression, always keep in mind how the player should feel when playing a given level, and try to communicate that emotional state in your writing.

Of course, not every game has levels, and so your Game Progression may not break down so easily into self-contained units. But most games have stages of some kind. Try to determine what the stages of your game are, and break down your Game Progression into these stages. For example, the original arcade game *Centipede* has a series of waves the player plays through. In that game, once the player kills all the segments of the centipede, he progresses to the next wave. The waves are cyclic, with each subsequent wave throwing a different centipede, either in terms of its length or speed, at the player. Also, from each wave to the next, the conditions under which certain enemies appear change. For instance, the flea never comes out in waves in which there is a twelve-segment centipede on the play-field. If one were to write a Game Progression for *Centipede* (which would not need to be very long at all), one would want to break it down by waves, clearly delineating how the game changes from wave to wave.

Free-form strategy games such as the *SimCity* series will not require a Game Progression section, since what happens during the game is entirely determined by the player's choices and the game mechanics. Pictured here: *SimCity 2000*.

Some games may not need a Game Progression section at all. For instance, a design document for a strategy game like *Civilization* or a software toy like *SimCity* could describe all of the relevant gameplay in the Game Mechanics, AI, and Game Elements sections. Since the levels in these games are randomly generated anyway, there is not much use in having a Game Progression section. However, if the game in question is to include certain scenarios which do start on predefined levels in specific configurations (as the *SimCity* games do), a Game Progression section would be the ideal place to describe these different scenarios and how they will challenge the player.

System Menus

The System Menus section is where you should detail the main menu and whatever other options screens the player will be presented with at various points outside of the game itself. These menus do not actually impact the gameplay in any significant way, and as a result should be separated into their own unique section. You should include descriptions of how the player will save his game and how he will load it later. Describe what type of interface the player will have with these menus: will he use mouse-pointer-based point-and-click, or will he use the Enter and arrow keys, or both? Try to be as complete as you think is necessary to ensure that the system menus are intuitive enough to allow the player to enjoy playing the game itself. Producers love to see that you have fully described the flow of these menus, so it may be important that you include a System Menus section, though, in my opinion, such a section is not truly required for a complete design document. It might even make sense to make the System Menus section into its own separate document, since they are so divorced from the gameplay proper.

One Man's Opinion

In the preceding pages, I have presented the format I like to use for game design documents. Let me repeat that it is by no means the industry standard format. Many great design documents have used formats wildly different from mine, both in terms of structure and in terms of how much detail they provided. But if you present a document structured as I have explained, you will not be laughed at or thought a fool. As I have stated previously, what is most important is that you communicate your vision for the game to the people reading your document. You are free to present your design information in whatever form makes the most sense to you while providing for maximum clarity and utility for your data.

Part of the reason why the design document format can vary so much from project to project is that games are not yet (nor do I think they ever will be) a standardized art form, as plays, movies, or symphonies are. Sure, within gaming there are certain genres or types of gameplay, and the design document format for a given genre, such as a first-person shooter, can be standardized. But even then, as the form of the shooter changes, as it implements new gameplay styles and mechanics, the structure of the document will need to adapt to these changes in order to communicate them effectively. One can hardly expect the design document for a first-person shooter such as *Half-Life* to be of the same form as one for a strategy game like *Alpha Centauri*. What the games accomplish and the experiences they provide are too radically different from each other, and hence their design documents must be different as well.

Inauspicious Design Documents

As I previously recommended, it may be useful to try to get your hands on some professional game design documents in order to give you an idea of what the industry expects in such specifications. However, you must be careful. It is likely that the document you obtain will not be any good. Many of the documents that have been used for published games and which were written by experienced professionals are truly terrible. By way of example, and in order to best teach you what to avoid, I will explore a few of the different types of horrible design documents, and why they fail so miserably at what they are supposed to accomplish.

The Wafer-Thin or Ellipsis Special Document

These thin little volumes, certainly none longer than thirty pages, startle and amaze the experienced game designer with their total and complete lack of any useful content whatsoever. They use meaningless descriptions like "gameplay will be fun" and "responsiveness will be sharp." In these documents, many comparisons to other games are made: "This plays like *Super Mario 64*" or "The game has a control scheme similar to *Quake*." While such comparisons can be slightly useful, as I have discussed, the writer of the Wafer-Thin Document almost always fails to go on to explain the control scheme of *Super Mario 64* or *Quake* in any detail, let alone the scheme to be used by the game in question.

Often these documents spend a lot of time, maybe half their pages, talking about back-story. Usually this back-story is very weak and poorly developed and is only tangentially related to the game being developed. The Wafer-Thin Document also spends a lot of time talking about how the menus will work. Not the in-game menus, but the system menus where the user selects what type of game he wants to play, sets his options, and so forth. Many mock-ups are made and options carefully listed. What exactly the options will affect in the game is seldom described in any detail, since the game itself is barely defined. Figuring out the menu system is something best pursued once the game is working, when the designer knows what sort of options might be important and what different gameplay choices the player will have; it is certainly far from the most difficult part of game design, nor the most important system to nail down first.

Wafer-Thin Documents are often constructed by managers who like to think they are game designers. The reason these can also be called Ellipsis Special Documents is that they are often littered with ellipses. For example, the worlds the player will encounter in the game will be described in the following manner: "Jungle World is a very hot and sticky place where the Garguflax Monkeys swing around and torment the player..." And that will be all the document provides in way of description for the world, ending at an ellipsis, as if to say "insert game design here." It is unclear whether the writers of these documents plan to come back and fill in at the ellipsis later or that perhaps they do not deem it worthy of their valuable time to actually explain how their game works. They just assume someone somewhere will fill it in and make them look good.

Another example of the content found in Ellipsis Special Documents might be: "The player will be given an option of many cool weapons. For example, the Gargantuan Kaboom does twice the damage of the player's other weapons and has a special effect. The Barboon Harpoon will allow the user to kill enemies at a distance with a nice camera effect. Other weapons will be just as fun and cool..." Here the writer of the Ellipsis Special fails to describe the weapons the game will have to any useful level of detail, and then, having listed two weapons, decides to leave the rest up to the imagination of the reader. Of course, readers are very usefully told that the other weapons will be "fun and cool." The writers of the Ellipsis Special mistakenly thinks that is all the description necessary to develop a game.

The only advantage to the Wafer Thin or Ellipsis Special Document is that it allows whoever gets to implement the design to pretty much take over the project and turn it into her own. I say this is a good aspect, since usually the ideas the manager included in the Wafer Thin Document are beyond ridiculous and do not make for viable gameplay. But one must be wary. Problems arise when the manager shows up six months later and complains: "But that's not what I wrote!"

The Back-Story Tome

Unlike writers of the Ellipsis Special Documents, the designer who writes the Back-Story Tome spends a lot of time working on his document. These books (it is hard to call them merely documents) usually stretch into the hundreds of pages—300-, 400-, even 500-page documents are not out of the question. There's a lot of information in there.

The first mistake these documents make is usually a poor table of contents and the lack of an index. In a design document, well-ordered information and a good table of contents can replace an index, but the absence of both is a huge error. The problems are compounded when the document is as long as *War and Peace*. The primary reason for the existence of game design documents is to allow team members to quickly look up information about a section of the game they are working on. If a programmer wants to know how the AI for a particular enemy is going to work, she needs to find that information quickly and easily. If she cannot find it, she may just make something up. Similarly, when an artist wants an idea of the textures that will be needed for a given area in the game, he wants to be able to find where that area is described as quickly as possible. Design documents are not read like novels. No one starts at the beginning and comes out at the end. Primarily, design documents are reference materials, and if team members cannot easily retrieve the data they are seeking, they are liable to give up.

However, once one starts hunting through one of these Back-Story Tomes, one is startled to find that, indeed, there is no information about the gameplay in there. It is all back-story. And at five hundred pages, it is far more back-story than most computer games will ever use. The history of all the characters in the game, the friends of those characters, and all the relevant parents and siblings are all described in minute detail. It may be very interesting stuff (though usually it is a disorganized mess), but in the end the reader is left with very little idea of how the game is supposed to function. A lot of games make storytelling one of their central concerns, and a story bible can be quite useful to game creation. In such a case, it makes sense to discuss the game's story in the design document to some extent. But first and foremost, a design document is supposed to contain the game's design, which is very different from a game's story. Though these Back-Story Tomes are very impressive in terms of weight and will probably impress the venture capitalists, the programmer who has to work with such a tome as his only guidance is going to end up designing the game himself.

The Overkill Document

Some designers think they can describe every last aspect of a game in the design document. It is certainly true that many design documents lack the necessary detail to be useful, as we found in the Ellipsis Special Document discussed above, but at the same time, going to an excessive level of detail can be a waste of the designer's time as well as the person who has to sift through all of that excess information. Furthermore, excessive documentation can lead to the illusion that the designer has created a complete, thorough document, when in fact he has gone into far too much detail about certain subjects while skipping other areas that need to be addressed.

For example, suppose that the game being documented has a number of characters who perform certain actions in the game-world. Say the game has townspeople, and they need to walk around, sit down and stand up, talk to each other, and sleep. The document should describe these behaviors in the AI section. A truly thorough document might break this down into separate animations: stand from sitting, sit from standing, idle sitting, idle standing, walk, converse with hand gestures, and so on. Probably this is not necessary, since a good animator and lead artist will be able to break this down better than a designer can. But some designers may go overboard and actually sketch or list the individual animation frames. This is absurd. There is no way to know in the design document stage how many animation frames will be required for a given animation. This sort of decision can only be made and adjusted during the game's production. Not to mention that listing animation frames is insulting to the animator who will only feel demoralized by this degree of micro-management. Furthermore, the design document should stick to gameplay design, and not veer into the territory of the art bible or other art documentation.

Another example might be what I call "balancing data." These are the actual statistics for the weapons, items, and characters found in the game. The design document should probably list what different attributes weapons and characters will have. For instance, a weapon might have a range, an accuracy, a number of shots, and a rate of fire. Furthermore, the design document might want to describe the qualities of a given weapon: "The Double Barreled Shotgun has a short range and a low accuracy, but does a large amount of damage in a large area." However, actually listing the values for a weapon's attributes is not very useful in the design document. Saying "Shotgun Accuracy: 2" does not really serve any purpose since the number "2" does not have any context and therefore no meaning. These values are best determined when the game is actually functioning, when a designer can balance the weapons as they will be used by the player and thus the designer can experiment with different settings to achieve the desired effects. Creating large tables full of data before this information is actually testable is by and large a waste of time.

As with animation minutia and precise balancing data, source code also does not belong in the document. Designers who start writing out algorithms in their design documents are going too far. It does not matter if the designer is also a programmer. There should be no code, not even pseudocode, in the design document. Including code will only serve to bloat the document and distract from omitted information which needs to be covered. If there is any useful information in the Overkill Document, it is so hidden in the river of useless data that team members will be too intimidated to look for it. The author of the Overkill Document thinks that he can preplan everything, and that he is far more talented than any member of his team. While such excessive attention to detail can be impressive to those who do not really know what they are doing, a design document that goes too far will only infuriate the team that has to work with it.

The Pie-in-the-Sky Document

These design documents often have noble intentions with grand ideas for truly magnificent gameplay. Sadly, the writers of them typically lack any technical grasp of what the computer is capable of or what a team of twenty people is likely to accomplish in a year and a half. As a result, these overambitious documents put forth fancy ideas with no basis in reality or feasibility and end up frustrating and infuriating the teams assigned to "make them happen."

Pie-in-the-Sky Documents include ideas such as "a fully modeled replica of Manhattan will be the player's primary game-world, complete with AI agents representing all of the city's seven million inhabitants in real-time." The authors of Pie-in-the-Sky Documents do not want to be bothered with messy details such as the reality that no existing computer system can simulate seven million humans in any sort of reasonable time frame (let alone real-time). Another feature suggested in a Pie-in-the-Sky Document might be "a natural language parser will be included that allows users to type in full, complex English sentences which the characters will respond to with their own dynamically generated dialog." The guilty designer does not want to hear that research institutions have been working for decades on natural language processors that still have trouble with short, simple sentences. Pie-in-the-Sky Documents are often combined with Ellipsis Specials into truly wretched design documents, where the guilty designer outlines a completely impractical project without bothering to go into much detail about it.

The Fossilized Document

Any of the above flawed design documents can also be a Fossilized Document. Indeed, a design document which does not necessarily suffer from any of the above problems and was once a fine reference tool will become a Fossilized Document over the course of a project if the designer is not diligent in her efforts to keep the document up to date. I know of no original game project whose design has not changed significantly during the course of its development, and when the design changes but the design document does not, that document starts to become a Fossilized Document.

Suppose a programmer on the development team looks something up in the Fossilized Document. Say the information that person finds is out of date. They may start implementing the old, long-since-modified functionality. At some point, a designer or producer who is aware of the changes that have taken place in the design will notice that the programmer is creating a system that is no longer appropriate, and will chastise the programmer for doing so. This creates frustration for both parties, not to mention wasting the programmer's time. Furthermore, whenever the programmer needs to know something about the design in the future, he will not trust the design document, and instead will go hunt down a designer or producer to find out how a given system is supposed to function. Of course, this defeats the purpose of the document, as the designer must stop whatever he is working on to explain the system to the programmer. This new system may be described correctly in the document, but the programmer is not going to get burned again by using the Fossilized Document. When the designer fails to update the document when design changes occur, the entire document becomes useless. No one can trust it, and as a result no one will bother to read it.

A Matter of Weight

It is often joked that design documents are not read, they are weighed. This is not surprising given the heft of many design documents and the lack of desire among team members to read them. Shockingly, this statement is often true. I once heard an ex-producer from a major gaming publisher talk about her experience with design documents and the project approval process. She said that the "decision-makers" would bring a scale to their "green-light" meetings. When it came down to two similar projects that were both relatively worthy of funding, they would take the design document for each project and place it on the scale. Whichever one weighed more would get accepted, the other rejected. Much as it pains me to tell you, if you are in the commercial gaming business and groveling for dollars at publishers, you need to make your document hefty. You need it to be impressive to pick up and flip through. Many will never read it at all. Others will read only the Overview and Table of Contents at the beginning. But everyone will pick it up and remark on its weight.

Of course, many of these super-thick documents contain a lot of information of negligible value toward the actual development of the project. They may be a stellar example of one of the failed types of documents I discussed earlier, such as a Back-Story Tome or an Overkill Document. It is your challenge as the game designer to make the document as practical as possible by providing only useful information in the document, while making it hefty enough to impress the suits. One might want to include a large number of flowcharts or concept sketches or choose to use a bigger font, all while not being too obvious. Indeed, a great game (though a simplistic one) can have a perfect design document only ten pages long. One wonders how many great, simple games have been cast aside by publishers who were unimpressed with the mass of their design documents.

Getting It Read

Once your design document is written, one of your biggest challenges may be getting anyone on the development team to read it. Often, many programmers, artists, or even other designers will not want to put the time into a careful reading of your document. Others may have been burned by bad design documents in the past and will jump to the conclusion that yours is of similarly poor quality. Keeping your document up to date, including only useful information, providing a detailed table of contents, and limiting yourself to practical, accomplishable gameplay elements will help. If your team members sample your document and find it to be of superior quality, they are more likely to return to it for reference when they are actually implementing a given system or working on a particular piece of art. As with any written document, you need to earn the trust of your readers if you hope to keep them reading.

Another key method of getting your design document read is to make it easily available to anyone who wants to read it. Keep it in the same source-control system that your team uses for asset management. You want your team members to be able to get the latest version of the design document as easily as they get the latest build of the game. Since you will be constantly revising and updating your document to keep it up to date with the project (and to prevent it from becoming a Fossilized Document), source control will be a valuable tool for keeping track of the previous revisions.

When you check in the latest version of the document, send your team an e-mail telling them that it is available and explaining what has changed. That way, people can easily skim over the changes. If one of the changes is relevant to their work, then they can get the latest version of the document off the network and read over the relevant updates. Updating your document does not do any good if no one knows you have updated it, or if people are still reading old revisions. It is probably a good idea to use a version number with your document, such as 1.3 or 2.7. Include this version number, along with the date, in a header on every page. Often people will print out a design document and not realize how old or fossilized it is. If they can quickly compare a date and a version number, they will know which version of the document they have and whether they need to get a new one.

Documentation is Only the Beginning

Some designers seem to think that a thorough design document is, by itself, enough to build a game. It also seems to be the case that companies have bought design documents from designers, with those designers moving on to write other design documents while another team actually executes their design. A design document is a rough outline, more the suggestion of a game than anything else, and without being involved in a game's creation until it goes gold master, one cannot truly be considered to have designed the game. A designer who takes any pride in his work will want to be there throughout the project, ready to change the design as necessary to make it the most compelling game possible and updating the document as the design is changed and revised (and rest assured it will be continuously changed and revised). A committed game designer will want to be there to balance the weapons, the AI, the controls, and certainly the levels, to make sure the game follows the focus through and the initial vision is realized.

If a designer writes a design document and then passes it on to others to actually build, the people who do the actual creation will change the design to match their own interests and artistic drives. The design document will be a springboard for their own act of creation, not the original designer's. The design document is an integral part of the game's creation, perhaps, but a design document is not all that is required. To claim any sort of meaningful authorship on the project, a designer

needs to be involved for the duration. In a way, writing the design document is the easy part of computer game design. Actually taking the document and creating a compelling gaming experience is much, much harder.

Chapter 18:
Interview: Jordan Mechner

The only complaint one could have about Jordan Mechner's work in computer games is that he has not made more games. Each of the games he has designed and spearheaded—**Karateka**, **Prince of Persia**, and **The Last Express**—has had a unique elegance and sophistication that one seldom finds in the world of computer games. But the game industry has had to do without Mechner for several periods of time while he pursued his other great love, filmmaking. Indeed, it is Mechner's knowledge of film that has helped to contribute to the quality of his games. But this quality does not come through the epic cut-scenes and barely interactive game mechanics that so often come about when developers attempt to merge film and gaming. Instead, Mechner has blended film and game techniques in unique and innovative ways, helping his titles to tell stories visually while still retaining the qualities that make them great games.

This interview was originally conducted around the release of **The Last Express** for **Inside Mac Games** magazine. For inclusion in this book, Mechner was kind enough to fill out the interview a bit, expanding it to cover the full breadth of his fifteen years in computer game development.

What initially attracted you to computer games?

Well, it was 1979, and I was a sophomore in high school. The first computer that I ever got a chance to play with was the PDP-11 that we had in our high school. But it was very hard to get any time on it, and the teacher who was in charge wouldn't let the students read the manuals, for fear that would give us the ability to go in and change grades and stuff like that. So it was this guessing game of trying to learn how to get the computer to do anything. So when a friend of mine showed me his new Apple II, it was just like a dream come true, to have a computer in your own house that you could use whenever you wanted. And it was completely open; you could pop open the top and see how it was made and you could read all the manuals that came with it. And of course, the irony was that at that time I didn't know of any manuals that explained assembly language. So I was just kind of looking through the assembly code of the computer's operating system to try to figure out what the different commands meant. Over the years I picked that up, and more books came out. It was just this great toy.

Did you always want to make games with the computer?

Well, I guess games were the only kind of software that I knew. They were the only kind that I enjoyed. At that time, I didn't really see any use for a word processor or a spreadsheet. I played all the games that I could find, and in my spare time I tried to write games of my own. That was just the first use that occurred to me.

So that was the origin of *Karateka*?

It took a few years to get there. The first really ambitious project I did was a game called *Asteroids*. That was my attempt to do for *Asteroids* what a game called *Apple Invaders* had done for the other most popular coin-op game of the time. I figured that if *Apple Invaders* was a big hit because it was exactly like the coin-op game, then I could do the same thing for *Asteroids*. But my timing was a little off. I actually finished an assembly language, high-resolution version of *Asteroids* and signed a deal with a publisher. But just about then Atari woke up to the fact that these computer games were ripping off its hugely profitable arcade franchises, so their lawyers scared everybody off and that *Asteroids* game was never published.

So then you did *Karateka*?

No, then I did a game that bore a strong resemblance to *Asteroids* except that instead of rocks you had brightly colored bouncing balls, and instead of wrapping around the edge of the screen they bounced off, hence its name: *Deathbounce*. I sent it to Broderbund (this was 1982, I was a freshman in college) and got a call back from Doug Carlston, who was at the time handling submissions as well as running the company. I was very excited to get a call from someone in the computer games industry. He said, "It looks like it's well programmed, we're impressed with the smoothness of the animation and so on. But it feels kind of old-fashioned. Take a look at our new game, *Choplifter*." Doug was kind enough to send me a copy of Dan Gorlin's *Choplifter*, which was the number one selling game at the time, along with a joystick to play it with. That was the game that really woke me up to the idea that I didn't have to copy someone else's arcade games, I was allowed to design my own!

Karateka came out of a lot of ideas all kind of converging at the same time. *Choplifter* showed me what was possible in terms of smooth scrolling and an original game design. Meanwhile, I was getting megadoses of exposure to cinema; Yale had about a dozen film societies and I was trying to

Karateka

see in four years every film ever made. *Seven Samurai* was my new favorite film of all time. My mom at that time was heavily into karate, and I had taken a few lessons during the summer down at the local dojo. Finally, I was taking film studies classes (always dangerous) and starting to get delusions of grandeur that computer games were in the infancy of a new art form, like cartoon animation in the '20s or film in the 1900s. So all those sources of inspiration got rolled into *Karateka*. What made the big difference was using a Super 8 camera to film my karate teacher going through the moves, and tracing them frame by frame on a Moviola. It was rotoscoping, the same trick that Disney had used for *Snow White* back in the '30s. That made the animation look a lot better than I could have done by hand and better than the other games that were out there. I worked on *Karateka* for a couple of years between classes, and sent it to Broderbund at about the end of my sophomore year. They were pleased and published it.

So one of your goals was to merge cinematic techniques with an action game to create a unique hybrid?

Very definitely. The accelerating cross-cutting to create suspense had been used by D.W. Griffith in 1915; I figured it should be tried in a computer game. The horizontal wipe for transition between scenes I lifted from *Seven Samurai*. The scrolling text prologue at the beginning. And silly things, like saying THE END instead of GAME OVER. I used the few techniques that I could figure out how to pull off in hi-res graphics on an Apple II.

Karateka's actually quite short. Was that a deliberate decision, to keep the game focused?

Well, it didn't seem short to me at the time. Actually, when I submitted it to Broderbund it only had one level: you'd enter the palace and have the fight. One of the first things they suggested to me was to have three different levels: you're outside, you're in the palace, then you're down below. I wasn't thinking in terms of hours of play, I just wanted to make it cool.

The ending is a pretty devious trick, where if the player approaches the princess in the "attack" stance she'll kick him. How did you come up with that?

It seemed like a fun little trick. You only have one life in that game: you get as far as you can, and if you're killed, it's "The End" and you have to start the movie from the beginning again. So I figured that most players, when they finally got to the end, would just run right into her arms. But it's not a total cheat,

Karateka

there's a little clue there, where she puts her arms out to you, and then if you run towards her she lowers her arms. So that's a sign that something's not right.

But I don't know that anybody ever played that game and did it right the first time.

Yeah, in retrospect that was pretty nasty. I don't know if we could get away with that today. The other thing that we got away with on *Karateka* was that if you played the flip side of the disk, if you put the disk in upside down, the game plays upside down. I was hoping at least a few people would call Broderbund tech support and say, "The screen is upside down, I think something's wrong with my monitor or my computer." That way the tech support person could have the sublime joy of saying, "Oh, you probably put the disk in upside down." And the customer would happily hang up thinking this was true of all computer software. I thought it was extremely brave of the publisher to increase the cost of goods by twenty-five cents just for a gag.

So did *Prince of Persia* grow out of your experiences on *Karateka*?

Well, there was a big gap between *Karateka* and *Prince of Persia* in terms of my own life. I finished school and I took a year off. I wasn't sure that I wanted to do another computer game. The most direct inspiration there was a game by Ed Hobbs called *The Castles of Doctor Creep*, which didn't get too big a circulation, probably because it was only available on the Commodore 64. My college dorm mates and I spent a lot of hours playing that game. It had these ingenious puzzles of the Rube Goldberg sort, where you hit one switch and that opens a gate but closes another gate, and so forth. So the one-sentence idea for *Prince of Persia* was to do a game that combined the ingenuity of *The Castles of Doctor Creep* with the smooth animation of *Karateka*. So when you ran and jumped you weren't just a little sprite flying through the air, your character actually felt like it had weight and mass, and when you fell on the spikes it felt like it really hurt.

Another inspiration was the first eight minutes of *Raiders of the Lost Ark*. I wanted to make a game with that kind of action feeling to it. And then there was the *Arabian Nights* setting. I was looking for a setting that hadn't been done to death in computer games, and a couple of animators at Broderbund, Gene Portwood and Lauren Elliot, suggested this one. I went back and reread the *Arabian Nights* and it seemed to offer a lot of promise. It had all those great story possibilities which have been absorbed into our collective unconscious—genies, the voyages of Sinbad, Aladdin's cave. It was just crying out to be made as a computer game.

You said you had taken some time off before making *Prince of Persia*. What finally made you want to come back and do another game?

That was the year I wrote my first film screenplay. It was optioned by Larry Turman, a very nice man who had produced about fifty films including *The Graduate*. We had a year of meetings with directors and studios and came close to getting it made, but in the end it didn't come together. Later I found out that for a first-time screenwriter, that's not considered a bad start at all. But I'd been spoiled by computer games, and I thought, "My God, I've just spent six months here in Los Angeles waiting for something to happen, and the film isn't even getting made." In compari-son, I knew that if I finished *Prince of*

Prince of Persia

Persia, it would get published. So I figured I'd better stick with that. At the point when all this good stuff had started to happen with the screenplay, I was about six months into *Prince of Persia*, and I'd put it aside for almost a year to focus on screenwriting. It was pretty scary going back to programming after so much time off; I was afraid I wouldn't be able to remember my own source code. But I went back, picked it up again, and finished it.

One thing about *Prince of Persia* is that it takes this finite amount of game elements and stretches them out over all of these levels. Yet it never gets dull or repetitive. How did you manage that?

That was really the challenge of the design. It was modular in that there were a finite number of elements that could be recombined in different ways. It's the same thing you try to do in a movie. You plant a line of dialog or a significant object, and fifteen or thirty minutes later you pay it off in an unexpected way. An example in *Prince of Persia* would be the loose floors. The first time you encounter one it's a trap: you have to step over it so you don't fall. Then later on, it reappears, not as a trap but as an escape route: You have to jump and hit the ceiling to discover there's a loose ceiling piece that you can knock down from below. Later on, you can use one to kill a guard by dropping it on his head, to jam open a pressure plate, or—a new kind of trap—to accidentally break a pressure plate so that you can never open it again.

It was necessary to make *Prince of Persia* modular because the memory of the computer was so limited. The smooth animation of the character, with so many intermediate frames and so many moves, was taking up a huge percentage of that 64K computer. When efficiency is not an issue, you can always add production value to a game by throwing in a completely new environment, or special effect, or enemy, but when you're literally out of RAM and out of disk space, you have to think creatively. Which in turn forces the player to think creatively. There's a certain elegance to taking an element the player already thinks he's familiar with, and challenging him to think about it in a different way.

Prince of Persia is really a simple game to control, especially compared to modern action games. Was that a design goal of yours?

Absolutely. That was a very strong consideration in both *Karateka* and *Prince of Persia*, and I spent hours trying to figure out how to integrate certain moves. Should it be up with the joystick, or up with the button? Personally, I have a strong prejudice against games that require me to use more than one or two buttons. That's a problem, actually, that I have with modern action games. By the time I figure out whether I'm using A, B, X, O, or one of those little buttons down at the bottom of the controller pad that you never use except for one special emergency move, I've lost the illusion that it's me that's controlling the character.

Ideally, you want to get the player so used to handling the joystick and the buttons that the action starts feeling like an extension of him or herself. The trick there, obviously, is that when you bring in a new movement that you haven't used before, you want

Prince of Persia

the player to somehow already "know" what button or what combination of actions is going to bring off that move. In *Prince of Persia* there were moves where I thought, "This would be great, but I don't have a button for it, so let it go. It would be cool, but it doesn't help the game overall." A major constraint was keeping the controls simple and consistent.

As far as game design, it seems that *Prince of Persia* was a logical extension of what you did in *Karateka*, and *Prince of Persia 2* was in turn an extension of that. But *The Last Express* seems to be off in a completely new direction. What provoked you to do something as different as *Last Express*?

I guess I don't think of *Last Express* as being off in a new direction. I was still trying to tackle the same problem of how to tell a story and create a sense of drama and involvement for the player. There are a number of proven action game formulas that have evolved since the days of *Prince of Persia*. Part of what interested me about doing an adventure game was that it seemed to be a wide open field, in that there hadn't been many games that had found a workable paradigm for how to do an adventure game.

So it wasn't the inspiration of other adventure games?

No, on the contrary in fact. If you look at the old Scott Adams text adventures from the '80s, it's surprising how little adventure games have progressed in terms of the experience that the player has: the feeling of immersion, and the feeling of life that you get from the characters and the story. So I guess it was the challenge of trying to revitalize or reinvent a moribund genre that attracted me.

What inspired you to set the game on the Orient Express in 1914?

In computer game design you're always looking for a setting that will give you the thrills and adventure that you seek, while at the same time it needs to be a constrained space in order to design a good game around it. For example, things like cities are very difficult to do. A train struck me as the perfect setting for a game. You've got a confined space and a limited cast of characters, and yet you don't have that static feeling that you would get in, say, a haunted house, because the train itself is actually moving. From the moment the game starts, you're in an enclosed capsule that is moving, not only towards its destination—Paris to

The Last Express

Constantinople—but it's also moving in time, from July 24th to July 27th, from a world at peace to a world at war. The ticking clock gives a forward movement and drive to the narrative, which I think works very well for a computer game.

The Orient Express, of course, is the perfect train for a story that deals with the onset of World War I. The Orient Express in 1914 was the "new thing"; it was an innovation like the European Economic Community is today, a symbol of the unity of Europe. At the time it was possible to travel from one end of Europe to the other, a journey that used to take weeks, in just a few days, without trouble at the borders and so on. On that train you had a cross-section of people from different countries, different social classes, different occupations—a microcosm of Europe in one confined environment. All these people who had been traveling together and doing business together, found themselves suddenly separated along nationalist lines for a war that would last four years and which would destroy not only the social fabric but also the very train tracks that made the Orient Express possible. To me the Orient Express is a very dramatic and poignant symbol of what that war was all about. And a great setting for a story.

So would you say your starting point for *Last Express* was: "I want to make an adventure game, what sort of story can I tell in that form?" Or was it: "Here's a story I want to tell, what type of game will allow me to effectively tell it?"

Definitely the latter. Tomi Pierce [co-writer of *The Last Express*] and I wanted to tell a story on the Orient Express in 1914 right before war breaks out: how do we do that? I didn't really focus on the fact that it was a switch of genre from *Prince of Persia*, or what that would mean for the marketing. It just became apparent as we worked out the story that given the number of characters, the emphasis on their motivations and personalities, the importance of dialog and different languages, that what we were designing was an adventure game. I consciously wanted to get away from the adventure game feel. I don't personally like most adventure games. I wanted to have a sense of immediacy as you're moving through the train, and have people and life surging around you, as opposed to the usual adventure game feeling where you walk into an empty space which is just waiting there for you to do something.

Was this your reason for adding the "real-time" aspect to *Last Express*, something we're not used to seeing in adventure games?

Of course, it's not technically real-time, any more than a film is. The clock is always ticking, but we play quite a bit with the rate at which time elapses. We slow it down at certain points for dramatic emphasis, we speed it up at certain points to keep things moving. And we've got ellipses where you cut away from the train, then you cut back and it's an hour later.

But still, it's more real-time than people are used to in traditional adventure games.

Or even in action games. I'm amazed at the number of so-called action games where, if you put the joystick down and sit back and watch, you're just staring at a blank screen. Once you clear out that room of enemies, you can sit there for hours.

You mentioned filmmaking back there, and I know in 1993 you made your own documentary film, *Waiting for Dark*. Did your experience with filmmaking help you in the making of *Last Express*?

It's been extremely helpful, but I think it can also be a pitfall. Film has an incredibly rich vocabulary of tricks, conventions, and styles which have evolved over the last hundred years of filmmaking. Some have been used in computer games and really work well, others are still waiting for someone to figure out how to use them, and others don't work very well at all and tend to kill the games they get imported into. The classic example is the so-called "interactive movie," which is a series of cut-scenes strung together by choice trees; do this and get cut-scene A and continue, do that and get cut-scene B and lose. For *Last Express*, I wanted the player to feel that they were moving freely on board a train, with life swirling all around them and the other characters all doing their own thing. If someone passes you in the corridor, you should be able to turn around, see them walk down the corridor the other way, and follow them and see where they go. If you're not interested, you can just keep walking. I think of it as a non-linear experience in the most linear possible setting, that is, an express train.

All of your games have featured cut-scenes in one way or another, and in *Karateka*, *Prince of Persia*, and *Last Express* they've all been integrated into the game so as to be visually indistinguishable from the gameplay. Was this a conscious decision on your part?

Absolutely. Part of the aesthetic of all three of those games is that if you sit back and watch it, you should have a smooth visual experience as if you were watching a film. Whereas if you're playing it, you should have a smooth experience controlling it. It should work both for the player and for someone who's standing over the player's shoulder watching. Cut-scenes and the gameplay should look as much as possible as if they belong to the same world. *Karateka* used cross-cutting in real-time to generate suspense: when you're running toward the guard, and then cut to the guard running toward you, then cut back to you, then back to the shot where the guard enters the frame. That's a primitive example, but one that worked quite well.

Same idea in *Last Express*: you're in first-person point-of-view, you see August Schmidt walking towards you down the corridor, then you cut to a reaction shot of Cath, the player's character, seeing him coming. Then you hear August's voice, and you cut back to August, and almost without realizing it you've shifted into a third-person dialog cut-scene. The scene ends with a shot of August walking away down the corridor, and now you're back in point-of-view and you're controlling it again. We understand the meaning of that sequence of shots intuitively because we've seen

The Last Express

it so much in film. A classic example is Alfred Hitchcock's *Rear Window*. The whole film is built around the triptych of shot, point-of-view shot, reaction shot, where about half the movie is seen through James Stewart's eyes. That's the basic unit of construction of *Last Express* in terms of montage.

On the other hand, in *Prince of Persia 2*, the cut-scenes were actually painted pictures that looked quite a bit different from the actual gameplay. I seem to recall not enjoying those quite so much...

I agree with you about that. There's a distancing effect to those cut-scenes, they make you feel like you're watching a storybook. But it was the effect we were going for at the time.

Right now there seems to be a trend away from full-motion video cut-scenes in computer games...

And rightly so, because the full-motion cut-scenes sometimes cost as much as the whole game and it's debatable whether they really improved the gameplay. Also, there's the problem that the quality of the cut-scenes in most cases was pretty low, if you compare it to good TV or good movies.

So you made a conscious attempt to do something different in merging a filmmaking style with a game-making style?

My hope is that *Last Express* offers something that hasn't really been offered by any other adventure game, or actually a game of any genre, which is to really find yourself in a world that's populated by people. Interesting, well-rounded characters, that are not just physically distinguishable, but have their own personality, their own purpose in the story, their own plans of action. And through the fairly conventional point-and-click mechanism, you're actually interacting with a world that's not just visually rich but richly populated.

So how did you go about designing the player's method of interacting with the game?

Our goal was to keep it as simple as possible. Point-and-click appealed to me because I always saw *Last Express* as a game that would appeal to a more mainstream audience of adults. People who don't usually play computer games and aren't particularly handy with a joystick aren't going to sit still to learn a large number of keys and what they all do. Pointing and clicking is something that adults in our society know how to do, so the challenge was to construct a game where you wouldn't have to know how to do anything beyond how to pick up a mouse and move it over the screen. The cursor changes as you pass over different regions to show you what you can do: you can turn left, you can talk to a different character. The specifics of how that works evolved as we tested it. During the development we worked out problems like: "Do 'up' and 'forward' need to be different-shaped cursors?" We decided yes they do. "Do 'look up' and 'stand up' need to be different?" We decided no, they can both be the up arrow. But the basic idea that it would be hot-spot based, point-and-click was very much a part of the original design.

So how much film did you shoot for *Last Express*? It seems like there is a monstrous amount of footage in there.

The whole project, because of its size, was a huge logistical challenge. The film shoot was actually only three weeks long. Which is not very much, when you consider that an ordinary feature film shoot takes at least four weeks, shooting an average of three screenplay pages a day. Whereas for three weeks, we shot about fifteen

The Last Express

screenplay pages a day. We had a few tricks that allowed us to move that fast: the fact that it was all blue-screen, the fact that we were shooting silent and had recorded the sound previously, and the fact that we were under-cranking, shooting seven and a half frames per second in some scenes, five frames per second in others. With the goal being to select key-frames and then reanimate them, as you see in the finished game. All that let us shoot a lot of material.

But in terms of keeping track of it . . . Just to give an example, the first phase of the shoot was in the train corridor. We laid out a fifty-foot track representing the corridor, with yellow lines on the blue-painted floor with a blue-painted cyc-wall behind it. And for three days we marched all thirty characters on the train up and down that corridor. The key moment, when a character walks toward the camera, is the moment of eye contact—friendly or unfriendly—the nuance of that glance being one of the things that brings you into the game as Cath, makes you feel that you're not just a phantom presence on the train but that people are reacting to you, even as they pass you in the corridor. For the first three days we just filmed corridor walks, and we had it basically down to a science. The camera was locked down for three days; it didn't move. If the camera moved, then we would have footage that didn't line up.

After three days in the corridor we moved to the restaurant, and again we had to do that in a very unusual way. Instead of shooting one scene at a time and covering each scene with a variety of camera setups, as we would in a film, instead we shot one camera setup at a time. From each camera setup we would shoot all the different scenes or actions that could possibly be seen from that angle in the course of the entire story. We would lock down the camera in each position, say, the "seated at the table looking straight ahead" view. We'd set up the other tables, and film every piece of action that could be seen from that view—August Schmidt walks in, sits down, orders dinner, the waiter brings him the food, he eats it, puts down his napkin, gets up, and walks away. Then with the camera set up from a different dining room angle, we'd have the same actors repeat the same actions. To make the shoot as efficient as possible was a bit of a jigsaw puzzle, figuring out which actors to bring in on which days and when to let them go, and is it more economical to move the camera one extra time so that we can send a bunch of actors home early, or should we leave the camera where it is and pay the actors for the whole day. That times nineteen days was a logistically very complicated film shoot. With a lot of the action being filmed from multiple angles, since in the game, you never know what angle the player's going to see it from.

And once it was all shot, it must have been a tremendous challenge to keep it all straight.

We did the editing on an Avid; without that I don't know what we would have done. We dumped it all onto huge hard drives on this Macintosh-based non-linear editing system, and selected the frames we wanted. We pushed that Avid system to its limits. At one point our film editor had to call tech support because the system was slowing down so much. When he told them how many effects he had, they were startled, and couldn't believe it was still functioning. We had more frame dissolves in just one of our scenes than they had anticipated anyone would ever have in a normal feature film. We were picking still frames and dissolving from one to another, so that every frame in the game was a special effect.

The official number is that we had forty thousand frames of animation in the game. In comparison to an animated feature film, however, that number is misleadingly low. In a typical dialog scene we're dissolving between still frames on the average of once every second or once every two seconds, whereas a conventional film runs twenty-four frames per second. So to get the equivalent in terms of how much action we really covered, you need to multiply forty thousand by twenty-four. Also, a lot of frames are reusable. You've got one hundred fifty frames of the character walking up the corridor towards camera, then one hundred fifty frames walking away from camera. Using just those three hundred frames, the train conductor character, say, might spend ten hours walking over the course of the game. When you walk into the dining room, you see six tables, and each table can have its own action going on independently. If you play the game from start to finish five times, the sixth time you might see two characters in the room together, whereas before they were always in the room separately. Just because the action unfolds a little differently. So the number of combinations of that footage is pretty much unlimited.

So what made you come up with the effect of dissolving between frames every one or two seconds used in *Last Express?* Why didn't you use the more traditional, full-motion style throughout the game?

From our point of view, full motion is basically an expensive special effect. It looks great, as in the corridors, as in the fights. But if we had decided to use that for the entire game, I think we would have ended up with something that was visually very flashy but not very deep. We're limited both by the amount of frames that can be kept in RAM, and by the number of CDs. But ultimately, you're limited by the processor's ability. When you walk into the restaurant and it's full of people, with a number of different animations happening on the screen at the same time, as well as multiple tracks of audio streaming from the CD, that's possible only because each character is only animating every few seconds.

But there's also an aesthetic disadvantage to full motion. Say the technological limitations could be overcome, and we had a thirty-second loop of a character eating dinner. Sooner or later you realize the character is repeating. So you say, "Why is it that when he takes a sip from his wine glass and then takes a bite of steak, the steak keeps getting replenished every time he eats it?" That's not helpful to the game, to have the player's attention distracted by following those little full-motion bits. When it gets down to it, we decided that what's important for the game is that the player believe the character is there, having dinner for an hour and fifteen minutes. And any time during that hour you can talk to him. The fact is that dissolving

The Last Express

between still frames gives just as good an impressionistic sense of "dining" as the full motion would, and in some ways better, because you don't have that glitch when the film loops. So, with this convention, once the player accepts it, it opens up the world and gives you the ability to tell this huge story that goes on for three days and three nights with thirty characters doing all kinds of things. It would have been a drastically smaller story had we stuck to full motion.

I noticed in the credits that for almost all the characters you have one actor doing the physical acting—what the player sees on the screen—and another doing the voice. Why did you decide to use different actors for the visual and audio aspects of the game?

Casting was a tremendous challenge with a cast where you've only got two Americans, and everybody else is French, Russian, Austrian, Serbian, Arabic... The Orient Express was a truly multilingual train. We made the decision to have the characters not just speak English with a foreign accent, as when they're talking to the American hero, but to also speak their native language, subtitled, whenever they would normally do so. When the two French conductors are chatting with one another off-duty, they'd naturally be speaking French. So casting American actors who can do a fake German or French accent just wasn't acceptable to us. We needed native speakers for each language. I think we were very lucky to get such a good cast both for the faces and for the voices. But to ask for the perfect face, the perfect voice, and the perfect nationality to be united in one person for each role would have been too much to ask—especially in San Francisco, on our budget! There again, the fact that we weren't doing full-motion lip-synching gave us the flexibility we needed in casting.

Tatiana is a case in point. We used three casting agencies and auditioned hundreds of actors in both L.A. and San Francisco, looking for the face and voice of a sixteen-year-old Russian princess. The actress who ended up doing the voice is Russian and lives in L.A., the one we filmed is American and lives in San Francisco. To find one actor who was that good for both, we would have certainly needed to go out of state, if not to Russia!

By the way, we recorded the voices first, and then created animated visuals to match, so the voice actors were free to create their own performance, as they would with a radio play or doing a Disney cartoon. It gives you a more natural voice performance than overdubbing. I think when you force actors to lip-synch to previously filmed action, you lose something in the performance.

Reality seems to have been a dominant goal in your design of the game, whether it's the native speakers for the voice acting or if it's the authentically modeled train cars. Why did you go to such great lengths to make the game as real as possible?

It's a matter of respect for the player. Whether it's a history world or a fantasy world, I think that players respond to the amount of detail and consistency that the creators of the game put into it. And even if the player doesn't pay enough attention to the conductors to figure out that one of them is close to retirement and the other one is a young married guy, or that they have opposite political views, even so, whenever you pass them in the corridor and overhear a little bit of one of their conversations, you get the subliminal feeling that you're hearing a real conversation between two real people. If we hadn't bothered, then whenever you walked by, you'd hear something artificial, and think, "You know, that sounds like something they just staged for my benefit." The fact that what you see in the game is just the tip of the iceberg, and that all the characters have their own history, and their own reality under the surface, you feel the mass of that, and the weight of it, though you don't actually see anything more than the tip.

Do you think computer games in general should strive for greater realism?

Well, realism is a bit of a loaded term. I don't mean to imply that games should be more realistic in terms of representing our world. Even something like *Super Mario Bros.*, which is completely a fantasy setting, has its own consistency. If a character can jump off a ledge and float to the bottom in one situation, you shouldn't have another situation where he jumps off and he gets crushed. As long as the creators actually took the time to think, "What are the rules for gravity in this world, and under what circumstances can you get hurt?" As long as the game plays by its own rules, players will accept it. In *Last Express*, we chose a real historical moment, and we were very conscious about trying to represent faithfully what was going on in the world at that time, and to respect that reality when drawing the constraints of our fictional world.

You use a very unique technique in *Last Express* where, though the actors were filmed, in the end they look like very well-crafted cartoons. Why did you decide to do it that way?

To begin with, I like the cartoon look aesthetically. I think the look of cartoon people against a 3D rendered background is very attractive. Films like *Snow White and the Seven Dwarfs* had technical reasons why they had to be flat—they were painted on cells—but they bring out the character nicely, and I think it's a look that has good connota-

The Last Express

tions for those of us who as kids wanted to step inside the cartoon and become one of the characters.

I think for computer games, there's another advantage to having the characters be cartoons, as opposed to live, filmed people. The experience of the computer game player depends on being able to put yourself into a fantasy world, suspend disbelief, and believe that what you're doing actually has an effect on these fictional characters. If you're watching a filmed live actor, intellectually you know that this is someone who was filmed on a sound stage, in a costume, with lights and cameras, and whatever he's saying and doing on the screen is what he did on the set. You know you're watching a cut-scene. Whereas with a cartoon, they're not real to begin with, so if you can believe that a cartoon character can walk and talk, why shouldn't he also be able to change his behavior in response to your actions as the player—for instance, run away when he sees you coming?

So it adds to the suspension of disbelief?

Or, at least, it doesn't break it, whereas filmed action would. And I think that's part of the reason why video cut-scenes haven't been successful in computer games at large. It's just not a good fit.

Finally, of course, there's one last reason why the cartoon style works in *Last Express*, which is a historical one. Most of the images we have, culturally, from 1914 come to us through drawings of the time: newspaper drawings, magazine advertisements, poster art by artists like Alphonse Mucha and Toulouse-Lautrec, which were in an Art Nouveau style which was really the forerunner of the modern comic book. So I think when we see someone in 1914 dressed as a cartoon, it feels right in a certain way, whereas if we saw a 1914 person as a 3D polygonal model, it wouldn't have that same resonance.

So do you think a game with a more modern setting could use the same cartoon-character approach to the visuals?

Well, I like the look a lot, and it could work in a lot of different situations. I don't think it needs to be a historical setting. But it was just one more reason why, for *Last Express*, it was too perfect to resist.

So since the characters ended up looking like cartoons, why didn't you just draw them from the very start, instead of filming actors and then making them look like drawings?

One reason was that, to get the high quality of animation and cell-type expression that you have in a Disney film, you need to spend as much money as Disney spends. As expensive as this game was by computer game standards, it's a tiny fraction of the budget you would spend on an animated feature. We wanted to assure consistency that the same character would look like the same character, whether they were seen from up close or far away, angry or happy, and from different, very difficult-to-draw angles. And to achieve that for forty thousand animated frames, there's just no way you're going to be able to do that on the budget we had.

The goal of our automated rotoscope was to take a black-and-white filmed frame and to turn that into something resembling a pen-and-ink line drawing, where an artist could pull up that frame and colorize it in less than two minutes. We got to the point where we had it set up like an assembly line. And not only that, but you could have two different artists working on the same character, and because the digitization and the rotoscoping were done automatically, it would yield very similar results. Anna looks like Anna, regardless of who colored her for that sequence.

We didn't want it to look like a processed film image, and we didn't want it to look exactly like a cartoon. If you see a character walking toward you down the corridor and you're not quite sure whether you're looking at a drawing or a processed filmed image, then we pretty much achieved our goal. And I think we did. Occasionally we have someone ask, "Did you draw all this by hand?" If they can't tell it was filmed, then it worked.

I thought one of the most innovative design elements in the game is the save-game system you used. Players never actually save their game, but _Last Express_ automatically remembers everything they do, and they can "rewind" to any point in their game they want, if they want to try something a different way. How did you come up with this system?

I'm glad you asked. I'm very proud of the save-game system. The funny thing is that some people, including some reviewers, just didn't get it. We still occasionally get a review where they say, "It's too bad you can't save your game." Our goal, of course, was an extension of the design philosophy that went into the point-and-click system; we wanted it to be very simple, very transparent, and intuitive. To have to think about the fact that you're on a computer, and you have to save a file, and what are you going to name the file, and how does this compare to your previous saved game file—to me that breaks the experience. The idea was that you'd just sit down and play, and when you stopped playing, you could just quit, and go to dinner, or use the computer for something else, or whatever. And when you go back to playing, it should automatically put you back to where you left off. And if you make a mistake, you should be able to rewind, like rewinding a videotape, go back to the point where you think you went wrong, and begin playing from there. And I think it works. The six different colored eggs were inspired by, I guess, _Monopoly_ where you can choose which piece you want: the hat, or the car... The idea was that if you have a family of six, everybody will have their own egg, and when someone wants to play they can just switch to their own egg and pick it up where they left it off. People who complain that you can only have six saved games, or that you have to use colors instead of filenames, are fixated on the conventional save-game file system; they've missed the point. An egg file isn't a saved game; it's essentially a videotape containing not just your latest save point, but also all the points along the way that you didn't stop and save. You can usually rewind to within three to five real-time minutes of the desired point.

Music also seems to have been effectively used in _Last Express_. It shifts depending on what's going on in the game, as opposed to music in most adventure games that just plays in the background, never changing. How did you approach the game's musical aspect?

We knew that music would be very important to the texture of the game, and finding the right composer was very important. And we found him: Elia Cmiral, a very talented film composer from Czechoslovakia, who, by the way, is not a computer game player, had never scored a computer game, and I think even to this day has never played a computer game. We approached it as a story, as situations, and once he understood that there were mutually contradictory situations possible in the same story—that in one outcome Cath gets stabbed and killed and in another outcome he gets past that and goes on with the story—he had no problem scoring the different variations. (Elia has since achieved success as a Hollywood composer with scores for *Ronin, Stigmata*, and other films.)

Actually, although the cliché is that the composer always wants to add more music and turn down the sound effects so the music can be louder, Elia is very disciplined about the role of music. For scenes where I thought he would put a big dramatic chord or at least a little bit of underlining, he'd say, "No, that's corny, it plays better without it." So he was really reducing the number of situations, saving the music for places where it could really add something. We don't have any wallpaper music in *Last Express*; there's no point at which music is just repeating in the background, waiting for you to do something. The real music of *Last Express* is the noise of the train. You become very attuned to subtle shifts in the ambience: a door opens, the train noise gets louder, or you hear a door close somewhere, or you hear a rumble of thunder in the distance, or the train slows down as it arrives at a station. All of that almost comes to the foreground in the sound track, so that when the music does appear it's really noticeable. And in the dramatic scenes, the cut-scenes, we scored those as you would in a film, using music, I hope subtly, to bring out the different characters and situations. The fact that Anna, the leading lady, is a violinist, gave Elia a major instrumental motif for the score. There's a few hours of gameplay on the second day where Anna is practicing in her compartment, and if you walk through the train you hear her playing Bach partitas, tuning up, playing scales, and so forth. Her character's main theme is a violin theme as well, and appears in different guises in different situations as the story develops.

It's a game you really wouldn't want to play with the sound off.

Certainly it would lose a lot without the sound. In *Last Express* the sound is more than just the dialog. Without the shift in ambient noise, the music, the sound effects operating as clues, the feeling of hearing a conversation so far away you can't quite make out the words and then getting closer to it, and then the effect of hearing conversations in foreign languages that you can't understand no matter how close you get, all of that's really integral to the experience of *The Last Express*. It's funny because people tend to focus on the graphics. But one of the more technically innovative things we did was on the sound track. Most people aren't aware of it, but we actually have six tracks of sound being simultaneously streamed off the CD and mixed on the fly. For example, you can have the train ambient noise, the sound effect of a door opening, two people talking, thunder rolling in the distance, and a bit of music trailing off from the last cut-scene, and all of that going at the same time. It really creates a very rich sonic tapestry.

Again differing from many other adventure games, *Last Express* offers a fairly non-linear experience for the player, where there seem to be multiple ways to get

through to the end. Do you think non-linearity in adventure games is important?

It's crucial, otherwise it's not a game. There are a couple of game models which I wanted to steer away from, one of which is where you have to do a certain thing to get to the next cut-scene or the story doesn't progress. Another is the kind of branching-tree, "Choose Your Own Adventure" style, where there's ten ways the story can end, and if you try all ten options you get to all ten of them. One of the puzzle sequences that I think worked best in *Last Express* is one of the first ones, where you encounter Tyler's body and you have to figure out what to do to get rid of it. There are several equally valid solutions, and each one has its own drawbacks, ripple effects down the line. For example,

The Last Express

if you hide the body in the bed, you risk that when the conductor comes to make the bed he will discover the body there, so you have to deal with that somehow. You can avoid that problem by throwing the body out the window, but if you do that, then the body is discovered by the police. And they board the train at the next stop and you have to figure out how to hide from the police when they're going compartment to compartment checking passports. Either way, your actions have consequences on the people around you. As another example, if you throw the body out the window, you may overhear François, the little boy, saying to his mom, "Hey, I saw a man being thrown out the window." And she'll say to him, "Shut up, you little brat, don't tell lies!"

I hadn't even noticed that.

The game is full of little things like that.

So is that why you don't tend to like other adventure games, because they're too set in "primrose path" style?

Some adventure games have great moments, but in terms of the overall experience it's rare that a game consistently keeps that high a level. In *Last Express* too, there are parts of the game that don't quite live up to the expectations set up by that first disposing-of-the-body puzzle. Defusing the bomb is one I wasn't so happy with. You just have to grit your teeth and follow the steps; there's no way around it. It's not a particularly clever puzzle. But again, the main concern was that the story would work overall, and that the overall experience would be satisfying.

I've heard many adventure game designers say that to effectively tell a story, you really need to limit the player's options, and force them on a specific path. Do you agree with this notion?

It's true, of course; it's just a matter of *how* you limit what the player does. The too-obvious-to-mention limit in *Last Express* is that you can't get off the train. Any time you get off the train, the game ends. The only way to win is to stay on the train all the way to Constantinople. So in that sense, yeah, it's the ultimate linear story. You're on a train, you can't get off. But given that, within the train you should be able to move around as freely as possible. There are some doors that we just had to close because they would have changed the story too much and they wouldn't have let us get to the ending we wanted to get to. What if you take the gun and go through the train and kill everyone? We decided you just can't do that. So there's definitely a trade-off. The more wacky, off-the-wall options you give the player, the more that limits the complexity and the power of the story you've set out to tell. Whereas if you want to keep a very ambitious, central narrative that's itself large in scope, then you have to start closing doors around that, to make sure the player stays in the game.

Every game approaches this challenge in a different way. With *Last Express*, the train motif gave us the metaphor that we needed to keep it on track. I think once people get the idea that they're on the train, time is ticking, and they have to do certain things before certain stops, and they have to get to Constantinople or else they haven't really made it to the end of the line; once they get that, the story works. It's a matter of finding a balance for what works for each particular story. What's right for one game might not be right for another. I wouldn't even begin to know how to use the *Last Express* engine to do a game that wasn't set on a train.

***Last Express* seems to have not sold well because of the lack of an adventure game market. Yet adventure games used to be very popular. I'm wondering if you had any idea what happened to all of the adventure game players?**

That's a good question, and I have to say that I was caught by surprise when I woke up to find the adventure game market was dead, because I'd never really thought that much in terms of genres. Even doing *Last Express*, the fact that *Prince of Persia* was an action game while *Last Express* was an adventure game, I just wasn't thinking about it that way, right or wrong. As a game player, I'm not a big adventure game player myself, for a lot of reasons. Usually the graphics weren't very good, the story lines were kind of arbitrary and contrived, the characters and the plot just didn't stand up in terms of the kind of story that I would want to see in a movie or a novel.

So with *Last Express* I wanted to do a game that would have what I saw as the qualities that were missing from most of the adventure games that were out there. So as a player, I guess I have to assume my share of the guilt for not supporting the adventure game market. I think I underestimated the degree to which the games market had been stratified by the different genres. You had people out there who saw themselves as action game players, as strategy game players, as role-playing game players, or as adventure game players. I never shopped for games that way, but I guess over a period of a few years there in the early '90s, even computer game publications started to stratify games according to genre. So did publishers, so did shops, and I guess I didn't see that coming.

So you don't have any ideas about why the adventure game market dried up?

Well, I can only look at my own experience as a player. I enjoyed playing adventure games back in the Scott Adams days, and then I kind of got bored with them. I think adventure game makers need to stop asking, "Where did the market go?" I think the question is, "Why do people no longer find these games fun to play?" Maybe it's something about the games themselves.

Your first two games, *Karateka* and *Prince of Persia*, were both solo efforts, where you did all of the designing, writing, programming, and even drew the art. How do you compare working with a large team on *Last Express* to working by yourself?

It's a lot more exciting and rewarding than working alone, because you have the chance to work collaboratively with a large team of talented people who are really dedicated and who excel in their own specialties. It was one of the most thrilling experiences of my

Karateka

professional life. The downside, of course, is that you spend all your time worrying about where the next payroll is going to come from. One thing that was really nice about the old days was that the cost of developing a game was negligible. Once you'd paid the two thousand dollars for the computer and you've got five blank floppy disks, it was basically paid for. Whereas with a large project there's a lot of pressure to meet budgets and schedules.

Computer games seem to be one of the only art forms that have shifted from being predominantly solo endeavors to being more collaborative efforts, at least for commercial titles. How do you think that affects the final games?

It's interesting. What I'm doing right now, writing film screenplays, reminds me more of programming than any other activity I've done in a long time. Like programming, writing screenplays is basically a matter of closing the door behind yourself in a room with a computer and nothing else. You're trying to create something from scratch. If you write a screenplay that gets made into a movie, at that point, like a modern computer game, you've got the whole circus, with highly specialized, skilled people, and it's a creative collaboration between hundreds or more, all of whom bring their own area of expertise. A big-budget movie, for all the daily chaos of production, lives or dies on the strength of the script that was written, often, years before. A modern game is a collaborative effort in the same way, on a very tight budget, with money being spent daily, usually with a publisher who's banking on being able to ship it by a certain date. There again, what makes it work or not is the strength of the concept, the initial vision, which usually predates the whole production. There's just no time to change your mind on the fly during production about what the game should be.

But that tends to limit what kind of game designer can be successful, doesn't it? One who needs to make radical changes throughout the project to find the ideal gameplay would have been more successful in 1982 than now. Now he wouldn't be working at all.

He just wouldn't be working on a big-budget, multimillion-dollar production. A game like *Tetris* I think is well within the means of anyone to dream up and program, and if it takes them a year to find just the perfect combination of rules that's going to make it endlessly addictive, that's fine, it's not that expensive. But you can't take on a project with the latest 3D engine and forty artists at your beck and call and think that halfway through you're going to get to say, "Oh, now I realize what this game really needs, I wish I'd thought of it a year ago."

We're at a pretty tough time in the industry. I'm not sure it makes much sense economically to be a developer. I think it kind of makes sense to be a publisher, but even then there's only room for a few. This is a scary time because the number of hits is small, but the size of those hits is bigger than ever. If you're a publisher with a *Myst* or a *Tomb Raider* that sells two or three million units, that's great; your other ten titles can be flops and you still survive. But if you're a small developer with only one title in production, as Smoking Car was, you absolutely need to hit the jackpot. Only a handful of titles each year sell upwards of half a million units, and that's the category you need to aspire to in order to justify the kind of budgets we're talking about.

And to make a game with *Last Express*'s production values you really need a large budget?

I think on *Last Express* we stretched the budget quite far for what we actually got up there on the screen. We saved a lot of money; we got people to work for less than their usual salaries or to defer salaries, we didn't spend a lot of money on the film shoot, we used a non-union cast and a non-union crew, and we didn't have any big names. So we pretty much saved money everywhere we could think of. And yet, just because of the nature of the project, the scale of the game, the number of people that were involved, and how long it took, it ended up costing a lot.

If you don't mind telling, just how much did the game cost?

About five million.

And the development took four years; was that your original intention?

It took two years longer than planned.

What made it take so much longer than you thought?

Tool development was one. To develop our own rotoscoping technology, we had to do a lot of tests, different types of costumes, makeup, processing to get it looking the way we wanted. That was one. And the 3D modeling; that model was huge, the train interior and exterior, and the number of rendered images was tremendous. 3D modeling and rendering, animation, and tool development were the areas that burst their boundaries. The film shoot itself actually came in on schedule and on budget; that was the easy part.

So, looking back, do you wish you had managed to get the project done in a shorter amount of time, on a smaller budget? Or are you satisfied that that's just how long was necessary?

Well, personally I took a bit of a bath on *Last Express*, financially. So in that sense, it probably wasn't a smart move. And I feel bad about our investors who also hoped the game would sell half a million units, and were disappointed. It's kind of like having purchased an extremely expensive lottery ticket.

On the other hand, I'm proud of the game, I'm glad we did it, and I don't think we could have done it much cheaper than we did. I'm happy with the finished game.

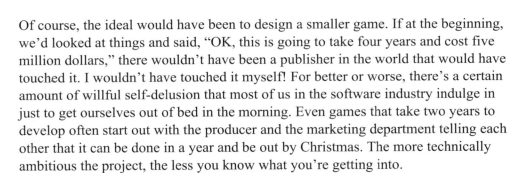

Of course, the ideal would have been to design a smaller game. If at the beginning, we'd looked at things and said, "OK, this is going to take four years and cost five million dollars," there wouldn't have been a publisher in the world that would have touched it. I wouldn't have touched it myself! For better or worse, there's a certain amount of willful self-delusion that most of us in the software industry indulge in just to get ourselves out of bed in the morning. Even games that take two years to develop often start out with the producer and the marketing department telling each other that it can be done in a year and be out by Christmas. The more technically ambitious the project, the less you know what you're getting into.

The film industry, by contrast, is relatively good at budgeting and scheduling shoots and doing them in just as long as they're supposed to take. The trade-off there is that they're not often trying things that are really new. When they do, like using a new technology for the first time, or filming on location in a war-torn country, or filming out at sea, they often experience the same kind of budget and schedule overages that are common in computer games. On *Last Express*, the whole production hinged on our development of this new rotoscoping process, so to a certain extent, at the beginning when we said, "Yeah, we'll develop it and it will take x months and cost this much," we were basically operating on blind faith, going forward assuming that we could resolve whatever problems there were and that it would work—which it did, eventually. It's very hard to make accurate time and cost projections when you are doing something for the first time. On *Last Express* we were doing maybe ten things that had never been done before, all at the same time. That was probably unwise.

Overall, unrealistic planning is not a good thing for developers; it doesn't really help us. One of my regrets about this project was that we were under so much financial strain from day to day that I was spending half my time worrying about the game and half my time worrying about raising money. That's the situation I put us in by undertaking such an ambitious project.

Last Express is the first of your personal projects where you didn't do any of the programming. Do you miss it at all?

One great thing about programming is that, when you're really on a roll, you can lock yourself in a room and have the satisfaction of making progress every day; it's just you and the machine. The times when I would miss that the most was usually when I'd just spent two days in back-to-back meetings. Why did these meetings have to happen and why did I have to be in them? On *Last Express*, we had four programmers working on the project, and although I often envied their lot, I had my hands more than full with the game design, script, artists and animators, casting and directing the actors on the voice recording and film shoot, working with the composer, sound designer, and editor, to list a few things that I actually enjoyed doing. At various points I did offer my services to the programmers, but since my last area of code expertise was in 6502 Assembly Language [on the Apple II] they decided they didn't really need me.

Last Express is an extremely unique game in both setting and design. In contrast, most of the rest of the new games coming out seem to be set in either fantasy or science fiction settings, and are all based on last year's big hit. How do you feel about the industry's trend toward "me too" games?

With the occasional magnificent exception, I think you're right about the majority of games. I don't know if the "me too" problem is primarily in terms of setting. I guess I feel it more in terms of genres. You can take _Doom_, and change the textures so that it's an express train in 1914, but I don't think that's really what the

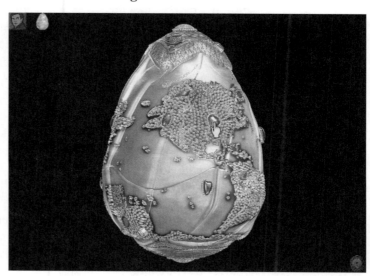

The Last Express

industry needs. What's more interesting to me is experimenting with game design itself, how the game is constructed, what the player is actually doing, trying to create a new form that works. That kind of experimentation was a lot easier to do when the publisher's stock price wasn't riding on the success or failure of the experiment. It's definitely easier to get backing for something that's a sequel or variation on a proven formula. The harder it is to describe or explain something new, the fewer people or companies you'll find who are willing to risk money on it. I think it's unfortunate, but I don't know what to do about it. It's pretty much an inevitable result of the cycle; when we go to the computer store as a shopper and look for the next game, let's be honest, what are we looking for? We're more inclined to look at things that are heavily promoted, that we've read about in magazines. So titles that come out with little fanfare are going to have a harder time reaching the bigger market. So in a sense, as a public, we're getting what we asked for. But as a game designer, yeah, I do miss it.

My friends who make films for a living always used to say: "Oh boy, I really envy you making computer games. There you've got the chance to do something really original. While down here in Hollywood all they want are retreads of last year's sequel." It's kind of interesting how the game industry now has the same set of problems that filmmakers have been complaining about for years. Maybe even worse. Along with bigger production values, bigger markets, and more glitzy award ceremonies, we've achieved a kind of genre paralysis, and it's become more difficult to break new ground.

So you just feel frustrated more than anything.

I guess resigned. I think every new art form goes through stages of its evolution. With computer games we've lived through the exciting early years, and now we're in the growing pains years. This definitely doesn't mean that innovation stops. Even in filmmaking, which is a hundred years old, every couple of years a film does come out that, whether because of societal changes or technological changes, could not have been made a few years earlier, and is a valuable step forward. It's just that you have to weed out hundreds of clones and mediocre films to find those few gems. I think we're in the same place with computer games. Every year, out of hundreds of new games, there's a couple that push the envelope in a new and interesting way. The best we can do is just keep trying to do that, and quit griping about the glorious bygone early years, 'cause they're over!

So how involved were you with the *Prince of Persia 3D* project?

My involvement was limited to giving them the go-ahead at the beginning, and offering occasional advice and creative consultation along the way. It was a Broderbund project. Andrew Pedersen, the producer, initiated it. It was his baby. He brought the team together and worked hard on it for two years. So I can't take credit for that one.

It's very difficult to take a 2D game and make it work in 3D instead, with full freedom of movement for the player.

That's the problem really. When you convert *Prince of Persia* to 3D over-the-shoulder, one problem is how do you keep the controls simple. And the other is how does the player know what kind of environment he's in. Because you only see what's right in front of you. A crude example is you're running toward the edge of a chasm. With a side view you can look at it and see if it's a three-space jump or a four-space jump and are you going to clear it or not. If it's too far, you know there's not even any point in trying. Whereas in a 3D over-the-shoulder game, you don't quite know how far it is until you try. And even then, when you fall you wonder, "Was I not quite at the edge? Or did I not jump in quite the right direction?" So it makes it a different kind of game. You gain in terms of visceral immediacy and, of course, the richness of the environment, but I think you lose something in terms of a clean strategy.

So you don't think that making every game 3D is necessarily the correct approach?

Well, you have to distinguish the real-time 3D graphics technology from a particular interface. I think there's a lot that can be done with real-time 3D graphics engines. *Doom*, the first-person shooter, was obviously the first prototype and that was the trend for a couple of years. And then *Tomb Raider* and *Super Mario* did the following camera. *Prince 3D* falls into that category. So I think the challenge is in finding new ways to present the action cinematically that will be as much fun as the old games but still have all the visual excitement of the new 3D games. I think there's plenty of ground yet to cover. *Prince 3D* had a few intriguing moments in it that I'd like to see pushed much further to invent the next big thing in 3D action games.

I read that you enjoyed *Tomb Raider* quite a bit. That seemed to be an attempt to put *Prince of Persia* into a 3D environment in order to produce something new and exciting.

I think the key word there is new. Yes, I was really excited by *Tomb Raider* as a player, because it was something that hadn't been seen before. But I think now that that's been done, we can more clearly see the pros and the cons of that type of game. If you want to do *Tomb Raider* today, you need to find a way to go beyond what they did in '96. You can't just do the same thing over and over.

So did you come up with any good solutions to 3D-space navigation in *Prince of Persia 3D?*

For me, *Prince of Persia 3D* is a bit on the complex side, in terms of the number of weapons and the number of moves. It's not the kind of game that I would design for myself. But they were aiming at a particular audience. I think the core audience as they saw it were people who were a lot more hard-core gamers than I was with the first *Prince of Persia*.

Do you find that your game designs change much over the course of a project?

With *Karateka* and *Prince of Persia* I had the luxury of letting the game evolve over time, since it was just me in a room with a computer, with no budget and no corporate bottom line. I thought *Prince of Persia* would take a year and it ended up taking three, and that was OK—that was what it was. *Last Express* was different because it was such a large project. With the machine that we constructed with hundreds of people and networked computers, every day was expensive, so changing the design in midstream was not an option. There I spent a lot more time at the beginning trying to work out the game in detail. You just have to pray that the original design is solid and doesn't have severe flaws that will reveal themselves down the line.

Prince of Persia

But your earlier games did change significantly over the course of their development?

Oh yeah. One example: *Prince of Persia* was originally not supposed to have combat. One of my bright ideas there was an answer to what I saw as the clichéd violence of computer games. I wanted the player to be an unarmed innocent in a hostile world full of spikes and traps. There would be lots of gory violence directed against the player, which it would be your job to avoid, but you would never actually dish it out. That was also a way of dealing with the fact that I didn't think there was enough computer memory to have another character running around on the screen at the same time. Luckily, I had stalwart friends who kept pushing me to add combat. When your friends tell you your game is boring, you'd better listen.

Shadow Man, the character, was a serendipitous accident because I thought, "There's no way to add another character in there, we don't have the memory for it." Only if the character looked exactly like the Prince, if he used the same animation frames. I can't remember who suggested it, but by shifting the character over by one bit and then exclusive ORing with himself you got a black shape with a shimmery white outline. So I tried that, and when I saw Shadow Man running around the screen I said, "Cool, there's a new character." So that suggested the whole plot device of the mirror and jumping through the mirror and having an evil alter ego who would follow you around and try to thwart you by closing a gate that you wanted to be open, or by dropping things on your head. And then there was the resolution, where you fight Shadow Man at the end, but you can't kill him, since he's yourself, and if you kill him you die. So you have to find a way to solve that. Call it Jungian or what you will, it was a way to take advantage of the fact that we didn't have that much memory.

So later on you must have found some more memory so you could put in the other characters.

A lot of the time that goes into programming a game like *Prince of Persia* on a computer like the Apple II is taking what you've done already and redoing it to make it smaller and faster. Eventually the stuff that was in there just got more efficient and left enough room to come up with a limited set of character shapes for the guards. If you notice, there's a lot that the guards can't do. They can't run and jump and chase you. All they can do is fight.

Your games have all been very visually appealing. How did you balance the games' visual appearance with the requirements of the gameplay?

I think along with what we already talked about with the simplicity of the controls and consistency of the interface, visuals are another component where it's often tempting to compromise. You think, "Well, we could put a menu bar across here, we could put a number in the upper right-hand corner of the screen representing how many potions you've drunk," or something. The easy solution is always to do something that as a side effect is going to make the game look ugly. So I took as one of the ground rules going in that the overall screen layout had to be pleasing, had to be strong and simple. So that somebody who was not playing the game but who walked into the room and saw someone else playing it would be struck by a pleasing composition and could stop to watch for a minute, thinking, "This looks good, this looks as if I'm watching a movie." It really forces you as a designer to struggle to find the best solution for things like inventory. You can't take the first solution that suggests itself, you have to try to solve it within the constraint that you set yourself.

So what made you decide to stop working in games and pursue screenwriting full time?

I've always sort of alternated computer games and film projects. I think there's a lot of value to recharging your creative batteries in a different industry. *Prince of Persia* would not have been as rich if I hadn't spent those couple of years after *Karateka* thinking and breathing film, writing a screenplay. The same with *Last Express*. That project came on the heels of doing a short documentary film in Cuba called *Waiting for Dark*. So, I don't know, never say never. Maybe one day I'll do another game, but right now the challenge of writing a screenplay and getting a good film made is a lot more exciting to me than doing another computer game. To me a compelling project is one that you have to talk yourself *out* of pursuing, rather than talk yourself into it.

One thing, though, computer technology is evolving pretty fast. A computer game now is so different from what a computer game was ten years ago, who's to say what we'll be doing in ten years?

So it's not that you prefer working in a more linear form. It's more of an alternate pursuit for you.

It's a different form, but a lot of the challenges are surprisingly similar. With a computer game, although it's a non-linear means of telling a story, you still have the fascinating mystery of what is it about a particular world or a particular set of characters that makes that game thrilling and gripping. What makes people say, "I want to play this game, I want to be Mario," and then look at another game that might be technically just as good and say, "I have no interest in being this character in this world." Same with a film. There's some mysterious chemistry between an audience and a storyteller that causes the audience to decide, even based just on the trailer, whether or not they want to live this particular story.

The two art forms are not all that dissimilar, when it comes to sitting down and wrestling with a set of elements and trying to get them into some kind of finite shape. The challenges of taking an established genre and breaking new ground with it somehow, of making it surprising and suspenseful, of economically using the elements at your disposal, are very similar whether it's a game or a film. The hardest thing with *Karateka* and *Prince of Persia* was coming back to it day after day, looking at something that had taken me a week to program and saying, "You know what? I got it working, but now I have to throw it out and find something different." Same with screenwriting. You have to be willing to throw away your own work repeatedly over the course of a long project, in order to arrive at that finite set of elements that works just right.

Jordan Mechner Gameography

Karateka, 1984
Prince of Persia, 1989
Prince of Persia 2, 1993
The Last Express, 1997
Prince of Persia 3D, 1999 (Consultant)

This interview originally appeared in a different form in Inside Mac Games *magazine, www.imgmagazine.com. Used with permission.*

Chapter 19:
Designing Design Tools

"Man is a tool-using animal . . . Without tools he is nothing, with tools he is all."

— Thomas Carlyle

An integral part of developing a good game is creating compelling content for that game. In order to create superior content, the design team will need to be equipped with well-designed, robust game creation tools. Therefore, one can conclude that designing a good game is about designing good game creation tools.

Other than the development environments the programmers use to compile the game's code, and the graphics packages the artists use to make the game's art, the most commonly used game creation tool is the level editor. What distinguishes this tool from the others I mentioned is that it is typically built specifically for a project or, at least, for the engine the team is using to power the game. It is the responsibility of the development team to make this level editor as powerful as it can be, to facilitate the job of the level designers and allow them to make the best game-world possible.

The simple levels found in early games such as *Defender* did not require a sophisticated level editor to be created.

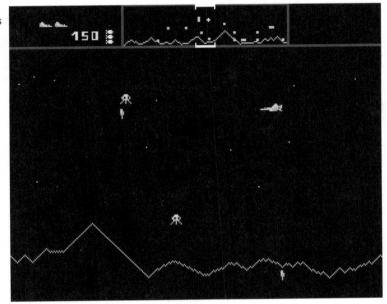

Of course, not every game has levels. Many of the classic arcade games from the early 1980s such as *Missile Command* or *Space Invaders* do not have levels as we think of them now. And the games that did, such as *Defender* or *Tempest*, certainly did not require sophisticated level editors to create their game-worlds. Games like *Civilization* and *SimCity* auto-generate the basis of a level and then allow the players and AI to build the rest themselves. Sports titles have levels that are quite simple and mostly require the construction of visually pleasing stadiums to surround the gameplay. I discuss the nature of levels in games in more detail in Chapter 21, "Level Design." Many modern games employ sophisticated levels, levels which have a tremendous impact on the shape and form of the gameplay that takes place on them. These games demand that their development team create an editor with which the level designers can build the game-world.

Surprisingly, many development teams fail to invest enough programming time in making their tools as good as possible. Usually teams have no idea what is standard in other tools used in the industry. Frequently, not enough time is invested in preplanning and thoroughly designing how a level editor will work. As a result of all of these factors, it is often many months before the level design tools are reasonable to use. Frequently a programmer is stuck with implementing or improving the level editor as "extra" work on an already full schedule, and is forced to use the trusty "code like hell" method of implementation to get it done in time. Often, key time-saving features are not added until midway through a project, by which time the game's designers are already hopelessly behind in their own work.

Desired Functionality

So what sort of functionality should a level editor include? Many might suggest an important part of any level editor is having hot keys hooked up to all the important functionality. Others would recommend plenty of configurable settings which allow different designers to turn on and off the features they prefer, when they need to use them. It goes without saying that a level editor should be stable enough that a designer can use it for a number of hours without it locking up, but these suggestions are all the obvious ones, the bare minimum that an editor should do to be useful. What sorts of features should be included to allow an editor to truly shine, to empower designers to do the best work possible?

Visualizing the Level

The most important objective for a world creation tool must be to allow the designer to see the world he is creating while simultaneously enabling him to make modifications to it. This is often called What You See Is What You Get (WYSIWYG) in the domain of word processors and desktop publishing packages, but is not something that level editors are universally good at. I will call such a WYSIWYG view the "player's view" since it represents what players will see when they play the game. The world the designer is crafting should be seen in this player's view window using the same rendering engine the game itself will employ, whether this means 2D or 3D, sprites or models, software driven or hardware accelerated. This seems to be the most important feature of any level editor. How can a designer hope to create a good looking world if he must first tweak the world's settings in the editor and then run a separate application to see how it looks in the game?

The designer should be easily able to move the camera in this player's view so that he can quickly maneuver it to whatever section of the map he needs to see in order to work on the level. This movement is probably best accomplished with a simple "flight" mode where the player can control the camera's position using simple movement and turning keys. In this mode the camera should move without colliding with geometry or other game-world objects. Though one may also want to provide a mode for the player's view where the designer can maneuver through the game-world as the player will in the final game, the editor should always allow the designer to move around the level unconstrained. In order to finely edit a level, the designer must be able to look closely at whatever he wants without having to worry that a tree blocks his way.

Every difference that exists in what the designer sees in the editor and what will show up in the game will make the levels look that much worse. Suppose the view in the editor is only available using 3D hardware accelerated rendering, while the game itself must run in a software mode in addition to hardware. This will create frustration for the designer, since he will not be able to easily tell how the level will appear in software. Sure, the level looks great with acceleration, but aliasing in the level's textures may be horrendous without the benefits of tri-linear filtering. Certainly having a hardware accelerated view in the editor makes sense since it will run much faster than a software view and will thereby allow the designer to work faster. But for games that need to run with and without 3D cards, the editor should be able to easily switch between an accelerated and unaccelerated view, so the designer can quickly and easily make sure the level looks good regardless of how it is rendered.

Of course, the world as it will appear in the game is not always the best view from which to edit that world. For this reason, level editors often need to include an "editing view" in addition to the player's view. The editing view is often top-down, but may also consist of a rotatable wire-frame view or multiple views. The last option is particularly useful for the editing of 3D game-worlds. For instance, the popular *Quake* engine editing tool Worldcraft, which was used to create all the levels in *Half-Life*, provides the player with the popular "tri-view" setup, with which the designer can see top-down (along the Y axis), from one side (along the X axis), and from another side (along the Z axis) simultaneously in three separate windows. The three side views appear in addition to a 3D "player's view" window. Having multiple views is of particular importance for editing complex, overlapping 3D architecture, such as one finds in *Quake* levels. In contrast to the player's view window, which exists in order to show the designer exactly what the level will look like in the game, the editing view's purpose is to allow the designer to easily modify and shape what he sees in the player's view window. Of course, the editor should allow editing views and a player's view to be all up on the screen simultaneously, and the changes made in one window should be instantly reflected in all the views.

In some cases there may not be a need for separate editor and player views. For instance, in a 2D world such as was found in my first game, *Odyssey: The Legend of Nemesis,* the player's view of the world may be perfectly suited to editing the levels. While I worked on the many levels for that game, not once did I wish for another view of the game-world. Similarly, in *StarCraft*, the representation of the world as it appears in the game is sufficiently clear to allow the designer to make modifications directly to it. For this reason, the *StarCraft* Campaign Editor provides

The view provided in the Zoner level editor for *Odyssey* was perfectly suited to editing a 2D world.

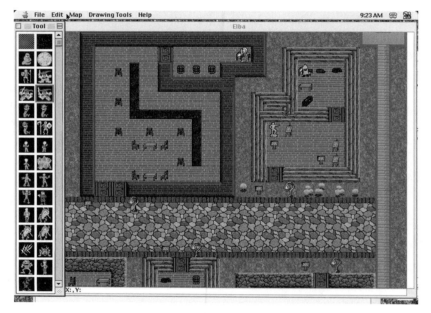

only a player's view window for the designer to edit in. However, for the *StarCraft* editor, it might have been beneficial to provide a separate editing view. Because of the isometric view the game uses, a view which can sometimes be confusing to look at, a strictly top-down view in which the designer could edit her level could have been quite useful in the placing and manipulating of units and other game elements. The *StarCraft* Campaign Editor does include a top-down "mini-map" of the level being created, but the designer cannot actually change the level using that view, nor is the mini-map large enough to allow for easy editing.

The Big Picture

I have argued that it is important for a game's level editor to allow the designer to see the level exactly as she will see it in the final game, but the player's view window does not always need to represent exactly what the player will see. It can be quite useful if the level editor can also show the designer various extra information about the level that will assist in that level's creation. For instance, suppose that the game being developed involves various monsters maneuvering the level on predetermined paths. Being able to see exactly where these paths go is key to understanding how the level functions, and being able to see exactly where these paths lead in the world the player will be navigating is important to making sure the paths are set up properly.

In many level editors, this sort of level functionality information is communicated in the editing view but not in the player's view, but it makes sense to display this data in both places. Certainly the player's view window should not always be filled up with this sort of level functionality information, but the ability to turn on and off the rendering of different data can be quite useful in setting up the level's behaviors. This is especially true for 3D games. Returning to the path example, why should the designer have to extrapolate in his head from the 2D top-down or side editing view exactly where a path will end up in the 3D view? Instead, the editor should just draw it for him, so there is no guesswork.

When working on *Centipede 3D*, a programmer was adding code that would prevent the player from traveling up slopes that were too steep. In order to debug this new slope-restriction code, he added functionality to the level editor that allowed it to toggle on and off lines that separated the different triangles which made up the landscape. These lines would change color depending on if a given edge could be crossed by the player or not. The triangles themselves were marked with a red X if they were too steep for the player to rest on. The programmer added this functionality primarily to aid in his debugging of the slope-restriction code, never realizing what a boon it would be to the level designers. Now the designers could see exactly where the player could and could not travel on the level. An even better side effect was the rendering of the triangle boundaries, which created a sort of wire-frame view of the landscape, functionality which had not previously been available in the editor. This then vastly simplified the editing of geometry, for now the designers could see exactly which triangles created which slopes and then modify the level accordingly. The addition of the wire-frame view and the slope-restriction markers led directly to better, more refined geometry in the final game. And the beauty of this functionality was that it could be turned on and off in the editor, so if the designer wanted to see how the level looked he could turn it off, and if he wanted to see how it functioned he could turn it on.

As with paths, it may also be useful if the designer can turn on and off the rendering of objects such as triggers and other normally invisible objects. Similarly, it can be enormously helpful to display the bounding information for the objects in the world (which often does not exactly match the visual composition of the object's sprite or model), so the player can easily observe how the bounding information will impact the ability of the player and NPCs to navigate the game-world. Marking off where the player can and cannot go can be quite useful as well. And again, each part of this functionality data should be easily toggled on or off via hot key, menu, or button, so that the designer has the choice of seeing exactly the data he needs for the problem he is working on. And the data should absolutely be rendered in the player's view window, so that the designer can see exactly how the trigger, path, slope restriction, or other object is placed in the game-world, without having to guess from a top-down view. By using a visually authentic view of the game-world which can also display game behavior data, the designer is able to work on a level's aesthetic qualities just as well as its gameplay attributes.

Jumping into the Game

For games where the player is manipulating a character through a world, it is important for the designer to be easily able to know how the level "feels" to navigate. To this end, in addition to having the player's view of the world represent what the player will see in the game, it can be quite useful to allow the designer to actually maneuver in this view as she would in the actual game. With this sort of addition, the designer is able to test whether the player will be able to make a certain jump, how it will feel to navigate a particular "S" curve, and whether or not the player's character moves smoothly up a set of stairs. In addition to this "gameplay" mode, the level editor should retain the unconstrained "flight" mode I mentioned previously.

The Vulcan editor for Bungie's *Marathon* engine was particularly well suited to allowing the designer to test the "feel" of the level while constructing it. The *Marathon* technology was similar but a bit better than *Doom*'s, and was licensed for use

Bungie's Forge level editor for the *Marathon* engine included a "visual mode" where the designer could actually maneuver through her level exactly as a player would in the game.

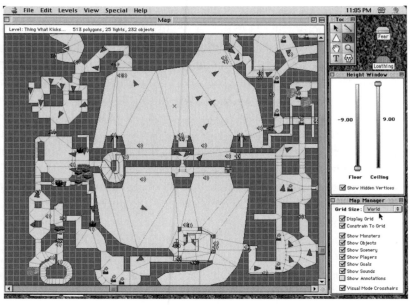

in a number of other games, including my game *Damage Incorporated*. Vulcan was subsequently revised, renamed Forge, and released with the final game in the series, *Marathon Infinity*. Vulcan/Forge allowed for a "visual mode" which functioned as a player's view window. In visual mode the designer could navigate the world just as the player would in the final game. The shortcoming of this was that the designer was unable to edit the world, aside from texture and lighting placement, while in this view. This was no doubt due to the speed of processors available when the editor was created, and the comparatively small size of affordable monitors at the time. Nonetheless, the visual mode in Vulcan was quite useful, and the switch from editing mode to gameplay mode was fast enough to allow the designer to make a change, see how it felt, and then switch back to make more changes as necessary.

Of course, one might conclude that the next logical step is to allow the designer to actually play the game in the player's view. In this way the designer can see how well different mechanisms function, and what sort of a challenge different adversaries will present. However, this opens the programmer up to a large amount of implementation difficulties. In order for game-world objects to function as they do in the game, many objects will move from the position they start out in when the player begins the level. For instance, an aggressive troll might run toward the player and attack. Do these moving objects then actually move in the level editor as well? And what happens if the designer saves the level in this new state? Surely that is a bad idea, since all of the locations in which the entities have been carefully placed will be changed. What a designer wants is to be able to quickly test a level at any given location, and once he is done playtesting have the level revert to its "unplayed" state. This may best be accomplished by allowing the designer to quickly enter a "test mode" and then allowing him to exit it just as quickly, instantly returning him to level editor functionality. The quicker this transition the better, for the faster and easier it is, the more likely the designer will want to go back and forth to test and re-test the playability of his level. If the designer has to wait a minute or longer to playtest, he will not be able to try as many different changes to the level before he runs out of time. For this reason, it makes sense to have a programmer focus on smoothing out and speeding up this transition as much as possible.

Any seasoned game designer will tell you that a large part of whether a game succeeds or fails is dependent on how well it is playtested and balanced. Even the most brilliant initial game design can be completely destroyed if the implemented game is not playtested thoroughly. I do not mean just for bugs, but for gameplay, for how the game feels to play, and for how it captivates the player. Playtesting is an iterative process which involves trying a type of gameplay, then modifying it, then trying it again, and repeating this loop until the game is fun. It can be very hard, then, to properly iterate through playtesting if the level editor does not facilitate the modification of the game's levels, and then easily allow the designer to try out what has been changed. The easier it is for the designer to jump into the game, the more likely she is to repeat the playtesting cycle again and again until the game is as perfect as possible. If the level editor does not facilitate such testing, the designer is likely to become frustrated or simply not have the time she needs to sufficiently balance the game.

Editing the World

The best development tools for a game are composed of a delicate mix of off-the-shelf programs and proprietary editors. A good team will know just how much to use of each so that they are neither wasting the time of their programmers by having them develop overly sophisticated tools when a good commercial package is better suited, nor unreasonably restraining the efforts of their designers by not allowing them to refine the game's content from within the level editor. Though no team should be forced to develop a game without a level editor, it is equally foolhardy to force the team to do all of the game's content creation from within proprietary tools.

It is important that the level editor actually allow the designer to modify all gameplay-critical aspects of a level. This would seem to me to be an obvious prerequisite for an editor, but I have heard so many stories of teams working with 3D Studio Max and "entity editors" that it bears mentioning. Often teams think they can get away with using an off-the-shelf tool such as Max to create all of their world geometry, and then create a level editor only for importing the meshes from Max and positioning the items, NPCs, and other game-world entities. This cannot lead to good levels. As the designer is placing creatures in the map, he needs to be able to simultaneously change the geometry to fit the placement of that creature. If a designer must exit the editor and then run a 3D modeling application (which are seldom known for their speed), modify the geometry in that program, and then re-import the level into the proprietary editor before she can test out her modifications, she will certainly be discouraged from making too many "tweaks" to the geometry. As a direct result, the geometry will not look as good in the final game, if it is playable at all. Not allowing a designer to edit the level's gameplay-critical architecture in the editor itself is tantamount to tying one arm behind her back. It is my experience that designers work best with both hands free.

When I started working on *Centipede 3D*, the level editor we had was really more of a game entity manipulator than a proper level editor. The geometry for a given level was derived from a grayscale, square height-map, with those used in *Centipede 3D* all consisting of 32 pixels square. Each pixel therein represented a height value on the landscape. These height-maps, which could be created in Photoshop or any other pixel-pushing tool, were a good way to create an initial version of a level's geometry. Unfortunately, in the version of the editor used at the start of the project, the height maps could only be modified in a paint program; they could not be edited in the editor itself. This was a shame, since looking at a top-down 2D representation of a 3D level is not exactly the best way to get an idea of how the level will end up looking. As a result, the levels that were created early in the project were simple and a bit flat. It was not that the level designers were not working hard to make the levels attractive, merely that there was only so much that could be accomplished with the tools provided.

However, midway through the project, functionality was added to the tool to allow the designer to edit the height-maps while in the level editor. The height-maps could still be created in Photoshop and brought into the game, and this remained the best way to make a first pass on the level's architecture. After that first pass, the geometry was easily manipulated in the level editor, where the designer was able to see the level in 3D while modifying the height-map. As a result, the designers were able to tweak the geometry until it was perfect. The change in the quality of the levels was dramatic. As always, time did not allow for us to go back and redo the earlier levels. Since the levels were made in the order they appeared in the game, anyone playing *Centipede 3D* will be able to tell at what point the level designers were given the new and improved tool. It was not that the designers could not create levels with the previous incarnation of the editor, it was just that level editing was so much more difficult that the levels failed to look as good as the designers wanted.

There is a lot to be said for being able to create fancy level geometry in a fully featured 3D package, and even level editors with sophisticated geometry editing capabilities would benefit from the ability to import externally created architecture. The key to creating quality game art assets, whether they are 2D sprites or 3D models, is being able to import from commercial packages. I do not know that anyone was ever forced to create 2D sprite artwork for a game using only an in-house tool. Yet, it seems that many unfortunate artists have only been allowed to model characters or other objects using proprietary modeling tools. I have discussed how important it is to allow the level designers to manipulate a level's architecture in the editor. But certainly forcing game designers or artists to model every game-world element in the level editor is a big mistake. Artists should be able to create game-world objects such as trees, weapons, or trash cans in their favorite modeling package and import them into the game. Simply put, there is no way a game's programming team is going to be able to code up an art editing package with all the power, robustness, and stability of a Photoshop, 3D Studio Max, Maya, Softimage, or any of a number of other popular off-the-shelf products. Without the many features found in these packages, artists will simply be unable to create the best quality art possible. Furthermore, most artists are already familiar with one or more of these packages, and so when they come on to the project they will be that much closer to being "up to speed."

At the same time, the team will need to be able to manipulate this art using proprietary tools. Having an in-house editor with which to set up animations, nodes on a skeleton, collision data, or other information is essential to making the art function properly within the game. Teams who attempt to avoid setting up any sort of art editing software will frustrate their artists, designers, or whoever gets stuck with configuring the art and its animations to work in the game. A proprietary art manipulation tool that does exactly what the game engine needs it to is a key ingredient in a bearable game development experience.

Scripting Languages and Object Behaviors

It seems to have become the norm for games to use a system where designers can set up and balance the enemy, weapon, and other game behaviors exactly as they need them, without involving a programmer. Many games now include scripting languages which, though relatively simple, allow for complex entity creation without requiring the game engine itself to be recompiled. These scripting languages provide many benefits to game development. Probably most important is that they encourage the creation of more unique behaviors in the game, whether these are reusable in-game entities such as NPCs or unique behaviors and events for different levels, such as NPCs carrying on a particular conversation while the player watches, as in *Half-Life*.

One great benefit of a properly designed scripting system is that it is completely portable to other systems. This means that when the game is ported from the PC to the Dreamcast, for instance, all of the enemy behaviors that have been scripted and debugged on the PC will be equally functional on the Dreamcast, provided the script interpreter and its associated functions are properly ported as well. In that vein, a robust scripting language is also more stable to work with than programming in C. The scripting language gives the script's author less opportunity to thoroughly crash the game, and when a script does something illegal the game can spit out a properly informative message instead of just locking up. Often the scripting languages are not as complex as actual C programming, and thereby allow designers with some programming savvy to take on the creation of unique world behaviors, thus freeing up harder-to-find programmers for more complex tasks. In most systems, scripts can also be loaded on demand, which means only the scripts that a particular section of the game uses will need to be resident in memory, thus freeing up more code overhead. An added bonus of a game having a scripting language is that it allows for complex user modification of that game. A well-designed and appropriately powerful scripting system will empower motivated players to make their own "mods" for the game for distribution to friends.

Scripting languages have their downside as well. First is the time involved in implementing a scripting system. If the language is to be actually useful to the game as described above, it will need to be very stable and provide its user with a lot of power, which is certainly non-trivial to implement. Debugging a problematic script can also be quite a lot of trouble, since no game developer is going to have the time to implement a symbolic debugger as nice as the one that comes with Visual Studio or CodeWarrior. Most of the time, the scripts are compiled at run time, and as a result can be significantly slower than C/C++ code. Again, no matter what the developer does in terms of optimizing performance of the scripts, he will not be able to match the compiling power of the C++ compilers made by Watcom, Microsoft, or Metrowerks. And finally, though one of the big advantages to scripting languages is supposed to be that they can be used by non-programmers, it often turns out that, if the scripting language is actually powerful enough to create AI for an NPC, the scripting language is going to be so complex that it requires a programmer to use it effectively. And if a programmer's time is being tied up in the creation of scripts, why stop her from just doing her coding work in C?

Of course, one of the main advantages of scripts is that they greatly simplify the balancing of gameplay. Instead of a programmer tweaking a number in the code and then waiting for the game to recompile, a designer can adjust a value in a script

Surreal Software's Riot Engine Level Editor allows the designer to tweak all sorts of settings for different game-world entities.

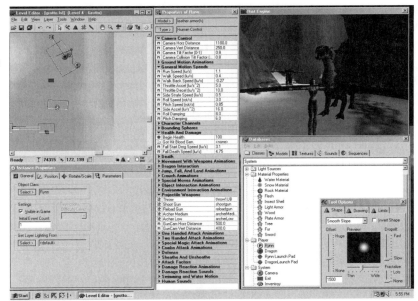

and just run the game. But what if one wants to achieve this benefit of scripts without having to implement a scripting system. What if, instead, the designer were able to adjust behavior parameters in the level editor itself? This is the approach taken by Surreal Software's Riot Engine. In Surreal's Level Editor, designers are given access to all the settings or "behavior variables" for a given AI, weapon, or other game-world entity. The behaviors themselves are coded in C++, with the programmers leaving "hooks" to all the crucial settings that determine how the game-world object will behave, such as how fast it moves, what its detect radius is, what objects it turns into when it is destroyed, and so forth. This provides much of the game-balancing benefit of scripting languages by empowering the designers to endlessly tweak the game while still taking advantage of the speed of a powerful C++ compiler and debugger. This functionality makes the level editor not just a tool for modifying the game's levels, but turns it into more of a gameplay editor, where the designer is able to change much of the game's content on the fly.

"Scripted events" in levels are another thing that game scripting languages do well. Each level in the game can have a unique script which sets up and triggers various unique behaviors on that level. Having complex, unique behaviors has recently become a much bigger concern of game developers, especially after Valve used scripted events to such great effect in *Half-Life*. Of course, there is a key difference between "scripted events" and the "scripting language" one uses to set them up. *Half-Life* had great scripted events, but apparently a difficult-to-use method for setting them up. Creating a solid and simple scripting system is the best way to ensure that the designers will make use of it. Instead of involving a separately compiled, text-based scripting language, level editors can include the ability to empower designers to easily set up complex game events. *StarCraft*'s Campaign Editor is an especially good example of this sort of functionality. Its "Triggers" editor allows designers to use a very familiar point-and-click interface to set up complex scripted events. Pop-up menus provide lists of all the commands available, and then further pop-ups show the designer all of the different parameters that can be passed to those commands. The whole system is easily comprehended by someone looking at it for the first time, with commands written in plain English. Thus, the Campaign Editor allows unique events to occur in *StarCraft* levels without involving the overhead of a full-blown scripting language.

Us Versus Them

Unfortunate as it may be, the development of the tools for a project often comes down to a battle between the programmers and the designers. Game programmers are often loath to work on tools for a variety of reasons. First, many of the programmers who wanted to get into gaming did so because they did not want to program databases, spreadsheets, or 3D modeling packages. They wanted to make games, and tools often seem too much like "real programming." There's also a perception that getting one's code in the game is more important than getting it in the tools. If the title is a big hit, the game will be played by millions of people. The tools for a given project will be used by ten, perhaps twenty people. When a programmer's friends ask her what she worked on while she was at that wacky game company, most programmers do not want to have to answer, "I worked on the tools." There is just no glamour there.

Further complicating matters is the perception that a programmer's time is more valuable than a designer's. So if a designer has to spend five times as long making a level because a programmer does not have the time to make the level editor better, well, that's OK. The level still gets made, right?

As I have stated previously, game developers should not be asking themselves the question, "Do the tools allow for the game's content to be created?" Instead, they should ask, "Do the tools allow for the game's content to be made well?" If a designer is constantly fighting with the level creation tools, he is not going to be able to invest time into truly refining the level. In fact, he may be so irritated at perceived programmer laziness that he throws his hands up in disgust and does not work on the level as much as he might otherwise. A good level designer will be inspired by a good tool set to do the best work he can, because he can see direct results. The example I used before about the level design tool and the resultant quality of the levels in *Centipede 3D* is a good lesson for game developers. With the creation of a superior level editing tool, level quality will improve dramatically.

A tools programmer should be able to take pride in having worked on a really good tool that facilitates the designer's work. The programmer responsible for a well-conceived and well-implemented level editor which greatly facilitates the creation of beautiful levels should feel that she played a vital role in the creation of those levels. For without the features of the level editor, the designer would not have been able to create the landscapes or structures he did. The designer must always make it a point to remember the programmer who made possible the creation of such levels and be suitably appreciative of her efforts.

Blizzard's *StarCraft* Campaign Editor automatically sets up transitions between different types of landscape textures, thereby saving the designer a lot of work.

At one point I added a texturing feature to the Riot Engine Level Editor. The Riot Engine employs tiling textures for its landscape, with transition textures available for when a grass texture meets a rock texture, for example. I added the functionality that allowed the editor to automatically place the proper transitions between two different texture types. Interestingly, this was a feature included in the level editor for my first published game of six years ago, *Odyssey: The Legend of Nemesis*. Indeed, this auto-transitioning functionality is found in many 2D terrain level editors, such as Blizzard's *StarCraft* Campaign Editor. Before I added the feature, the level designers at Surreal had to pick by hand the transition texture that was needed. Certainly the auto-transitioning feature was not absolutely necessary for the creation of levels. All of the levels for the game *Drakan* had been made without the use of the auto-transitioning tool, and certainly they were very beautiful levels with transitions in all the right places. The key difference is that those transitions took a lot of designer time to set up. Once I added the auto-transitioning tool the designers were delighted, since now a large and tedious part of their jobs had been all but eliminated. One even said, "Richard could take off the next month and we could keep paying him." He was appreciative of the feature I had added and was thoughtful enough to communicate his thanks to me. With praise like that, I am much more likely to keep adding nifty features to the editor.

The Best of Intentions

However, one must be careful. Sometimes when programmers are tasked with adding functionality to the editor, they may end up adding features that no one really needs. It is difficult for a programmer who, most of the time, does not make the game's levels and therefore does not spend a lot of time working with the level editor, to properly understand where that editor is lacking. Indeed, what a programmer may see as a cool feature turns out to be functionality no designer will ever want to use. When a programmer goes to a lot of trouble to implement a feature for the editor and then the designers fail to use it, resentment tends to grow in the programmer. Then when a designer comes to the programmer requesting a more practical and necessary feature be added to the editor, the programmer is likely to ignore her: "She never used the vertex-warping tool that I worked so hard on, so why should I work on this model-aligner for her? Forget it."

Anyone who has worked in the industry knows that, in a lot of ways, designers and programmers think differently. For this reason, it is very important for the designers and programmers to be in constant communication about what features the editor needs and how they can best be implemented. When developing an in-house tool set, the programmer has the tremendous advantage of having his user base down the hall. He does not have to guess what they want from the program; instead he can go ask them. Similarly, the designers have the advantage of being able to go to the editor's developer and make suggestions on how the tool should function. With a good flow of information between the parties involved, the tools cannot help but improve.

One possible technique for facilitating the creation of a good tool is to assign one programmer to be primarily responsible for the maintenance and improvement of the level editor. This programmer can then become quite familiar with the workings of the tool and can take pride in what a good application it is. If one programmer does most of the editor work, the designers will know which programmer they can turn to with their suggestions for improvements to the tool. That programmer will get a better sense of what the designers like and do not like. Of course, if the programmer assigned to working on the tool really wishes she was working on lighting effects or AI, the tool is going to suffer as a result. Finding a programmer who really wants to work on the tool is important if this strategy is to succeed.

Another useful tactic is to actually have a programmer make a complete, simple level using the tool. That way, the programmer can easily spot areas for improvement in the tool, and can finally understand what the designers have been complaining about for so many weeks. Without actually having to sit down and fully use the application they are creating, the programmer is likely to conclude that the designers are overemphasizing the problems with the editor (known in industry parlance as "whining"). But by actually having to use the tool he is working on, a programmer is likely to easily identify what shortcomings the editor has which can be trivially fixed through a few hours of coding. Designers frequently fail to understand the complexity of different programming tasks, and as a result make requests for nearly impossible features in the level editor, while thinking easily remedied problems are unfixable. Perhaps the best solution of all is to have a designer who is also a programmer, and thereby spends a lot of time working with the editor. This designer/programmer is directly motivated toward improving the tool she must work with every day, and is likely to do whatever she can to make it the best tool possible. Ten years ago I am sure this was not that uncommon, but for full-scale projects in development today it is fairly rare. Programming a level editor and designing levels have each become tasks which fully consume an individual developer's time, and the days of the designer/programmer often seem to be a thing of the past.

A Game Editor for All Seasons

A level editor does not actually need to be bug free. Bug-free software is the stuff one buys in stores, if one is lucky. Really great in-house tools can have plenty of bugs in them. What is important is that these tools be buggy in predictable ways. The bugs should occur in patterns that the designers can learn how to predict and teach themselves to avoid. Once a designer becomes adept at the tools he will know what not to do and will be able to easily work around the trouble spots. Proprietary level editor tools are one place in software development where the old joke, "Doctor, it hurts when I do this!" "Then don't do that!" really rings true.

Of course, if the tools used on a project are good enough, marketing may catch on and can come up with the bright idea, "Hey, we can release the tools with the game!" Indeed, shipping a game with its level editor and having users create add-on levels for your game can help to keep interest alive in a game long after it has been released. Hard-core fans will love to make "mods" for the game to circulate among their friends or the general public. For the tools to be released, they really will need to be relatively bug free, or at least much more stable than when they were only being used in-house. The possibility of releasing the level editor to the fans should function as an incentive to encourage the programming team to create the best tools possible. Of course, some publishers still fail to see the logic of having the fan community build add-ons and refuse to release the tools used for the game's creation. The argument they often give is that if users can build more levels themselves, who will want to buy the sequel? Of course, id Software, the company that popularized releasing level editors to the public, seems to be doing quite well financially, suggesting that protectionist thinking in terms of level editors is somewhat foolish.

It all comes down to what should be recognized as an axiom in the gaming industry: a game can only be as good as the tools used in its creation. A well-conceived level design tool can make the difference between a great game and a mediocre one. One can think of the ideal level editor as a place where the designer has total control of the game-world: of its architecture (where the player can go), of its aesthetic appearance (lighting, texturing, and sounds), and of its gameplay (NPC, item, and other entity placement, movement, and behavior). Of course, the best level editor in the world is not going to make up for a sub-par engine, a fundamentally flawed game design, or a demoralized development team. But those are topics for another chapter.

Chapter 20:

Game Analysis: The Sims

Designed by Will Wright
Released in 2000

B ased on its concept alone, *The Sims* is not a game that many people would identify as one they would want to play. Indeed, a focus group conducted early in the project's development was so unfavorable that the game's designer, Will Wright, had trouble getting any staff on the project. And why would

it be fun? "Control a collection of characters at home in a simulated suburbia." To hear that description of the game, it seems disturbingly too much like real, mundane, suburban life to possibly be entertaining. Indeed, all that is simulated in the game is home life—no going "out" to concerts or roller rinks for these "sims." But to hear someone talk about *The Sims* is to instantly become intrigued. "Well, I was trying to get my sim to flirt with this woman, but her husband became upset and decked my character!" So what is it that makes this game so brilliant and so fiendishly entertaining?

To summarize, the player starts playing *The Sims* by first creating the characters he wants to control by assigning quantities to different attributes: Neat, Outgoing, Active, Playful, and Nice. The player can then place these characters in a home, either pre-built or one he constructs himself. From there, it is the player's responsibility to make sure the house has all of the objects the sims will need to live: a bed, a toilet, a kitchen, a phone, objects for entertainment, and so forth. The Needs indicators help communicate what the sim requires to achieve happiness, including listings for Hunger, Energy, Comfort, Fun, and Social. The player also must see to it that his sim finds a way to bring in money to pay for all the nifty stuff the player purchases, a goal accomplished by looking at the job listings in the newspaper. In addition, the game has an elaborate social component, where other sims can be invited over, talked to, entertained, flirted with, and befriended. The game provides such an amazing breadth of areas for the player to explore, one is amazed that all of them are also quite deep in their functionality.

Abdicating Authorship

The Sims is a very good example of what Doug Church at a Game Developer's Conference lecture described as "abdicating authorship" in computer games. That is, instead of the game designer coming up with the game's story ahead of time, as is the case in 95 percent of adventure, role-playing, and action games made today, the authorship of the game's story is abdicated to the player. The player can then take the story in whatever direction he wants, no matter how prurient, dull, or hackneyed it may be. Indeed, at first the player may not even think of the experience as being a story, just as he may not think of his own life as a story. Yet it still is a story. In *The Sims*, the storytelling becomes more of a collaborative effort between the player, who directs the action, and the game designer, who provides the framework, tools, and space with which the player can work. Since the player is intimately involved in the creation of the story, that story becomes his, and as a result the player becomes that much more involved in the game. Instead of having his strings pulled by the game designer as has happened in so many other games, it is the player who is now pulling the strings. The feeling of empowerment is tremendous indeed.

The Sims provides a framework upon which players can author their own stories.

It is widely agreed that *The Sims* is a software toy and not technically a game, even though it is frequently called a game and discussed in the same breath as other titles which definitely are games. Indeed, *The Sims* is a toy because it does not present a definite goal to the player, though it may insinuate or imply one. There is no "winning" or "losing" *The Sims* beyond what the player defines those terms to mean. Perhaps the player will think he lost when his sim dies during a cooking fire. Or maybe the player will think he has won when his sim manages to build the largest, most extravagant house in the neighborhood and has reached the apex of her chosen career path. However, these victory/loss conditions are ones that the player is suggesting into the game, not ones that the game demands. This abdicates authorship to the player more than a goal-oriented game ever could. For instance, every time someone plays a racing game such as *San Francisco Rush*, the ending of the game is predetermined; once the player or one of his opponents crosses the finish line on the track, the game ends. Thus the end of the "story" that *Rush* is telling is predetermined. The player may be able to author how well his own car does in that race and what sort of tactics it uses to try to win, but how the story ends is a known, unchangeable quantity. Even a game like *Civilization*, which gives the player a great deal of freedom as to how he will play his game, still constrains the player by saying the game is over when the year 2000 rolls around, when the player wins the space race, or when he achieves military dominance. By setting up victory conditions, the game designer is authoring how the game will end. Since *The Sims* and other software toys do not dictate how the game must end, the player is left to decide when enough is enough. Some players, perhaps primarily the hard-core gaming aficionados, see this lack of winning and losing as a detriment to the game,

but for many players it would seem to make the playing experience all the more compelling.

Familiar Subject Matter

Of course, *The Sims* is not the original software toy, nor is it even Will Wright's first. His first success with the software toy genre came with *SimCity*. It too simulated a sophisticated system and allowed the player to truly control her city's destiny. Though *SimCity* is an excellent, entertaining title, *The Sims* is more compelling still. A lot of this has to do with the fact that the player of *The Sims* is controlling humans instead of a city. In other words, it follows Chris Crawford's insistence that games should focus on "people not things." In general, most players will find people to be much more interesting than things, and players will be able to form an emotional bond with a simulated person much easier than with a simulated city. After playing *The Sims* for a while, players will feel sad when their sim's amorous advances are rebuffed or when their house burns to the ground. Though certainly not as smart or interesting as actual humans, the simulated people in *The Sims* are close enough to being plausible that players will want to believe in their sims' virtual existences and will fill in the simulation's deficiencies for themselves.

Furthermore, almost all the players who play *The Sims* will have an intimate knowledge of the subject being simulated before they start playing. They will feel that they are something of an expert on this "suburban life" subject and think they will be able to play the game better as a result. For instance, players know by instinct that they should set up a bathroom with a shower, a toilet, and a sink. If the job were to simulate an alien life-form's daily life on another planet, players would have much less of an idea how to proceed and would need to figure out the life-form's culture before they could expect to succeed at the game. Because players already know so much about the subject matter of *The Sims*, they are that much more drawn into the game. From the moment she starts up the game, the player feels good because she is putting her real-world knowledge to use in creating these simulated lives. When Will Wright made *SimEarth*, he created a game involving systems that players knew very little about, and this may explain why so many people found the game to be quite difficult. For *SimCity*, players had a better sense of what was going on; while they may not have been experts on urban planning and dynamics, players at least thought they knew how a city should be laid out and were familiar with problems such as traffic, pollution, and crime. With *The Sims*, most players know infinitely more about the topic than they do about city planning. Hence, the game is that much more compelling to play. Its very familiarity draws the player in like nothing else can.

Of course, simulating a subject many of the players will be familiar with can be a challenge as well; if the designer gets it wrong, players will know instantly. In the alien-life simulator, who is to say what is accurate since the world and creatures are made up to begin with? This grants the designer more artistic license for how the world is constructed. However, in a reality simulation like *The Sims*, if the designer makes the wrong choice about what will provoke a sim to do what action, players will see the error and their suspension of disbelief will be shattered instantly. Working with a subject that players are intimate with may serve to draw them in, but if it is not done correctly it may drive them away as well.

Safe Experimentation

On first inspection, one might not think that what *The Sims* simulates is actually all that interesting. Indeed, for the suburbanites who are likely to own a computer to play the game and have the disposable income to purchase it, how different is the game-world of *The Sims* from real life? It would seem that the escapist and wish-fulfillment qualities many games possess are totally lacking in *The Sims*. Furthermore, *The Sims* does not even present "life with all the dull bits cut out." The player's sims still have to engage in the more mundane aspects of modern life, such as going to the bathroom, going to work, paying bills, and taking out the trash. Is this fun? Strangely, it is, since these more tedious chores lend an air of "realism" to the proceedings, which makes the player's successes or failures all the more meaningful.

Though the subject matter of *The Sims* may seem pedestrian, the game is so fascinating because it provides players with a safe world in which to experiment.

What *The Sims* really provides to the player is a test-bed for safe experimentation. While prudence may prevent the player from pursuing a career as a criminal or professional athlete in real life, the game will allow the player to take her sims in that direction with little risk to the player. While building a house is a major undertaking involving great financial risk for the purchaser, in *The Sims,* players can build lavish houses, spend money on frivolous trinkets for their sims, throw wild hot tub parties, or pursue homosexual relationships just to get a sense of what life might be like if they lived it differently. If these experimental lifestyles turn out to not work as well as the players had hoped, the only loss is for their sims, an effect considerably less serious than real-world bankruptcy or social ostracizing. Indeed, if the player avoids saving her game after a catastrophic event or decision, the loss is easily undone entirely. The life the player controls in *The Sims* may be one quite close to her own, but the ability to try new things without fear of serious repercussions makes the experience compelling and exciting.

Depth and Focus

A big part of what makes *The Sims* work is the range of choices the player is presented with for what he can do with his sims. Abdicating authorship is all well and good, but if the designer fails to provide the player enough meaningful choices, the player will find himself only able to author a very narrow range of stories. Indeed, it is the designer's responsibility in creating a software toy to design that toy with a broad enough range of possibilities that the appeal of playing with it is not quickly exhausted. And Wright did that expertly with *The Sims*, leaving the player with a constant feeling that there is so much more to do and see in the game-world, that one could never hope to do it all.

A player can concentrate on building her house, starting either with some of the pre-built houses or constructing one from the ground up. A robust set of house-construction and landscaping tools allows the player to create a very large variety of houses, with probably no two built-from-scratch houses ever being the same, even with hundreds of thousands of people playing the game. Once a house is built or purchased, players can concentrate on filling it up with all manner of interesting possessions which have a variety of effects on the inhabitants of the house. Of course, the player gets to construct the inhabitants as well, picking from a large range of personalities, body types, ages, ethnicities, and even hairstyles, with the option to make children or adults as well as males or females. Once the sims move into the house, the player is able to determine what they eat, what they study, what career they pursue, how they have their fun, and with whom they socialize. Whether it be house building, property acquisition and placement, character creation, or life control, any one of these components includes far more choices than most games provide. When all of these different systems are combined, the range of choices available to the player increases exponentially, creating a game with truly unprecedented depth.

Of course, what the sims cannot do in the game is significant as well. The sims cannot leave their homes except to go to work, and when they do the player cannot follow them. Being able to go to other places would be nice, but consider how much more complex the game would need to be to simulate the rest of the world. A massive amount of additional work would have been required, and had that sensible limitation not been made early on in the title's development it might never have been completed. By focusing on the home life, the game is able to "get it right" in a way it could not have had the game-world of *The Sims* been larger. In short, what would have been gained in breadth would have been lost in depth. If a designer spends all her time adding an unreasonable range of possibilities to the game, it is likely that any one of the features the game includes will be far shallower than if the designer knows how to focus her efforts.

The Sims also expertly captures the "just one more thing" style of gameplay. This type of gameplay is perhaps best exemplified by *Civilization*, where the player is constantly looking forward to the next technology to be discovered, the next unit to be built, or the next discovery of new territory. Similarly in *The Sims*, the player may be working on having his sims meet new people, trying to advance their careers, hoping to put an addition on the house, and thinking of someday having them raise a child, all at the same time. Because of these constant aspirations, there is never a good place to stop playing the game; there is constantly something on the horizon to look forward to. Hence the game is fabulously addictive, with captivated players devoting hour upon hour, day after day, and week after week of their lives to the game.

Interface

The best a game's interface can hope to do is to not ruin the player's experience. The interface's job is to communicate to the player the state of the world and to receive input from the player as to what he wants to change in that game-world. The act of using this input/output interface is not meant to be fun in and of itself; it is the player's interaction with the world that should be the compelling experience. But since the interface determines how the player interacts with the world, if that interface is not up to the task then at best the player will become frustrated and at worst the player will be unable to perform the action he wants.

The Sims' user interface is a beautiful example of how to do an interface correctly. It provides the player with a staggering amount of information about the game-world, while allowing the player to easily and intuitively make whatever changes she wants. Unlike many modern action games, the tutorial primarily provides the player with information about how to play the game, not how to manipulate the interface. The interface is so simple and intuitive that players pick it up with very little difficulty, no doubt the result of rigorous playtesting. The fact that help is embedded throughout the interface is key, allowing the player to click on any text item for an explanation of how it is important and why it is relevant.

The Sims has an extremely intuitive interface that includes multiple ways for the player to accomplish the same action.

A big part of the success of *The Sims'* input/output scheme is its similarity to systems the player is likely to understand before he ever starts playing the game. For instance, the buttons that determine the game's simulation speed look like those one would find on a tape player, something with which almost all players will be familiar. A large amount of the interface is reminiscent of Microsoft Windows, with the pointing and clicking the player does mirroring that OS wherever appropriate. Item manipulation is reminiscent of Windows as well; the player can use drag and drop to place objects, or simply click and click. The standard Windows "X" appears in the upper right-hand corner of dialog boxes to indicate that they can be closed, and the regular OK/Cancel button combinations are used wherever appropriate. While the functionality mirrors Windows in many ways, it is important to note that the appearance of the interface does not look exactly like Windows. All of the buttons are nicely drawn in a friendly art style that is a far cry from Windows' cold, utilitarian sterility. If the game used the actual dialog box art that Windows provides, the player would instantly be reminded of working with the file picker or some other Windows interface, not an experience he is likely to remember fondly, certainly not as a "fun" activity. However, by putting a new visual style on the behavior of Windows, the interface is intuitive and familiar to the player without actually reminding him of file management.

Another example of this is the "head" menu used throughout the game. When the player wants to have a sim perform an action on a particular object, the player simply clicks on the object in question. From there a floating head of her current sim appears, with a range of different actions the sim can perform surrounding it in a circle. The player then simply moves the mouse over to the action he wants and clicks on it. While moving the pointer around, the sim's head actually tracks the cursor, watching it wherever it goes. This menu functions identically to a pop-up menu in Windows, but with several distinct advantages. The first is that it does not look like a pop-up menu, and thereby the player does not associate it with boring Windows functionality. Second, the menu only lists the options that are available for the current object at that time. A normal pop-up menu would list all of the objects possible, with currently unavailable options grayed out. Third, by having the sim's head in the center, the menu brings the player closer to the core of what he is doing; he is directing the sim to perform a certain action. The directive he is giving to his beloved sim is more intimate than it would have been through a more sterile, bland, and standard pop-up menu.

Controlled Versus Autonomous Behavior

In the game, the player is able to direct his sims to perform certain actions: take out the trash, call up a friend, take a shower, and so forth. The sims will also, however, function on their own without the player's direction. The sims contain enough internal logic to tend to their most pressing needs, whether it is to eat, to go to the bathroom, to play a pinball game, or to read today's paper. As the player makes additions to the house or purchases further possessions, the sims will walk over to new objects and either applaud or complain about them, their reaction dependent on how much they like each particular object. This communicates to the player whether the sim is generally going to be happy with the new possession or if the sim would rather it were not there. Since the way the house is set up is a big component of the sim's total happiness, this provides crucial information to the player about how to best set up the house.

The autonomous behavior of the sims also allows the player to set up the house and then sit back and watch how the sims live in it. This makes the game more like *SimCity*, in which the player could only set up the framework of the city—its streets, its zones, its key buildings—and then see how the inhabitants of the city live in it. A player of *The Sims* can build a pleasant house that he thinks would be good to live in and then sit back and watch the sims inhabit it, using their default behavior. This provides yet another avenue for interesting gameplay.

The sims have some intelligence of their own, which frees up the player from having to worry about every last detail of their lives.

The sims generally do not have the foresight of a player, however, and as a result will perform better, be more productive, and be happier if the player smartly directs their every move. For instance, the sims will not try to improve their career-boosting skills of their own volition, such as improving their creativity by learning how to paint. So it is often in the player's best interest to override the sims' internal choices for what action to perform next, if he wants the sim to attain her full potential. However, the autonomous behavior avoids the player having to micro-manage every little decision. Sure, being able to tell the sims exactly what to do is a key part of the game, but if the player is controlling a number of sims at once, planning something for every one of them to do at a given moment can be quite a task. The sims' internal behavior helps to off-load this responsibility from the player when the player does not want to worry about it.

A Lesson to Be Learned

The Sims is perhaps the most original commercial game design released in recent years. The game does not take as a starting point any other published game, but instead seems to have emerged entirely from Will Wright's brain. To look at the game is to marvel at its creativity and innovation. There is so much that is done right in *The Sims*, an entire book could be devoted to an analysis of its design. The game is truly like a computerized dollhouse, providing us the ability to play-act real human scenarios in order to better understand them. The description of the dollhouse found in the game is quite illuminating:

Will Lloyd Wright Doll House

This marvel of doll house design is meant for everyone, allowing children as well as adults to act out fantasies of controlling little families. This incredible replica comes complete with amazingly realistic furniture and decorative items. Don't be surprised if hours upon hours are spent enjoying this little world.

What is perhaps most interesting and compelling about *The Sims* is the potential it has to teach us about our own lives. What is the relationship we have with the possessions we own? How does the space we live in affect our lives? How does jealousy start in a relationship?

Of course, no one would argue that *The Sims* is a completely accurate simulation of human motivations and activities, but does it need to be completely accurate to cause us to think about our lives in new and interesting ways? As we move our sims around and watch them interact, we may disagree with how the simulation models their behavior. But in that disagreement, we think about what we really would expect them to do, with that reflection shedding new light on the relationships we maintain in our real lives. This, it seems, is the potential of computer games—not to allow us to escape from real life or to even replace it, but to open up new areas of thought, to be able to see the world through a different set of eyes and come back to our own lives equipped with that priceless information.

Chapter 21:
Level Design

"We've always striven for 'immersion' in the gameplay, but as we've grown (well, changed at least) as designers, our sense of that has changed. While the details of this attempt vary from game to game, the core goal has been to provide a range of player capability in the world. With this breadth of capability, the player hopefully feels more involved in their decisions. An *Underworld* player can open a door with the key, by picking the lock, by breaking it down, or by casting a spell. If the player can choose their own goals, and their own approaches to an obstacle, then when they reach the goal it is far more satisfying. Flexible simulation of game elements is a powerful way to enable the player to make their own way in the world."

— Doug Church, talking about his game *Ultima Underworld*

As computer games have grown in size and scope, the tasks that in the past were performed by one person are now performed by multiple people. This division of labor is necessary for the timely completion of the sophisticated and massive games the publishers demand and the marketplace has come to expect. One of the unique roles that was created through this division of labor was that of the level designer. Once the core gameplay for a game is established, it is the level designer's job to create the game-world in which that gameplay takes place, to build spaces that are fun for the player.

The number of level designers required for a project is directly proportional to the complexity of the levels to be used in that project. For a 3D game with extremely detailed architecture which all must be built by the level designer, it is not unreasonable to have two levels per designer, perhaps only one. Sometimes the game's primary designer also serves as a level designer, and sometimes she merely oversees the team of level designers working on the project. For a 2D game, it is not out of the question for the game's lead designer to craft all of the game's levels.

Level design is where all the different components of a game come together. In some ways creating a level is like putting together a jigsaw puzzle; to build his levels, the level designer must make use of the game's engine, art, and core gameplay. Often level design is where a game's problems become most apparent. If the engine is not up to snuff, the levels will start behaving erratically in certain situations, or the frame rate will not be able to support the planned effects. If the art is made to the wrong scale or has rendering problems of any kind, these difficulties come out as the level designer starts placing the art in the world. If the title's gameplay is not able to support a wide enough variety of levels to fill out an entire game, or, even worse, if the gameplay just is not any fun, this problem will become apparent during the level design process. It is the level designer's responsibility to bring these problems to the attention of the team, and to see that the difficulties are resolved properly. Often this can result in the level designer being one of the least liked team members, since he must always be pestering people to fix problems, but if he instead tries to ignore the problems he encounters, the game will be worse as a result. The job of the level designer is one that comes with great responsibility.

With all the different aspects of the game's content to worry about, the level designer's job is certainly not an easy one. Beyond making sure all of the game's components are up to snuff, if the level designer's own work is not of the highest quality, then the game is likely to fail miserably. If the levels do not bring out the best aspects of the engine, the art, and the gameplay, it does not matter how good those component parts may be. Without good levels to pull it all together, the game will fail to live up to its potential.

Levels in Different Games

Joust made simple changes to its game-world to produce different levels.

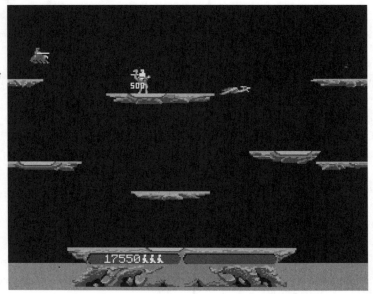

The definition of a "level" varies greatly from game to game. It most commonly refers to the game-world of side-scrollers, first-person shooters, adventures, flight simulators, and role-playing games. These games tend to have distinct areas which are referred to as "levels." These areas may be constrained by geographical area (lava world versus ice world), by the amount of content that can be kept in memory at once, or by the amount of gameplay that "feels right" before the player is granted a short reprieve preceding the beginning of the next level. Though many classic arcade games such as *Centipede* or *Space Invaders* took place entirely on one level, others such as *Pac-Man* or *Joust* offered simple variations on the game-world to prolong their gameplay. Thus, the different mazes in *Pac-Man* constitute its levels. In a campaign-based strategy game such as *StarCraft,* the levels or scenarios are defined by maps accompanied by objectives the player must accomplish, such as defend the Terrans against the Protoss forces in this amount of time. In a racing game, a level would be one of the tracks available in the game. In a sports game, say baseball, the levels would be the different stadiums featured in the game. Here the difference between the various levels is completely aesthetic, since in terms of play mechanics, a baseball game played in Wrigley Field is only subtly different from one played in Yankee Stadium.

Games such as *Civilization* and *SimCity* do have levels, but one key difference from the games described above is that the entirety of a player's game takes place on a single level. The base level is also often randomly generated, and from there it is largely the user's responsibility to construct the level as he plays. This is why these titles are often referred to as "builder" games. For these titles, the authorship of the level is almost entirely abdicated to the player.

This chapter deals primarily with games that use pre-built levels which have a major impact on the gameplay. Though sports titles and "builder" games may have levels, their construction is left up to the artists and players respectively, and therefore is not generally of concern to designers. For games like *Doom*, *Tomb Raider*, *Super Mario 64*, *Maniac Mansion*, *Pac-Man*, *StarCraft*, and *Fallout*, however, the design of the levels has everything to do with gameplay and therefore the designer must be intimately involved with their creation.

Level Separation

How a game is broken down into its component levels has a huge impact on the flow of the game. Players often play a game a level at a time. If a parent announces dinner while a child is playing a game, that child is likely to beg to be allowed to "just finish this level." In console games, frequently the player can only save her game between levels, which places further importance on the end of a level as the completion of a unit of gameplay. A level can function like an act in a play, a chapter in a book, or a movement in a symphony. It gives the audience a chance to see a discrete unit within a larger work, to understand what portion of the work has been completed and how much awaits ahead. Well-designed levels are set up such that difficulty and tension ramp upward toward the end of a level where some sort of a mini-resolution finally occurs. This may be through a boss monster to defeat or a special quest object to obtain. When the player finally sees that the level has ended, she knows that she has accomplished a significant amount of gameplay and should feel proud of herself.

Technical limitations often dictate where the end of a level must occur. Only so many textures, sounds, and level data can fit in memory at once, and when those resources are used up, the gameplay has to stop long enough for different level data to be loaded in. New technologies present the opportunity for more seamless environments. Even on the technically limited PlayStation, the developer Insomniac was able to avoid loading screens entirely in *Spyro the Dragon*, instead just having Spyro fly into the air for a second while the necessary data is swapped in, then flying back to earth in the new level. To the casual player watching *Spyro*, the break is much less jarring than seeing a "loading" screen come up. The *Spyro the Dragon* levels still have to be divided into sections between these non-loading screens, however, meaning that the gameplay in those levels is still limited to a certain amount of space. A good designer, of course, can take the memory constraints and use them properly to create levels that are fun and challenging to play while also fitting in the space available. Again, the designer must take the limitations of the hardware and embrace them.

Half-Life is another interesting example of level division. Here the team at Valve wanted to create a more seamless experience for the player, but were still using the limited *Quake* technology. *Quake* had featured thirty or so levels, each of which took a significant amount of time to load. In *Quake* the levels existed in separate universes from each other; never would a monster chase the player from one level to another, never would a player return to a previous level. The programmers at Valve came up with a system where, if the levels were small enough, they could be loaded in under five seconds. They also made modifications so that monsters could track the player across the boundaries between maps. The level designers at Valve were able to make their levels very small, much smaller than a standard *Quake* level, but then created a great quantity of them. The areas between two levels contain identical architecture, such that the player can run across the border between two of these levels and, aside from the brief loading message, not even know he had crossed a level boundary. The result is a much more seamless experience for the player. Evidently the team still felt the need for story arcs in the game, since text "chapter titles" appear briefly on the screen at key points during the game. But since the programming and design teams were able to create a near-seamless level loading system, the design team was able to separate the game into these storytelling units wherever it felt best, instead of where the technology dictated. The ideal for an immersive game like *Half-Life*, of course, would be to eliminate these load times entirely. Someday the technology will exist to cache in new level data as the player gets close to needing it. Until then, designers trying to create seamless environments must strive to keep the loading as short and unobtrusive as possible.

Level Order

The order in which the levels occur is also important to the overall flow of the game. Perhaps big shoot-out levels should be alternated with more strategic or puzzle-oriented levels. If a game places all of its strategic levels early in the game and then crowds the end with more action-oriented episodes, the game may seem unbalanced. At the very least, the designer should know how the order of the levels will affect the flow of gameplay, and should be aware of how moving different levels around will affect it. For example, if a game has thirty levels and six boss monsters, one logical way to place these adversaries in the game would be at the end of the fifth, tenth, fifteenth, twentieth, twenty-fifth, and thirtieth levels. The bosses certainly do not have to be on those precise levels, and each can be shifted slightly forward or backward in the level order without causing any serious problems. If the bosses were placed one each on the last six levels of the game, this would be obviously unbalanced. It would seem strange to the player that after twenty-four levels of no-boss-monster gameplay, suddenly he has to fight one every level.

The goal of the *Unreal* level designers was to create some cool levels, not necessarily to make them fit together as a whole.

The way the game is broken up into its different levels and the order in which those levels must occur differs from game to game. For a game like *Unreal*, as with the *Doom* and *Quake* series before it, the designers were only instructed to make some cool levels, with little concern for story (since none of these games really had one) or which events should happen before which other events. Some thought was put into at what point certain adversaries would first appear in the game, and hence the earlier levels were more restricted in which creatures they could use. Similarly, of course, the earlier levels had to be easier and the later ones had to be harder. But for the most part, the level designers just tried to make the coolest levels possible, almost working in a vacuum from the other designers. Certainly they would see each other's work and this might inspire them to make their own levels better, but none of the levels really had to match up thematically with the levels that came before or after it, and the lack of a story meant that this did not adversely affect the game.

In a game such as *Indiana Jones and the Infernal Machine*, however, the story plays a much larger role. In order for that story to work, the levels need to support it. Hence, for a more story-centric game, a great deal of preplanning is done by the game's design and story teams as to which story events need to happen in which levels. In what sort of environments should those levels take place? What types of adversaries will the player fight there? The order in which the levels appear in the game cannot be changed as easily as in *Doom*, since that would radically change the story as well. In order for the entire game to flow and escalate in difficulty appropriately, the type of gameplay found in each level must be planned ahead of time. The levels do not need to be planned down to minute detail, however, as this is best left to the level designer, who can place the individual encounters, objects, or minor puzzles as they best fit the level. A mini design document explaining what the level has to accomplish in order to function within the game's story will allow the level designer to know exactly what she must include in the level; from there she can fill in the details.

The Components of a Level

Once the levels a game needs have been decided on, possibly with some idea of how those levels must support the story, the next task is to actually create those levels. Regardless of its location in the game as a whole, the goal of every level is to provide an engaging gameplay experience for the player. When working on the levels for a game, it is important to constantly keep in mind the focus of the game. What is this game trying to accomplish? How important are the different aspects of the game? What will the level need to do to support the type of gameplay this game has? In addition, depending on the amount of pre-production design done on the levels, one may need to consider how this level may play differently than others. Is it a "thinking" level after an action-intensive one? Is this level more about exploration and discovery than building up the strength of the player character or characters?

A level for the sophisticated *Quake III Arena* engine requires significantly more work than one for a simpler 2D game. As a result, making changes to a Q3A level is significantly more time consuming.

Before level design begins, the design team should convene and break down the different gameplay components of the game, since each member must completely understand how the gameplay functions. Each level designer must understand how his level will use that gameplay before he starts building anything. In some games it is easy to radically change the layout of a level, such as in a tile-based game like *StarCraft*. If problems with the level arise, the level can be easily reworked. For a game using the *Quake III* engine, however, once a level is built it is very labor-intensive to radically alter it. Producers will be reluctant to invest another month of architecture construction time to rework a level because it is not playing well. Therefore understanding ahead of time the gameplay of the game and the level in question is important. One perhaps simplistic but still useful way to break down the components of a level's gameplay is in terms of action, exploration, puzzle solving, storytelling, and aesthetics.

Action

Action is the most obvious component of the levels for many games, and indeed for many titles the action element is the only justification for the level's existence. Of course there are some games that eschew the action component entirely, such as many adventure or puzzle games, but nearly all other games contain some action components, whether it consists of blasting demons in a shooter like *Doom*, incapacitating walking mushrooms in *Super Mario 64*, slaying mutants in *Fallout*, or speeding by the opponents' cars in *San Francisco Rush*.

Whatever your game's action component is, the level designer's job is to understand how much action the level contains and at what pacing this action component should be presented to the player. What percentage of your level should be action filled and exciting? How many battles will the player fight? Is the combat fast and furious or are there "breaks" or intermissions between major conflicts? Should the player's adrenaline be pumping during the entire level because of a constant fear of death? Of course, the amount of action is entirely dependent on what type of game you are making, but regardless, you need to have a clear idea of what amount of conflict the player will encounter.

For a game with a lot of action, the levels must be constructed keeping in mind how that action will play out. The level designer must keep in mind how the enemy AI functions and what types of maps will lead to the most interesting conflicts. What geometry will give the player lots of locations to duck and cover while dodging enemy fire? How can the levels be best set up to encourage the player to figure out her own strategy for defeating the opposition? Knowing what sort of action your game will have and how that action best plays out is critical to designing levels that bring out the best in the action gameplay.

Exploration

What will the player be doing when not in the heat of battle? Exploration is a major part of a lot of action/adventure titles such as *Tomb Raider* or *Super Mario Bros.*

Instead of just providing a bridge between different action set pieces, if properly designed the exploration can actually be a lot of fun for a player. It is often hard for the design team to see this after slaving away on a map for months. How much fun is exploring architecture with which you are already painfully familiar? Always try to keep in mind that for a player experiencing a map for the first time, the thrill of exploring a new virtual world can be quite stimulating. It may be important to constantly be showing your level to first-time viewers or playtesters, and getting their feedback on whether they enjoy exploring the level or not.

The designer must keep in mind how the player will explore the level to know how best to lay it out. What cool piece of art or architecture will the player see around the next corner? How excited or awe-inspired will the player be on finding new areas? Making exciting exploration a part of your game goes beyond creating exciting architecture for the player. It is also determined by how the level flows, and what the player will have to do to reach an exciting new area. Being dropped right into the middle of some nice architecture is much less satisfying than having to navigate a large area of the map to finally make it to an exploration payoff.

Part of making the exploration aspect of a game work is determining the flow of a level. Will the player need to explore several offshoots from a main, critical path, or will the player generally only have one way to proceed? Will the path the player must take to complete the level be obvious at first, or will the player need to experiment and look around quite a bit before they find it? Games that are very action-oriented will tend to put the player on a path which leads directly to the next conflict. Games that encourage the player to poke around may make the path less obvious.

As far back as *Super Mario Bros.* on the Nintendo Entertainment System, Miyamoto's games have included exploration as a key gameplay component.

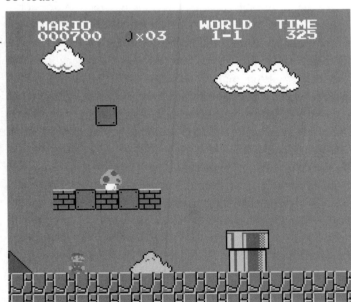

I once saw someone criticize Shigeru Miyamoto's games as being all about exploration, and therefore not very good games. The observation that exploration is the focus of the later *Mario* was a correct one. The mistake was in asserting that this is not a fun part of gameplay, as millions of Mario fans will refute. The challenge lies in making exploration entertaining and rewarding for the player, something Miyamoto's games do expertly.

Puzzle Solving

Sometimes progressing in a level involves more than just finding a path to the next area. Instead it may involve figuring out what needs to be accomplished in order to open a certain door or how a large obstacle can be cleared out of the way. Perhaps the worst examples of this are the "switch flipping" puzzles found in many first-person shooters. In these games, for no particular reason, the player needs to navigate through a large section of the map in order to flip a switch. This action opens a door which leads the player to another area where another switch is in need of flipping. And so it goes. This switch may instead be a key or any other object that opens a door or any other type of device that blocks the player's progress. This is the simplest form of a puzzle in an action/exploration game. Here the focus is mostly on the player exploring until he finds the puzzle, with the solution to the puzzle then being trivial. In the case of the switch, once it is found all the player needs to do is flip it.

More sophisticated variants on the switch/door combination can be situations which require the player to actually figure something out in order to progress. Perhaps a laser beam needs to be refracted around a series of corners in order for the player to progress. In order to refract it correctly, the player will need to move several reflective plates. The player must understand the simple physics of the situation which govern how the beam will behave when reflected in different ways. The focus here shifts from just finding the puzzle to finding it and then figuring out how to manipulate it correctly. The player's gaming experience is enhanced by this puzzle instead of it merely delaying the end of her game. Determining how much emphasis your level will have on puzzle solving is important to keep in mind, especially within the context of the game as a whole. A sure way to frustrate the player is to suddenly throw a bunch of arbitrary puzzles at her after the entire game up to that point has been more action-oriented.

Storytelling

Setting is a big part of storytelling, and levels are a vital component of establishing the setting for a game. Therefore, levels are an integral part of telling a game's story. If the story is more than something tacked on to an already completed game, it only makes sense for the game's levels and the story to work in synergy. Depending on

In a historical game such as *Gettysburg!*, the gameplay is very much tied to a particular story from history.

the type of storytelling that the game is employing, it may be necessary for the player to meet and converse with characters in the levels, such as in *Half-Life* or in almost any RPG. Setting up the levels to support the appearance of these characters becomes very important. In some games it is obvious that the levels were designed from the very start with the story in mind. For instance, in *Myth: The Fallen Lords*, the player's goals for a certain level are directly tied to the progression of the story. In a historical wargame such as *Gettysburg!*, the battles the player fights have to be tied to the story, since it could hardly be a historical simulation otherwise.

Knowing the story goals for a given level prior to constructing that level is crucial to communicating the story effectively. The story should still be loose enough to allow the level designer to be creative in making the best level possible. There are still concerns about gameplay, about balancing the right amount of strategy, action, puzzles, and exploration, and since it is nearly impossible to balance these components before the level actually exists, the level designer needs to not have his hands tied by an overly restrictive story. Indeed, it may turn out that the story needs to change in order to accommodate the gameplay needs of the level, but having an idea of what story needs to be told on a particular level is essential to designing that level so it fits properly into the overall narrative.

Aesthetics

How a level looks and sounds are probably the driving factors behind many level designers' work. I certainly would not dispute that a level's appearance is crucial to its overall success. At the same time, however, the aesthetic component becomes a problem when how the level looks becomes the designer's primary concern, a situation which usually has a detrimental effect on how the level plays. Suppose a level designer spends a lot of time creating a massive, gorgeous cathedral for a level, and the appearance of that cathedral is constantly at the forefront of his mind. What if it turns out that the cathedral is hard for the player to navigate, the AI agents easily get confused when trying to pathfind though it, and the whole structure is a bit more than the engine can handle, resulting in the level running slowly? If the cathedral looks great and its construction sucked up a lot of man-hours, who will want to cut it? It may translate into some fabulous screenshots on the back of the box; too bad it will not be any fun to play.

A big part of the level designer's job is to balance the appearance of the level with the other requirements of that level, as I have listed above. There is always an achievable middle ground where the level looks good, plays well, renders quickly, and suits the needs of the game's story. Level designers spend a lot of their time learning the "tricks" of a given engine or level editor. What can they do that will use the fewest polygons while still looking good? Often the solutions they come up with are not necessarily "real" but rather "faked." Of course the whole purpose of creating levels for a virtual world is creating "fake" content, so a level designer need not worry if an effect is achieved by "faking" something. If the player cannot tell it is faked, if he cannot see behind the magic curtain, that is all that matters. One of the principles behind all special effects is to create something that looks like something it is not. The level designer's job is to make the player see something that looks like something it is not, giving the level what *Unreal* level designer Cliff Bleszinski would call "schlack," a shiny and fancy coating over an otherwise uninteresting level.

The visual side of a level can have a big impact on the other concerns of a game's level as I have listed before. For instance, in order to make a level playable, the textures on a level should be laid out in such a way that the player can see where he should or should not be able to go. Instead of wondering if a particular slope is too steep for her game-world surrogate to climb up, a different texture can serve as a visual cue to the player as to which slopes are passable and which are not. Lighting can be used to conceal secret areas, or a big puzzle in the level may be figuring out how to turn the lights on. If certain special areas are supposed to be rewards for the player's diligent exploration, making those special areas look impressive is essential to maintaining the player's interest in the level.

A lot of time can be spent on the aesthetics of a level. The amount of time is directly proportional to the complexity of the engine and level editor being used as well as the desired visual effect of the level. In fact, it may be the case that all of the gameplay and story elements of the level can be set up first and then the visual appearance can be tweaked for weeks to come. Lighting can be endlessly adjusted, textures can be shifted or switched for other textures, and polygon faces can be adjusted to better represent the visual effect the designer is trying to achieve. All the while, the level designer must be fully aware of the effects changes in the level's appearance will have on the gameplay.

Balancing It All

Because a good level must balance action, exploration, puzzle solving, storytelling, and aesthetics, the work of the level designer is a bit of a balancing act. Even if the level may look better a certain way, how does that impact the story being told? Do the story requirements for the level mean that it cannot have much in the way of combat? Then how important is combat to the game, and can the level survive without it? Is the quantity of puzzle elements in the level preventing the player from being able to enjoy exploring it? The action, exploration, puzzle solving, storytelling, and aesthetic qualities of a game level all have interdependencies which the level designer must be constantly aware of and be constantly maintaining. The price of good level design is eternal vigilance.

Level Flow

For different types of games, what a level is expected to accomplish changes significantly. Consider action/exploration games such as *Super Mario 64*, *Tomb Raider*, or *Doom*. Though the gameplay in these three games is significantly different, the functions the levels serve in each is remarkably similar. In all these games, the player customarily plays through the level from a distinct beginning point to a separate end point. A big part of playing the level is exploring the spaces it contains, and as a result, once the player has played through the level, it is significantly less fun to play a second time. Furthermore, any encounters the player might have with characters or adversaries in these levels are carefully predetermined and set up by the level designer. Every time the player plays such a level, he will have roughly the same gameplay experience as the last time he played it. The flow of the level is more or less linear, with perhaps only a few choices of how to get from point A to point B.

RPGs offer roughly the same flow pattern as the action/exploration games discussed above, perhaps with a bit more non-linearity. The designer usually intends for the player to navigate to a particular location in a particular way. RPGs may tend to be a bit more non-linear than action/adventure games, usually allowing the player to choose the order in which different actions can be performed. Often "hub" style gameplay allows the player to branch off on different adventures while returning to a central location, such as a town. The player may also stay in the town to hone his skills for as long as he likes. In the end, though, RPGs offer similar level flow as action/adventure titles.

The level flow on a level of a real-time strategy game like *WarCraft* is less defined than in an action/ exploration game: combat encounters can take place all over the map.

In a level from a strategy game such as *WarCraft* or *Civilization*, however, the action is less canned and the level flow is less clearly defined. *WarCraft* and *Civilization* may be as different from each other as *Super Mario 64* and *Doom*, but the way they use their levels is the same. Exploration is not such a central part of the enjoyment of these strategy games, and the battles may take place on any part of the map. Different locations may provide specific strategic advantages when used correctly, but battles can start in one location and move to another, or certain sections of the map may go completely unexplored and unexploited by the player and his opponents. The gameplay on such a map is often significantly less predictable than on an action/exploration game's map. The level's flow is more nebulous.

Of course, there is at least one distinguishing characteristic that makes the level flow in *Civilization* significantly different from that of *WarCraft*. In *Civilization*, any one game consists of play on only one level. That is, the player starts a game of *Civilization* on one level and plays on that level until she wins or loses, while in *WarCraft* the player plays a series of scenarios on a series of levels. *Civilization* presents a much more continuous gameplay experience for the player, which may in turn make it that much more addictive. Whereas a game like *WarCraft* presents the player with an easy stopping point—the end of a level—a game like *Civilization* has no such breaks. Both types of games may include levels with unpredictable flows, where different players can play the levels significantly differently, but since a player in *Civilization* spends all of his time on one map, the overall feel of the game is radically different. Of course, the fact that *Civilization* is turn-based while *WarCraft* is real-time significantly changes the flow of the games as well, but that is a change in gameplay rather than a change in level design and usage.

Returning to our action/exploration games, if we were to take a multi-player death-match level from a game like *Quake*, we would see that the level's flow is much closer to that of a strategy game. That is, exploring the level is less important and combat can take place in completely unpredictable ways all over the map. Indeed, many players of multi-player death-match games will find a map they like and stick to it, at least for a while. The player will need to have explored the map thoroughly before he actually has a chance of winning a death-match on that map, certainly when playing with experienced players. Exploration and memorization of the map may be an integral part of the metagame in that such exploration leads to the player's victory in future games, but the exploration is only a means to an end, not an end in and of itself, unlike in a single-player game where exploration is a big part of the fun.

With the exception of racing games, sports games typically provide a very non-linear flow to their gameplay. The flow of a basketball game's levels more closely resembles a death-match or strategy game's levels than an action/exploration game's maps. Action takes place all over the level or court, with the player's movement flowing back and forth across the level, covering and recovering the same ground but in unique and unpredictable ways. Exploring the level is relatively unimportant, as the shape of the level is completely simple and typically the entire court or a very large chunk of it is on screen at once.

In a racing game, the player moves from a distinct start location to a distinct end location. This movement is quite similar to an exploration-oriented action game such as *Doom*, with the key differences that typically the race's start and end locations are the same (the track loops) and usually the race-path is repeated multiple times before the level is over. This flow is just as linear as in an action/adventure title, if not more so. Modern racing games such as *San Francisco Rush* or *Cruisin' World* incorporate some of the exploration elements of action/exploration games by making the levels look visually stunning and varied, making the first time the player rounds a corner an aesthetically thrilling experience. Older racing games (such as the venerable *Pole Position*) relied more on the challenge of navigating the track to entertain the player rather than the thrill of racing through new, fantastic locations. Many more modern racing games also include alternate paths or short-cuts that players can take for varied gameplay results. The flow is still in the same general direction, but some branching allows the player to concentrate on more than just how tightly he can take a given corner.

From my discussion of these gaming genres and the way that gameplay flows on their respective levels, one could divide the games into roughly two groups: those with more linear levels (action/adventure, role-playing, and racing games) and those with more non-linear, unpredictable gameplay experiences (strategy, sports, and multi-player death-match games). Of course, that is not to say that the two do not overlap. For instance, specific *StarCraft* levels do everything to encourage players to play them in a specific path, especially the small-team indoor levels. Similarly, many *Super Mario 64* maps allow for multiple viable paths the player can use to play them through. If the designer is creative enough in her efforts, the distinction between the two types of levels can be blurred, which can often lead to more varied and interesting gameplay.

Elements of Good Levels

As you design a level, there are a seemingly infinite number of details you must keep in mind. You must be concerned that you balance the elements of action, exploration, puzzle solving, storytelling, and audiovisual appeal. You must work with the artists and programmers to achieve the effects you want. For 3D levels, you must make sure the whole level is optimized so that it can run on the target system. Often you have to deal with unruly level design tools which seem to thwart your every attempt to make something cool.

Often a level designer will come up with a list of rules of thumb to follow while making a level, even if she does not write this list down. Every designer will have her own list of "dos" and "don'ts" that she keeps in the back of her mind, and this list can change significantly from project to project. Some games will have their own "design rules" established ahead of time and which the designers can then follow, but there are also rules which can apply to any project. Here I present a partial list of my own rules of thumb, which I use to attempt to make a level that is stimulating to play.

Player Cannot Get Stuck

This should be obvious. The player should never become hopelessly stuck when playing your level. There should be no pits that can be fallen into but not climbed out of, no objects which, when moved incorrectly, permanently block the player's progress, and no doors which fail to open if the player approaches them a certain way. Though this goal may seem perfectly obvious, it will actually consume a large amount of your time as a level designer. Consider a puzzle where the player has a certain amount of dynamite, and that dynamite needs to be used to blow a hole in a wall so the player can progress in the level. Well, what if the player uses up all his dynamite blowing up the wrong things? Without any more dynamite, the player is completely stuck. Similarly, suppose the player needs to talk to a particular NPC to get a particular object. What if, instead of talking to that character, the player kills him? Either the player's game must end nearly instantly, or there must be some alternate way to progress through the game. Designing your level in such a way that, whatever the player does, he can still finish the level, takes a lot of thinking and planning. As a level designer, you must always be asking yourself, "But what if the player tries it this way?"

Sub-Goals

As the player plays a level, he should have understandable sub-goals. Instead of playing through the whole level just trying to get to the exit or accomplish some large goal, the player should be able to recognize that there are various tasks he can accomplish which contribute to the final goal. A very simple example of this would be the different keys in *Doom*. The player knows that once he gets the blue key he is that much closer to finishing the level. In an arcade racing game like *San Francisco Rush*, instead of having just one finish line per track, most games have multiple "checkpoints" along the track at which the player is given a time bonus and informed of how well he is doing. In an RPG, the player may be working to defeat an evil force that is tormenting the land, but along the way he is able to go on various sub-quests for villagers who need his help. These various sub-quests lead the player toward the larger goal, and provide the player with positive feedback that he is, in fact, playing the game well. A sub-goal is useless if the player does not understand what he has accomplished. Therefore, it is also important to provide the player with some sort of reward for achieving the goal, whether it is audiovisual bells and whistles, a new weapon, bonus points, or more time on the racing clock. If the designer does not provide enough sub-goals on a particular level or if those sub-goals are so transparent that the player does not realize he has achieved them, the player may become confused as to what he is supposed to be doing and whether he is getting any closer to succeeding.

In racing games such as the *San Francisco Rush* series, players are given sub-goals through checkpoints which award more time. Pictured here: *San Francisco Rush: The Rock Alcatraz Edition*.

Landmarks

The more complex your level, the more the player is likely to get confused navigating it. Unless confusion is your goal, which it usually should not be, it is a good idea to set up memorable landmarks in your level to ease the player's exploration. A landmark is any unique object in your level that the player will recognize the second time she sees it, whether it is a particularly ornately decorated room, a large statue, or a steaming pool of lava. In terms of exploration, then, when the player returns to this landmark, she will know that she is returning to a location she has previously visited, and will thereby begin to understand the layout of the level. Landmarks do not necessarily need to be big red signs labeled "Checkpoint A," but can instead be worked into the story and setting of the level itself.

Critical Path

Even though I am a big proponent of non-linear gameplay, I am also a big fan of a nice critical path in a level. A critical path gives the player a sense of a direction he can go in order to complete the level. This direction may be a physical direction, such as "head North" or "head for the rainbow," or it can be a more ambiguous goal, such as finding a creature and defeating it or retrieving an important object. Always giving the player a primary goal to accomplish is crucial to making your level playable. The player should have a goal and, as I discussed, sub-goals that work toward achieving that primary goal. The player should always be aware of the goal and the related sub-goals, and should always have a sense of what he can do to progress in the level. Separate optional side-goals may be less obvious or hidden, but nothing frustrates a player more than having no idea what he is supposed to do. Having a clearly established critical path is a good way to help prevent the player from becoming confused.

Limited Backtracking

If your game relies on exploration for a large part of its gameplay value, it is probably a bad idea to make the player backtrack through large sections of the level that he has already explored in order to continue in the game. That is not to say that your level cannot have branching paths for the player to explore. It merely means that each branch should loop back to the main path without the player needing to backtrack along the same path. If your game is more of a role-playing or adventure game where creating the illusion of reality is important, the necessity of backtracking may be more acceptable. Certainly in an RTS or sports game, the player will be covering the same ground over and over again, but the appeal of a basketball game or *WarCraft* is not so tied to exploration as *Super Mario 64*, a title which does a very good job of eliminating the need for backtracking entirely.

Success the First Time

If most players are able to beat your level the first time they play it, you have probably made a level that is too easy. Nonetheless, the possibility should exist that a player could make it all the way through your level on the first try. I do not mean, however, that the player could make all of the right choices just by happenstance. Instead, you should provide enough data to the player that she has a reasonable chance of avoiding all the obstacles put in her path if she is observant and quick-witted enough. Whenever the player fails in your level, she should feel that she had a fair chance of avoiding that failure if she had only been more observant or had thought more before she acted. Nothing frustrates the player more than realizing that the only way to make it through the level is by trial and error combined with blind luck. Of course, your level can still be hard. Your clues as to what to do can be quite subtle, the monsters to be defeated can be really strong, or the choices to be made can be truly challenging, but if the player does everything perfectly, she should be able to get through your level the first time she plays it.

Navigable Areas Clearly Marked

The player should have a clear idea of where he will be able to go in the level. Slopes that the player will slide on should appear to be significantly steeper than the slopes that can be walked on. Textures may be used to differentiate between areas the player can navigate and those he cannot. It can be very frustrating to the player than when an area that appeared to be unnavigable turns out to be the only way out of a particular area. Another example might be a room with ten doors in it. The player tries three of these doors, and they are all locked. At this point, the player will probably conclude that the doors are there only for show and will stop trying any of the other doors. No information is given to the player to indicate that the other doors might be openable when the first three he tried were not. If it turns out that the only way out of this room is through one of the doors which happens to be the only one that was unlocked, I would suggest that this area has been poorly designed. The only way out of such a room is through tedious trial and error. The fun in a game may involve trying to get to certain areas or the thrill of running around in those areas, but there is little fun to be found in determining which areas the designer arbitrarily decided could be navigated and which could not.

Choices

This may seem obvious, but it is something level designers can often forget to keep in mind as they are building their levels. Good levels give the player choices of how to accomplish goals, just as good gameplay gives the player lots of choices for how she will play the game. Choices do not necessarily mean multiple paths through a level, though that may be a good idea as well. In a first-person shooter, choices could mean giving the player different options for how to take out all of the enemies in a room—plenty of different places to hide, different locations that the enemies can be shot from, and so forth. Such a setup creates a variety of different strategies that will successfully defeat the horde of advancing demons. Choices could also mean bonus objects that are challenging for the player to get, such as a rocket launcher in the middle of a pool of lava—the player has the choice to risk going for it or not. In a strategy game, interesting choices mean different places where battles may play out or different places a player can choose to rally his troops or gather up resources. In adventure games, the genre most notorious for not giving players enough options, choices mean multiple solutions to the game's puzzles, different characters to talk to, and plenty of different ways to move through the game. Players become frustrated when they feel that they are locked into just one way of playing the game, especially if that one way is not the way they would like to play it.

A Personal List

Certainly the list I have provided above is far from complete. As you work as a level designer, it makes sense to establish your own list of design goals to keep in mind while creating your level. As you work on levels that are received well by your peers or players, try to analyze the levels to see what you did well. Then try to abstract these accomplishments into a list of goals to keep in mind as you work on subsequent levels. This list does not necessarily need to be formally written down; just keeping a mental checklist may be sufficient. The options I listed here may be a start for your own list, or you may find yourself coming up with a completely differ-ent set of goals. Every designer approaches level design in her own way.

The Process

The process of constructing a level can vary greatly from designer to designer. What works for one person may not work for another. That said, I have found the follow-ing progression of steps to be one that works well for me. I may not always follow the steps precisely, but generally speaking, this progression produces more consis-tent and efficient results than just cranking out a level without any plan of what to do first or how to proceed.

step 1. *Preliminary*

Before starting to design a level for the game, ask yourself if the gameplay is in a close-to-final state. Is the game going to change so much that the level you design will no longer be fun to play? Or worse, will the level no longer be playable? For instance, suppose you are developing a third-person action/adventure such as *Tomb Raider*. Before you start making a level for the game, you need to determine how final the movement of the main character is. Will more moves for the character be added? Will the game's hero someday be able to do a double forward flip that will radically change the distance she will be able to jump? Often when you begin working on a level the game itself is far from complete, and some changes will probably be made to the main character's movement. But if the team is aware that radical changes to the player movement model will be made, having level designers start working on levels is a big mistake.

Before starting development on an action/ exploration game such as those found in the *Tomb Raider* series, it is important to have a clearly defined set of moves for the player.

On one project I worked on, we started working on the levels before the ability for the main character to jump had even been added to the game. As a result, once it was added, we went back and had to modify the levels to include areas that would use this jumping ability. Unfortunately, after the jumping had been in the game for a while, it became clear that the jumping was not that much fun, and that we would have to go back to the levels and remove a lot of the jumps we had put in. The end result was not nearly as clean as if we had known from the very beginning how the jumping would work. The problem here was that production had started on the levels before the game mechanics were sufficiently hammered out and implemented. As I discussed in Chapter 13, "Getting the Gameplay Working," you will probably need to have one level in progress while you work on implementing the gameplay, so you can test out different behaviors as they are added. But working on more than that one particular level is a waste of time which may be detrimental to the project in the long run. Furthermore, it may make sense to scrap the test level once the gameplay is firmly established, since that preliminary level usually turns out to be far from the best work you are capable of.

step 2. *Conceptual and Sketched Outline*

Before beginning work on a level, I think it is very important to understand what that level is going to need to do from a gameplay and story perspective. What sort of challenges will the player be facing here, and what sort of environments best facilitate those challenges? How exciting and nerve-racking is the gameplay in this level? Where will the player need to be rewarded? What story elements need to be conveyed through the level? At all times, but especially during the planning stage, you must keep in mind the game's focus and how your level will work to support that focus.

Once the designer has some grasp of what the level is supposed to accomplish, a pencil and paper sketch of the level's general layout is a very good idea. This avoids the perils of "designing yourself into a corner." Say you are designing a building in a military compound for a fully 3D first-person shooter. In your compound you need to include a room with a large generator. When you start making the architecture for the building, you first lay out all the halls, then start working on some of the cooler rooms before you finally get to the generator room. Then, whoops, it turns out you failed to leave as much space as necessary for the generator. The room is now too small to be able to be easily navigable. Unfortunately, the only way to make it big enough involves ripping up a lot of the halls you had made already. At this point, some designers would just move the generator room to a less-logical or less-optimal location rather than having to redo a lot of geometry they already spent time building. Of course, a level sketch might not always prevent this problem, but if done correctly it might point out to the designer how small the generator room was at a time when making it bigger only involves using the eraser. Changes to a sketch are much easier to make than changes to a fully constructed level. A sketch may also be valuable as something that you can show to your team leader, who may want to look it over to make sure you are on the right track with the rest of the team and the game as a whole.

step 3. *Base Architecture*

Once you are happy with your sketch, the actual construction of the level can begin. This construction stage varies in time and scope depending on the complexity of the level being created. For instance, a 2D, tile-based engine will allow for much quicker construction of a level than a 3D engine. Similarly, the complexity of the 3D engine being used will radically alter how much time is required to build out the level. An excellent map made with the *Doom* engine can be pounded out in a day or two. A level of similar quality made with the much more sophisticated *Quake III* engine can easily take weeks of hard work.

    At this point, keep in mind that you are just creating the base layout for your level. You are not adding niceties such as lighting or texturing, nor are you concentrating on making the geometry as pretty as possible. On this first pass you want to get the level to the point where the player can navigate through it and all of the locations the player will be able to go are accessible. This allows you to get a sense for whether the level's layout feels right.

As game engines become more sophisticated, the amount of time required to build a level increases dramatically. For example, a professional level using the *Quake III Arena* engine will easily take weeks to complete.

step 4. *Refine Architecture Until It is Fun*

At this point you need to repeat step three until your level starts feeling good and navigating it starts to be fun. For instance, if you are working on a first-person shooter, you should experiment with navigating your character around the 3D world, and see if the corners are fun to swing around, if the jumps are of just about the right difficulty, and if the areas come out at the size you had wanted them to. Take a look at the level as a whole and see if it makes sense and flows as you hoped it would. Once you actually spend time looking at and navigating the level as the player would, instead of just fiddling with it in the level editor, you stand a better chance of determining if your level is working out. If the level is not working out as you want, now is the time to make changes until it does.

step 5. *Base Gameplay*

Now that your level feels right in terms of player navigation, it is time to start implementing the gameplay your level will use. Certainly you had the gameplay in mind through all of the steps of this process, but now is the time to see if it will actually work out as you had hoped. The best designers can come up with ideas and sketches for levels that successfully translate into fun levels in the end. Others start with a sketch, build some architecture, and when it comes time to add the gameplay, find they need to make some significant modifications to what they have already built. With experience as a designer comes the ability to predict whether abstract ideas will turn out to be any fun or not. Before you become experienced, however, the process involves a great deal of trial and error.

Setting up the gameplay in a level from a game like *Duke Nukem 3D* consists of placing monsters and weapons, and configuring puzzles.

A level's gameplay consists of whatever actions the player is allowed to perform in that level. In a first-person shooter such as *Duke Nukem 3D*, this means placing the monsters the player will shoot and the items the player will pick up. In a role-playing or adventure game, this is expanded to include whatever puzzles the player will need to solve, the characters to which the player may talk, and the quests on which these NPCs send the player. In a real-time strategy game, the designer will need to figure out starting unit placement and quantities for the player and his opponent, as well as whatever reinforcements may appear later in the level. In a way, sports and racing titles have an easier time with this step, since their gameplay is the same from level to level and therefore does not need much setup for a particular stadium or track.

step 6. *Refine Gameplay Until It is Fun*

Of course, the gameplay is what makes or breaks the game, so it is absolutely essential that the designer repeat step five until the level is fun to play. Sometimes, refining the gameplay may take you all the way back to step number three. It may turn out that the area you thought would play well just is not suited to the capabilities of the AI. Or that the creature you thought would be able to spring out at the player from a fissure in a cliff does not really have enough space to hide. You may need to change the layout of your level to compensate for the problems you discover once you start implementing the gameplay.

For some designers, modifying existing level architecture to suit the gameplay can be quite a painful process. For instance, suppose a designer builds some architecture she is happy with from an aesthetic standpoint. If the gameplay then does not work in that space, the designer may be reluctant to go back and rework that geometry and may instead settle for substandard gameplay. Of course, this is the wrong choice to make. As painful as it may be, in order to get the best gameplay you may need to throw out some of your work. This is why I suggested only making base architecture without refining it too much; that way making radical changes to the level will not mean that too much work was wasted.

This is the step where your level really comes together and you start to get a sense of whether it is a success. Now you can take this space you created and really start to play in it. If you do not start enjoying yourself at this point, you may need to take a look at your level and ask yourself why it is not fun to play. In the worst case, you may realize that the level will never be fun, and as a result you need to start fresh. Ideally, however, this stage can be truly revelatory, as all of the work you put into the level starts to pay off.

step 7. *Refine Aesthetics*

Now that the level is playing well, you have an opportunity to make it look good as well. You may recall that in steps three and four we just set up base architecture, enough to allow the player to navigate and to give you a feel for the level. Now is the time to texture your level as needed, apply lighting effects, add decorative objects, and really flesh out your level from a visual standpoint. Many level designers spend the bulk of their time working on aesthetics for their levels, and certainly you should put in the time to make the level look as good as possible. But, as I have emphasized, it is crucial that you put off finessing the level until you are confident that the level plays well and that it accomplishes its gameplay objectives. Otherwise, you may waste your time making areas look nice which end up being scrapped. As you are finessing the level aesthetically, you must always remember not to break any of the gameplay you have already set up.

step 8. *Playtesting*

Now that all the parts of your level are in place, it is time to show it to some other people, let them play it, and get some feedback. Playtesting is a crucial part of game design, and level design is no different. These test subjects may include other members of your team, but should also include people less intimately involved with your project. A lot can be said for a fresh pair of eyes looking at your game and your level and giving you feedback on whether what you think is fun is also fun to them.

Playtesting a level can be as easy as handing over a level to someone, asking him to play it, and having him tell you what he thinks. Another useful method, especially for level testing, is to actually be there with the tester when he tries to play your level and observe how he plays it. Does he get stuck in locations you had not thought of? Does he have trouble finding his way around? Do the gameplay situations provide him with enough challenge? Watching other people play your level can be extremely educational and informative as to whether the level flows and plays well.

In the worst case, playtesting may reveal that your level is not as fun to play as you had thought, and that major reworking will be necessary to make it fun. As a designer you must not be resistant when someone tells you your level is hard to navigate or confusing or just no fun. Certainly, get a second and third and fourth opinion on it, but when you start hearing the same complaints from a number of different people, you need to realize that there may be some truth to what they are saying and that your level may need some serious reworking. Many designers who have invested a lot of time and energy in a level find it very difficult to then take criticism on their work. There is no denying that hearing someone tear apart a month's worth of work can be disheartening, but this is the purpose of playtesting. You need to take your testers' comments to heart, recognize the problems with your level, and start working on the level again. Thorough playtesting can often be the difference between a merely good level and a truly great one.

Process Variations

Of course, the process for level design I outline above is not the only way to make a level. Like the "dos" and "don'ts" of level design I described earlier, each level designer needs to find the method that works best for herself and her team. Many good designers use a method not entirely different from what I have outlined above, but with variations that better suit their own style of designing.

One potentially useful variation is to incorporate steps three through six. Instead of laying out the entire level, you can start with a particular room or area. Then, before moving on to set up the rest of the level, try to set up gameplay in just that area. Once you are happy with how well that section plays, move on to setting up the rest of the level, adding gameplay to the areas as you create them. This way, if an area has to be enlarged to make the gameplay work properly, less work is wasted since the areas around may not have been built yet. As I mentioned before, it is important to be careful to not design yourself into a corner. You do not want to spend a lot of time working on the gameplay for a specific area only to have to remove it later since the rest of the level no longer fits in the space available. If you are going to set up gameplay for particular areas before the entire level is built, it makes the most sense to build the architecture for an entire, discrete play-space, such as a specific building or structure. Then you can make the gameplay work in that entire area before moving on to the next.

Another useful idea is to incorporate playtesting earlier in the process, perhaps after step six. Once you have your level playable, have some people whose opinions you trust try playing the level. The aesthetics may not be fully refined yet, and you should certainly explain this to them as they play, but if you are able to get feedback at this early stage, you may be able to make important changes before you have spent a lot of time refining the aesthetics of the level. A possible drawback to testing the level this early is that others may not be able to understand that visually the level is not yet done. As a result they may get hung up on criticizing the appearance of your level instead of providing feedback about the gameplay. Be sure to communicate what type of feedback you are looking for at this stage and hope that the playtesters can see beyond the lack of fancy lighting effects. Testing at this early stage does not replace testing after the level is more final, but it may prevent some unpleasant surprises and can make the final testing go more smoothly.

Who Does Level Design?

Throughout this chapter, I have spoken as if you are responsible for all aspects of your level. Many development studios do still operate on the "one designer, one level" method of level design. This has many advantages, of course, since it helps to keep the levels focused. That one designer is constantly aware of what his level requires in terms of gameplay, art, and programming, and can keep that level on track. When it comes time to set up the level's lighting, for instance, the designer will remember that he thought that gameplay in one part of the level would play best in the dark with disorienting flashing light. Having one person working on one level from start to finish helps to ensure the level has a consistency of vision that can lead to great gameplay.

But the "one designer, one level" technique is not the only method which may work, and many developers have adopted more of a "team" approach to level design. If your team has one designer who is particularly good at making pretty architecture but is less skilled at getting the AI agents to work, it may make sense to have a different designer set up the gameplay on that designer's levels. One designer may be particularly good at lighting effects, while another may be adept at the scripted sequences. You may want the sound designer to set up your sound effects, since he will be better at correctly placing the audio effects he created. Of course, as with any task that is divided among several people, when putting multiple personnel on a single level, you need to make sure that they are all "on the same page" in terms of what that level is trying to accomplish. For instance, the architecture designer may have built a canyon that he thought would be ideal for an ambush, but when the designer who sets up the gameplay comes along, he may not notice that particular canyon and might set up encounters in less optimal locations. Communication between the different people working on a particular level is essential, just as it is between the programming, art, and design teams.

As I stated previously, as games become more complex, it becomes necessary to divide tasks that used to be accomplished by one person between multiple people. As games continue to become more complicated, designers will specialize more and more, and having multiple people working on a single level will become increasingly common. Keeping the game focused on such a project will be quite a challenge, which emphasizes the importance of project leaders and lead level designers. However, as people specialize in a particular area of level design, the possibility exists that they can become better at their specific area of expertise as a result. Furthermore, if one person sets up the AI and gameplay for all of the levels in the game, those levels as a whole may achieve a greater gameplay consistency than if each level designer was setting up his own gameplay. If managed correctly, these highly specialized level designers can lead to better levels in the final game.

Collaboration

As games have grown in complexity, the number of level designers required for a particular game has increased. Whereas one designer used to be able to truly control every last facet of a game's design, now a lead designer must find level designers she can trust to build levels which will make a significant contribution to the game's design. Though a lead designer may be able to look over the shoulder of these level designers and do her best to direct the efforts, in the end she has delegated a large part of the gameplay's creation to these invaluable members of her team. This can have both a good side, as more voices in the game's design may make the game a more robust experience, and a bad side, as the clearness of artistic vision becomes diluted by so many different people working on the project. Such are the perils of most modern commercial game development.

Chapter 22:

Interview: Will Wright

It is hard to measure the impact Will Wright's game *SimCity* has had on the industry. At the time of its release in 1989, the game was so radically different from any other piece of interactive computer entertainment that for many years the project had trouble finding a publisher. Now the game's influence can be seen in the countless "builder" games released every year. Sid Meier readily admits that *SimCity* was one of his primary inspirations in making *Civilization*. With his latest game, *The Sims*, Wright has come totally out of left field again with a game that he also had to fight to get made. While the majority of games released today take only evolutionary baby steps of improvement, with *The Sims* Wright has released something truly revolutionary that represents the most original game design to be seen in years. Talking with Wright is an experience in itself, as one is instantly made keenly aware of why he has developed such brilliant and innovative games.

How did you first become interested in game development?

I got totally into computers shortly after I bought an Apple II around 1980. I just got infatuated with games. As a kid I spent a lot of time building models, and I bought some of the very early games, such as the very first version of *Flight Simulator* with the wire-frame graphics. You had to write your own machine language patch to get it to run, that was funny. But just the idea that you could build your own little micro-world inside the computer intrigued me. So I saw it as a kind of modeling tool. At some point I just got so into these things that I decided I would try to make one myself, and that was right around the time the Commodore 64 was first coming out. So I bought one of those, figuring that it would be better to start on a new machine where everybody was on a level playing field, because other people had learned the Apple II years before I decided to do this. So, I bought a Commodore as soon as it came out and just dove into it, and learned it as quickly as I could. And that's what I did my first game on.

So how did you come up with the design for *Raid Over Bungeling Bay?*

Back then just about all the games were arcade games, you know. I had always loved helicopters, so I wanted to do a little helicopter game. And then I was looking at the Commodore. It was driven probably more by the technology than the game design side. I found that the Commodore had this really cool trick where you could redefine a character set, make it look like graphics, and then smoothly scroll it around the screen. So you could give the impression that you were scrolling over this huge bitmap, when in fact all you were doing is moving ASCII characters around on the screen. And when I saw that feature, I thought that would be really cool looking, because I knew the Apple couldn't begin to move that much in the way of graphics around the screen that smoothly. So I designed the game around that feature in a way.

I understand the game was much more popular in Japan than it was in the States.

I think that was right when piracy was probably at its peak. We sold around 30,000 copies in the U.S., which was average for a game like that. But then everybody I've talked to who had a Commodore back then had played it. Whereas the same game on the Nintendo in Japan sold about 750,000 copies. It was a cartridge system, so there was no piracy.

Do you still look back on the game positively?

Oh yeah. I look back on it with fond memories, it was a learning experience. It was one of those times where you realize that the last ten percent, getting the game out the door, that's the really hard part. And unless you plan for that last ten percent, it's just a killer. So I learned a lot of lessons from it. And back then programming wasn't nearly as elaborate as it is now. Every game was written by one person and that game was about eight thousand lines of machine language. So you could totally control the memory and totally control the machine. It was a good learning vehicle. It's kind of a shame that the programmers who learn to program nowadays are coming at it from a totally different point of view.

You mean because they're using higher level programming languages?

Oh yeah. Which isn't necessarily bad, I guess. But you still have the old hacks like myself. There were eight bytes of memory free on that machine when I finished that game, and I felt bad that I didn't use those last eight. And there are a lot of tricks you do when you're running out of memory, because the memory was the ultimate concern. There were some cool little tricks for that.

I read that the level editing tool for *Bungeling Bay* was your inspiration for *SimCity*.

It was a character set that actually described a bunch of islands with little roads and cities on them. And so there was such a big area that I developed my own little character editing program to draw this scene that I could scroll around really smoothly, like a paint program. I found that I was having so much more fun with the paint program than I was with the game that after I finished the game I kept playing with the paint program. And it eventually evolved into *SimCity*.

So you wouldn't cite any other games that inspired *SimCity*?

I'd say the biggest inspiration, if there had to be one, was the work of Jay Forester, who is considered the father of system dynamics, and one of the very first people to use a computer for simulation. So when I started getting the idea for *SimCity*, I started going to the library and reading. He did a lot of his work back in the

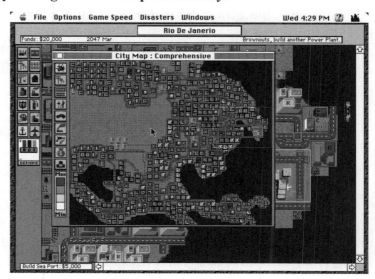

SimCity

'50s, working with very primitive computers and very primitive models, but yet he was the first person to try to simulate a city. And he did it with like twenty variables: one was population, one was production, one was birth rate, stuff like that. Very simple models.

System dynamics is a way to look at a system and divide it into, basically, stocks and flows. Stocks are quantities, like population, and flows are rates, like the death rate, the birth rate, immigration. You can model almost anything just using those two features. That was how he started system dynamics and that was the approach he took to his modeling. I uncovered his stuff when I started working on *SimCity* and started teaching myself modeling techniques. I also came across the more recent stuff with cellular automata, and *SimCity* is really a hybrid of those two approaches. Because his approach was not spatial at all, whereas the cellular automata gives you a lot of really interesting spatial tools for propagation, network flow, proximity, and so forth. So the fact that pollution starts here, spreads over here, and slowly gets less and less, and you can actually simulate propagation waves through these spatial structures. So *SimCity* in some sense is like a big three-dimensional cellular automata, with each layer being some feature of the landscape like crime or pollution or land value. But the layers can interact on the third dimension. So the layers of crime and pollution can impact the land value layer.

What made you think that such scholarly techniques could lead to something that people would find fun?

At that point I wasn't trying to build something that people would play for entertainment value. It's more like I was just having fun doing this on my own. At the same time I was reading about urban dynamics, just on the theoretical side. And having this little guinea pig city on my computer while I was reading about the subject made the subject so much more interesting. So I could read a theory and then try to figure out how to formalize it, code it, put it in the model, and see what the results of it were.

At what point did you start to think it might be something that other people could have fun with?

After about six months or so I started attaching some graphics to it. It was fairly abstract to begin with. And then I started thinking, you know, this might be an interesting game. I had actually done my first game with Broderbund Software, and I showed it to some people there and they thought it was pretty cool. They agreed to pick it up, and we had a contract for it and everything. And I worked on it for about a year to the point where it was where I wanted it to be. And they kept thinking it wasn't finished. They kept saying, "When is it going to be a game? When is it going to have a win/lose situation?" It was very unusual for its time, and this was about five years before it was actually released. This was around 1985, and we didn't actually release it until '89.

They didn't think it was enough of a game to fit in with their other products?

They just didn't see how they could possibly sell it. And I just left it there, and they left it there, and that was that.

So were you pretty discouraged?

I always thought it was a cool little thing I did, I never really thought it would be a mainstream thing. But I thought it would be worthwhile getting it on the market. So later I met my eventual partner, Jeff Braun, and I showed it to him. And he thought it was really cool. He really, really was into it. He, in fact, thought there was probably a big market for something like that. At that point, the two of us decided to start a company ourselves, and that's when we started Maxis.

So it had sat around, unpublished, for a number of years?

Yeah, for a couple of years. About the time we decided to start Maxis, the Macintosh had just come out, and the Amiga was coming out, and we decided we would rewrite the game for those computers. So we hired a couple of programmers, and I recoded the simulator in C. It had all been in assembly before. We had these other programmers helping on the graphical front ends on the Mac and on the Amiga, and those were actually the first versions that were released. We actually did go back and release the Commodore version about a month after we released those.

So originally *SimCity* didn't have a mouse-based, point-and-click interface?

No, actually it did. The Lisa had come out while I was doing it on the Commodore, and I actually had implemented a cursor-based system with icons. The interface was on a Commodore, but it still had that iconic, paint-program kind of feel. It looked like MacPaint in a way. So, in fact, it did have a similar graphic front end but at a much lower resolution.

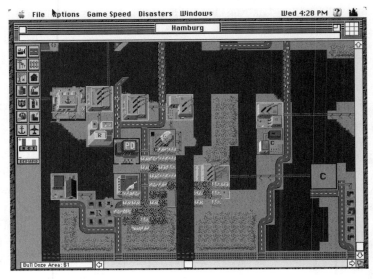

SimCity

Did the design change much from what you had originally done?

It got more elaborate, more layers were added, and there was higher resolution on the map, but it had the same basic structure for the simulation and the same basic sets of tools. But, for instance, there were only roads, there weren't roads and highways. The map was 80 by 90, instead of 128 by 128. Of course, the graphics were much lower resolution; they were about four pixels square for a tile, instead of the eventual sixteen. But the core of the model and the tuning of the model didn't actually change that much. And it actually didn't change all that much for *SimCity 2000* or *3000*.

So Maxis finally got it out to the market by self publishing it?

It's actually kind of interesting. After we had redone it on the Mac and the Amiga, we knew we could afford to produce it in the boxes and all that, but we had to have a distributor. And in fact we came back to Broderbund and showed it to them, and when they saw the Mac and Amiga versions they were much more impressed. Plus it was years later, at which point the market was getting into much more interesting games. At that point they offered to become our distributor, and so we had an affiliate publishing relationship with Broderbund. We were incurring most of the financial risk because we were the ones paying for the boxes and all that, so they weren't really risking that much on it. The people at Broderbund were really nice people and I hold no grudges against them at all. They helped us a lot in getting Maxis off the ground. And the Carlstons, the people who started Broderbund, were my role models for business people. They were just really nice people to deal with.

Did you come up with the term "software toy"?

I think I did, because I was giving a talk at the Game Developer's Conference, way back, and I decided that would be the name of my talk. It was "Software Toys: The Intersection of Creativity, Empathy, and . . . " something. Some high-falutin' sounding talk.

How would you distinguish between a software toy and a game?

Toys can be used to build games. You can play games with toys. But you can also engage in more freeform play with toys. It doesn't have to be a goal directed activity. I think of toys as being more open-ended than games. We can use a ball to play a game such as basketball, or we can just toss the ball back and forth, or I can experiment with the ball, bouncing it off of different things. So, I would think of toys as a broader category. Also, toys can be combined. I can strap Barbie to my R.C. car and drive her around, thus making up a new activity by combining toys. Games tend to be isolated universes where there's a rule set, and once you leave that universe the rule set is meaningless. Another way to think about it, and this is a more recent version of the same idea, is that I tend to think of the games we do in more of a hobby kind of way, whereas most games are thought about more in terms of a movie or cinematic form. Movies have a beginning and an end, there's a climax, there's one particular story line, and a lot of games are built more on that model.

Our games are more like a hobby, which you approach in a different way. Like with a model train set, some people get totally into the scenery and the details on the cliffs and the hills. Other people get into the little village in the middle. Other people get into the switching on the tracks. And sometimes these will play off of each other when a community builds around a hobby. You'll have certain people in the community who are very into certain aspects of the hobby and they have expertise which they can teach to other people. And you have sub-specializations within the community. People can create things and trade them, or they can just share ideas. I tend to think of hobbies as being a bit more community based than the cinematic model. That's more of a shared experience, it's a kind of cultural currency. "Oh, did you see that movie last night, what did you think?"

But with a software toy like *SimCity*, only one person is really playing it at any one time.

The community I'm referring to now more than ever is the online community. I can go online and I can start trading strategies with people, or I can upload my city or my family or my stories, or I can make skins for *The Sims*. And if someone gets really good at it they can have a standing in the community: "Oh, he makes the best skins." So there's this whole community on the web that develops around the game, with people creating things and sharing things.

Which is more possible now than when *SimCity* originally came out.

Back when *SimCity* came out, it was really just a few sporadic message boards on some of the online services like CompuServe or later AOL. It was mostly just chat discussions and things like that. There wasn't really a forum, where people could meet. It wasn't really a very involving online community. But even before we had our first web site, people were already uploading their cities to AOL and trading them. There were big sections with hundreds of cities trading. CompuServe was the first place where large collections of cities started to appear, not too long after the game came out.

The biggest complaint I've seen about *SimCity*, and I've seen this mostly from other game developers, is that since it is not a game and there aren't any goals, it doesn't hold the player's attention very well.

I think it attracts a different kind of player. In fact, some people play it very goal directed. What it really does is it forces you to determine the goals. So when you start *SimCity,* one of the most interesting things that happens is that you have to decide "What do I want to make? Do I want to make the biggest possible city, or the city with the happiest residents, or the most parks, or the lowest crime?" Every time you have to idealize in your head, "What does the ideal city mean to me?" It requires a bit more motivated player. What that buys you in a sense is more replayability because we're not enforcing any strict goal on you. We could have said, "Get your city to 10,000 people in ten years or you lose." And you would always have to play it that way. And there would be strategies to get there, and people would figure out the strategies, and that would be that. By leaving it more open-ended, people can play the game a lot of different ways. And that's where it's become more like a toy.

Simulations in general give you a much wider game-space to explore. There are probably no two cities in *SimCity* that are identical and created by different people. Whereas, if you look at a game like *Zelda*, I'm sure there are tens of thousands of saved *Zelda* games that are identical. Computationally you can look at this as the phase-space of the system, or how many variables does it take to describe a current state of the system. Another way of looking at that is it's how much creative exploration the player is allowed. How unique is your game from my game? In some sense that implies a certain level of creativity available to you. In some situations that can also be interpreted as how many different ways there are to solve a given problem. So if

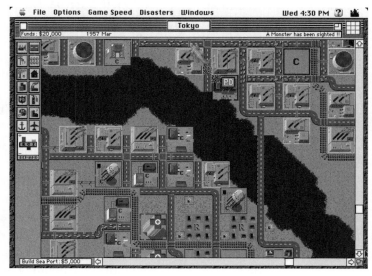

SimCity

we start with the same exact city that has a lot of traffic, there are a huge variety of ways that we can attack that problem successfully. In a lot of games there's a locked door and until you find that key you're not going to be able to unlock that door.

So it provides the player with a lot more variety.

There's a lot more variety, but also, because every player can take a unique approach, they can be more creative. And the more creativity the player can realize in a game, the more empathy they tend to feel with that game. Especially you see that in *The Sims*. If they spend all this time building up a family and running their lives for months, people really start to empathize with those characters because they have invested so much time in the creation of them. And the characters, in that sense, are a reflection not only of themselves, but it's a reflection of their current understanding of the game. Same with *SimCity*. You can look at somebody's city in *SimCity* at any time, and the design of the city is a reflection of what they understand about the model. From their understanding that was the best way to build a road network at that point.

But once they come to understand the game better...

It changes, exactly. You can go back to an old city and say, "Oh, right, that's when I thought highways really worked well, before I learned that they didn't." So in some sense it reflects your mental model of the game.

But if you play *Zelda* a second time...

Your mental model doesn't really evolve that much. You learn the surprises, but your model of the underlying mechanisms isn't really all that different once you've played the game through.

I'm a bit curious about the disaster feature in *SimCity*. It seems strange that players would want to spend a lot of time building something up and then just destroy it with a tidal wave or a fire.

Yeah, I always thought that was kind of curious myself.

You must have anticipated it, though, since you put it in the game from the very beginning.

No, actually, it wasn't in the original Commodore version. I later added it, though. When I first started showing the Commodore version, the only thing that was in there was a bulldozer, basically to erase mistakes. So if you accidentally built a road or a building in the wrong place you could erase it with the bulldozer. What I found was that, invariably, in the first five minutes people would discover the bulldozer, and they would blow up a building with it by accident. And then they would laugh. And then they would go and attack the city with the bulldozer. And they'd blow up all the buildings, and they'd be laughing their heads off. And it really intrigued me, because it was like someone coming across an ant pile and poking it with a stick to see what happens. And they would get that out of their system in ten minutes, and then they would realize that the hard part wasn't destroying it, but building it back up. And so people would have a great time destroying the city with a bulldozer, and then they would discover, "Wow, the power's out. Wow, there's a fire starting." And that's when they would start the rebuilding process, and that's what would really hook them. Because they would realize that the destruction was so easy in this game, it was the creation that was the hard part. And this is back when all of the games were about destruction. After seeing that happen with so many people, I finally decided, "Well, I might as well really let them get it out of their systems, I'll add some disasters to the game." And that's what gave me the idea for the disaster menu.

Plus you had the disasters randomly occur.

Yeah, that seemed obvious after I had the disaster menu, that they should randomly happen, but I didn't originally have that.

SimEarth seems to be a logical extension from *SimCity*. How did you come up with the idea for that game?

It was more my interest in certain subjects that drove me to it. I was very interested in certain theories, most notably the Gaia hypothesis, and also general environmental issues that a lot of times are counterintuitive. I thought it would be interesting to have a model of a global ecosystem. I learned a lot from *SimEarth*. Actually, I was very proud of the simulation of *SimEarth*, and pretty disappointed in the game design.

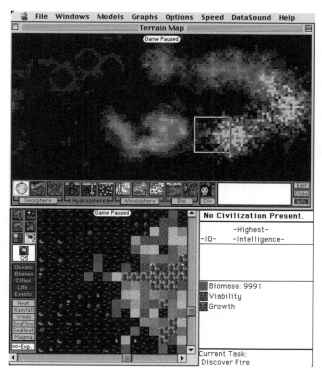

SimEarth

How do you mean?

It wasn't a terribly fun game. It's actually a very nice model, and we did a lot of research of the current climatic models, and I have still never seen anyone do an integrated model with an integrated lithosphere, hydrosphere, and atmosphere together like that. And we were getting some effects in the model that were real effects, that really show up, that even some of the more elaborate models that NCAR [National Center for Atmospheric Research] makes weren't capturing. But as far as the game goes, I started realizing that you can roughly look at all of our *Sim* games and divide them into one of two categories: the economic ones and the biological ones. And, in general, the economic ones have always done better.

Which ones would you include in that group?

SimCity, *SimTower*, *SimCity 2000*, *The Sims*, and *SimFarm*, though that's a bit of both. The biologicals would be *SimAnt*, *SimEarth*, and *SimLife*, roughly.

Why do you think the economic ones have been more successful?

I think it has a lot to do with how much control you have over the systems. The biological systems tend to be very soft, squishy things that you can do something to, and then it kind of reacts and adapts. It's not really clear what you did to it, because it'll then evolve around you. Whereas in the economic ones you have much better credit assignment. When something goes wrong, you can say, "Oh, it's because I forgot to do this. I should have bought one of those." I think people can reason through their failures and assign credit to the failures more easily with the economic models. Plus the idea that you have money and you make money this way and you spend money on that all seems very natural to people, whereas when you get into the complex things like diversity, food webs, and things like that, people just don't have an instinct for it.

And nothing's more frustrating than playing and not understanding why you're losing...

Right, exactly. And so in *SimEarth* people would be playing and all of sudden their planet would freeze up and they'd have no clue why it happened. And I, as the simulation engineer, couldn't tell them either!

One thing I like about *SimEarth* was how it could play tones that would communicate information about the state of your planet.

I always wanted to do more with that, but I never really got around to it. There's been some interesting work on data auralization. Instead of visualization, you can take complex data and map it to sound, because there are certain sound ranges that we're incredibly good at discriminating. There was actually some work done at the Santa Fe Research Institute in those areas. One of the things that they did that was remarkable was taking seismograph data, from earthquakes and whatnot, and mapping it into sound waves, using pretty much the same waveform just mapped to a different frequency. And they did the same thing with underground nuclear tests. From the seismograph, if you look at the waveforms, they're pretty much identical. It's really hard to tell any difference at all between the nuclear test and the earthquake. But when you map it to sound, there's a very definite tinniness to the nuclear test which you can instantly recognize. And it's interesting that, no matter how they mapped the waves visually,

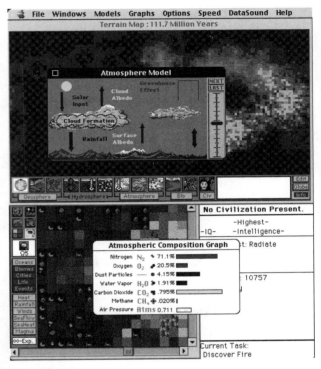

SimEarth

they couldn't find a way to discriminate between them. But as soon as they mapped it to sound it was obvious.

So you thought you could better communicate to the player the condition of their planet through sound?

Well, it was just kind of a stupid little experiment in that direction. At some point I'd like to sit down and do it right. The one that I thought worked pretty well was where it would map your atmosphere into tones ongoingly, starting at the North Pole and going to the South Pole. And if you left that in the background with the volume down, it was pretty useful, because you could tell changes from that much sooner than you could actually see them reflected on the visual graphs. And so, as a kind of threshold alarm, I thought that worked pretty well. Because you could actually be doing that subconsciously. After a while, you start getting used to this little tune, and then all of a sudden when the tune changes, it comes to the foreground of your mind. And it can be doing that while you're doing other things, so you don't have to be sitting there staring at the display all the time. I always thought that was pretty cool.

***SimEarth* is a pretty serious game compared to many of your other titles. Why did you opt for that approach?**

I didn't want to do too much anthropomorphizing in the game. One of the precepts of the game is that humans just happened to be the evolved intelligence on this planet. It could have just as easily been trichordates or something else. So I was really trying to avoid a human-centered approach to the game. And, really, the focus of the game was supposed to be on the planet. I'm trying to put myself back in my mind-set back when I worked on that, it was so long ago. I mean, it's one of those things that once you get into the subject you're just fascinated by it. I'm still to this day just blown away by continental drift and things like that, stuff that most people think sounds pretty boring. So it's kind of hard to express the passion I had for that subject. *SimAnt* was the exact same way. Still, I think ants are just the coolest thing around, and I don't think I clearly communicated that with the game.

***SimAnt* does seem to be a lot wackier than *SimEarth* or even *SimCity*.**

It's hard to take ants too seriously. Also, *SimAnt* really surprised me. It's the first time I did a game that appealed to a totally different demographic than I was expecting. *SimAnt* was actually a big hit with ten- to thirteen-year-olds. Parents would buy it, and the kids would play it, and the kids just loved it. Still to this day a lot of peo-

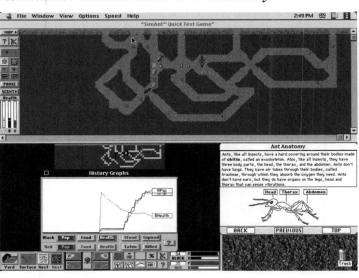

SimAnt

ple tell me, "I loved *SimAnt*, it was my favorite game." And it did very well. It's just that I was expecting it to be more older people that would appreciate how amazingly interesting ants are as an example of distributed intelligence. In some sense, I was trying to use a wacky approach to show how intrinsically interesting ants are as an information processing system. But in fact, I ended up appealing to twelve-year-olds who just loved playing with ants.

An ant simulator seems to be a pretty strange premise for a game. Why did you choose to do it?

I'd have to go into why I love ants. *SimAnt* always seemed obvious to me. I was always wondering why no one had ever done a computerized ant farm, and I kept expecting someone to do it for years but they never did. The time just seemed right. Most of my games have been influenced heavily by things that I have read. So, *SimEarth* was kind of inspired by James Lovelock and the Gaia hypothesis. *SimAnt* was definitely inspired by the work of Edward Wilson, who is kind of like *the* myrmecologist. He's written a lot of books. He actually wrote a Pulitzer Prize-winning book the year that *SimAnt* came out called *The Ants*, which was just an amazing resource. We used a lot of his books heavily in building the model for *SimAnt*. In fact, we probably couldn't have engineered the model without his work, as we probably could not have done *SimEarth* without James Lovelock's work.

Did you encounter any resistance to doing as unique and strange a game as *SimAnt*?

No, not at all. I think I met more resistance on *SimEarth* because everybody was expecting *SimCity 2* and I really didn't want to do *SimCity 2*, I wanted to do something different.

***SimAnt* seems to be a lot more of a game than *SimCity* or *SimEarth*.**

I think probably *SimAnt* was my slight overreaction to *SimEarth*. When *SimEarth* came out I realized at the end that, God, this is like sitting in the cockpit of a 747 in a nose dive. That's what it feels like to most players. So I wanted *SimAnt* to go in the opposite direction: something non-intimidating, something lighthearted, something fun, something where it was really clear what went wrong. Though I never could quite tell how successful it was, one of the things I really wanted to do with *SimAnt* was to have the idea that you have this light, easy to get into game, but you get more and more serious about it. That's why we had this little online database about ants, the little encyclopedia. And the idea was to get people interested enough, just through the game, that they would actually start reading this little encyclopedia and a lot of it would pertain to the gameplay. So you could actually learn new strategies for the game while at the same absorbing all this cool information about ants.

The game reminds me of a very strange wargame.

It's kind of like an RTS game. In *SimAnt* we did some wacky things. *SimAnt* in some sense was very experimental. There were some weird things in there, like the mystery button. On the interface, there's one button that has this big question mark, and it's the mystery button. Every time you press that button something very strange happens, and usually it's different. There are thirty different things that can happen,

and they're totally weird things. Like, all your ants die. Or your ants double. Or a giant rainstorm starts. Or you switch sides. Totally non-linear, random things happen when you click that button.

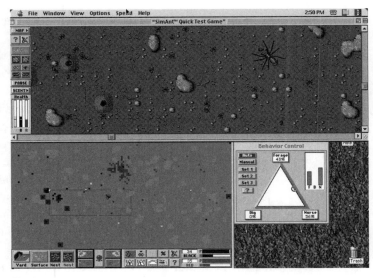

SimAnt

Kind of like the disasters from *SimCity* taken to an extreme...

It's almost meta-level disasters. Things that would all of a sudden erase your game, or give you twice the number of your opponents. Like the disasters in *SimCity*, what a lot of people would do is they would play and play and play for hours and when they were ready to stop, just before they would quit they would burn the city down just for the hell of it. In *SimAnt* people would play the game for a while and then, just before they quit, they would hit the mystery button to see what it did today.

Your next project was *SimCity 2000*. How did that come about?

Well, actually, before I did that, I had spent about six months working on the very first incarnation of *The Sims*. I had actually done a little prototype and some coding. At that point Fred Haslam was working on *SimCity 2000*. He was the guy who I ended up doing it with and who had done *SimEarth* with me. *SimCity 2000* wasn't going nearly as fast as everybody liked, and they didn't like the graphics and all this stuff, so I got dragged into it. At this point, the company was really depending on *SimCity 2000* being a best-seller and all that, so I basically dropped everything I was doing on *The Sims* and dove in with Fred. And, in fact, I took the code shell I had written for *The Sims*, and we actually ended up using it for *SimCity 2000*. In fact, if you go back and look at the source code for *SimCity 2000*, to this day the draw routines say DrawHouse and DrawYard, because it was the original code shell for *The Sims*. So then I got into that, and Fred and I, basically we started from scratch. Fred and I work together really well, and we did it in almost record time, for that complexity of a game. We did it in about twelve months flat.

So the idea was to improve on what had worked well in the original *SimCity?*

Roughly. Also, at that point, we had hundreds and hundreds of fan letters saying, "Oh, you should do *SimCity* again and add this and add that and add the other." And I read through all those letters. And there were a few things that were very common. And so we added the really common and obvious suggestions: altitude, mountains, a

SimCity 2000

water system, more road types, that type of thing. Beyond that it was all of the things I wished I could have done in *SimCity* that, now that computers were faster and graphics were better, we could do.

So, compared to *SimAnt,* it seems a lot less wacky. Was that because you were working with the company's prize franchise?

It was wacky enough I think, in its own way. It had the expected *SimCity* wackiness, plus a lot of things that were not in the original *SimCity*. We had a lot of hidden things in *SimCity 2000* that people didn't realize for a long time that helped its longevity. There was the Loch Ness Monster in there. It would only appear every two or three months that you played the game, and it would only appear for about four seconds. And so there were a lot of rumors about it. Two months after the game had shipped, people started saying they had seen this monster in the water, and most people didn't believe them because it was so infrequent. And it was almost a year after we shipped the game that someone actually managed to take a screenshot of it. And then you had Captain Hero. Only under certain weird conditions you would get this superhero that would fly around and fight your disasters for you. So we had a lot of stuff like that hidden in the game. The original *SimCity* didn't really have that level of depth.

Did you feel constrained since you were just doing a sequel?

Not really. At that point I was more in project management mode. I had a pretty clear idea of what the design would be, since we were basically just doing a sequel, which is always easier. It was more just making sure the engineering was good and the performance was decent. It was a pretty tight piece of code. The original *SimCity 2000* ran in 1.3 megs on a Mac. So, for what it was, it was actually pretty tight to work in that little memory.

Was *SimCopter* your next project?

That came quite a bit afterward, since I was actually working on *The Sims* in the background while I was working on *SimCopter*. So, at that point I had a programmer dedicated to *The Sims*. In fact, in *SimCopter*, the behavior of the people that walked around were actually using a very early form of Edith, which was the program-

SimCopter

ming language we developed for *The Sims*. A lot of people at Maxis decided we really wanted to try something where you were doing a 3D game inside of *SimCity*. So that was the original premise for *SimCopter*. They asked me: "Can you design a game where you're doing something in 3D in *SimCity?* Whatever it is, driving around, flying around, whatever." So *SimCopter* was the design I came up with. It was the first 3D game I ever did, and actually the first 3D game a lot of our team ever did as well. So we were definitely going up a learning curve a couple of years behind a lot of other people. The biggest problem with *SimCopter* I don't think was in the game design, it was in the graphics. They were really sub-standard for when it came out.

Did you like the way it turned out? Or did you not care so much since you were more interested in working on *The Sims*?

Well, I was actually concentrating on *SimCopter*. We didn't have a big enough team on it, we basically had four people doing it. And to do a 3D product at that point in time, that was just not enough at all. So I felt like I was really resource constrained on the product, plus we had this hard schedule that we absolutely had to make. For various reasons we could not miss Christmas, which meant we really couldn't aim too high. Had we had another six to eight months to work on it, graphically I think it would have turned out much, much better. The gameplay and tuning I'm still pretty happy with. It could have used a few more missions. But there was something really neat about having a city that you'd built in *SimCity* over many hours, and then all of a sudden being in it in 3D and seeing the people and the cars and flying around it. There was a real eerie quality to that. It worked well.

Now, you weren't involved at all with *SimCity 3000*. Were you just burned out on the whole idea of doing another city simulator?

Yeah, that's pretty much it. You hit the nail on the head with that. It was a running joke around Maxis that whenever the *SimCity* team would come to ask me for advice I would go running. They finally gave up. You know, the day they shipped *SimCity 3000* was one of the happiest days of my life. They proved that we have a team within Maxis that knows how to build *SimCity* without my involvement. And before, when *2000* came around, there was just nobody else to turn to. I had to work on it or it just wasn't going to happen. Whereas now we have the expertise in-house to do *SimCity*, a really great, talented team. The franchise is in good hands from my point of view.

So you were pleased to not have to be involved with that.

That's an understatement. Just doing one sequel for me was excruciating. Once I got into it, I had fun with *SimCity 2000*. But there are just so many games that haven't been done at all that I'd like to do, as opposed to going back and redoing games I've already done. Probably my favorite part of designing a game is the research and learning a new subject, and just totally diving into it. And, I've spent a lot of time reading about urban dynamics and city planning. I still love the subject, but I'm kind of burned out on the research in that area. There are so many other subjects I'd love to dive into and learn right now.

I do have one question about *SimCity 3000*. When I originally saw a prototype for the game it was fully 3D. But when it shipped it was back to the classic isometric viewpoint. Why did that change so radically?

Well, for a number of reasons, and it was a pretty hard decision to make. In retrospect, I'm convinced it was the right decision. Part of it had to do with user interface. A lot of people who play *SimCity*, who tend to be a much broader group, a lot of the more casual gamers, have a hard time moving around and controlling a 3D camera. And when you put on top of that the idea of editing a system and then give them a three-dimensional camera, it takes what used to be a very simple, Lego-like thing, and turns it into an AutoCAD. "What am I looking at? Oh, I see, I'm facing the building two inches away." It becomes that kind of experience. So that was part of it. The other part was the technology. Without going with really severe restrictions on what you could build, we just couldn't have a decent frame rate and have the level of detail that we could have in an isometric viewpoint. We're getting to the point today where it's pretty much feasible. But you deal with real RAM limitations of texture memory and real polygonal limitations. At the time that we were

SimCity 3000

working on it, there weren't enough people out there with 3D hardware to require that. So we would have had to have a software solution that was acceptable. There were a lot of reasons, but I'd say the two primary ones were performance and user interface.

So you actually started *The Sims* right after you finished *SimAnt*.

A long time ago, yeah. I also had a couple of projects that I started and then killed along the way.

Anything of interest?

Well, I had project Z. For a while there I had project X, Y, and Z. X was what we were calling *The Sims* for the longest time. Y was *SimCopter*. For Z, I wanted to do a simulation of the Hindenburg. And I really researched that and really enjoyed it. This was a really odd idea. But it was a combination of *Myst* and a flight simulator, if you can imagine that. It was going to be a very elaborately rendered, beautifully, meticulously drawn virtual Hindenburg that you could walk through and explore, every little nook and cranny. But it would also be completely functional, so every valve that you would turn would have the real effect, and every switch that you would flip would do what the real switch did. And you would find yourself all of a sudden, on the Hindenburg, over the Atlantic, heading to Lakehurst. You would be the only one aboard, you'd be on this ghost ship. Basically, history would keep repeating itself, and if you didn't do the right thing you would always blow up when you got to Lakehurst. And so it was going to be kind of a mystery game. And we were going to take the top ten or twenty theories for why the Hindenburg blew up, there are quite a few of them actually. And every time you started a new game it would pick one of those at random. So every time you played the game it wouldn't be the same reason why it blew up. So there'd be a totally different set of things you'd have to do to prevent it. In fact, you could also go up to the control cabin and pilot the thing, you could fly it around to different areas. You'd actually have to learn how to fly a zeppelin from scratch, which for one person is quite difficult.

That's really quite different from any of your other games.

Yeah. You know what really killed that project the most, the reason why I really gave up on it? It seems like a really minor reason, but it was the fact that the Hindenburg had a swastika on its tail. And even if we took the swastika off, a lot of people have this association in their mind of the Hindenburg as a Nazi symbol. Which is unfortunate, because the guy who designed and built the Hindenburg was one of the fiercest opponents of the Nazis, and he actually had to sign this pact with the devil to get the thing built. And so the Nazis actually paid for its final construction. So, anyway, that was one of my failed game designs.

So did *The Sims* stay pretty much the same throughout its development?

It definitely went through a focus change, from architecture to more about the people, but not a major one. In fact, I uncovered a tape, just before we finished *The Sims*, which I had forgotten I had. It was a tape of one of the very first focus groups we did back in '93. And on the focus group tape, the moderator describes the concept that I had written down of *The Sims*, and it's remarkably close to what we ended up shipping.

Did the focus group like the idea?

No, actually, this was probably the most negative focus group experience I have ever seen. It was actually quite remarkable. They universally hated it.

Was that why you couldn't get staff for the project at first?

Yeah, that was part of it, that certainly didn't help. It wasn't my idea to have the focus group in the first place. Our marketing people said, "Hey, let's have a focus group and make sure about this." Of course, when everybody in the focus group said, "There's no way I'd buy that," that made it a little more difficult for me to sell the idea.

So how did you finally get a chance to make it?

I convinced everybody to at least give me one programmer to work on it in the background. It was a guy named Jamie Doornbos, who was the eventual lead programmer. A really bright, young guy out of Stanford, a good science student. He was the one that was developing the behavior model with me in the background. We were trying to figure out how we could simulate an open-ended system where the behaviors were expandable and they had the level of intelligence that we would require for the game, so that they could basically live out their whole home life and we could simulate it reasonably. So Jamie and I probably spent a year and a half just working on the behavior model, as a little research project. At some point it just started really working out, and really looking pretty good. And that's the point at which I started getting more people on the team. And even then, I had to fight and kick and struggle for every person I got.

After your success with *SimCity*, it's surprising that no one trusted you.

But in fact, it's funny, because just recently I started on a couple of other back-burner type things. The last one I did, I started telling people this idea, and everybody said, "That's great, that's great, go do it, here's a programmer." And in a sense it was disappointing. It's much more satisfying when everybody says, "That sucks, no way that will work out" and then you go disprove them, rather than if everybody says, "Oh, that'll be great" and then if it doesn't turn out to be great... So in some sense I miss the struggle.

What was your original inspiration for *The Sims*?

I think the original inspiration for *The Sims* came from a book called *A Pattern Language* written by a Berkeley architecture professor named Christopher Alexander. It's a very interesting book, it's kind of controversial in the architecture world. It's almost like the Western version of feng shui. He's got two hundred fifty-six design rules, and each one looks at some aspect of human behavior and then derives a design rule that you can use. And the very first rules are where cities should be placed on a countryside. As you move up the rules, to rule ten or fifteen, it starts talking about the design of cities and neighborhoods, and circulation systems within cities. And then you move up to the higher rules and it's about how to design a

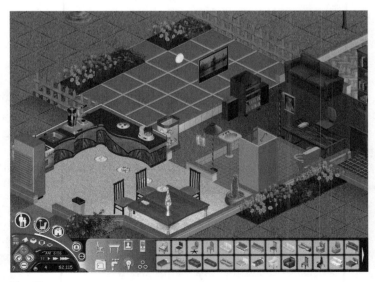

The Sims

neighborhood block and where you should put the schools and play-centers. And then it moves in closer, and it's about how you should place your house in the yard, and how you do private and public areas in the house. And as you move up to the highest level, it's about where you should put your flower planters on the window sill and how to place a park bench. So the rules go through all these different scales, but they're all based on aspects of human behavior. And they try to extrapolate. The fact that we like to have private spaces, and a lot of our activities at home we consider private activities, and other ones are public activities. And so the design of the house should reflect that. There should be some pretty clearly private areas in the house and more clearly public areas. So, that's the way he looks at an aspect of human behavior and then extrapolates a design rule from it. And then he gives examples of how you might implement that design rule. So basically he's coming up with one proposal for a grammar of design. And a lot of people have odds with the particular grammar he came up with, but I always thought his attempt was very noble.

So you thought you could come up with a simulation that would simulate his rules.

It wasn't even his rules I was after. What I was after was trying to get this linkage between human behavior and design. If you look at most architecture magazines nowadays they're about what textures are in this year, what colors, what fabrics, or what decorating styles. They have very little to do with human behavior. Architecture used to be about how you design spaces to facilitate human actions, tasks, and activities. He wrote an earlier book called *Notes on the Synthesis of Form* which drove home the point a little more clearly. He actually did a lot of third world design, where he would go in and study these tribes or cultures, fairly primitive people, and look at their activities. Which activities did they do together and what groups of people collaborated on these activities. And from this he was actually able to extrapolate some design rules for their culture. How their houses should be laid out and how their towns and villages should be arranged. And I just thought that was a very refreshing approach to architecture, getting back to the functional reasons for and requirements of architecture as opposed to the aesthetic and "architecture as modern art" sort of approach. If you look at a lot of these modern architecture books you see these houses in there that I would not want to live in. They're really cool looking, and they look really pretty, especially when they're empty and they're so stark. But I couldn't imagine living in them. There's this big disconnect.

So originally it had to do more with building your house?

It had more to do with enabling behavior and interaction through design. And in some sense it still retains that. Just with not quite the same amount of focus.

When I played the game, I got much more wrapped up in the interpersonal interactions.

Yeah, I think that's where the focus really changed. We didn't realize how engaging the social part of the game would be. The original concept was that you were trying to keep this family happy at home. The idea that you would have these visitors that you would develop these long-term relationships with was definitely a later concept.

So that just grew organically out of other aspects of the game?

It had a lot to do with the success of our behavioral model which was working better than we thought it would. Or, at least, people's interpretation of our behavioral model. Which is to say we were fooling them better than we thought we would.

So you're saying that people perceive the behavioral model as more impressive than it actually is?

In fact, that became also a big focus of the design. There was another book that became very influential later in the design, a book called *Understanding Comics* by Scott McCloud. And he makes some very good points that are very applicable to game design. One of the ones that we used the most is the idea that the activity is a collaboration, in this case, between the game designer and the player. And also that the level of abstraction that you present to the player gives them a very significant clue as to how much of this they should be modeling in their head versus on the computer. So, in fact, when somebody's playing *The Sims* and interpreting the expe-

rience, they may not realize it but they're doing a lot of the modeling in their head, not on the computer. The computer will sit there and it will pop up this gibberish conversation. Most people will actually sit there and roughly interpret what they're saying. They'll say, "Oh, I see, he's upset because she didn't take the trash out."

The Sims

And they'll be simulating in their heads the other side of the model to a greater level of detail than the computer ever could. People can't help but look at a sequence of events and overlay some kind of narrative on it.

We noticed that a while back, so we really decided to make use of that. And so when we designed their conversations and the iconic language and even their gestures, we tried to leave them open to interpretation so that the players can come in and have fairly creative interpretations of what they're seeing on the screen. And then later we were watching people play the game in early playtest sessions and some of the narratives they were creating were so entertaining and funny that that's what gave us the idea to put in the scrapbook feature. With that, they can actually record their particular narrative of what is going on and then share it.

Did you think *The Sims* was going to be such a big success?

I always thought *The Sims* seemed to have much more potential than *SimCity* ever did. I was never that confident about *SimCity*. And I'm not sure why I was that confident about *The Sims*, but just because it hit so close to home with human nature, I always suspected that people would like playing with people, as close as they could possibly get. And most games don't let you get that close to people, or if they do it's in a very scripted, linear format. It's not in an open-ended format.

Usually it's more in a *Zelda* sort of way, where you can talk to this character but they always say the same thing.

Exactly, and instantly the model breaks in your head and you say, "Oh, it's just a robot and it's repeating the same thing over and over." And if we could keep it open-ended, and we didn't try to get too close to the people and left the interpretation in there, people could reasonably believe that these were little creatures with desires and relationships and all these things.

Amongst all the praise, I've seen a lot of little complaints about the game. Like there aren't any weekends, or you can never play with your sims outside of the home environment. Do you often hear such complaints about your games?

That happens a lot. It's happened probably more with *The Sims* than any other title I've worked on, probably because more people consider themselves an expert on the subject than they do on ants or planet thermodynamics. It's hard to look at *SimEarth* and say, "Well, I really don't think ocean currents have that much of a thermal transfer rate with the atmosphere." But anybody can look at *The Sims* and say, "Well, I don't think we would slap her for that." We're more experts in that field, so that's kind of natural. The other thing though, is that, judging by the things that they feel that they're missing, people don't realize how much of it is actually clicking and working. Because there were so many hundreds of things that had to work before they were complaining about weekends. For weekends to be the big concern, that implies that a lot of the other stuff that we were sweating over is actually working.

Was deciding what to include and what to leave out a function of how much time you had to complete the game?

That was certainly a big part of it, although whenever we hit one of those situations we tried to leave the game open-ended so that we could expand it in that direction with a download. We haven't fully demonstrated how much we can expand the game with downloaded objects. Also, it's easy for people to say that they want weekends, but they're not thinking through all of the ramifications of it, which we did. And most people, when I sit and explain why we don't have weekends, all of a sudden they realize why not and say, "Oh, you're right, I guess I don't want weekends."

So how did you decide what limits to put on the simulation?

That very much was a resource issue. We could have put in the nightclub and the work and all that and added another year to the game's development. At which point it would have been past its best time. Another thing is, we could have done all that on a similar schedule, but done everything a lot worse. I figured I would much rather do the house really well than do everything poorly. Which I think is what would have happened, realistically, knowing how projects go.

So your advice to game designers is to focus their designs?

You also really have to understand what the core of the fun is going to be in the game. And if you're adding this stuff just so you can put more bullet points on the back of the box, but it's not actually making the game more fun, it's totally wasted effort. There's an old Japanese saying that I love, and it's about gardening: "Your garden is not complete until there's nothing else you can remove."

So you think that adage applies to game design?

Oh, very much. If you look at the amount of stuff we took out of this game, it would probably surprise you. Like the needs, for instance. You know, we have the eight needs. At some point it was twelve, and then it was ten, and then it was eventually eight. We were actually much more concerned with simplifying the game than we were with expanding it. And our interface. Our interface went through eleven iterations; total, complete redesigns of the interface. And each one ended up dropping a button here, a button there, or we found ways to combine functionality. I really thought that *The Sims*, if it was accessible, would appeal to a very wide audience, but it had to be incredibly accessible, through the interface. It couldn't be your standard strategy game interface, or we would turn off most of our customer base. So we went way out of our way to do that interface. Most people don't even realize how elegant parts of it are. I mean, parts of it are still fairly clumsy, but there are some things that we really sweated over, that are minor, minor details, but ended up making a huge difference. A lot of it is minor things that add up, like the pie menus. You can either click, drag, and release an object, or you can click, release, move over, and click again. So we're basically mirroring the Windows functionality that most people are used to.

Having the 3D head come up and respond, look in the direction you move the mouse. The fact that every single bit of text in the interface has embedded help. A lot of people don't realize this, but you can roll over any word down in that interface, and it will actually highlight as you roll over it, and if you click it comes up with a pretty elaborate explanation of what it is. So we did a lot of embedded help. And things like that just add up. There's no one thing that really makes it work. We probably ran a hundred playtesters through this thing in the last year of development. And these were things where one of the other designers or I would sit down and watch them play it for an hour and write notes about all the mistakes they made and misconceptions they had. So we did a lot of playtesting on the interface. If it turns out that five people made the same conceptual mistake that you rotate by doing this, or they were trying to drag an object by doing that, then we would try to figure out a way to solve that without breaking it for all the other people.

You've always had the iconic interface for your games, but yet each interface is quite a bit different than the one before it. Why is that?

It's really hard to just do an interface out of context. You really have to take a look at what the game needs, and how you're going to interact with things in the game. That's going to determine a lot of your interface. You also have to take a look at the environment you're living in, which is to say, what are the other applications and the other games doing? There were things that we did in *The Sims* to maintain consistency with *SimCity 3000*. Like the right button scrolling, where you right-click and drag, and the edge scrolling, we tried to mirror *SimCity* there. And in general you just learn. I think that each interface I've worked on for a game has been better than the last one. Also, as games reach a wider and wider audience of more casual people, that puts even more requirements on that interface. It just has to be that much easier if you're going to capture these people. It used to be hard-core computer people playing these games, and they would put up with anything. Now it's people who are much more casual, and if they find the interface frustrating in two minutes, they're going to put the game down.

In general, I'd say the PC designers, myself included, are still catching up to the console developers. This is something the console people learned a long time ago on the Nintendo and Sega because they were dealing with a casual, wide audience, younger kids for the most part. So they've had much more accessible, simple, and understandable interfaces long before we have on the computer side.

For *The Sims* you have a hybrid world with 3D characters walking around in an isometric world. Was that for the same reasons as in *SimCity 3000*?

Yeah, since the editing and building of the house and all that, if we had a full 3D camera and all that I don't think there's any way we would have made it as easy as it is now. Also we would have

The Sims

had some real graphic load issues. We could not have gotten the detail we had on the objects, if they were geometry.

Was there ever pressure to make the game 3D since so many other games were 3D?

About three years ago it seemed like everything was going to 3D, and if you weren't 3D you were just dead. At some point that kind of hysteria passed and people started looking at the top-selling games and realizing, hey, you still had *Age of Empires*, *SimCity*, and all these very good selling games that were not 3D. In fact, if you look at the top-selling games, a minority of them are 3D. So now the idea that consumers would accept a non-3D game is a given. There isn't this idea that it has to be 3D whether it makes sense or not.

I very much enjoyed the way the characters talk in *The Sims*. Was that a disc-space limitation, or did you go with the gibberish speak in order to leave it open to interpretation to the player?

Even if we had had five CDs worth of recorded voice, that stuff would have gotten really repetitive. And my biggest concern was that it didn't get repetitive and that you didn't hear the same string over and over and over. In fact, we recorded hundreds and hundreds of voice strings, each one with different emotional nuances. And we decided that the voice was entirely for the emotional content: you could tell if the person was flirtatious, upset, laid back, or tired by the tone of the voice and the cadence. But the way it works out is, because you don't get the semantics, because you're not hearing the words, you naturally sit there and imagine the words fairly fluidly. But the emotional context you get very easily. You know: "Wow, she sounds pissed."

So, yeah, I'm actually really happy with the way that worked out. You hear them talking over and over and over, but it's very hard to hear the exact repeats. Because in fact you are hearing a lot of the waveforms repeat eventually. But we actually designed that language so it was very hard to detect. And that was a long slow process, figuring out how to do that. Originally, we were planning to use a real language, but a really obscure one that people didn't understand. And we did a lot of tests with Navajo and Estonian. And they were still too recognizable. Even though you wouldn't understand the language, you would still recognize that, "Oh, that was the thing I just heard." A lot of it had to do with the number of hard consonants in an utterance, and also the cadence and rate at which it was going. It was a long process to get that figured out.

It seems remarkably progressive for a game to include the homosexual possibilities that _The Sims_ does. Why did you choose to allow that?

One of the things we knew that a lot of people were going to do with this game was model their real family. And the last thing I wanted to go in and do was say, "Oh, we're not going to recognize your family." So we wanted to give people a reasonably, fairly open-ended way to construct whatever family they came from or could imagine or wanted to play with. But we were dealing with an ethical and moral minefield that we had to thread very carefully. And there were a lot of things that we left out of the game on purpose. And there were a lot of things that we really wanted to have in the game at various levels, and homosexuality was one of the things that we really wanted to have in the game, in some way.

The Sims

What sort of things did you leave out on purpose?

There were a couple of things that became somewhat issues and we did slight modifications. One of them was the domestic violence issue. When the characters get upset, they can slap each other. I don't know if you've noticed, but there are two types of slap. There's one slap where they rear their arm back and then *whack* and it's as if they're breaking their jaw. And there's another one that's kind of an insulting British Army slap. Whenever you have people of the same gender slapping, they use the really hard slap, like a man slapping another man or a woman slapping another woman. But whenever you have a man slapping a woman, or a woman slapping a man they use the polite slap. Because before, when we had the strong-arm slap, and you had a husband slapping his wife, it rubbed a lot of people the wrong way, just from the domestic violence point of view. And that was one of those things where we were right on the edge and being very careful, but not losing the feature.

So it retains the emotional content without being too violent.

Right, and it doesn't make people think about serious domestic abuse. And, in fact, it was funny, because we also have an attack interaction. If they really don't like each other they can actually get in a fistfight. But because we did the fistfight like a cartoon fistfight, there's this big cloud and you see arms and legs poking out, no one had any problem with that. Even if it was a man and woman, it was always so cartoonish that it was never an issue compared to the slap. There were certain places that we just didn't want to go with the game at all. For example, pedophilia. And in general they don't kill each other. The Sims will not directly kill each other, though objects can kill them and various disasters can kill them. So, yeah, there were certain things we decided we would leave out, certain things we wanted to get in, and others that we had to be very careful how we treated.

With the inclusion of homosexuality, were there ever any concerns that senators who up until then had been concerned with violence would now be outraged by *The Sims*?

Actually, there was and it's very surprising to me that it hasn't materialized in the least. Not at all. There has just been no reaction to that, and it just really surprised me. I thought primarily if it came it would come from the Christian conservatives or some other group like that. Maybe they just don't play these games, maybe they could care less, I don't know. Yeah, but we've had absolutely no problems with that at all. We've had a couple of people on the bulletin boards, probably fourteen-year-old kids complaining, but you can tell their age by their spelling.

It seems like there were a lot of moral decisions you made in designing the game. For instance, the gameplay seems to be geared toward improving your career so you can get more stuff. It seems pretty materialistic.

Yeah, that was actually the intent. That's what most people interpret when they see the game, and even when they play it for a while they think it's very materialistic. It's only the people that play it a long time that start realizing the downside. Just about every object has some built-in failure state or maintenance requirement. If you keep buying stuff, it will eventually go bad or die or need to be cleaned or whatever. So in some sense it's like you're filling up your house with all these potential time-bombs. And so at some point you end up spending so much time fixing these things and doing this, that, and the other, that these objects you originally bought to save you time end up sucking up all your time. And this is pretty long into the gameplay that you start realizing this. But it was very definitely engineered that way. So in some sense it's the people who first start playing the game who say, "God, I can't believe how materialistic this game is." But then it's the hard-core players that say, "God, I'm not going to buy that much crap next time I play."

I guess it's open-ended enough that players can try to concentrate on the social aspects instead of object acquisition.

In some sense the social side has the same dynamic, where you make these friends, but the friendships decay over time. And your friends, once they decay to a certain point, will actually call you up and say, "Hey, you better invite me over, I haven't seen you in a while." So once you make about twenty friends, you'll start noticing that every day they're clamoring to come over, and that they're sucking up your time in a different way.

What can you tell me about the scripting language Edith?

Well, that was the thing that Jamie and I were working on for the longest time. It's a programming scripting language, it's visual, and we actually developed our own editor and debugger, all integrated with the game. So, in fact, you run this from within the game and you can program and debug and step through objects while you're playing.

So you can use it to add new objects to the world?

In fact, almost all the behavior in the game is in these objects, including the social interactions of the people, and it's all programmed in this language. The primitives of this language all sit atop C level code routines. The C level code routines are things like routing primitives, variable peeks and pokes, and things like that. But the language itself is very clean, and there are about thirty or forty primitives that it's all built out of. The main thing, though, is that it's all machine-independent tokenized code that travels with the object. Which means that you can drop a new object into the game and instantly the people know when to use it, when it's appropriate to use it, and how to use it. And the animations, sound effects, code, and everything is all contained within the object that you download.

So you created the language to make it easy to add new objects.

Yeah, that was the original specification of the language. We wanted to have a language we could write all the behavior in that was totally expandable, at the object level. That way the behavior of the people within the house is totally a function of the stuff in their house and we could always add new things, even Trojan Horse things, into the house.

Such as the guinea pig object.

Yeah, the guinea pig object is an example. Actually, in the design we were thinking that they should get sick, and we had planned to do sickness, but we just ran out of time. But then we realized, "Hey, we could just make that a download." Of course, nobody's going to download sickness, so we hid it in the guinea pig. It's funny, because some of the early reviews of the game said, "It's got all this stuff, but it doesn't have sickness. I don't know why." Of course, those are probably the same people that complained when we gave it to them. The reason we're releasing this language is that eventually I want the users to start making these things.

And you made it simple enough so that you wouldn't have to be a hard-core programmer to use it?

You'd have to know how to program, but you wouldn't have to be a hard-core programmer at all. I mean, this is a much simpler language than Visual Basic.

Doesn't it bother you that, with a tool like that, the game is never completely "done"?

Yeah, I think, again, if you go back to the hobby model, hobbies are never done. They're just a continually growing thing. And they grow pretty much as a function of the amount of people involved in it and how committed they are. And the more powerful tools they have, the stronger the hobby itself becomes, and it infects more people.

I also read a quote from you where you said: "The real long-term attraction of *The Sims* is as a storytelling platform." Now, when most game developers talk about stories in games, they're talking about them in that *Zelda* sense. To those people, something like *The Sims* doesn't have any story at all.

There's a big distinction between *Zelda* and *The Sims*. You're creating the story in *The Sims*; in *Zelda* you're uncovering the story. In some sense, the stories are just one aspect of player involvement. There are actually all these different levels. Some casual people will just play the game a few hours and have a good time and put it down. Other people will play it longer, and get into designing really cool houses, and maybe even uploading them on the web site, for people to see. Other people that get into the game even deeper will not only build interesting families and cool houses, but will use that to tell a story and upload it to share it with other people. And the even more hard-core people will start editing custom skins or wallpapers for the game and start sharing them. And then pretty soon they'll be able to create their own objects, custom objects, and put them on the web to share. So there are these different levels of player involvement. And each level higher is a much smaller number of people. But in some sense they're feeding the people beneath them. We have something like ten thousand homes on our web site that people have uploaded, but those ten thousand homes have been viewed over one hundred thousand times.

The Sims

So it's like a pyramid scheme.

Exactly. There are like thirty people out there making really good skins for the game. But there are probably thirty thousand that are downloading them and using them. So, for your really hard-core, talented fans, if you give them the tools and the ability to create content for the other ninety-nine percent, they will. And it will just benefit both sides. It gives them an audience to build these things for, and gives the audience cool stuff for the game that might eventually draw them in deeper. It'll increase the likelihood that these casual people eventually become those hard-core people.

So someday everyone on the planet has to be playing *The Sims*.

Right, so this is kind of like the zombie scheme, where the zombies go around, and then they start eating brains and turning the other people into zombies... At some point when it's five zombies against the world it doesn't look too good, but once you get a critical mass of zombies and they start converting other people into zombies fast enough...

On *The Sims* you are listed as just a game designer, while in the past you had served as both a programmer and a designer. Did you do any programming on the project?

I did quite a bit of programming in the Edith code. I didn't touch the C code in *The Sims*. It's probably the first project that I didn't do any of the C coding in. I did a lot of programming of the social interactions and stuff in Edith, but for the most part, even then, it was more a question of me going in and tweaking and tuning the algorithms the way I wanted. We had a really good team on *The Sims*, a really great team of engineers. So I didn't feel any need at all to go into the code.

It's not something you miss?

Oh, I kind of missed it. I enjoyed going into Edith and hacking stuff. But there was just so much to be done on the design side that I didn't have the time to waste programming. Not to say that programming is a waste of time, but I was never a great programmer. I was always persistent, and I could always make cool stuff out of computer code just because I was persistent. I mean, I know great programmers, and I'm not one.

So you didn't have any trouble communicating your vision for the design to the engineering team?

There were problems, but not for any lack of foresight or intelligence. Just because it was a complex thing. In fact, I didn't know what we were building for a long time myself, a lot of it was experimental. But yeah, in terms of the programming staff, I could always sit down and explain the dynamics I was looking for and be very confident of getting them.

You also made the transition from doing everything yourself on *SimCity* to working on a large team for *The Sims*. How big was the team?

It depends on what you count as the team. You know, there were probably sixty people who worked on it at some point, but what I would consider the team grew to about thirty.

So that's a pretty big shift from working in a small group. And the management required for that big a team is quite significant.

It is, and it has a huge amount to do with the quality of the people involved. And Electronic Arts also, they came in with a totally different orientation. Before they came in, I had about four or five people working on *The Sims*. And it was actually a very good little group and it was working out great, but I just couldn't get any more resources. When Electronic Arts came in, they came in and said, "What do you need?" And that was the point at which we just started really building the team up. But Electronic Arts also has a very strong concept of production, and what producers do. They have like ten levels of producers, and they put a very heavy load on the producers. So it's one of those things where if you get the right people in those slots, this stuff works pretty well; you can actually manage a pretty large team efficiently. If you get the wrong people in those slots, it's a total disaster, absolutely unmitigated disaster. At that point hiring practices become important, and how do you interview and make sure you get the right people, and how do you quickly find out if you don't have the right person. So it's a model that works with the right components and the right people, but if you get the wrong people, you've blown it.

We basically got the right people. At the same time, in our situation at Maxis, Electronic Arts brought in this one guy to run the studio, to replace most of our old management. His name was Luc Barthelet. And Luc and I hit it off from day one. We get along great. Luc is not your typical manager in any possible sense. I mean, he's very technically literate. So for *SimCity 3000*, they were having problems with the traffic model, and he came in and wrote the traffic code.

Really?

Yeah, the C level code. So it's unusual that you can have somebody running a studio that can also write some of the trickiest code in one of your simulations. And Luc's that kind of guy. There's really an art to management, and what Luc is great at is knowing exactly at what level you need to be concentrating on any given day. And so there was this point when it was crucial that we got this one feature in *SimCity 3000*. It was going to have a big impact on the success of the product, and that was the day he pulled out his compiler and started working on the traffic code. In most of the cases, it was, "How does the German distributor feel about this product?" and he'd be on the phone to the German distributor. You really have to pick your battles. And if you pick the right battles, you'll only have to win five percent of them. So anyway, there's this certain business savvy that certain people that Electronic Arts brought in had in abundance, that I was very impressed to learn from.

Were there guiding principles that people had to follow when designing and developing the Sim family of games?

Well, we basically always saw them as being for the most part non-violent, although we have broken that rule on occasion. But for the most part we've considered that one of our distinguishing features. A lot of our employees who work for us really want to work for Maxis because Maxis is known for their non-violent games. I don't want to sound like I'm making some moralistic statement, because I love *Doom* and *Quake* and those things myself. Some of my favorite games are wargames, I play wargames heavily. I just think that there are so many people making those games that we don't need to, and they're doing a good job of it too. So I'd rather be making games that nobody's making. But from the public's point of view, we do have this reputation for tending towards the more non-violent, more educational, more socially relevant games.

Do you ever feel constrained by making Maxis-style simulation games? Do you ever want to make _Raid Over Bungeling Bay II_?

In some sense _SimCopter_ was almost _Raid Over Bungeling Bay II_. There were a lot of Easter eggs hidden in _SimCopter_. In fact, you could get an Apache and lay waste to the city. In fact, if you had the Apache and you came across a nuclear power plant, you could blow up the entire city. Even in _The Sims_, a couple of times, I tried to get away from the political correctness here and there. So there are a lot of things we did in _The Sims_ that aren't terribly politically correct, that didn't even make sense, you know, more of the wacky side. We didn't try to let the Maxis thing constrain us, but the domestic violence thing was probably a good example. You'll see a lot of games where there's a much higher level of violence, much higher than a man slapping a woman. But we were sensitive to how people would be interpreting this, knowing that families would be playing it.

Your games always seem to have this strong educational component. I was wondering, how do you balance that with making the game entertaining?

SimCopter

I was never concerned with education until the game was fun. Any educational value a program might have is totally wasted if people won't play it. Probably the one game which I learned that the most from was _SimEarth_. _SimEarth_ was potentially the most educational game I ever made, but yet it wasn't fun. A surprising number of people bought it; I'm still surprised by the sales figures. I think most of them played it for two hours and then put it away. So I really think the fun has to come first. And the educational side, it's not something that you tack on, it's got to be fundamental to the design. In _The Sims_, it was all about learning to extrapolate design from behavior. That's a fairly deep lesson, it's not just a fact that I'm going to teach you. It's more like a way of looking at things. If the entire design is true to that, it might be educational at some deep level even though you might play the game for hours and not think of it as educational even once. One of the main things that *SimCity* teaches, it's not explicit but it's there, is the shape of chaos. The fact that the best-laid plans can always go wrong, and that the system is more complex than you think it is. Building a road to solve traffic doesn't always solve traffic, it frequently breeds traffic. Those types of lessons are hard to explain in other media. But when you've experienced them through a process like *SimCity*, you really get the lesson much deeper. It's experience rather than exposition.

Do you ever have to compromise realism to make the game fun?

Oh, all the time. There's also a frequent thing that we did in our games where we would decide to match expectation and not reality. In fact, nuclear power plants don't blow up. They just don't. But when everybody saw it, they said, "Oh, a nuclear power plant, can I make it blow up?" It's just what they thought of. So there are a lot of things we do just because people expect them to happen that way for fun, even though it's not realistic.

With the open-ended nature of your games, do you have to spend a lot of time in playtesting them?

We do, but it's invaluable time. You spend that time, or else you go spend months building the wrong thing and solving the wrong problems. We just had what we call "kleenex" testing on one little component of *The Sims* multi-player that we're working on. We have this one data display that's convoluted and twisted. And the programmer just got it implemented a few days ago, so we scheduled five people to come in today. We call them kleenex playtesters because we use them once and then they never come back, just because we want people who have never seen it before, with totally no preconceptions about it. We don't even tell them what it is, we just say, "Look at that, play with it" and have them describe to us what they're seeing and what that represents. We got some very consistent feedback from all five people today where we understood that three of the variables we were communicating they all understood, the other three they had no clue about. So for the last tester, we turned off the last three variables that everybody was having trouble with and it was perfect. We do this at every stage of the project now. It's not just at the end when we have the whole thing working, we do this with little components, even the art prototypes. And this was a lesson that was really driven home to me by the late Dani Berry. She's the one who did *M.U.L.E.* and all those things. She was drilling this into me years ago, that playtesting is probably the most undervalued thing that any game designer can use, and you really have to do it. And I started taking her advice and she was right. It's just invaluable.

For both *SimCity* and *The Sims*, you had trouble convincing anybody that they would be popular. Do you think there are many games out there with the same problem that never see the light of day? What do you recommend someone with a wacky game idea should do?

Oh, I'm sure they're all over the place. It's kind of depressing to think about it, how many wonderful masterpieces there are out there. For me, it's just that I am a very, very persistent guy. I think if you're really, really persistent, if you really want something, you can make it happen. It might take years. With *SimCity* it was like five years to actually get the first version out. With *The Sims* it was like seven. Aside from that, based on my track record, I don't know if I'm the one to be offering advice there. Whenever something unusual comes out like *The Sims*, I like to think that all of a sudden people say, "Hey, that was really off-the-wall, and it sold great!" Maybe that might help to green-light some other off-the-wall projects at other companies that were having problems getting approved. But I think realistically they're more likely to say, "Oh, we want a game just like *The Sims*."

Unfortunately, that's probably the lesson they're going to carry from it.

The Sims

Will Wright Gameography

Raid Over Bungeling Bay, 1984
SimCity, 1989
SimEarth, 1990
SimAnt, 1992
SimCity 2000, 1994
SimCopter, 1997
The Sims, 2000

Chapter 23:
Playtesting

"The common denominator, I would guess, is passion. Everyone says, 'Well, why aren't games better—why aren't there more really good games?' And I think that the answer is that what this industry doesn't do, amazingly, is play the games it makes. We create a game, we ask the teams to work all the hours God sends, and we don't give them time to play the game. That's really what makes the difference—sitting down and playing for hours and hours and hours."

— Peter Molyneux

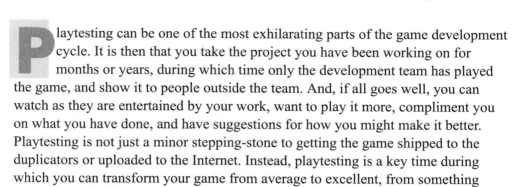

Playtesting can be one of the most exhilarating parts of the game development cycle. It is then that you take the project you have been working on for months or years, during which time only the development team has played the game, and show it to people outside the team. And, if all goes well, you can watch as they are entertained by your work, want to play it more, compliment you on what you have done, and have suggestions for how you might make it better. Playtesting is not just a minor stepping-stone to getting the game shipped to the duplicators or uploaded to the Internet. Instead, playtesting is a key time during which you can transform your game from average to excellent, from something which shows promise to a game that is truly great. No game ever came out of the developer's hands in absolutely perfect shape. Ideally, it is the playtesting cycle that gives your game the extra push to be the best it possibly can.

It is worth clarifying what exactly I mean when I say playtesting. This is not the same as debugging. Debugging is a more programming-oriented task in which all of the inherently broken aspects of the game are tracked down and fixed. This can be anything from the improper implementation of some game mechanics to graphical snafus to problems that actually crash the game. Certainly these bugs must be eliminated, but this is more a matter of concern for the programming team.

Playtesting is the design equivalent of bug fixing. When playtesters look at a game, they try to see if the game is any fun and try to find faults in the game mechanics themselves. This can be anything from a unit in an RTS game that is too powerful and allows the player who first acquires it to totally dominate the game, to the illogical nature of how one enemy AI agent attacks the player, to an unintuitive and difficult-to-use control system. It is in the playtesting stage that the game mechanics themselves are tested and refined. Unfortunately, some game developers focus entirely on fixing bugs and too little on determining if the game is actually any fun to play. As a result there may be nothing actually wrong with the game, and it may be completely stable on all the systems it is supposed to run on. Too bad that no one wants to play the game. Every player would rather have a game that plays really well and crashes occasionally than one that runs flawlessly but is not worth the time it takes to play it. At least the former game is fun some of the time, while the latter game is boring all of the time.

Finding the Right Testers

Finding the right testers is perhaps one of a game designer's biggest challenges in playtesting her game. Not just anyone will be able to playtest a game effectively. Almost any player can tell you whether he likes your game or not, but a surprisingly small number will be able to explain why they do not like it and what you might do to improve it. Of course, getting feedback from someone's general impression of the game can be useful: "that was fun" or "that was tedious" or "that was too hard" are all pieces of information you will be able to apply to your work in order to make your game better. Truly useful advice, however, comes in a more constructive form: "When I was fighting the twelfth clown on level three, I thought he was too hard to kill. I had no idea what I was supposed to do to kill him, or whether the attacks I was attempting were having any effect at all. I thought maybe I was supposed to roll the boulder at him, but I could not figure out how to do so." In this example, the playtester has provided the designer with very specific information about the problem and a detailed explanation of why he thought it was not much fun to play. Playtesters who can do that sort of analysis consistently are extremely rare, making a talented playtester a truly priceless asset for your team.

A key part of working with testers effectively is knowing them well enough to know how seriously to take their opinions and what biases they might have. Different testers will have different motivations which will necessarily color the opinions they give you. This is why picking a random person off the street to test your game can sometimes be ineffective, since you have no past experience with her and hence do not know whether you can trust her opinion or not. When you do have experience with a particular tester, you will be able to know if that person has any shortcomings. For example, some testers can be best described as "whiners" who complain about everything, even things that do not need fixing. Other testers may be shy, only saying, "Maybe you should look at the power of the Elephant Rider unit," when what they truly mean is, "Obviously, the Elephant Rider completely throws off the game." Try your best to understand the personalities of the testers you will be working with; it is key to effectively using the feedback they give you.

Who Should Test

There are various different types of playtesters a project may have, and it is a good idea to have some from each group working on your project. No one type of tester can provide all of the feedback you need for your project, hence the need for a variety of testers. Indeed, it makes sense for there to be a good number of testers, since having a broad range of opinions can be essential to getting beyond individual bias and understanding if your game plays well or not. While arguments can be made for keeping the size of your team small, especially in terms of designers and programmers, with playtesters more truly are merrier.

The first type of playtester is a member of the development team. Throughout the project, it is important to have your team members playing your game. This serves multiple purposes. First, it keeps them enthused about the project. They see to what end their art, sound, code, or level construction is being used. Second, as they see their work in action, they are better able to understand how it might be improved. And third, they can provide you feedback about how the game is working and what you might do to improve it. Towards the end of the project, in particular, as all of the art, most of the code, and the levels are completed, the members of the development team will be able to provide essential feedback about sections of the game that might need some last-minute improvements. Of course, members of the development team are very close to the project, and as a result may be far from objective in their comments about it. Furthermore, since they have been playing the game for so long, they will have trouble seeing it with a fresh set of eyes; their opinions will be skewed accordingly. Also, since they have contributed to the project, they may tend to like or dislike their own work for personal reasons. Similarly, they may like or dislike the ideas of other members of the team not because of the merits of the ideas themselves but rather because of their personal opinion of that person. Despite these drawbacks, getting playtesting feedback from the members of your team is essential.

The second type of playtester to have is the traditional playtester. This is someone who starts playtesting your game around the stage it enters "alpha" and is actually fully playable, and continues until the project ships. Often these playtesters spend half of their time tracking down bugs in the code, but they also provide vital feedback about how the game is playing, whether it is too easy or too difficult, if the controls are intuitive or obtuse, and so forth. On fully funded projects, these testers are typically paid employees who spend a full workweek playtesting your game and providing bug reports. Typically these testers love computer games and play a lot of them, both as part of their job and in their off time. Therefore, their opinions of how the gameplay needs to change are understandably skewed to the perspective of the hard-core gamer. Also, since these testers work on the project for such a long time, they can become used to certain inherent problems with the game, and may stop complaining about those shortcomings.

The third class of playtesters are first-impression testers. Will Wright, in his interview in Chapter 22, refers to these people as "kleenex testers" since at Maxis they are used once and then never used again. Wright used them extensively to test the GUI for *The Sims*. These are people who are neither on the development team nor testing the game full-time. Instead, these testers come in and play the game for a short period of time and provide their gut reaction as to how well the game plays. This may be for a few hours or a few days. These first-impression testers are useful because they see the game as a first-time player would. They can provide essential feedback about unintuitive controls, unclear presentation of information, or unfairly difficult portions of the game. The important point about first-impression testers is that you must keep bringing in new ones, since a human can only truly have a first impression of a game once; after that they are "tainted" by their knowledge of how the game works. Especially toward the end of the project, when the development team is extremely familiar with the game and the traditional playtesters have played it for a thousand hours or more, first-impression testers can be essential to making sure the game is not too hard to learn to play.

Many first-impression testers were used to refine and perfect the interface in *The Sims*.

The fourth type of playtesters are game designers or developers not actually working on your project. These are people whom you know and trust and whose opinions you respect. They may not be able to test your project full-time as traditional testers can, but the feedback they provide can be extremely useful. Fellow game designers who are not working on your project will be able to play your game and provide insight about its strengths and weaknesses in ways that other testers cannot. These testers understand game design in a way which allows them to analyze how your project may come up short and how it might be improved. Many experienced game designers will use these testers particularly early in the process, when they are still trying to get a sense of whether their new game design is truly compelling or not. These game designers turned testers will be better able to overlook the game's obvious shortcomings at this early stage, such as bugs or incomplete features, and look beyond to see if the game shows the promise of becoming a good game in the future. Steve Meretzky, in Chapter 10, mentions how useful the "Imp Lunches" were. At these lunches, the Infocom implementors would gather to discuss their different game design ideas. When a new Infocom title first became playable, other implementors would be the first to start testing the game, while there was still time to make any fundamental changes necessary. Of course, fellow game designers will typically be too busy to spend a lot of time playing your game and giving you feedback. Whatever feedback these fellow designers give you can be extremely helpful, both in helping you pinpoint problem areas you had not anticipated, as well as reassuring you that your design is on the right course, if it actually is.

The fifth class of testers that I find to be of particular value are non-gamers. All of the types of testers I have discussed thus far have, for the most part, been pretty big fans of games. They will have an especially high tolerance for the things that games traditionally do badly, such as having overly complex controls or simply being too hard to play. Having some people who are not very big gamers can provide fabulous feedback, pointing out fundamental problems that hard-core gamers will overlook and forgive. These testers can be literally anyone: the guy who comes to fix the coffee machine, a neighbor, a team member's parent, or literally someone right off the street. As long as they will be honest about what they think of your game, anyone's opinion can be valuable here. Combining the third group, first-impression testers, with non-gamer testers can be particularly useful in determining if an interface is too confusing or the game is too unforgiving. These testers will seldom be able to provide constructive feedback on how you might improve your game, but they will be able to point out fundamental problems in a way that other testers cannot.

Who Should Not Test

There are a number of people or groups of people whom you typically cannot trust as playtesters. These are people whose opinions are colored by their own personal motivations, or who may be unwilling to provide truly objective opinions. Though you may be forced to hear the feedback of these people, it is important to understand the motivations behind their comments so that you can apply their advice appropriately.

The first of these inappropriate testers is your boss. A key part of the game designer's relationship with a playtester is being able to get the playtester's feedback and then apply it as the designer sees fit, not as the playtester dictates. Playtesters often do not understand the game well enough to provide the best solution for a problem they encounter, and if your boss is the person who has found the problem it is likely she will try to impose a solution on you, even if it is not the best one for the situation. Some bosses may be wise enough to understand that, as the game's designer, you know how best to fix the problem. Nonetheless, getting advice from someone who is signing your paycheck cannot be the same as advice from someone who is in a less dominant position.

The second class of people ill-suited to testing your game is anyone from the marketing department. Marketing people have too many conflicting agendas when looking at your game and are unlikely to tell you what they actually think of it. Instead, they will attempt to figure out what the "target demographic" wants. As I have mentioned repeatedly in this book, it is extremely hard to anticipate what an audience other than yourself will like or dislike, yet this is what marketing people attempt to do. You do not want their second-guessing, which when it comes to gameplay is wrong as often as it is right, to muddle up your game.

A third group of people who should not test your game consists of people who are too close to you personally, be they your close friends from way back, your family, or your significant other. When these people look at your game, though they may claim they are being objective, their true agenda is often to strengthen their relationship with you. As a result they will be hesitant to criticize your game too harshly. Some friends may understand that the best way they can strengthen their friendship with you is to tell you the truth, but many will sugarcoat their opinions in a feeble attempt to make you like them more. It is true that many authors use their spouses as their first and most effective line of criticism, and if you can develop a relationship that is that honest it can be a wonderful thing. But the fact remains that many relationships are not that honest.

The fourth type of people that you do not want to have testing your game is idiots. Idiots tend to say idiotic things and have idiotic opinions, and as a result will not be of much help to you. It is best to notice and isolate idiots as soon as possible and, if you must work with them, learn to ignore everything they say. Of course, I am exaggerating; idiots certainly do not dominate testing teams. But every so often you will come across a tester whom you are better off ignoring completely.

The fifth group is testers who think that they are designing your game for you. These testers may have some useful suggestions, but mostly will try to get you to change aspects of your game not because they are wrong but simply because they would have done it differently. A truly good tester will recognize that you are the driving artistic force behind the project and that the game will reflect your individual preferences. They will suggest ways to strengthen the game, instead of ways to simply change it.

A sixth group to be wary of are extremely hard-core fans, particularly those who are fanatical about your game's genre or, in the case of a sequel, the previous version of the game. These testers will tend to see every difference in your game from other games in the same genre as being a serious design flaw and will, as a result, stifle whatever creativity you may try to incorporate in your new game. Appealing to the established fans of your franchise can be quite important for sequels, yet following every bit of their advice may result in a game that is not sufficiently different from its predecessors.

When to Test

When is the right time to start playtesting your game? As I have discussed earlier in this chapter, playtesting can be a key part of your game's development cycle from as soon as you get your game playable until it is finally released. That said, there are specific times when particular types of testing are best applied, and other times when certain types of testing may be ineffective or even pointless. Knowing when to use each type of tester is key to not wasting your testers' time.

Of course, your development team should be playing the game as much as possible through all the phases of its development. As I have mentioned, this is essential to keep them interested in the project and to enable them to do the best work possible. Assuming the game is not falling apart, a developer who knows exactly how he is contributing to the project and how that project is turning out will be better informed and motivated to do his best work possible.

Early playtesting is best done by people experienced in game development, whom you know very well, and whose opinions you hold in high regard. Early playtesting requires that the tester overlook many problems: the game crashes frequently, all of the art is place-holder, sections of the game are obviously incomplete, there is only one level to play, and so forth. Many people, when given such a game, will be unable to look beyond these extreme shortcomings. For instance, traditional testers, even if you tell them to ignore the large sections of the game that are missing, will most likely start pointing out the completely obvious bugs that need fixing. On the other hand, a friend who is also a game designer will be able to look at the work and see beyond its current shortcomings, seeing instead if the game shows promise. These designers have seen their own projects in the state yours is currently in, and understand why not everything works yet. These experienced professionals will be able to recognize and explain fundamental problems your game design contains better than anyone else.

It makes good sense to establish a small group of people whose opinions you trust and whom you can show your game to at various stages of development. These may be fellow game designers, as discussed above, or friends who understand the game development process and will be able to provide you with useful feedback. Over the course of the project, you may want to keep showing your game to this trusted group, so they can see how the game is progressing and give you their opinions on whether they like where the game is going and if they think that direction is the best one possible. Since these testers will work with you over the course of the project, they will have a better understanding of the game and why it has developed as it has.

As you are implementing the GUI and the controls, it will make sense to bring in some first-impression testers to experiment with these new controls. Set up a simple test level, area, or situation where the player can attempt to use the controls and GUI, and see how well these testers fare. This makes sense since the most important aspect of interface and control design is that these systems are as intuitive as possible, and the best way to determine that is by having some first-time players try them out. It should not take very long to determine if your I/O systems are intuitive, since if the player does not figure them out immediately, you will know your game needs work.

As the game becomes more complete, when a majority of the features are complete and a large section of the game is playable, it makes sense to bring in the traditional testers to go over the work. This period is typically called "alpha," though this definition varies from company to company. When they first start testing, the traditional testers will find a seemingly endless number of bugs in the code, as they try all manner of actions that the development team had never anticipated, but you should encourage them to look beyond the bugs and give you feedback about the gameplay itself if they can. Of course, getting feedback at this early stage is much better than in "beta" when, if the project is on a tight schedule, the focus will be less on refining the game and more on getting it out the door. At some point, you stop being able to make fundamental changes to the gameplay for fear it will break the game in some major way. As a result, you will need to make large-scale alterations while there is still plenty of time to track down all the bugs they may cause.

On projects with tight deadlines and "must ship by Christmas" edicts, management sometimes likes to think that they can speed up development by bringing in testers early, sometimes long before the game has even reached alpha. This way, they erroneously think, once the game finally gets to beta it will already have had most of its bugs removed and can be shipped immediately. Of course, what they fail to understand is that, before a game is "feature complete," it is likely to change fundamentally from a code point of view. As that code changes in major ways, old bugs are eliminated completely while new ones are introduced. If the testers point out bugs in old code and the programmers have to spend time fixing them, this is essentially wasted time since those bugs would have been eliminated completely later when chunks of the code were rewritten, and you are still left with the new bugs that the restructuring of the code will bring about.

To some extent, the same holds true for gameplay. When large parts of the game are missing, having testers report problems like "Levels 10, 12, and 17 have no enemies to fight and are therefore not much fun to play" is far from useful. Forcing designers to go through these meaningless bugs will waste far more time than it may save. It makes the most sense to bring in the traditional testers only when the game is in a state that is truly appropriate for testing. In the end, bringing them in too early will only delay the game's progress.

How to Test

How you have your playtesters work on your game is as important as who you have testing and when you have them do it. Game designers will often ruin the effectiveness of their playtesters by making a number of fundamental errors in how they interact with the testers. These are all problems that can be easily avoided, as long as the designer is conscious of the way he deals with his testers and what he does and does not tell them.

The most important part of interacting with playtesters is to actually spend most of your time watching them play instead of telling them how to play. Let them play the game their own way and see how they fare. The temptation to correct the playtester's actions is great and can be hard to resist. By the time the traditional playtesters start on the game, the designer has already played the game so much that she is intimately familiar with what the player is "supposed" to do in a given situation and how the game is "supposed" to be played in general. When watching over the shoulder of a playtester for the first time, the temptation is to say, "Go over there next," or "You want to use the strafe buttons for that," or "Why don't you try to get the power-foozle?" Watching someone stumble while playing a game the designer is intimately familiar with can quickly turn her into a teacher.

But the point of the playtesting is to see how the player will actually play the game without the game's designer coaching his every move. Certainly, the designer cannot fit in the box the game comes in or even be downloaded over the Internet. A certain amount of stumbling about and learning the controls is to be expected, and the best way to playtest is to let the testers do this initial exploration on their own. And if the player truly does get stuck or if he never seems to be able to master the controls, the designer needs to ask herself what is causing these problems. Is the game too hard or too confusing? How can it be made simpler so that the player has a fair chance of understanding it and learning how to play? These are the lessons a designer is supposed to take away from playtesting, but they are lessons which the designer is never going to learn if she corrects the tester's playing at every step.

While watching the testers play, the designer should try to observe the way in which they try to play the game. Players may not try the approach or solution the designer had thought of to a particular situation. The designer must then ask, does the game support what the tester is trying to do, and if not, could it and should it? The testing period is a time when the designer can add a breadth of content to the game that will allow the game to truly be accepting of multiple playing styles. Up until this point, the people playing the game have been limited to the development team and whatever preliminary testers may have been brought in. Now that there is a broader range of people playing the game, the designer will likely observe a broader range of playing styles than he had anticipated. The testing period is when the designer can make the game accepting of these playing styles, allowing players to truly play the game their own way on their own terms.

Of course, the designer cannot be present for all of the playtesting the game will undergo, not if the game is going to be thoroughly tested and released in a reasonable time frame. Often you will need to rely on what the testers report to you about their playing experiences. Though not as useful as watching the testers play first hand, this information can nonetheless be quite helpful. When you do get this feedback, it is crucial to truly listen to what the testers tell you. This may seem obvious, but it is surprising how many designers prefer to ignore the feedback they get on their game. Often most of a game's testing, particularly that done by traditional testers, takes place late in the development process, after a good deal of work has gone into the project. At this point the designer is probably fairly confident that the game is working as he wants it to work. Therefore, it can be difficult for the designer to hear testers contradict this, perhaps pointing out fundamental problems in the game that the designer has overlooked for months of development.

The designer's first defense is often to claim that the testers do not know what they are talking about. Excuses can range from the tester being a fool to the tester not being the target audience for the game to the tester just complaining for the sake of it. Granted, often testers do make suggestions for changes to the gameplay that are best avoided, and if only one tester out of ten suggests that a certain piece of gameplay needs to be changed it may be because of that tester's personal preference. But when the designer hears the same complaint from a number of different testers, he needs to realize that there probably is something wrong with the game that needs to be addressed. The designer must avoid dismissing the complaints of testers and to honestly look at each complaint they make to see if it has any merit. It is amazing the number of designers who will resist any and all suggestions the testers make. Often, these same designers come to regret their obstinacy later when the game is finally released, only to have players and members of the press complain about the same issues the testers had complained about earlier. Of course, once the game is released, it is too late to do anything about the problems.

Guided and Unguided Testing

One can divide the kind of testing being done on the project into two distinct classes: guided and unguided. Guided testing customarily happens earlier in the project, when the game is not yet completely functional. In that period, the designer knows what portions of the game are clearly incomplete, but wants to get some feedback on a section of the game he thinks is working fairly well. Then the designer may direct the testers to try a particular level or section of gameplay. Directed testing may also occur later in the project, when the entire game is functioning, but a particular section has just been changed or reworked. At this point the designer may need feedback on just that section, to see if the changes made fix an existing problem or break the game in some major way.

It is essential to allow and encourage your testers to do unguided testing as well. Give them the game, tell them to start playing it, observe what they do, and listen to their feedback. Many designers will often make the mistake of using only guided testing, usually having the testers test only the system on which they are currently working. When the testers bring up complaints about some other portion of the game, the designer will complain that he is not interested in working on that now, or that the problematic part of the game is already "done." Directed testing has its place, but if it is all the designer ever does, then he is likely to miss larger problems in the game that he may not have even realized were problematic. Undirected testing gives the designer feedback about the game holistically, something that is essential to resolving all of its problems.

Of course, even when you do direct your testers to test only a certain section of your game, often they will not be able to resist pointing out the other problems they see along the way. It takes an extremely disciplined tester to truly test only the system that the designer requests. Getting feedback on parts of the game that you are not currently working on may be frustrating but can be useful in the long run. When testers give you off-topic suggestions about how to improve the game, even if you do not want to address those issues immediately, be careful to take note of them to come back to later. Nothing is more frustrating than recognizing a problem in the game after it has shipped, only to realize that one of your testers had told you about the problem in plenty of time to fix it.

Balancing

The only time you can properly balance a game is when most of the game is done. Balancing your game ahead of time, before all of the gameplay is working and all the levels, if any, are made, can only be considered to be preliminary balancing. You cannot truly get a sense for how the entire game needs to function and how the difficulty must escalate over the course of the entire game until the game's content is complete. You can view your game as a collection of different systems that make up one large system. For a level-based game, each level can be considered to be a system in itself. Then, within each level, each combat encounter or puzzle can be considered to be a system itself. In order for the game to be balanced, all of these systems must be in place, since changing one system impacts how the other systems must be set up in order to achieve the overall balance you are seeking.

The time at which the game is largely complete and true balancing becomes possible usually coincides with the time when the game is in full-on testing. This works out for the best, since balancing and testing are closely intertwined activities. Balancing often involves changing some settings in the game and then playing it to see if those changes create the amount of challenge you are interested in. For each pass on the balancing, both you and the playtesters should try to play the game. Then the testers can give you feedback about just how effective your efforts to balance the game have been and, combined with your own analysis of the game's condition, you can make more changes and iterate through the process again. People who can successfully balance a game by themselves, without the input of other playtesters, are rare. Often designers who attempt to balance a game by themselves succeed in balancing the game only for themselves, usually resulting in the game being too hard.

The best way to balance the game is to break down different systems into groups of numbers that can be easily adjusted and tweaked. For instance, suppose you were making a melee combat action game of some sort. If the player uses a baseball bat in the game, that bat will have a number of different attributes associated with it, such as how much damage it does, how fast it attacks, how many times it can be used before it breaks, how much it costs to buy, how many hands are required to hold it, and so forth. Similarly, one can also break down enemy, player, and other system attributes into collections of numbers which can then be adjusted to vary the usefulness or challenge of that object. It is these values that you will continually adjust and massage in order to achieve the balance you are seeking.

As you are balancing, you must be keenly aware of how the different values you change affect each other. You may change one weapon in order to make one combat situation a lot of fun but end up making another location in the game actually unbeatable. The more complex your game, the more impact the changes you make may have on systems you might overlook. As you are balancing you must fully consider every part of the game that your changes are affecting and make sure you do not break the game. The only way to be truly sure you have not thrown off the entire game is by testing it thoroughly. As a result, making significant changes close to your ship date is a nerve-racking experience. What if the changes you make break something that no one catches before the game is sent to the duplicator?

Of course, the method for balancing I have described above necessitates that the data which affects the behavior of the game's different entities be accessible and modifiable by the designer. This means that the code needs to be written in such a way that makes changing this information easy. This last point may seem obvious, but I have seen many engines in which changing information such as weapon statistics was far from easy to outright impossible. From the very beginning of the game's development, the programmers must keep in mind how the designers will go about balancing the game at the end of the project. If, instead, they bury a collection of "magic numbers" in the code, the game will become "locked" in a particular state, making balancing it impossible. Though balancing can only take place once the game is largely complete, the programming team must start preparing for that balancing from the very beginning of the project or effective balancing will be impossible. If the designer is to have any chance of balancing the game well, this balancing information must be broken out of the code through configuration files, level editing tools, or other designer-accessible formats.

Your Game is Too Hard

While balancing your game you should keep one rule of thumb in mind at all times: your game is too hard. Regardless of the type of game you are making or how talented your development team may be, by the time your game nears completion and enters testing it will be too hard. This is usually because, up to this point, only the development team has been playing the game consistently. The development team has been working on the project anywhere from nine to eighteen months and during that time they have honed their gameplaying skills and have become quite good at the game, probably better than 90 percent of the players who will ever play the game. In order to keep the gameplay interesting for themselves, the development team has made the game somewhat challenging for themselves to play, which in turn means it will be too hard for 90 percent of the players out there.

The first comment testers will often make is, "This game is too hard." As I discussed above, your first reaction will be to ignore this complaint, to chalk it up to their incompetence or inexperience with the game. "They'll get better," you may say. And, unfortunately, that is true. If the game spends three months in testing, the testers will be just as good at the game as the rest of the development team. Then they too will probably stop thinking that the game is hard. It is entirely likely that the game will ship with the development team, including the testers, having no clue just how difficult it is.

As a designer you must be very careful to maintain an honest sense of how hard your game is, and during the balancing phase you must concentrate on making the game something that a first-time player will have a reasonable chance of succeeding at when he first starts playing. Always remember what the first impression of the testers was, and ask yourself if you have addressed the problems they immediately identified. If necessary, you should bring in new first-impression testers to see if the game is still too difficult.

Unfortunately, sometimes you may not always be able to make your game easier through balancing alone. You may have created a game design which, on a fundamental level, is hard to play. If you truly want your game to be something first-time players have an easy time getting into, you need to concentrate on this from the very beginning of your game design. My project *Centipede 3D* is a good example of how a game can become far more difficult than the development team ever anticipated. Attempts were made to balance the game to make it easier, but the gameplay was intrinsically designed to match that of the original arcade game. As a direct result, *Centipede 3D* did everything it could to make the player's game short and fast paced. Unfortunately, players of home games want their games to last a little longer than what they get for twenty-five cents at the arcade. As hard as the game was in its shipping version, it is chilling to think that before it went into the balancing phase the game was easily ten times as hard.

When designer Jason Jones was balancing the *Marathon* games, he had an interesting technique for making sure the game was not too hard. If he and other members of the development team could play through the entire game on its hardest setting using only the game's "fist" weapon, he figured that the game would be reasonably challenging for other players. Of course, other players get weapons far more powerful and easy to use than the fist, and they do not have to play it on the hardest difficulty setting. Jones handicapped himself in order to see how hard the game would be to a normal player. Techniques like this are smart to use. If the designer can win the game with both arms tied behind his back, other players will probably have a fair chance of playing it through with both arms at their disposal.

The *Marathon* games were tested for difficulty by forcing the development team to play through the game on the hardest difficulty setting using only the weakest weapon, the fist. Pictured here: *Marathon 2*.

In the end, balancing your game is often more of a "gut feeling" than anything else. Though you may always be able to assume that your game is too hard, there are not many other rules you can follow to balance your game. You need to be able to see your game holistically, to understand how players who have much less experience with the title than you will play it, and to realize what will challenge them without being unfair or even sadistic. Knowing how to balance a game is a skill that comes with experience, both from playing other games and from designing your own. In order to become truly skilled at balancing, you must do both as much as possible.

The Artistic Vision

I have mentioned at various points throughout this book the evil that is known as the focus group. It is important to understand the distinction between playtesting and a focus group. Focus groups are customarily a group of "off the street" people who are given a one- or two-hour presentation, often on a series of different games. Many times they are not allowed to play the games, as often the games have not even been developed yet. They hear about game concepts and, based on the descriptions, are asked whether they would be interested in buying such a game or not. Playtesters, on the other hand, are people whom members of the development team know or whom they at least have a chance to get to know. Knowing a person is crucial to understanding how seriously you should take their opinion. Furthermore, playtesters get to play the games in question, while focus group members often do not. As a result of these key differences, focus groups tend to be antithetical to the creation of original, creative games and encourage the development of safe, uninnovative games. One can only imagine how the focus group for games like *Pac-Man*, *Tetris*, or *Civilization* would go. We know from the interview with Will Wright in Chapter 22 that the focus group for *The Sims* went so poorly that the game was nearly canceled. It should be telling that focus groups are run by the marketing department, while playtesting is handled by the development team. One group's primary interest lies in making money for the company in the simplest way possible, while the second, it is hoped, is interested in producing compelling and stimulating games. Of course, the two motives need not necessarily be at odds, but

When released, *Tetris* was an extremely unique game. Chances are, an early focus group for the game would have gone terribly. Pictured here: classic mode in *The Next Tetris*.

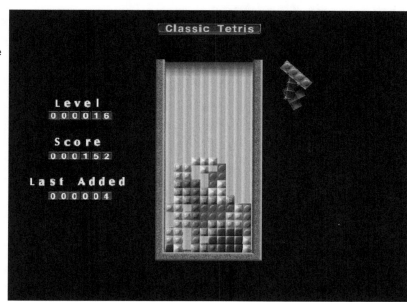

when one aims primarily for the former instead of the latter, one is likely to end up with neither.

As you are testing, it is important to remember that you cannot please everyone. Given a large enough testing team, there are bound to be people who do not like portions of your game, or even who do not like the entire game. If you start trying to make every single person on the testing team happy you often end up making the game less fun for other people. While you may have started with a game that a bunch of people liked a great deal and a few people thought was dull, if you start trying to please everyone you may end up with a game that everyone thinks is OK, but which no one is truly enthusiastic about. Given the choice, I always prefer to give a certain group of people an experience they truly love than try to give everyone something they like only marginally.

Testing should also not mean game design by committee. You do not have to take every suggestion that your development team presents and implement it. Some of these ideas may be perfectly reasonable but you may feel that they just do not fit with your game. That is a perfectly reasonable response to have. In the end, it may be that every single playtester you have tells you that some part of the game must change, but if you feel, in your gut, as an artist, that you do not want to change that portion of the game, then leave it as it is. In the end you must be the final arbiter of what happens in the game. A committee, whether it consists of executives, testers, or even members of the development team, can never have the unity of vision and certainty of purpose that can be maintained by a single person.

Conclusion

As I stated in the introduction, this book is not a definitive guide to computer game design. No book can be. But it has attempted to inform the reader of what I know about game design, in addition to sharing the thoughts of six of game design's most accomplished masters. Of course, none of the information in this book will amount to much if the reader is not prepared to use it to the right ends. As with any art form, computer games demand that their authors have a personal investment in their creations if the games are to be truly worthwhile. I feel that computer games have a great power to affect their audience, and a game designer has a tremendous responsibility to use that power wisely.

Art

The game development industry seems to be constantly involving itself with discussions of whether computer games qualify as an art form. Some other discussions center around whether computer games will ever be "legitimate" art. Such arguments are completely fruitless. We cannot make the public see us as legitimate merely by tooting our own horn and bragging of our accomplishments. Some people still fail to see film or jazz music or comic books as "legitimate" art and those forms have a body of work which, due in part to their age, dwarfs what computer games have produced. The question must be asked, "Would you do anything differently if computer games were or were not art?" Surely the best way to convince the public that we are legitimate is to act like it by producing works as compelling as those found in any other media.

Of course computer games are art. Could anything be more obvious? This is especially true if one uses the definition of art that I am most fond of, from Scott McCloud's magnificent book *Understanding Comics*: "Art, as I see it, is any human activity which doesn't grow out of either of our species' two basic instincts: survival and reproduction." It would appear that many game developers who constantly scream "games are art" have a certain insecurity complex and feel the need to justify working in games to their family or friends, to the public as a whole, or even to themselves. Such insecurities seldom lead to an artist working at his full capacity, since he is constantly going out of his way to prove himself. This seldom leads to great work; more often it leads to pretentious trash. When asked if he agreed with critics who said his films qualified as art, Alfred Hitchcock replied, "Oh, I'm very glad when they do, but it's not like taking page one of a script and then saying, 'I will now start a work of art.' It's ridiculous—you can't do it." Quality games are most likely produced when those developing them have no motives other than creating the most compelling experience for the player.

The Medium

So often, we in the game development community are envious of other media. In part, this may be game designers wishing for the respect that other media command in society, the "legitimacy" that I spoke of earlier. Others may secretly, subconsciously, or even openly wish they were working on something other than games. A game designer may say, "I want my game to have a similar effect on the audience as the movie *The Godfather*!" or "I want people to enjoy playing this game the same way they enjoy listening to The Jimi Hendrix Experience's *Electric Ladyland*!" But this is the wrong approach to take. The strength of our medium lies in what it does differently from other media and the emotions it can evoke in the audience that no other art form can. If we endlessly try to ape other media we will forever be stuck with second-class, derivative works. Surely Jimi Hendrix did not try to emulate a movie he had seen when he recorded *Electric Ladyland*. Similarly, Francis Ford Coppola knew he would have to radically alter Mario Puzo's book *The Godfather* in order to make a good movie out of it. Indeed, Coppola's mastery of film allowed him to create a movie significantly better than the book upon which it is based. Both have nearly the same story, characters, and even dialog, yet Coppola's telling of the story cinematically outdid Puzo's literary telling in nearly every way. Though the effect a game has on a player may be different than a book has on a reader, a film has on a viewer, or a song has on a listener, it is not necessarily a worse effect, merely a different one. Computer games have strengths of their own which we must master if we are to produce the best work possible. Surely our medium presents challenges for those who choose to work with it, challenges not to be found in other art forms, challenges we have a duty to face if we hope to be more than charlatans and conmen.

In his book *Understanding Media*, Marshall McLuhan is famous for saying, "...the medium is the message. This is merely to say that the personal and social consequences of any medium—that is, of any extension of ourselves—results from the new scale that is introduced into our affairs by each extension of ourselves, or by any new technology." McLuhan argues that while people concern themselves with the content of television shows or plays or music, a medium's true message comes not from the content but from the medium itself. Now, I certainly do not claim to be a McLuhan scholar, yet I cannot help postulating what the nature of our medium of computer games is, a medium which did not exist when McLuhan wrote those words. The inherently interactive nature of computer games creates a mass medium that encourages players to be active participants in art in ways other media cannot. I cannot help but conclude that the fundamental message of our medium is one of participation and empowerment.

Game designers make a product which either facilitates the interaction between others, in the case of multi-player games, or sets up an interaction between a single person and the computer, for solo games. In the latter case, it is somewhat incorrect to say that the true interaction takes place between the person and computer, since the computer is nothing more than a medium for the interaction; the interaction actually takes place between the player and the game's creator. When I spent weeks of my early life alone in the dark computer room in the back of my parents' house playing *The Bard's Tale* and *The Bard's Tale II*, I never thought of myself as being alone. In a way I was there with Michael Cranford, the games' creator, playing in the world he had made, exploring the piece of himself he had put into the game. This medium seemed so powerful I knew immediately that I wanted to work with it to create my own games, so I could put a part of myself in games for players to experience.

The Motive

I have talked at length in this book about why players play games, but perhaps the most important question you as a game developer should ask is why you make them. The film director Krzysztof Kieslowski said that no artist has a chance of understanding his work if he does not understand himself and his own life, and what events have brought him to where he is. As you embark on your life as a game designer, questioning your own motivations in your work is vital to effectively using your medium.

The first question a designer should ask himself is how he came to work in computer games. Was it happenstance? Did a friend in the business happen to know of a position that was open? Was he aimlessly searching the classifieds only to find an ad about game development to which he responded, "Hey, that might be fun"? Did he see game development as something cool to do, much hipper than his sorry friends who have to shuffle papers for a living? Did he really want to work in some other field, such as film or television, and when that career did not work out as planned he found that he could earn a living in the gaming business in order to pay the bills until something better came along? Or did gaming just turn out to be the profession which, given his skill set, would pay the most money?

As the reader might guess, none of the above are among the best motivations for working in games. There are people who come to gaming with more pure motivations, people who pursue it because it is what they want to do more than anything else. Of course, a designer might come into the world of game development with the wrong motivations only to find a passion for creating games stirred inside himself. Regardless of why he started working in games, what is essential is that now that he is developing games, he wants to truly make the best games possible.

I am continually surprised and disappointed by the number of people working in games for all the wrong reasons: because it is cool, because it pays well, because they do not have anything better to do. Game development may be more fun, stylish, and potentially profitable than many other professions, but these are side benefits that cannot distract from the true goal a designer must have: to make compelling interactive experiences. When other motives become a designer's primary guiding directives, her work is hopelessly compromised in a way that will hinder it from achieving its full potential.

The most likely person to make really brilliant games is a game designer with a dream. A dream that involves advancing the art of games beyond the more puerile and trivial concerns it may be seen wallowing in from time to time. A dream that involves a game-world so compelling players lose track of their regular lives as they play it. A dream which involves creating a work that captivates and involves players in the art as no other media can. A dream of computer games that enrich their players' lives for the better. Do you have such a dream?

Appendix

Sample Design Document: Atomic Sam

The following design document is for a simple console action game called *Atomic Sam*. The game itself is far from revolutionary and, from a design standpoint, part of its appeal is its simple nature. It is part of a project I was previously involved with that was never developed into a finished game. Despite this, the reader can consider the document to be "authentic," since it is written in the exact style and format I have used in design documents for projects which have been developed.

As a result of its simplicity, the design document for *Atomic Sam* is not very large. I have written documents five times the length of this one for other projects, and even those documents were not as big as others in the industry. Parts of this document were deliberately kept short, since it was not intended to be a complete design document, but rather to give its reader an idea of what *Atomic Sam* would be. In particular, certain sections have deliberately been kept short. For instance, the listing of enemy robots is much smaller than it would be if the document actually described all of the enemies in the game. Similarly, a full version of this design document would include descriptions of more projectiles for Sam to throw, more devices and contraptions for him to manipulate, and more of the characters he would meet in the game-world. The game might even be expanded to include more areas than just the five described here.

In fact, more detail could be used throughout the document. The way this document is written assumes that the author is going to be involved throughout the development process, guiding the design in the correct direction. As I have stated elsewhere in this book, as a game designer I am only interested in being involved with projects that I can see through from beginning to end. If this document were for a project that the author did not expect to be actively working on, it would make sense to add more detail throughout in order to be completely clear about the direction the project should take.

For example, the section about level design could be significantly more detailed. However, if one has a team of level designers who understand the gameplay and can be trusted with the responsibilities of designing a fun level, the descriptions contained in the document could be a sufficient starting point for level design. From this document, the level designers are given a great deal of freedom in terms of how to build their levels, a system that works well if the level designers are up to the challenge. Certainly, if you will be designing many of the levels yourself, you do not need to plan everything out in minute detail in advance. Many successful games have been made this way, including a number of the projects I have worked on. For instance, *Centipede 3D* had only a general notion of the AI, mushroom types, and power-ups designed before the level construction process began, and it was a system that ended up working quite well.

Of course, before writing a design document, the designer should have a good idea of the focus of the gameplay, as I have discussed elsewhere in this book. Here, for example, is the focus statement I had in mind when I started working on the design document for *Atomic Sam*.

Atomic Sam: Focus

Atomic Sam is a non-violent, fast-paced action game whose gameplay centers on defeating various villainous robots in creative and inventive ways, using a variety of projectiles and environmental devices. The story is one of a young boy separated from his parents for the first time who learns about the world through mentors, friends, and new experiences. Atomic Sam takes place in a unique "retro-future" with whimsical, non-sensical devices providing a unique backdrop to the unfolding of the story and action.

Armed with the direction provided by the focus, the game design grew organically from there into the design you will read below. As I have stated before, there is no set-in-stone format for design documents. It is the designer's responsibility to present the design in as much detail as is necessary, in a manner which clearly communicates that design to all the members of the team.

Atomic Sam

Design Document

Version 2.0

This document and Atomic Sam are TM and © 2000 Richard Rouse III, all rights reserved.
Atomic Sam character designed by Richard Rouse III and Steve Ogden

Table of Contents

I. Overview

Atomic Sam is an action game with a strong storytelling component. In it the player controls Sam, a young boy separated from his parents, who must battle his way through hostile environments and defeat the robots that try to prevent him from finding out what happened to his mother and father. The game is one of quick reactions and clever planning in a whimsical futuristic world, a setting which will appeal not only to children but to game players of all ages who enjoy fast-action gameplay. The game is suitable for any modern console system.

The player's main task in *Atomic Sam* will be to navigate young Sam through the various environments of the game while defeating the robots he encounters. Though the game is centered around this combat, it is a non-violent game from start to finish, with Sam incapacitating but not destroying the robots that try to stop him. Whenever Sam is defeated, he is always stunned or trapped, never actually killed. The whimsical and optimistic nature of *Atomic Sam* requires that the game not play up any sort of gore-factor and that violence be kept to an absolute minimum.

The game will reward the player's creativity by setting up situations where the player can use environmental objects to defeat the robots that come after him. Rube Goldberg-esque contraptions will be everywhere, providing whimsical ways for Sam to incapacitate the many mechanized adversaries he will face. Figuring out what to do in different situations will be just as important as quick reactions and manual dexterity.

Atomic Sam is easy to pick up and play with simple, intuitive controls. An in-game tutorial section at the beginning of the game will provide an easy way for new, inexperienced players to learn how to play the game. In each of the middle three sections of the game, Sam will be accompanied by special friends who will help him defeat the enemies he faces. All the while, these friends will tell Sam interesting stories about this world of the future.

The setting of *Atomic Sam* is in the Earth of the future, but not exactly the future as we imagine it now. This is the future as foretold in the first half of the twentieth century, a world where all of the optimistic predictions about how technology would change our lives have come true. Atomic energy has created a pleasant, trouble-free world, with robots answering to humans' every beck and call and mankind the happiest it has ever been. Yet, key advances from the latter half of the twentieth century are notably absent in this world. For instance, jet-propelled airplanes have not been popularized, and as a result citizens travel on giant propeller craft and zeppelins from one mammoth metropolis to another. Similarly, no one has ever heard of a compact disc, microwave, personal computer, or video game.

The game's story starts with Sam returning from school only to find his parents strangely missing. Setting out to find them at their office using the rocket-pack they gave him, Sam finds himself attacked by menacing robots along the way. Finding his parents not at their office either, Sam meets up with the mysterious Electric Priestess. She sends Sam to look for his parents in the underwater city of Benthos, the robot city called Harmony, and all the way to the Moon colony named New Boston. On the way, Sam gathers evidence and discovers that Max Zeffir, one of the world's richest men and also his parents' boss, had them kidnapped when they learned something they shouldn't have. Sam then goes to confront Zeffir in his giant propeller-driven and atomic-powered airship the Ikairus. Finally, Sam defeats him and is happily reunited with his parents.

Because of its whimsical nature and youthful protagonist, the most obvious appeal of *Atomic Sam* might appear to be to a young demographic. Parents will certainly be pleased that the game has the player capturing enemies rather than killing them, and that when the player loses in a particular situation, Sam is always incapacitated in some non-lethal manner. But due to its sharp, frantic gameplay, assortment of unique environments, and inventive adversaries, the game will also appeal to young adults. And with *Atomic Sam*'s retro-futuristic look and emphasis on story line, the game will also appeal to older players, those who may well remember how differently we thought of the future fifty years ago.

II. Game Mechanics

Overview

Atomic Sam is a third-person, floating camera 3D action game in the tradition of *Super Mario 64* or *Spyro the Dragon*. *Atomic Sam* is different, however, in that the gameplay focuses less on exploration but instead on the player battling his way through the levels, avoiding the robots and other adversaries that try to block his progress. That being the case, the game mechanics are designed in such a way as to allow the player intuitive and extensive control of his game-world character while enabling the player to appreciate the interesting and compelling game-world in which he is placed.

Camera

In the game, the player will control the character Atomic Sam. At all times, Sam appears in the center of the screen, with a "floating" camera above and behind the character, in an "over the shoulder" type of view. The camera will be at such a distance that the player has a reasonable view of Sam and his current environment. The camera will be "smart" enough to avoid penetrating objects in the world and will always give the player a clear view of Sam. If necessary, in tight situations, the camera will zoom up closer to Sam. If Sam is too large on the screen and prevents the player from viewing the world adequately, Sam will appear translucent to the player, thus giving the player a clear view of the world. This translucency is apparent only to the player, and has no effect on the game-world or how the enemies react to Sam.

The camera will try to stay behind Sam as much as possible while providing a smooth visual experience for the player. If Sam turns around in a hurry, the camera will slowly catch up with his new direction instead of suddenly jerking into the new position. If the player changes Sam's direction for only a brief period of time before returning to the original position, the camera's orientation will not change at all. This allows the player to make minor adjustments to Sam's positions without having the camera swinging around wildly.

In-Game GUI

The majority of the player's screen will be taken up by a view of the game-world with the player's character, Atomic Sam, near the center of that screen. A few other elements will be overlaid on top of this view in order to provide the player with information about Sam's status and goings on in the game-world.

- **Current Projectile + Count:** In the lower left corner will be displayed an iconic representation of Sam's currently readied projectile. Next to this will be a series of "chits" or "ticks" representing how many of that projectile Sam has in his inventory. More information about the projectiles used in the game can be found in the Projectiles description below and the Game Elements section.

- **Selecting the Current Projectile:** When the player presses and holds the Next Projectile button, the player will see a horizontal display of the projectiles in Sam's inventory along the top of the screen. The player can then scroll through this list and select the object he wants Sam to ready. The weapons will be represented as icons. Once the player releases the Next Projectile button, this display will disappear.

- **Flight Time:** Sam's rocket-pack has a limited amount of flight time. This will be represented by a horizontal bar next to an iconic picture of Sam's rocket-pack in the lower right corner of the screen. The bar will appear full when Sam's rocket-pack is fully charged and will slowly go down the longer Sam stays airborne. For more information about the rocket-pack and its functionality, see the Flying Movement section below.

- **Current Dialog:** Different people will talk to Sam during gameplay; the friends Sam has accompanying him on his adventures, the Electric Priestess via the radio she gave him, and other characters Sam encounters may all say things to Sam. All of this dialog will be prerecorded and played back to the player. In addition, however, in the upper left-hand corner of the screen a 2D cartoon representation of the character will appear with the text appearing next to it. This will be important for players playing with the sound off or who did not manage to hear the dialog as it was spoken. This GUI element will disappear a reasonable period of time after it appears, allowing enough time for the player to read the text. When the game is in a non-interactive cut-scene, however, the dialog will appear at the middle of the bottom of the screen, as it would in a subtitled movie.

Replaying and Saving

The player has no "lives" in *Atomic Sam*. When Sam is incapacitated by one of the robots or another adversary (always in a relatively non-violent way), the player is able to go back to the last checkpoint and play that section again as many times as he wants until he passes it. Checkpoints are scattered throughout the levels, and the game automatically and transparently remembers when the player has reached such a checkpoint. The checkpoints will be carefully placed so as to enhance the challenge of the game without making it frustrating for the player.

During the gameplay, the player will be able to save at any time. However, when the saved game is restored, it will only start the player back at the beginning of whatever level the game was saved on, instead of at the exact location (or checkpoint) Sam was at on that particular level. This encourages players to finish a given level before they stop playing the game.

Control Summary

The player will use a number of different controls to maneuver Atomic Sam and to navigate him through the game-world. These controls are discussed in detail below. First, however, is a summary of the different commands, which will give the reader an overview of Sam's capabilities. The controls are designed with modern console controllers in mind, and can be easily adapted for whichever system *Atomic Sam* is developed.

- **Up, Down, Left, Right (Analog Controller):** The player will use this control to maneuver Sam along the horizontal plane in the game-world. Utilizing its analog nature, if the player presses the control a little bit Sam will move slowly, while if he presses it all the way in a given direction Sam will move quickly in that direction.

- **Fly Up, Fly Down (Left and Right Back Triggers):** The player will use these controls to propel Sam vertically in the game-world.

- **Throw (Right-Pad Down Button):** This throws one of Sam's currently readied projectiles.

- **Next Projectile (Right-Pad Right Button):** The player uses this button to scroll through Sam's inventory of projectiles.

- **Action (Right-Pad Up Button):** The player uses this control to perform miscellaneous actions in the game-world, such as flipping a switch, talking to a character, or picking up a large object.

- **Look (Right-Pad Left Button):** The player uses this button to activate the camera-look functionality.

General Movement

While Sam is on the ground or in the air, the player can move Sam forward, backward, left, and right in the game-world. The player will control Sam's movement in these directions using the analog controller on the game-pad. Control is always relative to the camera's view of the world. Therefore, pressing forward or up on the controller will move Sam away from the camera while pressing backward will move Sam toward it. Similarly, pressing left or right will cause Sam to move in the corresponding direction in the game-world relative to the camera.

Moving in a Direction

When Sam starts moving in a direction, he will at first maintain his current facing before turning to move in the new direction. For instance, if Sam is facing away from the camera and the player presses to the left, then Sam will start side-stepping or side-flying in that direction. Only after the player holds that direction for a short period of time (approximately one second) will Sam then turn his whole body to face the new direction of movement. The same applies for moving backward from the current facing: at first Sam moves backward, and then after a second he will spin around 180 degrees and keep moving in this direction. This will allow Sam to reposition in small amounts in any direction without actually changing his facing.

Variable Movement Speed

Use of the console system's analog controller for movement in these directions will allow Sam to move either slowly or quickly in a given direction. If the player pushes the analog controller fully in a given direction, Sam will move in that direction at high speed. If the player presses it only a small amount in that direction, Sam will move much slower. This will give the player precise control over Sam's position in the world.

Flying Movement

Key to Sam's navigation of the game-world is the rocket-pack he wears on his back. The player has Fly Up and Fly Down buttons to control this rocket-pack, which allow Sam to move vertically in the game-world. Once in the air, Sam will hover at a given altitude if neither button is pressed.

Moving Up and Down

Sam will not move up and down at a constant speed. When the player presses up, at first Sam will move quickly, gaining speed the longer the player holds down the Fly Up button. This speed will eventually (after about a second of upward movement) reach a terminal velocity after which Sam will not gain any more speed. The downward movement functions in much the same way.

Stopping

When the player stops flying either up or down or in a given direction, Sam will not stop immediately, but instead will "coast" to a stop. Sam's animation when stopping

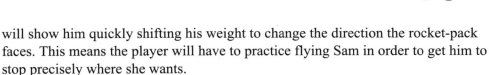

will show him quickly shifting his weight to change the direction the rocket-pack faces. This means the player will have to practice flying Sam in order to get him to stop precisely where she wants.

Flight Speed

Sam's pack is not an extremely fast device, providing a maximum speed approximately 1.5 times Sam's speed when he is jogging on the ground. Whenever the player maneuvers Sam to the ground Sam will return to a walking/jogging animation and will move at the slower speed associated with being on the ground.

Directional Flying

Sam can, of course, move forward, backward, left, or right while also moving vertically. The player can accomplish this simply by pressing the analog control in a direction while also pressing the Fly Up or Fly Down buttons. Sam will appear to pitch in the appropriate direction to correspond with his overall movement.

Burst Speed

The Fly Up and Fly Down buttons will both move Sam at the same maximum speed, but tapping either button twice quickly will result in a "burst" of speed in that direction, moving approximately 1.5 faster than the regular maximum speed for a short period. But moving at this high speed will also use up more of the rocket-pack's charge. This can be helpful for quickly dodging enemy attacks.

Limited Flight Time

The rocket-pack has a limited amount of flight time, however, though fortunately it can recharge simply through not being used. The rocket-pack's charge is used up whenever Sam is not standing on the ground, whether he is flying up, flying down, or just hovering. The amount of charge remaining in the rocket-pack will be represented by a small bar drawn on top of the game-world view in the lower right-hand corner of the screen, so the player will always be able to know when Sam's flight time is about to expire. The rocket-pack's charge will be decreased different amounts depending on how Sam is using his pack. The ratios of usage will be approximately as follows:

Usage	Charge Depletion
Flying Up	4
Flying Down	2
Hovering	1
Burst Up	6
Burst Down	6
On Ground	−3

Landing

Since the rocket-pack's charge is limited, the player must land Sam periodically in order to allow the pack to recharge. The player lands Sam simply by maneuvering him close to the ground or any flat surface he can stand on. Because Sam has a limited flight range, the player will have to plan Sam's movements accordingly in order to get Sam from one location to another. This will allow for puzzle elements in the levels where the player has to figure out how to navigate Sam to an area, given Sam's limited flying abilities. The "as the crow flies" route will often not be the route that Sam must take to reach a far-off platform.

Falling to the Ground

Having the rocket-pack run out of charge while Sam is in midair will not result in his death. Sam's outfit includes specially made shock-absorbing boots with extra thick soles which will allow Sam to land safely when falling from any height. But when his rocket-pack's charge runs out, Sam will plummet at a great speed, providing a very disorienting experience for the player when Sam falls from a great height.

Limited Altitude

The rocket-pack will also only be able to attain certain altitudes. If the player tries to fly Sam too high, the rocket-pack will start to sputter, indicating that Sam cannot fly any higher. Because of this limitation, the levels can have open skies without allowing the player to actually fly out of the levels.

Rocket-Pack Upgrades

Throughout the game, Sam will periodically find rocket-pack upgrades. These will either be attachments Sam can add on to his pack, or Sam may find game characters who will be able to tinker with Sam's pack in order to improve it. These changes will provide a variety of enhancements to Sam's flying ability.

- **Longer Flight Time:** Sam can fly for longer without having to land. This means Sam may have to acquire certain upgrades in order to reach certain locations.

- **Faster Burst Speed:** Sam can fly faster using the pack's "burst" functionality.

- **Faster Overall Speed:** The pack's maximum speed and acceleration are increased, allowing Sam to move vertically faster.

- **Improved Maneuverability:** The pack is better able to "stop on a dime." Instead of coasting to a stop, Sam can now stop as soon as the player lets go of the control stick.

Surfaces

Generally Sam can walk or land on any flat surface, whether it is the sidewalk or ground or a platform high in the air. Sam will be unable to land on surfaces that are significantly rounded or sloped. If Sam tries to walk up or land on a curved or sloped surface he will instead slide down the surface, stopping only when he reaches flat terrain.

There will be certain substances Sam will not be able to land or walk on. These include water, tar covered areas, or electrically charged floors. If the player navigates Sam onto such a surface while on foot, Sam will start an animation indicating the peril of the surface. For instance, if Sam comes up to an electrically charged floor, he will play an animation of starting to be shocked by the floor. If the player does not shift the direction of the controller to direct Sam out of the surface, Sam will quickly become incapacitated. Similarly, if the player tries to land Sam on such a surface while the rocket-pack still has charge remaining, Sam will start to be shocked, playing an animation early enough to indicate that the surface is perilous and to provide the player a chance to navigate him out of harm's way.

If the player runs out of charge while over such a surface, Sam will fall onto the surface and be incapacitated without any chance for the player to save him. Of course, whenever Sam becomes incapacitated, the player will have to start playing again from the last auto-save checkpoint. In order to succeed in the game, the player will need to avoid navigating Sam onto such surfaces and from letting the rocket-pack's charge run out while Sam is over such surfaces.

Picking Up Objects

Whenever Sam flies close to an object he can pick up, he will automatically pick it up if there is enough room in his inventory. The objects Sam can pick up include projectiles, rocket-pack enhancements, and the Electric Piranha. Sam will play an animation and a sound will be played to indicate that Sam has picked up the object.

Sam can also pick up certain larger objects but cannot add them to his inventory. Sam may need to move these objects for puzzles or may want to drop them on enemies to incapacitate them. The player can have Sam pick up these objects by pressing and holding the Action key while Sam is near them, and then can drop the object by releasing the Action key.

Throwing Projectiles

Key to dealing with the robotic adversaries Atomic Sam will face throughout the game are the different objects that Sam can find and throw. Though Sam will never find or use any sort of a gun, he will obtain different objects that can be hurled at enemies in order to incapacitate them.

Inventory

Sam will have a simple inventory which can hold up to fifty of each type of projectile. This is where projectiles Sam picks up will be automatically stored. The inventory is simple to use since the player cannot make room for another type of projectile by carrying fewer of another type of projectile. Sam cannot remove items from his inventory except by throwing them.

Picking Up Projectiles

In addition to starting the game with a small number of projectiles, Sam will find more projectiles throughout the game. Usually when Sam finds a projectile, he will find a group of them; for instance, ten Water Balloons or twenty Goo-Balls. Sam will automatically pick up these projectiles by maneuvering close to them. If Sam throws and misses with his projectiles, he may be able to retrieve them by going to where they landed, ideally after that particular encounter with enemies is over. In this way, players who are not very accurate at controlling Sam's throwing will get to retrieve their projectiles so they can try throwing them later.

Readying Projectiles

When a projectile is readied, the player will see Sam holding whatever his current projectile is, and an icon and counter in the lower right corner of the screen will reveal how many shots are left of that particular projectile. The readied projectile is the projectile that Sam is prepared to throw as soon as the player presses the Throw button.

The player will be able to select the "readied" projectile with the Next Projectile button. If the player quickly presses and releases this button, Sam will switch to the next available projectile in his inventory, if any. If the player presses and holds the Next Projectile button, the player will see a horizontal display of all the types of projectiles currently in Sam's inventory at the top of the screen, with the currently selected weapon appearing in the center. The player can then use the left and right directional controller to select previous and next projectiles, respectively, with the list of projectiles sliding left or right accordingly. The list will "wrap around" such that the player will be able to get to any projectile by pressing right or left repeatedly. Whatever projectile is in the center of the screen when the player releases the Next Projectile button will be Sam's new readied projectile.

Once selected, the player will see Sam holding whatever the current projectile is. If the player then does not throw the projectile or select a new readied one, after five seconds Sam will appear to put the projectile away. This is so that, visually, Sam does not appear to travel everywhere ready to throw a projectile. However, even if Sam does not appear to have a projectile ready, hitting the Throw key will instantly throw the readied projectile, just as quickly as if Sam had his arm out ready to throw.

Throwing the Projectile

The player will be able to throw Sam's current projectile by using the Throw button. The projectile will travel approximately in the direction the player is facing, though Sam will not have to be "dead on" in order to hit a target; the game will auto-target his shots at the closest adversary within the general direction Sam is facing. The current target will be labeled with a cross-hair so that the player always knows what target Sam will attack. It will be important to balance this auto-aiming so that it does not result in the projectile hitting targets the player did not want to hit, or in making the game too easy.

Throwing Speed and Distance

Releasing the Throw button will cause Sam to throw a projectile. A simple toss can be accomplished by a simple press and release of the Throw button by the player. However, if the player holds down the Throw button, Sam will be able to throw the projectiles faster and farther. This will be represented by Sam's arm starting to spin while the player holds down the Throw button, moving in a motion like a softball pitcher's windup, except continuing in a circle. Eventually, once Sam's projectile is going to leave his hand traveling at the maximum speed, Sam's arm will appear as a cartoon-style blur because it is revolving so fast. Though the auto-targeting will line up the player's shot with an adversary, if the player does not throw the projectile with enough force it may fall short of hitting this target. Part of the game's challenge for the player will be making sure the projectile is thrown hard enough to reach its intended target.

Projectile Capabilities

All of the projectiles in the game will be able to disable different types of enemies. For instance, the Goo-Ball projectile will cause enemies who are walking on the ground or on the walls to stick to the surface they are on, rendering them immobile. The Goo-Ball will be useless against flying adversaries. Another projectile, the Water Balloon, will be best used against non-waterproof robots, causing their wiring to short-circuit. Heavily armored robots or human adversaries will be invulnerable to the Water Balloon. The player will have to pick carefully the correct projectile to use in a given situation. A more detailed description of the capabilities of the projectiles can be found in the Game Elements section.

Electric Piranha

In addition to the projectiles and improved rocket-packs Sam will find in the game-world, the player will also find a special object which works in a passive way to protect the player against attacks. The Electric Piranha is a metallic green fish-shaped mechanism which, when found and picked up by Sam, will float or "swim" around him as if in orbit. This Piranha will be able to block incoming projectile attacks from adversaries by throwing itself in their path and "eating" the projectile. If the enemies attempt melee attacks while Sam has an Electric Piranha around him, the enemies themselves will be incapacitated when the Piranha sinks its teeth into the attacker. A Piranha explodes when it successfully defends Sam from an attack. Sam will be able to collect up to four of these Electric Piranha at any one time, and they will be key for his surviving particularly hairy situations.

Actions

The player will have a special Action button that will cause Sam to perform different actions in the game. The Action key will provide a variety of different actions, and the game will automatically determine what the correct action is for Sam in a given situation, if any.

Flipping Switches and Pressing Buttons

If Sam is near a button or a switch and the player hits the Action key, that button will be pressed or that lever will be thrown. The switch may do something as simple as opening a door or raising a platform, or it may perform a more complex action such as activating a crane or turning on a steam vent.

Pushing and Manipulating

Certain objects can be pushed by Sam, and pressing the Action key will allow him to do so. This may include crates, barrels, and balls of various kinds that may need to be pushed for a variety of reasons, including the blocking and unblocking of passageways.

Picking Up, Carrying, and Dropping

Sam will be able to pick up certain large objects using the Action key. This is different from the projectiles Sam will automatically pick up since he will not add these objects to his inventory, and while Sam holds one of these objects, he will be unable to throw any projectiles until he puts it down. When near such an object, the player can have Sam try to pick it up by pressing and holding the Action key. Once Sam has the object in his hands, he can carry it around with him, only dropping it once the player releases the Action button. While Sam is holding an object, particularly a heavy one, his movement may be slowed significantly. The player will want Sam to carry objects in order to aid in defeating adversaries. For instance, Sam could pick up a large anvil, fly with it up into the air, and then strategically drop it on a troublesome robot.

Talking

Some of the non-adversarial characters in *Atomic Sam* will be willing to talk to our hero, if only for a sentence or two. If the player wants Sam to talk to a character, he should press the Action key when near that character. These characters can fill in some of the back-story of the world of *Atomic Sam* while making the levels seem inhabited and interesting. Included among these characters will be "information robots," an invention of Sam's age which provide helpful advice to humans. Beyond just obtaining information, Sam will also want to talk to the characters who will be able to provide him with rocket-pack upgrades.

Reading

The player may see different informational signs or posters displayed on walls. In order to quickly zoom in and read these signs, the player can hit the Action key. These signs may include maps, which will help the player navigate the levels, or "tourist information," which describes the history of the area that Sam is in.

Interactive Combat Environments

In addition to throwing his projectiles at his enemies, Sam will also be able to defeat them by using parts of the level against them. The player can use the Action key to activate different events which will help incapacitate the various adversaries Sam is battling. The levels in *Atomic Sam* will be full of these contraptions, some of which may take on a Rube Goldberg-like level of complexity. Spotting and using these different setups correctly will be a major component of defeating the different robotic adversaries throughout the game. Indeed, the player will be unable to defeat certain adversaries without using these devices. In a way, these contraptions are "combat puzzles" in that the player must solve them in real-time in order to figure out the best way to defeat Sam's enemies.

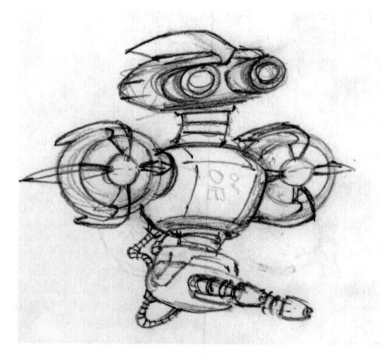

These contraptions will be designed and set up by the level designer in order to best suit the level in which they are going to be used. Some key devices may be repeated throughout a level, perhaps in different configurations. Some of the devices will be usable only once, while others can be used repeatedly. The use of devices that operate multiple times gives the player a better chance of figuring out how to use the device through trial and error. When creating these contraptions and environments, the level designer will need to set them up in such a way that the player has a fair chance of figuring out what they do and how to use them correctly.

A few examples of potential devices include:

- **Steam Vent:** A switch next to a hot steam vent may cause steam to shoot out, stunning or melting whatever is in its path. If the player waits until the precise moment when an adversary is in the path of the steam jet to flip the switch, the adversary will be disabled by the steam.

- **Fan:** A switch next to a large fan will be able to turn that fan on for a moment. This can be useful since it may blow whatever is in its path in a certain direction. For instance, if a steam vent is in operation across from a fan, a well-timed blast of the fan could force a creature into the steam vent.

- **Oil Drum and Lever:** Sam may come across a board laid across a steel box, creating a simple lever. A large, empty oil drum could then be placed on the lower end of the lever. If the player hits the Action key while Sam is near the higher end of the lever, this will cause Sam to press down on the lever, thereby causing the oil drum to flip through the air and possibly capture an enemy or two in the process.

If any of these devices are used incorrectly, they may backfire and end up hurting Sam. For instance, if Sam hits the steam vent switch when he is in the path of the steam, his rocket-pack may melt in the heat, sending him hurtling to the ground. Of course, a big part of using these contraptions effectively will be getting the enemy in the right place, and luring the robots and other adversaries into these traps will provide an interesting challenge for the player.

Looking

The player will have a Look button he can press. This functions similarly to Look buttons in other games such as *Super Mario 64*. While the player holds down the Look button, the camera will zoom in to be inside of Atomic Sam's head, and the player's forward/up, backward/down, left, and right controls will now pitch and turn the camera in those directions while Sam stays in one place. This will allow the player to get a clear view of Sam's surrounding environment, without Sam getting in the way of the visuals. This will be useful for examining puzzles and combat contraptions. As soon as the player releases the Look button, the camera will return to its normal gameplay mode.

Friends

Atomic Sam will not have to battle his way through all the game's levels alone. In each of the three intermediary game sections—Benthos, Harmony, and New Boston—Sam will meet game characters who will help him battle the robots and other adversaries he encounters. In Benthos, Sam meets Xeraphina the flying girl, in

Harmony he hooks up with Scrap the robot, and in New Boston he is helped by Dulo the Moonie. (For more information about these particular characters, consult the Game Progression section of this document.)

These friends will not be as good at defeating the robots as Sam, but they will be helpful in taking out some of the enemies, warning Sam about impending attacks, hinting at solutions to puzzles, pointing out items that Sam can pick up, indicating hidden areas, or showing the best direction to go next. The friends will talk to Sam frequently as they make their way through the levels, providing back-story, useful information, and amusing chitchat. These friends will never actually die or become captured during regular gameplay; they will always be able to fend off the enemy attacks directed against themselves. For more information about the AI for these friends, consult the Artificial Intelligence section of this document.

Speaking

A big part of making *Atomic Sam* an appealing and memorable character for the player will be the lines of dialog he speaks throughout the game. These won't occur just during cut-scenes, but also during actual gameplay. Not controlled by the player but added in order to color the gaming experience, Sam will have a variety of generic utterances he speaks as he defeats various adversaries. These will fit both his age and the optimistic retro-futuristic setting of the game. Some of these slogans will include: "You can't stop the future!", "Atomic is the answer!", "Infernal machine!", and "You're outdated technology!" Sam may provide useful, informative comments when he's running out of projectiles or his rocket-pack is close to being out of energy. Sam will also have lines of dialog specific to special events in the game, such as when he first walks on the Moon's surface or when he first encounters a particular boss monster. By keeping Sam talking during the actual gameplay, the player will grow fond of the character and will be even more concerned for his welfare in the game-world.

Cut-Scenes

Brief cut-scenes will be used in the game to help convey the story line to the player. The game's 3D engine will be used for these cut-scenes, so there will be a consistent visual appearance between the interactive gameplay and the non-interactive cut-scenes. The cut-scenes will include talking between Sam and different characters such as the Electric Priestess, the different friends Sam has accompanying him, or other characters he finds in the different areas to which he travels. For particularly short conversations consisting of only a few lines, conversations may happen during gameplay without the use of a cut-scene.

Cut-scenes may take place between or during levels. Between levels they will explain upcoming environments and challenges, usually through information provided by the Electric Priestess. Cut-scenes that briefly interrupt the gameplay mid-level will include short, conversational exchanges between Sam and the characters he encounters. These mid-level cut-scenes will be visually seamless with the gameplay environment; their primary difference will be the change in camera angles. When Sam first travels to a new area, the player will see Sam traveling by blimp, auto-gyro, monorail, or other means of transport to the different locations in the game. On the whole, the cut-scenes will be as short as possible in order to get the player back into the gameplay quickly.

Storytelling

An important part of *Atomic Sam* is the story, and various devices will be used to convey that story. One, of course, is the aforementioned cut-scenes. These will convey all of the key information the player needs to be successful in the game. However, since they are non-interactive, they will be strictly kept to a short length so that the player can quickly get back to the gameplay. In order to convey more story, more sections of the story will be revealed through devices used during the actual gameplay.

Environments

Of course, the environments (levels) themselves will provide a key storytelling component by conveying a sense of setting. Special care must be taken to make sure the levels fit with the world of *Atomic Sam* and do not conflict with any story components.

Friends

The friends Sam meets and who accompany him in the various worlds will share the information they have with Sam while they are flying around with him. The characters may explain the history of a particular environment or some interesting data about the world of the future. Sam, after all, is a young child and still has much to learn about life. Of course, these friends will only talk to Sam during non-combat situations, when the player is focusing on exploration instead of defeating threatening robots. All of the speech that the friends speak will appear on the screen via the in-game GUI, as discussed earlier in this document.

Radio

After they first meet, the Electric Priestess gives Sam a small radio which he can wear clipped to his ear. The player will hear information broadcast to Sam via this radio as he explores the levels. As with the friends, the Priestess may explain to Sam about the culture of the areas he is navigating and the nature of the adversaries he is facing. All of the dialog that the player hears over the radio will appear on the screen via the in-game GUI, as discussed earlier in this document.

Signs

As discussed earlier in the Actions section, Sam will also find static information displays which he will be able to read. These signs are yet another way to communicate the story of the world of *Atomic Sam*.

Levels

Atomic Sam is different from other console third-person action/adventures in that the gameplay focuses less on exploration and more on Sam's battling his way through the levels, avoiding the robots and other adversaries which try to block his progress. Certainly the levels will be interestingly designed and appealing to look at, but the player's motivation for continuing in a level will be more to confront the next interesting challenge than to merely uncover more of the level. Overall, the gameplay in the levels will be frantic and harried, and the player's split-second decisions and manual dexterity will be key to Sam eventually finding his parents. Sam will generally fight robots in two ways. The first way will be multiple robots at once, with all of the robots being of lesser power. The second way will be fighting a single, much more powerful or "boss" enemy. Usually the battles with the boss enemies will involve figuring out a particular method necessary to defeat the enemy, and will involve a bit more thinking than the battles with multiple adversaries at once. The method through which the player will maneuver Sam and the ways he will interact with his environment have been discussed earlier in this document.

That said, not all of the game will be frantic and combat-oriented. Between the battles with robots there will be calm, "safe" moments in the levels where the player can rest and regain his bearings. It will be in these calmer sections that the auto-save checkpoints (described later) will be included. This will allow the player to restart her game in a relatively safe area. Some of these "safe" sections may also require simple puzzle solving in order for the player to progress in the game.

Critical Path

All of the levels in *Atomic Sam* will have a definite "critical path" to them, a particular route the player is encouraged to travel in order to complete that level and move on to the next one. Though there may be bonus or secret areas off to the side, the critical path will remain strong throughout the levels. For each of the different sections of the game—Gargantuopolis, Benthos, Harmony, New Boston, and The Ikairus—the player will have to complete the levels within that section in a specified order; this will help to communicate the story line effectively, to build tension appropriately, and to ramp up difficulty over the course of a series of levels.

Training Level

The very beginning of the game will also provide a special "training" opportunity for players who want it. When Sam first returns to his apartment and finds his parents missing, he will decide to don his rocket-pack to go after them. The rocket-pack came with a helpful Instructobot, a pint-sized robot which speaks in robotic tones and instructs Sam how to use his rocket-pack. In fact, the Instructobot will encourage the player to experiment with the rocket-pack to get the hang of controlling it. In the safe environment of his house, the player will be able to experiment with Sam's different maneuvers before venturing into the more hazardous outside world.

The Electric Priestess' Home

The most "calm" section of the game is the Electric Priestess' bubble home. A mini-level where there is no combat, the bubble home acts as a "hub" between the worlds of Benthos, Harmony, and New Boston. In the Electric Priestess' home, the player will talk to the Electric Priestess and will be able to choose one of the different sections of the game to progress to next without any threat of harm. For more information about the Electric Priestess and the different worlds found in the game, consult the Game Progression section later in this document.

World Order

The player will get some choice in the order he experiences the game's different main areas or "worlds." After completing the Gargantuopolis levels at the beginning of the game, the Electric Priestess will present Sam with a choice of which area he will travel to next: Benthos, Harmony, or New Boston. Each of these areas will be fairly equivalent in difficulty, though due to the different challenges present in each area, different players may find one of the three harder or easier than the others. As such, the player can choose the one they find easiest first. (In the middle of a given section, the player will have the ability to instantly revert the game to the Electric Priestess' bubble home, from which the player can choose a different section, if the one he was playing proves to be too challenging or he simply grows tired of it.) For more on the flow of the game, consult the Game Progression section of this document.

III. Artificial Intelligence

Since *Atomic Sam* is based around interesting combat scenarios, the primary function of the game's AI is to support these conflicts, providing the player with a compelling challenge. The AI will also be essential for imbuing the friends Atomic

Sam encounters with some semblance of life, making them seem like more than just automatons.

Enemy AI

Many of the adversaries Sam faces will be robots. As such, the AI for these adversaries can be quite simple-minded while still being believable. Indeed, the simple-mindedness of some of his opponents will allow Sam to set traps for them using the interactive environments found in the levels. Not all robots will be simpletons, however. As the game progresses and the levels ramp up in difficulty, the robots will become more and more intelligent and thereby more and more challenging. Still later in the game, the player will fight human adversaries such as the Merciless Mercenaries. These human opponents will need to appear as intelligent in their combat decisions as a real-world human might be.

Player Detection

Different AI agents will have differing abilities to detect and track the player, which will in turn affect how much of a challenge they present to the player. Some robots will only be able to see in a very narrow cone in front of them, while others will have full 360-degree vision. Also, the distance of detection can vary from adversary to adversary; some can only see Sam when he is close to them, others can see him before Sam can see them. Some of the robots may have "super-vision," which allows them to see through walls and to always find Sam, regardless of how he may be hiding.

Some robots will also have very short memories. If Sam manages to run behind these robots, fully out of their field of vision, they may forget entirely about Sam and will return to an idle state. Other robots, once locked on to Sam's position, will never lose him. The player will need to figure out how well an adversary can detect Sam and use that to his advantage.

Motion

All adversaries will move in believable ways, employing a simple physics system to give the appearance that Sam's world is a realistic one. However, the feel of Sam's gameplay is one of a console action game, and hence does not need to rely too heavily on truly "authentic" motion systems. Indeed, the retro-future setting of *Atomic Sam* with its fantastic, implausible flying machines suggests a world that does not adhere to the laws of physics too closely.

Flying

Many of the adversaries Sam fights will be airborne, and it will be important to convey a sense of believable flight for these creatures. The type of flight motion involved will vary significantly depending on what type of flying equipment that enemy uses. An enemy kept aloft by a blimp will only be able to make slow turns and will not be able to move up or down very quickly. A creature with wings and propellers will be able to make turns, but will need to be able to bank to do so. Sam is the only character in the game who will have a rocket-pack, and this pack grants him a significant amount of maneuverability, something which will prove to be a great advantage over many of the adversaries he will face. Again, the flight model used by these creatures does not need to be truly authentic, but must be believable enough that the player gets a sense that the enemies Sam is fighting are truly flying.

Pathfinding

Detecting Sam is only the first part of the challenge for the robots. Once they have found Sam, the simpler robots may be too stupid to actually reach him. Pathfinding ability will vary significantly from the dumbest robot to the smartest. The dumbest robots will use a "beeline" technique and will be unable to maneuver around objects that get in their way. Somewhat smarter robots will be able to navigate around objects that they run into, but can still get hung up on corners. The smartest robots and the humans will always be able to navigate to the player, including opening doors and pushing obstacles out of the way as necessary. The player will need to exploit the deficiencies in the robots' pathfinding in order to succeed in the game.

Taking Damage

Many of the robots and other adversaries Sam faces will be incapacitated by a single hit from one of Sam's projectiles. Other, larger robots may take multiple hits before they are actually incapacitated. For instance, an electrical robot with heavy shielding may be able to survive three hits from water balloons before finally short-circuiting. Of course, different projectiles will have different effectiveness on different enemies, and some robots or enemies may be completely immune to certain attacks. See the Projectiles section under Game Elements for more information about the projectiles.

Combat Attacks

The AI agents in *Atomic Sam* will have a variety of attacks they can use to try to incapacitate young Sam. Many of the enemies will have multiple attacks to choose from in a given situation; for instance, an NPC may have a melee, close-range attack and several projectile, long-range attacks. The NPCs will be able to pick which attack is most effective, or, when several attacks may be equally effective, will pick one at random or will cycle through them in series.

Evading

The projectiles Sam throws travel at a slow speed, and as a result some of the smarter enemies will be able to dodge out of the way of incoming attacks. Of course, the AI agents will not be so good at dodging that the player never has a chance of hitting them, but just enough to provide an interesting challenge for the player.

Special Actions

To keep the challenges fresh and interesting to the player, there will be a variety of special behaviors that only the more advanced robots and human adversaries use. These will appear later in the game, and will force the player to adapt to them in order to succeed.

Taking Hostages

The battles the player fights with his enemies will often take place in inhabited communities, with non-hostile characters walking around to provide color. Some of the smarter AI agents will know to grab up some of these NPCs and hold them as hostages. Sam will now need to avoid hitting these hostages with his projectiles. If the player flies Sam up close to these hostages and presses the Action key, he will be able to snatch them away and fly them to safety.

Internal Repair Arms

As some of the robots take damage from Sam's projectile attacks, the more sophisti-cated robots will be able to repair themselves. A common way for this to work is that a special "repair arm" can spring from a compartment on the robot. This arm can then bend around the robot's body to weld broken parts back together. The effect is more cartoonish than realistic, but conveys the sense that the robot is repairing itself. Some robots may first retreat to a relatively safe location, such as around a corner or far from Sam. Others robots will be able to multi-task by having the repair arm work on them while continuing to fight Sam.

Collaboration

Some of the enemies, in particular the Merciless Mercenaries, will know how to work together. Many of the robots will be singular in their purpose (attack Sam) and will know nothing of the other robots who may simultaneously attack Sam. But the significantly more intelligent Mercenaries will know that working collaboratively will be much more effective in defeating Sam. For instance, while one Mercenary keeps Sam busy with attacks from the front, others may swing around to the flank and attack Sam from there. Of course, having the enemies work together will allow the enemies to provide a much greater challenge for the player.

Trash Talking

While Sam fights these adversaries, he will hear them making derogatory comments about him, suggesting he can never win against their superior numbers: "Admit defeat, human!", "Your success is statistically unlikely," and "Steel is stronger than flesh, relent!" Not all of the robots are able to speak English, and some may utter beeps and squawks as their means of communication. Others may be so cruel as to taunt Sam that he will never see his parents again.

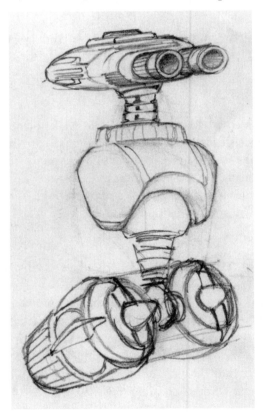

Falling into Traps

A big part of the game mechanics in *Atomic Sam* is the player using the environment to his advantage by triggering various traps and contraptions that will help to defeat the robots Sam faces. The AI will actually facilitate the player using the traps effectively, in part through the robots' lack of intelligence. In addition, designers will be able to set up these adversaries to have a tendency to maneuver into areas where the player will be able to incapacitate them if she is clever. For instance, if there is an empty oil drum set on a lever that the player can activate, the robots will have a tendency to fly by the potential trajectory of that oil drum.

Non-Combatant Agents

The various areas Sam travels to are places where the people of Sam's world live and work. As such, the areas will not only be inhabited by the enemies sent to capture Sam, but also by normal citizens. These citizens will not be very smart, and their inclusion in the levels is not in order to create the impression of a "real" environment. These citizens are mostly there for color, while also creating targets that Sam must be careful not to accidentally hit with his projectiles.

Fleeing

Often, at the first sign of trouble, these citizens will run away, trying to find cover away from the battles between Sam and the robots. Of course, the mere existence of flying robots or a boy with a rocket-pack will not be anything too exciting to the jaded people of the future; it is only when the fighting starts that the citizens will realize the dangerous situation they are in. The level designers will be able to set up paths for these citizens to walk along and positions they will try to flee to for safety.

Talking To and Helping Sam

Of course, certain citizens will be willing to talk to Sam, and may share information about the area Sam is currently navigating. Others may even be willing to give Sam objects, or to make improvements to Sam's rocket-pack. Citizens who will be able to help Sam will have a tendency to wave to Sam as he flies by, differentiating them from the citizens who are merely there to add color and variety to the game environment.

Friends

One of the most complicated pieces of AI that will be needed for *Atomic Sam* is that which will control the friends he meets throughout the game. These agents need to be able to follow along with Sam and provide him with help in key locations without ever getting lost or stuck. Making a teammate AI that can support the player without seeming stupid or canned will be quite a challenge, but will have a significant payoff in terms of gameplay.

Invincible

The friends that follow Sam through the levels will not be able to be killed or captured by the robots and other hostile creatures found in the levels. First, the enemy creatures will have a tendency to attack Sam instead of the friends, since indeed it is Sam that they have been sent to subdue. Second, the friend AI agents will be able to defend against any attack that does happen to come their way. Similarly, if Sam should happen to throw a projectile at a friend, the friend will easily be able to bat it out of the way, saying something to the effect of "You've got to be careful with those things!" The logistics in terms of the friend AI being defeated and what this does to the gameplay is simply too complex to deal with. It may be useful, however, for the friends to be temporarily stunned, only to return to full helpfulness within a few seconds.

Following Sam

The most important task these friend AI agents must be able to perform is to follow the player around the levels. This means the friends will have to be able to flaw-lessly follow the player through the potentially complex 3D environments that make up the *Atomic Sam* game-world. If the player ever turns around to find that a friend got stuck a distance back on some sort of structure, the gaming experience will be ruined.

The NPC will not necessarily be right on top of Sam at all times. Indeed, the flying friends will be able to fly in and out of frame, giving the player the sense that they are always close nearby without actually being on the screen constantly. Some-times the friends will be just in front of Sam, sometimes just behind him, but always close by.

Guarding Sam's Back

These friends will play a crucial role in the gameplay by pointing out enemies who may be attacking Sam from a given direction that Sam has not seen: "Watch out, Sam, it's coming up behind you!" In some cases, the AI agents will be able to use their own attacks or projectiles to help defeat an enemy before it gets too close to Sam, though in any given situation the agents will be far less successful than Sam. It is important that the player will still have to fight robots on his own and will not be able to just sit back and let the friends take care of everything for him.

Providing Advice

Similarly, the friends in *Atomic Sam* will be able to provide the player with advice about different enemies as they arrive: "That one looks like trouble!" or "I don't think water balloons will work on that one!" In certain situations in the levels, the friends will be able to point out secret areas or show Sam a cache of projectiles he might otherwise have overlooked. The player will be able to navigate Sam close to a given friend and then press the Action key, to which the friend will always provide an answer. Sometimes the answers will not be useful: "I'm glad I met you, Sam" or "You really showed that last robot!" Other times, having Sam talk to the friend will provoke them to provide a hint: "Take the fork to the left; that will get us there faster" or "The best way to take care of these climbing robots is to throw something sticky at them. Do you have anything like that?"

Storytelling

In addition to the snippets of advice the friends can provide, they will also be key in communicating elements of the story to the player. When Sam reaches a certain part of a level, a friend may start talking about the history of the area or about their own past. This provides additional story content to the game in a non cut-scene format, since Sam is still navigating the world while hearing about the story. The friends will be smart enough to only talk in "safe" situations when Sam is not actively being threatened by an enemy.

IV. Game Elements

Items

Sam's Projectiles

As Sam flies through the levels, he will be able to pick up a variety of different projectiles he can use in defeating his enemies. Different projectiles will work better or worse against different specific adversaries in different situations, and as such the player will have to constantly be selecting the most effective projectile for any given moment. The different projectiles are as follows:

- **Goo-Balls:** Greenish balls of a sticky substance which make ground-based or wall-crawling monsters stick to their surface. Depending on the strength of the creature, it may end up stuck there just briefly or forever.

- **Water Balloons:** Able to disable robots with exposed wiring by causing them to short-circuit. Robots with protective coverings may require multiple hits to short-circuit.

- **Magneto-Mass:** A powerful magnet attached to a heavy weight, which will stick to metallic flying robots and drag them down to the ground.

- **Spring-Cage:** A small black cube with six rods sticking out of it. On impact with a target the Spring-Cage will expand to surround the target, entrapping it in a strong cage. Works best against small flying adversaries; larger enemies will be able to smash out of the cage.

- **EM Disrupter:** A small sphere that, when thrown, will fly a distance and then activate, rendering all electrical equipment within a certain radius of the Disrupter immobile. Flying robots will plummet to the ground, robots that cling to the walls will fall off, and ground robots will grind to a halt. The EM

Disrupter does not work on humans or atomic-powered robots. The player will have to be careful when using the EM Disrupter while he has Electric Piranha (as described in the Game Mechanics section), as the device will also cause Sam's Piranha to cease functioning and clatter to the ground below.

- **Bubble Wand:** Similar to the bubble wands/rings used by children to blow bubbles from bottles, this wand produces much stronger bubbles which will envelop a target and prevent it from escaping, at least for a few minutes. One of the more effective of Sam's "throwable" objects in the game, the Bubble Wand won't work on enemies with sharp objects, spikes, or propellers on them.

- **Atomic Bola:** One of the most powerful projectiles in the game, this looks like a traditional bola: two black spheres connected by wire. But these bolas are powered, and when the bola starts to wrap around a target the engines in the bola-balls activate, causing the bola to wrap around the target many times, very tightly. The Atomic Bola will not work on any flying adversaries that have any sort of propellers or rotor blades on them.

Rocket Enhancements

The player will be able to get various improvements to Sam's rocket-pack throughout the game, either through having an NPC tinker with the pack and make an improvement, or through an add-on that Sam can find and simply install himself. These enhancements provide a range of improvements to Sam's abilities.

- **Burst-Master:** The Burst-Master is a simple modification to the pack that will cause it to have much faster speed when the player uses the pack's speed burst functionality.

- **Speedifier:** The Speedifier will cause the overall speed of the rocket-pack to improve, such that Sam can navigate the world at a higher speed than he could before getting the enhancement.

- **Gyromatic:** The Gyromatic will grant Sam much more stable flight using the rocket-pack, allowing him to stop and start much quicker, instead of having to coast to a stop. The Gyromatic is a simple "snap-on" attachment to the pack that Sam can easily install himself.

- **Atomic Compressor:** A simple box with a dial on it that can attach to the side of the pack, this device will provide Sam with a longer flight time. The device works using a unique method to "compress" the atomic energy the pack constantly generates, thereby allowing the pack to store more of it at any one time.

Miscellaneous

Atomic Sam will also include other miscellaneous devices that Sam is able to pick up. These devices have a variety of functionalities which will improve Sam's abilities to navigate and survive the levels.

- **Electric Piranha:** Throughout the levels Sam will find numerous Electric Piranha, small devices that will "swim" through the air around Sam and deflect attacks for him. The full functionality of the Electric Piranha is described in the Game Mechanics section.

- **The Spidersonic:** The Spidersonic kit allows Sam to stick to any vertical surface as a spider would. Using this kit, Sam can grab onto the side of a building and stop flying, allowing his pack time to recharge before he flies on to the next location.

- **Moon Suit:** Found in New Boston, this handy Moon Suit will allow Sam to travel outside of the Moon colony and survive on the surface of the Moon. Fortunately, Sam's rocket-pack and utility belt can both be placed outside the suit so that Sam will be able to continue to fly and throw projectiles, though both will be affected differently by the Moon's gravity.

Characters

Sam will encounter a variety of characters in *Atomic Sam*. These include both friends and allies as well as enemies and, eventually, the man who kidnapped his parents.

Atomic Sam

The player controls Atomic Sam, a ten-year-old with a rocket-pack who uses his wits and dexterity to evade countless robotic and human adversaries throughout the game, not to mention navigating tricky areas, all in order to find his parents. Sam is about three feet tall and wears brown jodhpurs with a red aviator's jacket, the latter with gold trim. He also has a brown leather belt with various pouches on it. The large, clunky, "moon boot" type boots that Sam wears are silver in color. On his back is mounted the atomic-powered rocket-pack he uses to fly. It is a fairly small, compact device that is several inches narrower than the width of his shoulders, and several inches shorter than the distance from his belt to his neck. Sam has short black hair and wears a pair of 1930s-style aviator goggles. Sam's abilities are covered throughout this document. Sam's personality is what would be expected of a ten-year-old boy of the bright future: optimistic and smart. At the same time, Sam is without his parents for the first time in his life, and is somewhat frightened of the world he must now explore on his own.

Friends

- **Xeraphina:** In Benthos, Sam will meet a twelve-year-old girl by the name of Xeraphina. A daughter of artists, Xeraphina has grown up entirely in Benthos, and has never seen the surface, a place she dearly longs to go. Xeraphina is able to glide around the city using a unique set of wings her parents invented, and will help Sam in his battles against his robotic adversaries. Xeraphina wears a tight-fitting light green outfit, with semi-translucent green shawls flowing around her body as she flies through the air. Her wings are made of a less translucent crystalline substance, are a darker jade green color, and are a good eight feet from tip to tip. Attached at her shoulder blades, they are a rigid construction, but flap slightly when she flies. She has a very friendly smile and wears her long brown hair in a bun behind her head, with a small paintbrush stuck through it to keep it in place.

- **Scrap:** In Harmony, Sam will meet Scrap, a shiny-new, recently constructed robot no more than a few weeks old. Scrap is a very friendly fellow who enjoys using his high-pitched voice to tell jokes whenever he can; puns are his specialty. In many ways, Scrap behaves like a robotic version of a ten-year-old, and dreads the day that he will be sent off to his work assignment, though he does not yet know what it is. Scrap is happy being a robot, but just wishes he would never have to "grow up," and dreams of a life traveling the world. Scrap is about Sam's size and is humanoid in form, except that he has four arms and a particularly small head. Scrap can use his pogo-stick-like legs to jump great distances, helping Sam to defeat his robotic adversaries in whatever way he can.

- **Dulo:** Dulo is Sam's parents' assistant. His general appearance as a Torso Moonie is described fully in the Moonie description below. In particular, Dulo wears special purple bracelets that he likes very much, which will help to make him stand out from the other Moonies, who all pretty much look the same, at least within the Torso or Bi-Header groups. Dulo is able to hop around and help Sam in defeating the robotic adversaries; his long tentacles are well suited to grabbing the robots out of the air and smashing them on the Moon's surface.

Other Characters

- **Electric Priestess:** The Electric Priestess is the mysterious woman who helps Sam to find out what happened to his parents and provides him with much useful information about the world. By the end of the story, the player learns that the Priestess is actually Max Zeffir's sister and was also one of his chief researchers. She lost her leg in a zeppelin accident due to Zeffir's lax safety standards. The Electric Priestess continues to love her brother, while despising the money-hoarding madman that he has become. The Priestess dresses in a long jade-green dress with a large black hat which partially obscures her face. She has only one leg remaining, the other having been replaced by a clunky, robotic prosthesis.

- **Ike:** In Harmony Sam meets Ike, an old robot assistant his parents had some years ago of whom they grew very fond. Unlike many owners, when Ike got old Sam's parents released him from his work for them instead of just shutting him off, and allowed him to return to Harmony to live out his time with other robots. Ike is quite smart, though his memory is failing, as is explained in the Game Progression section. Ike does not say much, but once his memory is activated he will speak with great love and respect for Sam's parents. Ike looks a bit older in design than many of the other robots Sam will find, with a boxy, clunky shape and a larger frame than many newer robots, such as Scrap. He is also quite slow moving because of his age. Ike moves around on tank treads, and was designed with only one arm, a long, five-jointed limb connected to his torso in the middle of his chest.

- **Tool:** Tool is the "robot doctor" whom Sam will need to locate in Harmony in order to save Ike. Tool is a huge robot who looks like he would be very violent and destructive. Instead he is very kind and caring, in a "gentle giant" sort of way. Tool is mute, and speaks only through a text display in the middle of his chest. Tool floats through the air a short distance above the ground using an anti-gravity unit he wears around his waist. When "operating" on robots, Tool does not use the massive arms and fists that are attached to his upper torso. Instead, a small compartment springs open in his chest from which small, spindly robotic arms pop out to do precision work.

- **Moonies:** "Moonies," as earthlings call them, average about four feet in height and hop around on the lower half of their bodies (they have no legs). For arms they have two tentacles, one on either side, which are quite long and strong, yet prehensile enough to use a human pen to write. Though the Moonies are asexual, there are two different physical varieties of the creatures; one with two heads that sit atop their bodies as humanoid heads do (which earthlings call "Bi-Headers"), and another that has no head at all, but instead has its eyes and mouth located on its torso (which earthlings call "Torsos"). The Moonies also have white bumps on their bodies which can glow when necessary, allowing them to maneuver through dark areas. This lighting is necessary for them to navigate on the Dark Side of the Moon, where they have lived for all their recorded history.

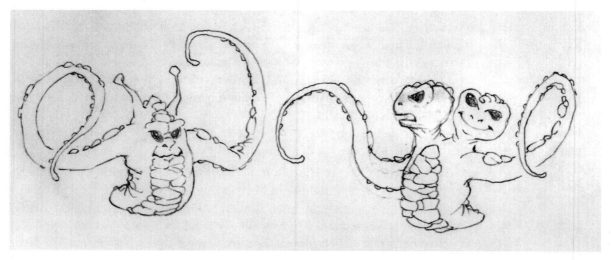

Enemies

Arctic Immobilizer Blimp The Arctic Immobilizer Blimp (AIB) is an easy to middle difficulty robotic adversary that Sam will have to disable or evade. Shaped like a cylinder, made of shiny, silvery metal, and suspended from a miniature zeppelin, the AIB floats through the air at a relatively slow speed, being propelled forward by a small rear propeller. Two metal claws extend from either side of the tube, and the AIB will wiggle these claws menacingly at Sam. The front end of the cylinder has four metal spikes which close over the front opening. The AIB will be able to move up and down (again, at slow velocity) in order to line up with Sam and attempt to attack him, but its slow speed will prevent the AIB from giving chase if Sam successfully evades it and flies away. Since the AIB flies, if Sam uses the Goo-Balls on it they will have no effect. One of the best projectiles for defeating the AIB will be the Magneto-Mass, which will quickly bring the enemy to the ground.

The enemy has two attacks, one a melee attack and the other a mid-range attack.

- **Claw Attack:** If in close range, the AIB will be able to slice at Sam with its two claws, possibly cutting off his rocket-pack. Sam will need to avoid getting in close range of the AIB in order to avoid this fate.

- **Freeze Mist Attack:** For the AIB's second attack, the four metal spikes that cover the front of the tube will fan outward, revealing a small nozzle. From this nozzle will come a liquid spray which will freeze whatever it contacts. The spray generates a cloud of mist in front of the AIB, and if Sam comes in contact with this cloud before it dissipates he will be frozen solid in a block of ice and plummet to the ground.

Arachnaught   The Arachnaught is a fairly easy robotic enemy. The Arachnaught looks approximately like a four-legged spider, with each leg being a three-jointed appendage with a spiked end. The legs all come together at a fairly small main body, which contains a curved vision-sensor that gives the creature a good range of sight. The Arachnaught cannot fly at all, but instead can climb up the sides of buildings just as easily as walking on the ground. The Arachnaught moves quite quickly, in a scurrying fashion. Since it crawls on surfaces, the Arachnaught will be impervious to Sam's projectiles that work on flying adversaries, while being particularly susceptible to the Goo-Balls projectile.

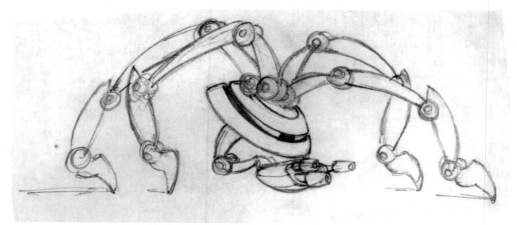

The Arachnaught has three attacks, one melee, one projectile, and one a short-range "tractor beam" like effect.

- **Claw Attack:** The Arachnaught will be able to attack with its sharp legs, devices that will easily allow it to slice off Sam's rocket-pack, thereby incapacitating him.

- **Sticky Web Balls:** The Arachnaught can shoot large, slow-moving globs of a uniquely sticky substance. If Sam is on the ground when hit by this substance, he will be stuck to the ground and immobilized. If Sam is in the air, he will be temporarily unable to throw any projectiles, as he attempts to struggle out of the sticky substance. If Sam runs into any surfaces with the web ball still on him, he will stick to that surface and become incapacitated.

- **Web Strand:** The Arachnaught's most fiendish weapon may well be its web strand attack. Using this, the Arachnaught can shoot a long strand of webbing towards Sam and, if it hits, can then pull Sam back towards itself. Then, once Sam is close, the Arachnaught can use its claws to rip Sam's pack off, thereby putting him out of commission. Sam will have to fly in the exact opposite direction of the web strand, only breaking free after five seconds of resistance.

Merciless Mercenary Though many of Sam's adversaries in the game will be various robotic constructions, Sam will encounter human foes on Max Zeffir's flying fortress, the Ikairus. Dubbed the Merciless Mercenaries (MMs), these humans are highly trained and will be quite difficult for Sam to evade or incapacitate. Dressed in black uniforms with red trim and fierce-looking steel helmets, the MMs are able to fly by an anti-gravity belt fastened around their waist. The belt allows them to float in the air, and in order to actually propel themselves, the MMs need to perform a "swimming" type motion. Many of Sam's projectiles will be useless against the MMs; the only effective weapon will be the Atomic Bola, which will wrap around the MMs' legs and prevent them from "swimming" any farther. The MMs are one of the more mobile adversaries Sam will encounter. For this enemy, running away will be hard since the MMs will be able to track Sam and move almost as fast as he does.

The MMs have a total of three attacks: one melee and two ranged.

- **Tri-Power Trident Melee:** The MMs carry gold-colored, metal tridents called Tri-Power Tridents, which have two functionalities. The first is as a simple melee attack, used if Sam gets too close. The sharp ends of the Tri-Power Trident will easily be able to rip Sam's rocket-pack right off.

- **Tri-Power Trident Ranged Attack:** The second attack of the Tri-Power Trident is to shoot a large, slow-moving mass of light blue, sparking energy into the air. This travels toward Sam, tracking him, but it alone will not hurt him. When it gets close enough to Sam, it stops moving and explodes into six miniature energy balls. These small balls hurtle at great speed in random directions outward from the main ball, and if they come into contact with Sam burst into a perfect energy sphere with Sam trapped inside. Unable to break out of the sphere, Sam is now immobile.

- **ElectroNet:** Finally, the Mercenaries have an ElectroNet which they will throw with their other arm (the one that does not have the Tri-Power Trident in it). This net, similar to Sam's Atomic Bola, has heavy black balls at its ends which propel it in the direction thrown. Of course, if the net manages to wrap around Sam, he is incapacitated.

Visionary At the end of Harmony city—the town that is the hub of robot manufacturing— Atomic Sam will face a fierce boss enemy. In appearance the Visionary is a giant eyeball-like mechanism, with two metal structures on each side, both of which have helicopter blades on them. These blades keep the Visionary aloft, giving it great maneuverability. The Visionary can travel up and down at speeds much faster than Atomic Sam can manage with his rocket-pack, though it is a bit slower at turning than Sam.

From the bottom of the eyeball emerge three steel tentacles, each with a different mechanism on its end. Each of these devices is the basis for one of the Visionary's three attacks.

- **Electric Blades:** One tentacle features three rotating blades that all point in the same direction like a claw. These blades continually rotate menacingly. Their real power, however, is to shoot an electric shock wave which can stun Sam into unconsciousness. The blades spin up to a high-speed whirlwind and then unleash the blast from their center. This ranged "beam style" attack will be tricky for the player to avoid; once the player sees the Visionary's blades start spinning at high speed, she must be careful to move Sam out of the path of whichever direction the blades are pointing.

- **Magnet:** One tentacle has a giant, U-shaped magnet on the end of it. By attracting the metal in Sam's rocket-pack, the Visionary can turn on this magnet to suck the player toward the robot. Sam will have to use all his dexterity to avoid getting too close to the enemy, where the robot will be able to rip Sam's rocket-pack off using the tentacle arm with the blade attachment.

- **Smog:** The third tentacle has a giant funnel on the end of it. From this funnel the Visionary can shoot a thick, black cloud of gas which will cause Sam to have an uncontrollable (and game-ending) coughing fit should he be so unfortunate as to fly into it. This smog cloud will hang in the air for some time after the Visionary shoots it, and the player will have to be careful not to fly into that cloud until it dissipates.

As with all the boss monsters in the game, most of Sam's regular projectiles will not be very effective against the Visionary. They may slow down the robot for a short time, but they will not permanently defeat it. The player will need to use the setup of the level itself in order to incapacitate the Visionary. This makes defeating the boss less a matter of dexterity, repetition, and perseverance, but more about understanding the puzzle, which, once figured out, is not that hard to repeat. Since the player is battling the Visionary at the end of the Harmony levels, the battle will take place in a robot factory. The Visionary emerges from a storage crate riveted to the ceiling at the top of the play area where Sam will battle the robot. Scattered about the area are various appropriate pieces of equipment used in a robot factory, as well as four high-powered fans. Sam will be able to turn on these fans by using his "action" ability near them. He will also be able to use his Action button to rotate the fans and change the direction they are blowing. By activating and blowing all of the fans upward beneath the storage crate, Sam can create a windy vortex which will be able to push the Visionary—since it is kept aloft by helicopter blades—back up into the case. Sam will then, by using a switch near the crate, be able to close the crate and trap the robot inside, hence defeating the creature.

Max Zeffir Zeffir is the founder and owner of Zeffir Zoom, and is widely considered to be the richest man on the planet. Zeffir started acquiring his fortune with his zipper company, Zeffir Zippers, and then moved on to virtually every other industry he possibly could. His companies include the aircraft manufacturer Zeffir Zeppelins, the clothing line Zeffir Zest, and the Zeffir Zeitgeist news network.

Max Zeffir is also the employer of Sam's parents and, as it turns out, the one who kidnapped them in order to keep them quiet. Sam will finally have a showdown with Zeffir in the end-game, where Zeffir will turn out to be quite a formidable opponent himself.

When the player finally meets Zeffir he will be wearing a 1920s-style "railroad baron" black pinstripe suit with an extra large top hat. Zeffir sports a stringy black mustache and a mischievous grin. Zeffir will battle Sam on his Negativity Platform, so named because it negates the effects of gravity. A circular disk which floats on the air and is much more maneuverable than Sam's rocket-pack, the platform features handrails that come up to Zeffir's waist, which he holds on to while the platform flies around.

Zeffir's combat will consist of two methods of attacking the player:

- **Robots:** Zeffir will battle the player by summoning robots to fight Sam. These will be all manner of robots that Sam has been fighting throughout the game, and they will emerge from various compartments throughout the large, domed room in which Sam and Zeffir battle. Sam will have to defeat these robots as he normally would in the rest of the game. Zeffir will bring out a maximum of three robotic adversaries at a time.

- **Tuning Fork:** Zeffir will also hold a six-foot-long tuning-fork-like device in his hand. When Zeffir strikes this bar on the bars of the Negativity Platform, it creates a sonic blast which he can aim at Sam. If the blast hits Sam, he will be temporarily stunned and have to stop flying and raise up his hands to cover his ears. This will make Sam particularly susceptible to robot attacks, since he will be unable to move or throw projectiles.

The player will be able to defeat Zeffir using a variety of different tactics, which can be used in different combinations.

- **Brute Force:** Once hit with a lot of projectiles of the right sort, Zeffir will finally be defeated. Only some of Sam's projectiles will work, however; the Magneto-Mass and Spring-Cage will be ineffective against Zeffir, while the others will slowly wear him down. It will take a lot of hits, however, and Zeffir will do his best to bring out more robots and to blast Sam with his Tuning Fork at the same time. As a result this is the most difficult of the ways to defeat Zeffir, but it is also the most obvious.

- **Disable Negaposts:** Zeffir's Negativity Platform is actually held aloft by four Negaposts which are on the ground in four opposite corners of the room. As Zeffir moves about on the Platform these posts glow. Sam will be able to take out one of the posts by hitting it with three water balloons. When the post goes out of commission, Zeffir temporarily loses control of his craft, only to regain it quickly. Sam will need to incapacitate all four posts before the Negativity Platform will actually stop working and clatter to the ground of the room, where Zeffir will surrender.

- **Get Zeffir's Ear Protection:** The player will notice that Zeffir is wearing a bulky pair of "ear protectors," large devices that look like headphones but which serve to block out the dangerous sound of the Tuning Fork. If the player is clever enough, he will realize that if he hits the Negativity Platform hard enough the ear protectors will be knocked off of Zeffir. They cannot be knocked off simply by pelting Zeffir with projectiles, however. The player will need to cause Zeffir to steer the Negativity Platform into a larger swinging girder that hangs from the top of the domed room. If Sam is simultaneously pushing the girder while Zeffir is flying toward it, the impact will knock the ear protectors right off. If the player then flies Sam down to where the ear protectors fell, Sam will put them on. Now Sam is immune from Zeffir's blasts and will have a much easier time defeating him, using either brute force or by disabling the Negaposts, as described above.

V. Story Overview

Atomic Sam is the story of a young boy, separated from his parents for the first time, who must rise to the challenge of discovering what has happened to them. Though *Atomic Sam*'s focus is as an action/adventure game, the humorous and touching story sets the game apart from many other console action games.

The setting of *Atomic Sam* is the Earth of the future, but not exactly the future as we imagine it now. This is the future as foretold in the first half of the twentieth century by magazines like *Popular Science* and *The Electrical Experimenter*, as well as by futurists like Norman Bel Geddes and Buckminster Fuller. Certain innovations that we see as obvious today never came to pass, such as jet airplane travel; instead, people still travel aboard giant propeller craft and zeppelins. Similarly, the personal computer and certainly the Internet are unheard of, while super-intelligent and always helpful robots are ubiquitous. Man has even colonized the Moon and found the extraterrestrial life which lives there, the "Moonies." It is in this whimsical and fun future that the story of *Atomic Sam* takes place.

One day, young Sam returns from school to his parents' apartment only to discover them mysteriously missing. Sam's parents are both scientists at Zeffir Zoom, a transportation company, but they always make it a point to be home when Sam returns from school. Distraught, Sam decides to go looking for his parents. He dons a red jacket and puts on the atomic rocket-pack they gave him for his birthday, and renames himself Atomic Sam, gaining courage through his new alter ego.

Sam travels through the city of Gargantuopolis towards his parents' office, but along the way is attacked by robots who try to block his progress. Sam finally reaches their office, only to find them missing from there as well, with only a mysterious note remaining. A friendly robot soon arrives, however, and escorts Sam to a towering building right next door. Sam travels up to the top floor and meets a strange woman who calls herself the Electric Priestess. She tells Sam that, though she does not know what has happened to his parents, she will help him find them. She offers Sam transportation to three locations where Sam may try to discover their fate.

Sam will travel to Benthos, the city beneath the sea. There he will meet Xeraphina, the flying girl, who will help Sam locate his parents' private office. Next is Harmony, the robot city, where Sam will try to look for Ike, the robot who was his parents' loyal assistant for years. Along the way Sam meets Scrap, a plucky young robot who strangely doesn't want to "grow up" and go to work. Finally, Sam travels to New Boston, the Moon colony, searching for another friend of his parents, Dulo the Moonie. At each of these locations, Sam is attacked by merciless robots out to defeat him and stop his inquiries. After having fully explored each of these areas, Sam finds a piece of a wax cylinder which, when all of its pieces are assembled, can be played back to reveal what happened to his parents.

The cylinder contains a warning message from Sam's parents: they think they have stumbled on a safety problem with the monorail system being developed by Max Zeffir, their employer. Unfortunately, Zeffir does not want to fix the problem because of its prohibitive cost and, as a result, has kidnapped Sam's parents to keep them quiet. The Electric Priestess will now be able to lend Sam an auto-gyro to take him to the Ikairus, Zeffir's massive airship. There Sam will battle still more robots before confronting and defeating Max Zeffir. Then, finally, Sam is reunited with his parents.

VI. Game Progression

Setting

Atomic Sam takes place on an Earth of the future, at an indefinite time, perhaps in the twenty-first century. This is not the future as our culture of the year 2000 envisions it now, but instead as people optimistically foresaw it in 1920s, 1930s, and 1940s America. Instead of jet planes transporting passengers across continents, the world of *Atomic Sam* is filled with zeppelins and "giant wing" propeller craft. In *Atomic Sam*, nuclear energy has not turned out to be a disappointment as it has in the second half of the twentieth century. Instead, it has fulfilled its tremendous promise of cheap, clean energy, and has been refined to the point where it can be used safely in a child's toy or in zeppelins.

This is a future that has conquered poverty through technology, a future in which the skyscrapers stretch to unprecedented heights, and there is enough room for all to live happily. Private planes and auto-gyros (a plane/helicopter hybrid) are not uncommon, and many land on the roofs of the towering skyscrapers. Rail travel is a very important part of this future, and high-speed monorails provide quicker travel between cities than slower zeppelins.

Intelligent robots are everywhere, and people can purchase robots either to be workers in their factories or butlers in their homes. Instead of running people out of work, however, these robots have increased everyone's leisure time, while in turn enhancing everyone's prosperity. This is not the bleak, troubling future found in so much science fiction of the last two decades, but an optimistic world where technology has set the human race free to be happy.

The advance in robots did create some interesting problems, however. Robots are now basically as smart as the smartest humans, with intelligences so developed that they have emotions and desires of their own. Certainly many robots are more physically strong and resilient than humans. Yet the robots have not risen up to conquer the humans, as many science fiction works might foresee. (All of the aggressive robots that Sam faces in the game are following the orders of a villainous human.) Instead, these robots are still obligated to follow the laws humans make, for reasons that are never fully explained. Indeed, robots have no rights and are treated very much as property by the humans, not unlike African slaves were treated in the first hundred years of United States history. For instance, if part of a robot breaks, it may be cheaper to replace the whole robot than to fix it. If this is the case, it is the prerogative of the owner of the robot to permanently shut it off if he so chooses, and few humans would question that decision as being the right one. *Atomic Sam* does include some hints of a robot "underground" which tends to the old robots in the most humane ways possible, as is explored in the Harmony section of the game.

In this future earthlings have managed to reach the Moon and have set up a Moon colony there called New Boston. This colony consists of a number of domed structures which provide a breathable atmosphere and Earth-like gravity. Moon walks are allowed for the residents, using space suits, of course, with many Moon residents finding such excursions to be a fun way to take a break from dome life.

When humans did finally reach the Moon, they were surprised to find a race of extraterrestrials there. These creatures had lived unnoticed on the Dark Side of the Moon for many centuries, only in the last thirty years revealing themselves to humans as the Moon colony was built. In addition to their generally strange appearance, the Moonies come in two varieties: the "Bi-Headers" and the "Torsos." The Bi-Headers have two heads on top of their bodies, while the Torsos have none, instead having a mouth and eyes on the front of their torsos. The Moonies do not breathe and are much denser creatures than humans, and as a result can survive in either Earth or Moon atmosphere. The Moonies, though not technologically advanced, are just as intelligent as humans, and on making contact with earthlings were quick to learn English. The Moonies and humans now live cooperatively on the Moon, helping each other in many different ways.

On first contact, the reaction of humans to the Moonies was one of shock and disbelief. Over time, however, humans came to realize that Moonies did not pose a threat and became quite friendly with them, in particular with the Bi-Headers. It seems that, since the Bi-Headers looked a bit more humanoid than the Torsos, that humans found them more acceptable. As a result, only the Bi-Headers are allowed in New Boston, while the Torsos must stay outside on the Moon surface. Humans found the Moonies to be great collaborators on scientific projects, using their unique way of thought to help advance technology. However, though both sets of Moonies are equally intelligent, only the Bi-Headers are allowed to work with humans in an academic capacity.

Though we now see many of the technological advances described above as either impossible, impractical, or undesirable, this is the world of *Atomic Sam*, where the illogical nature of the environment is part of its charm. On the other hand, while this future contains many advances we see as impossible today, it also doesn't include a lot of the advances we take for granted today. For example, in this future people have no idea what a personal computer is, and in turn, computer games surely don't exist. Though television exists, it is still on a tiny television screen and is vastly inferior to a movie theater experience. While in some ways the world of the twenty-first century in *Atomic Sam* is more technologically advanced than 1990s America, in other key ways it is certainly less advanced, giving it a unique "primitive future" look.

Introduction

The player controls the game's namesake, Atomic Sam. A normal though precocious boy ten years of age, Sam returns from school one day to find his apartment home ransacked and his parents mysteriously missing. Donning the atomic-powered rocket-pack given to him by his parents for his birthday, Sam renames himself Atomic Sam and vows to venture through Gargantuopolis to find his parents.

Gargantuopolis

Following this brief introductory cut-scene, the player gains control of Sam inside his parents' apartment. Here the player will be able to follow the instructions given to him by the Instructobot that came with his rocket-pack. These instructions will teach the player how to effectively control Sam. The player will also be able to skip by that section and proceed out into the city, trying to get to his parents' office deep in the city.

Gargantuopolis is a mammoth city of the future, with towering buildings creating something of a sense of claustrophobia, and Sam's rocket-pack is unable to fly him over their tops. Traveling through the city, Sam is attacked by a great variety of robots that try to prevent him from discovering what has happened to his parents. Where these robots came from and why they are trying to subdue Sam remains a mystery at this point in the game.

Sam's parents are atomic scientists at Zeffir Zoom—a company that works at harnessing atomic energy for increasingly fast modes of transportation. Upon reaching his parents' office at Zeffir Zoom's main research complex, a cut-scene will take over showing Sam finding a hastily written note left by his parents proclaiming, "Someone has to check on Sam!" Along with the note is a fragment of a wax cylinder used for voice recording. Since the cylinder is incomplete, Sam is unable to play it back at this point.

The Electric Priestess' Bubble Home

Distraught at having failed to find anything out about his parents' disappearance, Sam is suddenly approached by a friendly robot who quickly leads him to a nearby building. Here Sam takes the elevator to the top floor, where he meets a mysterious woman who calls herself the Electric Priestess. Quite a mysterious figure, the Electric Priestess lives alone in a sphere-like "bubble home" dwelling atop a high skyscraper. The ceiling of this bubble home is entirely glass, providing a breathtaking view of the surrounding city. In the home are numerous large steel doors which lead to various forms of transportation at the Priestess' disposal.

The Priestess explains to Sam that she knows of his parents' disappearance, and offers to help him. At this point in the story, why the Electric Priestess is helping

Sam is still unclear, but she seems quite concerned for his well-being. On hearing of Sam's concern about his parents she offers to help by guiding him to the other fragments of the wax cylinder. She offers Sam transportation to three different locations where she believes he may find more information about his parents and other fragments of the cylinder. She also gives Sam a miniature radio which he can hook on to his ear and which will allow him to stay in contact with her.

The player will now regain control and have a choice of navigating Sam through any of three doors that will lead to transportation to the middle three sections of the game: Benthos, Harmony, and New Boston. The player can play these areas in whichever order she chooses, though she must complete all of them before proceeding to the final area, the Ikairus. The Priestess will be happy to provide Sam with some background information about any of the areas before he goes there. Once the player selects one of the doorways, a brief cut-scene of Sam being transported there will follow, and then the player will regain control in the new area.

Benthos

First is Benthos, the city beneath the sea. The Electric Priestess sends Sam on her private, robot-operated auto-gyro to the undersea monorail which leads to Benthos. Benthos' population is made up primarily of two classes of people: undersea researchers and visual artists. The latter group mostly relocated to Benthos because of the solitary, remote lifestyle it provides. Benthos is a domed city, into which oxygen is pumped via ducts which float on the ocean's surface many miles above. Because of the low height of the dome, Benthos consists of smaller buildings than the mega-skyscrapers found in the surface cities. Scattered throughout the city are many sculptures that have been created by the artists who live there; the work is of amorphous, abstract, yet streamlined forms, many resembling "space age" versions of Picasso's sculpture work.

The Priestess informed Sam that his parents kept a private lab in Benthos, and Sam will set out across the city to look for it. As in Gargantuopolis, Sam will be waylaid by numerous mechanized adversaries who try to prevent him from reaching his parents' lab. Combat in Benthos will have less to do with flying to great heights as it did in Gargantuopolis, since the dome prevents anyone from flying too high. Flight will still be the key to fast maneuvering and effectively battling the robotic creatures Sam must defeat at every turn. In Benthos, Sam soon meets the flying girl Xeraphina, who will help him find his parents and tells him about Benthos.

Finally, Sam will make it to his parents' lab, a small office full of his parents' equipment and with a number of pictures of Sam on the walls. Once Sam reaches the office a cut-scene takes over to show Sam discovering another fragment of the important wax cylinder his parents made before they disappeared. With it in hand,

Sam will get back on the monorail and make his way back to the Electric Priestess' home, where he can proceed to the next area.

Harmony

From the Priestess' home, one of the doors will lead Sam to her private zeppelin that will take the player to Harmony. A good distance from Gargantuopolis, Harmony is a special "planned" community that includes both large green parks and industrial, metropolitan areas. Harmony is the city where most of the country's robots are built, and here the number of robot inhabitants greatly outnumber the humans. In Harmony, Sam will need to learn to differentiate between friendly robot natives and the more vicious adversaries who continue to try to stop his quest for his parents.

In Harmony, Sam will meet Scrap, a super-friendly robot who befriends Sam and helps him battle the robots who would block his process. Sam also hopes to find Ike, the old robot assistant of his parents. The Electric Priestess explains that Ike went to Harmony to retire among his own kind, and Scrap helps lead Sam to the senior robot.

However, on finding Ike, it turns out that the aged robot's memory has been damaged, leaving him with only two state-sanctioned options: be turned off forever or have a new head attached. Opting for the latter, Ike is soon to have a replacement head put on, a common procedure. But Scrap is afraid Ike will lose his memory of Sam's parents, since memories are often lost in the head-replacement procedures. Scrap suggests they try to find an "underground robot doctor," a fellow robot who works in secret to repair old robots, thereby saving their minds and memories from the junk pile.

Sam and Scrap will need to travel across more of Harmony to locate this robot doctor, and then lead him back to Ike. They eventually find one who is willing, a massive robot named Tool who agrees to do the necessary work. Of course, while traveling through Harmony, the player will still have to face ill-intentioned robots at every turn.

Once Tool is brought to Ike, a cut-scene takes over as Tool performs the procedure to restore the old robot's memory. Tool is successful, and Ike now remembers the wax cylinder fragment Sam's parents sent to him and will pass it on to Sam. With another piece of the puzzle in hand, Sam can board the Priestess' zeppelin and return to her bubble home.

New Boston

Finally Sam will be able to travel to New Boston, the Moon colony. Sent there on the Electric Priestess' private rocket, Sam will encounter the friendly extraterrestrials known by earthlings as "Moonies."

On some of their research projects, Sam's parents had worked with one of the Torso Moonies, a fellow by the name of Dulo. It is this Moonie Sam must find, since the Electric Priestess suspects that he has another piece of the wax cylinder. New Boston itself is another domed city—like Benthos—and its inhabitants are able to live much as they do on Earth. Earth-like gravity is maintained inside the dome, and a device called an Atmospherator generates breathable air for all the inhabitants. Some Bi-Header Moonies live inside New Boston, assisting with research projects.

When Sam inquires about Dulo, he will be told that Dulo, as a Torso Moonie, is not allowed inside the Moon colony, so Sam will have to acquire a space suit and go out onto the Moon's surface to find him. Shortly after going out on to the surface, Sam will meet Dulo. Dulo explains that, as a Torso Moonie, he was not able to work with humans. Sam's parents, however, noticed that Dulo had some special talents in their field of research, and as a result were willing to leave New Boston and travel to Dulo's home on the Moon's surface.

Dulo says that, yes, he too has a piece of the wax cylinder, but has stored it in his home, a good distance from the dome. Sam will go with Dulo to get the cylinder. Of course, throughout New Boston as well as on the surface of the Moon, more robotic adversaries will try to stop Atomic Sam from achieving his goals. Like Xeraphina and Scrap, Dulo will work with Sam in defeating the adversaries they encounter on the surface, helping to incapacitate the robotic nuisances. Once Sam reaches Dulo's home he will be able to get the fragment of the wax cylinder from him. Sam must then fight his way back to New Boston and return to Earth from there.

The Electric Priestess' Bubble Home

After Sam has completed each of the three areas, he will have collected all of the fragments of the cylinder he thinks he needs and will return to the Electric Priestess' bubble home. In a cut-scene, the Electric Priestess says that she is most impressed with Sam's work in recovering all the fragments of the cylinder. Unfortunately, when Sam tries to put it together, he finds that one piece is still missing. The Priestess then reveals that she has the final piece, with which Sam can fully assemble the complete cylinder.

Fortunately, the Priestess has a machine with which to play back the cylinder. On the cylinder Sam's parents explain the work they had been researching, and how it led them into conflict with Max Zeffir, the owner of their company, Zeffir Zoom, and the man who has abducted them. Sam hears his parents explaining that in their work for Zeffir Zoom they discovered a dangerous flaw in one of Zeffir's new monorail systems, something that would mean huge losses for the company in order to successfully redesign. Unfortunately, they relate, Max Zeffir himself became aware of the problem but refused to have it fixed, and needed to silence them so the monorail system could go ahead without delay.

With the cylinder's playback complete, the Electric Priestess reveals that, in fact, she is Zeffir's sister. She was the original head scientist for Zeffir Zeppelins, and lost her leg many years ago in a zeppelin accident which she blames on Zeffir's cost-cutting. She suspected all along that Zeffir was behind Sam's parents' disappearance, but felt she must have proof before she could reveal her suspicions to Sam. In fact, she explains, she has been a friend of Sam's parents for some time, and when they started to fear that they would be caught by Max Zeffir, they broke up the evidence, in the form of the wax cylinder, and scattered the pieces, putting one in their apartment, one in their office in Benthos, and mailing the remaining pieces to Ike, Dulo, and the Electric Priestess herself. The Priestess now concludes with certainty that it has been Zeffir sending robot minions to try to stop Sam from discovering the truth about his parents.

The Ikairus

His parents, the Electric Priestess reveals, are most likely being held captive aboard Zeffir's atomic-powered flying fortress the Ikairus. A constantly airborne, mammoth craft—its atomic power allowing it to fly indefinitely—the flying fortress is Zeffir's pride and joy, and is also where he resides. Kept aloft by some eighty propeller engines, the craft looks like a gigantic flying wing, and is large enough for other aircraft to land on.

The Priestess again lends Sam her private auto-gyro, which flies him to the Ikairus. On board the flying fortress Sam will have to battle still more robots in addition to the very challenging Merciless Mercenaries. The battles on the Ikairus take place in much more small and confined spaces, representing the corridors of the ship, and the player will need to adjust his fighting style accordingly. Finally, Sam will be able to confront the quite insane Zeffir. Zeffir not only has Sam's parents held captive, but he has also captured Xeraphina, Scrap, and Dulo. While Sam and Zeffir battle, Zeffir brags of what he will do to Sam's friends once he has defeated Sam. Finally managing to subdue Zeffir, Sam will at last be reunited with his parents, who are quite glad they gave him the atomic rocket-pack for his birthday.

VII. Bibliography

The following books were key points of inspiration for the setting and world of *Atomic Sam*. Those working on the game will find researching these books to be quite useful in getting a feel for what a "retro-futuristic" setting is all about.

Corn, Joseph J. and Brian Horrigan. *Yesterday's Tomorrows*. Baltimore: The Johns Hopkins University Press, 1984.

A great historical treatment of the various visions of future from the past century, including many invaluable photos and documents.

Moore, Alan and Chris Sprouse. *Tom Strong*. La Jolla, CA: America's Best Comics, 1999.

Moore and Sprouse's brilliant comic book *Tom Strong* is set in the "clean and friendly" world of the twenty-first century, following the adventures of "science hero" Tom Strong.

Motter, Dean and Michael Lark. *Terminal City*. New York: DC Comics, 1996.

Motter and Lark's future as seen in *Terminal City* is a bit bleaker and darker than *Tom Strong*, but with the same sort of retarded technological development. Both *Tom Strong* and *Terminal City* include brilliant visual design and amazing environments, perfect for a video game such as *Atomic Sam*.

Glossary

This section includes brief definitions of a number of the terms referred to in this book, and should be of particular use to readers less familiar with the jargon of the computer game industry. Some of the definitions veer close to talking about programming, and in these cases I provide only enough information to give the reader a general idea of what the term means. Those looking for more complete definitions are advised to pick up a book about computer game development from a programming standpoint, of which there are many.

A*:   The most popular pathfinding algorithm used by computer games, which finds short and effective paths consistently and quickly, though it is far from perfect. The basis of the A* algorithm is to search for a path by expanding valid nodes that are closest to the target location first in order to try to find the shortest path possible without searching too extensively. Of course, this can be found described in more detail in almost any book about programming games. *See also* Pathfinding.

Agent: *See* AI Agent.

AI: *See* Artificial Intelligence.

AI Agent: The entity that the artificial intelligence controls in a game; the agent of its actions. In a computer game, the AI agents include the monsters the player fights and the NPCs to which he talks. Many people make the mistake of referring to those creatures themselves as "AIs" but this betrays their lack of understanding of what AI means. Just as you would not say that a person walking down the street was an "intelligence," you should not refer to the agents in a game as the "AIs". See Chapter 9, "Artificial Intelligence."

Algorithm: In the land of game development this refers to a usually short piece of code designed to solve a particular problem, typically mathematical in nature. For instance, you might have an algorithm that determines whether one character in a 3D environment can see another one or not. Or you could say that the code that finds a walkable path from the first character to the second one is an algorithm. Or, in a game like *SimCity*, algorithms are used to calculate the population density in a given location based on the options the player has made in building his city.

A-Life: *See* Artificial Life.

Alpha: Customarily describes a game that is not yet close to being complete but which is playable all the way through. At this point, the design and content is largely done, and bug-fixing refining, and balancing are all that remain to be done to the title. This is often used by publishers to define the state of a project they have in development and is typically followed by the Beta state. Other developers may define Alpha differently, such as using it to mean any game that is in a playable state.

Arcade Game: Strictly speaking, a computer game that is found in an arcade environment. It may also refer to home conversions of the same games. More broadly, arcade game describes any game featuring the short and intense gameplay typical of these games. See Chapter 4, which contains an analysis of the arcade game *Centipede* and an exploration of the nature of the arcade game as a genre.

Art: In the context of game development, this is most often used to describe the graphical content of a game. It can also mean what all game developers engage in, the creation of computer games themselves, which qualify as art. The author's favorite definition of art comes from Chapter 7 of Scott McCloud's excellent book *Understanding Comics*: "Art, as I see it, is any human activity which doesn't grow out of either of our species' two basic instincts: survival and reproduction." Some game developers spend endless time debating whether or not computer games qualify as art, but these arguments are seldom productive or useful.

Art Bible: A document used in game development which includes concept sketches of game art assets and possibly some descriptive text. The art bible is used by a game's art team as a reference tool in the development of the game's graphical content, usually in order to maintain consistency.

Artificial Intelligence: The artificial intelligence in a game controls all of the entities or agents in the game which have the ability to react to the player or otherwise provide an unpredictable challenge for the player. Artificial intelligence in a single-player game typically fulfills the role that human intelligence provides in a multi-player game. Thoroughly defined in Chapter 9, "Artificial Intelligence."

Artificial Life: A system for artificial intelligence that tries to imitate biological life by assigning AI agents base behaviors and desires which cause them to perform specific actions by their "nature." This is the opposite of the type of AI typically used in most games, though artificial life was famously used in the computer game *Creatures*.

Assets: The content of a game, customarily used to refer to the art, sound effects, music, and possibly the levels. Code itself is seldom referred to as an asset.

Avatar: The same as a game-world surrogate, the player's avatar is whatever character represents him in the game-world. It may also be an icon used in chat-room-like situations. "The Avatar" is also the name of the character the player controls in the *Ultima* series of games.

Beta: The state games reach after passing through Alpha, and the last step before a game is published or otherwise released to the public. In Beta, changes made to a game are supposed to be strictly limited to bug fixes. Some developers define Beta to be when they first have what they consider to be a release candidate. *See also* Alpha *and* Release Candidate.

Bible: Used in the gaming industry to refer to various reference materials used during a game's development. *See* Art Bible *and* Story Bible.

Boss Monster: An enemy in a game, though not necessarily a "monster" per se, which is much larger or simply more difficult to defeat than the other opponents in the game. Typically boss monsters are placed at the end of levels and provide a climax for that level's gameplay.

'Bot: Short for "robot," this refers to artificial intelligence agents that are designed to appear to play similarly to humans, typically designed to work in first-person shooter death-match games. *Quake III Arena* and *Unreal Tournament* both feature 'bots as the player's only opposition in the single-player game.

BSP: Short for Binary Space Partition. A method for storing and rendering 3D space which involves dividing the world into a tree of space partitions, most famously used in id Software's games *Doom* and *Quake*.

Builder Games: One term used to describe games in which the player is responsible for building lasting structures in the game-world. In a sense, in builder games, the players are responsible for the level design. Examples of this type of game are *SimCity*, *Civilization*, *RollerCoaster Tycoon*, and *The Sims*.

Burn Rate: The amount of money a company, typically a developer, spends in a month to keep itself in business. This typically includes all of the employees' salaries, rent, utilities, and other persistent expenses. Sometimes publishers will try to fund a developer only to the extent of its burn rate, so that the developer does not have any spare cash and remains forever beholden to the publisher.

Candidate: *See* Release Candidate.

Capture the Flag: A game involving two teams, both of which have a flag. The flag is kept at a specific location and possibly guarded, while the players on both teams try to grab the other team's flag through stealth or brute force. In computer games, this is often a game variant offered in first-person shooter multi-player cooperative games, such as *Quake* or *Unreal*.

Choke-Point: A point in a game past which a player can progress only by passing through a particular area, completing a particular puzzle, or defeating a particular monster. Often the areas preceding and following a choke-point allow the player more freedom of play, while the choke-point presents a task the player absolutely must accomplish before proceeding.

Classic Arcade Game: Does not necessarily mean a game that is a classic, but any game which was released during the early period of arcade games or which exhibits the traits typical of those games. Classic arcade games include simple, single-screen-player games such as *Space Invaders*, *Centipede*, *Robotron 2084*, or *Pac-Man*. Classic arcade game is defined more fully in Chapter 4. *See also* Arcade Game.

Code: When used in reference to games, code is the lines of text that programmers enter into the computer and which the computer then compiles into the functional game. A talented programmer is sometimes referred to as a code-jockey.

Color: Beyond the obvious definition, in terms of game design this may also refer to the specific content and setting of a game. *Monopoly*, for instance, includes the street names of Atlantic City and a depression era real-estate mogul theme as a means of providing color. Color is separate from the gameplay itself.

Concept Document: Also known as a pitch document. This is a short document that includes text and concept sketches and that is used to initially sell the idea of a project to a publisher or other financier. A concept document gives the reader an idea of what the game will involve without including sufficient detail to actually develop the game. If accepted, the concept document is usually expanded into the design document.

Concept Sketch: A sketch of a particular game art asset which is used to show someone what the art will look like, approximately, before that graphic or model is actually created. May also be a sketch of a scene from the game as it will appear once the game is functional.

Creative Services: A deceptively titled wing of the publisher which is typically in charge of creating the box art and other advertisements and logos for a game.

Critical Path: The path that the player is expected and encouraged to follow when moving through a game or a particular level. Somewhat reminiscent of the yellow brick road in *The Wizard of Oz*.

CRPG: A computer version of a role-playing game. *See also* Role-Playing Game.

CTF: Typically refers to Capture the Flag multi-player games, though it may also refer to Valve Software's *Classic Team Fortress* game. *See* Capture the Flag.

Cut-Scene: A non-interactive portion of a game typically used to communicate to the player information about the game's story line, sometimes involving pre-rendered or live action full-motion video, other times using the game's real-time graphics engine. Cut-scenes often come between levels in a game, and are sometimes used as rewards for the player having finished a particularly challenging portion of the game.

Death March: When a development team, particularly the programmers, works every waking moment on a project for a long period of time, typically trying to make an unachievable deadline of some sort. Often the death march is entered into thinking it will be over soon enough, but it then drags on long beyond what anyone thought possible.

Death-Match: A multi-player game in which the players' only goals are to kill each other. Usually refers to games of that sort in first-person shooters such as *Doom, Unreal,* or *Duke Nukem 3D.*

Design Document: The textual reference used in developing a game which attempts to describe in detail every important aspect of the game's design. Sometimes referred to as the Functional Specification. Described more completely in Chapter 17, "The Design Document."

DM: *Depending on context, see* Dungeon Master *or* Death-Match.

Dungeon Master: The term for the Game Master used in conjunction with *Dungeons & Dragons* games. *See* Game Master.

Engine: The core code that handles the most basic functionality of the game, but not including the code which governs specific gameplay functionality. Sometimes the engine is split up into the rendering engine, the sound engine, the behavior engine, and so forth. Each of these components can be considered to be part of the game's engine as a whole. Engines are typically more general than a particular game, which allows them to be reused for multiple different projects. However, some developers use the term Engine to refer to the entirety of a game's source code. For example, id Software has licensed their *Quake* engine for use in a broad range of games, from *Half-Life* to *Soldier of Fortune* to *Heavy Metal: FAKK 2.*

Finite State Machine: *See* State-Based AI.

First-Person Shooter: The type of game exemplified by *Doom*, *Half-Life*, *Unreal*, *Marathon*, *Quake,* and *Duke Nukem 3D*. In first-person shooters, the player's perspective of the world is from the first person and her objective is to shoot everything in sight, though some first-person shooters offer some subtle variations on this goal.

Flight Simulator: Often shortened to flight sim, this is a type of game which attempts to model the flight of a real-world aircraft. The amount of realism involved varies from game to game; some games are extremely realistic and difficult, while others prevent the player from crashing entirely. Examples include *Microsoft Flight Simulator*, *F-15 Strike Eagle*, *Flight Unlimited*, and *Hellcats Over the Pacific*.

FMV: *See* Full-Motion Video.

Focus: A brief, three- to five-sentence description of the most important concepts guiding a game's development. Described in detail in Chapter 5, "Focus."

FPS: Depending on the context, this may refer to the first-person shooter genre of games or to the frames per second that the game's engine is currently rendering. *See* First-Person Shooter.

FSM: Stands for finite state machine. *See* State-Based AI.

Full-Motion Video: Any non-real-time graphics in a game which are displayed quickly in a sequential order to create a movie-like effect. Full-motion video can be of live actors, computer-generated environments, or a combination of the two.

Functional Specification: The sister document to the Technical Specification, in that it describes how the game will function from the user's perspective, as opposed to how the programmer will implement that functionality. In game development, typically referred to as the Design Document. *See also* Design Document.

Fuzzy Logic: A type of AI that introduces some degree of randomness into the decision making process. This means that, given the exact same inputs, an AI agent will make different decisions based on chance.

Game: *The Oxford Universal Dictionary* includes a number of definitions for "game." The definition we are most interested in for this book reads as follows: "A diversion of the nature of a contest, played according to rules, and decided by superior skill, strength, or good fortune." To rephrase, a game presents an entertaining challenge to the player or players, a challenge which the player or players can understand and may be able to succeed at using their wits, dexterity, luck, or some combination thereof. To expand, in order for that challenge to be meaningful, the player must be presented with a number of interesting choices for how to succeed at the game, and those choices must be non-trivial. And in order for the challenge to be truly meaningful, the game must define the criterion for success. This excludes "software toys" such as *SimCity* from being games. Of course, one could write an entire book about the nature of a game, but this is not that book.

Game Design: The game design establishes the shape and form of the gameplay in a game. The game design may be communicated through a design document, or it may only exist in the head of the implementors of the game. *See also* Gameplay.

Game Designer: The game designer is the person on a project who is responsible for establishing the form of the gameplay through the game design. *See also* Gameplay *and* Game Design.

Game Engine: *See* Engine.

Game Flow: The chain of events that make up the playing of a given game. A game can be said to flow between its action, exploration, puzzle-solving, and storytelling components. The proportional amount of time spent in each of these components and the pace at which the game takes place contributes to its overall flow.

Game Master: In a pen and paper role-playing game, the game master is the player who governs the actions of all of the other players in the game-world. The game master often has also dreamt up the adventures that the players are going on, and continues to dynamically create this story as the players navigate through it.

Game Mechanic: A specific way in which a part of the gameplay is implemented. For instance, the mechanic for doing an attack-jump in *Crash Bandicoot* is to hold down the "down" or "crouch" button while in mid-jump. The mechanic for sending a unit to a new location in *WarCraft* is to click on the unit in question with the left mouse button, move the pointer to the desired position on the map, and then to click there with the right mouse button. The gameplay as a whole is made up of a number of different game mechanics combined together.

Gameplay: The gameplay is the component that distinguishes games from all other artistic mediums. The gameplay defines how the player is able to interact with the game-world and how that game-world will react to his actions. One could consider the gameplay to be the degree and nature of a game's interactivity. Of course many different people have different definitions for gameplay, but as far as this book is concerned, gameplay does not include the game's story, graphics, sound, or music. This is easy to understand if one recalls that gameplay is what separates games from other artistic mediums; each of these components is found in literature, film, or theater. Gameplay also does not include the code used to make the game run, the game's engine, though that engine does necessarily implement the gameplay. The gameplay, however, could be implemented using a completely different engine while remaining identical.

Game-World: This is the space in which a game takes place. In a board game such as *The Settlers of Catan*, the game-world is represented by the board the game takes place on. For a sports game, the game-world is the real-world but is limited to the extent of the field the game is played on. For a role-playing game, the game-world is maintained within the imaginations of the game master and the players. For a computer game, this is a "virtual" space which is stored in the computer's memory and which the players can view via the computer screen. The actions the player makes in a game are limited to the game-world, as are the reactions of either the game itself or the other players.

GM: *Depending on the context, see* Gold Master *or* Game Master.

Going Gold: The time when a team completes a game and is thereby able to create the Gold Master which is sent to the duplicators. *See also* Gold Master.

Gold Candidate: *See* Release Candidate.

Gold Master: The version of the game, typically recorded onto gold CDs, which is going to be used by the duplicator to create copies of the actual shipping game. In other words, the final version of the game.

Graphical User Interface: This is any communications method the player has of interacting with the computer that is primarily graphical in nature. For instance, the Macintosh has always had a graphical user interface, as opposed to the text-oriented one available in MS-DOS or UNIX. Games use GUIs for starting up new games, loading saved games, and choosing other options from the main menu, but also for communicating information to the player not readily apparent from their view of the game-world: the player character's health, currently equipped weapon, amount of ammo, number of lives, score, and so forth.

GUI: *See* Graphical User Interface.

Heads Up Display: A type of graphical user interface which is overlaid on top of the player's game-world view. This may include the player character's health, a mini-map of the area, or radar of some sort, and typically communicates vital information to which the player must always have easy access. Heads up displays take their name from the displays used by jet fighter pilots, which constantly convey crucial flying information to those pilots while they are navigating the plane. *See also* Graphical User Interface.

High Concept: An idea for a game which attempts to merge disparate types of gameplay or setting into one game, without regard to whether those different ideas will work well together. An example might be making a first-person shooter which is also a racing game, or a wargame which includes a golf simulator. Usually synonymous with "bad concept."

HUD: *See* Heads Up Display.

IF: *See* Interactive Fiction.

IK: *See* Inverse Kinematics.

Input/Output: Often shortened to I/O, this refers to the systems a computer uses to allow the player to input information (typically a keyboard and a mouse) in combination with how it communicates information back out to the user (typically the monitor). In terms of computer games, the I/O refers to the controls with which the player manipulates the game and the way the game then communicates to the player the current nature of the game-world.

Interactive: An interaction is when two systems, be they a human and a human, a human and a computer, or a computer and a computer, are mutually active in a given process. For instance, a television show is not interactive, since only the television outputs data and completely ignores whatever the user/audience does. A conversation between two people is interactive, however, since both parties listen to what the other has to say and will then say something related or in response to that. As another example, a strict lecture is not interactive since the lecturer reads a prepared speech without any input from the audience. A discussion group, however, is interactive, since the professor or leader of the discussion will answer the students' questions and listen to and evaluate their ideas. Games are interactive since they allow both the player and the computer to determine the shape of that particular game. Computer games are not being especially interactive when they play long cut-scenes over which the player has no control.

Interactive Fiction: A term originally coined by Infocom, which is an alternate name for text adventures. Some people use interactive fiction to describe any games which use text to describe scenes and include a text parser, even if graphics are also included. *See also* Text Adventure.

Interactive Movie: A term coined by those working in games who wish to call their profession something more glamorous than what it is, similarly to how the comic book industry sometimes attempts to call some of its longer and more sophisticated works "graphic novels." Typically, interactive movies involve more and longer cut-scenes than your average game. Unfortunately, the makers of so-called "interactive movies" typically add more movie than they do interactivity, resulting in works which are almost always not very good movies and lack the interactivity to be good games.

Inverse Kinematics: An animation technique whereby a joint in a character's skeleton is moved to a desired location and the joints that depend on or are influenced by that joint are automatically moved to the correct location. For example, if animating a humanoid, the hand could be moved toward a door handle and the elbow and shoulder would automatically move to reasonable positions. *See also* Skeletal Animation.

I/O: *See* Input/Output.

Isometric: Isometric is defined to mean "equality of measure," particularly in reference to drawing objects. If one were isometrically drawing a cube from a distance with one of the points of the cube pointing directly toward the viewer, the lines of the cube would all be of the same length and would not use any foreshortening. Games such as *Civilization II*, *SimCity 2000*, *SimCity 3000*, and *StarCraft* are drawn isometrically. This allows a game to be drawn from a somewhat 3D overhead view which can then be scrolled around in all directions, without actually needing to involve a 3D rendering engine. The perspective on the world is technically wrong, but players do not seem to mind. Also referred to as a "three-quarters" view of the game world.

LAN: An acronym for a Local Area Network. These networks typically consist of a small number of computers in a specific area networked to each other but not necessarily to the Internet or other networks.

LAN Party: Held when a bunch of friends get together, bring their computers to one central location, and play multi-player games over them. Typically the fast "Ping" times allow players to have much faster and more lag-free games than are available over the Internet or other long-distance networks.

Linear: When the only way to get from point A to point B is via the line segment which connects them, we say that the movement is linear. Linear implies a lack of choice outside of a single dimension: forward or backward. In gaming, a linear game is one that does not give the player much choice in what he does. For some games, linear may mean no choice at all, since backward is often not even an option.

Lone Wolf: Term used to describe game developers who do practically everything themselves in the development of a game: the design, programming, art, sound, and writing. At the very least, a lone wolf developer must do all of the game's design and programming herself. A lone wolf does not typically develop commercially released software any more, though there are exceptions. For example, Chris Sawyer designed and programmed all of *RollerCoaster Tycoon* by himself, with a contractor completing the art to his specifications. Though he did not do the art himself, Sawyer can still be described as a lone wolf developer.

Massively Multi-Player: Strictly, a multi-player game involving a very large number of people playing it at once, at least 100 or more. Typically such games are also persistent and played over the Internet. *Ultima Online* and *Ever Quest* are examples of massively multi-player games. *See also* Multi-Player *and* Persistent.

Media: Go out and buy Marshall McLuhan's *Understanding Media*. Read it. Come back only when you fully understand it.

Metagame: According to Richard Garfield, creator of *Magic: The Gathering*, the metagame is "how a game interfaces with life." This means what the player takes to and brings away from a particular playing of a game and how that impacts his subsequent playings of that game. This is particularly applicable to multi-player games. Take, for example, a game of *Quake III Arena* on the Internet. If one player is known to play unethically through camping and other undesirable tactics, players will be likely to make a special effort to eliminate him in subsequent games. This means that the player may end up losing subsequent games because of his behavior in previous games. This interaction between the players from game to game is not part of the playing of the game itself, but is part of the metagame that the playing creates. For another example, in *Magic: The Gathering* the time a player spends preparing his deck before a game, though not part of the game itself, is part of the metagame.

Milestones: A term often used in contracts between publishers and developers. A milestone is an agreement of how much work on a project will be done at a specific date, with the publisher only paying the developer when that milestone (usually in the form of a current build of the game) is delivered to the publisher.

Mod: Short for "modification," mods are user-created add-ons or changes to an existing game. Mods were popularized by id Software's open-architecture policy which allowed players to make their own levels for *Doom*. Beyond levels, mods also often include new AI, new weapons, new art, or some combination of all three, potentially creating a radically altered gameplay experience from what was found in the original game.

MUD: Stands for Multi User Dungeon. MUDs resemble a text adventure with heavy RPG elements in their central play mechanics, with the important difference being that they take place in persistent, massively multi-player worlds. MUDs were set up and run by college students starting in the 1980s. Players of the games, when they reached a high enough experience level or rank, would become the creators of the games' content for other, more inexperienced players to explore. The primary interest many players have in MUDs is the social component, preferring to chat with people they have never seen before to going on *Dungeons & Dragons* style adventures. In many ways, *Ultima Online* is a carefully regulated graphical MUD. Another popular variant are MOOs, which stands for MUD, Object Oriented. In terms of game design, MOOs and MUDs are identical; only the way they are programmed and set up is different.

Multi-Player: A game that involves more than one player. Today, this typically also means "networked multi-player" where each player has his own computer and competes with the other players over a network, such as the Internet.

Non-Linear: Obviously, the opposite of linear. In terms of gaming, this means that the player is not locked into achieving different goals in a specific order or in achieving all of the goals she is presented with. Instead, the player is able to move through the game in a variety of paths and can be successful in a variety of ways. Non-linearity leaves the player with more choice to play the game her own way. *See also* Linear *and* On a Rail.

Non-Player Character: Any character in a computer game which is not controlled by the player. Typically this refers to game-world characters who are not hostile to the player, such as townspeople in an RPG.

NPC: *See* Non-Player Character.

NURBS: Stands for non-uniform rational B-splines. A 3D graphics technique for creating curved surfaces, a detailed explanation of which should be sought out in a 3D graphics programming book.

On a Rail *or* On Rails: A game is said to be on a rail when a player is forced to move through the game in a very specific, carefully controlled way, as if he were locked onto a rail that ran through the game. Games which are said to be "on a rail" or "on rails" are very linear games. A specific type of game called a "rail shooter" is on rails to such an extent that the flight path of the player's vehicle is completely predetermined, and the player is only able to shoot at targets as they pass by. *Rebel Assault* is an example of a rail shooter. *See also* Linear.

180 Degree Rule: A film technique for cutting a scene that says that the camera must always stay on one side of a line that extends between the two centers of attention in the frame. If the camera never rotates anywhere outside of those 180 degrees, the audience will not become confused by the scene's cuts from character to character.

Parser: In gaming, often refers to the input method used by text adventures. A parser takes natural language words or sentences the player enters and translates them into commands that the game logic can understand. Parsers can become quite sophisticated while still failing to understand many of the sentences that players attempt to use as commands. Natural language processing is a major field of AI research, one that is still far from perfect, so it is no wonder that parsers have as much trouble as they do. A more modern usage of the term parser is in reference to the interpreter for a game's scripting language. *See also* Text Adventure.

Pathfinding: This is the portion of the AI code which allows an agent to figure out how to get from one location to another in the game-world. Ideally, pathfinding allows the AI agent to avoid getting stuck on obstacles or other agents, yet pathfinding in many games is less than perfect. There are various algorithms, such as A*, that can be used for pathfinding which may have different results in terms of efficiency and the quality of the paths generated, though that is a topic better explored in a book about programming. *See also* A*.

PC: May refer either to a game's player character or to the Intel-based personal computer originally popularized by IBM and powered by MS-DOS. *Also see* Player Character.

Persistent: A persistent game is one which continues running and maintaining the state of the game-world regardless of whether a particular player is actively playing it or not. Often persistent games are also massively multi-player, and vice versa. MUDs were one of the first persistent games, while commercial products such as *Ultima Online* and *Ever Quest* have made persistent games quite popular to mainstream gamers. *See also* MUDs.

Pitch Document: *See* Concept Document.

Place-Holder: Typically refers to sounds or art used in a game while it is in development but which the development team plans to replace before the game is released to the public.

Platform: Often used to describe the different systems a game can be developed for. Popular gaming platforms past and present include the Apple II, Atari 800, Commodore 64, IBM PC, Commodore Amiga, Macintosh, Atari 2600, Nintendo Entertainment System, Sega Genesis, and the Sony PlayStation.

Player Character: This is the character the player controls in the game, such as Mario in *Super Mario 64*, Lara Croft in *Tomb Raider*, or the space marine in *Doom*. This term is a holdover from pencil and paper RPGs such as *Dungeons & Dragons*.

Player Surrogate: *See* Surrogate.

Playtesting: A term referring to the process of testing the gameplay of the game to see how well it plays. Playtesting is different from bug fixing or quality assurance in general since playtesting focuses on the performance of gameplay itself instead of general bug fixing. See Chapter 23, "Playtesting."

Port/Porting: The process of converting a game from one gaming platform to another, such as from the PC to the Macintosh, or from the Sony PlayStation to the Nintendo 64. Typically, games which are ported are completed on one system first, and only then brought over to the other system.

PR: *See* Public Relations.

Pre-Rendered: 3D graphics which are rendered into 2D sprites or images before the player plays the game. *Myst* features pre-rendered 3D graphics, while *Unreal* features real-time 3D graphics. *See also* Real-Time 3D.

Proposal: *See* Concept Document.

PSX: An abbreviation for Sony's PlayStation console. Actually based on an early name for the system, the PlayStation X. Nonetheless, the abbreviation stuck. However, Sony does not like you calling their newer system the PSX2.

Public Relations: A wing of the marketing department whose primary job is to hype a company's upcoming games in the press by readying press releases, screenshots, and other information. They also can be quite helpful in granting permission to use screenshots in books such as this one.

QA: *See* Quality Assurance.

Quality Assurance: This is the process of testing a game to make sure that it is bug-free and plays reasonably well. The quality assurance cycle or period is the time when a nearly complete project is extensively tested just prior to release. In large companies, the quality assurance department or team are the people who are going to perform that testing.

Rail, On a: *See* On a Rail.

Real-Time: Anything that is computed or rendered for the player while he waits, such as graphics and pathfinding. This differentiates something from being pre-computed before the actual gameplay is taking place. Can also differentiate a game from being turn-based. *See also* Turn-Based.

Real-Time Strategy: A currently popular genre of games, including such titles as *Command & Conquer*, *WarCraft*, *Total Annihilation*, and *Myth: The Fallen Lords*. This term is typically emphasized to differentiate these RTS games from turn-based strategy games such as *Civilization*, *X-Com: UFO Defense*, and *Alpha Centauri*.

Real-Time 3D: Describes 3D graphics which are rendered while the player is looking at them, so that as the player moves around the world, many different views of objects and configurations of the game-world can be generated on the fly. *Unreal* uses real-time 3D graphics while *Myst* uses pre-rendered 3D graphics. *See also* Pre-Rendered.

Release Candidate: A build of the game which the development team believes may be the one that can be shipped. A release candidate is generally tested for at least a few days, optimally a week or two, to determine if it is bug-free enough to be acceptable to the publisher. It is not uncommon for a particular product to go through five or more release candidates.

Role-Playing Game: Games based on the type of gameplay established by pencil and paper role-playing games such as *Dungeons & Dragons*. Those original non-computer-games were so titled because in them players took on the roles of characters of their own creation and guided them through a fantasy world. Much of the gameplay in RPGs depends on the players role-playing these characters who often had personalities different from their own. Ironically, most computer role-playing games often contain very little of the role-playing aspect of traditional RPGs, instead choosing to concentrate on the combat mechanics and fantasy setting.

RPG: *See* Role-Playing Game.

RT3D: *See* Real-Time 3D.

RTS: *See* Real-Time Strategy.

Scripted: In terms of a game, scripted typically refers to AI behaviors that are planned in advance to allow the AI agents to look clever in specific situations in a level. Scripted events play the same way every time a player plays a level. *Half-Life* used scripted events to produce very impressive gameplay effects that gave the illusion of a very smart AI system.

Sim: Short for simulator or simulation. *See* Simulation.

Simulation: In a game described as a simulation, the primary goal of the game's designer is to model a real-life system accurately and realistically, instead of simply making the game as fun as possible. This system could be anything, such as an aircraft of some kind, a race car, or a city.

Simulator: *See* Simulation.

Skeletal Animation: An alternative to vertex deformation for 3D animations. With a skeletal animation system, the game keeps track of an animating character's skeleton. The animation then controls this skeleton, moving the animating character's mesh to match the skeleton properly. A skeletal animation system has the advantage of causing animations to take up much less space than when they are animated using a technique such as vertex deformation, as well as often leading to superior looking animations. Furthermore, the skeleton can be controlled procedurally for inverse kinematics effects of various types. *See also* Vertex Deformation *and* Inverse Kinematics.

Skin: In gaming, skin refers to the texture set being used on a 3D player character in a game like *Quake III Arena* or *Unreal Tournament*. Players will get to choose what skin they play the game with either from the default collection that comes with the game, or by making their own and importing it into the game. This has recently become popular outside of the realm of first-person shooters in *The Sims*.

SKU: Stands for stock keeping unit or shelf keeping unit. It is the unique number associated with every bar code and used by stores to track their inventory. Each unique version of a game is sometimes referred to as a different SKU. If one game ships for a number of different platforms, say Macintosh and PC, then each version is a separate SKU. Similarly, *Thief* and *Thief Gold* are two different SKUs, though they are practically the same game.

Software Toy: A term coined by Will Wright of Maxis to describe that company's first product, *SimCity*. A software toy is quite similar to a game, except that it defines no criterion for success. The player is just left to play with the game as she wishes without ever "winning" or "losing." Yet a player may make a software toy into a game by defining her own personal conditions for success. *See also* Game.

State-Based AI: A type of AI which uses states for each of its agents. States include actions such as idle, walking, attacking, and so forth. The AI then switches the agent from one state to another depending on the conditions of the game-world. May also be referred to as a finite state machine or FSM.

State Machine: *See* State-Based AI.

Story Bible: A document that contains all the information available about the story elements of the game-world. Story bibles can be quite large, especially when working with properties with established histories, such as the *Star Trek* or *Ultima* universes. These documents are usually used as reference works for the developers during the game's creation. Described in detail in Chapter 15, "Game Development Documentation."

Surrogate: A term used to describe the entity that the player controls in the game, also known as the player character or the player's avatar. *See also* Avatar *and* Player Character.

TDD: *See* Technical Design Document.

Technical Design Document: This document takes the gameplay as described in the Design Document and explains how that gameplay will be implemented in more technical, code-centered terms. As a result, this document is often used primarily by the programming team. Described in detail in Chapter 15, "Game Development Documentation."

Technical Specification: Another name for the Technical Design Document. *See* Technical Design Document.

Text Adventure: Text adventures are devoid of graphics and describe the game-world to the player exclusively through text. Players are then able to interact with the game-world by typing in natural language sentences in the imperative form stating what they want their character to do next. The form was made extremely popular by Infocom in the early 1980s. *See also* Interactive Fiction.

Three-Quarters View: Typically refers to games that have an isometric view point. This view can be in any rendering system with an overhead view of the ground where the camera is oriented at a 45-degree angle from the plane of the ground. *See also* Isometric.

Turn-Based: Any game where the computer waits for the player to act before proceeding with its own actions. *Civilization*, for instance, is a turn-based strategy game, while *WarCraft* is a real-time strategy game. For some non-computer game examples, chess is a turn-based game while football (soccer) is real-time. American football is a bizarre hybrid of real-time and turn-based gameplay.

Turn-Based Strategy: *See* Turn-Based.

Vertex Deformation: A 3D animation system where the individual vertices of a model are moved one by one to new positions for each frame of the animation. This is the simplest 3D animation method to code for, but has many disadvantages over a skeletal animation system. Sometimes also called key-frame animation. *Also see* Skeletal Animation.

Virtual Reality: Technically, virtual reality, or VR, refers to advanced world-simulation systems at a minimum involving the user wearing a set of goggles with a small monitor or display device in each eyepiece. This allows the player to get a truly 3D, stereo-vision experience. Also, the VR headset allows the player to turn her head and have her view of the virtual world change accordingly, to match the new location at which she is "looking." VR systems may also involve wearing gloves or full-body suits which detect the user's motion and translate that into motion in the virtual world. Virtual reality is one of the most commonly misused terms in all of computer game parlance. Many game developers with inflated senses of what they are doing will refer to their RT3D first-person games as VR when, since they do not involve headsets, they are really nothing of the kind. Marketing people are particularly fond of misusing and abusing this term.

VR: *See* Virtual Reality.

Wargame: When used in reference to computer games, wargame typically refers to strategy-oriented games which employ gameplay based on pen and paper or board wargames such as those made by Avalon Hill. Computer wargames almost always simulate historic battles, typically feature hexagon-based play-fields, and use turn-based gameplay. Games which are set in historical wars but are not strategic in nature are not generally referred to as wargames. Classic examples of computer wargames include *Kampfgruppe* and *Eastern Front (1941),* while more modern examples include *Panzer General* and *Close Combat.*

Selected Bibliography

The following references have been a great help to me in solidifying my ideas about computer games. I list them here as a sort of "recommended reading" list for those who wish to continue to learn about game design outside the confines of this book.

Books

Bogdanovich, Peter. *Who The Devil Made It*. New York: Knopf, 1997.

A fascinating collection of interviews with classic film directors. Bogdanovich's interview style was my model for the interviews conducted in this book.

Campbell, Joseph. *The Hero with a Thousand Faces*. New York: Bollingen Foundation Inc., 1949. Reprint, Princeton: Princeton University Press, 1972.

Campbell's book is the definitive text on understanding the nature of myths, legends, and heroic stories from throughout the ages.

Crawford, Chris. *The Art of Computer Game Design*. Berkeley, CA: Osborne/McGraw-Hill, 1984.

Crawford's seminal work was the first book about computer game design and was the inspiration for this book. Despite its age in computer game industry terms, it remains largely relevant today. Though it is out of print, it can currently be read in a number of locations on the Internet, including www.erasmatazz.com.

Hague, James. *Halcyon Days: Interviews with Classic Computer and Video Game Programmers*. Issaquah, WA: Dadgum Games, 1997.

Hague's book is an invaluable source of information about what it was like to work in the gaming industry just as it was starting to establish itself. All information comes straight from the source through a series of interviews with a broad range of subjects, including many whose work is discussed in this book: Eugene Jarvis, Dani Bunten Berry, Dan Gorlin, Brian Moriarty, Ed Rotberg, Chris Crawford, and so on. The HTML-format book is available from Hague's company, Dadgum Games, at www.dadgum.com.

McCloud, Scott. *Reinventing Comics.* New York: Paradox Press, 2000.

_____. *Understanding Comics.* Northampton, MA: Kitchen Sink Press, Inc., 1993.

Though these books are technically about comics, they both provide tremendous insight about media and art of all kinds. It is fair to say that *Understanding Comics* fundamentally changed the way I think about art.

McLuhan, Marshall. *Understanding Media.* New York: McGraw-Hill Book Co., 1964. Reprint, Cambridge, MA: MIT Press, 1994.

The definitive book on media of all kinds, a work which takes on new meaning in the age of the Internet. McLuhan may be a bit obtuse in his writing style, but his insights are without peer.

Strunk, William and E.B. White. *The Elements of Style.* New York: Macmillan Publishing, 1959. Reprint 4th Ed., Boston: Allyn and Bacon, 2000.

The Elements of Style remains the last word on clear and concise writing, a book anyone writing a design document, script, or book about game design would do well to read.

Periodicals

Computer Gaming World (Ziff Davis Media)

A magazine that has been around almost as long as computer games themselves, *Computer Gaming World* remains informative and insightful.

Game Developer (CMP Media, Inc.)

The closest the gaming industry has to a professional journal, which covers all aspects of game development, including articles on game design.

Next Generation (Imagine Media, Inc.)

A hybrid computer game/console game magazine with an emphasis on cutting-edge game technology and, sometimes, the theory and people behind the games.

Web Sites

www.mpath.com/dani

A tribute page to the late Dani Bunten Berry, the tremendously gifted designer of the classic *M.U.L.E.* Includes some of Berry's writings about game design and reflections on her career.

www.costik.com

Greg Costikyan is best known for his pencil and paper game designs, including the classic games *Toon* and *Paranoia*, though he has also done a number of computer games. His web site includes an array of articles he has written, including the very interesting screed, "I Have No Words & I Must Design."

www.erasmatazz.com

Chris Crawford's current home on the web, centered on his interactive storytelling engine, the Erasmatron. Also includes a vast library of Crawford's writings about game design, including everything he ever wrote for the *Journal of Computer Game Design* and links to the full text of *The Art of Computer Game Design*. Required reading.

www.gamasutra.com

Gamasutra is the sister web site of *Game Developer* magazine. The site runs original content as well as some reprints from the magazine. Within its pages, a vast wealth of information is archived and searchable.

www.theinspiracy.com

The home page for Noah Falstein's game consulting company, The Inspiracy. Includes a number of articles by Falstein and transcripts of some of his talks at the Game Developer's Conference.

Index

Page numbers in **bold** indicate an image of that particular game.

About the Companion CD

The CD comes with a fully readable and searchable PDF version of this book, for those who prefer to read on their computers. It also includes an HTML document with a collection of links to various useful game design and development resources on the Internet, including all of those listed in the bibliography.

The CD also contains a wide variety of software, both demos as well as fully functional packages. All of the software included is used by professional game developers for various aspects of game creation, ranging from sound editing to 3D modeling to image manipulation to programming to interactive storytelling. It is included to provide the reader with useful and instructive companion materials for this book. There are fourteen packages in all, covering the full range of game development software, including:

- **DarkBasic**: Blending the power of DirectX and the remarkable ease of BASIC, DarkBasic is a language that gives absolute beginners unprecedented power to create professional software.
- **Erasmatron:** Chris Crawford's powerful interactive storytelling tool allows users to create their own complex interactive storytelling experiences.
- **Nendo:** Nendo is a fine 3D modeling and 3D painting package that is both simple enough for the novice and powerful enough for the professional.
- **Hugo & TADS:** Compilers, debuggers, and interpreters for creating sophisticated, immersive, and platform-independent text and graphical adventures.
- **SmartDraw:** Smart Draw is a terrific program for drawing flowcharts, level layouts, and other diagrams essential to game development.
- **SpriteLib:** SpriteLib is a free sprite graphics library for all multimedia developers. Containing well over 780 professionally drawn images in over a dozen sizes and themes, SpriteLib is the ideal tool for developing the latest generation of games.
- **Visual SlickEdit:** Visual SlickEdit is an award-winning source code editor that increases development productivity and improves software quality. It supports most languages out of the box and is extensible to support your favorite language as well.

The CD contains ReadMe.txt and ReadMe.html files, which are a good place to begin exploration of the CD.

System Requirements

The CD is a hybrid Windows/Macintosh disk and provides software for both platforms, though not all of the packages are available for both systems. The requirements of the different pieces of software differ from package to package. The base requirements for use of the CD are any system running Windows 95 or later, or any system with Macintosh System 7 or later.

CD/Source Code Usage License Agreement

Please read the following CD/Source Code usage license agreement before opening the CD and using the contents therein:

1. By opening the accompanying software package, you are indicating that you have read and agree to be bound by all terms and conditions of this CD/Source Code usage license agreement.

2. The compilation of code and utilities contained on the CD and in the book are copyrighted and protected by both U.S. copyright law and international copyright treaties, and is owned by Wordware Publishing, Inc. Individual source code, example programs, help files, freeware, shareware, utilities, and evaluation packages, including their copyrights, are owned by the respective authors.

3. No part of the enclosed CD or this book, including all source code, help files, shareware, freeware, utilities, example programs, or evaluation programs, may be made available on a public forum (such as a World Wide Web page, FTP site, bulletin board, or Internet news group) without the express written permission of Wordware Publishing, Inc. or the author of the respective source code, help files, shareware, freeware, utilities, example programs, or evaluation programs.

4. You may not decompile, reverse engineer, disassemble, create a derivative work, or otherwise use the enclosed programs, help files, freeware, shareware, utilities, or evaluation programs except as stated in this agreement.

5. The software, contained on the CD and/or as source code in this book, is sold without warranty of any kind. Wordware Publishing, Inc. and the authors specifically disclaim all other warranties, express or implied, including but not limited to implied warranties of merchantability and fitness for a particular purpose with respect to defects in the disk, the program, source code, sample files, help files, freeware, shareware, utilities, and evaluation programs contained therein, and/or the techniques described in the book and implemented in the example programs. In no event shall Wordware Publishing, Inc., its dealers, its distributors, or the authors be liable or held responsible for any loss of profit or any other alleged or actual private or commercial damage, including but not limited to special, incidental, consequential, or other damages.

6. One (1) copy of the CD or any source code therein may be created for backup purposes. The CD and all accompanying source code, sample files, help files, freeware, shareware, utilities, and evaluation programs may be copied to your hard drive. With the exception of freeware and shareware programs, at no time can any part of the contents of this CD reside on more than one computer at one time. The contents of the CD can be copied to another computer, as long as the contents of the CD contained on the original computer are deleted.

7. You may not include any part of the CD contents, including all source code, example programs, shareware, freeware, help files, utilities, or evaluation programs in any compilation of source code, utilities, help files, example programs, freeware, shareware, or evaluation programs on any media, including but not limited to CD, disk, or Internet distribution, without the express written permission of Wordware Publishing, Inc. or the owner of the individual source code, utilities, help files, example programs, freeware, shareware, or evaluation programs.

8. You may use the source code, techniques, and example programs in your own commercial or private applications unless otherwise noted by additional usage agreements as found on the CD.

Warning:
Opening the CD package makes this book non-returnable.